Jay Westbrook, early 21st century
Photo credit: Wyatt McSpadden

BANKRUPTCY'S UNIVERSAL PRAGMATIST

Festschrift in Honor of
Professor Jay Lawrence Westbrook

Christoph G. Paulus and John A. E. Pottow, Editors

Published in the United States of America by
Michigan Publishing
Manufactured in the United States of America

DOI: https://doi.org/10.3998/mpub.11499850

ISBN 978-1-60785-547-7 (paper)
ISBN 978-1-60785-548-4 (ebook)
ISBN 978-1-60785-565-1 (open access)

An imprint of Michigan Publishing, Maize Books serves the publishing
needs of the University of Michigan community by making high-quality
scholarship widely available in print and online. It represents a new model
for authors seeking to share their work within and beyond the academy,
offering streamlined selection, production, and distribution processes.
Maize Books is intended as a complement to more formal modes of
publication in a wide range of disciplinary areas.

http://www.maizebooks.org

FOREWORD

The Honorable Elizabeth Warren[*]

When Angie, Christoph, and John told me about their idea for this Festschrift, and the "JayFest" conference in Austin, I said I would do everything in my power to be a part of it. After all, Jay and Jay's scholarship are deeply woven into my own life.

Jay and I go back longer than a rule-against-perpetuities question. What brought us together was a commitment to understanding law, not just what law is on the books or the theoretical consistency of such laws but how laws affect real people with real problems and how those laws might be modified or shaped to make people's lives less (or more) painful. Together with Terry Sullivan, we decided to venture out from the protected world of academe, confronting instead the messy world of real life. We gathered data from actual bankruptcy courts and explored how this legal system actually worked (for better or worse) for people in financial distress who need help.

Our work was not always popular. The rising academic trend back then was economic theories of bankruptcy law; the best way to understand the system was to come up with an ever-more sophisticated model. We rebelled. The data we collected challenged the most widely accepted theories of the day. They also suggested that some of the most self-congratulatory descriptions of improvements in the

---

[*] United States Senate, Leo Gottlieb Professor of Law, *Emeritus*, Harvard University. The editors have corrected the author's formal academic title to comport with modern, gender-neutral language (which we have a vague suspicion the author might prefer).

bankruptcy system had not operated as promised. And in our text-book, we bucked the leading teaching tools by focusing on problem sets based on real-world problems rather than parsing the texts of famous Supreme Court opinions or grinding through multiple varia-tions in state law. Some of those who read our work or used our books were converts, while others were not. But we note that today, empiri-cal legal studies have blossomed and textbooks with problem sets are the rule, not the exception. Those are encouraging data points!

Jay deserves huge credit for this transformation, and I'm glad to see this public recognition. There are three things those who know Jay understand. First, he cares about getting it right. That's why he collects and analyzes data and wants to make sure he leaves no stone unturned, even if it means admitting that something he thought before was right is wrong. He's honest. Second, he cares about people. The law is not an abstract institution for Jay. It's something used by people, for people. Its content matters. Third, he is a great friend. Going back to our Texas days and beyond, Jay has always supported me and countless other colleagues in the field of commercial law, including inspiring a new generation (now maybe generations) of lawyers and scholars.

While I will always think of Jay as a great collaborator on our consumer work, I realize some of his biggest insights have come in international law. He was instrumental in developing what is now chapter 15 of the U.S. Bankruptcy Code, and his work is not just widely studied in this country but around the world. He is a man of wide-reaching interests, and so it is fitting that this book collects consumer, business, cross-border, and comparative commercial scholars from all around the globe into one place to present their own offerings inspired by the work of Bankruptcy's Universal Prag-matist, Jay Lawrence Westbrook.

To see in this volume some of the fruits of Jay's extraordinary leadership is a great joy. It is also a humbling reminder of the impor-tance of a commitment to press the boundaries of our understanding and to put those efforts in service to the people who will be deeply affected by the laws that emerge.

E.W.

"JayFest"

Austin, Texas, February 2-4, 2018

Convenors

Angela Littwin, *University of Texas*

Christoph G. Paulus, *Humboldt University*

John A. E. Pottow, *University of Michigan*

Hosts

International Insolvency Institute

Texas Law Review

University of Texas Law School

JayFest Program

Presenters

Prof. Stephanie Ben-Ishai, *Osgoode Hall Law School*
Prof. Susan Block-Lieb, *Fordham University*
Prof. Charles D. Booth, *University of Hawai'i*
Prof. Mechele Dickerson, *University of Texas*
Prof. (Emer.) Ian Fletcher, *University College London*
Dr. José Garrido, *International Monetary Fund*
Prof. Anna Gelpern, *Georgetown University*
Prof. Henry Hu, *University of Texas*
Prof. Melissa Jacoby, *University of North Carolina*
Prof. Edward Janger, *Brooklyn Law School*
Prof. Emily Kadens, *Northwestern University*
Prof. Jason Kilborn, *John Marshall Law School*
Prof. Robert Lawless, *University of Illinois*
Prof. Adam Levitin, *Georgetown University*
Prof. Jonathan Lipson, *Temple Law School*
Prof. Angela Littwin, *University of Texas*
Prof. Stephen Lubben, *Seton Hall Law School*
Prof. Ronald Mann, *Columbia University*
Prof. Bruce Markell, *Northwestern University*
Prof. Rosalind Mason, *Queensland University of Technology*
Prof. Luis Manuel C. Méjan, *Instituto Tecnológico Autónomo do México*
Prof. Charles Mooney, *University of Pennsylvania*
Prof. (Emer.) Christoph Paulus, *Humboldt University*

Presenters (cont.)

Hon. Katie Porter, *U.S. House of Representatives*
Prof. John Pottow, *University of Michigan Law School*
Prof. (Emer.) Harry Rajak, *Sussex University*
Prof. Iain Ramsay, *Kent Law School*
Prof. Irit Mevorach, *University of Nottingham*
Prof. Janis Sarra, *University of British Columbia*
Prof. Steven Schwarcz, *Duke Law School*
Prof. David Skeel, *University of Pennsylvania Law School*
Prof. Frederick Tung, *Boston University*
Prof. (Emer.) William Whitford, *University of Wisconsin*

Distinguished Keynote Speakers

Mr. Sean Hagan, Esq., *International Monetary Fund*
Rt. Hon. Leonard Hoffmann, Baron Hoffmann, PC GCB, *House of Lords* (Ret.)
Dr. Teresa Sullivan, President Emerita, University Professor, *University of Virginia*
Hon. Elizabeth Warren, *U.S. Senate*

Panel Chairs

Mr. Harold Burman, Esq., Hon. Charles Case II, Hon. Leif Clark, Hon. James Farley, QC, Hon. Allan Gropper, Hon. Clifton Jessup, Jr., Prof. Adrian Walters, Prof. Douglas Whaley

Lawyers' Roundtable Participants

Ms. Corinne Ball, Mr. John Barrett, Mr. Agustín Berdeja-Prieto, Mr. Donald Bernstein, Mr. Zack Clement, Mr. Richard Levin, Mr. Robert Millner, Hon. James Peck, Mr. Christopher Redmond, Ms. Carren Shulman, Mr. David Ward

ABI Distinguished Fellows

Prof. Abbye Atkinson, Hon. Samuel Bufford (Senior Fellow), Prof. Nathalie Martin (Senior Fellow), Prof. Andrew Dawson, Prof. Sally McDonald Henry, Prof. Pamela Foohey, Prof. Dalié Jiménez, Prof. Sara Sternberg Greene, Prof. Chrysten Ondersma, Prof. Ray Warner (Senior Fellow)

Planning Committee

Mr. Omar Alaniz, Mr. Charles Beckham, Mr. Michael Cooley, Ms. Deborah Langehennig, Mr. Stephen Lemmon, Mr. Berry Spears, Mr. William Stutts, Mr. William Wallander, Ms. Deborah Williamson.

Special Thanks and Consideration

JayFest would not have been possible without the International Insolvency Institute (Dr. Annika Wolf), American Bankruptcy Institute (Mr. Samuel J. Gerdano), *Texas Law Review* (Brittany B. Fowler, Andrew P. Van Osselaer, Weston B. Kowert, and Michael Cotton), Texas Law School (Dean Ward Farnsworth, Ms. Trish Do, and Mr. Thor Quick), and all the generous supporting law firms and sponsors as well as the co-publishing journals that agreed to grant copyright permission. Thanks also to Prof. Lois Lupica as well as Polly and Joel Westbrook.

And then, of course, there's Jay.

Sponsors

In addition to the primary hosts, *JayFest* was made possible financially thanks to the following:

Akin Gump Strauss Hauer & Feld LLP; AlixPartners, LLP; Alvarez & Marsal Holdings, LLC; Andrews Kurth Kenyon LLP; Baker Botts L.L.P.; Baker Hostetler LLP; BMC Group, Inc.; Bracewell LLP; Bridgepoint Consulting; Byrnie Bass; Cavazos, Hendricks, Poirot & Smitham, P.C.; Conway MacKenzie, Inc.; CR3 Partners LLC; Deloitte CRG; Dykema Cox Smith; Fears Nachawati; FTI Consulting, Inc.; Gardere Wynne Sewell LLP; Gray Reed & McGraw LLP; Harney Management Partners, LLC; Haynes & Boone, LLP; Hughes Watters Askanase, LLP; Husch Blackwell LLP; Jackson Walker L.L.P.; Jones Day; Jordan, Hyden, Womble, Culbreth & Holzer, P.C.; Kelly Hart & Hallman LLP; Kirkland & Ellis LLP; KPMG LLP; Lain, Faulkner & Co., P.C.; Latham & Watkins LLP; Law Office of Judith W. Ross; Locke Lord LLP; Mackinac Partners LLC; McGuire, Craddock & Strother, P.C.; McKool Smith; Munsch Hardt Kopf & Harr, P.C.; Neligan, LLP; Norton Rose Fulbright U.S. LLP; Okin Adams LLP; Pillsbury Winthrop Shaw Pittman LLP; Porter Hedges LLP; Pulman Cappuccio Pullen Benson & Jones, LLP; Rochelle McCullough, LLP; Ropes & Gray LLP; Simpson Thacher & Bartlett LLP; Strasburger & Price, LLP; Streusand, Landon, Ozburn & Lemmon, LLP; Thompson & Knight LLP; Tittle Advisory Group; Underwood Law Firm, P.C.; Vinson & Elkins LLP; Weil, Gotshal & Manges LLP; and Winstead PC.

PREFACE

Many chapters in this Festschrift have been written by III members in connection with the conference "Bankruptcy's Universal Pragmatist," which was held at the University of Texas School of Law in Austin, in February 2018, to honor Professor Jay Lawrence Westbrook's seventy-fifth birthday.

Jay Westbrook is perhaps the most renowned U.S. academic in the field of cross-border insolvency, as well as a leader in the related fields of corporate and consumer insolvency law. While analytically sophisticated, Jay has resisted the fad of economic analysis of law and remained a pragmatic, empirically based realist. His work has always been anchored in a desire to understand how the law actually works in the real world, and III is proud to sponsor this Festschrift.

The conference was attended by a who's who of insolvency experienced judges, academics, and practitioners with many travelling from overseas to honour Jay.

The chapters and the Festschrift represent a fitting tribute to Jay's impressive contribution to our field. The III is proud to have Jay as a member, he was made a III Outstanding Contribution Honouree in 2014.

Alan Bloom
International Insolvency Institute, President 2017–2019

CONTENTS

EDITORS'
INTRODUCTION

The idea behind a Festschrift is to honor a leading scholar whose outstanding contributions to a particular field of scholarship warrant—perhaps require—colleagues to join forces to pay their respect, homage, and obeisance to the honoree. By means of such a book in honor of that person, the contributors bow their heads, as it were, to acknowledge this person's eminent importance. It is hard to find anyone in the field of both national and international insolvency law who would fulfill these extremely high standards better than or even as good as Jay Westbrook does.

The breadth of topics in this Festschrift reflects to a good extent the enormous range of Jay's writings and interests. Throughout this all, as the Foreword by Elizabeth Warren makes clear, Jay has been willing to buck trends and avoid fads. For example, with his contributions about the fragile middle class, he has set completely new standards in scholarly work by incorporating facts and numbers from real-life cases. Terry Sullivan's Prologue recounts the early days of how cumbersome this data collection process was (portable copier machines and all), and Bob Lawless and Angie Littwin show how with just a few technological advances since then, consumer bankruptcy research is alive and well, still able to provide fresh insights on local legal culture. Adding to this pragmatism is Jay's emphasis on the requirement to look at others around the world to see how distant friends wrestle with the same problems. Building on Jay's work,

Steph Ben-Ishai shows how they do that near to the United States, explaining how Canada struggles with "non-banks" that seek to weasel around consumer protection regulations, while Jason Kilborn shows how they do it afar, looking at how the preoccupation with the moral hazard pendulum may be swinging differently in Eastern Europe and Russia than at home. Offering a rich sociological and institutional analysis, Iain Ramsay analyzes today's low-asset procedures in the United Kingdom that promised to provide cheap and nimble debt relief but may prove to offer nothing of the sort, whereas Emily Kadens goes backward in time to look at the persistence of fraud and concomitant skepticism one ought to have for the power of reputational discipline to rein in the "cunning and crafty."

With his work on corporate reorganization, Jay has brought needed focus on the levers and mechanisms of control that matter as much if not more than the content of any statute's text. Grappling with a recent issue close to Jay's heart, four colleagues take a hard look at systemically important financial institution (SIFI) resolution: Stephen Lubben sets the frame by providing a functional analysis and argues that it all boils down to special priorities, which may be poorly suited for the corporate bankruptcy paradigm; Ted Janger goes further and points out that the special treatment of financial contracts not only makes no sense but reverse-poisons the general insolvency regime; while Adam Levitin cheerfully notes that the inherently political nature of bailouts makes the allure of orderly, legalistic bankruptcy court resolution a pipe dream. Striking a friendly contrarian chord, David Skeel suggests that bankruptcy for banks can synthesize the baby's bathwater, not throw it out, by beefing up a role for regulators within the process.

Not everyone in the corporate realm inspired by Jay wants to talk about SIFIs, though, and so Jonathan Lipson looks at the "procedural concoction" of the U.S. Supreme Court *Jevic* case and, channeling Jay, argues it's not so much about priority as is commonly perceived but really about process and control. Henry Hu builds on earlier work (some with Jay) to examine the role—and absence—of disclosure for financially troubled non-bankrupt companies and the additional information asymmetries exacerbated by debt decoupling. Finally, John Pottow pays homage to Jay by trying to drive the final nail in the coffin on the executoriness doctrine by showing how the underlying opportunistic shenanigans can be brought to a halt by creative bankruptcy judges using the tools they already have in the Code.

Perhaps most significantly, with his writings about cross-border insolvency law, Jay has influenced entire generations of scholars in this field literally all over the globe. "Modified universalism" is a now-standard concept worldwide, and it is to Jay's credit not just that he coined the term but that he gave content to the idea in as "Jay" a way as possible: articulating an aspirational norm—but tempering it by pragmatic concession to the realities of the day. He is truly bankruptcy's universal pragmatist.

The late (and beloved) Ian Fletcher offers as his final scholarly contribution a moving tribute to Jay and then a characteristically "Ian" discussion of the rise of cross-border cooperation in England. He provides historical background to lay the context for how modified universalism came to take hold (and may be threatened) there. It is vintage Ian: thorough, painstaking, insightful, and full of little Ian-isms ("1978 and all that" in discussion of the U.S. insolvency record). It makes us miss him.

Following Ian, perhaps as an appropriate mentee, Irit Mevorach sketches out in convincing detail how modified universalism might be incorporated into customary international law. And Lennie (as he will let us call him) Hoffmann gives his own view on how this salutary concept has worked its way into English law, but may be under threat from the storm winds of the day. We made his remarks in the Epilogue not to end on a bummer note, but to underscore how quickly the weather can change in this dizzying-paced field and how much more work still needs to be done.

Shifting to the comparative, Luis Méjan discusses the triggering mechanisms for initiating insolvency proceedings, unpacking the roles of insolvency and imminence by canvassing many approaches from around the world. Chuck Mooney offers some "hot off the presses" insights from his Japanese Business Credit Project and finds that the interaction of secured credit law and insolvency law (as "credit enhancements" in his preferred parlance) may be much more regime-dependent than previously thought and require more work to understand. He thinks that work, and the work of international reform projects, is good work that needs to be done. Susan Block-Lieb's work segues nicely from this, where she looks at the role of soft law in international commercial law, teasing out the role of private (political) actors in the development of that soft law as well as the non-binary nature of soft law itself. This in turn segues into Ros Mason's focus on private international law (choice of law, for some) in international insolvency, an analysis that sagely anticipates where The United Nations Commission on International Trade Law (UNCITRAL) will likely next turn its efforts for Working Group V. Finally, Christoph G. Paulus gives us a sort of summing up of Platonic insolvency (fair weather), but then quickly returns to the real world of bad-weather insolvency regimes, with its combined patchwork of ad hoc solutions. Christoph struggles with what to do in a world of imperfect debtor-in-possession (DIP) financing, nationalization, weak legal institutions, and macro-economic crisis. And he does so with characteristic balance of the ideal and the pragmatic that would make Jay proud (at least so says John). All these authors acknowledge Jay's role in their work, and Christoph and John present their offerings in strictly egalitarian alphabetical order.

A Festschrift book is of course about writing. But it is not only his writing that makes Jay the outstanding scholar that he is. It is, additionally, his personality, his charm, and his empathy. Innumerable academics (including both the editors of this book) and practitioners owe their careers in no small part to encouragement from Jay. By writing a letter, by inviting to a presentation in Austin, by discussing on occasion at whichever conference Jay joins his two cents, Jay has spotted so many young professionals who have embraced his attention as an accolade from the master. He has, in his characteristically genteel but unrelentingly rigorous way, always offered a friendly hand to move people along in the scholarly pursuit of one thing:

what commercial law actually is and how it does and should actually work to help real people with real problems.

Jay's scholarship, teaching prowess, and mentorship are hard to match anywhere in our field. But ultimately what stands as the strongest testament to the man is the professional, and importantly, intertwined personal relationships he has made with so many around the world. Who has not had the pleasure of an animated conversation with Jay about the latest ridiculous opinion out of some court on the role of intellectual property rights in insolvency, or about how to conceive ideally the role of an automatic stay? But who also has not had that conversation over the course of a cool beer, a full-bodied glass of wine, or a wonderful but always-too-short meal?

We hope you enjoy reading these excellent scholarly contributions as much as we did editing and as much, we hope, as the authors did writing them—thinking of Jay's twinkling eye all along.

Christoph & John

PROLOGUE

Remarks of President Sullivan[*]

I have known Jay Westbrook since 1981. That was a long time ago. In 1981, Ronald Reagan was President. In 1981, Walter Cronkite was hosting the CBS Evening News. In 1981, Olivia Newton John was at the top of the pop charts. In 1981, the average sale price of a new home was $80,000, and a gallon of gas cost $1.30.

Having known Jay for nearly 40 years, I've learned a lot about him—as a scholar, as a colleague, and as a human being. There is one thing I've learned for certain: When duty calls, Jay Westbrook answers.

Jay's strong sense of duty has taken several forms over the years, both personal and professional. At least once, his sense of duty included actual military duty. In 1968, Jay was serving in the Texas National Guard when riots broke out in Washington, DC, following the assassination of Dr. Martin Luther King, Jr. The Texas Guard was called to Washington to help with peacekeeping, and Jay, called to serve, fulfilled his duty on the streets of the nation's capital.

Sometimes, Jay's sense of duty has led him to make noble—but, perhaps, impractical—decisions. On the day before he was supposed to get married, Jay broke his back in an accident. And he *still got married* the next day. For some men, the prospect of walking down the

* Teresa A. Sullivan, President Emerita and University Professor, University of Virginia. Adapted from remarks delivered on Feb. 2, 2018, six months before President Sullivan assumed *Emerita* status.

marriage aisle requires a stiff spine and a strong drink. Not Jay; he did it with a broken back.

Jay's sense of duty extends to his friendships—and even his involvement in the families of his friends. Jay is the godfather of my second son, and his wife Polly is the godmother. They have taken their godparent status seriously over the years. When my son was undergoing brain surgery in Dallas in 1997, Jay and Polly visited us in the hospital. Instead of flowers and get-well cards, they brought us hamburgers and Scotch. I'm fairly certain that bringing hamburgers and Scotch into the hospital broke several hospital rules. But Jay's duty as godfather called, and—hospital rules be damned—Jay was going to answer that call.

Jay's sense of duty extends to his role as a teacher and mentor. As a member of the Texas faculty since 1980, he has devoted endless amounts of time to working with his students, both inside and outside the classroom. He has helped many of his students find career positions around the country, after they graduated.

Jay's sense of duty includes a strong sense of honor. As an undergraduate student at UT-Austin, Jay left the Plan II Honors Program because he faced a situation involving what he believed to be a clear case of right and wrong, and he chose to stand up for what he believed to be right.

Many years ago, Jay felt a call of duty to understand and address the complex problems related to consumer bankruptcy, and he's been answering that call ever since—through his distinguished research and scholarship. As most of you know, Jay is a spectacular scholar, and in the annals of American bankruptcy law, he will stand forever as an influential and seminal figure.

It is my great fortune that Jay's interest in bankruptcy brought us together almost four decades ago, and our shared interest in that topic—together with our colleague Elizabeth Warren—became the seed of a remarkably productive research and writing partnership.

In 1984, Congress passed the Bankruptcy Amendments and Federal Judgeship Act to change the laws that regulated the American bankruptcy system. Around the time the amendments were taking effect, Jay, Elizabeth, and I were having lunch and, because the new regulations were somewhat confusing, we asked the question, "How could anyone ever know exactly what is true about bankruptcy?" To try to answer that question, we went to the federal courthouse in San Antonio and began pulling random samples of bankruptcy cases. This initial work led to a proposal for us to do this exercise across the country, to see how bankruptcy was affected by the exemptions that differ from state to state.

This was the mid-1980s. We had no digital recording devices, no Internet, no e-mail. We had to record all data by hand. It was important for us to go to every courthouse in every district. And when we went traveling around the country, we had to bring our own photocopier with us. In fact, every time we traveled by air, we had to buy a plane ticket for our photocopier so it could have its own seat on the plane.

We expected to find differences among the districts and among the states, and what we found was that the variations could often be traced to the behaviors and decisions of individual judges. These and other findings led us to write our first book *As We Forgive Our Debtors: Bankruptcy and Consumer Credit in America*.

We learned some useful lessons during our research, and occasionally we came away with different views of what we saw. For example, when we were reviewing a new report on consumer bankruptcy from another university, Elizabeth and Jay tended to skip over the tables and read only the text. I, on the other hand, tended to read the tables and skip the text. The three of us disagreed about the findings of this report. Eventually we discovered that we had come away with different conclusions because the information in the text and the data in the tables contradicted each other. There's a lesson there for the young scholars in the room: always look for the integration of the text and the tables.

Another thing we learned during our work together is that Jay Westbrook has a great sense of humor. When Jay, Elizabeth, and

I were drafting the chapters of our first book, my husband Doug reviewed the drafts and said, "I can really see Jay's influence in this writing. . . . Because there's *actual humor!*"

It's traditional to hold a Festschrift for a scholar in the year that he or she turns 75 years old. Jay reached that milestone in December 2018. Jay was in good company as he turned seventy five. Former National Football League quarterback Joe Namath also turned seventy five that year, as did politicians Newt Gingrich and John Kerry. So did the Watergate journalist Bob Woodward, and so did the pop singer Fabian.

Jay might be *most* amused to know that he and Keith Richards, the guitarist for the Rolling Stones with the famously licentious lifestyle, were born in the same year, which leads me to wonder about two questions: First, how in the world did Keith Richards survive long enough to make it to 75 years old? And second has anyone yet had a Festschrift for Keith Richards?

Jay: Congratulations on an extraordinary record of accomplishment over the course of your exemplary career. For nearly four decades, you have shined a bright light on the dark corners of bankruptcy law. And in the process you've distinguished yourself as the preeminent scholar in the field.

Thank you for your partnership and collegiality, and, more important, thank you for your personal friendship for so many years.

Consumer Protection Issues and "Non-Banks"
A Comparative Analysis
Stephanie Ben-Ishai[*]

I. Introduction

Non-bank financial institutions fill a big gap for millennials and others without a long and consistent credit history and confidence in capital markets. However, as will be shown in this chapter, non-bank financial institutions conduct business in Canada with far less oversight relative to their bank counterparts as a result of sweeping and loosely worded regulation. Various triggers, including the crisis at Home Capital, have reignited discussion about financial institutions and the regulations that govern them. Nearly a decade after the financial crisis, both Canadian and American regulatory responses to banks and non-bank financial institutions have had different effects—including on consumers.

This chapter argues that more work on the Canadian regulatory framework for Canadian non-bank financial institutions is necessary, including from a consumer protection perspective. It suggests that the post-2008 American regulatory approach offers a good model to

---

[*] Professor of Law and York University Distinguished Research Professor, Osgoode Hall Law School. Copyright © 54 Tex. Int'l. L. J. 327 (2019). Reproduced with permission.

ensure that Canadian non-bank financial institutions are more heavily scrutinized, and thus, ultimately Canadian consumers are better protected. The purpose of regulation for financial institutions after the financial crisis will be explored first. Then, Canada's financial regulatory institutions, including those with a mandate for consumer protection, will be explored, using recent incidents at Home Capital and Wells Fargo as illustrative examples. To distill key differences that Canada's regulatory agencies can implement, the Financial Consumer Agency of Canada (FCAC) will be compared with its American counterpart, the Consumer Financial Protection Bureau (CFPB).

II. 2008 Financial Crisis Response

A. Historical Underpinnings

Canada was the only country among the G8 to escape the financial crisis without a government bailout.[1] According to the World Economic Forum, Canadian banks were named the safest in the world.[2] Canada's ability to withstand economic ruin is rooted in tolerance for industry connection, state involvement, and differing routes of financial system development. Canada's financial resilience is partially explained through its history. Canada has not experienced a single bank failure; however, there were forty three non-bank financial institution failures from 1970 until present.[3] The removal of interest rate controls in 1967, and corresponding ability to adjust interest rates during inflationary periods, may be a contributing factor.[4] This earlier

---

[1] See Christopher C Nicholls, "The Regulation of Financial Institutions: A Reflective but Selective Retrospective" (2011) 50 Can Bus LJ 129 at 129.

[2] *Ibid.* at 129; Donald JS Brean, Lawrence Kryzanowski & Gordon S Roberts, "Canada and the United States: Different Roots, Different Routes to Financial Sector Regulation" (2011) 53:2 Bus History 249 at 251.

[3] Brean, Kryzanowski & Roberts, supra note 2 at 251; Canada Deposit Insurance Corporation, "History of Member Institutions Failing," online: <www.cdic.ca/en/about-cdic/resolution/Pages/history.aspx> [Institutions Failing].

[4] Brean, Kryzanowski & Roberts, *ibid.* at 265.

change may have led to a smaller shadow banking sector, and relatively lower exposures to highly structured, synthetic investments.[5] Fewer numbers of large banks enabled stability, which allowed higher equity returns with lower-risk funding practices while holding greater equity in Canada.[6]

B. Structure

The most significant differences between Canada and the United States during the financial crisis were their institutional structure of financial systems and the modes of financial sector regulation.[7] Five major banks predominantly dictate regulatory trends as a result of financial and political clout.[8] By contrast, the American "dual banking system" separated national and state banks, thus facilitating a clear demarcation ripe for intensified regulation.[9] Inherently, American regulation is rules-based and prescription-oriented.

In contrast, Canadian regulation is "principle-based" where financial institutions must meet both "intent and what is explicitly prescribed in legislation."[10] This approach suggests a more favorable environment for banks specifically as there is freedom for innovative responses to issues it faces. However, this approach may prove to be detrimental to non-banks as a function of the imbalanced, relative financial resources.[11] When facing instances of loan losses, banks possess the capital to navigate around this hurdles, while some non-bank institutions do not. The lack of guidance from the Canadian regulator may further exacerbate the financial hardships non-banks may face as this direction is what these institutions require.

---

[5] *Ibid.* at 266.

[6] *Ibid.* at 264.

[7] *Ibid.* at 260.

[8] The five major banks are the Bank of Montreal (BMO), the Bank of Nova Scotia (Scotiabank), Canadian Imperial Bank of Commerce (CBIC), the Royal Bank of Canada (RBC), and the Toronto-Dominion Bank (TD Bank).

[9] Brean, Kryzanowski & Roberts, supra note 2 at 261.

[10] *Ibid.*

[11] *Ibid.* at 265.

III. Who Regulates Non-Bank Financial Institutions?

Banking falls under the purview of the "Office of the Superintendent of Financial Institutions" (OSFI), but non-banking financial institutions can easily fall through the "regulatory cracks."[12] In addition to 87 banks, the OSFI regulates 44 trust companies, 18 loan companies, 68 life insurance companies, 13 fraternal benefit societies, and 155 property and casualty insurance companies.[13] A case study on Home Capital better situates the issue of non-bank financial institution regulation.

Home Capital is a publicly traded company which acts through its principal subsidiary, Home Trust Company, to offer mortgage lending, deposits, and credit cards.[14] Targeting the population who have been turned away from traditional banks for reasons such as poor credit history or self-employment, Home Trust offers uninsured mortgages which accounts for roughly 90% of its business.[15] Home Trust is a federally regulated trust company, and as such, is a non-bank financial institution that falls under the purview of the OSFI. As one of Canada's largest alternative mortgage lenders, Home Capital assumes only a small piece (approximately CAD twenty billion in mortgages) of the overall mortgage market, worth approximately CAD 1.1 trillion.[16]

[12.] See John Pazios & Matthew Underwood, "Musical Chairs: Who's Left Standing When the ABCP Music Stops?" (2009) 9 Asper Rev Intl Bus Trade L 65 at 75.

[13.] For a detailed list of these companies, see Office of the Superintendent of Financial Institutions Canada, "Who We Regulate," online: <www.osfi-bsif.gc.ca/Eng/wt-ow/Pages/wwr-er.aspx>.

[14.] See Armina Ligaya, "What Exactly Is Home Capital and Why Is It so Important to the Mortgage Industry?," The Financial Post (Apr. 27, 2017), online: <www.business.financialpost.com/news/fp-street/what-exactly-is-home-capital-and-why-is-it-so-important-to-the-mortgage-industry/wcm/8f536a80-78bb-4e36-8cff-91f1801145a7>.

[15.] Ibid.

[16.] Ibid.

When Home Capital announced the need for a $2 billion loan facility to aid in offsetting the CAD 600 million drop in high interest savings account deposits, the stock value dropped as much as 64.9% to $6.[17] Home Trust relies on deposits to help fund the company's mortgage lending. The drop in deposits directly impacted lending abilities, thus damaging investor confidence in the company's viability. Deposits started to dwindle back in 2015 when the Ontario Securities Commission accused the company and its officials of misleading shareholders as a result of broker frauds, which culminated in cutting ties with 45 brokers.[18] These brokers were found to be submitting altered and fictitious mortgage applications highlighting the emphasis on short-term thinking and a blindness to risk.[19] Despite this event occurring two years ago, its remnants have created an air of uncertainty for Home Capital. The OSFI announced that it was monitoring the situation and that it may move quickly to protect the alternative mortgage market confidence; however, the actions taken by OSFI remain unclear and ultimately a private action appears to have restored market confidence in the short term.[20] Ultimately, the lack of specific focus in the existing regulatory structure on non-bank financial institutions

---

[17] *Ibid.* For more information on how Home Capital ultimately received a $1 billion loan, see Janet McFarland et al., "Mayday at Home Capital," Globe and Mail (May 19, 2017), online: <www.theglobeandmail.com/report-on-business/home-capital-saga-real-estate/article34972594/>.

[18] Ligaya, supra note 14; Barbara Schecter, "The Home Capital Saga: A Timeline of Key Events and Allegations," The Financial Post (May 5, 2017), online: <www.business.financialpost.com/news/fp-street/the-home-capital-saga-a-timeline-of-key-events-and-allegations/wcm/fc4fc934-c114-45be-bbfe-b6d440f701a0>.

[19] See Lal Bakaran, "Home Capital Saga Highlights the Need for Strong Internal Auditing," The Globe and Mail (May 10, 2017), online: <www.theglobe andmail.com/report-on-business/rob-commentary/home-capital-saga-highlights-the-need-for-strong-internal-auditing/article34948959/>.

[20] *Ibid.*; Katia Dmitrieva, Kristine Owram & Doug Alexander, "Warren Buffett's Backing Boosts Home Capital Despite Investor Opposition," The Financial Post (June 29, 2017), online: <www.business.financialpost.com/news/fp-street/warren-buffetts-backing-boosts-home-capital-despite-investor-opposition>.

and confusion surrounding the role of the various regulators have negative implications for consumer protection.

IV. The Need for Effective Regulation

A combination of Canada's "principle-based" system and the U.S. "rules-/prescription-based" system may offer some guidance into the next step for an effective regulator. A mixed principle-and-rules approach has the advantage of enabling the regulator to possess a wider scope for action in face of innovation designed to avoid regulation.[21] This is currently in place in the United Kingdom and Australia.[22] This hybrid system does not necessarily equate to success, considering that the British banks still failed during the 2008 financial crisis, but it does offer a logical development of regulation which encompasses the innovative practices of financial institutions and better accounts for consumer protection concerns.[23]

An opaque and insulated regulator, like the OSFI, is beneficial as it can regulate unfettered by partisan politics, bank collusion, or rent-seeking.[24] In 2011, Brean, Kryzanowski, and Roberts suggest that this insulation, or lack of transparency, may be the best alternative.[25] This opacity goes against the generally held views about the benefits of transparency in regulating bodies.[26] While understanding that the OSFI operates in a "black box," its response and intervention process must be examined in more detail to truly identify the adverse ramifications for non-banks.

---

[21] Brean, Kryzanowski & Roberts, supra note 2 at 264.

[22] Ibid.; Fiona Haines, "Regulatory Failures and Regulatory Solutions: A Characteristic Analysis of the Aftermath of Disaster" (2009) 34:1 Law & Soc Inquiry 31 at 45; Deborah Healey & Rob Nicolls, "Should Stability Reign? The Consumer Downside of Foregone Competition in Retail Banking Markets" (2016) 32 BFLR 69.

[23] Brean, Kryzanowski & Roberts, supra note 2 at 264.

[24] See Anita Anand & Andrew Green, "Regulating Financial Institutions: The Value of Opacity" (2012) 57:3 McGill LJ 399 at 399.

[25] Ibid. at 404.

[26] Ibid.

V. The Office of the Superintendent of Financial Institutions

The OSFI is vital for federally regulated financial institutions (FRFIs) oversight by supervising deposit-taking institutions and conducting risk-based assessments of safety and soundness.[27] If material deficiencies are discovered, the agency can require necessary corrective measures.[28] Advanced regulatory frameworks must promote adoption of policies and procedures to manage risk while evaluating system-wide or sectoral issues that may negatively impact institutions.[29]

Structurally, the Minister of Finance "presides" over and is "responsible" for the OSFI, but practically, the Superintendent of Financial Institutions possesses the decision-making authority for this body.[30] The OSFI Act defers to the agency to create its own policy, considering factors such as risk management, interpretation of different requirements, and guidelines/rulings on certain matters.[31] It is neither the OSFI's role to regulate capital markets nor to advise investors on how to invest; instead, it is to "purely seek to ensure the safety and soundness of financial institutions that make promises to pay depositors and policyholders."[32] While formed to specifically address the oversight of regulations, the primary action that the OSFI undertakes is strictly bound to federally regulated deposit-taking institutions. That is to say, non-banking financial institutions, which are largely smaller in size than the Big Five banks, are treated with the same regulation, and thus decrease the OSFI's effectiveness for oversight.

---

[27] See Office of the Superintendent of Financial Institutions Canada, "Guide to Intervention for Federally Regulated Deposit-Taking Institutions," online: <www.osfi-bsif.gc.ca/Eng/Docs/Guide_Int.pdf> at 1 [Guide to Intervention].

[28] Anand & Green, supra note 24 at 403.

[29] Ibid.

[30] Ibid. at 419; Office of the Superintendent of Financial Institutions Act, RSC 1985, c 18 (3rd Supp), Part I, ss 3, 4(1).

[31] Anand & Green, supra note 24 at 420.

[32] Pozios & Underwood, supra note 12 at 85.

The potential collapse of federally regulated deposit-taking institutions triggers the OSFI intervention process, which considers the unique circumstances of financial institutions, including nature, scope, complexity, and risk profile.[33] If there are no significant problems with an organization, then the OSFI's responsibilities include assessing the financial condition and the operational performance of a financial institution.[34] For more severe cases, the OSFI has four different classification stages with varied oversight requirements, ranging from working with external auditors and the bank's management, to assuming temporary control of the assets and applying to the Attorney General for a windup order for the institution.[35]

The prescriptive language of the new OSFI guidelines is as burdensome on smaller institutions as they are on large ones, despite the OSFI's insistence that the new guidelines are not a "one size fits all."[36] The OSFI intervention process is specific to the economic climate and the pressures associated with maintaining a healthy economy; however, ramifications for consumers are not addressed by OSFI when federally regulated deposit-taking institutions fail. Clearly, there is still plenty of regulatory change required to address the specific needs of non-banking financial institutions.

VI. Canadian Deposit Insurance Company

The Canadian Deposit Insurance Company (CDIC) is tasked with ensuring the safety and soundness of deposits, including by requiring deposit-taking financial institutions participate in a reserve fund, of which banks must be contributing members, in the event

---

[33.] Guide to Intervention, supra note 27 at 1.

[34.] *Ibid.* at 3.

[35.] *Ibid.* at 5, 10; Office of the Superintendent of Financial Institutions Canada, "Supervisory Guide Applicable to Federally Regulated Insurance Companies (2015) at 5, online (pdf): <www.osfi-bsif.gc.ca/Eng/Docs/Insurance_guide.pdf>.

[36.] *Ibid.*

of collapse.[37] Consumer protection is not a specific consideration.[38] To be eligible for insurance, the deposit must be payable in Canada in Canadian currency and must be repayable no more than five years after the date of deposit.[39] Since its creation in 1967, the CDIC has handled forty three failures of member institutions.[40] Through monitoring and working with OSFI, the CDIC takes necessary action depending on the condition of member institutions.[41]

The CDIC has a variety of resolution tools available to it, with varying effects on consumer protection. The first is through the automatic reimbursement of funds for applicable deposits.[42] This tool is likely to be triggered only in the case of a small-to-medium-size bank.[43] If a bank fails and there is interest in its assets, the CDIC would assume control of the failing bank until its sale, merger, or restructuring could be completed.[44] Assuming control ensures that core banking operations continue and insured deposits are protected.[45] In situations where no private-sector solution exists for the failing institution, all or part of a bank's business is transferred

---

[37] See Canada Deposit Insurance Corporation Act, RSC 1985, c C-3; CDIC Overview, Canada Deposit Insurance Corporation, "An Overview of CDIC's History and Evolution" (2015) at 5, online (pdf): <www.cdic.ca/en/about-cdic/Documents/our-history.pdf>.

[38] *Ibid.*

[39] *Ibid.*

[40] Institutions Failing, supra note 3; Canada Deposit Insurance Corporation, "Resolution Tools," online: <www.cdic.ca/en/about-cdic/resolution/Pages/tools.aspx> [Resolution Tools]; Canada Deposit Insurance Corporation, "Protecting Your Deposits," online: <www.cdic.ca/financial-community/protecting-your-deposits/> [Protecting Your Deposits]. For a list of member institutions, see Canada Deposit Insurance Corporation, "List of Member Institutions," online: <www.cdic.ca/en/about-di/what-we-cover/Pages/list-members.aspx>; Robb Engen, "How CDIC Would Protect Your Deposits if Home Capital Goes Bankrupt" (May 8, 2017), online (blog): Boomer & Echo <www.boomerandecho.com/cdic-protect-deposits-home-capital-goes-bankrupt/>; Protecting Your Deposits, supra note 40 at 2.

[41] Guide to Intervention, supra note 27 at 1.

[42] Resolution Tools, supra note 40; Engen, supra note 40.

[43] *Ibid.*

[44] *Ibid.*

[45] *Ibid.*

to another bank, which is temporarily owned by the CDIC.[46] Once stable, the bridge bank would be sold to the private-sector buyer.[47] This option is similar to a forced sale in that the transfer would ensure that critical banking operations continue. The CDIC may also provide the member institution with loans, guarantees, deposits, or loss-sharing agreements in the event of an imminent collapse.[48] This process is generally completed on a stand-alone basis to assist in a private transaction. More flexible of the array of resolution tools, financial assistance may be employed concurrent to any of the other resolution tools.[49] Finally, authorities may trigger a bail-in framework, where long-term debt is converted to common shares while the institution remains operational, protecting taxpayers and depositors.[50] The bail-in process is the opposite of a bailout framework, which uses the taxpayers' money to save the failing institution.

VII. Financial Consumer Agency of Canada

A. Current Framework

The FCAC was designed to supervise financial institutions with a consumer protection lens, particularly in the financial services.[51] The agency is tasked with ensuring that entities are in compliance with legislative obligations, voluntary codes of conduct, and public commitments. It also conducts research, field-testing, and stakeholder engagement opportunities to provide information on

---

[46.] *Ibid.*

[47.] *Ibid.*

[48.] *Ibid.*

[49.] *Ibid.*

[50.] *Ibid.*; Ellen Roseman, "Most Canadians' Deposits Not at Risk if Bank Fails—But Check CDIC Protection," The Toronto Star (April 7, 2013), online: <www.thestar.com/business/personal_finance/2013/04/07/most_canadians_deposits_not_at_risk_if_bank_fails_but_check_cdic_protection_roseman.html>.

[51.] Guide to Intervention, *supra* note 27.

financial trends and emerging issues to the government.[52] For consumers directly, the FCAC promotes financial literacy.[53] The FCAC is led by a Commissioner who reports annually to Parliament through the Minister of Finance.[54]

The FCAC also has powers to receive and investigate complaints made about financial institutions.[55] In 2015–2016, 708 compliance issues were investigated.[56] Compliance issues with financial institutions are intended to be exposed with consumer complaints.[57] Banks are required to establish procedures to redress complaints made by customers with respect to fees, disclosure of information, and calculation for the cost of borrowing.[58] Complaint procedures must be readily available to customers and must include information on the process for the customer to access the FCAC.[59]

While legislation prescribes complaint systems to be easily accessible to consumers, the current Canadian framework does not allow for this. An outdated, convoluted website increases difficulty for consumers to find information about the complaint system to file documentation.[60] Further, the FCAC suggests first escalating the complaint within internal branches prior to filing a complaint, thus ultimately reducing the overall number of complaints to situations

---

[52.] See Financial Consumer Agency of Canada, "FCAC History," online: <www.canada.ca/en/financial-consumer-agency/corporate/history.html>.

[53.] *Ibid.*

[54.] See Financial Consumer Agency of Canada, "Supervision Framework" (2018) at 1, online (pdf): <www.canada.ca/content/dam/fcac-acfc/documents/services/industry/supervision-framework.pdf> [Supervision Framework].

[55.] See Anthony Duggan, Jacob S Ziegel & Jassmin Girgis, "Financial-Consumer Complaint Agencies" (2013) 54 Can Bus LJ 68; Financial Consumer Agency of Canada Act, SC 2001, c 9, s 121 [FCAC Act].

[56.] See Financial Consumer Agency of Canada, "Building for the Future: Annual Report 2015–2016" (2016) at 11, online (pdf) <www.canada.ca/content/dam/fcac-acfc/documents/corporate/planning/annual-reports/FCAC-annual-report-2015-16.pdf>.

[57.] See Jacqueline J Williams, "Canadian Financial Services Ombudsmen: The Role of Reputational Persuasion" (2005) 20:3 BFLR 41 at 44.

[58.] See Bank of Canada Act, RSC 1985, c B-2, s 455.

[59.] Williams, supra note 57 at 44; *Ibid.* s 456.

[60.] See Financial Consumer Agency of Canada, "FCAC Website," online: <www.canada.ca/en/financial-consumer-agency.html>.

of genuine concern.[61] However, while complaints that ultimately get filed with the FCAC may be of actual non-compliance, the current framework dissuades consumers from elevating it to the agency because of the seemingly overly-bureaucratic process.[62]

Redress for complaints must be incorporated into the corporate cultures of financial institutions through the "drip-down effect."[63] After an initial complaint to the financial institution, if the individual is dissatisfied, the next stage would be to speak to an individual more senior in the bank or an internal ombudsman. The internal ombudsman is an impartial body located within the bank whose responsibility is to report to the FCAC and investigate consumer complaints regarding process and bank misbehavior.[64] The issue lies in directing consumers to this impartial agent—the ombudsman—as a means for resolution and raises concerns of the differences in role between FCAC and an ombudsman.

The compliance role of the FCAC is contrasted with the appeal and redress role of an ombudsman. Regulators enforce requirements and utilize their own guidelines.[65] Regulators do not have the power to provide redress to customers of the institutions they regulate.[66] An ombudsman serves as a mediator between parties to bring about a mutually agreeable resolution. Based on the fairness of the circumstances, non-binding recommendations are provided; however, institutions generally abide by the recommendation due to their influence.[67]

Instead of merely monitoring consumer protection provisions to ensure compliance, the FCAC has the ability to compel banks to provide information to verify compliance.[68] While the limits

---

[61.] Williams, supra note 57 at 45.

[62.] *Ibid.*

[63.] *Ibid.*

[64.] *Ibid.* at 42.

[65.] *Ibid.*

[66.] *Ibid.* at 47.

[67.] *Ibid.*

[68.] *Ibid.* at 48.

to this are hazy, it raises the question of FCAC being more than a mere compliance-affiliated regulatory body. It is clear that while the FCAC has been granted a wide array of powers, it is not in the position to address the issues.[69] Consequently, while it has powers of an ombudsman to demand confidential information, it cannot act on this intelligence, thus addressing the issue of efficacy.

B. Shift to Supervisory Framework

The compliance framework became more supervisory in 2017, illustrating the FCAC's vision for more robust oversight.[70] Changes in this new framework are not immediate, but instead, need to be phased in over time, such as market conduct breach prevention, regulated entities must proactively identify, address, and monitor risks, regular FCAC updates on risks and responses, and continuing improving of supervisory and enforcement processes to remain efficient.[71]

Two tiers of classification will be brought in based on the level of market conduct risk inherent in entities under the new framework. Under the first tier, the nature of product/services offered by the entity requires compliance with market conduct obligations, including FRFIs offering retail products and services.[72] Each tier one entity is assigned an FCAC Senior Officer as their liaison with the Agency.[73] Intensity of supervision correlates to the size of the entity and the complexity of its business model.[74] The second tier encompasses banks and trust companies that do not offer retail products or insurance companies that restrict their business to the sale of insurance.[75] These entities engage in business activities that result in minimal

---

[69.] *Ibid.* at 50.

[70.] Supervision Framework, supra note 54 at 3.

[71.] *Ibid.*

[72.] *Ibid.* at 4.

[73.] *Ibid.*

[74.] *Ibid.*

[75.] *Ibid.*

risk of breaching a federal market conduct obligation[76] and require significantly less intensive supervision and monitoring. Within the supervisory framework, three prongs drive the mandate: promoting responsible conduct, monitoring market conduct, and enforcing market conduct obligations.

Promoting responsible conduct primarily assumes the form of providing Notices of Violations and Notices of Decision (for breaches of legislation/regulation) upon violation of FCAC guidelines.[77] FCAC rulings are binding for a particular situation and serve as a precedent for all future matters with similar material facts, thus serving to promote responsible behavior.[78] The FCAC also meets with senior officials of regulated entities to share priorities, build trust, and promote responsible market conduct, including through Annual Industry Sessions, and other public consultations.[79] Promoting responsible conduct applies directly to non-bank financial entities as outlined prerogatives may be imposed on these institutions without their express consent.

Market conduct profiles are created for tier one entities wherein the FCAC gathers information about an institution's business model and maintains a risk profile.[80] An FCAC Senior Officer devises an annual supervision plan for each regulated entity while focusing on how the entity manages risk, planned growth and change, and compliance culture.[81] The new monitoring framework specifically targets non-bank entities and works with them to address financial issues strategically. Profiles are shared individually or in aggregate with FCAC senior management and used to determine priorities for subsequent years.[82] Third-party intelligence and industry reviews are also components of the monitoring aspect of the new supervisory

---

[76.] *Ibid.*

[77.] *Ibid.* at 6.

[78.] *Ibid.*

[79.] *Ibid.* at 7.

[80.] *Ibid.* at 8.

[81.] *Ibid.*

[82.] *Ibid*

framework.[83] Ultimately, third-party intelligence amounts to consumers and merchants participating in consultations or by filing complaints to the FCAC Consumer Services Centre while industry reviews assess emerging issues on a specific topic to identify trends for policy discussions.[84]

Enforcement comprises the third prong of the new supervisory framework and primarily relies on the use of investigations.[85] Preliminary investigations determine basic information like whether a potential breach falls within its supervisory authority, if there is a potential breach, and if it is isolated or systemic. Investigations result in a Notice of Breach or a Compliance Report (which results in a Notice of Violation) which sets out the facts, an assessment and recommendations for enforcement action.[86] Actions plans detail corrective measures to be required to address a breach if a Notice of Violation is issued. This notice may include an administrative monetary penalty (AMP).[87] Regulated entities can pay the AMP or make representations to the Commissioner within 30 days, or do nothing.[88] The AMP can be a maximum of $50,000 for natural person or $500,000 for all other persons, per violation.[89]

Ultimately, while the FCAC appears to satisfy all of the criteria of an effective regulator, and the 2017 amendments may have a positive impact on consumer protection concerns raised by both bank and non-bank entities, its true efficacy is revealed when compared to its American counterpart, the CFPB. Despite the FCAC being in force and regulating from 2001, the CFPB has arguably had more meaningful impact on consumers and financial institutions, while only operating for less than half as long as its Canadian counterpart.

[83.] *Ibid.*
[84.] *Ibid.* at 10.
[85.] *Ibid.* at 11.
[86.] *Ibid.*
[87.] *Ibid.* at 11.
[88.] FCAC Act, supra note 55, s 22(3).
[89.] *Ibid.*, 19(2).

VIII. Consumer Financial Protection Bureau

A. Role

The CFPB has a plethora of roles in terms of supervision and oversight. In addition to traditional regulatory roles, the bureau may monitor risks to consumers to prevent unfair, deceptive, or abusive acts associated with consumer financial series or products.[90] Primarily, however, its role is to supervise covered persons for compliance with federal consumer financial law and take appropriate enforcement action to address violations.[91]

The CFPB has defined persons in a way that captures virtually any entity (natural or unnatural) that "engages in offering of providing a consumer financial products or services."[92] The CFPB has rulemaking power under 18 enumerated consumer financial protection laws with varying levels of supervisory and enforcement power.[93] However, to implement a specific rule, the bureau must consult with federal banking regulators or other appropriate federal agencies prior to proposing a rule to confirm its consistency with those agencies and their objectives.[94] The bureau may also participate in the judicial process by commencing a civil action against those who violate federal consumer financial laws or filing amicus briefs in court proceedings.[95] More common, their role is to analyze consumer complaints and conduct private investigations into alleged violations. Monetary

---

[90.] *Ibid.* at 845.

[91.] See Laureen E Galeoto, Karen Y Bitar & Gil Rudolph, "The Consumer Financial Protection Bureau: The New Sheriff in Town" (2012) 129:8 Banking LJ 702 at 702.

[92.] See Dodd—Frank Wall Street Reform and Consumer Protection Act, Pub L 111–203, HR 4173, section 1002(6).

[93.] See "Administrative Law—Agency Design—Dodd–Frank Act Creates the Consumer Financial Protection Bureau—Dodd–Frank Act, Pub L no 111–203, 124 Stat 1376 (2010) (to be Codified in Scattered Sections of the U.S. Code)" (2011) Harv L Rev 124:8 2123 at 2125 [Anonymous].

[94.] *Ibid.* at 2126; Michael B Mierzewski et al., "The Dodd–Frank Act Establishes the Bureau of Consumer Financial Protection as the Primary Regulator of Consumer Financial Products and Services" (2010) 127:8 Banking LJ 722 at 728.

[95.] Mierzewski et al., supra note 94.

penalties for violations can reach up to $1 million per day for every day a party knowingly violated a federal consumer protection law.[96] The CFPB, like the FCAC, also has a mandate for consumer financial literacy. Unlike the FCAC however, it may reform contracts and impose restitution for damages, which affects both non-bank and bank financial institutions.[97]

The CFPB structure is different than that of a traditional independent agency in two ways. First, while independent agencies are insulated from the executive branch, they must still report to Congress. The CFPB is insulated from both the executive and legislative branches, thus making it drastically different from the FCAC, which may be biased politically.[98] Second, independent agencies feature a board with multiple members, but the CFPB possesses a single director, again keeping it further removed from the influence of the political biases.[99]

The CFPB regulates large banks, large credit unions and their affiliates, and non-bank entities that offer financial products.[100] Any "service provider" of the large banks or non-bank institutions that provide a "material service" falls under the regulatory purview of the CFPB.[101] A recent regulatory example is the fiasco with Wells Fargo.[102] Officials within CFPB found 800,000 people who had taken out car loans had been unnecessarily charged for auto insurance, to a cost of $73 million to wronged customers.[103] Successful regulatory

---

96. *Ibid.*

97. *Ibid.* at 734.

98. Anonymous, supra note 93.

99. *Ibid.*

100. See Mierzewski et al., supra note 94 at 724 for acts that fall under the purview of CFPB; 726 for a list of covered persons; at 727 for those excluded from the purview of CFPB.

101. Galetoto, Bitar & Rudolph, supra note 91.

102. *Ibid.*

103. See Gretchen Morgenson, "Wells Fargo Forced Unwanted Auto Insurance on Borrowers," *The New York Times* (July 27, 2017), online: <www.nytimes.com/2017/07/27/business/wells-fargo-unwanted-auto-insurance.html>.

enforcements, such as this one, depended in large part on an effective and easy mechanism for individuals to submit complaints.

B. Complaint Database

Unlike the Canadian institution, the American version does not recommend speaking with the institution and its internal hierarchy first when submitting a complaint. The first stage is to submit the complaint to an online form, which is extremely clear and accessible to the general public.[104] The complaint must address the type of problem being experienced, details of the occurrence, the company that the complaint is directed to, and the individuals involved.[105] Specific details, such as dates and amounts, are required along with any documents to support the exchange.

Unlike the FCAC, American consumers can follow the status of their complaint through an online portal that tracks progress.[106] The complaint is forwarded to the company, who reviews the complaint and communicates as needed and reports back about steps undertaken to rectify the issue.[107] Likely the most unique and pro-consumer stage in the complaint process is that the complaint is published on the Consumer Consent Database, and with consent, descriptions of the exchange are published after removing all personal information.[108] Complaints are publicly available after the company responds or after 15 days.[109] Also, 97% of complaints sent to companies receive timely responses.[110]

---

[104] See Consumer Financial Protection Bureau, "Consumer Complaint Database," online: <www.consumerfinance.gov/data-research/consumer-complaints/> [Complaint Database].

[105] See Consumer Financial Protection Bureau, "Submit a Complaint," online: <www.consumerfinance.gov/complaint/getting-started/>.

[106] See Consumer Financial Protection Bureau, "Learn How the Complaint Process Works," online: <www.consumerfinance.gov/complaint/process/>.

[107] *Ibid.*

[108] *Ibid.*

[109] Complaint Database, supra note 104.

[110] *Ibid.*

C. Shortcomings

Comparatively, it appears that the American CFPB is several steps ahead of its Canadian counterpart in terms of regulation and pro-consumer behavior, but there are several shortcomings to the American regulator as well. A common criticism is that this body reduces profit-making ability, and thus impacts the competitiveness of U.S. firms relative to their foreign counterparts.[111] While the individual institution is undoubtedly safer due to capital constraints, these constraints make for a more illiquid market overall. Banks must hold a higher percentage of their assets in cash, which consequently decreased the total amount they are able to hold in market securities.[112] The impact of this is that banks will not be able to play the market maker so prospective buyers will have more difficulty finding counteracting sellers.[113] In turn, prospective sellers will find it more difficult to find counteracting buyers.[114] This may affect Americans in the form of higher unemployment, lower wages, and slower increases in wealth and living standards.

The most common criticism of the CFPB is rooted in what some may consider its strength: independence. The only way for the Director of the bureau to be removed is by the President for cause.[115] "The Director enjoys significantly more unilateral power than any single member of any other independent agency . . . other than the President, the Director of the CFPB is the single most powerful official in the entire United States Government."[116] The Trump administration

---

[111] See Will Kenton, ed., "Dodd–Frank Wall Street Reform and Consumer Protection Act," (last updated: Feb. 18, 2019), online: Investopedia <www.investopedia.com/terms/d/dodd-frank-financial-regulatory-reform-bill.asp>.

[112] *Ibid.*

[113] *Ibid.*

[114] *Ibid.*

[115] See Gillian B White, "What Will Happen to the Consumer Financial Protection Bureau?, " The Atlantic (Oct. 11, 2016), online: <www.theatlantic.com/business/archive/2016/10/court-rules-consumer-financial-protection-bureaus-structure-is-unconstitutional/503660/>.

[116] *Ibid.*

is currently arguing before the Federal Appeals Court that the CFPB director should be made accountable to the President to ensure that the agency won't engage in extreme departures from executive policy.[117]

IX. Canada versus the United States

Ultimately, the CFPB has several advantages over the Canadian counterpart in terms of structure, policy, and process. When banks were "upselling" customer products in the United States, the fines were far more punitive. American regulatory actions are intended to serve as a message for the industry. The CFBB was set up in light of the 2008 economic crisis and in its five-year existence, it has recovered more than $11.8 billion dollars and handled 1.1 million complaints.[118] Their website makes it easy to submit complaints and includes a searchable public database with complaints and encourages whistleblowers. Undoubtedly, Wells Fargo is a bank, but had a non-bank entity partaken in similar conduct, the American system ensures that a similar fine would have been imposed.

In Canada, the FCAC is more obscure. In the recent TD Bank scandal, where agents were encouraged to upsell products to meet internal quotas, FCAC did not mimic CFPB's behavior.[119] The FCAC was aware of what the Big Five banks were doing and had only conducted

---

[117.] See Daniel Fischer, "Trump Administration Switches Sides, Argues CFPB Structure is Unconstitutional," Forbes (Mar. 17, 2017), online: <www.forbes.com/sites/danielfischer/2017/03/17/trump-administration-switches-sides-argues-cfpb-structure-is-unconstitutional/#446d94de3105>; Donna Borak, "House Republican: President Trump Fires CFPB Director Richard Cordray," CNN (Apr. 5, 2017), online: <www.money.cnn.com/2017/04/05/news/economy/cfbp-director-cordray-republicans/index.html>.

[118.] *Ibid.*

[119.] See Armina Ligaya, "Consumer Banking Watchdog to Review Consent Practices after Report of Aggressive Sales Tactics at TD," Financial Post (Mar. 15, 2017), online: <https://business.financialpost.com/news/fp-street/consumer-banking-watchdog-to-review-consent-practices-after-report-of-aggressive-sales-tactics-at-td>.

a special investigation after a delay.[120] In comparison, the CFPB pursued Wells Fargo promptly upon being notified of its misbehavior.[121] If found guilty in Canada, the fine could only go up to $500,000, not $500 million like in the U.S..[122] If the situation is especially serious, the FCAC may opt to name the institution publicly; however, in 16 years of existence, it has only named institutions twice and has only issued 27 fines.[123] Further, the FCAC has not carried out "mystery shopper" exercise since 2005 as they claim that there are "better ways to make sure the banks actually comply with the legislation";[124] however, it was mystery shopping that helped U.S. regulators identify allegations of discrimination that led to a $10.6 million settlement.[125]

X. Conclusion

The United States, while historically lagging in regulation capable of protecting consumers in a financial crisis, has recovered in a consumer-conscious fashion with empowered regulators. The Canadian system, effective in its regulation to prevent widespread financial ruin, places less emphasis on consumer protection and the increasing number of non-bank financial institutions. The difference in oversight focus for banking and non-bank financial entities is a prime example as to how consumers are placed in a vulnerable position, as seen in the case of Home Capital. The CFPB is several strides ahead of Canada in protecting the general population as seen with its emphasis on punitive retribution. The Canadian regulator must be in a mindset to encourage complaints and oversight with

---

[120.] *Ibid.*

[121.] See Jennifer Wells, "Can Our Financial Watchdog Actually Protect Us?, " The Toronto Star (Mar. 17, 2017), online: <www.thestar.com/business/2017/03/17/can-our-financial-watchdog-actually-protect-us.html>.

[122.] See Alan Freeman, "Canada's Financial Watchdog Is a Joke," iPolitics (Mar. 17, 2017), online: <www.ipolitics.ca/2017/03/17/canadas-bank-regulator-is-a-joke/>.

[123.] *Ibid.*

[124.] *Ibid.*

[125.] *Ibid.*

accessible, plain language systems, available processes to communicate, and additional funding to encourage autonomous, effective regulating. Innovative and transformative regulatory practices must be encouraged to flourish alongside innovative and transformative developments in increasing access to banking services for all Canadians.

Soft and Hard Strategies

The Role of Business in the Crafting of International Commercial Law

Susan Block-Lieb[*]

What motivates the choice between hard law and soft law in the drafting of international commercial law, and what role does business play in the preference between the two?[1] Most of the existing international relations ("IR") and international law ("IL") commentary—from positivists, rational institutionalists, and constructivists—focuses exclusively on states' interests in producing hard or soft law for international coordination and leaves out

---

[*] Cooper Family Professor in Urban Legal Issues, Fordham Law School. This Essay replublishes, with permission, portions of a longer article by the same name, Susan Block-Lieb, *Soft and Hard Strategies: The Role of Business in the Crafting of International Commercial Law*, 40 Mich. J. Int'l L. 433 (2019).

[1] I use the phrase "international commercial law" in this Essay to refer to a subset of international private laws governing commercial transactions involving trade in goods and services, including the laws governing the transport of such goods, and the payment and financing for the payment of such goods. The phrase is sometimes used to cover the laws governing a broader range of financial transactions than those dedicated to the purchase of goods; it is also mostly limited to transactions between businesses, and thus excludes consumer protection laws. I do not look to resolve either ambiguity in this Essay. This cluster of issues currently engages the lawmaking efforts of several global lawmakers: the "United Nations Commission on International Trade Law" (UNCITRAL), the "International Institute for the Unification of Private Law" (which refers to itself as UNIDROIT), and the Hague Conference on Private International Law. For deeper analysis of these international organizations and their lawmaking efforts, see Susan Block-Lieb & Terence C. Halliday, Global Lawmakers: International Organizations in the Crafting of Global Markets (2017). This usage modernizes the phrase "trade law" initially used by UNCITRAL. *Id.* at 1 n.1.

any question of private interests in the promulgation of soft international law. Although this analysis is widely applied to a variety of international and transnational laws, whether public or private,[2] this commentary mostly ignores businesses' interests in international lawmaking.[3]

The focus on states' interests in the choice between soft and hard international law is not surprising: for over 100 years, conventional IL theory has asserted that international law is made wholly by states negotiating in their own national interests and that businesses influence states' international lawmaking efforts only indirectly through domestic channels.[4] From this perspective, states may or may not incorporate these market interests made known to them through

---

[2.] *See, e.g.*, Andrew T. Guzman & Timothy L. Meyer, *International Soft Law*, 2 J. Legal Analysis 171, 172 (2010) ("Language included in the Universal Declaration of Human Rights, the Helsinki Final Act, the Basle Accord on Capital Adequacy, decisions of the UN Human Rights Committee, and rulings of the International Court of Justice (ICJ), are thought to impact states because of their quasi-legal character."); Gregory C. Shaffer & Mark A. Pollack, *Hard vs. Soft Law: Alternatives, Complements, and Antagonists in International Governance*, 94 Minn. L. Rev. 706, at 752–65, 790–98 (2010) (drawing examples from WTO trade law, international laws governing genetically modified food, finance, environmental protection of biodiversity, human rights, and trade in cultural products).

[3.] For counterexamples of commentary focused on business' intervention in global lawmaking efforts, see, e.g., Block-Lieb & Halliday, *supra* note 1; John Braithwaite & Peter Drahos, Global Business Regulation 27 (2000); Melissa J. Durkee, *The Business of Treaties*, 63 UCLA L. Rev. 264 (2016; Melissa J. Durkee, *Persuasion Treaties*, 99 Va. L. Rev. 63 (2013); Melissa J. Durkee, *International Lobbying Law*, 127 Yale L. J. 1742 (2018); Gregory C. Shaffer, *How Business Shapes Law: A Socio-Legal Framework*, 42 Conn. L. Rev. 147, 172 (2009). For counterexamples of commentary focused on businesses involvement in transnational private standard setting, see, e.g., Non-State Actors as Standard Setters (Anne Peters et al. eds., 2009).

[4.] 1 L. Oppenheim, International Law: A Treatise 341 (1905) ("Since the Law of Nations is a law between States only and exclusively, States only and exclusively are subjects of the Law of Nations."); *see also* Oona A. Hathaway, *Between Power and Principle: An Integrated Theory of International Law*, 72 U. Chi. L. Rev. 469, 470–83 (2005) (surveying foundations of international legal theory including the primacy of the state); *Developments in the Law: Extraterritoriality*, 124 Harv. L. Rev. 1226, 1228 (2011) (tracing notion of the primacy of nation-states in international lawmaking to the Treaty of Westphalia in 1648).

domestic channels; economic actors are viewed as helpless to press their case in international settings.

Increasingly, however, this concentration on states as the only legitimate influence in the making of law, whether domestic or international, has been criticized as "an outdated theory."[5] Recent scholarship has begun to question the primacy of nation-states and their national interests in the making of international law.[6] Some of this criticism is the result of empirical work demonstrating that the state-centric focus of conventional IL theory is either inaccurate or at least incomplete.[7] These empirical studies find that businesses influence IL indirectly at the domestic level, to be sure, but also more directly by accessing "international organizations" (IOs) and "transnational regulatory networks" (TRNs) both as observers and as participants in the lawmaking process.

In our book, Terence Halliday and I demonstrate broad involvement within the "United Nations Commission on International Trade Law" (UNCITRAL) by delegations of non-state actors.[8] Our observations involve three case studies within UNCITRAL (insolvency, secured transactions, and international transport law),[9] but others have studied non-state influences across a broader range of international lawmaking.[10] For example, John Braithwaith and Peter Drahos study thirteen areas of global business law and found that

---

[5] Durkee, Business of Treaties, *supra* note 3, at 267.

[6] See, e.g., Braithwaite & Drahos, *supra* note 3, at 27 (2000) (widely studying global business regulation and concluding, among other things, that "[t]he most recurrently effective actors in enrolling the power of states and the power of the most potent international organization (e.g. the WTO and IMF) are large U.S. corporations."); Durkee, Business of Treaties, *supra* note 3 (studying role of business actors in treaty formation generally and in particular in case of Trans-Pacific Partnership and Cape Town Convention); Shaffer, *supra* note 3, at 172 (concluding that "[b]usinesses play a critical role in international and transnational law, which has spread, directly or indirectly, to most regulatory areas.").

[7] Gregory Shaffer & Tom Ginsburg, *The Empirical Turn in International Legal Scholarship*, 106 Am. J. Int'l L. 1 (2012).

[8] Block-Lieb & Halliday, *supra* note 1.

[9] *Id.* at 4–7, 96–150.

[10] Durkee, Business of Treaties, *supra* note 3, at 266.

business actors invariably took leading roles in the formation of this law.[11] Based on two additional case studies (the Cape Town Convention on securing international interests in mobile equipment, like aircraft and rolling, stock, and the Trans-Pacific Partnership, a free trade agreement), Melissa Durkee similarly contends that businesses "form transnational coalitions, address their concerns directly to international lawmakers who are not subject to domestic political checks, and assume lawmaking roles previously held only by states."[12]

Although conventional analyses of hard and soft international laws fail to account for the distinct goals of soft international law in private, commercial contexts, commercial law contexts present an important locus of international law study.[13] Specifically, emphasis on international commercial law provides a basis for examining the role that business interests can and do play in producing and implementing hard and soft commercial laws and the special usefulness of soft international law to private, commercial entities.

This chapter proceeds to fill these gaps in two steps. Section 1 analyzes existing commercial law treaties and concludes that virtually none of these commercial law treaties constitute "hard" international law because nearly all commercial law treaties rely on national courts for enforcement. It also details the soft international law that complements these "nearly hard" commercial law treaties.

---

[11] Braithwaite & Drahos, *supra* note 3.

[12] Durkee, Business of Treaties, *supra* note 3, at 268. Unlike Halliday and I, who focus both on UNCITRAL's hard and soft international law products, Durkee concentrates her analysis on the business of treaties—that is, the involvement of business actors in treaty negotiations and the effect of this participation in the content and the success or failure of this hard law. *Id.* at 287–88.

[13] Others have written on the distinct role that soft international law plays in regulating global financial institutions and financial markets. *See, e.g.*, Chris Brummer, Soft Law and the Global Financial System: Rule Making in the 21st Century (2nd ed. 2015); International Investment Law and Soft Law (Andrea K. Bjorklund & August Reinisch eds., 2012); The Changing Landscape of Global Financial Governance and the Role of Soft Law (Friedl Weiss & Armin J. Kammel eds., 2015). On the distinction between commercial, financial, and other sorts of economic law, see *supra* note 1.

Section II considers the implications of commercial lawmaking for international settings and, in particular, state and non-state (that is, business) interests in the production of international versions of such laws.[14] State sovereignty interests vary depending on the type of international commercial law reform proposed, whether regulatory or otherwise; business' autonomy interests also vary along this axis. These interests may diverge,[15] although the interests of states and businesses are also interconnected and subject to change based on assertions of influence.[16] Soft law may aid in bridging these differences in various ways—through its gap filling, advocacy, and socializing functions. Businesses are uniquely capable of fulfilling these functions of soft international law, capabilities explored both with reference to various international commercial laws and with regard to broader theoretical concerns.

I. International Commercial Laws and Their "Legalization"

IL and IR scholars often view only precise obligations subject to enforcement by an international court or other binding dispute

---

[14.] Soft law commentators mostly consider the role of soft international law in mitigating conflicts between states, and thus as complementing or supplementing hard international laws. *See, e.g.,* José E. Alvarez, *Reviewing the Use of "Soft Law" in Investment Arbitration* (N.Y. Univ. Pub. Law & Legal Theory Research Paper Series, Working Paper No. 18-46, 2018), https://papers.ssrn.com/sol3/papers.cfm?abstract_id=3258737##; Guzman & Meyer, *supra* note 2; Shaffer & Pollack, *supra* note 2. Shaffer and Pollack also have written extensively on the potential for hard and soft international laws to interact as antagonists. See Shaffer & Pollack, *supra* note 2, at 743–52, and 788–98. When Shaffer and Pollack view this antagonism as between actors, they mostly talk in terms of states' interests diverging. *But see* Shaffer, *supra* note 3. In this chapter, I too hold out the possibility that states hold divergent interests from business and other private participants in international lawmaking.

[15.] For discussion of the hard and soft laws as antagonists, see Shaffer and Pollack, *supra* note 2, at 765–84, 788–98.

[16.] *See id.* at 722–27 (noting that soft law commentators focus more on the ways in which hard and soft laws interact as complements).

resolution mechanism as sufficiently legalized to qualify as hard international law.[17] According to this test, hardly any international agreements on topics of commercial law would constitute hard international law, specifically the aspect of their test regarding delegation and objectively certain enforcement of international treaties.[18] This is not because there is a dearth of commercial law treaties to have entered into force, however.

There are numerous long-standing private law treaties governing a wide range of procedural topics. The New York Convention (1958),[19] which governs enforcement of foreign arbitral awards, is a multilateral treaty that enjoys nearly unparalleled ratification by countries around the Globe. The Hague Conference on Private International Law promulgated a number of treaties on topics that range from service of process, evidence, enforcement of choice of court clauses, and so on.[20] In addition to this international commercial law governing procedural topics, there are more than a handful of

---

[17] Kenneth W. Abbott & Duncan Snidal, *Hard and Soft Law in International Governance*, 54 Int'l Org. 421 (2000) (developing the concept of "legalization" in distinguishing between hard and soft international law); see also Kenneth W. Abbott et al., *The Concept of Legalization*, 54 Int'l Org. 401 (2000) (expanding upon the definition of "legalization"); Christine Chinkin, *Normative Development in the International Legal System*, in Commitment and Compliance 21, 30 (Dinah Shelton ed., 2000) (adopting a similar six factor test for soft/hard law).

[18] As noted above, Kenneth Abbott and Duncan Snidal distinguish among harder or softer international instruments on the grounds of their "legalization"—that is, (i) the precision of the rules; (ii) the obligation they create for implementing states; and (iii) whether the rules delegate resolution of disputes arising under their terms to a third-party decision-maker or enforcement agent. *See supra* note 17.

[19] Convention on the Recognition and Enforcement of Foreign Arbitral Awards, June 7, 1958, 330 U.N.T.S. 3 [hereinafter New York Convention].

[20] The Hague Conference on Private International Law (sometimes referred to as "HCCH") describes itself as "The World Organisation for Cross-Border Cooperation in Civil and Commercial Matters." *See* Hague Conf. on Priv. Int'l L., www.hcch.net/en/home (last visited Mar. 20, 2019). Perusal of the international instruments it has promulgated over the past century clarifies that the term "matters" refers to litigation between private parties and that its core mission involves coordination of the procedural rules followed in such litigation. For a list of these instruments, see *Conventions, Protocols and Principles*, Hague Conf. on Priv. Int'l L., www.hcch.net/en/instruments/conventions (last visited Mar. 20, 2019).

treaties governing the substance of specific commercial transactions, such as the International Convention for the Unification of Certain Rules of Law relating to Bills of Lading, commonly referred to as the Hague Rules (1924),[21] the United Nations Convention on Contracts for the International Sale of Goods, also known as the CISG, (1978),[22] and the Convention on International Interest in Mobile Equipment, known as the Cape Town Convention (2000).[23]

All of these conventions, whether procedural or substantive, rely on national courts for their enforcement.[24] Without international provision for their enforcement, these conventions would not be

---

[21.] International Convention for the Unification of Certain Rules of Law Relating to Bills of Lading, Aug. 25, 1924, 120 L.N.T.S. 187 [hereinafter Hague Rules]. Nearly 100 years has passed since the Hague Rules entered into force, and enormous changes in the shipping industry have rendered many of its provisions out dated. *See* Block-Lieb & Halliday, *supra* note 1, at 99–100. As a result, states have sought to revise it, but treaty revision is exceedingly difficult with a treaty that has been agreed to as broadly as the Hague Rules have. The most successful of these revisions, the Visby Protocols, have been ratified by dozens of nations. For discussion of the Visby Protocols, see Block-Lieb & Halliday, *supra* note 1, at 99–107. But dissension is widespread, especially among less economically developed nations. UNICTRAL sought to redress states' concerns with the Hague Rules lack of modernity and carrier focus with its production of the Hamburg Rules in the late 1970s, and several states' ratification of this draft treaty mean that these too have entered into force. Block-Lieb & Halliday, *supra* note 1, at 100. Technical advances in the shipping industry and shifts in the economics of shipping prompted subsequent pressure for modernization of the Hague-Visby Rules with a new draft convention on international transport. Block-Lieb & Halliday, *supra* note 1, at 102–04. UNCITRAL recently promulgated its United Nations Convention on Contracts for the International Carriage of Goods Wholly or Partly by Sea, Dec. 11, 2008, www.uncitral.org/pdf/english/texts/transport/rotterdam_rules/Rotterdam-Rules-E.pdf [hereinafter, the "Rotterdam Rules"]. Although roughly 20 countries have signed this convention, only 3 have ratified it. As a result, the Rotterdam Rules have not (yet?) entered into force. For discussion of the Rotterdam Rules, see Block-Lieb & Halliday, *supra* note 1, at 236–41.

[22.] United Nations Convention on Contracts for the International Sale of Goods, Apr. 11, 1980, 1489 U.N.T.S. 3 [hereinafter, "CISG"].

[23.] Convention on International Interests in Mobile Equipment, Nov. 16, 2001, T.I.A.S. No. 06-301.2, 2307 U.N.T.S. 285 [hereinafter, the "Cape Town Convention"].

[24.] *See, e.g.*, Durkee, *Persuasion Treaties, supra* note 3. The "Cape Town Convention" (CTC) creates an international registry for international interests in mobile equipment, however. By internationalizing implementation of its mandatory rules and setting up this international registry, the Cape Town Convention may limit the grounds on which national courts can undermine enforcement of its mandates.

sufficiently legalized to be considered hard law under the definition set out by Abbot and Snidal. Moreover, the CISG widely permits private parties otherwise subject to its terms to simply decide
that they do not like these provisions and thus opt out by saying as
much in their contract. This kind of opt-out provision, sometimes
also referred to as a default rule, while ordinary in some domestic
law contexts, is unusual in international law and is highly controversial in some academic circles.[25] A convention that can be avoided
through a contractual opt-out would hardly seem an "obligation"
in the sense many IL and IR scholars understand. Moreover, nearly
all of these treaties govern contractual relationships of one kind or
another. As a result, the obligations that they impose are conditional
on the conclusion of some initial private agreement.

International commercial law consists of more than just these
"nearly hard" multilateral conventions. IOs have also widely promulgated non-binding legal texts concerning commercial and financial
markets, mostly in the form of precisely drafted model laws or model
legal provisions but also sometimes in the form of broad statements
of principle offered to guide future legislation or regulation on a
topic. States have implemented some of this soft international commercial law, for example, by enacting domestic legislation based on
these international models or inspired by these principles.[26] Examples of this soft international law demonstrate the breadth of this
range of commercial topics.

---

[25] *See generally* Gilles Cuniberti, *Is the CISG Benefiting Anybody?* 39 Vand. J. Transnat'l L. 1511 (2006); Clayton P. Gillette & Robert E. Scott, *The Political Economy of
International Sales Law*, 25 Int'l Rev. L. & Econ. 446 (2005); Paul B. Stephan, *The Futility of Unification and Harmonization in International Commercial Law*, 39 Va. J. Int'l L.
743 (1999). The CISG is not unique in this regard. For example, the draft Rotterdam
Rules would allow parties to enter into "volume contracts" that would not, based
on such an agreement, otherwise get subjected to specified mandatory provisions
in this draft convention once it enters into force. United Nations Convention on
Rotterdam Rules, *supra* note 21, art. 80.

[26] For collections of essays on these topics, see, e.g., International Investment
Law and Soft Law, *supra* note 13; The Changing Landscape of Global Financial Governance and the Role of Soft Law, *supra* note 13.

In our recent book *Global Lawmakers*, Terence Halliday and I found that UNCITRAL has relied on soft law instruments since its inception in issue areas as varied as commercial dispute resolution, e-commerce, procurement, project finance, insolvency, and secured transactions law.[27] We also found that, over its 50-year history, UNCITRAL "invented" and adopted many types of soft law when drafting international standards, including rules; model laws and model legal provisions; model contract provisions; recommendations; legal guides; notes; legislative guides; practice guides; and reports.[28] Some of UNCITRAL's soft laws supplement existing commercial law treaties: for example, its Arbitration Rules and Model Law on Arbitration, which fills in gaps of New York Convention. Other soft laws promulgated by UNCITRAL, however, sit alone such as, for example, its various legislative guides on topics of insolvency and secured transactions law, which do not supplement a convention or other hard international law.

UNCITRAL is not unique in its reliance on soft international law on commercial and financial topics.[29] Although the "International Institute for the Unification of Private Law" (UNIDROIT) promulgated only draft conventions between its re-emergence after World War II and the 1990s, it has increasingly relied on soft law formats such as model laws and principles.[30] So, too, the Hague Conference on Private International Law, which, until recently, worked exclusively on producing draft conventions and protocols, promulgated a set of Principles on Choice of Law in International Commercial Contracts in 2015.[31] The "United Nations Conference on Trade and Development" (UNCTAD) and other IOs that focus on reforming

---

[27.] Block-Lieb & Halliday, *supra* note 1, at 65–82.

[28.] Block-Lieb & Halliday, *supra* note 1, at 80–82.

[29.] *See* Block-Lieb & Halliday, *supra* note 1, at 80; Susan Block-Lieb & Terence Halliday, *Contracts and Private Law in the Emerging Ecology of International Lawmaking*, *in* Contractual Knowledge: One Hundred Years of Legal Experimentation in Global Markets 350 (Grégoire Mallard & Jérôme Sgard eds., 2016) [hereinafter, "Block-Lieb & Halliday, Emerging Ecology"].

[30.] *See* Block-Lieb & Halliday, *Emerging Ecology*, *supra* note 29, at 352.

[31.] Block-Lieb & Halliday, *Emerging Ecology*, *supra* note 29, at 383.

sovereign debt lending and restructuring practices have similarly published principles on responsible sovereign lending and borrowing,[32] although in the past UNCTAD legislative projects mostly centered on producing draft conventions.[33] The G20, and the numerous lawmaking IOs and TRNs it relies on to build out its financial architecture project, have endorsed principles on a wide range of financial and economic issues.[34] Indeed, some commentators promote soft international law as preferable to hard law for addressing problems in international regulation of financial institutions and financial markets, despite—and possibly because of—the fact that it is not enforceable.[35]

That international commercial law rarely satisfies the test for legalization as set out in IL/IR scholarship is hardly surprising.

---

[32] Anna Gelpern, Hard, Soft, and Embedded: Implementing Principles on Promoting Responsible Sovereign Lending and Borrowing (2012), https://unctad.org/en/PublicationsLibrary/gdsddf2012misc2_en.pdf (written for United Nations Conference on Trade and Development (UNCTAD)); Matthias Goldmann, Responsible Sovereign Lending And Borrowing: The View from Domestic Jurisdictions (2012), https://unctad.org/en/PublicationsLibrary/gdsddf2012misc3_en.pdf (a comparative survey written for UNCTAD); Juan Pablo Bohoslavsky & Matthias Goldmann, An Incremental Approach to Sovereign Debt Restructuring: Sovereign Debt Sustainability as a Principle of Public International Law, 41 Yale J. Int'l L. Online 13, 23–26 (2016).

[33] Block-Lieb & Halliday, *supra* note 1, at 377–80.

[34] For discussion of the G20's high-level principles on financial consumer protection, financial inclusion, financial education, and other topics, see Susan Block-Lieb, *Consumer Financial Protection, Inclusion, and Education: Connecting the Local to the Global, in* Law Between Buildings: Emerging Global Perspectives in Urban Law 82 (Nestor Davidson &Nisha Mistry eds., 2017). For discussion of other aspects of the G20s financial architecture project, see, e.g., Brummer, *supra* note 13; Sungjoon Cho & Claire R. Kelly, *Promises and Perils of New Global Governance: A Case of the G-20*, 12 Chi. J. Int'l L. 491 (2012); Martin Gelter & Zehra G. Kavame Eroglu, *Whose Trojan Horse? The Dynamics of Resistance Against IFRS*, 36 U. Pa. J. Int'l L. 89, 102–03 (2014). So far, clubs of nations like the G20 and G7 have produced "leaders' declarations," which endorse "high-level principles," but nothing "harder."

[35] *See* Brummer, *supra* note 13, ch. 3, *A Compliance-Based Theory of International Financial Law* (exploring why "most agreements, rules and standards used for promulgation of international financial law [are] non-binding" but entered into solemnly and complied with by means of reputation sanctions, market discipline, and institutional disciplines, and how the "dominant explanations" of "soft law effectiveness" fall short in explaining global financial markets).

Domestic private laws, like many governing commercial transactions, get implemented and enforced differently than their domestic public law counterparts. While public laws set mandatory obligations, private laws may condition obligation on voluntary agreement of one sort or another. While mandatory public laws are mostly enforced by states, private laws are often self-enforcing, albeit with the assistance of state-sponsored courts.

None of this should be understood as an argument to disregard the focus on precisely stated, independently enforceable obligations when assessing international commercial law. Emphasizing and examining the distinctions between hard and soft international commercial laws assist in understanding that the role of open-ended, non-binding texts may hold distinct implications for commercial contexts, and particularly for the business actors to which they apply. These distinctions hold sovereignty and autonomy implications for the participants in national and transnational commercial lawmaking, and for the implementation and enforcement of these laws once promulgated, as more fully discussed in the next two sections.

II. International Implications: Distinguishing Sovereignty and Autonomy Effects of International Commercial Laws

How do state and business interests interact in the production of international commercial law? Under what circumstances are states' sovereignty interests and business' autonomy interests consistent, and when do they diverge? How does this interaction of interests affect businesses that look to influence international commercial lawmaking, not just through domestic channels, but also in an international setting? And how has this interaction affected the choice between hard and soft laws governing international commercial markets? Each of these questions is analyzed next.

The following sections generally describe the sovereignty and autonomy interests involved in the making of international commercial laws. Sovereignty and autonomy interests vary with the type of commercial law involved, but there may be more issue-specific national and market interests at stake. Together these interests are applied to the list of international commercial laws set out in Part 1.

A. International Commercial Law and Its Implications for Sovereignty and Autonomy

Section 1 identified two broad types of international commercial law treaties: procedural and substantive. Since the latter decades of the nineteenth century, jurists have viewed multilateral conventions on matters of procedure to be the most promising avenue for international agreement governing commercial transactions on the grounds that they were "apolitical," or at least removed from the politics of substance.[36] Consistent with this expectation, more than several procedural treaties have entered into force, including the New York Convention on the enforcement of arbitral awards.[37] Like domestic commercial common laws, procedural treaties minimally affect states' sovereignty interests. They bind domestic courts in specified ways but may not otherwise constrain states. Procedural treaties also lightly touch private, commercial parties' autonomy interests. They limit some litigation practices but strengthen others by enabling the recognition and enforcement of foreign judgments; the substance of commercial rights and obligations is otherwise untouched by procedural treaties.

[36.] *See, e.g.,* Ralf Michaels, *Globalizing Savigny? The State in Savigny's Private International Law and the Challenge from Europeanization and Globalization, in* Aktuelle Fragen zu politischer und rechtlicher Steuerung im Kontext der Globalisierung 119, 124 n.21 (Michael Stolleis & Wolfgang Streeck eds., 2007), https://scholarship.law.duke.edu/faculty_scholarship/2812 (describing the "private international law" analysis of Story and Savigny as intentionally "apolitical,"); Daniela Caruso, *Private Law And State-Making in the Age of Globalization,* 39 N.Y.U. J. Int'l L. & Pol. 1, 20 (2007) (same).

[37.] *See* New York Convention, *supra* note 19.

The existence of hard, or mostly hard, procedural international law is, thus, explained to a large extent by an analysis of its limited intrusions on the sovereignty interests of states and the autonomy interests of private, commercial actors. Treaties governing the enforcement of awards or judgments and other procedural matters encroach only, or at least mostly, on the judicial authority within a nation-state. As a result, they intrude less on the sovereignty of ratifying countries than treaties governing substantive areas of law. Treaties on the recognition and enforcement of judgments also impinge lightly on the autonomy of the commercial actors located in these countries, especially where the treaty enforces choice of court and choice of law provisions in the parties' contract. International laws governing the enforceability of international arbitral awards are even less intrusive on sovereignty and autonomy interests given that treaties on arbitral enforcement are limited to a single, procedural issue and that the private parties whose disputes are governed by such treaties contractually agreed to arbitrate in the first place. Both sorts of international procedural laws mirror the logic of domestic commercial common law in that both sorts of commercial laws focus on the enforcement of the contracts between private, commercial actors.

And yet, broad agreement on a multilateral convention governing the recognition and enforcement of judgments has evaded international agreement, despite international consensus on the enforceability of arbitral awards. There is also a substantial body of soft international law on the procedures to be followed in litigating commercial claims before domestic courts and in international arbitration proceedings. The details of this hard and soft international law are discussed next with an eye to explaining the relative absence of hard law on the recognition of foreign judgments and presence of soft international laws on topics of commercial procedure.

There are also several treaties on topics of commercial law that extend beyond procedure and reach to substance. Two of these substantive commercial treaties govern topics that, under national law, would count as common law or a commercial code because they govern contracts of one form or another.[38] Another of these treaties is both regulatory and "code-like," in that private parties must first opt in to the contracts governing these international interests before its mandatory rules apply.[39]

Once parties opt in to these international laws through contract, each of these substantive treaties constrains commercial actors' freedom to contract in specified ways, but these constraints are, in turn, limited. Only the *international* commercial transaction specified in the convention is implicated; purely domestic transactions continue to be governed by the relevant domestic law. In addition, contracting parties may opt out of one of these conventions—the CISG—through the simple expedient of choosing some other applicable law.[40]

Because these substantive treaties are triggered by, and potentially limited by, private contracts, most of the obligations under them are borne by private parties. States' obligations under these substantive commercial law treaties are relatively limited: domestic courts are obligated not to enter judgments inconsistent with the rules set out in the treaty; once they are satisfied, the treaty governs the transaction. Further, domestic legislatures are obligated not to produce laws inconsistent with the treaty provisions. Like other types of contracts, the contracts subject to these substantive commercial law treaties are self-enforcing.

A focus on national interests in minimizing the impositions on sovereignty of commercial law treaties assists in understanding why global lawmakers succeeded in promulgating these nearly

---

[38.] These include contracts for the international sale of goods in the case of the CISG and contracts for the carriage of goods by sea in the case of the Hague-Visby Rules. Hague Rules, *supra* note 21; CISG, *supra* note 22.

[39.] Cape Town Convention, *supra* note 23. The Cape Town Convention is also at least "conditionally regulatory," in that the international interests it governs are valid and effective against non-parties to the contract on the basis of satisfying the registration requirements set out in the treaty and one of the appended protocols. *See, e.g.,* Roy Goode, *Private Commercial Law Conventions and Public and Private International Law: The Radical Approach of the Cape Town Convention 2001 and Its Protocols,* 65 Int'l & Comp. L.Q. 523 (2016).

[40.] CISG, *supra* note 22, art. 6.

hard, code-like conventions, but—as with the explanation of international lawmaking on procedural matters—does not tell the full story. There is also a growing body of soft international law governing international contracts and commercial transactions, including international contracts for the sale of goods, which gets detailed in the following. The purpose of this supplementary soft law on international contracts is similar to the soft international law on topics of commercial arbitration and conciliation—one complements the other by providing a gap-filling function.[41]

Finally, international commercial law implicating national commercial regulation would create maximal imposition on state sovereignty. This is because a "regulatory" treaty would constrain three distinct aspects of sovereignty: a state's judiciary would be obligated to decide enforcement actions brought before it, whether by public or private parties, consistent with the rules set out in the treaty; its legislature could not enact legislation inconsistent with the treaty provisions; and its executive would be required to enforce treaty obligations in the same way as with obligations under domestic commercial regulation.

Not surprisingly, the only international commercial legislation that approaches a regulatory topic is insolvency law and possibly intellectual property law, depending upon the breadth of the definition of commercial law. If we expand the circle slightly to include both international commercial and financial laws and open up the possibility for consideration of regulations governing securities, capital markets, and financial institutions, we find additional international texts—but few if any international or multilateral conventions. On these topics, global lawmakers have produced hard international law only on the regulation of intellectual property, with the Agreement

---

[41.] *See, e.g.*, Kenneth W. Abbott & Duncan Snidal, *Pathways to International Cooperation*, in The Impact of International Law on International Cooperation: Theoretical Perspectives, Eyal Benvenisti & Moshe Hirsch eds., at 51–53 (2004) (analyzing three "pathways to cooperation" through the interaction of hard and soft international law); Shaffer & Pollack, *supra* note 2, at 722–27, 733 (analyzing range of IL and IR scholarship that views hard and soft international law as "complements").

on Trade-Related Aspects of Intellectual Property Rights ("TRIPS" or the "TRIPS convention").[42] International insolvency law,[43] and the international law governing banking, securities, and other financial regulatory topics, are all formulated as soft law.[44]

The lack of hard, or nearly hard, international legislation on these regulatory topics is, thus, mostly explained by the breadth of the intrusions on the sovereignty of any country bound to such a mandate. Hard international law that governs banking regulation or the regulation of capital markets would tread on all three "sovereign toes" in that domestic versions of these types of laws involve national legislation enforced by national regulators or other executives through national courts. Hard international law governing intellectual property or insolvency laws would not tread on national executives' interests in regulatory enforcement to the same extent since these laws are mostly self-enforced by the private parties, but it would tread, in some way, on all three branches of national government. In addition, depending on how they are drafted, international commercial laws implicating national commercial regulations may constrain private parties' freedom to contract, although these autonomous interests may already be severely limited by the governing domestic regulation. Moreover, because commercial regulation mostly sets mandates, private parties may not be able to opt out—regardless of whether such regulations impose international or national obligations.

A focus on the sovereignty and autonomy interests at risk with international commercial regulation may explain the absence of

---

[42] Agreement on Trade-Related Aspects of Intellectual Property Rights, Apr. 15, 1994, Marrakesh Agreement Establishing the World Trade Organization, Annex 1C, 1869 U.N.T.S. 299 [hereinafter, "TRIPS"].

[43] UNICTRAL Legislative Guide on Insolvency Law, U.N. Sales No. E.05.V.10 (2005); UNCITRAL Legislative Guide on Insolvency Law: Part Three: Treatment of Enterprise Groups in Insolvency, U.N. Sales No. E.05.V.10 (2012); UNCITRAL Legislative Guide on Insolvency Law: Part Four: Directors' Obligations in the Period Approaching Insolvency, U.N. Sales No. E.13.V.10 (2013).

[44] See, e.g., supra note 34 (discussing predominance of soft international law in this context).

hard international laws on these regulated issue areas, but what explains the presence of soft international laws in substantive areas on which domestic regulation is commonplace, such as insolvency law or the regulation of financial institutions and financial and capital markets. Existing commentary posits complementary or antagonistic roles for soft laws layered with hard laws,[45] but these analyses do not explain stand-alone soft laws that neither bolster nor compete with pre-existing hard international law. This earlier commentary also focuses nearly exclusively on states' interests, but our focus on international commercial law forces consideration of the interests of sub-national actors (such as regulators) and non-state actors (such as the businesses and transactions to which the soft law texts are directed). Puzzles remain regarding the extent of reliance on soft international law in these commercial contexts and the possible influence of business actors in this decision-making.

B. The Roles That Soft Law Plays in International Commercial Lawmaking and the Centrality of Private Business Interests to These Roles

Soft laws play important roles in the development of international commercial law—some complementary and some antagonistic. Rather than simply focusing on interactions between hard and soft international laws, or on consensus or dissensus among states' interests in such laws, this chapter looked at the involvement and influence of business interests in the making of international commercial law and particularly at the role soft laws play in this context.

In the realm of international commercial and financial law, soft laws play at least three distinct roles: gap filling, advocacy, and socializing. Identification of these roles is not itself novel,[46] but discussion of them through the lens of business influence's impact on these functions does lend a distinct perspective. Although we may discuss

---

[45] *See, e.g.*, Shaffer & Pollack, *supra* note 2, at 722–27, 788–98.
[46] *See, e.g.*, Shaffer & Pollack, *supra* note 2, at 722–27.

these functions without reference to businesses' access to international efforts to craft agreed-upon standards for conduct in global commercial and financial markets, this discussion would ignore an important reality: Just as "business entities have become deeply involved in designing, negotiating, and implementing a number of *treaties* in the private law,"[47] they are also embedded in designing, negotiating, and implementing the *soft law* governing international commercial law.[48] Private, commercial actors' involvement is not limited, moreover, to the process of global lawmaking itself; businesses and the professionals, professional associations, and IOs that represent their interests are also engaged, after the fact, both in terms of incremental work to "harden" these soft standards in subsequent rounds of lawmaking and in implementing these standards with practices "on the ground." Although sovereign states might be expected to focus on the absence of obligation in soft international law, regardless of its function, autonomous, non-state actors are more likely to emphasize soft laws' effectiveness in coordinating activity, its flexibility in the face of changing markets, technology and the resulting political economy, and the legitimacy it provides in validating otherwise purely private action.[49]

When businesses seek to influence the adoption and implementation of gap-filling soft international laws, they bring their distinct capabilities to the table. *Gap-filling* soft laws are understood to extend the subject matter reach of pre-existing hard law instruments with reference to topics implicated in a treaty but left unsaid. The drafting of gap-filling soft laws involves the drafting of more precise detailing information that got left out of the treaty in order to ensure international agreement on an enforceable obligation. To

---

[47] Durkee, *supra* note 3, at 266 (emphasis added).

[48] *See supra* Part III.

[49] For a more general discussion of the interaction of public and private incentives in international lawmaking, see Jürgen Basedow, *The State's Private Law and the Economy Commercial Law as an Amalgam of Public and Private Rule-Making*, 56 Am. J. Comp. L. 703, 719 (2008) (looking to "identify the conditions that favor the emergence of private rules as well as those that make state law indispensable").

emphasize gap-filling soft laws merely as producing greater detail in the international commercial law on a topic is to focus solely on the implementation of this form of soft law through the subsequent production of some harder sort of international law. Yet businesses hold a distinct edge in the implementation of gap-fillers in that this sort of soft law often is relied on by private parties in constructing their contracts and possibly also in standardized networks of contracts. UNCITRAL's Arbitration Rules, for example, set unenforceable standards for the conduct of arbitration proceedings. This guidance may thereafter become enforceable when the contents of the Rules are incorporated into arbitration clauses in private contracts. The contracts themselves are enforceable under national laws of general application, while the arbitral awards that result from the arbitration proceedings committed to in such contracts are themselves likely to be enforced as a result of the New York Convention.

Private actors' involvement and influence also affect the implementation of soft law intended to prompt *socializing* on an area of financial regulatory law.[50] To be sure, soft laws' effect on the conduct of central banking practices will mostly be socialized by public actors charged with regulating these functions under national laws.[51] But to a varying degree across national regulatory landscapes, private actors' involvement may well be critical to the success of the socializing of the global standards set out in soft international law, especially where central banking functions are held by private banks or where self-regulation governs financial markets. Public and private actors coordinate their interactions through IOs with "highly developed"

[50.] For discussion of concept of "modeling" and the interaction of epistemic communities of like-minded actors, see Braithwaite & Drahos, *supra* note 3, at 539; *see also* Shaffer &Pollack, *supra* note 2, at 726 (discussing importance of Braithwaite and Drahos to understanding of complementary relationship between hard and soft international law and regulation).

[51.] Michael S. Barr, Who's In Charge of Global Finance?, 45 Geo. J. Int'l L. 971, 992 (2014) (detailing working methods of Financial Stability Board as involving both development of independent reports and "ensuring global compliance" in part through "peer reviews on a country-by-country and regional basis").

governance structures.[52] Together the "vertically integrated regulatory system" that Prof. Chris Brummer likens the global financial architecture project to may work on three distinct levels, as has been suggested by TLO theorists:[53] it may vertically link international and transnational organizations not only to national regulators, but also to commercial and financial entities "on the ground."[54] While socializing soft laws may interact with existing, or lead toward eventual, hard international laws, they need not. Where the socializing occurs among tightly bound epistemic communities of actors, there is little need for the formal obligations that hard law would bring. Their commonalties converge action toward a singular goal despite the absence of a credible threat of enforcement.

Finally, soft laws aimed at *advocating* the need for further international or national laws on a topic may also rely on a combination of public and private actions. The Hague Conference promulgated its Choice of Law Principles as soft law and not as a draft treaty because preliminary work on the topic convinced the Conference that the time was not ripe for such a convention. It also promulgated the Principles because, notwithstanding this lack of state interest in pursuing the topic, private parties and organizations representing

---

[52.] Brummer, *supra* note 13, at 116 ("Despite their soft law foundations, the standard-setting bodies that drive standard setting and international agendas typically possess highly developed institutional structures, each with its own mix of membership rules, decision rules, and decision-making processes.").

[53.] For discussion of the international, national, and local coordination and concordance envisioned by TLO theory, see Transnational Legal Orders, ch. 1, at 31–34 (Terence C. Halliday & Gregory Shaffer eds., 2016), at 42–48.

[54.] *See, e.g.*, Eric Helleiner, *Regulating the Regulators: The Emergence and Limits of the Transnational Financial Legal Order, in* Transnational Legal Orders, *supra* note 53, at 231–57, 249 ("Major shifts in the content of regulation in the period—including the new emphasis on 'macroprudential' regulatory philosophy—can be attributed in large part to new ideas and consensus formation among experts in transgovernmental networks, many of which have become more skeptical of neo-liberal ideas in finance, as well as of transnational private lobbying.") (citation omitted); Carola Westermeier, *The Bank of International Settlements as a Think Tank for Financial Policy-Making*, 37 Pol'y & Soc'y 170, 183 (2018) (analyzing Bank of International Settlements both "as a host to central bankers, financial politicians and other actors in financial governance and as a provider of knowledge to these networks").

various business interests persisted in the commercial benefits of predictable enforcement of contract clauses choosing the applicable governing law. This divergence between states' sovereign and businesses' autonomous interests were negotiated through the soft law format.[55]

III. Conclusion

Empirical research increasingly demonstrates that businesses' influence on international commercial law may involve more than simply pressing the State Department or a foreign ministry to pursue their interests in international negotiations. In the wake of these findings, this chapter sought to "update" theoretical understanding regarding the primacy of states' involvement in the making and implementation of international law by focusing on one sort of international law—specifically, international commercial law. The chapter explored the role that businesses and other private actors play in the construction and implementation of these international texts. In theorizing about private, commercial actors' roles in these processes, it emphasized and compared the distinct interests and abilities of public and private actors in the choice between hard and soft international laws.

The conventional way to conceive of business access in the lawmaking context is as lobbying or legislative influence. With this depiction, domestic businesses press the state in which they reside to design international agreements on topics of commercial law consistent with their commercial interests. But, while commercial actors may well look to influence global lawmaking in this way, indirectly through the portal of state action, studies show that businesses also make their transnational commercial interests known

---

[55] Advocacy through soft law can be both positive (pressing for the subsequent adoption of some harder international law) and negative (making the case for revisions to or reversals from existing international law instruments). For examples and analysis of antagonistic soft international laws, see Shaffer & Pollack, *supra* note 2, at 788–98.

more directly to global lawmakers. That businesses exercise their influence in both national and international settings suggests that hard and soft international laws can serve distinct purpose for states than for businesses, depending on the type of international commercial law at issue. It also suggests that the decision to promulgate soft or hard international commercial laws may not depend exclusively on state-centric factors or on commercial interests filtered through a state's perception of its national interests.

Although international law conventionally gets divided between public and private, between procedural and substantive, the chapter described commercial law as falling into a three-part typology: (i) judicial enforcement of private contracts, judgments or arbitral awards; (ii) "bottom-up" legislative codification of commercial practices; (iii) "top-down" regulation of commerce. When viewed this way, the role of business in influencing the production of international commercial law should not be limited to consideration of activities that resemble lobbying. This sort of influence pertains to legislative or regulatory proposals, but not all commercial law is regulatory in format. Businesses may exert influence through contracts, including networks of standardized contracts, and through their dispute resolution practices, including transnational litigation. These additional forms of business influence on commercial law deserve distinct consideration.

This chapter identified three purposes of soft international commercial law: its gap-filling; advocacy; and socializing functions. It linked soft law's gap-filling function to international laws that resemble common law or code approaches at domestic commercial law. Its socializing function, by contrast, was applied predominantly to regulatory commercial law contexts in that soft law can guide TRNs of regulators and civil society toward consensus on a desired range of administrative practices. Soft law advocacy looks not only to plan for subsequent lawmaking within IOs, but also at national and local decision-making: domestic legislators, domestic courts, and others involved in the design and conduct of dispute resolution mechanisms.

States may object less to the influence of private interests in the context of soft international commercial law than with hard law. Soft international law may look "redundant" or harmless because it is not "legalized" in the way that IL/IR scholars describe. Yet, perhaps states should be warier of business interests' access to the making of soft international laws, although soft laws lack legalization. Resolution of the divergences between state and non-state interests by means of soft law channels may obscure business influence, making it harder to detect, and that may be the point.

Walking on Thin Ice

The Formative Era of Judicial Cooperation in Cross-Border Insolvency: An English Perspective

Ian F. Fletcher[*]

I. Preliminary—A Personal Tribute

During the past half-century (down to the time of writing), revolutionary processes have been actively at work reshaping the hitherto obscure and antiquated realm of international (cross-border) insolvency. Throughout these heady years, the name of Jay Westbrook has been inextricably linked with the seminal events and initiatives which have propelled this revolution to ever greater heights. It has been both a privilege and a pleasure to have observed these momentous developments and, on occasion, to have participated in them. From that vantage point, I can unhesitatingly affirm that no individual has more richly deserved the high esteem in which he is regarded by his fellow academics, as well as by those judges, legislators and practitioners in the field of insolvency law who currently enjoy the fruits of his unstinting devotion to the cause of delivering efficient and effective frameworks in which to operate in the modern era of fluid international commerce.

[*] Professor of Law *Emeritus*, University College of London. Professor Ian Fletcher, QC, passed away July 21, 2018.

Our professional paths converged soon after the publication in 1990 of the edited papers of a colloquium on cross-border insolvency which I had chaired at the university where I was then based.[1] Our shared interest – nay, passion – for the study of insolvency law, particularly in its international and comparative aspects, has brought us together countless times since then, as academic colleagues, co-panellists and collaborators, but above all as friends. Other contributors to this celebratory collection will doubtless inject their own insights into the multi-faceted impact which Jay has had upon the theory and practice of bankruptcy law in its domestic context, notably through the series of groundbreaking studies of the law concerning debt and bankruptcy based upon innovative, multi-disciplinary empirical studies.[2] For the purposes of this tribute, I call attention to the remarkable sequence of groundbreaking contributions he has made to the development of a modern, sophisticated approach to the development of principles by which to conduct multi-jurisdictional bankruptcy cases. A notable indication of Jay's established stature as an authority on these matters was his appointment by presiding Judge Tina Brozman as *amicus curiae* in the landmark case of Maxwell Communications Corporation plc,[3] in a ruling (subsequently affirmed on appeal) which signalled a willingness by the respective judges in London and New York to achieve a commercially sensible, value-preserving solution despite the lack of any formal legislative framework on which to base their intuitive cooperation. That case served as a catalyst for a major initiative promoted jointly by INSOL International and the United Nations Commission on International Trade Law (UNCITRAL) to establish international standards by which such proceedings could in future be governed. In the ensuing project undertaken by UNCITRAL which resulted in the adoption

---

[1.] I. F. Fletcher (Ed.), Cross-Border Insolvency: Comparative Dimensions. The Aberystwyth Insolvency Papers (1990), published by the United Kingdom National Committee of Comparative Law.

[2.] Notably, As We Forgive our Debtors (1989) and The Fragile Middle Class (2000).

[3.] Re Maxwell Communications Corporation plc 170 BR 800 (Bankr. S.D.N.Y. 1994); aff'd 186 B.R. 807 (S.D.N.Y. 1995); aff'd 93 F.3d 1036 (2nd Cir. 1996).

in 1997 of the Model Law on Cross-Border Insolvency, Jay served as co-head of the U.S. delegation which played a crucial role in bringing the project to its speedy and triumphant conclusion.

The successful completion of the Model Law led in turn to an initiative by the American Law Institute (ALI) to establish an authoritative apparatus for use within the three North America Free Trade Agreement (NAFTA) countries, the United States, Canada, and Mexico. The ALI's goal was to enable courts in those countries to understand each other's bankruptcy laws and to resolve cross-border cases arising under the auspices of NAFTA. To serve as United States Reporter and leader for this ambitious project the ALI naturally turned to Jay Westbrook, who duly presided over the complex and delicate task of designing a user-friendly, comparative statement (in three volumes) of the laws of the three systems involved, complemented by a fourth volume in which agreed principles of cooperation in transnational insolvency cases were set out together with explanatory commentary.[4] In a master stroke, an appendix was included in Volume 4, "Guidelines for Court-to-Court Communications in Cross-Border Cases," a text which was rapidly embraced and adapted by courts and practitioners in many lands. Typically, while fulfilling his mandate to produce a text suitable for use within the context of NAFTA, Jay had ensured that it also had the capability to serve as a model for wider application. This far-sighted ambition was subsequently realised after 2006 through the setting up of a joint project by the ALI and the International Insolvency Institute aimed at developing the NAFTA Principles, together with the Guidelines for Court-to-Court Communications, into a form suitable for acceptance and application in jurisdictions across the world. This time, Jay acted as co-chair for the Global Principles project on behalf

---

[4.] Each of the four volumes bears the main title Transnational Insolvency: Cooperation among the NAFTA Countries, followed by the appropriate subtitle. The fourth volume bears the subtitle Principles of Cooperation among the NAFTA Countries. All four volumes were published for the ALI in 2003 by Juris Publishing Inc.

of the ALI, supporting and encouraging the two non-American academics who served as joint Reporters.[5] Such was the quality of the original NAFTA Principles and Guidelines that the task of restating and reformulating them so as to be suitable for use by courts in the world at large proved to be far less daunting than might otherwise have been the case. The joint Reporters, and their legion of international advisers and consultants, were profoundly conscious that they were 'standing on giants' shoulders'.

II. The Problem Stated

For as long as human societies have engaged in trade with each other questions have inevitably arisen as to methods of resolving disputes between counterparties, including in cases where a defaulting party has entered into a state of insolvency. The locally generated laws under which one of the parties habitually conducted their commercial activities would almost inevitably differ in some respects from the corresponding laws of the state to which the counterparty 'belonged'. Hence the vital questions 'whose court can hear the case?' and 'whose law governs?' have been constant features of the slowly evolving doctrinal literature of what has come to be known as private international law. That title is seriously misleading, however, as it too readily suggests that there is a single corpus of internationally agreed and applicable legal rules whereby cross-border disputes between non-state parties may be conveniently resolved. Nothing could be further from the truth. Until very recent times, and in many respects even to this day, each sovereign country has maintained its own, indigenous tradition of private international law, whereby the manifest differences of the conflicting laws which happened to

---

[5] The present author was one of the joint Reporters for the Global Insolvency Principles project, together with Professor Bob Wessels. Copies of the final Report (2012) are obtainable from the American Law Institute, and may also be viewed online on the website of the International Insolvency Institute at www.iiiglobal.org/sites/default/files/alireportmarch_0.pdf, last accessed 1/1/2018

be engaged in a given case were in turn subjected to home-made rules and methods of solution, thus rendering the outcome heavily dependent on the venue in which proceedings happened to take place. The resulting mosaic of autonomously generated systems of private international law was appropriately described as being in 'a state of chaos' by Professor Otto Kahn Freund, who advocated a sustained international effort to establish a more orderly and harmonious environment for the resolution of civil and commercial disputes.[6]

In practice, however, having regard to the traditional mode of conducting business between sovereign states, such a desirable goal could only be achieved incrementally, mainly by means of treaties and conventions negotiated between state parties prepared to accept some mutually agreed 'middle way' in place of their established national rules and practices. Such international instruments inevitably require the allocation of substantial time and resources to the conduct of negotiations, and are ultimately dependent on a willingness by the participants to accept a compromise as the basis for the final agreement. Historically, prior to the second half of the twentieth century, in the sphere of bankruptcy law the achievements had been confined to a rather limited number of bilateral treaties, and a handful of multilateral agreements of a regional character: the goal of securing a genuinely global bankruptcy treaty was viewed as impossibly remote.[7] It may also be observed that in an era of

---

[6.] O. Kahn-Freund, General Problems of Private International Law (1974, III) 143 Hague Rec. des Cours 147.

[7.] For surveys of the early history of treaties concerning bankruptcy law and related commercial matters, see K. Lipstein, 'Early Treaties for the Recognition of Foreign Bankruptcies', in I. F. Fletcher (Ed.), supra n.1, Ch. 14 at 223–36; J. M. Dobson, 'Treaty Developments in Latin America', Ibid. Ch. 15, at 237–62. See also J. H. Dalhuisen, Dalhuisen on International Insolvency and Bankruptcy (Matthew Bender, 1986), Pt.III, Ch. 1; O. Kahn-Freund, General Problems of Private International Law (1974, III) 143 Hague Rec. des Cours 147, Ch.II, esp. at 187–96. A classic delineation of the subject is that by K. Nadelmann, 'Bankruptcy Treaties' (1944) 93 U. Pa. L. Rev. 58, reproduced with permission in Conflict of Laws, International and Interstate (1972) at 299.

steadily expanding international commerce the practical value of a bankruptcy treaty concluded between a limited number of participating states is severely limited. In practice, such an instrument is unlikely to furnish a satisfactory solution in cases where, as so frequently proves to be the case, the parties and interests randomly brought into competition by the circumstances of a particular debtor's failure extend beyond the combined frontiers of the states in question. In the absence of a clear, treaty-based direction as to the course to be followed a national judge is likely to adhere to the principles inculcated by the judicial oath, and seek to apply the rules of the home forum, with their inbuilt alignment with local values and expectations.

While the aforementioned approach inevitably has the propensity to favour local parties over the claims and interests of 'foreigners', a troubled judicial conscience might be somewhat assuaged by the maxim that 'strangers who come to the forum must take the local law as they find it'.[8] While this may serve as a 'facts-of-life-based' rejoinder to any foreign creditor thereby encountering a less favourable treatment in their debtor's insolvency than they might have expected under the corresponding laws of their home state, it scarcely provides a tenable justification in cases where the debtor, taking advantage of the opportunity to engage in systematic trading in a foreign country in competition with others who operate in accordance with the laws of that country, subsequently retreats beneath the protective mantle of its 'home' state's insolvency regime to the potential detriment of parties who trusted in its trading presence within their jurisdiction and framed their expectations accordingly. Although reason and justice might furnish powerful arguments for the redress of this unhappy state of affairs, it was not until the second half of the twentieth century that enlightened counsels could begin gradually to prevail over the predominantly isolationist and parochial attitudes that had previously shaped the conduct of international

---

[8.] A sentiment traditionally summed up by the aphorism: 'When in Rome, do as the Romans do.'

insolvency cases. There were however certain notable exceptions to those antediluvian practices, attributable to early manifestations of a spirit of judicial activism which was to flourish in more recent times.

III. Early Judicial Initiatives: The English Judges Break New Ground

The early history of English law reflects a markedly distinctive character as against that of its continental European counterparts. The English judiciary were far less reliant upon the doctrinal treatises written by university scholars extrapolating the received legal literature ultimately derived from Roman law, but instead ascribed authority to case precedents, and to a limited canon of books compiled by indigenous authors who also subscribed to the same, case-based philosophy. By the eighteenth century, the English courts were able to synthesise the traditions of the common law itself with those of the Law Merchant to develop a practical, market-friendly system of commercial law in tune with evolving mercantile practice and expectations. In this context, early judicial rulings in cross-border insolvency cases of first encounter appear to have been decided on an almost intuitive basis, giving rise to precedents which served to enhance confidence among those engaging in international trade. Their decisions signalled that the English courts, at least, would not simply and mechanically deliver judgments favouring the interests of local, English parties as against claims advanced by 'aliens'. Thus in the landmark case of *Solomons v. Ross*, decided in 1764,[9] Dutch merchants trading from Amsterdam with various English counterparties had been adjudicated bankrupt in Holland, and 'curators' (equating to trustees in bankruptcy) had been duly appointed. Prior to the adjudication, an English creditor of the bankrupts had commenced

---

[9] *Solomons v. Ross* (1764) 1 Hy. Bl.131n, 126 E.R. 79, also reported in Wallis and Lyne, Irish Chancery Rep.59 (note) (1839). See also *Jollet v. Deponthieu* (1769) 1 Hy. Bl. 132n, 126 E.R. 80 (Camden LC).

proceedings to levy execution upon a debt owed to the Dutch merchants by another English counterparty. Bathhurst J ruled that the title of the curators, to whom the bankrupts' estate had passed upon adjudication, had priority over the attaching creditor, whose writ of execution was only obtained after the date of the Dutch adjudication. Inevitably, this ruling entailed the acceptance (tacitly) of the instantaneous, extraterritorial operation of the Dutch bankruptcy law and of its effect upon the bankrupt's property. In so doing, Bathhurst J, together with his fellow judges who subsequently decided similar cases in similar fashion, appear to have been influenced by the proposition – widely accepted in mercantile law at that period – that the transmission of title to personal (i.e. movable) property must be governed by the laws of the country where that person is domiciled ('*mobilia personam sequuntur*').[10] Such were the circumstances in which, in the absence of any relevant legislative authorisation or guidance, the English judiciary took the initiative in extending their cooperation to the foreign insolvency representative seeking to collect a bankrupt's movable property and administer it in accordance with the insolvency law of the bankrupt's 'home' country.[11]

A further extension of the judges' international sensibility was to occur early in the nineteenth century, when once again the central issues for consideration were the suitability of the forum in which insolvency proceedings had been opened, and the extent to which the effects of those proceedings should be recognised and given effect, including the international recognition of any purported

---

[10] See *Hunter v. Potts* (1791) 4 Term Rep.182, 100 E.R. 962 at 967, per Kenyon LCJ, and *Sill v. Worswick* (1791) 1 Hy. Bl. 665, 126 E.R. 379 at 393, per Lord Loughborough.

[11] It must be acknowledged that judges in the nineteenth century refrained from applying the same principle of automatic divesting of a bankrupt's estate in the case of English immovable property – see *Waite v. Bingley* (1882) 21 Ch.D. 674, Hall V-C. However if the bankruptcy proceedings themselves were being conducted in the bankrupt's domiciliary forum, and hence qualified for recognition under English law, the court could assist the foreign trustee to claim the immovable property on behalf of the estate, for example, by appointing him as receiver of the property with express power to sell and to deal with the proceeds in accordance with the foreign bankruptcy law: Re Kooperman [1928] W.N. 101; 72 Sol. Jo. 400 (Astbury J).

discharge of the debtor's unsatisfied liabilities. As to the first of these questions, we have already seen that English law had already adopted the position that the appropriate forum in which bankruptcy proceedings should take place was that of the debtor's 'domicile' (as perceived and attributed according to English standards and criteria). The second question posed a further jurisprudential challenge in the realm of private international law, because it potentially required the court before which recognition was sought to allow parties and property within its own jurisdiction to be affected by legal proceedings conducted under the laws of a separate, sovereign state. Upon what principles should such acceptance be accorded? The answer was delivered, ultimately by the Privy Council, in the remarkable case of *Odwin v. Forbes* (1814–1817).[12]

A sugar trader, Forbes, had conducted his business in London with various counterparties. On becoming insolvent he underwent bankruptcy proceedings in London and subsequently obtained a certificate of discharge releasing him from the bankruptcy debts. Some of the creditors, who had had notice of the proceedings, nevertheless refrained from lodging proof for their debts. According to English law (then as now), discharge releases the bankrupt from all provable debts, irrespective of whether the creditors had participated in the proceedings. Forbes subsequently resettled in the English colony of Demerara (notable for sugar production) and began to rebuild his fortunes. Thereupon the creditors who had absented themselves from the English bankruptcy proceedings sought to bring suit in the court of Demerara to enforce their original claims. Forbes pleaded the certificate of discharge by way of defence, and it therefore became an issue for the court of the colony to determine whether the discharge obtained through the English proceedings could furnish a complete answer to a suit brought in an overseas jurisdiction. By an irony of history, the colony of Demerara had previously been a Dutch possession which had only recently passed under English

---

[12.] *Odwin v. Forbes* (1817) 1 Buck. 57 (PC).

control under an arrangement whereby the former Romano-Dutch laws were to retain the force of law, albeit the administration of justice would henceforth be conducted by English colonial officials. The English judge presiding over the case, Jabez Henry, happened to be a man of deep scholarly learning and he quickly perceived that the English discharge, despite being granted by the court of the colonial Mother country, could not enjoy extraterritorial effect as of right in a foreign country to which legal autonomy had been conceded. The matter therefore fell to be resolved by reference to the rule of Romano-Dutch law concerning the recognition of the effects of foreign insolvency proceedings. Upon investigation, it transpired that the Dutch law would accord such recognition provided that it could be shown that reciprocal recognition was available, *mutatis mutandis*, under the law of the country where the discharge had been granted. Conveniently, the earlier English precedents already discussed had in several instances demonstrated the willingness of English courts to recognise and give effect to Dutch bankruptcy proceedings. Thus Forbes' defence was upheld, not on the basis that the English colonial court would meekly enforce the original order of the 'home' court in London, but only after confirming that the recognition rule of the foreign system would recognise the efficacy of the discharge. Once again, despite the total absence of any legislative provisions to control the court's approach to its intellectually challenging task, judicial resourcefulness proved equal to the challenge.

As a postscript to the case, it may first be noted that in a near-contemporary decision by the U.S. Supreme Court it was held that a foreign discharge in bankruptcy was no defence to an action by a creditor residing in the United States unless the creditor had consented to the foreign court's exercise of jurisdiction over the claim.[13] It is also significant, for the purposes of the present contemplation of the role played by judicial activism in the evolution of cross-border insolvency, that the presiding judge in the Demerara court before

---

[13.] *Ogden v. Saunders*, 25 U.S. (12 Wheat.) 213 (1827).

which the initial hearing of *Odwin v. Forbes* took place, Jabez Henry, was subsequently inspired to publish what may be claimed to be the earliest treatises on the subject written by an English common lawyer. First, in 1823 he published in London a full account of the judgment of the court over which he had presided in 1814, incorporating extensive references to the English and foreign legal authorities on which the court had drawn in arriving at its conclusion.[14] Later, in 1825, he published a fourteen-page tract entitled *Outline of Plan of an International Bankrupt Code for the Commercial States of Europe*,[15] which contains a series of propositions suitable to provide the basis for an international treaty to be concluded among the major European commercial powers. The proposal was considerably ahead of its time, and no such project was seriously undertaken until well into the twentieth century. Among the chief points advanced by Henry were the need for an internationally agreed standard for the test upon which bankruptcy proceedings should be opened, and likewise as to the effect of the opening with respect to the divesting of the bankrupt's property. Henry also proposed a standard jurisdictional test for operation of the bankruptcy laws based on the location of the bankrupt's domicile, and he was particularly prescient with regard to the need to counteract forum shopping by debtors seeking to evade their creditors by means of a fraudulent change of domicile. These arguments bear a striking alignment to observations made by Henry himself in the course of his judgment in *Odwin v. Forbes*, where he observed that the whole amount of the plaintiff's claim and demand originated from a contract concluded in London, which was also the agreed place of payment. Moreover the defendant's domicile

---

[14.] J. Henry, The Judgment of the Court of Demerara in the case of *Odwin v. Forbes*, to which is prefixed a Treatise on the Difference between Personal and Real Statutes, and its effect on foreign judgments and contracts, marriages and wills (London, S. Sweet, Chancery Lane, 1823). (The transcript of the judgment occupies pp. 87–178.)

[15.] Published in London printed by Cox and Bayliss, Great Queen Street. The pamphlet bears no date but was published at some time between 1823 and 1827. See K. Nadelmann (1961) 10 I.C.L.Q. 70.

at the time of incurring the debt, and also at the time of his English bankruptcy, was in England. Henry accordingly concluded that in Forbes' case England was, 'by intention and in fact', 'the seat of the affairs and fortunes (*sedes rerum ac fortunarum*) of the defendant and his late partners'.[16] For good measure, he added, 'This is not the case of a man, who after contracting debts in one country removes to another and there obtains a discharge.'[17]

A. Ancillary Insolvency Proceedings

Until the mid-nineteenth century insolvency proceedings coming before the English courts were restricted to cases of personal bankruptcy involving either individuals, or persons trading in partnership. Such matters were governed by successive iterations of statutes bearing the title 'Bankruptcy Act'. With the evolution, from 1844 onwards, of legislation permitting the formation of joint stock companies a parallel branch of insolvency law was developed under the auspices of successive Companies Acts in which provision was made for the winding-up of companies under various circumstances including insolvency. As was also true of the bankruptcy statutes of that era, the Legislature omitted to give any consideration to the cross-border aspects of corporate insolvencies, even though it was the case that many companies were formed for the purpose of conducting business wholly or mainly overseas, with the consequence that many of their assets – and also their creditors and shareholders – might be located outside the jurisdiction of the English courts. In an age when international transport and communications were slow and unreliable, the logistical difficulties confronting the liquidator of such a company were substantial and in some cases insuperable. Correspondingly,

---

[16] Op. cit supra n.14, at 164–65. It may be observed that, in thus attributing the jurisdictional propriety of the English proceedings conducted at the debtor's 'seat of affairs', Henry was anticipating by more than 150 years the jurisdictional rules developed by the authors of the conventions and regulations produced by the Council of Europe and the European Union, and also embraced by the UNCITRAL Model Law on Cross-Border Insolvency, utilising the concept of the debtor's 'centre of main interests'.

[17] *Ibid.*, at 170.

foreign-formed companies might establish a trading presence in England giving rise to a similar order of problems for any foreign liquidator appointed under the laws of the company's 'home' country.

During the final quarter of the nineteenth century, the English judges developed a practical approach to the resolution of many of the difficulties alluded to previously, despite the absence of any clear legislative direction or authorisation for that purpose. Initially, by deploying the equitable remedy of injunction the courts acted to defeat efforts by creditors in English insolvency proceedings to gain priority over other domestic creditors by means of foreign acts of execution whereby they obtained part of the assets of the debtor which should properly be distributed under the collective procedure.[18] Secondly, utilising the doctrine of hotchpot, the courts ensured that creditors who might not be personally amenable to the injunctive powers of the English court could be denied the right to participate in the collective process of distribution until they had honestly accounted for what they had so far received through their foreign executions.[19] Next, in a characteristic display of common law pragmatism, a workable solution was devised to the logistical problem of winding-up an insolvent company or partnership whose business affairs had been conducted in a different jurisdiction to that in which it had been originally incorporated. The judges coolly formulated the concept of 'main' and 'ancillary' proceedings whereby, in the words of Vaughan-Williams J (subsequently affirmed by the Court of Appeal) the court would:

> Ascertain what is the domicile of the company in liquidation; let the court of the country of domicile act as the principal court to govern the liquidation; and let the other courts act as ancillary, as far as they can, to the principal liquidation.[20]

[18.] Re Oriental Inland Steam Co. (1874) L.R. 9 Ch. App.557 (CA).

[19.] *Banco de Portugal v. Waddell* (1880) 5 App. Cas. 161 (HL).

[20.] Re English, Scottish and Australian Chartered Bank [1893] 3 Ch. 385, at 394, per Vaughan-Williams J. See also Re Commercial Bank of South Australia (1886)

The open-minded approach of the English judiciary towards the pursuit of cross-border cooperation was articulated by North J who explained:

> The winding-up here will be ancillary to a winding-up in Australia, and if I have control of the proceedings here, I will take care that there shall be no conflict between the two courts and I shall have regard to the interests of all the creditors and all the contributories, and shall endeavour to keep down the expenses of the winding-up as far as possible.[21]

Notably the judges of the late Victorian era did not allow the fact that there were no express provisions in the relevant legislation to deflect them from acting upon their resolve to facilitate practical solutions that were manifestly for the benefit of all creditors in all the jurisdictions concerned.[22] They, and their successors in the twentieth century, were to continue in the same spirit when confronted by fresh challenges for whose resolution the Legislature had conspicuously failed to make suitable provision. Among these un-provided-for cases were those in which an English court might be invited to exercise a winding-up jurisdiction in respect of a foreign-formed company having materially significant connections with England such as to render it appropriate for such a winding-up to take place there, either on a stand-alone basis or, as in the situations discussed immediately earlier, if main and ancillary proceedings were considered appropriate, under circumstances such that the main proceeding would be in the company's state of incorporation. The omission from the successive versions of the companies legislation of any provision expressly authorising the English court to wind up a 'foreign' company was elegantly finessed by a judicial extrapolation of a provision first enacted as s.5(7) of the Joint Stock Companies Amendment

---

33 Ch.D. 174 (North J); Re Federal Bank of Australia [1893] W.N. 77 CA, affirming Vaughan-Williams J); Re P. MacFadyen & Co [1908] 1 K.B. 675 (Bigham J).

[21.] Re Commercial Bank of South Australia (1886) 33 Ch.D. 174, at 178, per North J.

[22.] See Re P. MacFadyen & Co [1908] 1 K.B. 675 (Bigham J).

Act 1848 and reiterated in almost identical terms in every subsequent Act.[23] The original purpose of the section had been to enable the courts to exercise, subject to certain modifications, their new jurisdiction to wind up companies formed and registered under the Act itself also with respect to domestic companies which had previously been formed utilising various other non-statutory devices. Such companies were conveniently designated as 'unregistered companies' by the terms of s.5(7) of the Act of 1848. By logical extension, any company not formed under the registration process under the English companies legislation could be classified as an 'unregistered company' and hence a foreign-formed company, even if formed under legislative provisions analogous to those available in England, could be brought within the ambit of the jurisdiction to wind up 'unregistered' companies.

At first, the courts made use of this conveniently liberal reading of the scope of the statutory provisions to facilitate the operation of the binary system of 'main' and 'ancillary' proceedings in cases where the company's principal connections lay between England itself and one of its overseas colonies, such as Australia or India.[24] In such cases, cross-border coordination of proceedings was more readily achievable because the colonial legislation under which such companies were formed was essentially modelled upon the corresponding statutes of the Mother country. In due course, however, the English courts began to encounter cases involving companies formed under the laws of countries with no such ties of legal kinship, notably in the wake of the Russian revolution of 1917 when the

---

[23] See Companies Act 1862, s.199; Companies Act 1908, s.268(1); Companies Act 1948, s.399(1). The final iteration of the provision within the companies legislation was as s.666(5) of the Companies Act 1985, superseded by the entry into force of s.221(1) in Part 5 of the Insolvency Act 1986. The definition of 'unregistered company' is supplied by s.220(1) as follows: 'For the purposes of this Part, "unregistered company" includes any association and any company, with the exception of a company registered under the Companies Act 2006 in any part of the United Kingdom.'

[24] See, e.g., Re Commercial Bank of India (1868) L.R. 6 Eq. 517 (Ld. Romilly MR); Re Mercantile Bank of Australia [1892] 2 Ch. 204 (North J); and also cases listed above in fn. 20.

wholesale nationalisation of Russian enterprises, including banks and financial institutions, by the Soviet authorities resulted in a situation where the Russian-formed companies had undergone dissolution under the law of their original incorporation (Tzarist Russia), leaving behind 'orphan assets' located in England and elsewhere In the absence of any diplomatic or legal framework to allow cooperation between Soviet Russia and its 'capitalist enemies', English courts concluded that the most appropriate course in such a case was to entertain a petition for the winding-up in England of the Russian company as an unregistered company so as to enable a distribution of its orphan assets to take place according to the English law scheme of distribution, in which (in principle) all claimants, both local and foreign, were entitled to participate.[25] The 'inconvenient conceptual truth' that, according to established principles of English conflict of laws, there was no extant legal entity to be made the subject of a winding-up order because the company had already been dissolved under the law of its state of incorporation was calmly overcome by the judicial fiction that the very act of presentation of a winding-up petition caused the company to undergo a miraculous revivification, thereby rendering it amenable to undergo an English winding-up.[26]

B. Jurisdictional Nexus

One further, and vital, stroke of judicial innovation was required in order to complete this remarkable saga of Praetorian jurisprudence. For rather obvious reasons, the statutory provisions governing the winding-up of unregistered companies made no reference to the circumstances under which it would be appropriate or permissible

---

[25] See Re Russian Bank for Foreign Trade [1933] 1 Ch. 745 (Maugham J); *Russian and English Bank and Florence Montefiore Guedalla v. Baring Bros. & Co. Ltd* [1936] A.C. 405 (HL).

[26] *Russian and English Bank and Florence Montefiore Guedalla v. Baring Bros. & Co. Ltd* [1936] A.C. 405 (HL).

for an English court to exercise its jurisdiction for the purpose of winding up a foreign company. It therefore became a task for the courts themselves to articulate the parameters within which this power would be exercised in an international context. Essentially, this involved a progressive development of a principled test for jurisdictional *nexus* between the company and the English court, to withstand potential criticism that the winding-up was taking place in a jurisdictionally inappropriate forum. The readiest justification might be claimed in cases where the foreign company had built up a substantial business operation including the maintenance of one or more established places of business or branch offices in England, and a fortiori if the company had taken the additional step of completing formal registration as an 'overseas company' so as to render it readily amenable to legal process before the English courts.[27]Progressively however the courts began to extend their concept of what species of engagement on the part of the foreign company would suffice to render it legitimate to exercise their winding-up jurisdiction. The need to prove that the dissolved foreign company had previously done business in England was relaxed so that it sufficed to show that there were assets of the company within the jurisdiction of the court and persons here claiming as creditors whose claims could not be entertained by the courts of the company's state of incorporation.[28] Further liberalisation took place in a series of decisions from the 1970s onwards, culminating in the substitution of the conveniently elastic expression 'sufficient connection' as the basis for the exercise of the English court's discretionary jurisdiction. In 2001 the Court of Appeal confirmed the legitimacy of this test, and hence the correctness of previous decisions at first instance which had employed it, in the case of *Re Latreefers Inc.*[29]

---

[27] The current legislative provisions concerning the registration of overseas companies are contained in Part 34 of the Companies Act 2006 (ss.1044–59).

[28] *Banque des Marchands de Moscou v. Kindersley* [1951] 1 Ch. 112 (CA) (see at 126–28 per Lord Evershed MR).

[29] Re Latreefers Inc. [2001] B.C.C. 174; [2001] 2 B.C.L.C 116 (CA).

Delivering the judgment of the court, Morritt LJ identified three 'core requirements' as comprising the principles on which English courts exercise their jurisdiction to wind up a foreign company. These are the following:

1. There must be a sufficient connection with England and Wales which may, but does not necessarily have to, consist of assets within the jurisdiction.
2. There must be a reasonable possibility, if a winding-up order is made, of benefit to those applying for the winding-up order.
3. One or more persons interested in the distribution of the assets of the company must be persons over whom the court can exercise a jurisdiction.[30]

The aforementioned formulation, which remains the *locus classicus* concerning the operation of the jurisdiction to wind up foreign companies, conveniently allows a considerable margin of appreciation for the court in its evaluation of the precise nature of the company's contacts with England and its law, and it must always be borne in mind that the jurisdiction is a discretionary one, enabling the court to decline to make a winding-up order if there are grounds for suspecting that ulterior, and less-than-legitimate, purposes lie behind the petitioner's bid to invoke the assistance of the English court in this way.[31]

[30.] Re Latreefers Inc. [2001] B.C.C. 174; [2001] 2 B.C.L.C 116 (CA) at para 20 of the judgment, per Morritt LJ. In the same paragraph, express approval is confirmed of the previous first instance decisions delivered in the following cases: Re Compania Merabello San Nicolas SA [1973] Ch. 75 (Megarry J); Re Eloc Electro-Optieck and Communicatie BV [1982] Ch. 43 (Nourse J); *International Westminster Bank plc v. Okeanos Maritime Corp.* [1988] Ch. 210 (Peter Gibson J); and Re Real Estate Development Co. [1991] B.C.L.C. 210 (Knox J).

[31.] See, e.g., *Banco Nacional de Cuba v. Cosmos Trading Corp.* [200] B.C.C. 910; [2000] 1 B.C.L.C. 813 (CA), and also Re Real Estate Development Co (previous fn.). In both cases, the court concluded that the circumstances were such as to render it unjustifiable for a winding-up order to be granted.

IV. The 'High Summer' of English Common Law Assistance: Sustained Legislative Neglect

We have seen that, from the mid-eighteenth century onwards, English courts contrived to play a positive and constructive role in the management of cross-border insolvency cases despite the complete absence, from the legislation in force at any given time, of any explicit provisions relating to the conduct of international cases. Even in the fundamental matter of the basis on which foreign insolvency proceedings were to be recognisable by English courts so as to enable assistance to be given and, where necessary, enforcement to be authorised of such orders as might be made in the foreign proceedings, the English Legislature signally failed to provide clear statutory rules. It is true that the Bankruptcy Acts of the late nineteenth century included a requirement that 'very *British* court . . . having jurisdiction in bankruptcy or insolvency . . . shall severally act in aid of and be auxiliary to each other in all matters of bankruptcy'(emphasis added).[32] Those provisions were of restricted scope however, being by definition applicable only to courts within the British Empire which were amenable to the legislative authority of the Crown, and they were moreover confined to cases of personal bankruptcy. No equivalent provisions were ever included in the successive iterations of the companies legislation. It was only during the course of the extensive reform and recasting of the legislation relating to personal and corporate insolvency, resulting in the Insolvency Act 1986, that Parliament consciously addressed the issue of international cooperation in post-imperial terms.

---

[32] See Bankruptcy Act 1869, s.74; Bankruptcy Act 1883, s.118; Bankruptcy Act 1914, s.122 (all repealed).

A. A Belated Legislative Contribution

Section 426 of the Insolvency Act 1986 bears the marginal heading 'Co-operation between courts exercising jurisdiction in relation to insolvency'. Despite that open-ended statement, the section is actually of carefully restricted scope, covering two specific constituencies of application. Firstly, the domestic constitutional composition of the United Kingdom itself is the subject of provisions to ensure that insolvency proceedings opened in any part of the UK are effective and enforceable in any other part of the Kingdom.[33] Secondly, assistance in genuinely 'international' cases is authorised by the provisions of s.426(4)-(5) and (10)-(11). Subsection (4) states that '[t]he courts having jurisdiction in relation to insolvency law in any part of the United Kingdom shall assist the courts having the corresponding jurisdiction in any other part of the United Kingdom *or any relevant country or territory*' (emphasis added). It is only when we turn to subsection (11), which supplies the definition of those last six words, that we discover how narrow is the scope for international assistance established by s.426. The only external jurisdictions covered by the section are (a) any of the Channel Islands or the Isle of Man and (b) any country or territory expressly designated for this purpose by Ministerial order. Since 1986 only three such orders have been made, nominating a total of just 20 jurisdictions, all of them current or former members of the Commonwealth. Notable omissions include all member states of the European Union (with the exception of the Republic of Ireland), as well as major global trading partners including the United States. Thus the practical value of this legislative provision authorising judicial cooperation is tightly circumscribed, thereby necessitating a continued operation by the English courts of the established common law rules of recognition and assistance, augmented in more recent years by the impact of the international initiatives which are considered in Section 5 here.

[33.] Insolvency Act 1986, s.426(1)-(3), (6)-(9), (12)-(14).

Despite these limitations, it is appropriate to identify certain distinctive features of the s.426 provisions which are in contrast with the common law alternative. Firstly, the statutory assistance can only be invoked by means of a request issued to the UK court by a court in a 'relevant country or territory'.[34] At common law, as was seen in Section 3 earlier, a foreign liquidator or trustee in bankruptcy can apply directly to the English court for recognition of their appointment and for appropriate assistance in their mission to collect and administer the debtor's assets for the benefit of creditors. On the other hand, the criterion for common law recognition of foreign insolvency proceedings – that they have been opened in the country of the debtor's domicile (construed as the state of incorporation in the case of corporate debtors) – can nowadays appear unduly restrictive in view of the more fluid modes of operation adopted by both individual and corporate debtors – as vividly exemplified by the liberal approach developed by English law itself to enable its winding-up jurisdiction to be exercised on the basis of a company's 'sufficient connection' with this country. There is no indication in the language of s.426 to suggest that the English court's assistance can only be obtained if the debtor is shown to be domiciled in the overseas country or territory from which the request is made. In one respect, moreover, the terms of s.426(5) endow the English courts with a unique power not otherwise available under any of the alternative bases on which their assistance may be sought. This is the power to respond to a request for assistance made by a court in a relevant country or territory by applying 'the law which is applicable by *either* court in relation to comparable matters falling within its jurisdiction' (emphasis added). This authorisation for the English courts to administer 'ambidextrous' assistance under s.426 is a continuation of a facility included in the Bankruptcy Acts of former times, and now made available also to cases of corporate insolvency.[35] The essential point to emphasise however is that this statutory authority to exercise an enhanced

---

[34.] Insolvency Act 1986, s.426(5).

[35.] See legislative provisions listed above in fn. 32.

quality of assistance is in practice confined to requests made by courts in the twenty overseas jurisdictions which have been favoured by inclusion in a ministerial order. All other instances of assistance in cross-border insolvency cases have continued to be dependent on the common law rules and principles which had evolved over the preceding centuries, and more recently to the newly developed arrangements to be described in the following.

B. 1991-1997: Seven Years That Changed the World

Even in s.426 of the Insolvency Act 1986 there is no provision which could provide statutory authority for the English court to engage in some form of dialogue, or two-way correspondence, with the court from which the request has been made, with a view to deciding the appropriate nature and form of the assistance to be provided. It is quite possible that, in 1985–1986 as the new legislation was being drafted and enacted, the concept of direct court-to-court communication simply did not enter into the contemplation of those having conduct of the parliamentary process. However, within less than a decade of the Insolvency Act entering into force, international events in the shape of high-value, multi-jurisdictional insolvencies were destined to expose these historic limitations and to present the English judiciary with a major challenge to their capacity to devise innovative responses to the changing needs of international commerce.

Within the space of a few months in 1991 two major international insolvencies occurred: that of Maxwell Communications Corp plc ('the Maxwell Case') and the even more complex insolvency of the Bank of Credit and Commerce International ('the BCCI case'). In each of those cases, the nature of the respective corporate structures, and the manner in which their global businesses had been conducted, necessitated that the English courts would be centrally involved in the process of resolving their affairs, but that they would have to do so in collaboration with courts in other, sovereign jurisdictions having their own traditions and procedures for dealing with cross-border insolvency cases. Under circumstances of extreme urgency, and with immense sums of money at stake, the lack of any pre-agreed framework for resolving such multi-jurisdictional cases left courts and practitioners with no option but to improvise solutions 'on the hoof'.

In the *BCCI* case a group of banking companies operated in sixty nine countries across the world utilising a structure built around three principal corporate entities, two of which were incorporated in Luxembourg and one in the Cayman Islands. The group's centre of operations was located at various times in London and latterly in Abu Dhabi, but the Bank of England had regulatory oversight of the principal banking entity – BCCI SA – by virtue of its being an author-ised institution carrying out substantial operations in England. The group collapsed in the summer of 1991 and provisional liquidators were appointed on the application of the Bank of England. Initial investigations revealed the enormous magnitude of the group's liabil-ities, exacerbated by evidence of wholesale fraud in the conduct of its operations. The English High Court accordingly made a winding-up order, conscious of the fact that it was exercising jurisdiction over a Luxembourg bank, not an English one, and that delicate questions would inevitably arise as to the relationship between the English court and the Luxembourg court, and also with numerous other courts in countries where the bank's operations had been conducted. In the absence of any international agreement governing complex insolvencies of this kind, it became the task of the practitioners appointed by the court as liquidators to liaise with their counterparts in the many affected jurisdictions with a view to devising a workable strategy for coordinating the burgeoning mass of concurrent pro-ceedings in such a way as maximise the ultimate return for creditors. By their endeavours, within a relatively short time frame a coordi-nated sequence of judicial proceedings was arranged in Luxem-bourg, the Cayman Islands, London, New York, and Washington DC, the ensuing judgments providing a basis on which the convoluted affairs of the group could be administered on the basis of a single, agreed plan – the pooling agreement – by an international team of liquidators mainly drawn from the same, global firm of accountants. All this was achieved without the judges in the respective courts having direct contact with one another, although the judgments themselves display a concerted desire to play a positive role in facilitating the best possible outcome under the circumstances.[36]

In the *Maxwell* case an English company, managed by a board of directors in London and quoted on the London stock exchange, had its principal assets in the form of shares in valuable American companies. Those assets greatly exceeded in value the company's non-U.S. assets. The company was massively overindebted, and in December 1991 multiple defaults on its debt obligations were imminent. The directors filed a petition under chapter 11 of the U.S. Bankruptcy Code in the Bankruptcy Court for the Southern District of New York, which accepted jurisdiction on the basis that the English company had property in the United States.[37] Although the filing brought into operation an automatic stay, pursuant to section 362 of the U.S. Bankruptcy Code, on all proceedings against MCC this would not have prevented action being taken in England by creditors who were not subject to the jurisdiction of the U.S. court. Accordingly MCC presented a petition to the English High Court for an administration order. The petition was heard by Hoffmann J (as he then was), who made the order and appointed joint administrators. This development had the potential to bring about a 'turf war' between rival insolvency procedures, given the numerous differences between a chapter 11 restructuring and an English administration. That undesirable outcome was averted by the imaginative initiative of the administrators, sympathetically supported by the judicial orders

[36.] See, e.g., successive judgments of the English courts in Re Bank of Credit and Commerce International SA [1992] B.C.C. 83 and 86 (Brown-Wilkinson VC); Re Bank of Credit and Commerce International SA (No.2) [1992] B.C.C.715 and 720 (Nicholls V-C, and CA); Judgment and Order of the District Court of Luxembourg, Sixth Chamber (1431.12P) (M. Welter, Vice-President), 3 January 1992; *U.S.A. v. BCCI Holdings (Luxembourg) and others* (Docket No. CR 91-0655) United States District Court for the District of Columbia (Green, District Judge) 24 January 1992.

[37.] Bankruptcy Code (11 USC), section 109(a).

made by Hoffmann J and his U.S. counterpart, Judge Tina Brozman, who had conduct of the case in the New York court. A melding of the two insolvency procedures was accomplished by the expedient of Judge Brozman recognising the English administrators as the corporate governance of MCC duly constituted under the law of the company's incorporation, and thereupon designating the administrators as the debtor-in-possession for the purposes of the chapter 11 proceeding. To allay any concerns about the process being conducted by non-U.S. practitioners, a distinguished Connecticut insolvency lawyer, Richard Gitlin, was appointed examiner in accordance with section 1104(b) of the Bankruptcy Code. Thereafter the process was conducted in binary fashion, with each significant stage being submitted to authorisation and approval by the appropriate constituencies of engaged parties, and by the respective courts.

As in the BCCI case, the successful outcome of this pioneering venture into unprecedented legal territory was crucially dependent on the willingness of the two judges to take risks in the interests of securing an economically more favourable outcome for creditors. This ultimately required them to place complete trust in each other's integrity, despite the fact that they were not personally acquainted and were unable to enter into direct communication with each other. Subsequently, both judges are on record as acknowledging that they would have welcomed the opportunity to establish direct contact in order to discuss how best to move the matter forward, but that in the absence of any formal authorisation in the legislation of their respective countries they felt constrained from doing so. Under the circumstances, they confined themselves independently to articulating clear declarations of mutual respect and goodwill in the course of judgments delivered at various stages of the proceedings.[38] In extrajudicial presentations made in the immediate aftermath of the *Maxwell* saga, the two judges were able to affirm their belief that clear

---

[38.] See, e.g., Re Maxwell Communications Corp. plc (No.2), *Barclays Bank v. Homan* [1992] B.C.C. 757 at 767, per Hoffmann J, aff'd CA *ibid.* at 767–78; Re Petition of Brierley, 145 B.R.151, 27 C.B.C. 2d 828 (Bankr. S.D.N.Y. 1992) (Judge Tina Brozman).

authorisation to engage in court-to-court communication would be a welcome facility in international cases, provided that suitable safeguards and guidelines were also established. Their considered opinions, borne of experience, were to provide influential support for the movement to enable such authorisation to become established in law, as discussed in the next section.

V. The American Breakthrough – 1978 and All That

A vital contribution to the reshaping of the architecture of cross-border insolvency in the final years of the twentieth century came about during the course of the wholesale reform of the bankruptcy law of the United States, culminating in the Bankruptcy Reform Act 1978 which established the current U.S. Bankruptcy Code.[39] Most celebrated among the reforms, and undoubtedly the most widely studied by the global insolvency community, has been the innovative chapter 11 entitled 'Reorganization'. Less noticed at the time of enactment, certainly by most non-American scholars, were the provisions numbered as section 304–306 within chapter 3 of the Code (titled 'Case Administration'). These three sections brought about a revolution in the American courts' approach to international insolvency cases, and in particular to the giving of active assistance to the conduct of foreign insolvency proceedings. Previously, there were no legislative provisions on which the courts could base such assistance, and the resources of the American legal system were mainly inaccessible save in those cases where the foreign administrator was able to procure the opening of a full-scale bankruptcy proceeding under U.S. law, with all the additional costs and complexities that this would entail. Moreover, the very fact of making application to the U.S. court for that purpose, or indeed for the more limited purpose of seeking to

---

[39.] Bankruptcy Reform Act 1978, 11 U.S.C., replacing the Bankruptcy Act 1898 with effect from October 1, 1979.

claim property located in the United States, could constitute a voluntary submission to the full panoply of American civil jurisdiction, thereby placing at risk the assets of the foreign insolvent estate in the event that U.S. litigants successfully brought action in their domestic courts. For this reason, prior to 1978, many foreign administrators elected to forego the prospect of seeking to claim property located in the United States for fear that this might result in a net depletion of the value of the estate which they already had under their control.[40] By section 306 of the Bankruptcy Code, a concept of 'limited appearance' was established whereby '[A]n appearance in a bankruptcy court by a foreign representative in connection with a petition or request under section 303, section 304 or section 305 of this title does not submit such foreign representative to the jurisdiction of any court in the United States for any other purpose'.[41] Significantly, this vital provision, affording a foreign representative a genuine, rather than a merely theoretical, right of access to invoke the assistance of the U.S. courts, has been replicated in Art.10 of the UNCITRAL Model Law.

The centrepiece of these groundbreaking provisions included in the 1978 reforms was the creation by section 304 of a new procedure known as 'a case ancillary to a foreign proceeding'. The procedure made available a broad range of assistance to a foreign representative without the need for formal bankruptcy proceedings to be commenced in the United States (although if necessary such proceedings could be resorted to by using section 303(b)(4)). In many cases, the required

---

[40.] See, e.g., the notorious case of the Herstatt Bank during the years 1974–1975., in which the interested parties in the liquidation of a German bank opted to settle proceedings pending before the court in New York before the court could adjudicate upon the legal issues, and Herstatt's German liquidator decided upon advice to stay out of the proceedings and did not enter an appearance. Comments on the case were published by Becker in (1976) 62 A.B.A.J. 1290 and in (1983) 11 Intn'l Bus. L. 239, and also by Nadelmann in (1977) 52 N.Y.U.L. Rev. 1. The opinion of Professor Nadelmann was considered to have strongly influenced the decision to include section 304–06 in the Bankruptcy Code of 1978.

[41.] Note that with the enactment of Ch. 15 of the Bankruptcy Code in 2005, and the consequential repeal of section 304, the references to that section in section 306 were deleted, although the section itself remains in force.

assistance would be of more limited scope, such as the obtaining of an injunction to restrain parties from pursuing action against property involved in the foreign proceedings, or to obtain turnover of property claimed by the foreign representative on behalf of the estate. Significantly, the legislature also included a less precisely worded provision empowering the U.S. court to order 'other appropriate relief'.[42] Crucially, an ancillary proceeding could be sought by a foreign representative without it being a precondition to show that some kind of treaty was in force between the United States and the state in which the foreign proceeding was taking place, or that demonstrable reciprocity operated between the two systems of insolvency law. In a remarkably magnanimous gesture, the U.S. legislature was opening the doors of its bankruptcy courts and their repertoire of assistance without demanding any *quid pro quo* of the state whose officer was requesting their assistance. The granting of relief was however a matter for the discretion of the U.S. court, to be exercised in accordance with the terms of section 304(c)(1)–(6), which included ample scope for the court to scrutinise the inherent qualities of the foreign system of justice, and to ensure that claim holders in the United States would be treated fairly and non-prejudicially under the law governing the foreign proceeding. Those guidelines enabled the U.S. courts to develop a series of precedents controlling the exercise of their discretionary powers, including a doctrine whereby the court would not insist that the foreign insolvency law must match, in every material particular, the process and outcome that would operate in a U.S. proceeding in comparable circumstances. Provided that the court was satisfied that there was 'substantial similarity' between its own system and that of the foreign state, discretionary assistance could be made available.[43]

---

[42] 11 U.S.C. § 304(b)(3). Note the somewhat differently worded provision for the granting of 'additional relief' included in the assistance provisions of the UNCITRAL Model Law as art.21(1)(g).

[43] See, e.g., the cases of Re Culmer 25 B.R. 621 (Bankr. S.D.N.Y. 1982); *Cunard Steamship Co. v. Salen Reefer Services AB*, 773 F.2d. 452 (2nd Cir. 1985); Re Axona International Credit and Commerce Ltd, 88 B.R. 597 (Bankr. S.D.N.Y. 1988). Contrast

Unquestionably, section 304 transformed the ethos of cross-border assistance, not merely in the United States but progressively across the commercial world. Among the American judiciary it engendered an 'assistance culture' which has had a far-reaching impact on the theory and practice of international insolvency. In an historic 'first', the U.S. Congress had enacted authorisation for judges actively to assist their foreign counterparts, thereby setting an example to legislators elsewhere. For their part, taking inspiration from the examples furnished by such cases as *Maxwell* and *BCCI*, American bankruptcy judges began to give thought to the possibility of engaging in direct communication with their foreign counterparts, in the interests of devising the optimum way to manage cross-border proceedings in the real-time context under which insolvency matters have to be conducted. Initially, such experiments were arranged in cases straddling the frontier between the United States and Canada, where the potential difficulties posed by differences of language, legal culture and time zones were less of a concern. Thus it was that in the years immediately after 1993, when a joint initiative was undertaken between UNCITRAL and INSOL International to promote the development of an international framework for the conduct of cross-border insolvency cases, the U.S.-Canadian experience was to furnish a powerful inspiration to the working party tasked with the elaboration of what duly became the Model law on Cross-Border Insolvency, adopted by the United Nations in May 1997.[44] In addition to proclaiming, in the opening paragraph of the Preamble, the

---

Re Hourani, 180 B.R. 58 at 64 (Bankr. S.D.N.Y.1995); Re Tam, 170 B.R. 838 (Bankr. S.D.N.Y. 1994).

[44] For background material and documentation of key stages in the evolution of the Model Law, beginning with the Vienna Colloquium of April 1994, see [1995] 4 International Law Review, Special Conference Issue; [1996] 5 I.I.R. 139–69; [1997] 6 I.I.R. 139–60; 236–51. Full documentation of the working sessions of UNCITRAL Working Group V can be accessed at www.uncitral.org/uncitral/en/commission/working_groups.html (accessed 15 November 2017). Materials from the numerous colloquia relating to insolvency convened by UNCITRAL since 1994 can be accessed at www.uncitral.org/uncitral/en/commission/colloquia_insolvency.html (accessed 15 November 2017).

objective of promoting '[C]ooperation between courts and other competent authorities . . . involved in cases of cross-border insolvency', the Model Law adopts two expressions from the terminology associated with section 304 – 'foreign proceeding' and 'foreign representative', defined in article 2(a) and (d), respectively – as key factors governing eligibility to seek access, recognition and assistance under the substantive provisions embodied in the text. Also of vital importance, in the context of a text designed to be adopted on a worldwide basis by states representing a wide spectrum of legal traditions, are the provisions in articles 25–27 inclusive which impose a matrix of duties of cooperation and direct communication 'to the maximum extent possible' between courts, between courts and foreign representatives, and between foreign representatives. Articles 25(2) and 26(2) each specify that a court or a person or body administering an insolvency proceeding is entitled to communicate directly with, or to request information or assistance from, foreign courts or foreign representatives, as the case may be.

One may note at this point that a constructive role was also played during the elaboration of the text of the Model Law by the representatives of the United Kingdom, together with other representatives of Member States of the European Union which by 1997 were in the process of finalising the text of what was to become, by May 2000, the European Regulation on Insolvency Proceedings.[45] The Europeans were instrumental in procuring the transplantation into the Model law of the newly coined connecting factors – 'centre of main interests' and 'establishment' of the debtor – which supply functional tests for determining internationally accepted standards for the exercise of jurisdiction to open insolvency proceedings. The same two concepts, according to article 2(b) and (c) of the Model Law, supply the tests for identifying the status of a foreign proceeding as either a 'main' or a 'non-main' proceeding for the purposes of recognition under the Model Law.

---

[45] Council Regulation (EC) No.1346/2000 of May 29, 2000, on Insolvency Proceedings [2000] O.J. L.160/1, which entered into application on May 31, 2002.

A. The English Judges Bite the Bullet

Following the adoption of the Model Law by UNCITRAL on 30 May 1997, it was anticipated that many of the states which had played a leading role in the project would quickly set an example to the rest of the world by enacting legislation to incorporate the Model Law into their domestic systems. Disappointingly, during the early years between 1997 and 2004 a mere seven states or territories had risen to the challenge. Notably, neither the United States nor the UK managed to bring enacting legislation into force until 2005 and 2006, respectively.[46] During that over-lengthy hiatus, English courts were placed in an uncertain position in their conduct of cross-border cases. Primary legislation had indeed been enacted in the form of the Insolvency Act 2000, s.14 of which was an enabling provision to confer on the Secretary of State for Trade and Industry the power to make regulations in the form of a statutory instrument enacting the Model Law. But for a further five years the power remained unused. Cases came before the courts in which it would clearly be advantageous to establish communication with the judge having conduct of concurrent proceedings in another country, yet in the absence of express legislative authority to do so the judges refrained from taking that vital first step onto the ice. In April 2003 however Lightman J, sitting in the Chancery Division, took the pioneering decision to engage with his opposite number, Judge Drain sitting in the Southern District of New York, in an effort to resolve a potentially value-destructive jurisdictional contest between the two courts in the case of *Cenargo International plc*. Having obtained the consent of all interested parties in the proceedings before them, and with arrangements in place to enable their legal representatives to

---

[46.] In the United States, enactment of the Model Law, as Ch. 15 of the Bankruptcy Code, was finally accomplished by the Bankruptcy Abuse Prevention and Consumer Protection Act 2005 (S.256), which simultaneously repealed section 304. In the U.K., statutory instruments giving the Model law the force of law in each part of the Kingdom were brought into force from April 4, 2006 (England, Wales and Scotland) and April 12, 2007 (Northern Ireland): SI 2006/1030 and SRNI 2007/115, respectively.

listen to the telephone discussion (of which a full record was also made), the judges engaged in an historic discussion which resulted in a commercially sensible resolution of the 'turf war'.[47] Initially, Lightman J's fellow judges were cautious in their response to invitations made by counsel appearing before them to enter into similar transatlantic conversations, while leaving open the possibility that 'in an appropriate case' they might be prepared to do so.[48] In the years since 2006, when the Model Law had received belated legislative enactment, English courts have shown a greater willingness to follow where Lightman J. so boldly led.[49]

VI. The Indian Summer of the Common Law, 2006-2012

From 2005 onwards, the list of states enacting the Model Law steadily began to grow.[50] It seemed possible to conclude that the campaign to promote judicial cooperation, including communication, in

---

[47.] Re Cenargo International plc (No.862 of 2003), April 14, 2003 (directions hearing before Lightman J in conference with Judge Drain (unreported, but discussed in S. Shandro and R. Tett, 'The Cenargo Case: A Tale of Conflict, Greed, Contempt, Comity and Costs', in INSOL World, Fourth Quarter, 2003, 33, and by Sir Gavin Lightman, 'Recent Developments in Insolvency Law – A Judicial View', in Sweet and Maxwell's Company Law Newsletter, Issue 19/2005 (Oct. 31, 2005), 1–3 at 3.

[48.] See the remarks of David Richards J (as he then was), declining to engage in a telephone conference with the U.S. judge at the stage at which the proceedings were at that time, while acknowledging that such inter-court communications could serve a useful purpose at a later stage, as and when appropriate: Re T&N Ltd [2004] EWHC 2878 (Ch); [2005] B.C.C. 982, at 988–89.

[49.] For reported examples of judicial communication, see *Perpetual Trustee Co. Ltd v. BNY Corporate Trustee Services Ltd* [2009] EWHC 2593 (Ch); [2010] B.C.L.C. 237 (Henderson J); Re Lehman Brothers Holdings Inc, 422 B.R. 407 (Bkcy. S.D.N.Y. 2010); Re Lehman Brothers International Europe [2013] EWHC 1664 (Ch); [2014] B.C.C. 132, at paras [15]-[17] of the judgment, per David Richards J.

[50.] See the official list of enacting states, recording the dates of enactment, maintained by UNCITRAL and displayed at www.uncitral.org/uncitral/en/uncitral_texts/insolvency/1997Model_status.html (accessed Nov. 17, 2017, at which date the Model Law had been adopted in 43 states in a total of 45 jurisdictions).

cross-border insolvency was well on the way to gaining worldwide acceptance. The question remained whether there was still a role for the alternative traditions of assistance and cooperation developed on a case by cases basis by the common law systems. In the case of the United States, the enactment of chapter 15 of the Bankruptcy Code was the occasion for shutting down alternative grounds of assistance based on section 304 together with the doctrine of comity, leaving chapter 15 as the single gateway for access by a foreign representative. In the UK, on the other hand, care was taken in drafting the provisions of the Cross-Border Insolvency Regulations 2006 to ensure that s.426 of the Insolvency Act 1986 continues to apply in relation to such cases as fall within its scope,[51] and no provision was included which could bring about the abrogation of the accumulated precedents of the common law. Provision was also made to ensure that in any case where the Model Law conflicts with an obligation of the UK under the European Insolvency Regulation, the latter shall prevail.[52] The survival of the common law 'heritage' in this area is especially welcome, as there are situations where, by their own self-imposed limitations as to scope, neither the European Regulation nor the Model Law are applicable, whereas at common law recognition and assistance could be forthcoming.[53] Moreover, it must not be forgotten that the English common law, via the Privy Council, furnishes the ultimate fountain of authority for the laws of a number of Commonwealth countries and territories, not all of which have to date enacted the Model Law but retain the practices assimilated over the years from the common

---

[51] See Cross Border Insolvency Regulation 2006, S.I. 2006/1030, Sched.1, art.2(a), (b); 15.3;18(b).

[52] Ibid., art.3.

[53] An example of such a case was Re Phoenix Kapitaldienst GmbH [2013] Ch. 61 where assistance in the form of granting a clawback remedy under s.423 of the Insolvency Act 1986 was granted to a German liquidator of an investment company in circumstances where neither the Model Law nor the EU Regulation could apply. The decision was subsequently declared by Lord Collins to have been wrongly decided as having 'involved an impermissible application of legislation by analogy': Singularis Holdings Ltd v. PricewaterhouseCoopers [2015] A.C. 1675 (PC), at paras 50 and 94–98 of the judgment.

law precedents on recognition and assistance. It is therefore especially significant that the latter-day decisions which have most influenced the state of the common law concerning such matters have been delivered by differently composed panels of senior English judiciary sitting in London as the Privy Council. These are, respectively, the *Cambridge Gas* case[54] and the *Singularis* case.[55]

The *Cambridge Gas* case was decided by the Privy Council in May 2006.[56] In that case, a company formed in the Isle of Man ('Navigator') had entered into chapter 11 restructuring in New York, resulting in a confirmed plan under which the shares in the company were to be vested in the creditors and the equity interests of the previous investors extinguished. As the shares in Navigator were situated in the Isle of Man, such vesting would require the assistance of the Manx court, which was duly sought by Letter of Request sent by the New York court. The equity holders challenged the propriety of such assistance before the Manx courts, from whose decision final appeal lay to the Privy Council which concluded that it lay within the powers of a common law court to grant the assistance sought. In delivering the single judgment of the Privy Council, Lord Hoffmann explained that by the traditional principles of English common law there should ideally be 'a single bankruptcy in which all creditors are entitled and required to prove' and that, in order to attain the ideal of universality, upon recognition of the validity of the foreign proceedings the active assistance of the court should be forthcoming.[57] In considering what the limits of such assistance should be, Lord Hoffmann expressed doubt whether at common law it would be possible to replicate the approach authorised by

---

[54] *Cambridge Gas Transport Corp v. The Official Committee of Unsecured Creditors of Navigator Holdings plc* [2006] UKPC 26; [2007] 1 A.C. 508 (PC).

[55] *Singularis Holdings Ltd v. PricewaterhouseCoopers* [2014] UKPC 36; [2015] A.C. 1675 (PC).

[56] It should be noted that the decision of the Privy Council was delivered some six weeks after the entry into force of the Cross-Border Insolvency Regulations, which gave the UNCITRAL Model Law the force of law in England and Wales and Scotland.

[57] [2007] 1 A.C. 508 at paras 16–20 of the judgment, per Lord Hoffmann.

s.426(5) of the Insolvency Act 1986 and apply the law of the foreign state concerned. But he firmly asserted that

> the domestic court must at least be able to provide assistance by doing whatever it could have done in the case of a domestic insolvency. The purpose of recognition is to enable the foreign office holder or the creditors to avoid having to start parallel insolvency proceedings and to give them remedies to which they would have been entitled if the equivalent proceedings had taken place in the domestic forum.[58]

It may be noted that the previous passage is also reflecting the spirit and intent of the UNCITRAL Model Law, and it is further relevant to observe that in enacting the Model Law the UK Legislature had gone out of its way to list numerous remedies available under English and Scottish domestic law, including several that are otherwise exclusively available to the office holder in insolvency proceedings conducted pursuant to the insolvency legislation, which can be made available to a foreign representative without the necessity to open formal insolvency proceedings under domestic law.[59] Thus, in articulating the proposition that common law assistance could include the granting of assistance by analogy based upon domestic legislation 'as if' it had been expressed to apply to foreign cases, Lord Hoffmann's remarks were effectively synchronising the common law with the latest policy position embodied in legislation enacted by Parliament. However, after a few brief years in which the *Cambridge Gas* decision stood as a shining example of the ability of the common law to develop to meet the changing circumstances of international commerce, the changing composition of the judicial personnel constituting the Privy Council and Supreme Court brought about a reversal of fortune, and a radical recasting of the possibilities of granting assistance.

[58.] *Ibid.*, at para 22 of the judgment, per Lord Hoffmann.
[59.] See Cross Border Insolvency Regulation 2006, S.I. 2006/1030, Sched.1, arts.21, 23.

Although the broad proposition embodied in the *Cambridge Gas* decision was enthusiastically received and emulated by many judges both in England and in the wider Commonwealth, the euphoria was destined to be of relatively brief duration. The first high-level challenge to Lord Hoffmann's vision of the spirit and purpose of common law assistance was delivered in the UK Supreme Court in October 2012 in the case of *Rubin v. Eurofinance SA*.[60] The case involved a separate, but related point of law to the *Cambridge Gas* decision, as it raised the question of enforceability in England of a default judgment delivered by a foreign court in which insolvency proceedings were being conducted in circumstances which met the recognition criteria of English law. The foreign court, exercising its own powers under domestic law, had issued a judgment against a party alleged to have benefited from a voidable transaction with the insolvent debtor. The defendant in those proceedings had chosen not to defend or enter an appearance, and relied upon the English law precedents which held that a foreign judgment against a non-submitting defendant cannot be enforced in England. By a majority of 4–1, the Supreme Court ruled that the default judgment could not be enforced in England, but Lord Collins, delivering the judgment of the majority of the court, went further and delivered the incidental observation that *Cambridge Gas* had been 'wrongly decided'.[61] Lord Mance, while agreeing with the majority on the actual point under appeal, expressly reserved his position on the correctness of the *Cambridge Gas* decision, pointing out that 'this was not argued before the Supreme Court',[62] Nevertheless the resulting uncertainty as to the true legal position regarding cross-border assistance meant that the matter would inevitably be brought back before the courts for direct consideration.

[60.] *Rubin v. Eurofinance SA* [2012] UKSC 46; [2013] 1 A.C. 236 (SC).

[61.] *Ibid.*, at para 132 of the judgment, per Lord Collins (see also paras 35–131).

[62.] *Ibid.*, at para 178 of the judgment, per Lord Mance. See also the dissenting judgment of Lord Clarke, at paras 191–205.

In November 2014, the Privy Council delivered the final judgment in the *Singularis* case, and in doing so brought about a severe diminution of the common law doctrine of assistance and its scope to play a constructive role in the resolution of complex, multi-jurisdictional insolvencies for the foreseeable future. The case came in the form of an appeal from the courts of Bermuda, whose assistance was being sought by the liquidators of related companies incorporated in the Cayman Islands. The Cayman liquidators needed to gain access to information held by the companies' former auditors, whose accountancy firm happened to be based in Bermuda. Although both Caribbean jurisdictions are members of the Commonwealth (and are indeed listed in the schedule to s.426 of the UK Insolvency Act for the purposes of obtaining assistance from courts in the UK), no direct statutory powers to grant assistance to each other in insolvency matters are currently in force in the two jurisdictions, and neither of them has yet enacted the UNCITRAL Model Law. Moreover, differences between their respective laws governing corporate insolvency result in a more extensive power to gain access to material and information relating to an insolvent company under the law of Bermuda than would be available under Cayman law. The Privy Council concluded that this discrepancy between the discovery powers contained in the two laws was fatal to the liquidators' case and they proceeded to re-state the principles of cross-border assistance in heavily circumscribed terms which have effectively emasculated the doctrine in the context of present-day business practices. Exceptionally, all five members of the Board of the Privy Council delivered separate judgments embodying their individual formulations of the state of the law, but all five were agreed that the Bermudian courts had no power to grant assistance to a foreign liquidator where the form of assistance requested was not available under the law of the jurisdiction in which the insolvency proceedings were 'anchored'. In contrast to the 'substantial similarity' doctrine developed by the U.S. courts in former days when operating section 304, today's judges operating under English law are required to confirm that absolute congruency exists between the discovery and assistance laws of the two jurisdictions involved, thus effectively resurrecting, in a new context, the long-discredited 'double actionability' doctrine that for a hundred years bedevilled the English approach to 'foreign tort' cases until questioned and mitigated by the House of Lords in the celebrated case of *Boys v. Chaplin*.[63]

The most detailed articulation of the new limits on modified universalism as a basis for providing assistance is to be found in the judgment of Lord Sumption.[64] Lord Collins in his separate, concurring, judgment delivered a sustained denunciation of the *Cambridge Gas* decision and of its core philosophy, namely the courts' practice of applying remedies of domestic law 'as if' the Legislature had intentionally made them applicable to foreign insolvency cases. In no fewer than four places in his judgment, the 'application by analogy' basis of common law assistance is denounced in the strongest possible terms as involving 'a fundamental misunderstanding of the limits of the judicial law-making power'; 'a plain usurpation of the legislative function'; 'profoundly contrary to the established relationship between the judiciary and the legislature'; and 'profoundly unconstitutional'.[65] With respect, as was noted previously, Lord Hoffmann's seminal formulation in *Cambridge Gas* of the scope of assistance was delivered in a judgment which post-dated the legislative authorisation, in enacting the Model Law for the UK, for the judges to make available to a foreign representative a significant number of remedies which are normally available only to an insolvency

---

[63] *Boys v. Chaplin* [1971] A.C. 356 (HL), an example of 'judicial legislation' importing the 'proper law of the tort doctrine', as evolved by U.S. courts, to mitigate the double actionability rule first propounded by Willes J in *Phillips v. Eyre* (1870) L.R. 6 Q.B. 1. It is pertinent to note that one of the most influential advocates of the adoption of the 'proper law' doctrine was the late Dr. J. C. Morris, who served as the principal editor of Dicey and Morris on the Conflict of Laws between 1949 and 1980, since which date the General Editor of the work has been Lawrence Collins (now Lord Collins of Mapesbury).

[64] *Singularis Holdings Ltd v. PricewaterhouseCoopers* [2014] UKPC 36; [2015] A.C. 1675 (PC), at paras 19–25, per Lord Sumption.

[65] *Ibid.*, at paras 36, 64, 83 and 108 of the judgment, per Lord Collins.

administrator appointed in domestic proceedings under the Insolvency Act 1986 or the Bankruptcy (Scotland) Act 1985.[66]

Moreover it is hopefully not impertinent to point out that the function of the Privy Council is to serve as the court of last recourse from those jurisdictions around the Commonwealth that continue to value the additional qualities of judicial wisdom and experience that are traditionally associated with the senior judiciary of the United Kingdom, who simultaneously comprise the benches of the Privy Council and the Supreme Court. It is therefore deeply disappointing to encounter the somewhat complacent passage at paragraph 42 of the judgment in which Lord Collins notes that, thanks to the operation within the UK itself of the UNCITRAL Model Law and s.426 of the 1986 Act, in conjunction with the very broad (judicially developed) jurisdiction to wind up foreign companies, the practical effects of the wholesale contraction of the common law assistance powers effected through the *Singularis* ruling are likely to be minimal. This, alas, consigns the offshore territories and dependencies such as Bermuda, the Isle of Man, and the Cayman Island to an unenviable limbo as the Privy Council has apparently renounced its constitutional responsibilities to ensure that the common law can continue to serve the ends of justice in today's globalised, and highly sophisticated, world of commerce and finance.[67]

A. Envoi

As will be evident from the preceding account of the jurisprudential arc that has been traversed by English law over two and a half centuries in its response to the challenges of cross-border insolvency, the present writer deeply regrets the recent, collective decision by the senior judiciary of the United Kingdom to relinquish the distinguished role of standard bearers for the creative approach to resolving

---

[66.] See above, n.59 and text thereto.

[67.] See the insightful account of the common law on judicial cooperation in the British Atlantic and Caribbean World by Chief Justice Ian Kawaley (Chief Justice of Bermuda) in (2015) 3 NIBLej 10.

the complex, and ever-changing, challenges posed by cross-border insolvency cases. Faced with the fluid and resourceful strategies devised by those engaged in international commerce (not always entirely for the best and most honourable of motives), it ill serves the cause of international justice for a leading jurisdiction such as the UK to revert to its 'classic' and 'traditional' rules and principles, and to insist that their application must be rigidly and inflexibly maintained. That way, surely, lies stagnation. One can but hope that, in time, a new generation of English judiciary will be prepared to revisit this aspect of our law and that they will do so mindful of the golden tradition in which some of the most eminent judicial minds of former generations have succeeded in advancing the common law. One may conclude by quoting the words of two of the most distinguished representatives of that tradition. Thus Lord Macmillan, in the landmark case of *Donoghue v. Stevenson*[68] affirmed that

> The grounds of action may be as various and manifold as human errancy; and the conception of legal responsibility may develop in adaptation to altering social conditions and standards. The criterion of judgment must adjust and adapt itself to the changing circumstances of life.

In the same spirit is the celebrated dictum of Lord Atkin in *United Australia Ltd v. Barclays Bank Ltd*[69]:

> When the ghosts of the past stand in the path of justice clanking their medieval chains, the proper course for the judge is to pass through them undeterred.

Mais où sont les juges d'antan?[70]

---

[68] *Donoghue v. Stevenson* [1932] A.C. 562 (HL), at 619.
[69] *United Australia Ltd v. Barclays Bank Ltd* [1941] A.C. 1 (HL), at 29.
[70] With apologies to François Villon.

Corporate Distress, Credit Default Swaps, and Defaults: Information and Traditional, Contingent, and Empty Creditors

Henry T. C. Hu[*]

I. Introduction

Financially troubled companies, endemic to our economic system, are likely to become more pervasive. Since October 1, 1979, more than a thousand large public companies became so distressed that they ended up in bankruptcy.[1] In 2016, the average Standard & Poor's

---

[*] Allan Shivers Chair in the Law of Banking and Finance, University of Texas Law School. This chapter is based in part on my presentations at the February 2018 University of Texas Law School conference in honor of Jay Westbrook and the March 2018 Brooklyn Law School symposium on corporate control. I have benefited much from the comments of conference/symposium participants and from the assistance of Michael Davis, Jacob McDonald, Vaughn Miller, Scott Vdoviak, Alicia Vesely, Helen Xiang, and Lei Zhang. A substantially identical version of this chapter was published in the corporate control symposium issue: Henry T. C. Hu, *Corporate Distress, Credit Default Swaps, and Defaults: Information and Traditional, Contingent, and Empty Creditors*, 13 Brook. J. Corp. Fin. & Com. L. 5 (2018), available at http://ssrn.com/abstract=3302816. Reproduced with permission. Copyright © 2018 by Henry T. C. Hu. All rights reserved.

[1] See A Window on the World of Big-Case Bankruptcy, UCLA-LoPucki Bankruptcy Research Database, http://lopucki.law.ucla.edu/ (last updated Aug. 2018).

credit rating for U.S. corporate debt fell to junk levels.[2] In April 2018, the International Monetary Fund reported that the U.S. market for leveraged loans had reached almost $1 trillion[3] and that two-thirds of loans extended in 2017 were rated "B" or lower.[4] In May 2018, Moody's stated that a prolonged environment of low growth and low interest rates has caused "striking changes in nonfinancial corporate credit quality."[5] Such deterioration in credit quality leaves corporations especially vulnerable as interest rates return to normal.

The task of protecting debt and equity investors in companies in danger of bankruptcy will thus be increasingly important. The academic literature has largely focused on the role of substantive corporate law in doing so, in particular the doctrine of "duty shifting" present in the substantive law of many states. Under this doctrine, when a corporation is sufficiently distressed—but not bankrupt (and thus not subject to the alternate mandates of federal bankruptcy law)—management must shift its focus from the interests of shareholders to the interests of bondholders or the enterprise as a whole. A vast academic literature is devoted to this doctrine, including a work that I co-authored with Jay Westbrook.[6]

In contrast, the role of disclosure with respect to such troubled, non-bankrupt companies has received little academic attention.[7]

---

[2] Patrick Gillespie, Junk Territory: U.S. Corporate Debt Ratings near 15-Year Low, CNN Money (Mar. 24, 2016), http://money.cnn.com/2016/03/24/investing/us-corporate-debt-rating-junk-15-year-low/index.html.

[3] Int'l Monetary Fund, Global Financial Stability Report: A Bumpy Road Ahead 12 (2018).

[4] Id. at 15.

[5] Jeff Cox, Moody's Warns of "Particularly Large" Wave of Junk Bond Defaults Ahead, CNBC: Corp. Bonds (May 25, 2018), www.cnbc.com/2018/05/25/moodys-warns-of-particularly-large-wave-of-junk-bond-defaults.html.

[6] Henry T. C. Hu & Jay Lawrence Westbrook, Abolition of the Corporate Duty to Creditors, 107 Colum. L. Rev. 1321, 1340 (2007). By mid-2006, over 150 law review articles had cited the seminal 1991 duty shifting case, Credit Lyonnais Nederland, N.V. v. Pathe Commc'ns Corp., No. Civ. A. No. 12150, 1991 WL 277613 (Del. Ch. Dec. 30, 1991).

[7] The earliest academic work that deals in a material way with the disclosure aspects of distressed but not bankrupt companies appears to be Richard H. Mendales, Looking under the Rock: Disclosure of Bankruptcy Issues under the Securities

This chapter explores some important informational asymmetries in this context, which are curious in their origin, nature, and impact. Disclosure matters for companies that are already in bankruptcy are different and extensively discussed elsewhere.[8]

This chapter explores two types of asymmetry that undermine the robust informational base needed by investors in such troubled companies. The first type is simple and direct: asymmetry with respect to information about the company itself that the company does not fully convey to investors. This chapter suggests that there is fresh evidence for the belief that troubled companies may prove lax in securities law compliance and for a long-standing explanation for such laxity. In addition, the chapter offers two new explanations rooted in securities law developments.

Building on the existing analytical framework for decoupling, the chapter also examines a less obvious category of asymmetries: "extra-company" informational asymmetries flowing from credit default swap (CDS) and CDS-driven "debt decoupling" activities of third parties.[9] Such third-party activities can be determinative of a company's prospects, but reliable public information on the presence, nature, and magnitude of such activities tend to be scant. Here, even the company itself, not just investors, may not have the

---

Laws, 57 Ohio St. L. J. 731 (1996). More recent academic works in this space do not try to offer an integrated overview but instead center on particular situations, such as the "final period" incentive pattern discussed in Part I(B).

[8.] A company in bankruptcy is generally subject to two disclosure regimes, one under federal bankruptcy law and one under federal securities law. As to federal securities law, an "SEC-lite" disclosure regime is sometimes available. See, e.g., Application of the Reporting Provisions of the Securities Exchange Act of 1934 to Issuers Which Have Ceased or Severely Curtailed Their Operations, Exchange Act Release No. 9660, 1972 WL 121308 (June 30, 1972); David J. Barton, SEC Disclosure, Filing Requirements for Public Companies in chapter 11, J. Corp. Renewal, Jan. 2009, at 1. As to works on disclosure matters for companies in bankruptcy, see, e.g., Kelli A. Alces, Limiting the SEC's Role in Bankruptcy, 18 Am. Bankr. Inst. L. Rev. 631 (2010); Dennis F. McNally, Relaxed SEC Reporting Requirements for Domestic Companies in Bankruptcy, 26 Cal. Bankr. J. 324 (2003); 7 Collier on Bankruptcy 1125.02 (Alan N. Resnick & Henry J. Sommer eds., 16th ed., 2011).

[9.] See Part II.

requisite information. This chapter largely examines such CDS and debt decoupling matters through the lens of four examples, the three most important and recent of which have not previously been considered in the academic literature.

Part I centers on information about the troubled company itself. Troubled corporations can be lax in securities compliance (*Part I(A)*). Woody Allen said, "Showing up is 80 percent of life."[10] Fresh evidence, found in an unexpected source, suggests that many troubled companies simply do not show up: they do not even bother to file the required Securities and Exchange Commission (SEC) periodic documents. Moreover, when they do show up, a surprising number embarrass themselves with misrepresentations.

The chapter then turns to a long-standing explanation for the laxity and offers two new ones. After briefly setting forth the existing "final period" explanation, the chapter refers to new empirical work from an unlikely source that is consistent with the underlying intuition (*Part I(B)*). The chapter then shows how two aspects of current securities law, by lessening the threat of private enforcement, can also contribute to laxity. First, requirements for class action certification in Rule 10b-5 litigation are more difficult to meet in the troubled company context (*Part I(C)*). Second, recent cases have created uncertainty as to private enforceability of an important disclosure item—the "Management's Discussion and Analysis" (MD&A)—of particular salience to troubled companies (*Part I(D)*).

Part II centers on extra-company informational asymmetries flowing from CDS and CDS-driven debt decoupling activities of third parties. The highly counterintuitive and unusually complex incentives that such third parties may have can be determinative of the ultimate change in control: bankruptcy. But even the company itself, not just investors, may not have reliable and timely information on the presence, nature, and magnitude of such activities and incentives. Unlike traditional creditors, "empty creditors with a negative

---

[10.] Yale Book of Quotations 17 (Fred R. Schapiro ed., 2006).

economic ownership" as well as certain other buyers of CDS protection can have strong incentives to intentionally cause corporations to go bankrupt even when bankruptcy would make little sense. Such third parties may profit not only from actual defaults on financial covenants—at just the right times—but also from manufacturing "faux" defaults or seizing on real, but largely technical, defaults. The chapter begins consideration of such CDS and net short creditor matters with a brief overview of the existing analytical framework for decoupling, a framework that addresses the impact on corporations of third-party CDS activities and associated terminology such as "empty creditors" and "empty creditors with a negative economic ownership." (*Part II(A)*).

The chapter then examines four significant real-world examples of such matters. The first example (Radio Shack) shows the impact of a CDS *seller* being, in effect, a contingent creditor of the pertinent company and taking steps consistent with this status. The second example (Norske Skog) shows how certain empty creditors can have exceptionally complex, dynamic, counterintuitive, and certain difficult-to-detect incentive patterns. The third example (Hovnanian) shows a CDS *purchaser* seeking to create what can be described as a "faux" default: an artificially manufactured covenant default that *benefits* the pertinent company and extracts funds from the CDS *seller*. The final, perhaps most consequential, example (Windstream Services) involves an alleged empty creditor with negative economic ownership that might be seizing on what some observers view as a real, but largely technical default, in order to cause financial distress, if not bankruptcy, to a going concern (*Part II(B)*).

This chapter is a brief work consistent with the space constraints of this *Festschrift* volume and the previously referenced corporate control symposium issue. It is meant as an initial, exploratory foray. It is not intended to identify all factors undermining the informational base associated with troubled companies and, apart from a few ideas mentioned in passing in the Windstream discussion and in the Conclusion (and the cross-reference to my other commentary), does not explicitly address the matter of solutions.[11]

II. Informational Asymmetries as to the Company

A. Overview: The Robust Informational Base and Troubled Company Laxity in Compliance

With the usual public company, disclosure and market forces animated by disclosure play crucial roles in protecting investors. The SEC's core goal has always been to ensure a robust informational base that investors can use in their decision-making and that can help deter managerial misbehavior.[12] In the 1970s, the efficient market hypothesis (EMH) provided a social science foundation for the disclosure philosophy.[13] An efficient market supported by good information would facilitate the market for corporate control. The stock price would reflect lazy and incompetent management, and a low stock price would encourage changes in control.[14]

Many troubled corporations do not bother to even facially comply with federal securities disclosure requirements. In Woody Allen terms, many don't show up. New evidence, found in a current

---

[11] As an example of the former, the chapter does not deal with the lack of public clarity as to whether management has come to the legal conclusion that its duty had shifted to the interests of creditors or the enterprise. As another example, the chapter leaves aside the contours of the disclosure requirements in the MD&A context and elsewhere. In particular, the uncertainties in the "duty to correct" and "duty to update" can result in material information not being made available in advance of the next periodic report. As to this "interim nondisclosure" issue, see generally Bruce Mendelsohn & Jesse Brush, The Duties to Correct and Update: A Web of Conflicting Case Law and Principles, 43 Sec. Reg. L.J. 67 (2015); Mitu Gulati, When Corporate Managers Fear a Good Thing Is Coming to an End: The Case of Interim Nondisclosure, 46 UCLA L. Rev. 675 (1998).

[12] See, e.g., Henry T. C. Hu, Efficient Markets and the Law: A Predictable Past and an Uncertain Future, 4 Ann. Rev. Fin. Econ. 179, 180–81 (2012).

[13] Id. at 181.

[14] Id. at 200.

working paper on the entirely different matter of forum shopping, suggests the significance of this issue. Jared Ellias compiled a data set consisting of all large companies that filed for bankruptcy reorganization between 2001 and 2012 with debt that traded in public or private markets and for which prices could be observed.[15]

The vast majority of the 285 firms that filed for bankruptcy in Delaware, the Southern District of New York, and other jurisdictions were public companies (i.e., subject to SEC disclosure requirements): 83%, 86%, and 89%, respectively.[16] But in the year preceding bankruptcy, only a minority of the companies continued to comply with SEC disclosure requirements: 35%, 39%, and 36%, respectively.[17]

There is also evidence of laxity when troubled companies not in bankruptcy do show up. Deloitte identified 519 public companies with assets of at least $100 million that filed for chapter 11 between January 1, 2000, and December 31, 2005.[18] Deloitte looked at SEC final "Accounting and Auditing Enforcement Releases" (AAERs) that alleged financial statement fraud that occurred *before* the bankruptcy filings, apart from releases that dealt solely with auditors.[19]

Deloitte found, first, that the bankrupt companies were three times more likely than comparable non-bankrupt companies to have been issued such AAERs.[20] Of the 519 companies that filed, 9% were issued AAERs for such pre-bankruptcy behavior versus 3% for companies that had not. Second, companies that were issued AAERs for such pre-bankruptcy behavior were more than twice as likely to file bankruptcy as those not issued one.[21]

---

[15] Jared A. Ellias, What Drives Bankruptcy Forum Shopping? Evidence from Market Data, J. Legal Stud. (forthcoming 2018) (manuscript at 7), available at http://ssrn.com/abstract=2795824.

[16] *Id.* at 17.

[17] *Id.*

[18] Deloitte Forensic Ctr., Ten Things about Bankruptcy and Fraud: A Review of Bankruptcy Filings 2 (2008).

[19] *Id.* at 3.

[20] *Id.* at 5.

[21] *Id.* at 2. Admittedly, the Deloitte figures can be explained in other ways. For instance, they may reflect the SEC's finding it easier to target companies that have filed for bankruptcy, even with respect to pre-bankruptcy disclosures.

Finally, *post-bankruptcy* attitudes to disclosure compliance may be reflective of *pre-bankruptcy* attitudes. One practitioner noted, for instance, that companies in chapter II "often comply . . . only very loosely" with SEC periodic disclosure requirements.[22]

B. Explanations for Laxity: The Final Period Problem

With healthy corporations, managements have strong incentives to cause their corporations to comply fully with SEC disclosure requirements. Such transparency may help increase the stock price and contribute to continuing access to the capital markets. The value of the executives' stock options and securities holdings would tend to be enhanced, as would their human capital from reputational effects.[23]

People can do surprising things on their final day of work. Janet Yellen, on her last day as the Chair of the Federal Reserve Board, effectively ousted four of the directors at Wells Fargo.[24] On his last day as President, in what *The New York Times* characterized as "a shocking abuse of presidential power," Bill Clinton pardoned Marc Rich, a fugitive financier.[25]

To the extent that existing literature addresses SEC compliance at troubled corporations not in bankruptcy, it focuses on the managerial final period problem. Jennifer Arlen and William Carney posited a model that predicted that fraud on the market generally occurs when agents fear they are in their last period of employment, and found empirical evidence that such frauds generally result from

---

[22] Barton, supra note 8, at 1.

[23] Such factors would not apply if, for instance, a leveraged buyout was afoot.

[24] See, e.g., John Heltman, Fed Drops Hammer on Wells Fargo as Four Board Members Ousted, Am. Banker (Feb. 2, 2018), www.americanbanker.com/news/fed-drops-hammer-on-wells-fargo-as-four-board-members-fired; Letter from Elizabeth Warren, U.S. Senator, to Janet Yellen, Chair, Fed. Reserve Bd. of Governors (July 28, 2017) (on file with U.S. Senate), www.warren.senate.gov/files/documents/2017-7-28_Wells_Fargo_Fed_letter.pdf.

[25] Opinion, An Indefensible Pardon, N.Y. Times (Jan. 24, 2001), www.nytimes.com/2001/01/24/opinion/an-indefensible-pardon.html.

last period agency costs.[26] They suggest that when a firm is ailing, a manager's expectations of future employment no longer serve as a constraint.[27] Building on Arlen and Carney, Mitu Gulati states that a variety of nonlegal sanctions serve to police disclosure in all but a small subset of cases, and that these cases are composed primarily of situations in which management perceives itself to be facing the final period of its managerial life.[28] These situations include takeovers and bankruptcy.[29]

At the time of those articles, there was sparse empirical evidence of CEO career and compensation changes arising from bankruptcies. The first study, published in 2016, suggests that the intuitions expressed in the earlier articles were well-founded. Analyzing 322 chapter 11 filings in the period from 1996 to 2007 by large public U.S. companies, the authors found that 86% of the CEOs left the firm (voluntarily or otherwise) within the year of filing and that only about one-third of the incumbent CEOs either left for a new executive position or remained CEO of the restructured firm after emergence from bankruptcy.[30]

C. Explanations for Laxity: The Requirements for Class Certification in Rule 10b-5 Actions

The threat of class actions under Rule 10b-5,[31] the central antifraud provision of securities law, is a key incentive for companies to provide fulsome and accurate information. The requirements that plaintiffs must meet to bring class actions have the effect of reducing this threat for troubled corporations.

[26.] Jennifer H. Arlen & William J. Carney, Vicarious Liability for Fraud on Securities Markets: Theory and Evidence, 1992 U. Ill. L. Rev. 691, 691 (1992).

[27.] Id. at 702.

[28.] Gulati, supra note 11, at 736.

[29.] Id.

[30.] B. Espen Eckbo, Karin S. Thorburn & Wei Wang, How Costly is Corporate Bankruptcy for the CEO? 121 J. Fin. Econ. 210, 211 (2016).

[31.] 17 C.F.R. § 240.10b-5 (2018).

For private plaintiffs to bring a lawsuit under 10b-5, the plaintiffs must, among other things, establish reliance. For a class to be certified, a court must conclude that "common" questions of fact or law predominate over particular questions pertaining to individual plaintiffs. Requiring proof of individualized reliance on a misstatement or omission from each member of the proposed class would make it impossible to satisfy this requirement.[32]

Rule 10b-5 class actions became possible when courts effectively did an end-run around the reliance requirement. In particular, the Supreme Court adopted the "fraud-on-the-market" doctrine in *Basic v. Levinson*.[33] Under this doctrine, rooted in the EMH, there was no need for individualized proof of reliance. Instead, there would be a rebuttable presumption that the plaintiffs had relied: after all, "in an open and developed securities market, the price of a company's stock is determined by the available material information regarding the company and its business."[34]

Critically, to invoke the presumption, the plaintiff must show that the shares involved were traded in an informationally efficient market. The leading case of *Cammer v. Bloom*[35] set out five factors to consider

1. the average weekly trading volume of the shares;
2. the number of securities analysts following and reporting on the company's stock;
3. the number of market makers and arbitrageurs;
4. the company's entitlement to use a Form S-3 registration statement for public offerings; and
5. empirical facts showing responsiveness to unexpected events and financial releases.[36]

---

[32] *Halliburton Co. v. Erica P. John Fund, Inc.*, 134 S. Ct. 2398, 2407–08 (2014).

[33] *Basic Inc. v. Levinson*, 485 U.S. 224, 224 (1988).

[34] *Id.* at 241 (quoting *Peil v. Speiser*, 806 F.2d 1154, 1160 (3d Cir. 1986)).

[35] *Cammer v. Bloom*, 711 F. Supp. 1264, 1286–87 (D.N.J. 1989).

[36] *Id.*; see *Freeman v. Laventhol & Horwath*, 915 F.2d 193, 199 (6th Cir. 1990) (summarizing the Cammer factors).

Additionally, whether a security is traded on an organized exchange has sometimes been a factor. One court, after citing the *Cammer* factors, noted the relevance of securities being traded in "national secondary markets such as the New York Stock Exchange."[37] Some courts have concluded as a matter of law that stocks trading in an over-the-counter market do not trade in an efficient market.[38]

The foregoing factors reduce the chances of class action certification with troubled corporations. First, many of these factors correlate with firm size: in general, larger firms are more likely to have higher weekly share trading volume, greater numbers of securities analysts, and greater numbers of market makers. Empirical studies suggest that analyst coverage increases with firm size.[39] One fund manager interested in small company stocks estimated that about 15% of companies he held had no sell-side analyst coverage.[40] In 2017, Reuters estimated that the number of companies in the Russell 2000 benchmark for small cap stocks without formal attention from Wall Street research firms increased 30% over the preceding three years.[41]

The emphasis on size has a disparate impact on investors seeking class certification in troubled companies. Larger firms tend to be more stable financially. Among other reasons, larger firms tend to be more diversified, have greater market power, and better access to capital markets.[42] Empirical academic studies consistently show the importance of

---

[37] Freeman, 915 F.2d at 199.

[38] See Victor E. Schwartz & Christopher E. Appel, Rebutting the Fraud on the Market Presumption in Securities Fraud Class Actions: Halliburton II Opens the Door, 5 Mich. Bus. & Entrepreneurial L. Rev. 33, 51 (2016).

[39] See, e.g., Lihong Liang, Edward J. Riedl & Ramgopal Venkataraman, The Determinants of Analyst-Firm Pairings, 27 J. Acct. & Pub. Policy 277, 278–79 (2008); Huai-Chun Lo, Do Firm Size Influence Financial Analyst Research Reports and Subsequent Stock Performance, 6 Acct. & Fin. Res. 181, 181 (2017).

[40] David Randall, Funds Target "Unknown" Stocks as Wall Street Cuts Analyst Jobs, Reuters, Aug. 7, 2017, www.reuters.com/article/us-usa-funds-research/funds-target-unknown-stocks-as-wall-street-cuts-analyst-jobs-idUSKBN1AN22I.

[41] Id.

[42] Panayiotis Theodossiou, Emel Kahya, Reza Saidi & George Philippatos, Financial Distress and Corporate Acquisitions: Further Empirical Evidence, 23 J. Bus. Fin. & Acct. 699, 704 (1996).

firm size in predicting the likelihood of default.[43] An industry participant noted in 2015 that only fifty seven of the Standard & Poor's 500 (an index of large company stocks) were considered non-investment grade, and that companies rated at junk-grade levels tend to be small.[44]

Second, a number of the *Cammer* considerations relate to financial health. The right to use an S-3 registration statement is such a factor. One requirement for using the S-3 is that neither the company nor any of its subsidiaries have, within a specified period, (a) failed to pay any dividend or sinking fund installment on preferred stock, or (b) defaulted on any debt or any rental on long-term leases, which defaults in the aggregate are material.[45] Trading on an organized stock exchange such as the New York Stock Exchange or NASDAQ is another financial health-related factor. Both such exchanges rely on a variety of financial metrics with respect to initial listings.[46]

Third, as noted, many troubled companies do not even file the requisite periodic SEC documents. If a company is not doing so, the cost for a securities analyst to follow the company would rise, thus discouraging coverage. Moreover, the company would not be entitled to use an S-3 registration statement. One S-3 requirement is that the company has filed in a timely manner all required Securities Exchange Act of 1934 (Exchange Act) reports.[47]

[43.] See, e.g., James A. Ohlson, Financial Ratios and the Probabilistic Prediction of Bankruptcy, 18 J. Acct. Res. 109, 110 (1980) (using a sample of U.S. firms and stating that the firm size was one of four factors found statistically significant in affecting the probability of failure); Julie Fitzpatrick & Joseph P. Ogden, The Detection and Dynamics of Financial Distress, 11 Int'l Rev. Fin. 87, 87 (2011) (using a sample of U.S. firms and finding that firm size was the most important of six variables examined in forecasting five-year failure); Clive Lennox, Identifying Failing Companies: A Re-evaluation of the Logit, Probit and DA Approaches, 51 J. Econ. & Bus. 347, 347 (1999) (studying a sample of U.K.-listed companies and finding company size among the most important determinants of bankruptcy).

[44.] Sam Ro, There's Not Much Junk in the S&P 500, Bus. Insider (Oct. 20, 2015), www.businessinsider.com/speculative-grade-companies-in-the-sp-500-2015-10 (quoting Barclays' Jonathan Glionna).

[45.] 17 C.F.R. § 239.13(a)(4) (2018).

[46.] PricewaterhouseCoopers.

[47.] 17 C.F.R. § 239.13(a)(3)(ii) (2018).

This failure to file creates a problem extending beyond the particular factors a judge considers. The basis for the *Basic* "fraud-on-the-market" theory is that the information provided to the market is, in effect, processed by the market as an unpaid agent of the investor.[48] If *no* information is being provided (at least in SEC periodic reports), a foundational assumption of *Basic* is missing.

This has an ironic result. A company, by failing to file SEC periodic reports, reduces the chances of a securities class action being brought against it. *Not* showing up can have rewards.

D. Explanations for Laxity: New Uncertainties as to Enforcement of the "MD&A"

For all public corporations, the MD&A section of the quarterly Form 10-Q and annual Form 10-K[49] is widely considered to be the primary form of narrative disclosure that is reviewed, together with financial statements, for investment decision-making.[50] Because of the substantive content required, the MD&A addresses matters with particular resonance for troubled corporations. Uncertainties that have recently become manifest on the private enforceability of the MD&A, most notably in the Ninth Circuit, undermine the robustness of the informational base for troubled companies.

[48.] *Basic Inc. v. Levinson*, 485 U.S. 224, 244 (1988) (citing In re LTV Sec. Litig., 88 F.R.D. 134, 143 (N.D. Tex. 1980)).

[49.] The MD&A is set out as Item 303 of Regulation S-K. 17 C.F.R. § 229.303 (2018). As to the disclosure items required by Forms 10-Q and 10-K, see Regulation S-K, 17 C.F.R. § 229.10 et seq. (2018).

[50.] See Orin E. Barran et al., MD&A Quality as Measured by the SEC and Analysts' Earnings Forecasts, 16 Contemp. Acct. Res. 75, 80 (1999) (noting "a growing body of evidence suggests that the SEC and users of financial reports view the MD&A as particularly important. . . ."); Bernd Hüfner, The SEC's MD&A: Does It Meet the Informational Demands of Investors? A Conceptual Evaluation, 59 Schmalenbach Bus. Rev. 58, 58–59 (2007) (noting how, of all disclosure items in the annual report, sell-side financial analysts in the U.S. most frequently use the MD&A when preparing their reports).

The SEC has stated that

> The MD&A requirements are intended to provide, in one section of
> a filing, material historical and prospective textual disclosure ena-
> bling investors and other users to assess the financial condition and
> results of operations of the registrant, with particular emphasis on
> the registrant's prospects for the future.[51]

The MD&A is expressly "intended to give the investor an opportunity to look at the company through the eyes of management."[52]
The MD&A requires disclosure of, for instance, "known trends or any
known demands, commitments, events or uncertainties" reasonably
likely to result in the company's liquidity changing materially and
"known material trends, favorable or unfavorable" in the company's
capital resources.[53] More generally, the MD&A "shall focus specifically
on material events and uncertainties known to management that
would cause reported financial information not to be necessarily indicative of future operating results or of future financial condition."[54]

The MD&A is thus seemingly tailor-made to the needs of investors in troubled corporations.[55] Empirical evidence is consistent with
this. Using a sample of 354 firms that filed for bankruptcy between

[51] Management's Discussion and Analysis of Financial Condition and Results of
Operations; Certain Investment Company Disclosures, Securities Act Release No.
6835, Exchange Act Release No. 26,831, Investment Company Act Release No. 16,961,
54 Fed. Reg. 22,427, 22,428 (May 24, 1989).

[52] Concept Release on Management's Discussion and Analysis of Financial Condition and Operations, Securities Act Release No. 6711, Exchange Act Release No.
24,356, 52 Fed. Reg. 13,715, 13,717 (Apr. 24, 1987).

[53] 17 C.F.R. § 229.303(a)(1)–(2)(2018).

[54] Id. § 229.303(a) (Instruction 3 to para 303(a)).

[55] Certain narrative disclosures can arise for troubled companies from Financial
Accounting Standards Board (FASB) requirements. Notably, the FASB now requires
company management to perform its own independent "going concern" evalua-
tion, separate from the long-standing obligations on this matter on the part of out-
side auditors. Fin. Acct. Standards Bd., FASB Accounting Standards Codification,
Accounting Standards Update No. 2014–15, Presentation of Financial Statements—
Going Concern (Subtopic 205-04), Disclosure of Uncertainties about an Entity's
Ability to Continue as a Going Concern, 205-40-50-12, at 10 (2014).

1995 and 2012, a study found that both the management's explicit mentions in the MD&A that the firm may be unable to continue as a going concern, as well as the MD&A's overall linguistic tone, provided significant explanatory power in predicting whether a firm would cease as a going concern.[56]

However, recent U.S. Court of Appeals cases have introduced uncertainty as to a key issue: whether the omission of information required under the MD&A gives rise to liability under Section 10(b) and Rule 10b-5 thereunder.[57] In cases in 2015 and 2016, the Second Circuit held that an omission can give rise to such liability.[58] But in 2014, the Ninth Circuit held that "Item 303 does not create a duty to disclose for purposes of Section 10(b) and Rule 10b-5."[59] The Second and Ninth Circuits together handle more federal securities law cases than the rest of the circuits combined.[60] The U.S. Supreme Court granted certiorari to resolve this split in the circuits.[61] But this was not to be the Supreme Court announced on October 17, 2017, that the parties would settle.[62]

[56.] William J. Mayew, Mani Sethusraman & Mohan Venkatachalam, MD&A Disclosure and the Firm's Ability to Continue as a Going Concern, 90 Acct. Rev. 1621, 1621–22, 1627 (2015). On August 24, 2014 (i.e., after the period covered by the study), the FASB issued Accounting Standards Update No. 2014-15, which requires management to assess a company's ability to continue as a going concern and related disclosures in certain circumstances. Daghan Or et al., Going Concern: FASB Defines Management's Going Concern Assessment and Disclosure Responsibilities, PricewaterhouseCoopers 1 (2014), www.legalexecutiveinstitute.com/wp-content/uploads/2016/09/25.-PwC-us2014-07-going-concern.pdf.

[57.] See Brief for the United States as Amicus Curiae Supporting Respondents at 1, Leidos Inc. v. Ind. Pub. Ret. Sys., 137 S. Ct. 1395 (2017, (No. 16-581).

[58.] Ind. Pub. Ret. Sys. v. SAIC, Inc., 818 F.3d 85, 94 (2d Cir. 2016); Stratte McClure v. Morgan Stanley, 776 F.3d 94, 101 (2d Cir. 2015).

[59.] In re NVIDIA Corp. Sec. Litig., 768 F.3d 1046, 1054 (9th Cir. 2014) (citing Oran v. Stafford, 226 F.3d 275, 288 (3d Cir. 2000)).

[60.] Monica Loseman et al., 2017 Year-End Securities Litigation Update, Gibson Dunn 17 (Feb. 1, 2018), www.gibsondunn.com/wp-content/uploads/2018/02/2017-year-end-securities-litigation-update.pdf.

[61.] See Leidos, Inc. v. Ind. Pub. Ret. Sys., 137 S. Ct. 1395, 1396 (2017).

[62.] Order, Leidos, Inc. v. Ind. Pub. Ret. Sys., 138 S. Ct. 369 (2017) (staying proceedings pending settlement); Order, Leidos, Inc. v. Ind. Pub. Ret. Sys., 138 S. Ct. 2670 (2018) (dismissing writ of certiorari for mutual agreement of the parties).

The failure of the Supreme Court to adopt the Second Circuit approach undermines compliance with the MD&A. The Acting Solicitor General, in his amicus brief, suggested that the Ninth Circuit approach would exempt from Section 10(b) liability "conduct that is clearly fraudulent," preventing defrauded investors from obtaining compensation, and would prevent the SEC from obtaining various sanctions available under Section 10(b) but not available under other securities law provisions.[63] With troubled companies, this impact becomes especially significant: the substantive content in the MD&A is particularly salient, and, as noted earlier, troubled companies appear to be lax in SEC compliance to begin with. What ameliorates this situation somewhat is that many companies, as a matter of prudence, may assume the possibility of MD&A liability. This is because, in many situations, plaintiffs will have the flexibility to bring MD&A claims in the Second Circuit.[64]

III. Extra-Company Informational Asymmetries: CDS and Debt Decoupling

A. Overview

The fate of a company has traditionally depended largely on company-specific issues and the regulatory environment it operates in. Not surprisingly, SEC disclosure requirements thus focus on such matters as the quality and integrity of company management,

---

[63.] Brief for the United States as Amicus Curiae Supporting Respondents, supra note 57, at 32. But see Joseph A. Grundfest, Ask Me No Questions and I Will Tell You No Lies: The Insignificance of Leidos Before the United States Supreme Court 5 (Stanford Law Sch. and Rock Ctr. for Corp. Governance, Stanford Univ., Working Paper Series No. 229, 2017) (2017), www.ssrn.com/abstract=3043990.

[64.] As to the grounds on which plaintiffs may be able to bring claims in the Second Circuit, see, e.g., Edward J. Fuhr, Scott H. Kimpel & Johnathon E. Schronce, Client Alert, Supreme Court Will Not Consider Leidos Case after Apparent Settlement, Hunton & Williams 2 (Oct. 17, 2017), www.hunton.com/images/content/3/3/v2/33768/supreme-court-will-not-consider-leidos-case.pdf.

the competitiveness of its goods and services, its access to financing, and its regulatory environment. The fate of a troubled company, however, does not necessarily flow largely from such "company-specific" matters. For instance, in modern capital markets, CDS and other "debt decoupling" activities on the part of third parties may be critical to the company's survival. "Extra-company" informational asymmetries flowing from such financial innovations are necessarily important as well.

The exploration of such extra-company informational asymmetries begins with a brief summary of the analytical framework for decoupling (*Part II(B)*). This is followed by a close examination of four recent examples where such third-party activities appear to have significant impact (*Part II(C)*).

B. Debt Decoupling and Public Information

Classic conceptions of "debt" and "equity" are clearly understood. Ownership of debt conveys a package of economic rights (to receive payment of principal and interest), contractual control rights (to enforce, waive, or modify the debt contract), other legal rights (including rights in bankruptcy), and sometimes disclosure obligations. Similarly, ownership of equity conveys a package of economic rights, voting rights, and other rights, as well as disclosure and other obligations.

These classic conceptions assume that the elements of these packages of rights and obligations are normally "bundled" together. With debt, the holder's contractual control rights (such as in a loan agreement) are linked to the holder's economic rights to interest and principal. With equity, the holder's voting rights are usually linked to the holder's economic interest: the familiar "one share, one vote" is an example.

These foundational conceptions no longer hold. Today, through the use of derivatives and other means, debt holders and equity holders can, if they wish, easily separate components of these packages. Sophisticated, lightly regulated hedge funds have been especially active in this arena. And, importantly from the standpoint of this chapter, often the activities can occur without any public disclosure. Within the analytical framework that Bernard Black and I introduced in 2006 and refined and extended in a series of articles that I sole- or co-authored through 2015, the term "decoupling" was coined to refer to this separation.[65]

It is decoupling on the debt side and associated derivatives such as CDS, that are particularly pertinent to distressed corporations.[66] Notwithstanding the new reality made possible by debt decoupling and CDSs, law and contracting practice generally assume an immutable link between the debt holder's control rights and its economic interest. That is, both law and credit agreements are predicated on the creditor's being interested in keeping a solvent firm out of bankruptcy and (intercreditor conflicts aside) in maximizing the value of an insolvent firm.

Today, this can prove dangerously naïve. This chapter is narrowly focused on decoupling related to troubled companies that are not in bankruptcy. And for simplicity, I focus on CDS-based techniques for decoupling.

[65.] The initial decoupling article was Henry T. C. Hu & Bernard Black, The New Vote Buying: Empty Voting and Hidden (Morphable) Ownership, 79 So. Cal. L. Rev. 811, 816 (2006). Among the subsequent articles are Henry T. C. Hu & Bernard Black, Hedge Funds, Insiders, and the Decoupling of Economic and Voting Ownership: Empty Voting and Hidden (Morphable) Ownership, 13 J. Corp. Fin. 343, 343 (2007); Hu & Westbrook, supra note 6, at 1330, 1401-02; Henry T. C. Hu & Bernard Black, Equity and Debt Decoupling and Empty Voting II: Importance and Extensions, 156 U. Pa. L. Rev. 625 (2008) [hereinafter Hu & Black, Penn-Debt and Equity Decoupling]; Henry T. C. Hu & Bernard Black, Debt, Equity and Hybrid Decoupling: Governance and Systemic Risk, 14 Eur. Fin. Mgmt. 663 (2008) [hereinafter Hu & Black, EFM – Debt, Equity, and Hybrid Decoupling]; and Henry T. C. Hu, Financial Innovation and Governance Mechanisms: The Evolution of Decoupling and Transparency, 70 Bus. Law. 347 (2015) [hereinafter Hu, Financial Innovation and Governance Mechanisms].

For a brief 2015 summary of the analytical framework for decoupling (debt, equity, and hybrid), see Hu, Financial Innovation and Governance Mechanisms, at 350-81.

[66.] For a more detailed analysis of debt decoupling than is set out in this chapter and discussion of the closely related phenomenon of "hybrid decoupling," see, e.g., Hu & Black, EFM—Debt, Equity, and Hybrid Decoupling, supra note 65, at 679-94.

Debt decoupling and CDSs have made "debt governance" perhaps less efficient and definitely more opaque and complex. This is especially so when there are hidden parties or when there are counterintuitive incentive patterns.

Consider, for instance, one technique for becoming what the framework refers to as an "empty creditor." A creditor holds the shaky debt of a troubled company and has the formal contractual control rights set out in the credit agreement, including the protections provided by various affirmative and negative covenants.

However, say that this creditor has approached a derivatives dealer and has purchased protection against the default of that company under a CDS. Under the terms of a simple CDS, when a "credit event" (e.g., default on a debt obligation or bankruptcy) occurs with respect to the "reference entity" (e.g., that company), the seller of the CDS protection must, in effect, compensate the buyer of the CDS protection. The relationship of the CDS buyer to the CDS seller is roughly akin to the relationship of a homeowner to the insurance company that provides fire insurance on the home.

I coined the term "empty creditor" to refer to this kind of creditor.[67] That is, an empty creditor retains the control and other formal rights flowing from the credit agreement yet has partly or fully hedged its economic risk to the debtor.[68]

Highly counterintuitive incentive patterns can occur. For instance, what if that creditor has decoupled by buying a huge amount of CDS protection relative to the debt it holds? That is, what if the creditor had extended a $50,000,000 loan to a company but bought CDS protection naming that company as the reference entity

---

[67.] See, e.g., Henry T. C. Hu, "Empty Creditors" and the Crisis, Wall St. J. (Apr. 10, 2009), www.wsj.com/articles/SB123933166470307811 [hereinafter Hu, Empty Creditors and the Crisis] (on the origins of the term); Hu & Westbrook, supra note 6, at 1402 n. 310 (same).

[68.] See, e.g., Hu & Black, EFM—Debt, Equity, and Hybrid Decoupling, supra note 65, at 680. A creditor need not rely on CDSs to hedge. For instance, a creditor can also hedge by being long one class of a company's debt, and short another. They can also hedge through strategies involving the company's common or preferred shares. See id. at 681, 683–86.

in the amount of $200,000,000? This creditor may actually *benefit* from the company's filing for bankruptcy. After all, the payoff from the CDSs the creditor holds on the company's bankruptcy may well be greater than any loss that creditor suffers on its loan. In this circumstance, that creditor has negative exposure to a firm's credit risk. The creditor is over-hedged.

In 2008, the analytical framework for decoupling called such *over*-hedged empty creditors "empty creditors with negative economic ownership"; this year (2018), some practitioners appeared to refer to such persons as "net-short debt activists."[69] This extreme category of empty creditors would have incentives to use contractual control rights not to protect the value of their loans but, subject to reputational concerns and legal and other constraints, to harm the company, such as by helping grease the skids to bankruptcy.[70] In contrast, traditional creditors often waive breaches of the loan agreement, agree to out-of-court restructurings, and work with troubled debtors in manifold other ways that would redound to the benefit of both the creditors and their debtors.

Even a creditor that does not have a negative economic interest would have lessened incentives to cooperate with a troubled debtor. For example, an empty creditor with merely zero economic interest would be indifferent as to whether the company survives.[71]

Neither the identity of the parties who buy or sell CDS protection as to a troubled company nor the net economic ownership, positive or negative, of such parties is, generally speaking, publicly available. This is notwithstanding the increased transparency of the CDS market as a result of the Dodd-Frank Act of 2010.

The Depository Trust & Clearing Corporation maintains a centralized electronic database for "virtually all CDS contracts outstanding

---

[69] *Id.* at 682. As to a 2018 use of the term "net-short debt activist," see Joshua A. Feltman, Emil A. Kleinhaus, & John R. Sobolewski, The Rise of the Net-Short Debt Activist, Wachtell, Lipton, Rosen & Katz 1 (Aug. 1, 2018).

[70] See, e.g., *id.* at 679–86.

[71] See, e.g., Hu, Financial Innovation and Governance Mechanisms, supra note 65, at 370–71.

in the global marketplace."[72] Access is restricted to derivatives dealers and other market participants, and subscribers can obtain data such as the gross notional and net notional amounts and trade volumes as to the CDS outstanding for particular companies.[73] However, no information is available on, say, any particular hedge fund's CDS holdings. Thus, as will be illustrated shortly, even such sophisticated parties would instead have to rely on market chatter and media reports to get a sense of what a hedge fund's CDS exposures to a company might be.

The scarcity of public information compromises not only debt governance but also the robustness of the informational base needed by investors. The informational deficiencies abound, involving both "hidden non-interest" and "hidden interest." If a creditor has decoupled and the troubled company or the capital markets are generally unaware of this, that creditor has a "hidden non-interest"; that is, the creditor does not have the economic interest that the debtor and the capital markets think it has. Investors, the capital markets, and the troubled company itself would thus have an overly optimistic view as to the willingness of those creditors to help the company survive.

Where, unbeknownst to investors and capital markets, there are empty creditors with negative economic ownership, the gap between perception and reality may be especially large. Here, their misunderstandings of the incentives of the creditors do not involve questions of *degree*, but instead, the fundamental matter of *direction*.

There are additional informational deficiencies in debt governance that extend to a party that has no contractual relationship

---

[72] Trade Reporting Repository: Overview, Depository Trust & Clearing Corp., www.dtcc.com/derivatives-services/trade-information-warehouse/trade-reporting-repository.

[73] Press Release, Depository Trust & Clearing Corp., TIW Market Reports Give Clients Insights into Global CDS Contracts: A Conversation with Chris Nardo, Director, DTCC Data Pro (Mar. 17, 2017), www.dtcc.com/news/2017/march/17/tiw-market-reports-give-clients-insights-into-global-cds-contracts.

whatsoever with the troubled company: the CDS seller. The CDS seller is, in a very rough sense, a contingent creditor of the troubled company. That is, the CDS seller is exposed to the credit risk of the company. If the company goes bankrupt, that seller must pay up (to the CDS buyer).

This "hidden interest" that the CDS seller has in the troubled company can raise informational concerns for investors. The CDS seller only has a hidden interest in the troubled company until the maturity of the CDS. Under certain circumstances, the CDS seller may deem it worthwhile to become an actual creditor of the troubled company, not because of the CDS seller's optimism about the company, but because it wants to get the company through to the maturity of the CDS. An announcement by the company of new financing, unadorned by fulsome disclosure of the CDS seller's status as the new creditor, has the potential of sending an unduly positive message to investors.

One key takeaway of the foregoing from the standpoint of this chapter can be summarized. The scarcity of public information as to the identity and interests of these hidden interests and hidden non-interests, and thus the possibility of counterintuitive incentives, undermines the robust informational base needed by investors, the capital markets, and troubled corporations themselves.

We now turn to some recent examples involving third-party CDSs and other debt decoupling behavior. These examples yield new insights as to the informational asymmetries now possible with troubled companies.

C. Illustrative Examples from 2008 Through 2018

From 2007 to 2008, when the term "empty creditor" was coined and debt decoupling was incorporated into the overall decoupling framework, the real-world evidence for debt decoupling was more limited than that for equity decoupling. Subsequently, far more such evidence became available. In a 2015 article, I showed that debt decoupling and the related "hybrid decoupling" phenomenon appeared to have played roles in, among other things, three of the iconic corporate disasters of the 2008 global financial crisis: American International Group (AIG), Chrysler, and General Motors.[74] For instance, Goldman Sachs's apparent status as an "empty creditor" of AIG might help explain its decision to ask for an additional $1.5 billion in collateral from AIG, notwithstanding the possible impact on AIG's survival.[75] Five days later, AIG had to be bailed out.

The chapter turns now to closer examination of what are likely to be four recent examples:

(1). *RadioShack* (2014–2015): survival, at least as a temporary matter, due to financing arranged by Standard General, an alleged seller of CDS protection that would soon expire;

(2). *Norske Skog* (2016): survival, as least as a temporary matter, dependent on approval of an exchange offer (1) objected to by BlueCrest, an alleged *purchaser* of CDS protection, and (2) supported by GSO Capital Partners (GSO), an alleged *seller* of **short-term** CDS protection and alleged *purchaser* of **longer-term** CDS protection;

(3). *Hovnanian* (2017–2018): financing obtained at exceptionally favorable terms from GSO, an alleged buyer of CDS protection, in return for Hovnanian deliberately triggering a credit event by defaulting on certain debt held by its own subsidiary; and

(4). *Windstream Services* (2015–2018): an alleged empty creditor with negative economic ownership uses an alleged breach of a covenant in a bond indenture to cause a going concern to go into bankruptcy to the detriment of the company and the company's normal creditors.

[74.] See Hu, Financial Innovation and Governance Mechanisms, supra note 65, at 369–72.

[75.] This example was initially advanced in abbreviated form in Hu, Empty Creditors and the Crisis, supra note 67, and discussed in greater detail in Hu, Financial Innovation and Governance Mechanisms, supra note 65, at 370–71.

1. RadioShack *(2014-2015): CDS Seller as Contingent Creditor and Incentives to Keep Firm Out of Bankruptcy*

In late 2014, RadioShack, an electronics retailer, was near bankrupt-cy.[76] But on October 3, 2014, RadioShack announced a financing plan that would stave off a filing and help it stock stores through the 2014 holiday season.[77] The new financing came from investors including Standard General LP, a hedge fund that was RadioShack's largest shareholder.[78] In spite of this new financing, RadioShack filed for bankruptcy on February 5, 2015.[79] Neither RadioShack's Form 8-K filed on October 6, 2014, nor the initial press reports mentioned any CDS-related matters.[80]

Later press reports, however, suggested that much of the new financing came from hedge funds who had sold CDS protection.[81] In bankruptcy proceedings, the unsecured creditors alleged that those who provided the late 2014 financing had "reportedly sold" CDS pro-tection, "betting that the company would not default on its bonds—at least not until December 20, 2014"—"[i]f the company defaulted before that date," the CDS sellers would have suffered "massive

---

[76] Drew FitzGerald & Matt Jarzemsky, RadioShack Gets a Lifeline, Wall St. J., Oct. 4, 2014, at B3.

[77] See *id.*; see RadioShack Corp., Current Report (Form 8-K) 2 (Oct. 6, 2014); Drew FitzGerald & Matt Jarzemsky, Lifeline for RadioShack Only Buys a Little Time, Wall St. J., Oct. 6, 2014, at B3 [hereinafter FitzGerald & Jarzemsky, Lifeline for RadioShack].

[78] FitzGerald & Jarzemsky, Lifeline for RadioShack, supra note 77.

[79] Phil Wahba, RadioShack Pulls the Plug and Files for Bankruptcy, Fortune (Feb. 5, 2015), http://fortune.com/2015/02/05/radioshack-bankruptcy-filing/.

[80] See RadioShack Corp., Current Report (Form 8-K), supra note 77; FitzGerald & Jarzemsky, RadioShack Gets a Lifeline, supra note 76; FitzGerald & Jarzemsky, Life-line for RadioShack Only Buys a Little Time, supra note 77.

[81] Jodi Xu Klein, RadioShack Kept Alive by $25 Billion of Swaps Side Bets, Bloomb-erg (Dec. 18, 2014), www.bloomberg.com/news/articles/2014-12-18/radioshack-kept-alive-by-25-billion-of-swaps-side-bets. See also Michael Aneiro, What's Keeping Radio Shack Afloat? Credit Derivatives, Barron's (Dec. 19, 2014), www.barrons.com/articles/whats-keeping-radio-shack-afloat-credit-derivatives-1419003199; Mike Kentz, CDS allegations surround RadioShack, Reuters, Dec. 15, 2014, www.reuters.com/article/radioshack-cds-idUSL1N0TZoV720141215?feedType=RSS&feedName=bondsNews.

losses."[82] The 2014 financing, they alleged, allowed these investors to avoid having to pay out on their CDSs by "orchestrating when RadioShack would default."[83]

Standard General disputed the allegations of the unsecured creditors and dismissed them as "conspiracy theories" and a "red herring."[84] Indeed, Standard General noted that it had *bought* some CDS protection to hedge certain RadioShack bonds it held.[85]

Diligent RadioShack investors, on reading both the initial press reports and the Form 8-K relating to the new financing, would have assumed that traditional creditor incentives were animating the Standard General-arranged financing. If Standard General was indeed a CDS seller with CDS maturing on December 20, 2014, and investors knew of this additional "contingent creditor" status, investors might have assessed the implications of the new financing differently. Although later press reports mentioned the possible role of CDS sellers, the absence of verifiable quantitative information on the actual CDS positions of Standard General limited the value of those reports.

2. Norske Skog (2016): Time-Varying Incentives to Keeping
   the Firm Out of Bankruptcy and Pushing the Firm into
   Bankruptcy

RadioShack is a relatively simple tale involving allegations that, by virtue of their CDS positions, certain hedge funds had incentives to, and did take steps to keep the firm *out of* bankruptcy—at least for a while. In contrast, Norske Skog is a complex and surprising saga.

[82.] Motion of Official Committee of Unsecured Creditors for an Order, Pursuant to Section 105(a) of the Bankruptcy Code, Bankruptcy Rule 2004, and Local Bankruptcy Rule 2004-1, Authorizing and Directing the Examination of the Debtors and Certain Third Parties at 12, In re RS Legacy Corp., Case 15-10197-BLS (Bankr. D. Del. Mar. 17, 2015), Doc. 304.

[83.] *Id.* at 12–13.

[84.] Preliminary Response of Standard General L.P. to Motion of Official Committee of Unsecured Creditors for an Order, Pursuant to Section 105(a) of the Bankruptcy Code, Bankruptcy Rule 2004, and Local Bankruptcy Rule 2004-1, Authorizing and Directing the Examination of the Debtors and Certain Third Parties at 6, In re RS Legacy Corp., Case 15-10197-BLS (Bankr. D. Del. Feb. 5, 2015), Doc. 503.

[85.] *Id.* at 4.

In late 2015, the debt of Norske Skog, a troubled Norwegian paper company, reached "unacceptable" levels: €1 billion, the most immediate maturity being certain unsecured notes maturing in 2016 and 2017.[86] GSO, an affiliate of Blackstone (the world's largest private equity firm), and Cyrus Capital Partners (Cyrus) owned a large position in the unsecured notes, and Blackstone itself owned 11% of Norske Skog's equity.[87] Norske Skog sought approval for an exchange offer that would, among other things, effectively extend the maturity of the unsecured notes to 2019 and thus address immediate liquidity issues.[88] GSO and Cyrus backed the exchange offer. Holders of the secured debt, including the hedge fund BlueCrest, objected.[89]

Why would these two sets of creditors, GSO and Cyrus on the one hand, and the secured creditors on the other, take opposing positions on a transaction that would alleviate Norske Skog's urgent problems? There are grounds to believe that the answer may lie with the CDS positions of the key players.

GSO and Cyrus. Citibank, as trustee for the secured noteholders (including BlueCrest), sued Norske Skog to enjoin the exchange offer.[90] Relying on reporting by Bloomberg, Citibank alleged that GSO and Cyrus were not participating in the exchange offer "to ensure Norske's long-term economic viability."[91] Instead, Citibank alleged, two

---

[86] Press Release, Norske Skog Commc'ns & Pub. Aff., Norske Skog Launches Exchange Offer to All Holders of 2016 and 2017 notes (Nov. 17, 2015) (on file with Norske Skog), www.norskeskog.com/Show-news.aspx?Action=1&NewsId=258&M=NewsV2 &PID=3264; Sally Bakewell, Swaponomics II: Blackstone, BlueCrest and the Great Paper Caper, Bloomberg (Feb. 19, 2016), www.bloomberg.com/news/articles/2016-02-19/ swaponomics-ii-blackstone-bluecrest-and-the-great-paper-caper.

[87] Gavin Jackson & Miles Johnson, Hedge Funds Spar Over Norske Skog Debt Restructuring, Fin. Times (Feb. 25, 2016), www.ft.com/content/ea90717a-dbad-11e5-98fd-06d75973fe09.

[88] See Press Release, Norske Skog Commc'ns & Pub. Aff., supra note 86.

[89] Robert Smith, "No Winners" in Norske Skog Debt Ruling, Reuters, Mar. 11, 2016, www.reuters.com/article/norske-skogsind-restructuring/no-winners-in-norske-skog-debt-ruling-idUSL5N16I2CN.

[90] See Amended Complaint for Declaratory and Injunctive Relief, *Citibank, N.A. v. Norske Skogindustrier, ASA*, No. 16-cv-850 (RJS) (S.D.N.Y. Mar. 7, 2016), Doc. No. 60.

[91] *Id.* at para 4; see Luca Casiraghi, Why Blackstone Would Prop Up Troubled Paper Giant, Bloomberg (Dec. 21, 2015), www.bloomberg.com/news/articles/2015-12-22/

starkly different CDS-related motivations were at play: first, **"to avoid a large payout** to their counterparties under the credit default swaps if Norske does not default on its debts *in the short-term*," and, second, to **"earn a large pay out** from their counterparties if Norske *eventually goes bankrupt*."[92] A BlueCrest trader filed a declaration stating that he believed GSO had a "large steepener trade," wherein GSO *sold* short-dated CDS protection but also *bought* long-dated protection.[93] With these two different types of CDS positions, GSO would benefit from Norske staying alive for a few years but then defaulting.

BlueCrest. Norske's CEO claimed that the secured noteholders would benefit massively from the company's insolvency. He claimed that the secured notes' "principal investor" held a CDS short position "in the range of 120m–130m nominally."[94]

If the respective allegations on the part of both sides are to be believed, this Norske Skog situation is more complex and involves more counterintuitive behavior than RadioShack. First, while both RadioShack and Norske Skog allegedly had CDS market participants incentivized to see to the survival of the firm in the short term, Norske Skog also had CDS market participants that would benefit from the destruction of the firm. In the terminology of the analytical framework, with Norske Skog, there were "empty creditors with negative economic ownership."

Second, the incentives of certain of the empty creditors with negative ownership are especially counterintuitive. BlueCrest was an

---

swap-o-nomics-why-blackstone-would-prop-up-troubled-paper-giant; see also Bakewell, supra note 86.

[92] Amended Complaint for Declaratory and Injunctive Relief at 16, *Citibank, N.A. v. Norske Skogindustrier ASA*, No. 16-cv-850 (RJS) (S.D.N.Y. Mar. 7, 2016), Doc. No. 60 (emphasis added).

[93] See Supplemental Declaration of Deniz Akgul in Support of Plaintiff's Request for a Preliminary Injunction at Ex. A, 3, *Citibank, N.A. v. Norske Skogindustrier ASA*, No. 16-cv-850 (RJS) (S.D.N.Y. Feb. 26, 2016), Doc. No. 52-1; Smith, "No Winners," supra note 89; see also David Wigan & Robert Smith, GSO's Win-Win on Norske Skog CDS, Reuters, Apr. 28, 2016, www.reuters.com/article/norske-skog-cds-idUSL5N17V5TX [hereinafter Supplemental Declaration of Deniz Akgul].

[94] Smith, "No Winners," supra note 89.

empty creditor with negative economic ownership, both in the short term and in the long term. In contrast, by virtue of highly customized CDS positions, GSO would allegedly benefit *both* from the firm not going bankruptcy *in the short term* as well as from the firm going bankrupt *in the long term*. Thus, GSO's immediate incentives were diametrically opposed to their incentives in the long run. It is only with respect to the long term that GSO was an empty creditor with negative economic ownership.

The greater complexities associated with Norske Skog render even more pressing investors' need for quantitative data on the CDS positions of the key players. Yet, as with RadioShack, the true CDS positions were unclear. BlueCrest claimed that there had been "materially incorrect statements" regarding its CDS positions.[95] Norske's counsel stated that the secured creditors' group that included BlueCrest had been unwilling to disclose their CDS positions.[96] As for the details of GSO's positions, it is notable that even Citibank, a major derivatives dealer, had to rely on Bloomberg stories.[97]

We may never find out the true CDS positions of these key players. A March 2016 court ruling effectively precluded the exchange offer, and Citibank's case settled before trial.[98] GSO and Cyrus then altered their plans to provide the needed liquidity for Norske Skog.[99] In June 2016, the CDS protection that GSO sold settled and in December 2017, Norske Skog filed for bankruptcy.[100]

---

[95] Supplemental Declaration of Deniz Akgul, supra note 93, at para 5.

[96] See *id*. at Ex. A, 6.

[97] See Amended Complaint, supra note 90, at 4, 16.

[98] *Citibank, N.A. v. Norske Skogindustrier ASA*, No. 16-cv-850 (RJS), 2016 WL 1052888 (S.D.N.Y. Mar. 8, 2016); Smith, "No Winners," supra note 89.

[99] See Robert Smith, GSO and Cyrus help Norske Skog get round debt exchange block, Reuters, Mar. 21, 2016, https://de.reuters.com/article/norske-skog-restructuring-idUKL5N16T3SZ; Press Release, Norske Skog Commc'ns & Pub. Aff., Norske Skog launches amended exchange offer; equity and liquidity initiatives; trading update and outlook (Mar. 18, 2016) (on file with Norske Skog), www.norskeskog.com/files/filer/Arkiv/PR/201603/1996060_5.html; Press Release, Norske Skog Commc'ns & Pub. Aff., Norske Skog—successful participation level for the 2017 exchange offer (Apr. 6, 2016) (on file with Norske Skog), www.norskeskog.com/files/filer/Arkiv/PR/201604/2001252_5.html.

[100] Miles Johnson & Robert Smith, The Mystery Trader Who Roiled Wall Street, Fin. Times (June 4, 2018), www.ft.com/content/5e23e516-5cdc-11e8-ad91-e01af256df68.

3. Hovnanian *(2017-2018): Incentives to Create a Faux Default*

RadioShack and Norske Skog involved the complex, counterintuitive, and opaque incentives flowing from key debtholders' CDS positions. Investors in both companies may not have had sufficient information to understand such incentives and assess how such incentives could affect the companies' fates. The Hovnanian situation also involved GSO and the unique incentives created by CDSs. However, while the behavior in Hovnanian certainly has long-term implications for the viability of the CDS market and the pocketbooks of the specific CDS players involved, the behavior has almost nothing to do with the fates of companies or, indeed, anything else in the real world. Because of this, the discussion will be very brief as to Hovnanian.

Beginning in early 2017, GSO purchased $333 million of CDS protection on the debt of Hovnanian, a home builder.[101] At that time, there was a material risk that Hovnanian would not be able to repay its debt, and if that had come to pass, GSO stood to gain. However, Hovnanian's financial prospects began to improve in the first half of 2017 and by the end of July, GSO was likely to face large losses on its CDSs.

GSO allegedly saw a way out. Since Hovnanian's new-found health was such that it was unlikely to default on its obligations, GSO could try to "manufacture" a default that, as a purely technical matter, would trigger a "failure-to-pay" credit event payout on GSO's CDSs. GSO and Hovnanian struck a deal. GSO would provide below-market financing to Hovnanian if Hovnanian would default on an interest payment on $26 million of debt held by a Hovnanian subsidiary.

[101.] Amended Complaint at 2, *Solus Alt. Asset Mgmt. LP v. GSO Capital Partners L.P.*, No. 18 CV 232-LTS-BCM (S.D.N.Y. Feb. 1, 2018), Doc. No. 75; Declaration of J. Larry Sorsby in Opposition to Plaintiff's Motion for Preliminary Injunction at Ex. 13, *Solus Alt. Asset Mgmt. LP v. GSO Capital Partners L.P.*, No. 18 CV 232-LTS-BCM (S.D.N.Y. Jan. 22, 2018), Doc. No. 43-13 (letter from Harrison Denman of White & Case on behalf of an ad hoc group of investment funds that had sold Hovnanian CDSs, sent to J. Larry Sorsby CFO of K. Hovnanian Enterprises on Nov. 11, 2017).

This was, in effect, a faux default. This manufactured default did not cause any financial distress for Hovnanian. No outside creditor of Hovnanian would be affected. It was a win-win for Hovnanian and GSO: below-market financing for the former and a CDS payout for the latter.

This win-win gaming of the literal terms of the CDSs would come at the expense of the CDS sellers. Solus Alternative Asset Management, one such seller, sued, but the court refused to grant a preliminary injunction.[102] Regulators, the International Swaps and Derivatives Association, and outside observers expressed concern at the threat such gaming behavior may pose to the integrity and viability of the CDS market. On May 30, 2018, the manufactured default was called off after GSO and Solus settled.[103]

4. Windstream Services (2015-2018): Incentives to Use a Possible Technical Default to Cause Financial Distress

Windstream Holdings (Holdings) is a publicly traded company, and its only asset was its equity interest in Windstream Services (Windstream), a telecommunications company based in Arkansas. In April 2015, Windstream spun off Uniti Group (Uniti), a wholly owned subsidiary.

This spin-off involved Windstream contributing substantial assets to Uniti in return for Uniti securities and cash.[104] In connection with the spin-off, Holdings and Uniti entered into a lease transaction whereby Holdings leased a large portion of the assets that Windstream contributed to Uniti.[105] This occurred notwithstanding

---

[102.] Memorandum Opinion and Order Denying Motion for Preliminary Injunction, *Solus Alt. Asset Mgmt. LP v. GSO Capital Partners L.P.*, No. 18 CV 232-LTS-BCM (S.D.N.Y. Jan. 29, 2018), Doc. No. 69.

[103.] Joe Rennison, "Manufactured" Credit Default Called Off after Legal Challenge, Fin. Times (May 30, 2018), www.ft.com/content/c184dd72-6457-11e8-90c2-9563a0613e56.

[104.] Windstream Services, LLC's Corrected Proposed Findings of Fact and Conclusions of Law, at 1, 2, 5, 6, No. 17-cv-7857 (JMF) (S.D.N.Y. June 18, 2018) [hereinafter Windstream FF+CL].

[105.] Counterclaim Defendant and Counterclaim Plaintiff Aurelius Capital Master, Ltd.'s Proposed Findings of Fact and Conclusions of Law, at 1, No. 17-cv-07857 (JMF) (S.D.N.Y. June 21, 2018) [hereinafter Aurelius FF+CL].

the possible applicability of a covenant prohibiting certain sale-and-leaseback transactions in the indenture of certain senior notes issued by Windstream.[106]

For two years, no one complained about the spin-off and lease. But on September 21, 2017, Aurelius Capital Master (Aurelius), the largest holder of the senior notes, privately sent Windstream a notice of default alleging that these 2015 transactions were impermissible under the indenture. In October 2017, after being sued by Windstream in Delaware Chancery Court, the indenture trustee filed suit in the Southern District of New York against Windstream on the same grounds. Rather than litigating the question of whether the transactions violated the indenture, Windstream announced a series of exchange offers and consent solicitations that Aurelius believed were designed to obtain a waiver of the Aurelius-noticed default.[107]

Why did Aurelius initiate action against Windstream over an alleged covenant breach that occurred two years earlier? If the court agrees that a covenant breach occurred, the decision could trigger cross-defaults on an estimated $5.7 billion in debt, and Windstream may have to file for bankruptcy.[108] As the secured notes' largest holder, this would seem to be against Aurelius's economic interest.

But Aurelius is likely not a traditional creditor and has very different incentives. According to Windstream, Windstream became aware in the summer of 2017 that an unknown hedge fund was acquiring a substantial position in its notes, with the intent to call a default. It soon learned from industry sources that the unknown

---

[106.] Plaintiff-Counterclaim Defendant U.S. Bank Nat. Ass'n Proposed Findings of Fact & Conclusions of Law (Corrected), at 11–12, No. 17-cv-07857 (JMF) (S.D.N.Y. June 15, 2018).

[107.] Aurelius FF+CL, supra note 105, at 1–2.

[108.] Katia Porzecanski, Dan Wilchins & Allison McNeely, Citadel-Led Creditor Group Agrees to Windstream Debt Swap, Bloomberg (Jul. 26, 2018), www.bloomberg.com/news/articles/2018-07-26/citadel-led-creditor-group-said-to-agree-to-windstream-debt-swap.

fund was Aurelius and that Aurelius intended to characterize the 2015 transactions as a violation of the indenture's sale-and-leaseback covenant.[109]

Critically, Windstream claims that Aurelius had "also acquired a sizable position in CDS on Windstream's debt.[110] Windstream proffered the testimony of Michiel McCarty, the head of a boutique investment bank as follows:

> McCarty will testify that Aurelius's conduct was not consistent with how a typical economic creditor of [Windstream] would behave. Aurelius's conduct appears calculated to *reduce* the prospects of payment in full at maturity. Aurelius's conduct would only be economically rational if it profits more from its CDS position if [Windstream] defaults than if [Windstream] successfully pays off the bond at maturity, creating an incentive for Aurelius to destroy value to other noteholders.[111]

Similarly, Windstream suggests that Aurelius's October 20 and 24, 2017, letters urging other Windstream noteholders to reject Windstream's consent solicitations and exchange offers should have, but did not, acknowledge Aurelius's skewed incentives.[112] For instance, Windstream stated:

> While the October 24 Letter characterized Aurelius as a "Windstream Noteholder," it neglected to inform that market of the material information about Aurelius's CDS position (giving Aurelius a short-position as to [Windstream]), and Aurelius's financial motives for disseminating the letter.[113]

[109.] Windstream FF+CL, supra note 104, at 14–15.

[110.] *Id.* at 15.

[111.] Windstream Services, LLC's Trial Witness List & Test. Summ. at 15, *U.S. Bank Nat'l Ass'n v. Windstream Services, LLC*, No. 17-07857-JMF-GWG (S.D.N.Y. Oct. 12, 2017), ECF No. 158-2.

[112.] Windstream FF+CL, supra note 104, at 28.

[113.] *Id.* at 39–40.

The consent solicitations and exchange offers were successful.[114] The litigation, which was pending as of time of writing the version of this chapter published in the corporate control symposium issue, was anticipated to focus on whether the 2015 transactions constituted a default under the indenture, and whether the subsequent exchange offers and consent solicitations violated the indenture.[115] (A brief afterword on the February 15, 2019 court decision and consequent Windstream bankruptcy filing is now in the Conclusion.)

If Aurelius's CDS positions are as McCarty and Windstream claim, then Aurelius falls squarely within the decoupling framework's definition of "empty creditor with a negative economic ownership." The framework clarifies the Windstream situation in a number of ways.

First, most obviously, the framework helps explain Aurelius's behavior and how timely and granular information on the presence of empty creditors like Aurelius can be important to understanding the debtor's financial prospects. The incentives McCarty ascribes to Aurelius are precisely the counterintuitive incentives that the framework posited for such extreme empty creditors. In the two years following the 2015 transactions, not one of Windstream's other creditors had noticed a default, presumably because no other creditors were net short.

Windstream had limited information on any empty creditors in its midst. In the summer of 2017, Windstream was initially aware only that some unknown hedge fund was acquiring a position in its notes with the intent of calling a default. Afterwards, when it learned that Aurelius was the fund in question, Windstream appeared not to know the precise extent and nature of that fund's CDS positions. Windstream' CFO, Bob Gunderman, filed an affidavit that he "heard from market analysts that Aurelius had purchased [CDS] as to [Windstream], with respect to which Aurelius would profit if [Windstream]

[114.] *Id.* at 44.
[115.] Aurelius FF+CL, supra note 105, at 2–3.

experienced an Event of Default."[116] The affidavit of Steve Cheese-
man, a Citi investment banker who advised Windstream on the
Aurelius crisis, stated that he "developed an understanding based on
various sources of information, including conversations with market
participants, that Aurelius . . . held a significant CDS position referencing Windstream."[117]

Second, Windstream might illustrate the framework's long-
standing concern over the weaponization of "technical defaults" by
empty creditors with a negative economic ownership.[118] A 2008 Hu
and Black article pointed out that financial covenants are traditionally written on assumptions that creditors need protection in order
to get repaid and that creditors thus care about the borrower's success.[119] We noted that, because of debt decoupling, some creditors
will not care and, indeed, that some "may seek to use the 'technical default' provided by a covenant violation as leverage toward" the
borrower's demise.[120] In terms of private ordering, debtor companies
would be well-advised to craft financial covenants carefully, including recognizing the possibility of net short creditors.

Third, Windstream illustrates the need to determine whether
empty creditors with a negative economic ownership should be entitled to exercise control rights under standard credit agreements, or
if the agreements themselves should be drafted to expressly limit
control rights for such creditors. In the *debt* decoupling context,
the framework has raised the possibility of curbs on the contractual

---

[116.] Aurelius Obj. to Excerpts in the Direct Test. Aff. of Bob Gunderman at 2, *U.S.
Bank Nat'l Ass'n v. Windstream Services, LLC*, No. 17-07857-JMF-GWG (S.D.N.Y. Oct.
12, 2017), ECF No. 187-3.

[117.] Aurelius Obj. to Excerpts in the Direct Test. Aff. of Stephen John Cheese-
man at 3, *U.S. Bank Nat'l Ass'n v. Windstream Services, LLC*, No. 17-07857-JMF-GWG
(S.D.N.Y. Oct. 12, 2017), ECF No. 187-4.

[118.] It is not necessary for the purposes of this chapter to determine whether in
fact the covenant breach alleged in Windstream should be characterized as merely
involving a "technical default" with little consequence or should be characterized as
involving something more substantial. The author does not take a position on this
issue.

[119.] Hu & Black, EFM–Debt, Equity, and Hybrid Decoupling, supra note 65, at 685.
[120.] See *id.*

control rights of creditors who hold zero or negative economic interests in companies not in bankruptcy.[121] For companies in bankruptcy, the framework raised the prospect of forcing disclosure in bankruptcy proceedings of significant disparities between nominal debt holdings and actual economic exposure, and of courts overriding a creditor vote tainted by some creditors voting with little, no, or negative economic ownership.[122] Disclosures in this general spirit were mandated on December 1, 2011, when amendments to Rule 2019 of the Federal Rules of Bankruptcy Procedure became effective.[123]

In the *equity* decoupling context, the framework called for corporate law to disallow voting by empty voters with negative economic ownership.[124] In the 2012 TELUS case, the Supreme Court of British Columbia found that a hedge fund was an empty voter with a negative economic ownership under the Hu-Black analytic framework, and found that this status was relevant to the court's consideration of the hedge fund's objection to the company's proposed dual class recapitalization.[125]

Finally, the Windstream net short creditor situation shows that the presence of CDSs held by third parties can sometimes result in "real-world" victims. The acceleration of $5.3 billion in debt from the Aurelius-noticed default and consequent bankruptcy would hurt the traditional creditors, the company itself, and the nearly 13,000 employees employed by the company and its subsidiaries.[126] This pattern also occurred with respect to the Norske Skog situation. This

---

[121] See *id.* at 685–86.

[122] *Id.* at 684.

[123] See Fed. R. Bankr. P. 2019; Hu, Financial Innovation and Governance Mechanisms, supra note 65, at 372–73 (noting the impact of the subject parties being required to identify their "disclosable economic interests" under the new Rule).

[124] Hu & Black, Penn-Debt and Equity Decoupling, supra note 65, at 701–03.

[125] TELUS Corporation (Re), 2012 BCSC 1919, para 342, 365, & 366 (2012); Hu, Financial Innovation and Governance Mechanisms, supra note 65, at 375–81. The author prepared the affidavit cited by the court as an expert to assist the court and not as an advocate for any party pursuant to the strict requirements of Rule 11-2(2) of the British Columbia Supreme Court.

[126] See Windstream FF+CL, supra note 104, at 1.

is in direct contrast to the Hovnanian situation. In Hovnanian, the only losers from the manufactured default were the CDS sellers. In fact, Hovnanian (and all of its stakeholders) actually benefited from the existence of third-party CDS activities.

IV. Conclusion

This chapter shows some key factors undermining the informational base needed by investors in distressed companies. It focuses on informational asymmetries that are curious in some way, those that in source, nature, or degree may be new or unfamiliar, including those that arise from new capital market developments. The impact of the true, faux, or technical defaults that can arise from third-party CDS activities and other debt decoupling may necessitate steps to better address certain "extra-company" information critical to investors.

Insufficient incentives contribute to the tendency of distressed-company managements to simply decline to file required SEC reports. The SEC has already shown itself willing to enact "bad boy" deterrents, including by way of the required biographical disclosures for directors and certain officers.[127] An incremental change, applicable to those who had served as, for instance, the chief executive officer or chief financial officer of a company that had failed to file required SEC reports, could be made to the required biographical information. If the CEO or CFO knows they will have to disclose such outright non-compliance failures in some future job, they may hesitate to shirk that responsibility. In certain more extreme cases involving laxity in SEC compliance, the SEC could seek to bar certain securities fraud defendants from serving as a director or officer of a public company, either permanently or for a specified period of time.

[127.] See, e.g., Regulation S-K, 17 C.F.R. § 229.401(f) (Item 401) (requiring disclosure of various legal proceedings "that are material to an evaluation of the ability or integrity" of any person nominated to become a director or officer).

If the Supreme Court does not soon rule on the private enforceability of the MD&A requirements, the SEC could consider trying to move a few of the more "objective" aspects of the MD&A disclosure requirements to Form 8-K. No one, including the Ninth Circuit, disputes that Form 8-K omissions are actionable by private plaintiffs.[128]

The extra-company information needs flowing from CDSs and the debt decoupling phenomenon pose real challenges. The absence of public information on the CDS positions of individual entities is one concern. But benefit/cost considerations aside, change in disclosure rules relating to derivatives positions of individual holders may prove difficult. For instance, unlike major foreign jurisdictions, the U.S. has yet to address the long-standing "hidden (morphable) ownership" problem relating to equity derivatives positions under Section 13(d) of the Exchange Act.[129]

An incremental, if less satisfying, alternative to systematic reform in this area might be to again look to Form 8-K. The SEC could add to the current list of occurrences triggering a Form 8-K filing. One trigger might be a troubled company's top management becoming aware of a major creditor having become an empty creditor with negative economic ownership, whether through CDSs or by other means.

I have written elsewhere, however, that a variety of regulatory, industry, judicial, and corporate self-help measures should be considered in responding to credit default swap abuses, such as abuses flowing from empty creditors with negative economic ownership.[130] The 2019 court decision in favor of Aurelius on all counts and Windstream's follow-on bankruptcy filing illustrate the importance of considering such measures.

[128.] See, e.g., In re Atossa Genetics Inc. Sec. Litig., 868 F.3d 784, 797 (9th Cir. 2017).

[129.] See Hu, Financial Innovation and Governance Mechanisms, supra note 65, at 358–60, 366–69.

[130.] As one example, see, e.g., Henry T. C. Hu, Reform the credit default swap market to rein in abuses – Windstream's fight with Aurelius highlights the complexities of 'empty creditors,' Fin. Times (Feb. 24, 2019), https://www.ft.com/content/1fcd2f34-2e14-11e9-80d2-7b637a9e1ba1.

Informational asymmetries can now materially hinder investor decision-making and market efficiency in the context of troubled companies not in bankruptcy. Addressing these asymmetries starts with a fuller understanding of how they arise. With today's debt-laden companies and the return of normal interest rates, opportunities to go further should not be missed.

Baby Lehman

A Functional Approach to Non-SIFI Resolution

*Edward J. Janger**

B ecause this is a conference in honor of Jay Westbrook, the "pragmatic functionalist," this chapter is a celebration of pragmatic
functionalism; it is also about how to facilitate the value maximizing
resolution of financial institutions whether or not they are systemically important. To celebrate Jay, and his method, I use his "functional
approach" to develop a set of "pragmatic" recommendations regarding the resolution of non-bank financial institutions. Significantly,
these recommendations apply whether or not the debtor is a systemically important financial institution (a "SIFI"). I advocate a reversal of the current resolution paradigm. Current reform efforts seek
symmetry of forum: resolution of all non-bank financial institutions
in a bankruptcy forum. At the same time, they promote asymmetry
with regard to financial instruments: prescribing disparate treatment
of financial instruments depending on whether the party is a bank,
SIFI or anybody else. In this piece I argue for asymmetry of forum

* David M. Barse Professor and Associate Dean of Research and Scholarship,
Brooklyn Law School. The substance of this chapter is reproduced with permission from Norton Journal of Bankruptcy Law and Practice, Vol. 27 No. 5 (Oct. 2018),
with permission of Thomson Reuters. Copyright © 2018. Further use without the
permission of Thomson Reuters is prohibited. For further information about this
publication, please visit https://legal.thomsonreuters.com/en/products/law-books
or call 800.328.9352.

but symmetric treatment of instruments. SIFIs should be treated like banks, but bankruptcy treatment of financial contracts needs to work better for smaller non-systemic financial institutions as well.

As I have written previously, at the center of discussions about financial institution bankruptcy is the asymmetric treatment of certain financial contracts (swaps, repos, and various types of derivatives) for different types of financial institutions that are subject to different resolution regimes: (1) These "qualified financial contracts" or "QFCs" are given "short-stay" treatment for banks under the "Federal Deposit Insurance Act" (FDIA); (2) they are given "safe harbor" treatment under the Bankruptcy Code for non-banks; and finally, they are subject to a complex hybrid approach for SIFIs under Dodd-Frank.[1] This asymmetry creates opportunities for various forms of opportunism, and in particular, it undercuts the ability of debtors and regulators to stop runs and limit contagion. In this chapter, I suggest that Jay's functionalism points the way toward a harmonized treatment of financial contracts across resolution regimes that will help preserve both firm value and financial system stability. The key is to protect the benefit of the counterparty's bargain, rather than its formal rights.

Any analysis of contracts in bankruptcy starts with Jay's functional approach.[2] But the analysis in this chapter is functional in a broader sense as well. In addition to examining the Bankruptcy Code's provision on contracts and financial contracts, it explores the functions served by (1) regulators, bankruptcy judges, various types of financial institutions (Banks, SIFIs, non-bank financial institutions, etc.), as well as (2) the function of various types of financial contracts themselves, within the financial system. This functional analysis leads to a set of

---

[1] See generally Edward J. Janger & John A. E. Pottow, Implementing Symmetric Treatment of Financial Contracts in Bankruptcy and Bank Resolution, 10 Brook. J. Corp. Fin. & Com. L. 155 (2015–2016).

[2] See Jay Lawrence Westbrook, A Functional Analysis of Executory Contracts, 74 Minn. L. Rev. 227 (1989); Michael T. Andrew, Executory Contracts in Bankruptcy: Understanding "Rejection," 59 U. Colo. L. Rev. 845 (1988); Jay Lawrence Westbrook & Kelsi Stayart White, The Demystification of Contracts in Bankruptcy, 91 Am. Bankr. L.J. 481 (2017).

principles for balancing concerns about the safety and soundness of the financial system against concerns about value preservation. Finally, the chapter seeks to show how Jay's functional approach to executory contracts can be used to inject a measure of pragmatism into the treatment of financial contracts in chapter 11 that will help preserve asset value for financial institutions without undercutting the market for financial products. Put succinctly, *a debtor that (1) continues to perform its obligations and can credibly assure its counterparties that they will receive the benefit of their bargain (2) should be legally protected from a run. Moreover, (3) this principle should apply, regardless of the debtor's status as a Bank, SIFI, non-systemic financial institution, or ordinary debtor who happens to be a financial contract counterparty.*

Getting to this simple solution, however, requires cutting through a lot of path dependence in the current regulatory structure. In particular, it requires us to reevaluate the lessons of Lehman Brothers. As will be explained next, one set of lessons involved the need for SIFIs to maintain adequate capital and liquidity to respond to a financial shock. A second set of lessons involved the need to structure a SIFI so that that capital can be effectively deployed to stop a run. These are questions principally for the regulators. However, a third lesson learned was that chapter 11 of the U.S. Bankruptcy Code is not a hospitable place for financial institutions to resolve, whether or not they are SIFIs.

Because Lehman was a SIFI, legislative and regulatory energy has been devoted almost solely to SIFI specific reforms: Title II of the 2010 Dodd-Frank legislation; and proposed, pending, legislation seeking to make bankruptcy work better for "too-big-to-fail" (TBTF) non-bank financial institutions.[3] After offering a bit of history, this chapter broadens the focus beyond SIFIs and users asks three interrelated functional questions: What is the proper role of bankruptcy courts in administering financial institution bankruptcies? What is

---

[3.] Dodd–Frank Wall Street Reform and Consumer Protection Act (Dodd–Frank Act), Pub. L. No. 111-203, section 201 to 214, 124 Stat. 1376, 1442-1518 (2010) (codified at 12 U.S.C. §§ 5381 to 5394 (2012) (hereinafter "Dodd–Frank Act").

the proper role of QFCs in the financial system? And, what should we do to balance the imperatives of these two systems?

The pragmatic answer is that the SIFI focus with regard to financial industry bankruptcy teaches us the wrong lessons. Bankruptcy courts have an important role to play in financial industry bankruptcies, but not for SIFIs. For a variety of reasons, it is unlikely that a larger financial institution (a SIFI) will ever find its way into bankruptcy court. But smaller institutions (non-SIFIs) will use bankruptcy, and for them, the treatment of financial contracts is highly problematic. Some financial contracts play a crucial role in the financial system, as so-called, "safe assets." Because they need to function in the financial system like money, preferential treatment for those contracts may be justified. However, the safe harbors should be narrowly tailored, giving this special treatment only where the instruments are commonly viewed as money substitutes. In this regard, instead of focusing on SIFIs, and proliferating institution specific resolution regimes, we should seek symmetric treatment of these instruments across fora, specifically seeking to assure that financial contract counterparties can receive the benefit of their bargain, without undercutting the value maximizing and firm-level run-stopping goals of chapter 11, and in a manner that will limit financial contagion within the broader financial system.

I. History—Safe Harbors, Lehman, and the SIFI-Specific Response

The financial crisis of 2008 demonstrated that the Bankruptcy Code and bankruptcy courts are not well equipped to address the bankruptcy of financial institutions.[4] This is largely a result of the paradoxical tension between two policy imperatives: (1) preserving stable financial markets for certain financial instruments and (2) preserving

---

[4] Edward R. Morrison, Mark J. Roe & Christopher S. Sontchi, Rolling Back the Repo Safe Harbors, 69 Bus. Law. 1015, 1045–46 (2014).

the safety and soundness of financial institutions. The road to Lehman was paved much earlier, at a time when TBTF meant something entirely different from what it does today. It was an assumption rather than an imperative. It referred to the fact that it was simply inconceivable that a large main line investment bank might fail.[5] It was assumed that large financial firms were simply failure proof. The concern, instead, was with the possible failure of smaller financial institutions.[6] The history, thus, starts with an initiative to protect certain financial products and ends with a focus on how to protect certain financial institutions. Consistently lacking is a holistic approach that takes the interaction between legal fora, financial institutions, and financial instruments into account.

A. The Bankruptcy Safe Harbors–Protecting Financial Products from Bankruptcy Courts

Dating back to the 1980s, a key concern of large financial firms was the perceived inability of bankruptcy courts to prevent a small financial institution's bankruptcy from disrupting the clearance of certain

---

[5.] Kenneth Ayotte & David A. Skeel, Bankruptcy or Bailouts? 35 J. Corp. L. 469, 470, 481 (2010).

[6.] In re Grafton Partners, 321 B.R. 527, 532-33 (B.A.P. 9th Cir. 2005) (Klein, J.) ("Public Law 97-222 was a package of amendments designed to protect the carefully-regulated mechanisms for clearing trades in securities and commodities in the public markets from [the] dysfunction that could result from the automatic stay and from certain trustee avoiding powers."). See also, H.R. Rep. No. 97-420, at 1-2 (1982), quoted in In re Grafton Partners, 321 B.R. at 536. The House Report states:

> The commodities and securities markets operate through a complex system of accounts and guarantees. Because of the structure of the clearing systems in these industries and the sometimes volatile nature [of] the markets, certain protections are necessary to prevent the insolvency of one commodity or security firm from spreading to other firms and possibly threatening the collapse of the affected market. The Bankruptcy Code now expressly provides certain protections to the commodities market to protect against such a "ripple effect." One of the market protections presently contained in the Bankruptcy Code, for example, prevents a trustee in bankruptcy from avoiding or setting aside, as a preferential transfer, margin payments made to a commodity broker.

H.R. Rep. No. 97-420, at 1-2.

financial products and the securities clearance process. This led to the adoption of the so-called "safe harbors" for financial contracts.[7] Ostensibly designed to address systemic risk in the financial system, these safe harbors exempt QFCs[8] from bankruptcy's automatic stay and insulate any pre- and post-petition payments under those contracts from avoidance. The safe harbors were thought to serve a dual purpose: (1) to insulate the securities clearance process from the consequences of a bankrupt broker-dealer, and (2) to protect the liquidity of certain "money-like" financial instruments.[9] The original concern was that if a small broker dealer were to fail, this would disrupt the clearance of trades and ripple through the financial system. Financial instruments that form the backbone of the money market might lose their key financial attributes if closeout was delayed. It was understood that the effect of these provisions might be to allow a small broker dealer to fail, but SIPC was available to protect investors, so the risk was tolerable.[10] It was never anticipated that one of the largest financial institutions in the country might fail.[11]

B. Lehman

Lehman changed all that by calling attention to a different and distinct risk to the financial system: the failure of a large, non-bank, financial institution—a SIFI. When Lehman failed, instead of stabilizing the financial system, the safe harbors deprived the bankruptcy

---

[7.] See 11 U.S.C. §§ 546(e), 562, 555, 559.

[8.] Charles M. Mooney Jr., The Bankruptcy Code's Safe Harbors for Settlement Payments and Securities Contracts: When Is Safe Too Safe? 49 TEX. INT'L L. J. 245, n. 2 (2014).

[9.] For a discussion of "safe assets," see Anna Gelpern & Erik F. Gerding, Inside Safe Assets, 33 Yale J. on Reg. 362 (2016).

[10.] Over time, and particularly with the enactment of Bankruptcy Abuse Prevention and Consumer Protection Act in 2005, this "safe harbor" treatment was expanded to cover a wider variety of financial instruments. Also, a number of Bankruptcy Court opinions expanded the scope of the safe harbors beyond bank-to-bank transactions.

[11.] Edward R. Morrison, Mark J. Roe & Christopher S. Sontchi, Rolling Back the Repo Safe Harbors, 69 Bus. Law. 1015, 1029–30 (2014).

courts of the automatic stay, the tool usually used to stop runs.[12] Because they were not subject to bankruptcy's automatic stay, Lehman's QFC counterparties could (1) declare a default based on Lehman's bankruptcy; (2) exercise early termination rights under those contracts; (3) net out their positions; and (4) sell any collateral that they might hold.[13] In short, the counterparties could "run." The Bankruptcy Code had no power to stop them.[14] Even contracts that were "in the money" could be terminated without paying damages, as a result of so-called "walkaway" clauses. Unable to protect its assets, Lehman bled out—destroying much of the value of its derivatives portfolio along the way and taking much of the economy with it. In short, the safe harbors actually accelerated the financial contagion, fueling first the run on Lehman and then a systemic bank run.[15]

C. The SIFI-Specific Response to Lehman

In the wake of Lehman, reforms were put in place to address the possibility that another SIFI might fail. Title II of the Dodd-Frank Act extends the regulatory authority of the Federal Deposit Insurance Corporation (FDIC) to cover SIFIs—non-bank entities that are nonetheless TBTF. Included in that authority is supervisory power that requires a SIFI to engage in resolution planning by developing a "living will" that will show how the institution would be resolved

---

[12] See 11 U.S.C.A. § 362(b).

[13] See infra n. 15; see also Mark J. Roe & Stephen P. Adams, Restructuring Failed Financial Firms in Bankruptcy: Selling Lehman's Derivatives Portfolio, 32 Yale J. on Reg. 362, 385–87 (2015).

[14] See Mark Roe & David Skeel, The Derivatives Market's Payment Priorities as Financial Crisis Accelerator, 63 Stan. L. Rev. 539, 553 (2011) ("Prior to its collapse, Lehman owed J.P. Morgan about $20 billion. Four days before Lehman's bankruptcy, J.P. Morgan froze $17 billion of Lehman cash and securities that J.P. Morgan held, and then demanded $5 billion more in collateral. . . . Because of the exception from the Code's automatic stay.. J.P. Morgan could immediately liquidate the collateral in Lehman's bankruptcy.").

[15] Roe & Skeel, Financial Crisis Accelerator, 63 Stan. L. Rev. at 553.

in an orderly fashion in bankruptcy.[16] Also, Dodd-Frank creates an "Orderly Liquidation Authority" (OLA)—a special resolution regime that can be used to resolve the institution should bankruptcy prove inappropriate.[17] By all accounts the regulatory efforts by the FDIC to provide supervision and the exercise of resolution planning have been salutary: corporate structures of large financial firms have been rationalized and capital levels at systemically important banks have improved. But all of the regulatory energy has remained focused on SIFIs.

A lurking problem remained, however: the continued unsuitability of bankruptcy courts as a venue for SIFI resolution. This unsuitability arose from two competing concerns, the safe harbors and the need for speed: (1) because of the safe-harbor treatment of QFCs, there was no way for the bankruptcy court to stop a run, and (2) in the absence of the safe harbors, bankruptcy courts would not be able to act quickly enough to calm the financial markets. Some believe that, with a few tweaks to the Bankruptcy Code, bankruptcy courts can be adapted to the needs of SIFI resolution.[18] This view is reflected in the bankruptcy focus of the FDIC's resolution planning process and in proposed legislation to either add special provisions to chapter 11 or adopt a new chapter 14, to facilitate SIFI resolution.[19] Jay, John Pottow, Adam Levitin and I are dubious. Each of us has raised the concern that bankruptcy courts will never be an appropriate venue for SIFIs, because of the need for (1) speed; (2) because of the need for liquidity support; (3) because of the need for regulatory supervision; and (4) because international recognition may simply

---

[16.] See, FSB Guidance, available at www.federalreserve.gov/newsevents/pressre leases/files/bcreg20170324a21.pdf and FDIC Guidance, available at www.fdic.gov/resauthority/2017faqsguidance.pdf.

[17.] See Dodd–Frank Act section 201–214.

[18.] This view is reflected in the work of Mark Roe and others. See Mark Roe et. al., Harvard Law School Bankruptcy Roundtable (2017), available at http://blogs. harvard.edu/bankruptcyroundtable/tag/choice-act/ (last visited Aug. 24, 2018).

[19.] Stephen D. Adams, chapter 14 Proposal in the Senate (2014), available at https://blogs.harvard.edu/bankruptcyroundtable/2014/06/17/the-chapter-14-proposal-in-the-senate/ (last visited Aug. 24, 2018).

not be feasible in bankruptcy court.[20] As a result, the OLA is likely to remain the only appropriate resolution forum for SIFIs. This point will be further developed in the next section.

So, if bankruptcy will not likely be used to resolve SIFIs, is there any need to change the Bankruptcy Code to deal with financial institution resolution? The answer is yes, but the preferred reforms are different where non-SIFIs are involved. The next section explains the current efforts to protect the financial system by creating an orderly regime for SIFI resolution and shows that this set of reforms gets a lot of things right. However, by focusing solely on SIFIs, it gets a number of important things wrong, that, together, could cause significant damage to the financial system if left unremedied.

II. A Functional Approach to Financial Institution Resolution: Forum vs. Institution

To understand the current efforts to address SIFI resolution, it is worth taking a moment to lay out the broader institutional outline of

---

[20.] On this point, Jay has been both pragmatic and adamant. Bankruptcy courts are not, as a practical matter, the right place to handle the insolvency of a G-SIB. There are a number of reasons for this: (1) the need for administrative supervision; (2) the need for preparation and expertise by those administrative supervisors; (3) the need for coordination among global regulators; (4) the need to assure global recognition of resolution orders; and (5) the fact that the stakes are just too high to try something new. This is just to name a few, and he is certainly right. As a practical matter, those firms will never use it; those firms will always go the "administrative" route. But OLA is not available for non-SIFIs, and proposed reforms to the Code do not apply to non-SIFIs. While making the world safe for Lehman, they have ignored the existence of many baby Lehmans. In short, once the experts and regulators and Congress are finished creating a gold-plated regime for SIFIs that are too big to, and hopefully will never, fail, they will have left a significant gap in the architecture. Bankruptcy will still not work for ordinary non-systemically important, non-bank, financial institutions— the institutions most likely to need it. This is also the position of the National Bankruptcy Conference. See National Bankruptcy Conference, Resolution of Systemically Important Financial Institutions (Mar. 17, 2017), available at http://nbconf.org/wp-content/uploads/2015/07/NBC-Letter-re-Resolution-of-Systemically-Important-Financial-Institutions-March-17-2017.pdf (last visited Aug. 24, 2017).

financial institution resolution, before and after Dodd-Frank. Before Dodd-Rank, the applicable legal regime and resolution forum for a financial institution was determined by the type. Banks were subject to administrative resolution.[21] Non-banks were resolved in bankruptcy.[22] Post-crisis, SIFIs are now subject to a hybrid regime under Dodd-Frank.

A. Judicial vs. Administrative Resolution: The Function of the Administrative Track

Prior to the 2008 financial crisis, banks were resolved administratively by the FDIC under the FDIA and everybody else used bankruptcy.[23] There were functional reasons for singling out banks for administrative oversight and resolution. First, banks hold insured deposits. Second, banks operate with high leverage and hold particularly liquid assets that are subject to runs. Third, a bank run at one institution might easily spread to another institution, because the financial system is tightly linked. The practice for resolving banks is fairly familiar. The regulators arrive on Friday, and over the course of the "FDIC Weekend" divide the assets of the bank into two piles, "good" and "bad."[24] The good assets are quickly sold to another bank, while the government steps in and backs up the liabilities related to the bad assets. The process happens quickly and is designed to minimize the disruption to the financial system. The focus of the bank resolution regime is on protecting the public fisc and maintaining the stability of the financial system.[25]

---

[21] Federal Deposit Insurance Act (FDIA), 12 U.S.C.A. §§ 1811 to 1835a.

[22] 11 U.S.C.A. § 109.

[23] Janger & Pottow, Symmetric Treatment, 10 Brook. J. Corp. Fin. & Com. L. at 155–56.

[24] Janger & Pottow, 10 Brook. J. Corp. Fin. & Com. L. at 157.

[25] Department of the Treasury, Treasury Proposes Legislation for Resolution Authority, Treasury Press Releases (2009), available at www.treasury.gov/press-center/press-releases/Pages/tg70.aspx (last visited on Aug. 24, 2018); R. Christian Bruce, Treasury Releases Legislative Proposal on Resolution Authority for Nonbank Firms, Bloomberg Law (2009); Ben Bernanke, The Right Fix for the Fed, Washington Post (2009), available at www.washingtonpost.com/wp-dyn/content/article/2009/11/27/AR2009112702322.html?noredirect=on (last visited on Aug. 24, 2018).

There were a number of reasons that bankruptcy was thought unsuitable for banks. First, bankruptcy (by contrast to the FDIA) is a relatively slow party-driven court supervised process. Bankruptcy focuses on creating breathing space to maximize the value of firms for their creditors without government involvement. The debtor files for bankruptcy; the court puts in place a governance structure to administer the firm in bankruptcy (the debtor, committees, etc.); decisions are made whether to liquidate, sell the firm, or recapitalize; and then value is distributed. This process can sometimes be accomplished in weeks, but it sometimes takes a year or more; the idea of accomplishing it in a weekend for a complex firm seems folly. This concern led to the adoption of the safe harbors and created a paradox. For financial firms, bankruptcy is too slow for the clearance process. But it is also too fast for resolution, because the safe harbors provide for no stay. There isn't even the two-day, short-stay, moratorium of bank resolution to allow for an orderly transfer of assets.

B. The Lesson of Lehman: Expanding the Administrative Track for SIFIs through OLA and Resolution Planning and the Financial Institutions Bankruptcy Act

This was the first lesson of Lehman: SIFIs should be treated more like banks. They, too, operate at high leverage, and are subject to runs. Unlike banks, their deposits are not insured, but the failure of Lehman and the resulting systemic bailout showed that even where an institution was not bailed out, the public fisc was still at risk.[26] So Congress extended the FDIC's regulatory authority, resolution power, and the short stay to include SIFIs through the granting and

---

[26.] Dep't of the Treasury, Report to the President on the Orderly Liquidation Authority and Bankruptcy Reform (2017), available at https://home.treasury.gov/sites/default/files/2018-02/OLA_REPORT.pdf (last visited Aug. 24, 2018) (hereinafter "Treasury Report"); Taxpayer Protection and Responsible Resolution Act of 2014, S.1861, 113th Cong. section 1407 (2014) (hereinafter "chapter 14 Proposal");Financial Institution Bankruptcy Act of 2014, H. 5421, 113th Cong. section 1187 (2014) (hereinafter "Subchapter V Proposal").

The Bank/SIFI Approach: OLA

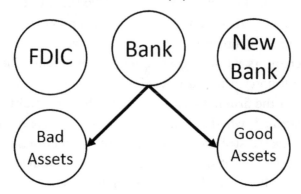

creation of the OLA. This new regulatory authority allowed the bank regulators to regulate the safety and soundness of SIFIs and provided an administrative track for resolution would allow the FDIC to implement the traditional weekend resolution for SIFIs that would not formerly have fallen under their authority.

But there was a twist, the OLA could only be used if the regulators deemed bankruptcy unsuitable. The next step for the regulators and Congress was to make orderly SIFI resolution possible in bankruptcy. This required changes to both SIFIs themselves, through regulation, in the form of "resolution planning" for SIFIs and to the law, through SIFI-related amendments to the Bankruptcy Code.[27]

1. Resolution Planning: Bail-in and SPOE

The first step toward making the post-Lehman resolution structure work was to mandate changes to the SIFIs themselves through mandated resolution planning or "living wills." SIFIs were required to explain to their regulators how they would respond to a significant financial shock in one of their operating businesses, and, if necessary, how they would resolve in bankruptcy. This resolution planning process had two prongs. The first prong was "bail-in." SIFIs would be structured as "clean" holding companies, and the

---

[27.] Treasury Report; chapter 14 Proposal; Subchapter V Proposal.

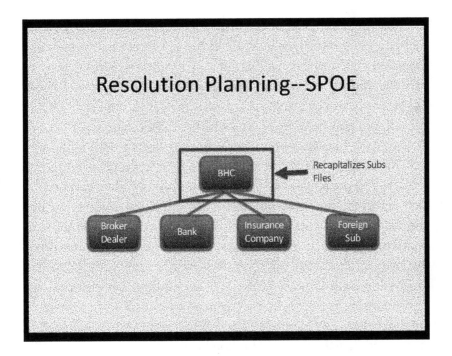

"operating companies" (OpCos) would look to the "Bank Hold-ing Company" (BHC) as a source of strength. The parent would be required to maintain sufficient capital and liquid assets to "bail-in" a troubled subsidiary by downstreaming sufficient capital and liquid assets to stop a run. Second, orderly resolution in bankruptcy would occur through "single point of entry" (SPOE). Once the sub or subs have been recapitalized, the BHC (but only the BHC) might need to file for bankruptcy itself. While Dodd-Frank Act does provide for an administrative process for resolution, the planning process requires the SIFI to plan for an orderly resolution in bankruptcy in the first instance.

2. Why Bankruptcy Doesn't Function Well for Financial
   Institutions and SIFIs in Particular: Speedy Transfer
   and Confidence

This requirement that resolution planning focus on bankruptcy brings into focus the various ways in which the traditional bankruptcy process is ill-suited to financial institutions. The Bankruptcy Code is well equipped to stop runs on ordinary firms. The automatic stay stops collection efforts on the petition date. This gives the debtor time to right the ship, either by recapitalizing the firm or by selling it, either as a going concern or piecemeal. Where contracts are involved, the debtor is given the opportunity to choose whether to breach the contract and discharge the breach claim or, perform the contract, and honor it in full. The problem is that this process is complicated and takes time.

As noted previously, financial institutions are characterized by high leverage, runnable liabilities, and illiquid assets. A savings and loan is the classic example, holding a portfolio of illiquid real estate mortgages, financed by demand deposits. If depositors run, the institution comes up short. Where ordinary sized firms are involved, private capital may be available to fund a reorganization. This financing is referred to as "debtor-in-possession" financing—a DIP Loan. However, where a large financial institution is involved, it is assumed that the firm will be "too big to DIP."[28] Also, where SIFIs are involved, there is a risk of contagion, both among banks (if a firm does not honor its financial obligations to other highly leveraged financial institutions), and within product markets (if there is a run on a particular type of instrument). This creates a need for speedy reassurance of the markets. Bank regulation seeks to solve the leverage problem through regulation of leverage and liquidity—capital requirements. When that is not enough, Bank insolvency law—as represented in the FDIA—places the emphasis on speedy resolution by arranging a speedy transfer of assets through bridge bank transaction, usually over the weekend. After all, a bank rarely has much in the way of fixed assets, or firm-specific assets. Therefore, the transfer

---

[28.] Frank H. Pearl, Too Big To Fail, Too Big To Bail: A Plan to Save the U.S. Auto Industry (2008), available at www.brookings.edu/research/too-big-to-fail-too-big-to-bail-a-plan-to-save-the-u-s-auto-industry/ (last visited Aug. 24, 2018); Michelle M. Harner, Final Report of the ABI Commission to Study the Reform of chapter 11 at 94–110 (2014), available at https://digitalcommons.law.umaryland.edu/cgi/view-content.cgi?article=1096&context=books (last visited Aug. 24, 2018) (hereinafter "ABI Commission Report"); Treasury Report.

can be accomplished quickly. Thus, resolution is a three-step process. If a bank fails, (1) the run is stopped briefly, (2) temporary liquidity is provided by an external source—the government or the bank's parent holding company, and (3) the valuable assets and liabilities are then transferred/sold to a solvent institution, and life continues as before. By acting quickly, contagion is stopped by making sure that the markets are confident that the obligations will be honored. The key attributes of SIFI resolution post-Lehman are (1) administrative supervision; (2) public liquidity support because SIFIs are too big to DIP; (3) speed; and (4) transfer.

The problem with bankruptcy for SIFIs turns on the ability to accomplish a transfer with sufficient speed to calm the markets and stop a run. On the one hand, a chapter 11 bankruptcy case is too slow to accomplish an orderly winding down of a financial institution in a weekend. On the other hand, even if a bankruptcy judge was prepared and equipped to execute a bridge bank transaction in a weekend, that would not be sufficient to stem a run. Many, if not most of the assets and liabilities held by financial institutions fall under the bankruptcy safe harbors; these contracts are exempted from the automatic stay and subject to early termination rights.[29] Instruments are not subject to the stay, so transactions clear—unless the institution runs out of money. Then the music stops. Without the benefit of the automatic stay there is no way to stop a run, nor, as a practical matter is there an ability to preserve asset value through a restructuring in place or an orderly value preserving sale. As Lehman demonstrated, because of the safe harbors, there is no way to stop the firm from bleeding out, and this in turn can cause broader contagion by other means.

3. Duct Tape for SIFIs

In the absence of legislation, the FDIC has managed to put in place a partial contractual solution for SIFIs. The so-called "ISDA Universal

---

[29.] ABI Commission Report at 95–110.

Stay Protocol" was negotiated between the International Swaps and Derivatives Association (ISDA) and the Financial Stability Board (FSB) to cause all SIFIs to agree, as a contractual matter to the same "short-stay" treatment in bankruptcy that would be available under the OLA, and to allow treatment in bankruptcy that would be consistent with the treatment in other resolution regimes.[30] Under the protocol, if a SIFI filed for bankruptcy, any safe-harbored instruments subject to the protocol would be subject to a two day stay, similar to that available under the FDIA.[31] The hope is that the combination of the SPOE structure, administrative supervision and the stay protocol would allow a bankruptcy court to effectuate a quick transfer of assets and an orderly resolution. Needless to say, it has not yet been tested.

4. The Legislative Fix (Forthcoming?)

While the ISDA Protocol is a partial solution, concern remains about the power and capacity of bankruptcy courts to implement a quick transfer of assets within the short window provided by the Protocol. This has led to a number of legislative proposals to facilitate the resolution of SIFIs by bankruptcy courts: a new chapter 14 of the Bankruptcy Code for SIFI bankruptcies; or a new subchapter V to be added to chapter 11. The proposals have different names, but the basic approach is consistent. The key provisions of these bills include a short stay, provisions for providing liquidity support, and provisions that preclude termination upon transfer to a creditworthy financial institution. While there a number of differences between the bills—such as the degree of administrative supervision and/or the extent to which the administrative track remains available—all

---

[30] ISDA Universal Resolution Stay Protocol (2015), available at www.isda.org/protocol/isda-2015-universal-resolution-stay-protocol/ (last visited on Aug. 24, 2018) (hereinafter "ISDA Universal Resolution Stay Protocol") (the purpose of the protocol is "to support the resolution of certain financial companies under the United States Bankruptcy Code.").

[31] ISDA Universal Resolution Stay Protocol.

share provisions that would modify the safe harbors to render them symmetric with their treatment under the FDIA.

C. The Lessons of Lehman—So Far

So, the lessons of Lehman, as embodied in Dodd-Frank's resolution planning provisions, and OLA, as well as in the proposed changes to the Bankruptcy Code, have been a series of SIFI-specific reforms that are based on the following assumptions: (1) SIFIs can be subjected to administrative supervision both in resolution planning and resolution itself; (2) SIFIs are too big to DIP, so the focus must be on a speedy transfer of the assets of the bank to a solvent entity within the short-stay window.

III. The Function of Bankruptcy Courts and The Canard of SIFI-Specific Resolution

The regime described previously is all well and good, as far as it goes. But it has a crucial flaw. All of the post crisis reforms are aimed solely at SIFIs.[32] In particular, the legislative proposals. Aimed at the Bankruptcy Code apply only to financial institutions with assets in excess of $50 Billion.[33] This focus on making bankruptcy safe for SIFIs has it exactly backward. While bankruptcy needs to work for financial institutions, as a practical matter, it will never be used for SIFIs. This is where Jay's pragmatic functionalism comes into play. As he, and a number of us have pointed out, it is unlikely that bankruptcy courts will ever be used to resolve a SIFI. Indeed, Title II of Dodd-Frank recognizes that where SIFIs are involved, an administrative solution

---

[32] FDIC, Title I and IDI Resolution Plans, available at www.fdic.gov/regulations/reform/resplans/ (last visited Aug. 24, 2018); see also chapter 14 Proposal; Subchapter V Proposal.

[33] See, e.g., Financial Inst. Bankruptcy Act of 2017, H.R. 1667, available at www.congress.gov/bill/115th-congress/house-bill/1667/text (last visited Aug. 24, 2018).

to resolution may be essential.[34] This is because (1) bankruptcy courts may not be able to act with sufficient speed to accomplish a traditional FDIC, weekend takeover; (2) the complexity of many BHCs, including entities that operate under multiple regulatory schemes, makes it unlikely that a court could provide the coordination necessary; and (3) the international aspects of a SIFI bankruptcy require coordination among bank regulators that simply is not possible in a party-driven bankruptcy process. For these reasons, we think it unlikely that if another SIFI found itself in financial difficulty that the FDIC would chance bankruptcy.

This does not mean that the bankruptcy will not be used for financial institutions. It just means that it is unlikely to be used by identified SIFIs. It also does not mean that the existing flaws in the Bankruptcy Code do not have systemic risk implications. The problem is that the concerns about SIFIs are different from those for non-SIFIs. In this section, I explain (1) why bankruptcy needs to work for non-SIFIs and (2) how it should be fixed.

A. SIFIs Are not the Only Source of Systemic Risk

On the one hand, not all financial institutions are SIFIs, and regardless of what happens to SIFIs, non-bank financial institutions have no alternative but to use bankruptcy. More importantly, SIFIs are not the only source of systemic risk in the financial system. For example,

- **Not all SIFIs are identified as such.** The proposed amendments identify a SIFI as any financial institution with liabilities of over $50,000,000,000.[35] Regulators maintain a list of institutions that fall into this category, but needless to say, the category is fluid, and, at any given time the categorization may be over or underinclusive. So, not all systemic risk will be situated in identified institutions, and, since $50,000,000,000 is just a number, systemic risk may come from unanticipated places.

---

[34] Dodd–Frank Act, Title II.
[35] Dodd–Frank Act, Title II.

- **SPOE may fail.** The SIFI-focused regulations are designed to facilitate a SPOE restructuring, where operating firms never enter bankruptcy. The BHC is required to maintain sufficient capital to recapitalize the OpCos. Therefore, only the holding company will file.[36] The holding company's assets are then resolved in a bridge bank transaction. Unfortunately, there is no guarantee that the SPOE approach will be sufficient to stop a run at the operating firm. If the operating firm still fails, it will need to make use of bankruptcy.
- **Operating firms may fail.** Not all financial institutions, and particularly those that have not been regulated as SIFIs, use a BHC structure. Thus, an OpCo with significant financial assets may fail, and bankruptcy may be its only recourse.
- **Stealth financial institutions.** Not all financial institutions look like financial institutions. Enron, for example, was generally thought to be an energy company, or a trading company, not a bank, or an investment bank. But its failure shook the economy. Significant elements of the GM and Chrysler bankruptcies involved their financial subsidiaries, GMAC and CMAC.[37]
- **Ordinary firms with derivatives portfolios.** Finally, real businesses make use of derivatives and other financial assets as part of their operating business, for business related reasons. For example, an airline may maintain a portfolio of jet fuel hedges to manage its exposure to fuel prices.[38] Early closeout of its derivatives may be the death nell for the business.

As a result, even if it is unlikely that an identified SIFI will ever again find itself in bankruptcy, Lehman demonstrated that there is a deep

---

[36.] Fed's Final TALC (2016), available at www.pwc.com/us/en/industries/finan cial-services/regulatory-services/library/feds-final-rule-TLAC-2016.html (last visited Aug. 24, 2018).

[37.] John Heltman, FSOC gives up effort to designate MetLife as SIFI (2018), available at www.americanbanker.com/news/fsoc-gives-up-effort-to-designate-metlife-as-sifi (last visited Aug. 24, 2018.

[38.] Hemal Gosai, Part Two: Fuel Hedging in the Airline Industry (2017), available at https://airlinegeeks.com/2017/09/18/part-two-fuel-hedging-in-the-airline-industry/ (last visited Aug. 24, 2018.

problem with the way the Bankruptcy Code deals with financial assets. The Code needs to be fixed so that it can work for firms that hold such assets, whether or not they are SIFIs. The problem is that many of the assumptions that drove the SIFI-specific reforms break down when non-SIFIs are involved.

B. Size Matters: Smaller Institutions Can and Should Be Handled Differently

The SIFI focus of both Dodd-Frank and the proposals for financial industry bankruptcy has led to a sector-specific approach predicated on implementing an administratively supervised SPOE bankruptcy. This focus on systemically important institutions is premised on a set of assumptions that are likely to be inaccurate for non-SIFIs.

- **Too big to DIP**—First, where SIFIs are involved, it is assumed that the financial firm is going to be too big to DIP. In other words, the liquidity needs of the firm are going to be so large that no private financing will be available to provide the liquidity needed to honor the firm's obligations on its financial contracts.
- **Resolution planning**—Second, where SIFIs are involved, it is assumed that the firm is already on the radar screen of the prudential regulators. As a result, the firm will have been required to engage in resolution planning and will have created the clean holding company structure necessary to effectuate an SPOE restructuring, and that the prudential regulators will be involved in supervising the bankruptcy, and, under Dodd-Frank, an administrative alternative.
- **Need for speed**—Third, because of these preceding assumptions, there are two further assumptions with regard to speed. In order to limit the effect on financial markets, it is assumed that the resolution must be accomplished quickly, either over a weekend or in 48 hours. Second, it is assumed that such speed is feasible, because of the resolution planning that has already taken place.
- **Focus on transfer**—Fourth, the focus is on transfer. One assumption about financial firms is that they are basically repositories of

contracts—that there are no firm-specific investments. Therefore, little is lost if financial assets are simply transferred from one firm to another.

For non-SIFI firms, none of these assumptions are correct, or at least they are not attributes should be assumed. Taking them in order, the inaccuracy of these assumptions leads to an inappropriate set of prescriptions:

- **Too big to DIP**—Where non-SIFIs are involved, the assumption that the firm is too big to obtain private financing to maintain operations may not always be the case. This is true for two reasons: the firm may not be all that large; and, in many cases the firm's derivative portfolio may be balanced. In other words, while the notional liability may be large, the net liability on a day to day basis may be considerably smaller. As a result, where smaller firms are involved, private institutions may be able to provide financing to stand behind the firm's financial contracts, allowing the firm to continue to perform. In other words, it may be possible to protect the benefit of the counterparty's bargain without rushing to accomplish everything over the weekend. In some cases, where the firm can be recapitalized, it may not even be necessary to transfer the contract.
- **Resolution planning**—Where non-SIFIs and stealth SIFIs are involved, the firms will not have been subjected to resolution planning, so it may not be feasible to disentangle their various assets quickly. As a result, a speedy transfer, which is the *sine qua non* of the FDIA and OLA structures may not be feasible, at least not in bankruptcy court.
- **Need for speed**—However, because the firm may be able to arrange DIP financing, it may be possible for the firm to continue to honor its obligations under the QFC without interruption. Where this is possible, then the need for "speed" may not be as great. If a creditworthy backstop for the financial contracts can be arranged in a short time, additional time may be taken to determine how to maximize the value of the portfolio and the firm.
- **Focus on transfer**—Finally, once the analysis is broadened beyond SIFIs, the types of institutions involved becomes much larger.

Financial institutions come in a wide variety of flavors. Some have significant operations behind their financial assets. Other debtors may be operating financial firms. Indeed, many non-financial firms may have significant QFC exposure if they have engaged in significant hedging strategies. In all of these cases, there may be reasons to continue the firm in operation, provided that the run can be stopped, and the firm can fulfill its obligations on its contracts. For example, a large airline might want to preserve its jet fuel hedge portfolio, or an automobile company may have significant positions with regard to raw materials. In all of these cases, the focus on transfer may be misguided.

For many smaller financial institutions, quick liquidation and transfer of assets may be the best solution. However, this will not always be the case. For example, an otherwise viable institution may be subject to a transitory shock. Or, for any number of reasons, a financial firm may be worth more if assets are kept in place then if they are disbursed. If it is feasible to protect derivative counterparties within the context of an ongoing case, it may not be as important to ensure that the derivatives are transferred quickly. Neither may it be desirable. For example, where the safe-harbored contracts are in the form of jet fuel hedges held by an airline, the preferable approach might be to leave the derivatives in place, while safeguarding the counterparty by guarantying critical vendor treatment.

C. The Proper Function of Bankruptcy Courts

Thus, current regulatory reform efforts misconstrue the function of bankruptcy courts in financial firm bankruptcies. They seek to make bankruptcy work for SIFIs that have been subject to regulatory supervision and resolution planning. They assume that the institutions that enter bankruptcy will be too big to DIP but will be amenable to speedy resolution through bail-in and quick transfer of financial assets. These assumptions are wrong in virtually every particular. First, SIFIs are unlikely to find themselves in bankruptcy court, ever. Second, the smaller non-SIFI financial institutions that do use bankruptcy come in many shapes and sizes and will not have been subject to resolution planning or administrative supervision. More importantly, many of these institutions, may be small enough to DIP, and therefore to continue to honor their financial contract obligations during a restructuring. Since the institutions are not so large, this may be sufficient to calm the financial markets, without having to resolve all issues within a weekend.

This suggests a very different role for bankruptcy courts than is envisioned under current proposed legislation. First, making the provisions of proposed chapter 14 or subchapter V only applicable to identified SIFIs ensures that they will never be used. Second, for the firms that do use bankruptcy, the focus should be on stopping runs and quickly assuring counterparties of the benefit of their bargain, rather than focusing on speedy transfer.

IV. The Function of Financial Contracts and Safe Harbors in the Financial System

Thus far we have focused on the function and role of bankruptcy courts. In this section, the focus shifts to the function of financial contracts—from institutions to instruments, and in particular to the function of the safe harbors. The scope and shape of the safe harbors is inextricably tied to the purpose served in the economy by QFCs: (1) why do we give special treatment to certain contracts, and (2) what shape should that treatment take.

A. The Function of QFCs

The starting point in a functional analysis of the safe harbors is to ask why certain financial contracts are given preferred treatment? In the financial system, not all money takes the form of currency, or even currency denominated obligations. For example, various measures the "money supply" as measured by the federal reserve include the supply of financial assets redeemable at par on demand.[39] This measure is sometimes referred to as MZM or money with zero maturity. Significantly, it includes money held in money market mutual funds. Gelpern and Gerding have pointed out that this creates a need for safe, money like, assets.[40] For instruments that play this role in the economy delay in the ability to gain access to these funds could have significant consequences. This does create a need to treat these types of instruments specially in bankruptcy. However, not all financial instruments fit this description. When the definition of QFC was amended in 2005, it was expanded to cover instruments far beyond those that are included in the money supply. In this regard, Roe and Morrison have argued that the scope of safe harbors should be limited to repos secured by treasury securities rather than other speculative collateral, arguing that beyond that category, the safe harbors are just being used as a mechanism for creating a contractual opt-out from bankruptcy treatment.[41]

B. The Function of the Safe Harbors for QFCs

Thus, the purpose of the safe harbors is to allow these "safe assets" to continue to function as money-like safe assets. To do this, it is important that financial markets recognize that even if a counterparty on a QFC files for bankruptcy, the debtor will continue to perform its obligations under the contract. This is the same problem that is faced when a bank fails. Here, it is worth taking a lesson from the bank resolution regime. There is no special treatment for financial contracts

---

[39] Federal Reserve Bank of New York, The Money Supply (2008), available at www.newyorkfed.org/aboutthefed/fedpoint/fed49.html (last visited Aug. 24, 2018).

[40] Gelpern & Gerding, Inside Safe Assets, 33 Yale J. on Reg. at 398 (2016); Anna Gelpern & Erik F. Gerding, Private and Public Ordering in Safe Asset Markets, 10 Brook. J. Corp. Fin. & Com. L. (2015). A significant reason that the federal government felt the need to create the Toxic Asset Relief Program (TARP) was concern that without government intervention, these money-like assets would no longer trade at par. This would have been referred to as "breaking the buck."

[41] Edward R. Morrison, Mark J. Roe & Christopher S. Sontchi, Rolling Back the Repo Safe Harbors, 69 Bus. Law. 1015, 1029–30 (2014).

under the FDIA. They are stayed for 48 hours, just like everything else.[42] This has not proven a problem for financial markets. The short delay has not led to financial catastrophe.

Therefore, a second concern about the current bankruptcy safe harbors is that under current law, there is no stay, not even a short one, and the filing of bankruptcy operates as a default under the agreement. This triggers the right to early withdrawal. In this regard bankruptcy treatment is more generous than the treatment accorded to these contracts when banks and SIFIs fail. It also makes it impossible, as in Lehman, to achieve an orderly transfer of a bank's assets. That was the problem in Lehman, where two days might have made a considerable difference.

V. Conclusions: The Implications of Functional Analysis for Financial Institution Bankruptcy

This functional analysis of QFCs and the safe harbors leads to some important conclusions about the shortcomings of the current regime for resolving non-systemically important financial institutions in bankruptcy. First, if one zeroes in on the reason for the special treatment given to QFCs, the category of QFCs has been expanded well beyond the appropriate boundaries to include assets that are not "safe" at all, for example, repos secured by highly volatile subprime mortgages, or other volatile collateral. These assets would not ordinarily be held in a money market fund, but they are nonetheless entitled to safe-harbor treatment. Second, the experience with bank resolution suggests that at the very least, short-stay treatment would be preferable to the current regime, which allows counterparties to treat bankruptcy as a default. These basic points are made in revised

---

[42.] ABI Commission Report.

World Bank Standard C.10.4 (and its footnote). These implications are applicable to SIFIs and non-SIFIs alike.

When the analysis is extended to non-SIFIs that are not too big to DIP, a bankruptcy regime that, like bank resolution, focused on preserving the benefit of the bargain, rather than treating bankruptcy as a default would be preferable to the current regime.

Thus, for those instruments that need safe harboring, the safe harbors should be modified to match the OLA regime. Instead of a right to immediate termination, there should be a short stay that lifts unless one of three things happen within the "short-stay" window: (1) transfer; (2) assumption; or (3) a finding that QFCs are improperly classified. Much has been written about the "FDIC weekend." The bankruptcy approach should be designed to match that approach: the debtor and the court would have a short period to protect the benefit of the counterparty's bargain; or they face lifting of the stay.

During the stay, the counterparty's interest could be protected in a number of ways. First, the DIP Lender would be required to provide liquidity to perform the obligations under the contract. Second, acceptable counterparties would be identified in advance through a list, published by the FDIC, or through transparent and readily available financial attributes. These reforms are pragmatic. They assure that non-bankrupt financial counterparties receive the benefit of their bargain. Most importantly, these guaranties could be incorporated into the existing Code with relatively minor amendments.

- **Short stay:** 362 (b) would be modified so that the safe harbors would not allow early termination, but instead, a short stay of termination so that would lift automatically after 48 hours, unless the contracts were transferred to a creditworthy counterparty, or were guaranteed by a creditworthy party.
- **Preserving the benefit of the bargain:** 365 would require timely performance of obligations on QFCs (along the lines of 365(d)). 365 would also incorporate special provisions regarding adequate assurance of future performance.

- Acceptable counterparties identified by list or credit rating.
- DIP lender could provide credit enhancement or take second loss position.

- **No default on bankruptcy:** So long as these conditions were met, the filing of a bankruptcy petition would not constitute a default under the QFC.

The key intuition here is again, to channel Jay, QFCs are just "contracts." If the debtor wishes to preserve their value, they need to be performed. The key is to have provisions in place that will assure that the counterparty is receiving sufficient assurance of performance, either by the debtor (with an appropriate financial backstop) or a solvent assignee. So long as the counterparty is getting the benefit of their bargain, they should have no standing to complain, and, so long as this assurance is provided quickly, it should be possible to prevent contagion.

The Dark Side of Reputation

Emily Kadens[*]

I. Introduction

In 2017, the English journalist Oobah Butler wanted to test his theory about "society's willingness to believe absolute bullshit."[1] He had previously had a job writing false TripAdvisor reviews: "Restaurant owners would pay me $13, and I'd write a positive review of their place, despite never eating there."[2] Using this experience, he set out to create a website for an entirely fictitious restaurant and, through the manipulation of reputation built on TripAdvisor posts, to make it the highest rated restaurant in London. The ostensible site of the restaurant was the shed in which Butler lived in the non-descript London suburb of Dulwich.[3]

[*] Professor of Law at the Northwestern University Pritzker School of Law. With thanks to the William G. and Virginia K. Karnes Research Professorship for research funding, and to Lisa Bernstein, Erin Delaney, Jeremy Edwards, Jerome Farrell, Sue Helper, Bruce Markell, Sheilagh Ogilvie, Destiny Peery, and Annie Prossnitz. And with abiding gratitude to my colleague and good friend, Jay Westbrook, in whose honor this chapter was written. This piece was originally published as Kadens, Emily, *The Dark Side of Reputation,* 40 Cardozo L. Rev. 1995 (2019). Reproduced with permission.
[1] Oobah Butler, I Made My Shed the Top-Rated Restaurant on TripAdvisor, Vice (Dec. 6, 2017, 5:20 PM), https://www.vice.com/en_us/article/434gqw/i-made-my-shed-the-top-rated-restaurant-on-tripadvisor [https://perma.cc/CQQ5-HLFH].
[2] *Id.*
[3] *Id.*

Needless to say, Butler succeeded. He posted fake pictures of meals; enlisted his friends to write glowing reviews; and within a few weeks he was inundated with phone calls and e-mails requesting bookings for months in advance. In May 2017, the restaurant debuted at the bottom of the heap, ranked 18,149. By November 1, "The Shed at Dulwich" was ranked number one with "89,000 views in search results" in one day.[4] Eventually, Butler decided to end the charade and see what would happen if he booked actual diners. He served them microwaved frozen dinners at "a hastily-assembled collection of chairs outside of my shed, and they left thinking it really could be the best restaurant in London—just on the basis of a TripAdvisor rating."[5]

Reputation is the foundation of theories of private ordering. These theories contend that commercial actors will act honestly because if they do not, they will get a bad reputation and others will not want to do business with them in the future.[6] But economists and scholars of networks increasingly realize that reputation has its defects.[7] Mixed in with trustworthy and useful reputation information on which commerce of all sorts relies is inaccurate, distorted, misguided, or outright fraudulent information. If TripAdvisor ranks The Shed at Dulwich as the best restaurant in London, people are

---

[4] *Id.*

[5] *Id.*

[6] See, e.g., Douglas W. Allen & Dean Lueck, The "Back Forty" on a Handshake: Specific Assets, Reputation, and the Structure of Farmland Contracts, 8 J.L. Econ. & Org. 366, 369 (1992) ("Punishment to cheaters, through lost future trade, encourages cooperation between the contract parties"); W. Bentley MacLeod, Reputations, Relationships, and Contract Enforcement, 45 J. Econ. Literature 595, 609 (2007) ("individuals . . . choose to be trustworthy because of the effect upon their reputation and the future rents they would receive from keeping their reputation intact"); Barak D. Richman, Firms, Courts, and Reputation Mechanisms: Towards a Positive Theory of Private Ordering, 104 Colum. L. Rev. 2328, 2335 (2004) ("if a party cheats any other party, that party's misconduct becomes known throughout the community; and no one will transact with any individual known to have cheated in the past. Thus, . . . the prospect of future beneficial transactions induces cooperative behavior.").

[7] *See infra* Part I.

willing to believe that it is.[8] And such inaccurate information threatens the effectiveness and efficiency of the reputation-based governance of the market.[9]

Much of the existing literature about reputation's flaws focuses on unintentional distortions caused by biases, the requirements of social niceties, and the dearth of fully representative information. This chapter, by contrast, approaches the problem of the distortion of reputation from the dark side. It uses a rich set of sixteenth- and seventeenth-century English court cases and merchant correspondence to examine how the deliberate manipulation of reputation, and, importantly, people's failure to verify the gossip and rumors creating such reputation, enabled fraud.[10] It turns out that reputation was "a complex process,"[11] even in interconnected early modern markets in which merchants did business face-to-face and participated in

---

[8.] Jonathan Silberstein-Loeb, *Reputation or: How I Learned to Stop Worrying and Love the Market, in* Reputation Capital: Building and Maintaining Trust in the 21st Century 23, 25 (Joachim Klewes & Robert Wreschniok eds., 2009) ("People believe in reputation, true or false, presumably because the costs of corroboration are too high, yet reputation is often forged of untrustworthy stuff.").

[9.] Eric Goldman, *Regulating Reputation, in* The Reputation Society: How Online Opinions Are Reshaping the Offline World 51 (Hassan Masum & Mark Tovey eds., 2011) ("[W]ell-functioning marketplaces depend on the vibrant flow of accurate reputational information"); Marcel Fafchamps, *The Enforcement of Commercial Contracts in Ghana*, 24 World Dev. 427, 428 (1996) ("Enforcement mechanisms based on reputation are vulnerable to disinformation: they do not operate well unless a complementary mechanism ensures the accuracy and veracity of the shared information.").

[10.] *See* Mark Granovetter, *Economic Action and Social Structure: The Problem of Embeddedness*, 91 Am. J. Soc. 481, 491 (1985) ("The trust engendered by personal relations presents, by its very existence, enhanced opportunity for malfeasance."); Peter Kollock, *The Emergence of Exchange Structures: An Experimental Study of Uncertainty, Commitment, and Trust*, 100 Am. J. Soc. 313, 319 (1994) ("[R]isk creates a breeding ground not only for trust but for exploitation as well.").

[11.] *See* Christopher McKenna & Rowena Olegario, *Corporate Reputation and Regulation in Historical Perspective, in* The Oxford Handbook of Corporate Reputation 260, 272 (Timothy G. Pollock & Michael L. Barnett eds., 2012) ("A second shortcoming of the historical literature is *the tendency to take for granted the power of reputation and to depict it as an uncomplicated phenomenon*, rather than as a complex process whose power to regulate may be weak or indeterminate.").

active gossip networks.[12] Even being caught, tried, and found guilty of a serious fraud did not necessarily undermine one's business and perceived trustworthiness in these networks, which raises questions about how much the merchants depended upon reputation when making decisions about whom to trust.[13]

The English merchants were aware of the potential for fraud based on the manipulation of indices of reputation. The trials of fraudsters were public; friends and business partners were summoned to give depositions; and word got around town.[14] And yet, many merchants—just as diners, book buyers, moviegoers, hotel patrons, or purchasers of goods online today—preferred not to incur verification costs and instead chose to trust easily-obtained, but also easily-falsified information. The result was a windfall for scammers.

This chapter seeks to contribute to the literature challenging the role of reputation in disciplining commerce. The historical disputes discussed here, which arose in the supposedly privately ordered zone of the premodern merchant,[15] add nuance to our understanding of how commerce works in the real world. Part I briefly reviews some of the problems the economic and network theory literature has identified with reputation. Part II turns to the history and demonstrates how trust could be cheaply manufactured due in part to potential partners' failure to look beyond superficial indicia of reputation. Part III then

---

[12.] *See* Daniel Defoe, The Complete English Tradesman 246–47 (1726) (discussing the commonality of merchant gossip); Letter from George Lowe to John Quarles, National Archives (U.K.), SP 46/176/fo201 (May 10, 1597) (reporting that the only thing merchants were talking about was other merchants' financial situations).

[13.] *See* Silberstein-Loeb, *supra* note 8, at 27–28 ("Reputation may be too ambiguous and easily perverted to hold companies to account, for even when a firm is caught behaving badly, its reputation may emerge unscathed.").

[14.] *See, e.g.,* Emily Kadens, *Cheating Pays,* 119 Colum. L. Rev. 527 (2019) (describing the early seventeenth-century case of a cheating grocer, the large number of deponents, and the spread of gossip throughout London and into the provinces about his frauds).

[15.] *See* Barak D. Richman, Stateless Commerce: The Diamond Network and the Persistence of Relational Exchange 133–34 (2017) (providing an overview of the law merchant theory and its influence); Bruce L. Benson, *The Spontaneous Evolution of Commercial Law,* 55 S. Econ. J. 644, 646–47 (1989) (on the concept of the privately ordered medieval law merchant).

considers why reputation might have been so susceptible to manipulation even in the face-to-face networks of early modern merchants.

II. The Known Unreliability of Reputation

Reputation presumably supports higher levels of trade because actors with good reputations will succeed and actors with bad reputations will fail.[16] As a consequence, anyone who wishes to remain in business will strive to maintain a good reputation. The fly in this theoretical ointment is that reputation information is itself subject to distortions, and "any distortions in reputational information may effectively distort the marketplace itself."[17] Aware of this problem, economists and network theorists have begun studying the unreliability of reputation.

Reputation, to use the dictionary definition, is "[t]he esteem in which someone is held or the goodwill extended to or confidence reposed in that person by others."[18] Reputation thus arises from the perceptions and opinions of other people.[19] Depending on the situation, it results from an observation or experience communicated directly to others or from gossip passed from person to person further and further from the original source.[20] Gossip, however, has its own social dynamic and motivations,[21] of which accuracy is not necessarily one.[22]

[16.] See Goldman, supra note 9, at 53 ("[R]eputational information can play an essential role in rewarding good producers and punishing poor ones.").

[17.] Id.; see Silberstein-Loeb, supra note 8, at 25 ("Reputation may distort markets because it is often a red herring."); Robert E. Scott, A Theory of Self-Enforcing Indefinite Agreements, 103 Colum. L. Rev. 1641, 1644 (2003) (pointing out that reputation-based governance works only under quite "stringent" and limited conditions).

[18.] Reputation, Black's Law Dictionary (10th ed. 2014).

[19.] Goldman, supra note 9, at 51.

[20.] Silberstein-Loeb, supra note 8, at 24 ("Reputation is largely gossip.").

[21.] Sally Engle Merry, Rethinking Gossip and Scandal, in 1 Toward a General Theory of Social Control 271, 276–77 (Donald Black ed., 1984).

[22.] See Diego Gambetta, Godfather's Gossip, 35 Eur. J. Soc. 199, 211 (1994) (maintaining that reputation does not have to be true); Silberstein-Loeb, supra note 8, at 25 ("[N]either reliability nor truth are necessary conditions for reputation. A reputation may be founded on falsely held beliefs.").

Furthermore, reputation is "an evaluation made without a concrete empirical referent,"[23] and that untethered evaluation is sensitive
to many warping effects. One of these is common social etiquette.[24]
A gossiper will share information in a way that conforms to the perceived preferences of his listeners.[25] If the speaker senses that the listener likes Jane, the speaker will shade the gossip he has to share so
that it sounds more positive, and the opposite is also true. Relatedly,
when this gossip occurs among the members of a closed network
with a set of shared preferences, the shading creates an echo effect,
reinforcing the biased view of the facts selectively communicated.[26]

The speaker's own biases and fears can also impact the reputational
information she conveys. If Jane is a member of a disfavored group, the
gossiper's implicit or explicit biases can color how she perceives Jane or
her actions and describes them to others.[27] Conversely, if the gossiper
fears retaliation from Jane if she says something negative but truthful,
then she will shade her gossip to sound misleadingly positive.[28]

In addition, conveying reputation information is not costless.[29]
Consequently, the motivations of the people who choose to take on
the cost of being reputation-creators matter. Psychologists believe
that those who spread online and word-of-mouth reputation information are often motivated to incur this cost to satisfy altruistic or

---

[23] Ronald S. Burt, Brokerage & Closure: An Introduction to Social Capital 175
(2005); see Gambetta, *supra* note 22, at 211 ("In gossip . . . there is no truth test
involved; truth, as established by evidence, is not part of gossip.").

[24] Burt, *supra* note 23, at 171.

[25] *See id.* at 170–71; Ronald S. Burt & Marc Knez, *Kinds of Third-Party Effects on
Trust*, 7 Rationality & Soc'y 255, 260 (1995) (C will shade stories and gossip about B to
fit what A seems to want to hear).

[26] *See* Burt, *supra* note 23, at 172 (discussing echo effect); Abbey Stemler, *Feedback
Loop Failure: Implications for the Self-Regulation of the Sharing Economy*, 18 Minn. J.L.
Sci. & Tech. 673, 693 (2017) ("[I]nitial confederate or fake positive reviews on Sharing
Economy platforms can amplify the herding effect.").

[27] Stemler, *supra* note 26, at 697–98 (discussing the problems of discrimination
in reputation systems).

[28] *Id.* at 691–92.

[29] Yonathan A. Arbel, *Reputation Failure: Market Discipline and Its Limits* 17–19
(Univ. of Alabama, Legal Studies Research Paper No. 3239995, 2018), https://papers.
ssrn.com/sol3/papers.cfm?abstract_id=3239995 [https://perma.cc/2X3W-VPP7].

vengeful needs.[30] The result is a biased perspective in which highly positive and negative experiences lead people to share their views, but "middling experiences" do not.[31] Online reviews, for example, tend to be overwhelmingly positive or negative, with few reviews in the middle.[32] This "regression to the extreme" creates reputations that do not reflect a normal distribution of perspectives.[33]

Shading, bias, and the unrepresentative perceptions of those with extreme views do not mean that the gossip shared is outright false. But gossip also does not have to be objectively true. It just has to be believable.[34] As discussed further in Part II, false but convincing gossip creates a false but convincing reputation. In the last several years, for instance, false but believable (and believed) online reviews have created a significant problem for the reliability of online rating systems and the reputations they create.[35]

---

[30] *Id.* at 20–23.

[31] *Id.* at 21–22.

[32] *Id.* at 32; *see* Chrysanthos Dellarocas, *Designing Reputation Systems for the Social Web, in* The Reputation Society, *supra* note 9, at 3, 6 ("[I]t has been documented that users are generally more likely to post feedback when they have had extreme (either very good or very bad) experiences than when they have had average experiences.").

[33] Arbel, *supra* note 29, at 29.

[34] *See* Gambetta, *supra* note 22, at 211 ("Plausibility is more relevant than truth."); Silberstein-Loeb, *supra* note 8, at 25 ("[N]either reliability nor truth are necessary conditions for reputation. A reputation may be founded on falsely held beliefs.").

[35] *See, e.g.,* Caroline Beaton, *Here to Help; Why You Shouldn't Always Trust Negative Online Reviews*, N.Y. Times, June 15, 2018, at A3 (reviewing research on the unreliability of online reviews); Mark Bridge, *For Sale: Five-Star Amazon Reviews*, Times (Apr. 30, 2018, 12:01 AM), https://www.thetimes.co.uk/article/for-sale-five-star-amazon-reviews-hsq5t6dwr [https://perma.cc/6JG6-5XTL] (describing Amazon review farms that generate fake reviews); Robin Henry & Sanya Burgess, *Our Little Book Roots Out the Amazon Chart Cheats*, Sunday Times (Oct. 11, 2015, 1:01 AM), https://www.thetimes.co.uk/article/our-little-book-roots-out-the-amazon-chart-cheats-c66ptc9p796 [https://perma.cc/2LHF-8CWT] (detailing fake gardening book pushed to the top of Amazon's gardening bestsellers list by fake reviews); Ryan Kailath, *Some Amazon Reviews Are Too Good to be Believed. They're Paid For*, NPR (July 30, 2018, 12:03 PM), https://www.npr.org/2018/07/30/629800775/some-amazon-reviews-are-too-good-to-be-believed-theyre-paid-for [https://perma.cc/8UM4-B5AZ] (describing process for obtaining fake reviews); Simon Parkin, *The Never-Ending War on Fake Reviews*, New Yorker (May 31, 2018), https://www.newyorker.com/tech/annals-of-technology/the-never-ending-war-on-fake-reviews

Gossip, whether by word of mouth or by online reviews, speaks reputation into being.[36] Negative gossip sows the seeds of doubt even if the recipient of the information suspects the motivations of the speaker.[37] By contrast, positive gossip and appearances sow the seeds of trust, sometimes even when the recipient of the information should know better. None of this is new. Shading, manipulating, and falsifying reputation also occurred in the premodern era, a time of face-to-face, credit-based trade conducted within dense social networks in which individual merchants had access to information— some of it accurate, some of it false, and not all of it verified—about the trustworthiness of potential trading partners.

III. Case Studies of Reputation Fraud

This part describes three cases from the early seventeenth century to illustrate how fraudsters used superficial indices of wealth to create a reputation for creditworthiness and thereby gain the trust of

---

[https://perma.cc/G7RD-QAYC]; Laura Stevens & Jon Emont, *To Game Amazon, Sellers Use Scams, Clicks & Dirty Tricks*, Wall St. J., July 28, 2018, at B1–B2 (reviewing the methods, including fake reviews, to improve online ratings on Amazon); David Streitfeld, *The Best Book Reviews Money Can Buy*, N.Y. Times, Aug. 26, 2012, at BU1 (discussing fake Amazon book reviews); Emma Wollacott, *Amazon's Fake Review Problem Is Now Worse Than Ever, Study Suggests*, Forbes (Sept. 9, 2017, 12:13 PM), https://www.forbes.com/sites/emmawoollacott/2017/09/09/exclusive-amazons-fake-review-problem-is-now-worse-than-ever/#449a6eec7c0f [https://perma.cc/GY89-NNH5] (describing study flagging many recent Amazon reviews as fake).

[36.] *See* Defoe, *supra* note 12, at 232 ("To say I am broke, or in danger of breaking, is to break me."); Thomas Starkie, A Treatise on the Law of Slander, Libel, *Scandalum Magnatum*, and False Rumours 12 (1813) ("Before mercantile convenience . . . had created what is termed credit, an imputation of insolvency could produce little prejudice, yet after the establishment of commerce, it might largely contribute to its own verification.").

[37.] Defoe, *supra* note 12, at 233–34 ("[A]nd tho' I know the Devil is a Liar, a Slanderer, a Calumniator, . . . yet there is a secret lurking doubt (about [the person gossiped about]), which hangs about me concerning him; the Devil is a Liar, but he may happen to speak truth just then."); Beaton, *supra* note 35 ("[P]eople may see negative reviews as more informative, and therefore more valuable."). *Cf.* Gambetta, *supra* note 22, at 209 ("Gossip does not work well if the receiver suspects ulterior motives behind the transmitter's story.").

sophisticated merchants. In every instance, the victims could have dug a little deeper and discovered the speciousness of these reputational indicators, but they did not. Instead, blinded by what looked like a promising business opportunity, they trusted unwisely and ended up scammed out of significant sums of money. These stories support the concern expressed in current literature that the ease with which reputational information can be falsified, the willingness of potential partners to trust, and their reluctance to incur costs to ensure that they base their decisions on accurate data will limit the ability of reputation to discipline the market.

The three cases that follow come from the records of the Court of Star Chamber, a court with a bad rap in history textbooks due to its involvement in a number of highly politicized and procedurally questionable cases during the early seventeenth century.[38] For most of its existence, however, the Star Chamber played a useful role as a court of equity dealing with criminal misdemeanors and perversions of justice.[39] The regulation of trade and the punishment of fraud constituted two of the Star Chamber's more important areas of jurisdiction.[40]

The cases do not deal with reputation in its broadest sense of "information used to make a value judgment about an object or a person,"[41] but rather with the narrower subset of commercial reputation. For the premodern merchant, commercial reputation was virtually synonymous with creditworthiness. As Daniel Defoe, the writer of novels and commercial tracts, explained in 1726, "[a]s a good

---

[38.] Thomas G. Barnes, Shaping the Common Law: From Glanville to Hale, 1188-1688, 152-53, 158-62 (2008).

[39.] J. H. Baker, An Introduction to English Legal History 118-19 (4th ed. 2002). *See also* John A. Guy, The Court of Star Chamber and Its Records in the Reign of Elizabeth I 7, 52-53 (1985) (explaining that the court's regular membership consisted of the Privy Council—the king's closest ministers and advisors, many not trained in law—as well as the chief judges of the Courts of King's Bench and Common Pleas and the Chief Baron of the Exchequer).

[40.] *See* 1 Thomas G. Barnes, List and Index to the Proceedings in Star Chamber for the Reign of James I (1603-1625) 34-36 (Thomas G. Barnes & Staff of the Legal History Project, American Bar Foundation, eds., 1975).

[41.] Randy Farmer, *Web Reputation Systems and the Real World, in* The Reputation Society, *supra* note 9, at 13.

name is to another man, . . . the same is credit to a tradesman . . . "[42] It is, he continued, "the life and soul of his trade . . . "[43] Defoe defined creditworthiness as "[h]onesty; a punctual dealing, [and] a general probity in every transaction,"[44] which closely aligns with a modern economist's definition of reputation in the context of contract enforcement as "a person's propensity to keep promises or . . . their reputation for trustworthiness."[45] Just as it is today, having good credit in premodern England was the difference between being able to do business on trust and do business solely on a cash basis.[46]

A premodern merchant's creditworthiness was something less than the sum of all the perceptions others had of him. The successful merchant could have good credit and yet be thought of poorly in other respects. For instance, at the end of the sixteenth century, the London merchant John Quarles had good credit in the England-to-Germany cloth trade carried out by the Merchant Adventurers, the monopolistic trading company of which he was a part.[47] That is, he could buy and sell on credit and others would take his bills of exchange and promissory notes. But because he associated with an unpopular, monopoly-busting non-member and assisted that interloper's trade, he was not always personally well thought of by the other Merchant Adventurers.[48]

---

[42] Defoe, *supra* note 12, at 226.

[43] *Id.* at 225.

[44] *Id.* at 420; *see* Letter from George Lowe to John Quarles, National Archives (U.K.), SP 46/176/fo203 (Oct. 16–17, 1597) (explaining the need to pay debts when asked in order to avoid being discredited); Letter from George Lowe to John Quarles, National Archives (U.K.), SP 46/176/fo210 (June 4, 1597) (same).

[45] MacLeod, *supra* note 6, at 609.

[46] Defoe, *supra* note 12, at 417 ("[I]f a man has ten thousand pounds in money, he may certainly trade for ten thousand pounds, and if he has no credit he cannot trade for a shilling more."). *See* Letter from George Lowe to John Quarles, National Archives (U.K.), SP 46/176/fo62 (Oct. 16–23, 1594) (discussing fear of bad debts due to rampant bankruptcies among English merchants in Germany, forcing merchants to do business in cash only because everyone was afraid to trust and give credit).

[47] Thomas Leng, *Interlopers and Disorderly Brethren at the Stade Mart: Commercial Regulations and Practices amongst the Merchant Adventurers of England in the Late Elizabethan Period*, 69 Econ. Hist. Rev. 823, 834 (2016) (discussing Quarles's credit).

[48] *See* Letter from George Lowe to John Quarles, National Archives (U.K.), SP 46/176/fo177 (Mar. 1, 1597); Letter from George Lowe to John Quarles, National

The cases in this part all concern alleged bankruptcy bust-outs. The bust-out remains one of the most common bankruptcy frauds in the United States today,[49] but these cases show that it has roots deep in English history. As a U.S. federal appellate court described the scam in 1976:

> A bust out begins with the formation by the malefactors of a seemingly legitimate wholesale business. The fledgling business's first goal is to establish a favorable credit rating. This task is accomplished by a number of devices which can include temporarily putting cash into the business in order to create a strong balance sheet, bribing credit rating agencies, and inflating financial statements so as to vastly overstate the business's assets and net worth. Also, bills for the company's initial purchases are promptly paid—thus furthering the deception through enhancement of the company's credit standing. As the business becomes more established, its promoters order considerable amounts of additional merchandise although they have no intention of paying for these goods. A huge inventory, most of it not paid for, is built up. The principals then busy themselves disposing of their purchases at substantial discounts or secreting the unsold portion for later below-cost covert sales. In other words, they "bust out" the business. The company is then petitioned into bankruptcy with the mulcted creditors left to pick over the meatless carcass of an assetless enterprise. The con men, or at least those whose names are legally associated with the bankrupt company, suffer a loss of their credit standing and "good" name. In return, they and their co-conspirators reap handsome monetary benefits for having arranged in advance the demise of a local wholesale outfit.[50]

Other than the use of credit agencies, seventeenth-century bust-outs operated exactly the same way.

Archives (U.K.), SP 46/176/fo205 (May 24, 1597) (reporting that members of the Merchant Adventurers speak badly about Quarles).

[49] Stephanie Wickouski, Bankrupcty Crimes 10 (3rd ed. 2007) (on commonality of bust outs today).

[50] United States v. Crockett, 534 F.2d 589, 592 (5th Cir. 1976).

The bust-out depends upon creditors relying on indices of credit-worthiness that turn out to be false. As a result, the court documents in the historical cases described below tend to be fairly explicit about the role reputation, and the abuse of reputation, played in enabling and encouraging the trades that ended up going bad.

Section II.A discusses a paradigmatic bust-out case from 1612 in which otherwise experienced merchants were willing to extend more credit to an existing debtor whose creditworthiness they had good reason to suspect.[51] They were "hoping against hope"—trusting blindly without doing due diligence.[52] In Section II.B, two other cases show how easily a buyer could dupe potential new contracting part-ners using superficial, but false, reputation signals.[53] Only after it became apparent that they had been cheated did the sellers make further, relatively simple inquiries and learn that the debtor was not who he seemed.

A. Hoping against Hope

Around December 1609, William Barkam found himself in some trouble. Barkam was a mercer—a dealer in cloth and dry goods—in the small Norfolk market town of Thetford, about eighty miles northeast of London.[54] He purchased his wares from London mer-chants, and by the end of 1609 he already owed £235 to one group

---

[51] *See* generally *Brearly v. Moore* (Star Chamber), National Archives (U.K.), STAC 8/69/1 (1612).

[52] *See* Rowena Olegario, A Culture of Credit: Embedding Trust and Transpar-ency in American Business 6 (2006) (quoting lawyer from 1839 that "[i]n the oper-ations of a rich and rapid commerce, great confidence must be often reposed in others, without the minute caution necessary to a perfect protection against fraud or unfairness.").

[53] *See generally Hales v. Moxon* (Star Chamber), National Archives (U.K.), STAC 8/173/9 (1607); *Campe v. Llewellyn* (Star Chamber), National Archives (U.K.), STAC 8/105/5 (1610). The name Llewellyn is spelled several different ways in the docu-ments related to this case. The spelling has been normalized here for clarity.

[54] Bill of Complaint, *Brearly v. Moore* (Star Chamber), National Archives (U.K.), STAC 8/69/1, fol. 3r (Nov. 25, 1612).

of merchants and £600 to another group for various wares.[55] These were not negligible sums. Six hundred pounds in 1609 would be worth about £106,400 today.[56] Barkam was so worried about his solvency that he began hiding from his creditors. Concerned that he was "verie like to become a bankrupte," he turned to local notable Edward Moore, to whom he also owed some small debts, for assistance.[57] Moore was a chapman—a regional middleman serving as the intermediary between London wholesalers and provincial traders[58]—and a man of substance in Thetford. He was styled a "gentleman,"[59] suggesting that he was a member of the local landed gentry.[60]

According to the complaint, which is our only significant source of information about the case, Moore had a plan to take advantage of Barkam's trouble and convinced Barkam to go along.[61] He took Barkam to London, where he gave him £100 (£17,740 today) with the instructions to buy as many goods as he could, using the money to pay about 20% down and taking the rest on credit. Moore estimated

---

55. *Id.*

56. *See Five Ways to Compute the Relative Value of a UK Pound Amount, 1270 to Present,* MeasuringWorth, https://www.measuringworth.com/calculators/ukcompare [https://perma.cc/2RVL-QGG3] (last visited Mar. 19, 2019) (enter "1609" under initial year, "600 pounds" under initial amount, and the desired year; then, select "calculate").

57. Bill of Complaint, *Brearley. v. Moore* (Star Chamber), National Archives (U.K.), STAC 8/69/1, fol. 3r (Nov. 25, 1612).

58. *See* David Hey, Packmen, Carriers and Packhorse Roads: Trade and Communications in North Derbyshire and South Yorkshire 200–02 (1980).

59. Thetford Borough Council Records, Norfolk Record Office (Norwich, England), T/C1/9 (no foliation) (Jan. 31, 1613) (notation linking Barkam and Moore, who is styled "gent").

60. Robert Bucholz & Newton Key, Early Modern England 1485–1714: A Narrative History 160 (2nd ed. 2009).

61. Bill of Complaint, *Brearley v. Moore* (Star Chamber), National Archives (U.K.), STAC 8/69/1, fol. 3r (Nov. 25, 1612) (Moore told Barkam that he was "a foole to greive or be sadde, for if he woulde be Ruled by . . . Moore, he . . . would advise such a course for [Barkam], that woulde make . . . Barkam a man in the worlde againe, for that [Moore] coulde att any tyme make fooles of londyners (meaninge [the plaintiffs]) & other the saide then Creditors of the said Barkam.").

that with the £100, Barkam should be able to "take up foure or five hundred powndes worthe of wares more upon Creditt & truste."[62]

Barkam returned to his existing creditors and used Moore's cash to buy additional goods, largely on credit, in his own name and without any indication that Moore was involved. He then immediately transferred the wares to Moore's warehouse, where Moore took the goods, leaving Barkam wares worth only £30.[63] Moore sent Barkam back to the London suppliers twice more, once with £40 and another time with £30, to buy more goods on credit.[64]

When the creditors finally grew suspicious, and it became clear that they would imprison Barkam for the debt and sue him for their money, Moore persuaded Barkam to flee to the "Northerne p[ar]tes of this kingedome" where the creditors would not find him.[65] Before Barkam left, however, Moore had him make a fraudulent transfer of all his assets, worth over £100, to a strawman "but to the proper use & benefitt of . . . Edward Moore" in exchange for a "sixpence in silver."[66] Barkam then disappeared, leaving no assets for his creditors to seize.[67]

What is interesting about this case is that Barkam was able to scam the same people from whom he had made purchases in the past, men to whom he already owed a great deal of money. He apparently looked quite different to the creditors when he came to them with ready cash. Either they did not know about his existing financial troubles, despite the fact that he had been keeping himself hidden from them to avoid having to confess he could not make payments,[68] or the creditors' concerns were sufficiently assuaged when Barkam reappeared seemingly flush with cash.[69] Without doing any additional investigation into the source of the

---

62. *Id.*

63. *Id.*

64. *Id.*

65. *Id.*

66. *Id.*

67. *Id.*

68. *Id.*

69. Amar Bhide & Howard H. Stevenson, *Why Be Honest if Honesty Doesn't Pay*, 68 Harv. Bus. Rev. 121, 123–24 (1990) ("When the expected reward is

sudden new funds, and without asking Barkam to pay down his existing debt, the various creditors extended him another £460 in credit.[70] Whether due to their gullible willingness to trust Barkam or to their greed, the creditors permitted the scam to succeed. This case demonstrates that when fraudsters can manipulate the information on which trust is based, that same information becomes a tool to enable cheating.[71]

It is, of course, possible that fraud of this nature was so uncommon as not to have been within the ordinary contemplation of these creditors. Where misconduct is unlikely, trust is not misplaced. Bust-outs and fraudulent transfers, however, were a well enough known risk to be go-to claims to make in order to get jurisdiction in Star Chamber.[72] That court sat in public sessions,[73] meaning that anything that came out about the parties and their nefarious deeds could quickly become common knowledge amongst traders. The three cases described in this section involved allegations—true or not—of bust-outs and fraudulent transfers brought in the Star Chamber over the course of only a few years between 1607 and 1612. Each case involved merchants connected to the London cloth trade. While this was not a closed network, the world of London merchants was not so large that Barkam's creditors would plausibly have had no inkling that such frauds were occurring in their trade.

---

substantial . . . reference checking goes out the window. In the eyes of people blinded by greed, the most tarnished reputations shine brightly.").

[70.] Bill of Complaint, *Brearley v. Moore* (Star Chamber), National Archives (U.K.), STAC 8/69/1, fol. 3r (Nov. 25, 1612).

[71.] *See* Granovetter, *supra* note 10, at 491 ("The more complete the trust, the greater the potential gain from malfeasance.").

[72.] *See infra* Section II.B (discussing cases that claim to be bust outs but probably are not); *see also* Guy, *supra* note 39, at 58–60.

[73.] Barnes, *supra* note 38, at 152 (2008) ("Star Chamber did not meet in secret. All trials in the court were public, in a chamber of Westminster Palace, the Camera Stellata. . . . In fact, perhaps even more than Shalcespeare's Globe, Star Chamber trials provided one of the most engrossing spectacles in the capital. A notable case between great persons would draw in scores of spectators, so many that they crowded in almost to the bar of the court.").

To finish the story, after sending Barkam away, Moore had his apprentice inform the creditors that "Barkam was Bankrupte, run awaie & fledd & had nothinge wherew[ith]all to satisfie his saide debtes."[74] Then he waited. Once the creditors realized that neither Barkam nor his assets were anywhere to be found, Moore approached them with an offer to buy up Barkam's debt. Three of the largest creditors agreed to compose for four shillings in the pound and to sign a release freeing Barkam from any remaining debts owed to them.[75] Three others, however, refused to be drawn into Moore's scheme and chose to sue instead, thus leaving us this record of early modern malfeasance.

The Star Chamber books recording the court's rulings are lost. Indeed, this case may never even have gotten past the pleading stage, as no interrogatories or depositions are extant. Nonetheless, we can make some assumptions about the truth of the complaint based on Moore's answer. After alleging that the plaintiffs paid Barkam, "[a] man utterlie decayed both in his estate and Creditt and one destitute of all conscience," to confess to the scam,[76] Moore said that the frauds with which he had been charged "were Comitted and donne" before the most recent general royal pardon granted in 1609 and not afterwards,[77] as claimed by the plaintiffs. As such, while he appears to

---

[74] Bill of Complaint, *Brearley v. Moore* (Star Chamber), National Archives (U.K.), STAC 8/69/1, fol. 3r (Nov. 25, 1612).

[75] *Id.* A pound consisted of twenty shillings.

[76] Answer of Edward Moore, *Brearley v. Moore* (Star Chamber), National Archives (U.K.), STAC 8/69/1, fol. 2r (Nov. 16, 1613).

[77] *Id.*; *see also* Cynthia Herrup, *Negotiating Grace*, *in* Politics, Religion and Popularity in Early Stuart Britain 124, 126 (Thomas Cogswell, Richard Cust & Peter Lake eds., 2002).

[G]eneral pardons were broadly framed acts of grace available to anyone who fell within their purview. . . . [They] could be purchased directly from the office of the Lord Chancellor. . . . Monarchs issued general pardons when, where and as they chose. . . . The specific contents of each pardon was different, but the scope was always broad: most forgave all save the worst of felonies, suits already in progress and transgressions that closely touched the finances of the crown. The customary instrument for such grace was a royal proclamation. . . .
Id.

admit to the acts alleged in the complaint, he contended that those acts were "clearelie p[ar]doned and remitted."[78]

The bust-out is an "endgame" fraud. Presumably, having scammed his creditors out of their money, the fraudster should not assume that people will be lining up to do business with him in the future. And yet, in each of the three cases discussed in this Part II, at least the mastermind of the fraud seemed to have remained in business. Barkam is still in Thetford in January 1613, when he is recorded as making a cession of property to Thomas Stegold—the original strawman—in the presence of Moore.[79] That is all we know about him, but given how little remains in the Thetford archives from the period, this does not necessarily mean very much. Moore, by contrast, prospered. Two years after the lawsuit, in 1614, he was elected mayor of Thetford, a position of social and economic prominence that he subsequently held several more times.[80] It is entirely possible that instead of paying with his good name for making "fooles of londyners,"[81] his reputation in this provincial town was improved by scamming the big city merchants.

B. Trust and Do Not Verify

Reputation is not an end in itself. In commerce, it serves to assist the recipient of the reputation information in deciding whether to trust some person or entity and thus to engage in trade.[82] The remaining

---

[78.] Answer of Edward Moore, *Brearley v. Moore* (Star Chamber), National Archives (U.K.), STAC 8/69/1, fol. 2r (Nov. 16, 1613).

[79.] *See* Thetford Borough Council Records, *supra* note 59; Bill of Complaint, *Brearley v. Moore* (Star Chamber), National Archives (U.K.), STAC 8/69/1, fol. 3r (Nov. 25, 1612).

[80.] Thomas Martin & Richard Gough, The History of the Town of Thetford, in the Counties of Norfolk and Suffolk, from the Earliest Accounts to the Present Time 256–57 (1779).

[81.] Bill of Complaint, *Brearley v. Moore* (Star Chamber), National Archives (U.K.), STAC 8/69/1, fol. 3r (Nov. 25, 1612).

[82.] Mark Eisenegger, *Trust and Reputation in the Age of Globalisation*, in Reputation Capital, *supra* note 8, at 11, 11–12 (arguing that we do business with people because we trust them, and reputation establishes that trust).

two cases in this section detail how fraudsters manipulated superficial indices of reputation to build that necessary trust.

1. Campe v. Llewellyn

In the 1610 case *Campe v. Llewellyn*,[83] the plaintiffs claimed that the London merchant Maurice Llewellyn set up Paul Barrowe, his young former apprentice, in a nice house in a fashionable area and gave him two well-stocked shops selling cloth in the Royal Exchange, the commercial heart of London at the time. The goal, so the plaintiffs claimed, was to convince cloth merchants like themselves that "Barrowe was reputed to be a man of good Creditt and abilitie" so that they would sell him wares on credit.[84] Llewellyn, they alleged, even provided Barrowe with money so that he could pay cash for a third of the purchase price of goods he bought from the creditors, "the better Creditt mighte be geven unto the said [Paul] Barrowe and to drawe on [the plaintiffs] and others to truste him."[85] Anxious to make sales, the merchants permitted this appearance of wealth to draw them in. When Barrowe could not pay his debts, and the merchants discovered that he had made a fraudulent transfer of his assets to Llewellyn,[86] they realized that they had been deceived, for Barrowe turned out to be "a man of smale or noe estate, creditt, or hability att all."[87]

Although allegedly a bust-out, the evidence suggests this story was not all it seemed. The real scam may have been Llewellyn's manipulating Barrowe into making a fraudulent transfer of his assets to Llewellyn's use and to the disadvantage of Barrowe's creditors.[88] Nonetheless, the possible falsity of the bust-out claim should

---

[83.] Bill of Complaint, *Campe v. Llewellyn* (Star Chamber), National Archives (U.K.), STAC 8/105/5, fol. 12r (Feb. 8, 1610).

[84.] *Id.*

[85.] *Id.*

[86.] *Id.*

[87.] *Id.*

[88.] Answer to Interrogatory 8, Deposition of Thomas Hathwait, *Barrowe v. Llewellyn* (Court of Chancery), National Archives (U.K.), C 24/359, fol. 5r (Apr. 23, 1611) (describing Llewellyn's machinations to convince Barrowe to make the fraudulent transfer).

not obscure the message of the merchants' pleading. They based their decisions about Barrowe's creditworthiness on how successful he looked. The fact that he appeared to be rich meant that he must be rich.

These merchants were not rubes. They included men prominent in the cloth trade: a leading member of the Merchant Taylor guild and one-time sheriff of London;[89] a merchant who later served as King Charles's silk purveyor;[90] a draper wealthy enough to leave £1500 to his children and fund the construction of almshouses (that still exist) at his death in 1613;[91] and two leading foreign merchants.[92] Nonetheless, their complaint gives no sense that they felt they had acted unreasonably in permitting themselves to be misled by Barrowe's illusory reputation signals, and they expected the court to sympathize with their plight.[93]

The court may indeed have sympathized. Although the opinion does not exist in *Campe*, the Star Chamber found Llewellyn guilty in a related contemporaneous lawsuit for fraudulently arranging for Barrowe to be executed on for a debt to Llewellyn that he did not, in fact, owe.[94] Despite this, Llewellyn remained in business, and he was repeatedly asked to be a guild warden, including in the months

---

[89] Nigel Victor Sleigh-Johnson, The Merchant Taylors Company of London, 1580–1645, 92, 127 n.1 (June 1989) (unpublished PhD dissertation, University College, London) (Richard Hearne was a plaintiff against Barrowe, as were his former apprentices Walter Eldred and Samuel Paske).

[90] Thomas A. Mason, Serving God and Mammon 93 (1985) (naming Walter Eldred, plaintiff against Barrowe, as silkman to King Charles).

[91] Will of Lawrence Campe, National Archives (U.K.), PROB 11/123/33 (proved Dec. 29, 1613).

[92] *See* Bill of Complaint, *Att'y Gen. v. Munsey et al.* (Star Chamber), National Archives (U.K.), STAC 8/25/23 (Feb. 1620) (Leonard Sweers and Abraham Becke, plaintiffs against Barrowe, among a large number of major merchants and foreign traders, sued for the export of bullion from England).

[93] Bill of Complaint, *Campe v. Llewellyn* (Star Chamber), National Archives (U.K.), STAC 8/105/5, fol. 12r (Feb. 8, 1610).

[94] Bill of Complaint, *Barrowe v. Llewellyn* (Star Chamber), National Archives (U.K.), STAC 8/56/2, fol. 37r (Nov. 18, 1610); *see* Report of the Star Chamber Judgment, *Barrowe v. Llewellyn* (Star Chamber), British Library (U.K.), Stowe MS 397, fol. 38v (1615).

after the original bust-out allegations had become public.[95] Barrowe similarly remained in the good graces of his guild, which elected him to a lower office in the guild in 1613 and twice in the years after the lawsuit gave him substantial loans.[96]

2. Hales v. Moxon

Perhaps Barrowe's creditors could not have obtained more accurate information about his trustworthiness. Some evidence that he was a reasonably successful trader prior to getting involved with Llewellyn means that his existing reputation would have been both good and not predictive of his future malfeasance.[97] The 1607 case *Hales v. Moxon*[98] is also allegedly, though likely not actually, a bust-out. Unlike the murkier facts in *Campe*, however, the rich detail in the *Hales* case file provides precise information about how the debtor's reputation first formed with his trading partners and how they failed to take simple extra steps to investigate his identity and creditworthiness.

As the complainants tell it, the story behind this alleged bust-out is quite straightforward. For a period of about one year beginning in November 1605, eighteen different Suffolk clothiers individually sold

---

[95.] *See* Minute Book 1608–1622, Worshipful Company of Leathersellers (London, England), fol. 43 (describing Llewellyn's refusal to serve as warden from 1616 to 1617); *see also* Retha M. Warnicke, *A Dispute among the Freemen of the Draper's Company in Elizabethan London*, in 1 Guildhall Studies in London History 59, 64 (1974) (discussing a mid-sixteenth-century arbitrator accused of fraud and later kicked off the London Court of Alderman and fined for misbehavior, "but, interestingly, that expulsion and his participation on the board of mediation the previous year did not seriously damage his reputation, as he was elected master of the Drapers' in 1566").

[96.] *See* Minute Book 1608–1622, *supra* note 95, at fol. 63 (mentioning Barrowe's election to warden of the yeomanry and his receipt of a loan of £50 in 1613); Liber Curtes: Accounts and Inventories, 1584–1647, Worshipful Company of Leathersellers (London, England) at fol. 181 (Barrowe being approved for another loan of £50 in 1617).

[97.] *See* Answer to Interrogatory 22, Deposition of Thomas Hathwait, *Barrowe v. Llewellyn* (Court of Chancery), National Archives (U.K.), C 24/359, fol. 9r (Apr. 23, 1611) (discussing Barrowe's prior trade).

[98.] *Hales v. Moxon*, National Archives (U.K.), STAC 8/173/9 (1607).

a total of 147 Suffolk-made cloths to Thomas Moxon,[99] a young man whom they apparently believed to be a reputable citizen of London and member of the Merchant Adventurers.[100] Most of these sales were made on credit with anywhere from 2% to 44% of the purchase price paid upfront, but in four instances with no money down at all.[101] Ultimately, Moxon's total debts to these clothiers amounted to £1343 (about £275,500 today),[102] and he also had other creditors not involved in this lawsuit.[103] Once Moxon took possession of the cloth, he passed it on to a Merchant Adventurer, John Skynner, who exported it in his own name or that of his business partner, William Burton.[104]

About a year into his buying spree, Moxon fled the country, unable to pay his debts. According to the complainants, Skynner sent him away, emptying his cash box and borrowing money from his neighbor in order to provide Moxon with funds to disappear.[105] By

---

[99.] Star Chamber Cause List, Huntington Library (San Marino, Cal.), Egerton Papers, EL 2765, fol. 2r (no date) (court papers with notes on the oral argument in the *Moxon* case).

[100.] Bill of Complaint, *Hales v. Moxon* (Star Chamber), National Archives (U.K.), STAC 8/173/9, fol. 68r (Mar. 9, 1607) (alleging that Moxon was "in shewe and profession a Marchant adventurer"); *see* Report of the Star Chamber Judgment, *Hales v. Moxon*, British Library (London, England), Stowe MS 397, fol. 15v (1610) ("Moxon pretending himselfe to bee a Merchant where in truth hee was not").

[101.] Bill of Complaint, *Hales v. Moxon* (Star Chamber), National Archives (U.K.), STAC 8/173/9, fol. 68r (Mar. 9, 1607) (listing the sales prices and the amount still owed).

[102.] Star Chamber Cause List, Huntington Library (San Marino, Cal.), Egerton Papers, EL 2765, fol. 2r (no date) (court papers with notes on the oral argument in the *Moxon* case). For the conversion, see *Five Ways to Compute the Relative Value of a UK Pound Amount*, *supra* note 56.

[103.] Bill of Complaint, *Skynner v. Moxon* (Court of Chancery), National Archives (U.K.), C 8/8/87, fol. 1r (April Apr. 27, 1607) (referring to attachments made by Moxon's other creditors); Bill of Complaint, *Lyndall v. Skynner* (Court of Exchequer), National Archives (U.K.), E 112/95/589 (1608) (suit brought by different creditors of Moxon's).

[104.] Bill of Complaint, *Hales v. Moxon* (Star Chamber), National Archives (U.K.), STAC 8/173/9, fol. 68r (Mar. 9, 1607).

[105.] Answer to Interrogatory 19, Deposition of William Judson, *Hales v. Moxon* (Star Chamber), National Archives (U.K.), STAC 8/173/9, fol. 22r (Mar. 22, 1609) ("Skynner hath Confessed that the *said* Thomas Moxon had of him at suche the tyme of his de*p*arture all the money that hee the *said* Skynner had in his Cashe and alsoe some money that hee borrowed to gyve him in his purse when hee soe wente awaye"); Answer to Interrogatories 18, 19, Deposition of Hanamiell Wardell,

this time, most of the cloth was gone, sold abroad by Skynner and Burton. What little remained Skynner attached for a debt Moxon supposedly owed him.[106] The clothiers were left with nothing, ultimately causing them to sue. Various branches of the dispute ended up working their way in separate, virtually simultaneous actions through Common Pleas, King's Bench, Chancery, and Star Chamber.[107] Yet another case against Skynner by different Moxon creditors was brought in the Court of Exchequer.[108]

The clothiers gave Moxon, a man whom none of them seemed to have known previously, so much credit because they had heard that he had a good reputation and then made assumptions about him that increased their trust level.[109] They obtained this information with little investment, and it turned out to be false.

According to the depositions in the case, Moxon's reputation was built by a game of telephone. The Suffolk clothiers were interested in doing business with him, so they asked one of their London factors what he knew about Moxon. This factor asked another London factor, George Massy, who had known Moxon for years.[110] Massy shared his belief that Moxon was an honest dealer.[111] The factors and clothiers

---

Hales v. Moxon (Star Chamber), National Archives (U.K.), STAC 8/173/9, fol. 26v (Apr. 11, 1609) ("[T]he said John Skynner . . . did confesse unto this deponent that hee had sente unto the sayed Thomas Moxon . . . all the money which the sayed John Skynner then had & some alsoe that hee borrowed of his neighboure for the said Moxon to take in his purse.").

[106.] Bill of Complaint, *Skynner v. Moxon* (Court of Chancery), National Archives (U.K.), C 8/8/87, fol. 1r (Apr. 27, 1607).

[107.] Answer to Interrogatory 18, Deposition of John Skynner, *Hales v. Moxon* (Star Chamber), National Archives (U.K.), STAC 8/173/9, unpaginated (May 6, 1607) (discussing suits in King's Bench and common pleas); Bill of Complaint, *Skynner v. Moxon* (Court of Chancery), National Archives (U.K.), C 8/8/87, fol 1r (Apr. 27, 1607).

[108.] *Lyndall v. Skynner* (Court of Exchequer), National Archives (U.K.), E 112/95/589 (1608).

[109.] Bill of Complaint, *Hales v. Moxon* (Star Chamber), National Archives (U.K.), STAC 8/173/9, fol. 68r (Mar. 9, 1607).

[110.] Answer to interrogatory 17, Deposition of George Massy, *Hales v. Moxon* (Star Chamber), National Archives (U.K.), STAC 8/173/9, fol. 54v (May 15, 1609).

[111.] Answer to Interrogatory 7, Deposition of George Massy, *Hales v. Moxon* (Star Chamber), National Archives (U.K.), STAC 8/173/9, fol. 54r (May 15, 1609).

also questioned Skynner and Burton about Moxon's estate.[112] They may have believed that Skynner was Moxon's partner; at the least, he seemed to them to be Moxon's close associate.[113] Skynner assured them that Moxon was "an honest, conscionable dealer" whom he would trust with £500 in credit.[114] He also told them that Moxon was "a man of very good sufficiencie and estate," who had property in the north of England, and could, if he wanted, have a wife who would bring a dowry of £800.[115] When one of the clothiers, John Ranson, expressed some doubt about Moxon's creditworthiness, Skynner and Burton allegedly berated him, accusing him of doing irreparable and unjustified harm to Moxon's good name and credit.[116]

What Skynner did not tell the people who inquired about Moxon is that Moxon was not a citizen of London; he was not even a native-born citizen of England.[117] Instead, Moxon was born and grew up in

---

[112.] Answer to Interrogatory 3, Deposition of Hanamiell Wardall, *Hales v. Moxon* (Star Chamber), National Archives (U.K.), STAC 8/173/9, fol. 25v (Apr. 11, 1609).

[113.] Answer to Interrogatory 2, Deposition of Hanamiell Wardall, *Hales v. Moxon* (Star Chamber), National Archives (U.K.), STAC 8/173/9, fol. 25r (Apr. 11, 1609).

[114.] Bill of Complaint, *Hales v. Moxon* (Star Chamber), National Archives (U.K.), STAC 8/173/9, fol. 68r (Mar. 9, 1607); Answer to Interrogatory 6, Deposition of Hanamiell Wardall, *Hales v. Moxon* (Star Chamber), National Archives (U.K.), STAC 8/173/9, fol. 68r (May 14, 1609). *Cf.* Defoe, *supra* note 12, at 255 (also using the example of whether "I would trust him with five hundred pound" when talking about giving a reference).

[115.] Bill of Complaint, *Hales v. Moxon* (Star Chamber), National Archives (U.K.), STAC 8/173/9, fol. 68r (Mar. 9, 1607).

[116.] *Id.*; Answer of John Skynner and William Burton, *Hales v. Moxon* (Star Chamber), National Archives (U.K.), STAC 8/173/9, fol. 67r (Apr. 29, 1607); Answer to Interrogatory 8, Deposition of Hanamiell Wardall, *Hales v. Moxon* (Star Chamber), National Archives (U.K.), STAC 8/173/9, fol. 26r (Apr. 11, 1609) ("Skynner & Burton, hearinge of the doubt made by the sayed John Ranson, sente for him & this deponent and verye sharpelye reproved the sayed Ranson for discreaditinge of the said Thomas Moxon and then greatlye commended boathe his the said Moxons sufficiencye and honestye . . . .").

[117.] He was, in fact, naturalized by a private act of Parliament in 1601. David Dean, Law-making and Society in Late Elizabethan England, The Parliament of England, 1584–1601 221 (1996) (mentioning Moxon's naturalization); *see* Surrejoinder of Thomas Moxon, *Moxon v. Iles* (Duchy Chamber), National Archives (U.K.), DL 1/220/164, fol. 2r (Oct. 18, 1604) (acknowledging that he was naturalized by an act of Parliament).

Antwerp, where his father, who was a Merchant Adventurer from Yorkshire, was living and trading.[118] Skynner later claimed that he did not know whether Moxon really was a Merchant Adventurer. Like everyone else, he had just assumed that Moxon was.[119]

All of this new information mattered a great deal to the creditors. When they assumed he was a citizen of London and a Merchant Adventurer, he had credit in their eyes and seemed trustworthy. Once they found out he was foreign born and not a citizen of London, most of them refused to trust him any further.[120]

It was only after the creditors and their factors began to fear something was amiss, because Moxon had disappeared, that they made more thorough inquiries about him. In addition to learning that he was not a citizen of London, not a Merchant Adventurer, and "Alien borne,"[121] they also discovered at the Customs House that Skynner and Burton had exported all of the cloth in their own names and that Moxon had never exported anything.[122]

None of this information had been secret. The creditors could have inquired earlier about Moxon's exports at the Custom House. They could have asked other Merchant Adventurers about him. They could have investigated his guild membership, which was a prerequisite to citizenship in London.[123] They could have spoken to merchants and factors from Yorkshire who knew something of Moxon's history.[124] They could, in other words, have obtained more reliable

---

[118.] Surrejoinder of Thomas Moxon, *Moxon v. Iles* (Duchy Chamber), National Archives (U.K.), DL 1/220/164, fol. 2r (Oct. 18, 1604).

[119.] Answer to Interrogatory 20, Deposition of John Skynner, *Hales v. Moxon* (Star Chamber), National Archives (U.K.), STAC 8/173/9, unpaginated (May 15, 1609).

[120.] Answer to Interrogatory 5, Deposition of William Judson, *Hales v. Moxon* (Star Chamber), National Archives (U.K.), STAC 8/173/9, fol. 53r (May 15, 1609).

[121.] Bill of Complaint, *Hales v. Moxon* (Star Chamber), National Archives (U.K.), STAC 8/173/9, fol. 68r (Mar. 9, 1607).

[122.] *Id.*

[123.] *See* Robert O. Bucholz & Joseph P. Ward, London: A Social and Cultural History, 1550–1750 77–78 (2012).

[124.] *See* Replication of Alexander Lyndall, *Lyndall v. Skynner* (Court of Exchequer), National Archives (U.K.), E 112/95/589 (1609) (suit by Yorkshire merchants over Moxon's debts and referring to Moxon as a foreigner).

data about Moxon, either prior to dealing with him or at least before extending him considerable amounts of credit. But they did not bother.[125] Instead, the creditors relied on cheaply obtained information, taking the word of a few people—people who may either have had something to gain from deceiving them or may have been telling them what they wanted to hear.[126] That information turned out to be inaccurate.

Ultimately, the court sided with the complainants, fining the defendants and ordering them to make restitution of the money owed, with interest, and to remain in prison until they had done so.[127] Moxon was also to stand in the pillory at Westminster (where the court sat) and at Cheapside (the main commercial thoroughfare) with a paper hung around his neck detailing his fraud.[128] Yet despite this ruling, Burton and Skynner seem to have remained in business.[129] Moxon disappears from the record, so we do not know what happened to him in the aftermath of the lawsuit. He may have returned to his usual business abroad, or he may have fled to his property in Yorkshire.

These stories illustrate the dark side of reputation. The exact same indicia of trustworthiness that facilitate honest trade and private ordering can, if false, also facilitate fraud. When people choose to rely on those indicia alone without checking the facts, they set themselves up to be victims.

[125.] Answer to Interrogatory 8, Deposition of George Massy, *Hales v. Moxon* (Star Chamber), National Archives (U.K.), STAC 8/173/9, fol. 54r (May 15, 1609).

[126.] *See* Silberstein-Loeb, *supra* note 8, at 24–25 (discussing unreliability of reputation information).

[127.] Exchequer Memoranda Rolls and Enrolment Books, National Archives (U.K.), E 159/444, fol. 226r–226v (1610) (recording fines of £100 for Skynner and Moxon and £50 for Burton).

[128.] Report of the Star Chamber Judgment, *Hales v. Moxon* (Star Chamber), British Library (U.K.), Stowe MS 397, fol. 16r (1610).

[129.] Grocers Company Orders of the Court of Assistants, Guildhall Library (U.K.), MS 11,588 vol. 3, fol. 250 (May 27, 1623) (recording Burton as taking out a loan in 1623); Ironmongers' Company Court Minutes, Guildhall Library (U.K.), MD 16967/2, fol. 71r (Dec. 25, 1609) (listing Skynner as a "bachelor," which was a status in the guild hierarchy).

IV. Mixed Reputational Signals

Material from other cases and commercial correspondence from the late sixteenth and early seventeenth centuries provide a number of explanations why reputational information might have been susceptible to manipulation and why it did not serve the disciplinary function assumed by the private ordering theories even in the sorts of dense networks to which the traders in the bust-out cases belonged. These explanations both parallel and add to the defects already noted in the economic and network theory literature.[130] First, reputation is historical information. It may not accurately predict future behavior. Second, accurate information may be scarce or secret, leaving those not "in the know" to rely on inaccurate assumptions. Third, although reputations are presumed to be slow to change within closed groups, in fact gossip may be fickle, and it can influence the listener in subtle ways. Fourth, in trade, actors need to trust, and they cannot always verify what they perceive to be the good reputation of their potential partner. Sometimes they trust unwisely. Finally, the alleged fraudster who produces a convincing counternarrative may succeed in creating questions and confusion about which available reputational information is most accurate.

A. Reputation Is Backward Looking

First, reputation, by definition, is based on prior behavior that may not correctly foretell future behavior.[131] In the case of Thomas Moxon, for instance, even if Skynner and the creditors' agent, Massy, had no nefarious intentions in praising Moxon to the cloth sellers, the information they had to offer concerned only their past interactions with Moxon. As Skynner kept protesting in the lawsuit, he believed his

---

[130.] *See supra* Part I.

[131.] Goldman, *supra* note 9, at 58 ("[R]eputational information relies on the accuracy of past information in predicting future behavior, but this predictive power is not perfect.").

own assertions to the creditors that they could trust Moxon, because he had found him trustworthy before.[132] But if Moxon decided to commit fraud, that historical data became not just useless, but in fact affirmatively harmful. It allowed Moxon and his accomplices to build up a positive reputation for Moxon that they could then manipulate to their benefit.

B. Scarcity of Information

Second, the person with accurate information about another may want to hoard that information, leaving less accurate or incorrect information to circulate. Perhaps the hoarder seeks a competitive advantage, perhaps she is protecting her friends, or perhaps she is protecting herself. Such was the case in 1582, for example, when the merchant Martin Delafallia refused to divulge the name of the person who passed forged bills of exchange to him because if he did, the forger would be ruined and Delafallia would not be paid the money the forger owed him.[133]

The late sixteenth-century correspondence between the London merchant John Quarles and his agent George Lowe, based in Stade, Germany, also offers insight into the keeping of commercial secrets.[134] In one letter, Lowe reported to Quarles that the credit of

---

[132] Answer of Skynner and Burton, *Hales v. Moxon* (Star Chamber), National Archives (U.K.), STAC 8/173/9, fol. 67r (Apr. 29, 1607):

> John Skynner saieth that the said Moxon was a Merchant and a dealer of good Creddytt in buyeng, transporting, and selling of clothes long before the *defendant* had any acquaintans, familiarity, or dealinges with him. And afterwardes by Reason of such his Creddytt and of the good Report that other Merchantes gave out of his sufficiency and honest dealing, This def*endant* did sometymes deale with him . . . .

Id.; see also Silberstein-Loeb, *supra* note 8, at 27 (noting that a person with a good reputation can leverage it to cheat).

[133] Answer of Martin Delafallia, *Alldersey v. Delafalia* (Star Chamber), National Archives (U.K.), STAC 5/A4/16, fol. 1r (Feb. 15, 1582); *see* Olegario, *supra* note 52, at 21 ("The mere whiff of trouble . . . could bring creditors to his door, demanding that he pay his debts immediately.").

[134] *See* Leng, *supra* note 47, at 828.

Robert Burleyghe, another merchant, was poor, but asked him to keep that knowledge secret.[135] This secret was not costless to others. When Burleyghe failed shortly after, Lowe noted that he had avoided doing business with him because he had known his credit to be worthless. But other merchants had not realized this, and suffered for their lack of knowledge.[136]

Refusing to share information could by itself create a negative impression. In 1726, Daniel Defoe wrote in his *Complete English Tradesman* about the practice of checking into the credit of a potential new partner by first making enquiries about him "and of his circumstances among his neighbours and fellow tradesmen, perhaps of the same profession, or employment."[137] Defoe saw no good coming from these inquiries. The competitor may have wanted to disparage the object of the inquiry in order to drive business away from him,[138] while the man who praised him did not want to be responsible if he ended up proving untrustworthy.[139] And yet, remaining silent and refusing to divulge what one knew was "downright giving him the worst character" one could, for the interlocutor would interpret the silence as a polite way of refraining from spreading negative gossip, even though that might not be the case.[140]

[135.] Letter from George Lowe to John Quarles, National Archives (U.K.), SP 46/176/fo122 (Feb. 26, 1596). This letter also asks Quarles to conceal information about goods Lowe purchased secretly. *Id.*

[136.] Letter from George Lowe to John Quarles, National Archives (U.K.), SP 46/176/fo299 (Mar. 29, 1597). This letter is incorrectly catalogued as missing and dated [1660]. It is, in fact, located in Part II of the letters with the stamp "300" on the verso of the first page. *See also* Letter from George Lowe to John Quarles, National Archives (U.K.), SP 46/176/fo225 (Aug. 3, 1597) (Lowe asking that news about Quarles shop being shut up be kept secret); Letter from George Lowe to John Quarles, National Archives (U.K.), SP 46/176/fo138 (July 8, 1596) (concealing purchases); *see also* Letter from George Lowe to John Quarles, National Archives (U.K.), SP 46/176/fo154 (Aug. 15, 1596) (concealing ties to an unpopular merchant).

[137.] Defoe, *supra* note 12, at 247.

[138.] *See id.* at 247; *see also id.* at 246 ("[N]o men are apter to speak slightly and coldly of a fellow-tradesman, than his fellow tradesmen . . . .").

[139.] *Id.* at 248.

[140.] *Id.* at 248–51.

C. Fickleness of Reputation

The third reason fraudsters could easily manipulate reputation was that reputation could change quickly with the infusion of a new piece of, perhaps entirely false, information. Defoe claimed that "the loss of credit is never repair'd,"[141] but in this he seems to have been mistaken. New gossip could chase away perceptions created by earlier gossip, and facts could correct fictions. The Lowe-Quarles correspondence provides examples of both situations. In two letters, Lowe told Quarles to ignore reports that his credit was impaired, that this was just malicious gossip, and that his trade was, in fact, doing just fine.[142] In another letter, Lowe reported that gossip had rumored him to be in financial trouble but that his quick return from a business trip had been all it took to change the narrative about him.[143]

Similarly, Maurice Llewellyn, in denying the allegations of fraud made by Paul Barrowe's creditors, accused Barrowe of spreading spurious accusations of misconduct against him and claimed that those accusations had ruined his credit at the Royal Exchange.[144] And yet, within a few months after the case against him became public knowledge, Llewellyn was elected warden (or governor) of his guild—a position of significant trust and authority.[145]

By contrast, the 1620 case *Grigg v. Wheeler* shows how easily a few convincing negative words could destroy a reputation.[146] Grigg claimed that he bought cattle from Wheeler, who ended up cheating

---

141. *Id.* at 235.

142. Letter from George Lowe to John Quarles, National Archives (U.K.), SP 46/176/fo124 (Feb. 28, 1596); Letter from George Lowe to John Quarles, National Archives (U.K.), SP 46/176/fo126 (Mar. 9, 1596) (assuring Quarles that the rumors are untrue and his credit is good).

143. Letter from George Lowe to John Quarles, National Archives (U.K.), SP 46/176/fo173 (Feb. 1, 1597).

144. Answer of Maurice Lewellyn, *Barrowe v. Llewellyn* (Star Chamber), National Archives (U.K.), STAC 8/56/2, fol. 35r (Nov. 27, 1610).

145. *See* Minute Book 1608–1622, *supra* note 95, at fol. 43 (recording Llewellyn's refusal to serve as warden in 1611).

146. *See* Bill of Complaint, *Grigg v. Wheeler* (Court of Chancery), National Archives (U.K.), C 2/Jasl/G9/36, fol. 1 (Oct. 31, 1620).

him by repossessing the cattle a short time later and refusing to return Grigg's bond or earnest money. Wheeler justified his actions to the community by claiming that he believed Grigg was going to defraud him.[147] The result of Wheeler's gossip was that, whereas before Grigg had dealt with Wheeler Grigg's "word & Creditt was currant & would passe in the Countrey w[i]th and amongest his neighbours for twenty, thirtie, or fortie poundes, or much more. . ., nowe they make it verie scrupulous to take [his] word or p[ro]mise, yea scarcely his bond for a matter of five poundes."[148] A few negative words from Wheeler, and Grigg saw his reputation ruined among people he had presumably known for most of his life.

Defoe himself provided ample evidence of the fickle nature of gossip. He told the story of a spurned lady who used innuendo to turn her former fiancé's reputation from good to bad, causing a run by his creditors that ultimately nearly bankrupted him.[149] And he pointed out that even if the recipient of the rumor knew that the person conveying the gossip was "a Liar, a Slanderer, a Calumniator," the hearer still wondered, perhaps the liar "may happen to speak truth just then, he may chance to be right, and I know not what there may be in it, and whether there may be any thing or no, but I will have a little Care."[150] In other words, when reputation arises from gossip and appearances "without a concrete empirical referent,"[151] it may sometimes be as ephemeral as the gossip itself.

D. Need to Trust

Ultimately, commerce relies on trust. At some juncture in the process of trade, each person is forced to take a risk and trust the other without having either complete information or the possibility of

---

[147.] *Id.* ("[H]ee thought in his conscience hee shold have bin cheated & cousoned both of ye monie and Catall.").

[148.] *Id.*

[149.] Defoe, *supra* note 12, at 237–44.

[150.] *Id.* at 234.

[151.] Burt, *supra* note 23, at 175.

verification.[152] These junctures, in which parties must rely on mere reputation, introduce opportunities to cheat because the trust bestowed on another may be given unwisely.

Fraudsters know how to play on the willingness to suspend disbelief. In 1601, for example, Attorney General Edward Coke brought suit against a certain "John Kellam al[ia]s Gray al[ia]s Cotton" for defrauding a respectable but vulnerable widow whom he had convinced that he possessed alchemical powers.[153] He gained her trust by showing her "strange peeces of pap[er] wrytten some with Figures, some w[i] th Cyphers, and Certaine strange Invented characters & wordes," by giving her talismans and tokens that seemed mysterious, and by maintaining "a Contynuall fyer w[i]th stills uppon ytt that burned Six weekes night and daie and sett upp Certaine Instrumentes as yf he were about some such strange worke."[154] Misled by these appearances, the widow kept handing over more and more money.

Not only widows, but also world traders paying small fortunes settled for trusting rather than verification. Around December 1608, a group of wealthy Amsterdam merchants subscribed to a maritime insurance policy, insuring part of the cargo in an English ship sailing from Livorno, Italy, to Spain for £2200—roughly £399,000 today.[155] In all, the cargo was said to be worth £8000—or approximately £1,451,000 today. This astonishing sum was merited by the rich silks, gold velvets, and other expensive merchandise said to be aboard the ship. And what evidence did the insurers have of this unusually expensive cargo? The bill of lading listed these wares, and they had been laded aboard the ship packed the way silks and velvets were normally packed, and the shippers had impressed upon the crew the

---

[152] Niklas Luhmann, *Familiarity, Confidence, Trust: Problems and Alternatives*, in Trust: Making and Breaking Cooperative Relations 94, 95 (Diego Gambetta ed., 1988) ("[T]rust is a solution for specific problems of risk.").

[153] Bill of Complaint, *Att'y Gen. v. Kellam* (Star Chamber), National Archives (U.K.), STAC 5/A1/18 (Feb. 20, 1601).

[154] *Id.*

[155] Bill of Complaint, *Att'y Gen. v. Goodlake, Povey, & Webbe* (Star Chamber), National Archives (U.K.), STAC 8/12/6 (July 19, 1613). *See Five Ways to Compute the Relative Value of a UK Pound Amount, supra* note 56.

costly nature of the freight. These indicia of authenticity apparently sufficed even though no objective party had ever actually seen the goods. Not surprisingly, the true cargo was waste paper and soap. But the insurers only discovered this long after the ship "accidentally" sunk (as planned and instigated by the shippers) and the insurance benefits were paid out.[156]

E. Counternarratives

Finally, a credible counternarrative can raise questions about the reputation value of existing information.[157] For instance, while their creditors might be spreading gossip that Moxon and Skynner, the alleged perpetrators of a bust-out, were dishonest, the story as the accused related it sounded quite different. In their telling, the debts reflected an unfortunate, but not fraudulent, confluence of circumstances. In this version, Moxon, who mostly did business on the continent, came to know Skynner on his trips to London. Moxon would assist with Skynner's exports abroad, and, when Moxon needed help in London, he expected the same assistance from Skynner in turn. This help became particularly pressing between 1604 and 1606 when Moxon was often required to go to Yorkshire to prosecute a lawsuit seeking to reclaim land he had inherited from his father. During his absences, Skynner acted as his London agent with the clothiers and their factors and shipped Moxon's purchases abroad in his own name. But the lawsuit was costly, and Moxon found himself overstretched. He went overseas for a short time to try to get his affairs in order, not to defraud his creditors.[158]

[156.] Bill of Complaint, *Att'y Gen. v. Goodlake, Povey, & Webbe* (Star Chamber), National Archives (U.K.), STAC 8/12/6 (July 19, 1613).

[157.] *See* Burt, *supra* note 23, at 175 (discussing how gossip can transmit "more than one truth" about a person); Gambetta, *supra* note 22, at 211 ("Plausibility is more relevant than truth. A convi[n]cing story gets repeated because of its appeal not its truthfulness.").

[158.] Answer of Thomas Moxon, *Hales v. Moxon* (Star Chamber), National Archives (U.K.), STAC 8/173/9, fol. 66r (May 9, 1608).

This explanation is perfectly plausible and accounts for the evidence offered at trial. The lawsuit in Yorkshire did happen, and it generated a great deal of paper, so it likely was expensive.[159] Skynner never denied doing business with Moxon or attesting to his honesty.[160] And the practice of shipping goods in another merchant's name was not unusual, and may have had something to do with Moxon's legal status.[161]

Faced with both sides of the story, could the parties' contemporaries have known for sure whether the defendants committed fraud or were rather the victims of a fraud on the court by the plaintiffs? If the facts communicated were ambiguous, the reputational information derived from them could also be ambiguous. Perhaps Skynner and Moxon were fraudsters who should never have been trusted again; and perhaps Moxon was an unfortunate debtor and his friend Skynner an innocent associate whose deep pockets looked very attractive to Moxon's creditors. Moxon and Skynner's future reputations may have depended upon whom one talked to.

In sum, therefore, reputation fraud could occur because reputation was, and is, formed from a complex web of information, misinformation, and absence of information. What a trader does not know might cause him to make bad decisions, but what he thinks he does know might do the same. He may hear good things about bad people, and bad things about good people. At some point, however, traders have to trust to do business, and they then open themselves up to the possibility of fraud.

[159.] See Bill of Complaint of Thomas Moxon, *Moxon v. Iles* (Duchy Chamber), National Archives (U.K.), DL 1/218/44 (no date); Answer of the Defendants, *Moxon v. Iles* (Duchy Chamber), DL 1/219/92 (no date); Rejoinder of the Defendants, *Moxon v. Iles* (Duchy Chamber), DL 1/220/164, fol. 1 (1604); Surrejoinder of Thomas Moxon, *Moxon v. Iles* (Duchy Chamber), DL 1/220/164 fol. 2; Depositions, *Moxon v. Iles* (Duchy Chamber), DL 4/48/59 (1604–1605); Depositions, *Moxon v. Iles* (Duchy Chamber), DL 4/47/1 (1604–1605).

[160.] Answer to Interrogatory 4, Deposition of John Skynner, *Hales v. Moxon* (Star Chamber), National Archives (U.K.), STAC 8/173/9 (unpaginated) (May 6, 1607).

[161.] Answer to Interrogatory at 4, Deposition of Edward Misselden, *Hales v. Moxon* (Star Chamber), National Archives (U.K.), STAC 8/173/9, fol. 59r (May 22, 1609).

V. Conclusion

We do not know how often commercial fraud occurred in pre-modern commerce. But we know that it did happen, and that it happened at least in part because merchants could not verify the honesty of all their partners. They could try to avoid the need for trust by using contractual mechanisms, such as requiring the debtor to name sureties, put up pledges, or give his bond or bill of exchange to guarantee payment.[162] But sureties could dispute their liability or disappear. Bonds and bills could be lost, forged, or used fraudulently against the debtor. At some point, therefore, the English merchants would have had to rely on mere reputation. Unfortunately, that reputation evidence could be falsified, reinterpreted, misinterpreted, and hoarded. Fraudsters took advantage of such distortions of reputation to cheat.

This ability to make the data say different things should raise questions about any notion that reputation alone suffices to incentivize honesty. It may also help explain why the English court records contain plenty of commercial fraud cases. The availability of public enforcement permitted traders to rely on questionable reputation information and then sue for damages ex post when the information turned out to have been bad, instead of expending time and money doing perhaps costly due diligence before entering into contracts. And the potential for reputation fraud may also help explain why some early modern commentators were less optimistic than many modern economists about the potential of self-regulating commerce.

[162.] Defoe, *supra* note 12, at 421 (stating that if a man has credit "then he may borrow again whenever he will, he may take up money and goods, or any thing, upon his bare word, or note," but if he does not then he "must give bondsmen, or *mainprize*, that is, a pawn or pledge for security, and hardly be trusted so neither"); Sheilagh Ogilvie, Institutions and European Trade: Merchant Guilds, 1000–1800, 287–89 (2011).

As the lawyer John Stone observed in his seventeenth-century lecture on the 1571 Elizabethan bankruptcy statute, "as the Number of Merchants hath increased, so have their cunning and crafty dealings increased, so as now a dayes it falls out, that we had more need to make Laws against them, than for them."[163]

[163.] John Stone, The Reading upon the Statute of the Thirteenth of Elizabeth, chapter 7: Touching Bankrupts 3 (1656); see *Twyne's Case*, (1602) 76 Eng. Rep. 809, 815; 3 Co. Rep. 80b, 82a ("[F]raud and deceit abound in these days more than in former times.").

The Rise and Fall of Fear of Abuse in Consumer Bankruptcy

Most Recent Comparative Evidence from Europe and Beyond

*Jason J. Kilborn**

L aw is fundamentally a social science. Its theories usually can and should be tested based not just on the behavior of appellate courts but also on anthropological evidence of the actual frontline form and effect of law's regulation of human behavior. Jay Westbrook has led the charge in an enormously fruitful campaign of discovery of such evidence in the United States.[1]

Our federalist legal system offers a natural laboratory for comparison of different approaches and outcomes in a checkerboard of state

---

* Professor of Law, UIC John Marshall Law School, jkilborn@uic.edu. Copyright © 96 Tex. L. Rev. 1327–53 (2018). Reproduced with permission.

[1]. See, e.g., Teresa A. Sullivan, Elizabeth Warren & Jay Lawrence Westbrook, As We Forgive Our Debtors: Bankruptcy and Consumer Credit in America 17–20 (1989) (describing the methodology behind the authors' Consumer Bankruptcy Project, a study of debtors in ten federal judicial districts across the United States); Teresa A. Sullivan, Elizabeth Warren & Jay Lawrence Westbrook, The Fragile Middle Class: Americans in Debt 7–11 (2000) (discussing Phase II of the Consumer Bankruptcy Project, which focused on debtors in sixteen federal districts); Teresa A. Sullivan, Elizabeth Warren & Jay Lawrence Westbrook, Consumer Debtors Ten Years Later: A Financial Comparison of Consumer Bankrupts 1981-1991, 68 Am. Bankr. L.J. 121, 122–24 (1994) (same).

and federal districts and their various actors' often widely divergent approaches to key issues. This is surprisingly true even in the supposedly unified federal consumer bankruptcy system. Opportunities for comparative analysis are supercharged, however, when one moves outside the United States and beyond the Anglo-American context on which most consumer bankruptcy scholarship has focused.

Almost exactly 20 years ago, Jay extrapolated his research on U.S. consumer bankruptcy to the new frontier of emerging consumer insolvency systems in Europe. In so doing, he launched a field of scholarship that would yield rich rewards. Before the turn of the twenty-first century, there was all but nothing in Europe to compare with Anglo-American consumer bankruptcy practice.[2] By the late 1990s, however, the first consumer discharge procedures were emerging in Northern Europe and had produced a foundation of operational results for comparison. Jay was among the first Americans to seize this new opportunity.

In a short commentary on one of the earliest comparative consumer bankruptcy conferences in Europe, Jay noted the potential of comparative perspectives on the topic.[3] At that time, he was studying judicial discretion and a resulting pernicious phenomenon that he referred to as "local legal culture," marked by persistent disparate treatment of similarly situated consumer debtors across the United States.[4] The comparative conference offered Jay a chance to extrapolate his U.S. findings to the few emerging consumer

---

[2] When U.S. reformers were looking for comparative ideas for revision of the U.S. bankruptcy law in the 1970s, they concluded "the bankruptcy experience of other countries is not a useful resource." Comm'n on the Bankr. Laws of the U.S., Report of the Commission on the Bankruptcy Laws of the United States, H.R. Doc. No. 93-137, at 66 (1973).

[3] Jay Lawrence Westbrook, Local Legal Culture and the Fear of Abuse, 6 Am. Bankr. Inst. L. Rev. 25, 33–34 (1998).

[4] See Teresa A. Sullivan, Elizabeth Warren & Jay Lawrence Westbrook, The Persistence of Local Legal Culture: Twenty Years of Evidence from the Federal Bankruptcy Courts, 17 Harv. J.L. & Pub. Pol'y 801, 803–07 (1994) (applying the concept of local legal culture to bankruptcy law); Westbrook, supra note 3, at 26–27 (elaborating upon the concept of local legal culture).

discharge regimes in Europe and to develop hypotheses as to the causes of the phenomenon of local legal culture. He noted that even the sparse European data revealed the emergence of local legal culture as a consequence of judicial discretion, particularly in determining (1) whether certain debtors should have access to a discharge and (2) the duration of the payment plan imposed on debtors as a *quid pro quo* for earning discharge relief.[5]

In light of his U.S. research, augmented by this limited set of comparative observations, Jay tentatively suggested a cause for the discretion producing these local legal culture disparities on both sides of the Atlantic: he attributed this syndrome to a powerful fear of abuse by debtors of the benefit of consumer discharge relief, a benefit that was radical and revolutionary in Europe and still somewhat controversial in the United States.[6] He optimistically predicted "[f]urther research over the next several years in the various countries that have adopted these new laws could yield a rich harvest of new evidence and perhaps unexpected variations."[7]

This commentary was published just as I was beginning my academic career, and it inspired everything I have done since then. It is extremely gratifying to be able to celebrate Jay's career in this symposium issue by adducing recent comparative evidence in support of his thesis in that early commentary and by providing a small taste of the "rich harvest of new evidence"[8] from the most recent developments in consumer bankruptcy in Europe and beyond. As Jay predicted, European authorities have been extremely concerned about debtors abusing the new discharge regimes, and common impediments to relief have been far more obvious and imposing than the nuanced effects of discretion and the resulting local legal culture. Twenty years after Jay identified this fear of abuse, however, a thaw is manifest in the icy European attitude, as evidenced in particular by

---

5. Westbrook, supra note 3, at 25, 32–33.
6. *Id.* at 28.
7. *Id.* at 33–34.
8. *Id.* at 34.

developments over just the past few months. Fear of abuse—and discretionary or statutory mechanisms for making the path to discharge narrower and more onerous—appears to be diminishing with time and experience. This message needs to be broadcast more effectively, as several projects for new consumer discharge laws reveal a resurgence of fear of abuse or at least reticence to embrace the notion of discharge relief. Thus, the vicious cycle repeats itself.

This chapter presents the most recent evidence of these propositions in three segments. Part I discusses three regimes that exemplify the trends discussed previously—that is, extremely fearful, highly discretionary procedures that abruptly reversed course on fear of abuse after a decade or two of operation but retained significant court discretion (Denmark, Slovakia, Poland). Part II announces some of the most recent developments, including notable harbingers of both a softening of fear of abuse and a reining-in of discretion across Europe (Austria, Russia, Croatia, Romania). Part III looks to the future of several nascent personal insolvency regimes-in-waiting, which evidence a return to square one and a high degree of fear or resistance to discharge (Bulgaria, China, Saudi Arabia). Like Jay's commentary, mine here is designed primarily to stimulate interest in and discussions of developments of which many followers of English-language legal scholarship will be unaware[9] but which hold great potential for revealing important cross-cultural trends about this important area of legal and social policy.

I. From Fear and Discretion to Acceptance and Greater Standardization

A. Denmark, 1984-2005

The first story is a bit dated, but it is both closely connected to Jay's early foray into comparative consumer bankruptcy and perfectly

---

[9.] See *id.* at 25–26 (noting that the value of the paper "will lie in stimulating discussion by referring the reader to a very interesting series of papers about consumer bankruptcy that many will not have read").

revealing of the trend away from the discretion and fear he described. Denmark was the bellwether, adopting the very first consumer "debt adjustment"[10] law in Europe in 1984.[11] The Danish law was structured very much like the Norwegian law that caught Jay's interest,[12] as a persistent problem of local legal culture plagued Danish practice for two decades and led to the only major reform of this law in 2005. This syndrome of local legal culture resulting from judicial discretion was fairly clearly born of a powerful fear of abuse of this radical departure from the traditional *pacta sunt servanda* notion that debts must be paid. Trailblazing Danish lawmakers were expressly hesitant to undermine individual-payment morality, so they imposed strict, discretionary access controls at both the entry and exit points to discharge relief.

Simply to gain access to the relief process, debtors had to clear two hurdles. First, they had to exhibit "qualified insolvency," which implied a clear and doubt-free inability to regain financial footing in the foreseeable future, by reducing profligate living standards and redoubling efforts to service debts in full.[13] Second, as in Norway,[14] each court had to be convinced that offering relief in any particular case was subjectively appropriate in light of a series of enumerated factors, such as the debtor's efforts to manage debt problems and the makeup of the debt load (preferably relatively few fines, penalties, and "irresponsible" debts, such as debts for luxury consumption).[15] Predictably, the highly subjective and probing inquiries prompted by

---

[10.] This is the usual language used to name these laws in continental Europe, eschewing both the stigma and the suggestion of an easy way out implicit in the word "bankruptcy."

[11.] Lov nr. 187 af 09.05.1984 om gældssaneringslov [Law No. 187 of 9 May 1984 on consumer debt adjustment], af konkurslov afsnit IV, kapitel 25–29 [at Bankruptcy Act Section IV, chapters 25–29] (Den.) [hereinafter Konkurslov].

[12.] See Westbrook, supra note 3, at 32–33 (discussing the discretionary elements of Norwegian bankruptcy law, which produced local variations similar to those observed in the United States).

[13.] Konkurslov, supra note 11, section 197.

[14.] See Westbrook, supra note 3, at 32 (discussing the Norwegian law's requirement that the debtor's bankruptcy be "permanent in nature").

[15.] Jason J. Kilborn, Twenty-Five Years of Consumer Bankruptcy in Continental Europe: Internalizing Negative Externalities and Humanizing Justice in Denmark, 18 Int'l Insolvency Rev. 155, 168 (2009).

these two tests produced widely and persistently divergent results among debtors based on little more than the location of the governing court. In 2002, for example, while the court in Odense admitted approximately 66% of its 161 debt adjustment applications, "the court in Roskilde admitted only 39% of its 139 applicants, and the court in Copenhagen admitted a mere 25% of [its] 828 applications."[16] For debtors who navigated past this Scylla, the Charybdis of court confirmation of debtors' five-year debt adjustment plans presented an equally daunting and equally divergent challenge. While the court in Århus closed 41% of its 244 cases with a confirmed plan, "the courts in Ålborg and Randers confirmed plans in only 19% and 15%, respectively, of the 136 cases closed" by each of these courts, and "[a]s in most years, the Copenhagen court had a miserly success rate of only 13% of its 8,689 closed cases."[17]

For the few lucky debtors who cleared these two procedural hurdles, more local legal cultural variation plagued their pursuit of earned relief. Like the Norwegian law that Jay learned about,[18] the Danish law also left completely to court discretion the terms of debtors' payment plans to earn their discharge—both the length in years and the budget allocated to debtors for family support.[19] Unlike in Norway, the Danish courts quickly coalesced around a standard five-year term, but courts differed widely in their assessment of proper budgets to support, as the statute directed, a "modest" lifestyle. Some courts allowed supplementary budget items beyond a basic allowance (for things like eye and dental care and household appliance rental), while others did not.[20] Even the amount of the basic budget allowance varied widely and was not based on variances in local cost of living,

---

[16] Id. at 174–75.

[17] Id. at 175.

[18] See Westbrook, supra note 3, at 33 (discussing the Norwegian courts' discretion regarding payment plans).

[19] See Kilborn, supra note 15, at 172, 177 (stating that Danish law originally left questions of disposable income and plan length "open to individual case-by-case and court-by-court discretion" and that budgetary practices "varied widely" among local courts).

[20] Kilborn, supra note 15, at 177.

as this allocation varied by 40%–50% among otherwise similar districts.[21] These varying perspectives on appropriate sacrifice and thrift led some debt counselors to suggest that their pre-bankruptcy clients engage in in-country bankruptcy tourism, moving what we would now call their "center of main interest" (i.e., their home residence) from a miserly region to a more generous (reasonable?) region.[22]

After nearly 20 years of frustration with these overly restrictive and divergent court demands, the Danish government stepped back from fear of abuse and launched a reform process that culminated in 2005. While the reform did not deal directly with the regional variations in admission and plan confirmation rates, it relaxed access criteria and standardized plan terms.

In a technical but crucial about-face, the initial presumption of restricted access was reversed. That is, while debtors were originally presumed *not* admissible unless the court was convinced that the totality of the circumstances militated *in favor* of relief, after 2005 the presumption is *in favor* of admission unless consideration of a slightly reformulated list of factors "suggests decisively against" relief.[23] Also, at least for former small-business entrepreneurs, the "qualified insolvency" test was modified expressly to provide admission for debtors whose economic situation is "unclear,"[24] and the payment term for a discharge plan for these former small-business entrepreneurs was set by Justice Ministry regulation at three years, rather than the standard five years for consumers.[25]

---

[21] See Betænkning nr. 1449 af august 2004 om gældssanering [Report No. 1449 of August 2004 on Debt Settlement] 144 (Den.) (reporting that in 1997–1998, budget allowances for singles varied from 2,500 to 3,500 kr. and for couples from 4,000 to 6,000 kr.); Dommerfuldmægtigforeningen & Advokatrådet, Redegørelse Vedrørende Ændringer i Konkurslovens Bestemmelser om Gældssanering [Statement Regarding Changes to the Bankruptcy Act's Debt Settlement Provisions] 34 (1999) (Den.) (same).

[22] Kilborn, supra note 15, at 174.

[23] Konkurslov, supra note 11, section 197(4), 231a(4).

[24] *Id.* section 231b, 236a(2).

[25] Bekendtgørelse nr. 894 af 22.9.2005 om gældssanering [Executive Order No. 894 of 22 September 2005 on Debt Settlement] section 2 (Den.).

For all debtors, the reform dealt head-on with the local legal cultural problem of vast differences in court parsimony in discharge plans. The Justice Ministry was tasked with establishing uniform, nationwide basic budgetary allowances, and the Ministry took a much more humane approach to debtor support. The new budget guidelines exceeded the upper range then applied by the courts in most debt adjustment cases by nearly 20%, and additional types of income were exempted entirely from distribution to creditors, such as state transfer payments for children.[26]

As Jay predicted, however, local legal culture is quite sticky. The Danish courts have continued their rigorous watch at the gates into and out of the discharge procedure. In the decade following the reform, fewer than half of all petitions for admission to the personal discharge procedure were granted (fewer than 40% in 2009 and 2010).[27] While the reasons for these rejections are not reported, anecdotes from other jurisdictions suggest that most of the rejected applications involve paperwork errors rather than merit-based judgments. Of an average of just over 5,000 cases closed per year during this period, only about 30% (an average of about 1,680) concluded with an approved plan. Though again looking on the bright side, excluding the cases rejected at the entryway, this represents a 70% confirmation rate for admitted cases.[28]

B. Slovakia, 2006-2017

When Jay attended the comparative conference in 1997, Denmark's personal discharge regime and similar ones in neighboring

---

[26.] Kilborn, supra note 15 at 1, 176–78.

[27.] See Danmarks Domstole, Statistik for Skiftesager m.v.: Modtagne Sager om Insolvensskifte m.v., www.domstol.dk/om/talogfakta/statistik/Documents/Skiftesager/ [https://perma.cc/F6HX-JUNN] (reporting the number of debt adjustment applications received and the number of debt adjustment applications declined). Calculations were based on ten years of data from 2006 to 2016 (on file with author).

[28.] Kilborn, supra note 15, at 173.

Scandinavia were effectively the only games in town.[29] Since then, the dam has broken and new consumer discharge laws and experience have flooded into virtually every country in Europe,[30] often through multiple iterations and amendments of new laws.[31] Much of the intervening experience has been analyzed elsewhere,[32] so this chapter will focus on the very latest developments.

The most exciting and bold departure from a system historically both quite discretionary and quite fearful of abuse occurred in Slovakia, whose consumer discharge system was entirely overhauled effective March 1, 2017.[33] This amendment was preceded by a long period of disappointment with the original quite restrictive law. The Slovak consumer discharge provisions were added to the Law on Bankruptcy and Restructuring 2005 with a delayed effective date of January 1, 2006.[34]

[29.] See Westbrook, supra note 3, at 31. Though Jay notes emerging systems in France and Germany as well, in 1997 the French law offered no discharge to consumers and the German consumer bankruptcy reforms would not become effective until 1999. See Jason J. Kilborn, Expert Recommendations and the Evolution of European Best Practices for the Treatment of Overindebtedness, 1984–2010, at 13 n.69, 14 (2011).

[30.] But see discussion infra subpart III(A) (addressing Bulgaria's hesitance to adopt consumer debt discharge procedures).

[31.] See, e.g., Gerard McCormack et al., Study on a New Approach to Business Failure and Insolvency: Comparative Legal Analysis of the Member States' Relevant Provisions and Practices 333–48 (2016) (reviewing the variations among consumer discharge laws in EU member states).

[32.] See generally, e.g., Kilborn, supra note 29 (tracing the evolution of consumer bankruptcy systems throughout Europe); World Bank, Report on the Treatment of the Insolvency of Natural Persons (2013) (discussing laws of insolvency of natural persons throughout the world).

[33.] See Radovan Pala & Michal Michalek, Long-Awaited Changes to Restructuring Rules in Slovakia, Taylor Wessing LLP (Feb. 1, 2017), https://united-kingdom. taylorwessing.com/en/insights/rcr-update/long-awaited-changes-to-restructuring-rules-in-slovakia [https://perma.cc/FH6E-G8DF] (discussing the enactment of an amendment to Slovakia's bankruptcy law).

[34.] Zákon, č. 7/2005 Z.z. o konkurze a reštrukturalizácii a o zmene a doplnení niektorých zákonov z 9. decembra 2004 [Law on Bankruptcy and Restructuring and on Amendment and Supplementation of Several Other Laws of December 9, 2004] (Slovk.), http://ec.europa.eu/internal_market/finances/docs/actionplan/transposition/slovakia/d7.3-ml-sk.pdf [https://perma.cc/UN5B-VXKB].

A surprisingly imposing barrier to relief prevented all but a few cases from making their way past the admissions stage for the first decade of this new law. To access relief, debtors had to pay the equivalent of about $800 (€663.88) in filing and trustee fees and demonstrate that they had assets to liquidate that would produce the equivalent of about $2,000 (€1,659.70) in distributions for creditors.[35] Debtors who cleared this hurdle faced yet another: like most European consumer insolvency laws, the Slovak regime required debtors to earn their fresh start by complying with a three-year payment plan imposed by the court.[36] The amount of payment demanded of debtors was subject to the all-but-unfettered discretion of the court, guided only by a frightening suggestion that the payment obligation could be "up to 70% of the debtor's net income."[37]

Few debtors managed to clear the entry barrier to this new system, though those who did so seem largely to have succeeded in obtaining relief. It took seven years of operation for this new procedure to produce 100 cases admitted to the three-year payment plan phase, though 484 debtors had applied for such relief and only about 200 cases were fully administered (leaving a significant and persistent backlog).[38] By the end of 2016, the total number of discharge applications over the ten-year life of the regime had risen to 1,855, with administered cases still lagging far behind at 685, of which 478 had been admitted to the payment plan phase.[39] This methodical

---

[35.] *Id.* section 171(1) (repealed Mar. 1, 2017); Vladimír Kordoš & Filip Takáč, Resurrection of Personal Insolvencies in Slovakia? Eurofenix, Spring 2017, at 34.

[36.] Kordoš & Takáč, supra note 35, at 34.

[37.] *Id.*

[38.] These figures derive from annual bankruptcy case statistics published by the Slovak Ministry of Justice. See Konkurzné konania na okresných súdoch SR, Ministerstvo Spravodlivosti Slovenskej Republiky (Slovk.), www.justice.gov.sk/Stranky/Informacie/Statistika-konkurznych-konani-OS.aspx [https://perma.cc/5J5Q-772X] [hereinafter Slovak Bankruptcy Statistics] (reporting discharge application and administration statistics in Slovakia from 2006 through 2012).

[39.] See *id.* (reporting discharge application and administration statistics in Slovakia from 2006 through 2016).

approach to case evaluation was apparently fairly successful, as only a handful of cases over the eleven-year life of this original procedure ended in default or withdrawal, and most admitted cases seem to have concluded with a granted discharge about three years later, suggesting that courts had exercised their discretion in imposing relatively judicious payment obligations.[40]

Digging a bit deeper reveals a stark local legal culture issue at the admissions stage. The admissions figures just mentioned produce an admissions rate of 70% of all administered cases from 2006 through 2016. But in examining district-level rates among the eight districts adjudicating these cases, stark differences emerge. In the last six years of the original regime, the court in the capital region of Bratislava admitted 100% of administered cases, with the high-volume courts in Banská Bystrica and Žilina not far behind. The district court in Trenčín, in contrast, admitted only 33% of administered cases during this period (fewer than 20% before 2015).[41] The small number of cases makes these figures less compelling, but the differing admissions practices of these decision makers seem to fairly clearly reflect very different attitudes toward, most likely, quite similar debtors. Payment-plan practices likely also differed dramatically. Over the entire 11-year period under the original law, only 2 debtors emerged with a discharge from the process in Trenčín, compared with 5 in Bratislava and 38 in Banská Bystrica (percentages are difficult to determine here, but judging by any perspective, the ratios of success vary wildly across districts).[42]

The Slovak government set out in 2016 to rectify this sad situation and align Slovak practice with regimes that are more accommodating to debtors. The legislature quickly took up and adopted the Justice Ministry's bold revision of the bankruptcy law in November 2016,

---

[40.] See *id.* (compiling bankruptcy proceeding outcome statistics in Slovakia from 2006 through 2016).

[41.] See *id.* (providing discharge application and administration statistics by district from 2011 through 2016).

[42.] See *id.* (reporting discharge statistics by district from 2006 through 2016).

effective March 1, 2017.[43] Departing from the European standard and all but abandoning fear of abuse, the new Slovak regime offers debtors a free choice between asset liquidation and immediate discharge or a five-year payment plan,[44] parallel to the U.S. choice between chapters 7 and 13 of the Bankruptcy Code. Debtors must be represented by the publicly supported Centre for Legal Aid,[45] and the now reduced €500 application fee can be lent by the Centre (for repayment in installments over three years) to debtors unable to pay the fee immediately.[46] To make liquidation an even more attractive option, the range of debtors' property exempt from liquidation has been expanded with a homestead exemption of €10,000 in unencumbered value in a home.[47]

In stark contrast with recent U.S. practice, Slovak lawmakers embedded in their new system a clear preference for quick liquidation-and-discharge relief, actively discouraging debtors from pursuing the payment plan route. For debtors who choose to preserve their nonexempt assets and propose a payment plan, the reserved budget for family support must cover the debtor's family's housing and basic needs (still undefined in the law[48]) and offer creditors a minimum 30% dividend (and at least 10% more value than a

---

[43.] See Kordoš & Takáč, supra note 35, at 34 (describing the implications of the amendment).

[44.] Zákon, č. 7/2005 Z.z. o konkurze a reštrukturalizácii a o zmene a doplnení niektorých zákonov [Law on Bankruptcy and Restructuring and on Amendment and Supplementation of Several Other Laws] (Slovk.), www.noveaspi.sk/products/lawText/1/59304/1/2 [https://perma.cc/WKK2-D6D6] (current version).

[45.] Id. section 166k.

[46.] Centrum Právnej Pomoci, Osobný bankrot 4–5 (2017) (Slovk.), www.centrumpravnejpomoci.sk/wp-content/uploads/2014/03/Bro%C5%BE%C3%BAAra-OB-02_2017.pdf [https://perma.cc/NFR3-4WHV].

[47.] Zákon, č. 7/2005, supra note 44, section 167h(4). The Justice Ministry issued a press release on the new law and homestead exemption. Dostupnejší osobný bankrot, Ministerstvo Spravodlivosti Slovenskej Republiky (Mar. 1, 2017) (Slovk.), www.justice.gov.sk/Stranky/aktualitadetail.aspx?announcementID=2179 [https://perma.cc/XK7U-3L7G].

[48.] See Silvia Belovičová, New Personal Insolvency Regime in Slovakia, 0-1-CEE! Cent. Eur. Legal News & Views Blog (Dec. 16, 2016), www.ceelegalblog.com/2016/12/857/ [https://perma.cc/7MQ7-98WR] (noting that debtor living

liquidation would produce).[49] For debtors whose disposable income does not appear sufficient to meet these thresholds, the statute directs the trustee to recommend that the debtor file a petition for bankruptcy liquidation.[50]

By the end of November 2017, the Centre for Legal Aid had registered nearly 63,000 consultations with debtors interested in the new discharge procedure.[51] Over 8,000 petitions were filed in the first nine months of availability of the new processes, 7,800 seeking liquidation and discharge, and slightly more than 200 proposing a five-year payment plan.[52] The courts quickly accelerated their formerly languid administration process, granting admission to 6,454 bankruptcy cases and 117 payment plan cases.[53] Of these, about half of the bankruptcy cases have already closed with a discharge, while a payment plan has been confirmed in forty cases.[54] In the nine months from March to November 2017, the number of petitions for bankruptcy exceeded the entire number filed in the 11-year period of the old law by a factor of four. The number of cases admitted in the first 9 months of the new procedure was 13.5 times as large as the total number admitted over the previous 10 years, and 17 times as many discharges have been granted.[55] The new Slovak system is a unique example of the modern European retreat from fear of abuse and embrace of standardized, low-burden personal discharge.

---

expenses are to be determined by trustees and courts, "and let's hope they will use their discretion wisely").

49. Zákon, č. 7/2005, supra note 44, section 168c(4)–(5).

50. Id. section 168c(7).

51. Rok 2017 na ministerstve spravodlivosti, Ministerstvo Spravodlivosti Slovenskej Republiky (Dec. 19, 2017) (Slovk.), www.justice.gov.sk/Stranky/aktualitadetail.aspx?announcementID=2285 [https://perma.cc/2YWG-NALA] [hereinafter 2017 at the Ministry of Justice].

52. Id.

53. Id.

54. Id.

55. See Slovak Bankruptcy Statistics, supra note 38 (reporting bankruptcy admission and discharge statistics in Slovakia from 2006 through 2016); 2017 at the Ministry of Justice, supra note 51 (reporting bankruptcy admission and discharge statistics from March through November of 2017).

C. Poland, 2009-2015

A somewhat similar story played out in Poland, though over a shorter period of time. Poland's first consumer discharge law was adopted much later than the Slovak version, and it ran into serious trouble immediately. Effective at the end of March 2009,[56] the Polish Law on Bankruptcy and Rehabilitation was supplemented to allow consumers to seek discharge relief, but, again, fear of abuse compelled legislators to place two major obstacles in the way of access to this relief. First, debtors had to establish that their insolvency resulted from exceptional circumstances entirely beyond their control.[57] As if this were not sufficient to bar access to all but a small handful of applicants, admission also required a demonstration of sufficient assets to cover the costs of administration, which varied from case to case and were estimated at between €1,000 and €5,000.[58]

In the nearly four years from March 2009 through the end of 2012, just over 2,160 consumer debtors applied for discharge relief under the new law, but only sixty (2.8%) were admitted into the system.[59] The Justice Ministry was not pleased. The Ministry proposed a reform, expressing its feeling that these statistics "and legislative experiences of other countries show, the current restrictive approach envisaged in Polish law should be liberalized."[60] A little over a year later, a bill was on the floor of the legislature with an explanatory statement reminding

---

[56] Marek Porzycki & Anna Rachwał, Consumer Insolvency Proceedings in Poland 5 (Instytut Allerhanda, Working Paper 12/2015, 2015).

[57] Prawo upadłościowe [Bankruptcy and Reorganization Law] (2003 r. Dz. U. Nr 175, poz. 1361), Art. 1 (Pol.); Katarzyna Kołodziejczyk, Consumer Bankruptcy in Poland, Money Matters, no. 14, 2017, at 20, 20.

[58] Kołodziejczyk, supra note 57, at 20.

[59] See Ewidencja spraw upadłościowych (w tym upadłości konsumenckiej "of") za lata 2005–2015, Informator Statystyczny Wymiaru Sprawiedliwości (Pol.), https://isws.ms.gov.pl/pl/baza-statystyczna/opracowania-wieloletnie/download,2853,56.html [https://perma.cc/GAN4-WSXM] (reporting bankruptcy applications and admissions in Poland from 2009 through 2012).

[60] Ministerstwo Sprawiedliwści, Rekomendacje Zespołu Ministra Sprawiedliwości ds. nowelizacji Prawa upadłościowego i naprawczego 270 (2012) (Pol.) (original in Polish).

lawmakers of the many benefits of consumer discharge law, observing that the Polish approach had failed due to the cost and qualification barriers noted previously and aiming to "reduce or completely remove" these barriers.[61] The bill traveled through the legislative process quickly, and legislators put fear of abuse behind them as they passed the liberalizing amendments into law at the end of August 2014, effective December 31, 2014.[62] Meanwhile, statistics on the operation of the old law came to an ignominious end, with a total of 2,735 applications submitted over nearly six years and only 120 successfully admitted—an ultimate aggregate admission rate of just 4.4%.[63]

From 2015 forward, Polish debtors have been free to seek discharge relief so long as they did not cause their insolvency "intentionally or as a result of gross negligence."[64] For debtors with limited assets, administration costs are initially covered by the state treasury (and the costly formality of publication of case information in newspapers was scrapped in favor of electronic publication to reduce expense).[65] After liquidation of the debtor's assets, Polish practice still follows the European norm of imposing a payment plan on debtors to earn their discharge, but both the term (up to three years, down from five in the earlier law) and payment amount are still left to unfettered court discretion.[66] In a powerful move away from fear of abuse, however, the law explicitly recognizes that many debtors will lack payment capacity beyond meeting their basic needs, so it provides for an immediate discharge if the court finds that this is

---

[61] O zmianie ustawy – Prawo upadłościowe i naprawcze oraz niektórych innych ustaw [Bill Amending the Bankruptcy and Reorganization Law] (2014 Nr 2265) (Pol.) (original in Polish).

[62] Porzycki & Rachwał, supra note 56, at 5.

[63] See Informator Statystyczny Wymiaru Sprawiedliwości, supra note 59 (presenting applications and admission statistics from 2009 through 2014).

[64] O zmianie ustawy – Prawo upadłościowe i naprawcze, ustawy o Krajowym Rejestrze Sądowym oraz ustawy o kosztach sądowych w sprawach cywilnych [Amendment to the Bankruptcy and Reorganization Law] (2014 r. DZ. U. poz. 1306), Art. 4914(1) (Pol.) [hereinafter Prawo upadłościowe] (original in Polish).

[65] Id., Art. 4917(1), Art. 49116(2); Porzycki & Rachwał, supra note 56, at 10, 29.

[66] Prawo upadłościowe, supra note 64, Art. 49114, Art. 49115.

"clearly shown."[67] For cases where a payment plan is imposed, it can be amended for improvements in the debtor's payment capacity, but only for "reasons other than an increase in remuneration for work or services personally performed by the debtor."[68] This provides a creative incentive for debtors to maximize their productivity immediately following insolvency proceedings.

As in Slovakia, Polish debtors eagerly accepted the invitation to this newly liberalized relief. Already in the first year of the new Polish law, more than 5,600 debtors applied and 2,153 were admitted— nearly 20 times as many admitted cases as in the previous six years combined.[69] Those figures nearly doubled again in 2016, with almost 8,700 applications and 4,447 admission orders, and the acceptance rate rose above 50% for the first time.[70] Many applications are still being rejected, but largely for incorrect completion of the forms,[71] and the average four-month processing time for cases suggests that the admission rate will rise as the crush of new cases makes its way through the procedure. Fear of abuse is in definite retreat in Poland.

II. Most Recent Developments: Less Discretion, Less Fear of Abuse

A. Russia, 2015-2017

Only two years old, the new Russian consumer bankruptcy system has already encountered and addressed the same cost impediments that hindered the operation of the Slovak and Polish systems. It also

---

[67.] *Id.* at Art. 49116(1) (original in Polish).

[68.] *Id.* at 64, Art. 49119(3) (original in Polish).

[69.] See Informator Statystyczny Wymiaru Sprawiedliwości, supra note 59 (providing applications and admission statistics from 2009 through 2016).

[70.] *Id.* Admissions leveled off in 2017 at just over 5,500, though with a sharp turn upward in the last three months of the year. 2017 upadłość konsumencka, Centralny Ośrodek Informacji Gospodarczej, www.coig.com.pl/2017-upadlosc-konsumencka-lista_osob.php [https://perma.cc/SR3D-WPAU].

[71.] Informator Statystyczny Wymiaru Sprawiedliwości, supra note 59.

confronted an unexpected form of resistance when lower courts creatively interpreted the new law to prohibit use by most consumer debtors. Here again, in a decisive rejection of fear of abuse, the Russian Supreme Court last year put the system back on track to achieve its primarily rehabilitative purposes.

In the transition back to a market-based economic system following decades of stagnation under Communism, Russia adopted a consumer bankruptcy law in December 2014, with a delayed effective date of October 1, 2015.[72] This law carried few of the hallmarks of fear of abuse seen elsewhere. Though it appears to follow European standards by requiring debtors to relinquish both nonexempt asset value and some amount of future income, the income expropriation period seems to last only six months, and debtors are entitled to a nondiscretionary exemption of a statutorily determined portion of their income.[73] So far so good.

The ironic problem, as in Slovakia and Poland, seems to be money, as debtors have struggled to afford the costs of the procedure. In the first year of the law, of an estimated avalanche of 670,000 potential overindebted applicants, only 33,000 debtors petitioned for relief, only 14,800 cases were opened, and fewer than 500 made their way completely through the complex, ten-month-long average procedure.[74] Lawmakers first thought cost barriers were keeping the sea of applicants back, so in November 2016 they reduced the filing fee from 6,000 rubles to a nominal 300 rubles (from about $244 to $12 at Purchasing Power Parity exchange rate [PPP]), effective January 1, 2017.[75] But by the end of the second year of the new law's operation,

---

[72.] Jason J. Kilborn, Treating the New European Disease of Consumer Debt in a Post-Communist State: The Groundbreaking New Russian Personal Insolvency Law, 41 Brook. J. Int'l L. 655, 686 (2016).

[73.] Id. at 698–700, 710–11.

[74.] Nataliia Shvabaėr, Zhizn' vzaĭmy, Ros. Gaz. (Nov. 7, 2016) (Russ.), https://rg.ru/2016/11/07/sredi-rossijskih-grazhdan-okazalos-bankrotov-bolshe-chem-sredi-kompanij.html [https://perma.cc/47DW-PL7X].

[75.] Georgiĭ Panin, Kakie vazhnye zakony vstupiat v silu s 2017 goda, Ros. Gaz. (Dec. 28, 2016) (Russ.), https://rg.ru/2016/12/28/kakie-vazhnye-zakony-vstupiat-v-silu-s-2017-goda.html [https://perma.cc/2YEA-JQTA].

the total number of consumer cases commenced had little more than doubled to just over 40,000.[76]

The reduction in filing fees was merely a drop in the bucket compared to the real problem: the cost of the required "financial administrator," set by statute at 25,000 rubles (about $1,000 at PPP) but in reality often higher, and other administrative expenses reportedly boost the total cost of a personal bankruptcy filing to at least 100,000 rubles in Moscow ($4,000 PPP) and at least 60,000 rubles in provincial regions (about $2,500 PPP).[77] This is in addition to the logistical challenge of filing a bankruptcy case in the often distant commercial courts, only one of which is located in each "subject" (governmental region) of Russia's expansive territory.[78]

Both the cost factor and another less obvious obstacle to relief were revealed as serious doctrinal problems when one of the first cases under the new law made its way to the Russian Supreme Court.[79] Two months after the effective date of the new law, the Commercial (*Arbitrazh*) Court in the remote Western Siberian Tyumen Oblast opened a personal bankruptcy case only to close it five months later on two grounds, both related to the absence of any substantial asset value in the case.[80] First, the court felt that the absence of sufficient asset value to offer even a partial distribution to unsecured creditors undermined the very purpose, in its view, of the bankruptcy law—that is, to offer proportionate satisfaction of creditors' claims from the debtor's assets.[81] Second, insufficient asset value to pay

[76] Tat'iana Zamakhia, Dobrosovestnym grazhdanam predlozhili spisat' dolgi, Ros. Gaz. (Nov. 8, 2017) (Russ.), https://rg.ru/2017/11/08/dobrosovestnym-grazh danam-predlozhili-spisat-dolgi.html [https://perma.cc/LVG2-P67P].

[77] Tat'iana Zykova, Bol'she ne dolzhen, Ros. Gaz. (Jan. 12, 2017) (Russ.), https://rg.ru/2017/01/12/chislo-bankrotov-v-rossii-za-poslednie-3-mesiaca-vyroslo-na-27.html [https://perma.cc/8RL9-VG29].

[78] Kilborn, supra note 72, at 691–93.

[79] Opredelenie Verkhovnyĭ Sud Rossiĭskoĭ Federatsii ot 23 ianvara 2017 [Decision of the Russian Federation Supreme Court of Jan. 23, 2017], N. 304-ēS16-14541, Delo N. A70-14095/2015. 2017 (Russ.).

[80] Id. at 2–3.

[81] Id. at 2.

administrative costs constitutes a basis for case closure under Article fifty seven of the Law on Insolvency, and the court held that funds could not be advanced by a nondebtor to cover these costs.[82]

The Supreme Court struck back at these philosophical constraints on the new law and dealt another blow to fear of abuse of consumer discharge. Consumer bankruptcy has other purposes, the Court asserted, beyond satisfying creditors. Access to legislatively prescribed relief cannot be restricted simply on the basis that the debtor has no asset value to offer creditors, and this cannot be equated to "bad faith," more specific evidence of which is required to deny a discharge.[83] And while debtors must, indeed, somehow cover the administrative costs of the proceeding (which at the time were much smaller than now, with only a 10,000 ruble fee for the financial administrator), the Court pointed out that the law contained no provision forbidding debtors from seeking help from third parties in covering these fees.[84]

For debtors without generous friends, the law does indeed still require full payment of administrative costs,[85] which clearly remains a deterrent for many debtors, as it was in Slovakia and Poland. Fortunately, the Ministry of Economic Development has already proposed a simplification of the procedure—mainly exclusion of the costly financial administrator—for cases involving debtors with limited debts and assets (less than 900,000 rubles of debt, about $37,000 at PPP, fewer than ten creditors, and income less than the statutory minimum livable income).[86] This further step away from fear of abuse has been met with some resistance, so this will be a developing

---

[82] *Id.*

[83] *Id.* at 3 (original in Russian).

[84] *Id.* at 4.

[85] Federal'nyĭ Zakon o Nesostoĭatel'nosti (Bankrotstve) [Federal Law on Insolvency (Bankruptcy)], N 127-FZ. st. 57(1) (Russ.); see also Zykova, supra note 77 (noting that the administrator can request case closure at any point if his fees and expenses are not paid by the debtor).

[86] Elena Berezina & Irina Zhandarova, Vernut' vse, Ros. Gaz. (Mar. 13, 2017) (Russ.), https://rg.ru/2017/03/13/grazhdanam-uprostiat-bankrotstva.html [https://perma.cc/ZV55-Z7HH]; Zykova, supra note 77.

story to watch in 2018 and beyond. Incidentally, lawmakers in neighboring Ukraine have long agitated for a personal bankruptcy law as well, but to date, they have not progressed beyond the stage of a draft bill, the most notable of which has been pending for two years.[87]

B. Austria, 1995-2017

Perhaps the biggest change ushered in at the start of the new year is a major withdrawal from fear of abuse at the culmination of a long-fought battle in Austria. This is one of the small handful of consumer discharge regimes that was already in operation beginning in 1995, before Jay wrote his commentary, and it exemplifies the fear of abuse that he discerned in Europe at the time. For over twenty years, the Austrian procedure imposed three classic European hurdles to deter feared abuse by consumer debtors. After decades of criticism by counseling centers and other observers,[88] each of these three obstacles was cleared away by near-unanimous legislative reform effective November 1, 2017.[89]

First, like in Poland and Russia, the Austrian law originally required debtors to pay at least the administrative costs of the proceeding. For those unable to do so immediately upon applying for relief, such debtors had to comply with another prerequisite: a mandatory attempt to work out their debt problems privately through an out-of-court negotiation with creditors.[90] This negotiation was, unsurprisingly, very seldom successful, so in the reform it was finally

---

87. Natal'ía Mytskovskaía, Kak stat' bankrotom: novyĭ zakon mozhet pomoch' yzbavyt'sía ot nevyplachennykh dolhov, Komsomol'skaía Pravda v Ukrayne (Nov. 15, 2017) (Ukr.), https://kp.ua/print/economics/592146-kak-stat-bankrotom-novyi-zakon-mozhet-pomoch-yzbavytsia-ot-nevyplachennykh-dolhov [https://perma.cc/K28J-M8A5].

88. For example, ASB Schuldnerberatungen, Schuldenreport 2016 14, 18 (2016) (Austria) (calling for overdue reforms in Austrian insolvency law); Christiane Moser, Österreich: Reform des Privatkonkurses überfällig, Das Budget, no. 78, 2016, at 6, 6 (Austria) (noting that Austria is lagging behind in private bankruptcy reform).

89. Clemens Mitterlehner & Christa Kerschbaummayr, Reform of Personal Bankruptcy Procedure in Austria, Money Matters, no. 15, 2017, at 8, 8.

90. Konkursordnungs-Novelle 1993 [Bankruptcy Amendment of 1993] Bundesgesetzblatt [BGBl] No. 974/1993, section 183(2) (Austria), www.ris.bka.gv.at/Dokumente/BgblPdf/1993_974_0/1993_974_0.pdf [https://perma.cc/B79C-HTTF].

scrapped.[91] Austria thus joins Sweden in having abandoned mandatory debt counseling and negotiation as a prerequisite for formal
consumer insolvency relief.[92]

Second, like virtually every European consumer discharge regime,
the Austrian procedure requires both a liquidation of nonexempt
assets and a payment plan. Historically, most such plans were
accepted by a vote of creditors. Debtors had to propose to pay creditors an amount equal to five years' worth of their projected nonexempt income, and they could string out those payments over as many
as seven years to lighten the burden.[93] Such a plan is accepted by
an affirmative vote of creditors who represent a majority in number
and amount of the claims of all voting creditors.[94] While the great
majority (70%) of Austrian personal insolvency cases in the past have
concluded with such a court-mediated payment plan,[95] low-income
debtors have been largely shut out of the process by the unique final
minimum-payment hurdle discussed in the following passages. With
the reform to allow low-income debtors realistic access to relief, the
necessity to propose a payment plan for creditor voting has now
been limited to debtors with substantial nonexempt income. That
is, debtors with little or no nonexempt income can proceed immediately to the final stage, a court-imposed earned discharge period.[96]

[91.] Philipp Wetter, Austria: Major Changes in Personal Bankruptcy Law,
Schoenherr (July 4, 2017), www.schoenherr.eu/si/publications/publication-detail/
austria-major-changes-in-personal-bankruptcy-law/ [https://perma.cc/32US-3T5X].

[92.] Jason J. Kilborn, Out with the New, In with the Old: As Sweden Aggressively
Streamlines Its Consumer Bankruptcy System, Have U.S. Reformers Fallen Off the
Learning Curve? 80 Am. Bankr. L.J. 435, 458 (2006).

[93.] Konkursordnungs-Novelle 1993, supra note 90, section 193(1), 194(1).

[94.] Insolvenzrechtsänderungsgesetz 2010 [IRÄG 2010] [Insolvency Law Amendment 2010] Bundesgesetzblatt [BGBl] No. 29/2010, section 147(1) (Austria), https://
www.ris.bka.gv.at/Dokumente/BgblAuth/BGBLA_2010_I_29/BGBLA_2010_I_29.
html [https://perma.cc/3JXX-4ALX].

[95.] Georg Kodek, Handbuch Privatkonkurs: Die Sonderbestimmungen fur das
Insolvenzverfahren natürlicher Personen 384 tbl.C.3 (2015).

[96.] Insolvenzrechtsänderungsgesetz 2017 [IRÄG 2017] [Insolvency Law Amendment 2017] Bundesgesetzblatt [BGBl] No. 122/2017, section 193(1), 194(1) (Austria),
www.ris.bka.gv.at/Dokumente/BgblAuth/BGBLA_2017_I_122/BGBLA_2017_I_122.
html [https://perma.cc/LWF7-RPRE].

This earned discharge period and its culmination were the subjects of the third and most substantial reform. Neither the length of this period nor the amounts demanded from debtors were ever subject to any notable degree of court discretion. Originally, debtors formally assigned to a trustee all of their actual income in excess of an objective statutory "existence minimum" amount for seven years.[97] An additional requirement echoed the sentiment of the Russian Tyumen Oblast Court discussed previously regarding the purpose of bankruptcy: at the conclusion of this seven-year period, Austrian debtors received a discharge only if they had paid off administrative costs and produced a dividend of 10% of unsecured creditors' claims.[98] Debtors who missed this mark only slightly could hope for a hardship discharge at court discretion, perhaps after an additional three-year period of toil and sacrifice, but the discharge could be and sometimes was denied to debtors who failed to produce a satisfactory dividend for creditors.[99] Many more low-income debtors were doubtless deterred from even attempting to obtain discharge relief, knowing they likely could not cover costs and produce the minimum 10% dividend for creditors.[100]

As of November 1, 2017, in a tectonic shift from longtime fear to full acceptance of consumer discharge, Austrian legislators scrapped the 10% minimum dividend, softened the requirement to cover administrative costs, and reduced the earned discharge period from seven to five years.[101] At the conclusion of the now five-year period, the court enters a discharge regardless of whether the debtor has covered costs and produced a dividend for creditors.[102] Administrative costs that cannot be covered by debtors are advanced from the state Treasury, to be collected from the proceeds of liquidation of

---

[97] Konkursordnungs-Novelle 1993, supra note 90, section 199(2).

[98] Id. section 194, 213.

[99] Id.

[100] See ASB Schuldnerberatungen, supra note 88, at 14–15 (discussing the 10% minimum); Kodek, supra note 95, at 165–202, 249–338.

[101] Insolvenzrechtsänderungsgesetz 2017, supra note 96, section 199(2), 213(1).

[102] Id. section 213(1).

debtors' nonexempt assets or collection of nonexempt income.[103] If the debtor's asset value and five years of nonexempt payments have not managed to cover administrative costs, the debtor remains liable to cover those costs only "if and when he is in a position to do so without impairment of his [and his family's] necessary support."[104] Even this obligation prescribes (i.e., is barred by a statutory limitations period) three years after the conclusion of the proceedings.[105] The Czech Republic now stands alone in the European Union with a law that requires a minimum dividend to unsecured creditors (30%) for consumer debtors to earn their discharge.[106] Perhaps not enough time has passed for fear of abuse to abate since the Czech consumer discharge became available in 2008, but one hopes the Czech Republic will follow Austria's example in far less than the twenty-two years it took for Austria to do so.

C. Croatia 2016, Romania 2018

The two newest consumer discharge procedures in Europe reveal a bit of unfortunate backpedaling toward fear of abuse, though there is good reason to expect that discretion will be exercised sparingly and within relatively narrow boundaries in these two latecomer systems. Both will be unfolding stories to watch in the years to come.

1. Croatia

Croatia was the most Recent European Union Member State to adopt a consumer bankruptcy procedure, effective January 1, 2016.[107] It

---

[103.] Insolvenzordnung [Insolvency Code] Bundesgesetzblatt I [BGBl] no. 122/2017, as amended, section 184(1)–(2) (Austria) www.ris.bka.gv.at/GeltendeFassung.wxe?Abfrage=Bundesnormen&Gesetzesnummer=10001736&FassungVom=2017-10-31 [https://perma.cc/WEG7-86U2].

[104.] *Id.* section 184(3).

[105.] *Id.*

[106.] Kilborn, supra note 29, at 30, 37.

[107.] Zakon o stečaju potrošača [Law on Consumer Bankruptcy], NN 100/2015 (1936) (Croat.); Emir Bahtijarevic & Ema Mendusic Skugor, New Insolvency Legislation to Thoroughly Change Bankruptcy Procedures in Croatia, CEE Legal Matters, Feb. 2016, at 88, 88.

immediately took two steps backward toward fear of abuse by adopting the prereform Austrian procedure, minus the minimum dividend to creditors. Not learning from the repeated failures of these processes in neighboring regions, Croatian legislators reimposed two futile access restrictions just abandoned by Austria, along with what seems like a fairly menacing multiyear payment obligation.

First, Croatian debtors can gain entry to the in-court discharge procedure only after engaging a counseling center to propose an out-of-court settlement plan to creditors.[108] When the counseling center inevitably concludes that this effort is doomed to failure, it issues a certificate to that effect, which the debtor must present within three months with a petition for bankruptcy relief.[109] The state agency that oversees these counselors, the Financial Agency (FINA), has released statistical data on the first two years of the new Croatian procedure indicating that a total of 1,159 debtors have engaged counseling centers to initiate the out-of-court process.[110] These debtors had an average of only six creditors and mostly quite small debts, but in only *one* case were all creditors somehow convinced to sign onto the debtor's proposed settlement plan (and in only sixteen cases was an agreement reached even with *some* of the debtor's creditors).[111] Certificates of failure had thus been issued to 795 debtors, with the same result most likely awaiting most or all of the remaining applicants.[112]

Second, to gain access to the formal discharge procedure, debtors must again present a settlement plan to creditors in an in-court process. Only after that effort inevitably fails again, a liquidation of the debtor's nonexempt assets ensues, and like in Austria, Croatian

---

108. Ozren Ivković & Marko Kruc, Schonherr, Croatia: Consumer Bankruptcy Act Introduces Consumer Bankruptcy into the Legal System (2016), https://www.schoenherr.eu/uploads/tx_news/Croatia_Consumer_Bankruptcy_final_pdf3.pdf [https://perma.cc/W45U-U3KL].

109. *Id.*

110. Financijska agencija (Fina), Pregled zbirnih podataka iz Sustava provedbe Stečaja potrošača za razdoblje od 1.1.2016. do 03.04.2018. godine 2 (2018) (Croat.), http://www.fina.hr/lgs.axd?t=16&id=19566 [https://perma.cc/J4YR-U2LM].

111. *Id.* at 2, 7.

112. *Id.* at 7.

debtors are relegated to an additional "behavior checking" period of between one and five years.[113] While the law appears to leave the precise duration of this period to judicial discretion, it seems likely that courts will in most cases choose the maximum five-year term. This was the result in the very first personal bankruptcy case in Croatia, where a 51-year-old former entrepreneur with no assets and only pension income was assigned a five-year term from which she filed an appeal for a reduction to a year and a half.[114] During this period, debtors are subject to a nondiscretionary requirement of turnover of all income above the statutory exemption. The Croatian statutory minimum income figures seem far less livable than their Austrian equivalents, with one Croatian journalist characterizing them as "neoliberal euthanasia."[115] This likely explains why only a fraction of the expected 10,000–20,000 potential debtors have applied for relief.[116] In this respect, the newest European consumer discharge system may reveal something of a resurgence of fear of abuse, though not in the guise of judicial discretion.

2. Romania

Meanwhile, the latest European consumer discharge system to actually begin operations has just come online in Romania as of January 1, 2018. While the Romanian legislature unanimously adopted its Law no. 151/2015 "on the insolvency procedure of natural persons" in

---

[113.] Ivković & Kruc, supra note 108.

[114.] See Ljubica Gatarić, Prva u osobni bankrot otišla propala poduzetnica iz Krapine, Večernji list (Oct. 17, 2016) (Croat.), www.vecernji.hr/vijesti/prva-u-osobni-bankrot-otisla-propala-poduzetnica-iz-krapine-1121543 [https://perma.cc/7FKP-QUE9] (reporting the details of Croatia's first personal bankruptcy case).

[115.] See Leo Buljan, Možete li preživjeti s 800 kuna mjesečno? Ako potpišete osobni stečaj, bolje da naučite!, Portal Dnevno (June 26, 2014) (Croat.), www.dnevno.hr/novac/mozete-li-prezivjeti-s-800-kuna-mjesecno-ako-potpisete-osobni-stecaj-bolje-da-naucite-126174/ [https://perma.cc/APA5-RYJR] (original in Croatian) (citing minimum income figures of $133 per month for the debtor, $80 for an adult family member, and $53 for each child (not at PPP)).

[116.] See Ivković & Kruc, supra note 108 ("According to the Ministry, somewhere between 10,000 and 20,000 of the indebted citizens might take advantage of this opportunity.").

June 2015,[117] the government pushed back the effective date several times.[118] This delay was attributable in part to government efforts to constrain discretion in evaluating debtors' capacities to support settlement plans with creditors and to endure a multiyear earned discharge period.

The Romanian law adopts the French approach[119] of routing debtors through standing insolvency commissions, which evaluate whether cases should be directed to a negotiation with creditors and a potential five-year payment plan, or, for debtors whose financial situation is "irremediably compromised," to a liquidation-and-discharge procedure.[120] In performing the sensitive and critical evaluation of debtors' payment capacities that determines which path is pursued, the insolvency commissions are not left to their own devices; rather, the Ministry of Justice directed the chair of the central insolvency commission to publish detailed criteria for determining a "reasonable standard of living" for debtors in insolvency proceedings. These criteria must be based on a list of national economic benchmarks, including cost-of-living indices, various family and household compositions, and transportation and housing guidelines.[121] The publication of these criteria seems to have been delayed as of this writing, but the effort to constrain discretion and contain fear of abuse is manifest.

[117.] Legii 151/2015 privind procedura insolvenței persoanelor fizice [Law on the Insolvency Procedure of Natural Persons] publicată în Monitorul Oficial al României, Partea I, nr. 464/26.06.2015 (Rom.); Mihaela Condrache & Liviana Andreea Nimineț, Personal Bankruptcy and the Romanian Realities, Stud. & Sci. Res., no. 22, 2015, at 7, 8.

[118.] See, e.g., Ordonanță de urgență pentru prorogarea termenului de intrare în vigoare a Legii nr. 151/2015 privind procedura insolvenței persoanelor fizice [Government Emergency Ordinance for the extension of the entry into force of Law no. 151/2015 on insolvency procedure of natural persons] publicată în Monitorul Oficial al României, Partea I, nr. 962/24.12.2015 (Rom.).

[119.] See Kilborn, supra note 29, at 34–35 (tracing the development of France's commission-based approach to processing debtors' cases).

[120.] Condrache & Nimineț, supra note 117, at 9–11.

[121.] Hotărâre 419/2017 pentru aprobarea Normelor metodologice de aplicare a Legii nr. 151/2015 privind procedura insolvenței persoanelor fizice [Decision Approving Methodological Norms for the Application of Law on the Insolvency of Natural Persons] publicată în Monitorul Oficial al României, Partea I, nr. 436/13.06.2017, art. 2 (Rom.).

If Romanian institutions embrace the French approach to the notion of "irremediably compromised" debtors (as seems highly likely), many if not most debtors will be routed to an immediate liquidation-and-discharge procedure.[122] The insolvency commissions can send particularly low-income, elderly debtors to simplified proceedings, which require a simple observation period of three years before a final discharge is granted.[123] For all others, the asset liquidation is followed by a payment period, during which a court-determined proportion of the debtor's income in excess of reasonable living expenses must be paid to creditors.[124] This proportion is determined in accordance with the published budgetary guidelines for a "reasonable standard of living."[125] The duration of the payment period is determined by the percentage of debts paid off—as little as one year if 50% of debts are paid within that time—but given the finances of most debtors, the most common objectively determined term will be five years for debtors unable to produce at least a 40% dividend.[126] These nondiscretionary and sensitive terms for earning discharge relief reflect further relaxation of fear of abuse at the most recent launch of a consumer insolvency system.

III. Consumer Discharge-in-Waiting: Fear of Abuse Manifest in Laws in Development

In countries that have not by this point followed the personal bankruptcy trend sweeping across Europe, one would expect to find a

---

[122.] See Kilborn, supra note 29, at 34–35 (describing the increasing number of cases administered under France's "personal recovery" procedure for debtors whose financial situation is "irremediably compromised"); Jason J. Kilborn, Determinants of Failure . . . and Success in Personal Debt Mediation, Transnat'l Disp. Mgmt. Nov. 2017 at 1, 11–12 (discussing the growth of France's bankruptcy commission regime).

[123.] Legii 151/2015 privind procedura insolvenței persoanelor fizice, supra note 117, arts. 65–70.

[124.] Id. art. 57(1)(b).

[125.] Id. art. 3(25) (original in Romanian).

[126.] See id. art. 72 (prescribing the procedure for determining the duration of a debtor's payment period).

great deal of resistance to the notion of offering such relief. A resurgence of fear of abuse is fairly obvious in the last European straggler, Bulgaria, where proposed bills reflect this fear in objective, but all-but-insurmountable, barriers to relief. Beyond Europe, advanced-stage proposals developing in China and Saudi Arabia confirm that newcomers to personal discharge approach the policy conversation with great hesitancy.

A. Bulgaria

In 2000, household debt was hardly a blip on the social policy radar screen in Bulgaria. By 2008, household debt had exploded and while still not reaching the worrying levels of some other European states, had risen to and remained at a level that caught the attention of policymakers.[127] Concerned Bulgarian legislators finally introduced a bill in February 2015 to provide "protection against overindebtedness of natural persons" in the form of a cost-free, European-style procedure of asset liquidation followed by a three-year earned discharge period of relinquishment of nonexempt income.[128] The explanatory note to the bill commented that "[t]he public interest requires 'eternal debtors' to be given an opportunity to engage anew in socially beneficial activity," consistent with European practice.[129]

This controversial bill made no progress before another was introduced on July 21, 2017. The tone and approach of this new bill are quite different from its predecessor's: debtors are deemed overindebted and allowed access to relief only if they have worked

---

[127.] See Miroslav Nikolov, Households Indebtedness: State-of-the-Art, Money Matters, no. 14, 2017, at 7, 8 fig.3 (illustrating the sizeable growth in Bulgaria's household debt between 2000 and 2008); Bulgaria Household Debt 2000–2016, CEIC, www.ceicdata.com/en/indicator/bulgaria/household-debt [https://perma.cc/STW7-L7ZN] (reporting that Bulgaria's household debt "reached an all-time high" in December of 2008).

[128.] Proekt, Zakon za zashtita pri svrŭkhzadŭlzhenost na fizicheskite litsa [Draft, Law of Protection Against Overindebtedness of Natural Persons], 554-01-30 ot 12/02/2015, arts. 3(2), 6, 16, 26 (Bulg.).

[129.] Id., Notes at 12 (original in Bulgarian).

consistently during three of the preceding five years, their debts do not exceed 150,000 Bulgarian levs (about $95,000), and they nonetheless appear unable to pay their debts with *ten* years of expected income.[130] In such cases, the earned discharge period would be ten years on minimum income.[131] Moreover, during this ten-year period, debtors are prohibited from entrepreneurial activity as members or directors of companies.[132] Excluding retired people and long-term unemployed debtors and calling on ten years of earning capacity is sure to produce a remedy for very few maladies. One suspects Bulgaria is still some distance from a consumer discharge law of any kind, let alone an effective one. One can just picture the fear in legislators' eyes!

B. China

A most exciting recent development in China comes not from a central government project, but from a controlled provincial experiment. While China is in principle a highly centralized state, central authorities often afford significant autonomy to regional governments to pursue large-scale trial runs of new policies. Nowhere is this trend more powerful and more obvious than in the "special economic zones" developed during the period of "reform and opening" initiated by Deng Xiaoping in 1979.[133] Deng's famous "southern tour" in 1992 took him to one of the most prominent of these zones, Shenzhen, just to the north of Hong Kong.[134]

This hotbed of economic development and local initiative appears to be the likely future birthplace of personal bankruptcy law in China. In June 2014, a subgroup of the Shenzhen Bar Association began developing a personal bankruptcy bill for the Shenzhen

---

[130]. Bill, Zakon za zashtita pri svrŭkhzadŭlzhenost na fizicheskite litsa [Bill, Law of Protection Against Overindebtedness of Natural Persons], 754-01-46 ot 24/07/2017, arts. 4(1), 5 (Bulg.).

[131]. *Id.* art. 22(1), 30.

[132]. *Id.* art. 31.

[133]. Arthur R. Kroeber, China's Economy: What Everyone Needs to Know 5 (2016).

[134]. *Id.* at 7.

228 JASON J. KILBORN

Special Economic Zone.[135] A draft law emerged by September 2015, with some unique and intriguing provisions that suggest Shenzhen authorities are stepping lightly into this new legal terrain.[136]

A preliminary review of the proposed law, working from this author's rather rudimentary foundation in Chinese, reveals what seem to be fairly rigorous and restrictive requirements for accessing the procedure and obtaining relief. To access the personal liquidation process, debtors must submit evidence of five years of income and expenditures (which presumably indicate their payment ability and substantiate their claimed inability to clear their debts timely), and their current standard of living must not exceed a level corresponding to the local minimum wage.[137] The draft law seems to require the debtor to pay creditors the value of any nonexempt property—including disposable income—the debtor reasonably anticipates receiving over the next two years, which must in any case suffice immediately to cover administrative costs.[138]

The discharge provision is a bit puzzling, but it seems to require a minimum distribution to creditors of at least the amount distributed to them by the debtor during the two-year period preceding the debtor's filing an application for liquidation; otherwise, a discharge is conferred only by the (extremely unlikely) unanimous vote of the creditors' committee.[139] This provision could spell trouble for any

---

[135] Shenzhen Jingji Tequ Geren Pochan Tiaoli cao'an Jianyi Gao Fu Liyou (深圳经济特区个人破产条例草案建议稿附理由) [Shenzhen Special Economic Zone Personal Bankruptcy Regulation Draft Proposal with Accompanying Reasoning] (Lu Lin (卢林), ed., 2016) (China) [hereinafter Shenzhen Draft Bankruptcy Proposal]; see also "Shenzhen Jingji Tequ Geren Pochan Tiaoli" Dashiji (《深圳经济特区个人破产条例》大事记) ["Shenzhen Special Economic Zone Personal Bankruptcy Ordinance" Retrospective], Jiangsu Huijin Bankr. Liquidation Firm Ltd. (Mar. 3, 2016), www.js-hj.com/content/?190.html [https://perma.cc/MAC3-AMC7] [hereinafter Jiangsu Huijin] (China) (providing a timeline of the development of the Shenzhen bankruptcy proposal).

[136] Jiangsu Huijin, supra note 135.

[137] Shenzhen Draft Bankruptcy Proposal, supra note 135, arts. 95, 103.

[138] Id. arts. 111, 113–16, 120.

[139] Id. arts. 158–59. This unique discharge provision seems to be based on the discharge provision of the Taiwan Consumer Insolvency Act of 2008. Xiaofeizhe

potential discharge procedure, and it suggests a deep fear of abuse by opportunistic debtors. Indeed, since 2013, the current nationwide approach to defaulting debtors in China has been a Supreme Court blacklist banning some debtors from using such "luxuries" as airplane and high-speed-train travel and hotels.[140] Time will tell whether the Shenzhen draft or something like it becomes law and, if so, how it is applied by Chinese courts who seem to be both wholly unaccustomed to and quite skeptical of the concept of relief for defaulting debtors.

C. Saudi Arabia

The Saudi Ministry of Commerce and Industry delivered a bombshell when in April 2015 it released a policy paper on an initiative to revamp the Kingdom's insolvency law.[141] That paper projected that a new procedure would encompass all private individuals, including ordinary consumers, and would offer an automatic discharge of unpaid liabilities following a liquidation and waiting period of 12 months.[142] Another comment expectedly but ominously noted that "Shari'a compliance would be an important element when choosing public policies and the underlying rules."[143] This is ominous because no school of Islamic Law (shari'ah) seemed to support or even accept

---

Zhaiwu Qingli Tiaoli (消費者債務清理條例) [Consumer Debt Clean-Up Regulation] (amended Dec. 26, 2010), art. 133 (Taiwan, officially Republic of China), https://law.moj.gov.tw/LawClass/LawParaDeatil.aspx?Pcode=B0010042&LC-NOS=++80+++&LCC=2 [https://perma.cc/X5FR-ZEW9].

[140.] See Yongxi Chen & Anne Sy Cheung, The Transparent Self under Big Data Profiling: Privacy and Chinese Legislation on the Social Credit System, 12 J. Comp. L., no. 2, 2017, at 356, 362, 370 (describing travel restrictions on judgment defaulters and public disclosures of public credit information); Yuan Yang, China Penalizes 6.7m Debtors with Travel Ban, Fin. Times (Feb. 15, 2017) (reporting that a man surnamed Liu "almost lost his bride after the man's father . . . was named on the local television as being blacklisted"), www.ft.com/content/ceb2a7f0-f350-11e6-8758-687615182 1a6 [https://perma.cc/FUF3-AQSU].

[141.] Ministry of Commerce & Indus., The Kingdom of Saudi Arabia Insolvency Law Project, Policy Paper (2016) (Saudi Arabia), http://mci.gov.sa/LawsRegulations/Projects/Pages/ippd.aspx#1 [https://perma.cc/BV7Y-PQGH].

[142.] Id. section 4.1–4.5.

[143.] Id. section 1.2(b)(iii).

the notion of discharging debts without the consent of creditors.[144] An imprint of the name of a Western law firm (Clifford Chance) on every page of the English portion of the policy paper offered reason for hope, however, so the announcement of a potential Islamic discharge was both confusing and exciting.

As it turned out, the Western law firm had apparently not sufficiently appreciated the implications of shari'ah compliance. The ultimate draft law released in September 2016 indeed adhered to Islamic Law and did not offer a nonconsensual discharge.[145] The explanatory note to the new draft makes no mention of the Western concept. The provisions on liquidation do apply to ordinary individuals, but the "rehabilitation" article is quite clear that following a liquidation of nonexempt assets, the debtor "is not discharged from his liability for remaining debt except for under a special or general discharge from creditors."[146] In other words, perfectly consistent with Islamic Law, the new Saudi bankruptcy law offers individual debtors a discharge only with the consent of creditors, which one suspects is unlikely to be forthcoming. The current draft is reportedly on its way to becoming law in early 2018,[147] leaving Saudi Arabia without consumer discharge. While adherence to Islamic Law may not be fairly equated with fear of abuse, there is a congruent reticence here to allow debtors to evade their obligations over creditor opposition—a reticence that appears likely to persist indefinitely in the Kingdom.[148]

[144.] Abed Awad & Robert E. Michael, Iflas and chapter 11: Classical Islamic Law and Modern Bankruptcy, 44 Int'l Lawyer 975, 981, 997, 999 (2010); Jason J. Kilborn, Foundations of Forgiveness in Islamic Bankruptcy Law: Sources, Methodology, Diversity, 85 Am. Bankr. L.J. 323, 347 (2011).

[145.] Ministry of Commerce & Indus., Mashru' Nizam al-Iflaas [Draft of the System of Bankruptcy] (2016) (Saudi Arabia), http://mci.gov.sa/MediaCenter/elan/Documents/01.pdf [https://perma.cc/9E8P-KWSR].

[146.] Id. art. 160.

[147.] Saudi Arabia Advisory Council Approves Draft Bankruptcy Law, Reuters (Dec. 13, 2017), www.reuters.com/article/saudi-bankruptcy/update-1-saudi-arabia-advisory-council-approves-draft-bankruptcy-law-idUSL8N1OD2IP [https://perma.cc/YF5A-8PYH].

[148.] The same is true elsewhere in the region, as the new United Arab Emirates bankruptcy law does not apply to nonmerchants at all, leaving overindebted

IV. Conclusion

Virtually none of the developments described here would have a counterpart in U.S. experience. Even the advent of the infamous means test for constraining access to quick chapter 7 relief is of a very different nature than the aggressive constraints on consumer discharge access witnessed in Europe over the past twenty years. Following these comparative developments (in English) has allowed policymakers and academics worldwide to explore more deeply and in greater detail the fear of abuse that Jay observed in the United States and Europe in the late 1990s, along with its gradual but definite abatement in recent years. Comparative analysis has greatly enriched the conversation about the proper balance of relief, restriction, and responsibility with the "rich harvest of new evidence" that Jay predicted. I am thrilled to have been part of that harvest and to say, once again, thanks, Jay!

---

consumers, particularly those who write NSF checks, still subject to arrest and imprisonment. See Qanun al'iiflas al-qanun al-aitihadaa raqm (9) lisanat 2016 [Bankruptcy Law] (Official Gazette Sept. 29, 2016, effective Dec. 29, 2016) (U.A.E.), www.mof.gov.ae/En/Lawsandpolitics/govlaws/pages/federalbankruptcy.aspx [https://perma.cc/M4KQ-A5DQ]; Issac John, Why UAE's New Bankruptcy Law Is a Boon for Business, Khaleej Times (Mar. 1, 2017), www.khaleejtimes.com/business/economy/uae-bankruptcy-law-boom-bust-bonanza [https://perma.cc/N64T-T98S].

Local Legal Culture from R2D2 to Big Data

Robert M. Lawless and Angela Littwin**

I. Introduction

If you ask Teresa Sullivan, Elizabeth Warren, or Jay Westbrook about the early years of their groundbreaking Consumer Bankruptcy Project (CBP), they eventually will tell you about R2D2, their mobile photocopier. They carted R2D2 across the country to copy the bankruptcy court records that formed the backbone of their examination of the lives of consumer bankruptcy filers. Courthouses charged twenty-five cents per page for photocopies, so it was cheaper to bring R2D2, although they had to purchase a separate airplane ticket for "him." Journeying to courthouses across the country resulted in several anecdotes, such as the time R2D2 "made a break for it" on Grand Avenue in Chicago by sliding out of the back of the station wagon rented for the purpose of transporting the machine or when they had to lug R2D2 up three flights of stairs in Danville, Illinois[1] In 1981, gathering data on consumer bankruptcy filers in three states took a tremendous amount of time and effort.

* Max L. Rowe Professor of Law, University of Illinois College of Law. The coauthors' names appear in alphabetical order.

** Ronald D. Krist Professor of Law, The University of Texas School of Law. Copyright © 96 Tex. L. Rev. 1353–76 (2018). Reproduced with permission

[1.] Telephone Interview with Professor Jay Lawrence Westbrook, Benno C. Schmidt Chair of Business Law, Univ. of Tex. Sch. of Law (Jan. 20, 2018).

Once they had the data, analyzing it posed another hurdle. At the time of the first study, Westbrook had just obtained his first Apple II Plus, which was an order of magnitude slower than even today's cell phones. To analyze their data, they used the campus mainframe. They could access it by telephone but had to hire a graduate student who knew how to operate it.

Fast-forwarding to today, we obtained a database with over 12.5 million records on every U.S. bankruptcy case that was pending sometime during the government fiscal years 2012–2016. We added Census Bureau data to estimate demographic and other characteristics by matching debtor zip codes to those in the Census database. We analyzed these data and obtained our results within weeks of formulating our analysis plan. We did this all without having to raise money or leave our offices.[2] Our world of ready data availability and computers to analyze them compares to photocopier R2D2 about the same as the world of science-fiction R2D2 compares to the U.S. Space Shuttle program (a contemporary of photocopier R2D2).

We do not use the term "groundbreaking" lightly when describing the early CBP. Sullivan, Warren, and Westbrook changed the nature of the consumer bankruptcy field. They shattered myths such as the idea that debtors were marginalized workers rather than part

---

[2.] That said, we both believe in the value of researchers leaving their offices to interact with the systems they are studying and to generate their own data. Lawless is a coprincipal investigator on the current CBP, which gathers court-record data and surveys consumer bankruptcy filers on an ongoing basis. See, e.g., Pamela Foohey, Robert M. Lawless, Katherine Porter & Deborah Thorne, "No Money Down" Bankruptcy, 90 S. Cal. L. Rev. 1055, 1071 (2017) (analyzing data from the 2007 and 2013–2015 CBP). Littwin has collected qualitative and quantitative data for analysis in recent years. See, e.g., Angela Littwin, Adapting to BAPCPA, 90 Am. Bankr. L.J. 183, 189 (2016) (reporting data from fifty-three interviews with consumer bankruptcy attorneys); Angela Littwin with Adrienne Adams & McKenzie Javorka, The Frequency, Nature, and Effects of Coerced Debt Among a National Sample of Women Seeking Help for Intimate Partner Violence, Violence Against Women (forthcoming 2020). We are both nonetheless glad that we did not have to carry a copy machine up three flights of stairs.

of the middle class.[3] They developed the dominant framework of why consumers file for bankruptcy, as reported by the debtors themselves: job loss, medical problems, and divorce.[4] They were the first research team to discover that fewer than half of chapter 13 cases receive a discharge.[5] Most importantly, Sullivan, Warren, and Westbrook created the norm of empirical research in the field, making it unacceptable to write about consumer bankruptcy without engaging in real-world analysis.

One key contribution of Sullivan, Warren, and Westbrook was putting "local legal culture" on the scholarly map. Along with Professor Jean Braucher, who was writing contemporaneously,[6] the CBP researchers realized that debtors experienced a theoretically federal and theoretically uniform consumer bankruptcy law very differently based on where they lived.[7]

In some areas of the country, such as Alaska, Connecticut, and Indiana,[8] the overwhelming majority of debtors were filing under chapter 7 of the Bankruptcy Code[9]—the quicker and cheaper consumer chapter that provides the majority of bankruptcy debtors the relief they need. Under chapter 7, debtors liquidate all of their

---

[3.] Teresa A. Sullivan, Elizabeth Warren & Jay Lawrence Westbrook, The Fragile Middle Class: Americans in Debt 238–52 (2000).

[4.] *Id.* at 73–74.

[5.] Teresa A. Sullivan, Elizabeth Warren & Jay Lawrence Westbrook, As We Forgive Our Debtors: Bankruptcy and Consumer Credit in America 17, 217 (1989) (reporting that only one-third of chapter 13 debtors in their database completed their bankruptcy plans).

[6.] Jean Braucher, Lawyers and Consumer Bankruptcy: One Code, Many Cultures, 67 Am. Bankr. L.J. 501, 503 (1993).

[7.] Teresa A. Sullivan, Elizabeth Warren & Jay Lawrence Westbrook, The Persistence of Local Legal Culture: Twenty Years of Evidence from the Federal Bankruptcy Courts, 17 Harv. J.L. & Pub. Pol'y 801, 810–11 (1994). The Bankruptcy Code also incorporates some elements of state law, most notably state exemption law. 11 U.S.C. § 522(b) (2012). But the researchers found a wide variety of practices within states, which suggested that state law could not be driving regional differences. Sullivan et al., supra note 7, at 828–29; Braucher, supra note 6, at 515–16.

[8.] Sullivan et al., supra note 7, at 825 tbl.3.

[9.] 11 U.S.C. § 701–27 (2012).

nonexempt property and receive a discharge of most unsecured debts.[10] The liquidation requirement has little bite because very few chapter 7 filers have unencumbered, nonexempt assets that a bankruptcy trustee can sell to pay creditors.[11] Most chapter 7 debtors receive their discharge within a few months.[12]

In other areas of the country, such as Alabama and the Western District of Tennessee, most debtors were filing under chapter 13,[13] which requires debtors to pay all of their disposable income over a period of three to five years.[14] Chapter 13 does provide tools for some consumers trying to save their homes[15] and a broader discharge than chapter 7 (although Congress has narrowed this discharge since the time of the original CBP research).[16] Still, the differences in chapter 7 and chapter 13 were highly improbable sources for the huge variation in chapter choice bankruptcy scholars observed around the country.

Although the Bankruptcy Code leaves the decision of which chapter to use mostly in the debtor's hands,[17] the scholars argued that

---

[10] *Id.* section 523, 727.

[11] Dalié Jiménez, The Distribution of Assets in Consumer chapter 7 Bankruptcy Cases, 83 Am. Bankr. L.J. 795, 797 (2009); Lois R. Lopica, Am. Bankr. Inst. Nat'l Conference of Bankr. Judges, The Consumer Bankruptcy Creditor Distribution Study 6, 44–45 (2013).

[12] Dov Cohen & Robert M. Lawless, Less Forgiven: Race and chapter 13 Bankruptcy, in BROKE: How Debt Bankrupts the Middle Class 175, 175 (Katherine Porter ed., 2012); Katherine Porter, The Pretend Solution: An Empirical Study of Bankruptcy Outcomes, 90 Texas L. Rev. 103, 116 (2011).

[13] Sullivan et al., supra note 7, at 825–26 tbl.3. Consumers may also file under chapter 11, but only a tiny percentage of consumer debtors use this option. See Admin. Office of the U.S. Courts, Caseload Statistics Data Tables, www.uscourts.gov/statistics-reports/ caseload-statistics-data-tables [https://perma.cc/4AN2-2LMN] (showing statistically that a minimal number of nonbusiness filings fall under chapter 11 while the majority fall under chapter 7 and chapter 13).

[14] 11 U.S.C. § 1325(b)(4) (2012).

[15] *Id.* section 1322(b)(5), (c).

[16] *Id.* section 1328(a)(2) (incorporating some but not all of the nondischargeability provisions in section 523(a)).

[17] In 2005, Congress added the means test to prevent high-income debtors from filing under chapter 7. Bankruptcy Abuse Prevention and Consumer Protection Act of 2005, Pub. L. No. 109-8, section 102(h), 119 Stat. 23, 33–34 (2005). The change appears to have had little effect on the ratio of chapter 7 to chapter 13 filings.

the results of this choice and other choices[18] were, in fact, driven by local legal culture. As Professor Westbrook explained:

> The evidence strongly suggests that the "choices" given to debtors are often exercised in fact by creditors, lawyers, by judges through lawyers, and by judges through debtors. The average consumer debtor, faced with an extraordinarily complex statute at a moment of financial and personal crisis, will be guided by lawyers and pressures exerted through lawyers.[19]

Sullivan, Warren, and Westbrook identified local legal culture as "systematic and persistent variations in local legal practices" that arose because of "perceptions and expectations shared by many practitioners and officials in a particular locality."[20] Persistence over time was a key feature of their conceptualization, and their foundational article on the topic examined local culture features that persisted across 1970, 1980, and 1990.[21] Braucher similarly defined local legal culture as the "context created by" a locality's "administrative practices of judges and trustees, and prevailing professional attitudes,"[22] although she did not emphasize persistence. The CBP researchers and Braucher each used qualitative data to develop portraits of the

---

Chrystin Ondersma, Are Debtors Rational Actors? An Experiment, 13 Lewis & Clark L. Rev. 279, 295–303 (2009).

[18.] Bankruptcy chapter is not the only debtor choice guided by local legal culture. Sullivan, Warren, and Westbrook also studied filing rates and proposed payments to creditors in chapter 13 plans. Sullivan et al., supra note 7, at 811. Braucher additionally studied repayment rates in chapter 13 cases. Braucher, supra note 6, at 530–34. We focus on chapter choice in this chapter for two reasons. First, once a debtor decides to file for bankruptcy, the choice of chapter influences—and frequently determines the outcome of—the other choices in the case. Second, most of the recent research on local legal culture has focused on chapter choice because of the disturbing racial trends associated with that decision. See infra subpart II(B).

[19.] Jay Lawrence Westbrook, Local Legal Culture and the Fear of Abuse, 6 Am. Bankr. Inst. L. Rev. 25, 30 (1998).

[20.] Sullivan et al., supra note 7, at 804.

[21.] See generally Sullivan et al., supra note 7.

[22.] Braucher, supra note 6, at 503.

complex interactions among judges, trustees, and debtor attorneys that shaped local legal culture.[23]

Authors working with the databases from the CBP since that time have produced findings on local legal culture, but the focus has shifted to race. Specifically, beginning with the 1991 CBP, researchers documented a disturbing trend. Black debtors, and sometimes Latino debtors, were overrepresented in chapter 13, the chapter that takes more time,[24] costs more money,[25] and has a significantly lower discharge rate.[26] These patterns remained even when controlling for income, homeownership, and a variety of other factors associated with chapter 13.[27] Research from the 2007 CBP additionally controlled for judicial district and found that the correlations between chapter 13 and black debtors remained significant.[28] An article based on the 2007 and 2013–2015 CBPs found that judicial districts with high chapter 13 rates significantly correlated with the overrepresentation of black debtors in chapter 13—and that the effect of judicial district became more pronounced once researchers controlled for debtor financial variables associated with chapter 13.[29]

The current study adds to this recent work with new methods. Using a public database collected by the Administrative Office of the U.S. Courts (AO), we analyzed chapter choice in consumer bankruptcies filed from fiscal years 2012–2016.[30] We developed three sets of factors expected to influence chapter choice in a consumer bankruptcy case: (1) case characteristics, particularly features of the debtor's economic situation that make chapter 7 or chapter 13 more

---

[23.] See infra subpart II(A).

[24.] See supra Part I.

[25.] Lois R. Lupica, The Consumer Bankruptcy Fee Study: Final Report, 20 Am. Bankr. Inst. L. Rev. 17, 58 fig.4, 69 fig.7 (2012).

[26.] Sullivan et al., supra note 5, at 222; Sara S. Greene, Parina Patel & Katherine Porter, Cracking the Code: An Empirical Analysis of Consumer Bankruptcy Outcomes, 101 Minn. L. Rev. 1031, 1042 (2017).

[27.] See infra Part II.

[28.] Cohen & Lawless, supra note 12, at 185.

[29.] Foohey et al., supra note 2, at 1088.

[30.] See infra subpart III(A).

appropriate; (2) a debtor's geographic community based on demographics of her zip code; and (3) judicial district. We analyzed both geographic community and legal district to shed light on an ambiguity in the scholarship of local legal culture—what does "local" mean? Is it the debtor's neighborhood or the debtor's legal neighborhood that counts?

Our results support and extend the prior research. Race, once again, matters. More specifically, race, case characteristics, and judicial district are the only variables that matter. We find that case characteristics are significantly associated with each bankruptcy chapter in the expected ways. For example, real property correlates with chapter 13, almost certainly because of the tools chapter 13 provides for saving debtors' homes.[31] Unsecured debt correlates with chapter 7, which provides a more effective mechanism for discharging it.[32] At the community level, the most interesting point is what we do not find. Although most of the community variables we tested are statistically significant when the regression includes only case and community variables, once we add judicial district to the regression, the only variable that retains its statistical significance is race, specifically the percentage of the debtor's zip code that is black. The disappearance of significance for most of the community variables once we add district fixed effects suggests that the "work" of local legal culture is being done at the legal level rather than at the community level. Finally, most judicial districts in the United States are statistically significant at a very high level. The pattern we find among judicial district chapter 13 rates both confirms and complicates the conventional wisdom of chapter 13 as a southern phenomenon.

This chapter makes several contributions. First, we use observational data on the universe of bankruptcy filers. All of the recent CBPs are surveys of a national random sample, which means that participation in them is voluntary. Thus, researchers using the CBP

[31.] See 11 U.S.C. § 1322(b)(5) (2012) (providing an option to cure a mortgage in default).

[32.] Foohey et al., supra note 2, at 1093 tbl.5.

data could never rule out nonresponse bias, the possibility that study participants somehow differed from debtors who chose not to participate.[33] Second, although the prior research, especially that of the early CBP and Braucher, leaves little doubt that local legal culture exists, the phrase contains ambiguities. This study considers competing definitions of "local" and thus provides quantitative evidence suggesting that legal boundaries may be more relevant than geographic ones. Third, our finding that race is the only community-level variable that retains significance when we add judicial districts to the regression provokes more questions than it addresses. This unsettling result, combined with the importance of judicial districts, suggests directions for future research. Legal professionals and their attitudes need further examination. A return to the qualitative methods of Braucher and the early CBP may be a particularly fruitful line of inquiry.

The rest of this chapter proceeds as follows. Part II is a literature review. Part III provides our methodology, results, and interpretation of findings. Part IV concludes with more directions for future research.

II. Literature Review

A. What Is Local Legal Culture? Definitions and Origins in the Literature

The first study to probe local legal culture, although it did not use the term, was Stanley and Girth's seminal Brookings Institution study. They found wide variation in chapter XIII rates—the predecessor to chapter 13—among the seven districts they studied.[34] Chapter XIII cases ranged from 76% of all filings in the Northern District of

---

[33] Jean Braucher, Dov Cohen & Robert M. Lawless, Race, Attorney Influence, and Bankruptcy chapter Choice, 9 J. Empirical Legal Stud. 393, 423–24 (2012).

[34] David T. Stanley & Marjorie Girth, Bankruptcy: Problem, Process, Reform 74–75 (Brookings Inst. ed., 1971).

Alabama to 52% in Maine to 11% or fewer in four districts.[35] Their "unit of locality" was district, but they did not study any districts within the same state,[36] limiting their ability to identify judicial district or state as the level of locality for the effect.

Sullivan, Warren, and Westbrook began to fill this gap by examining the variation between judicial districts within the same state, using survey and court-record data from ten judicial districts studied in the CBP. They argued that because bankruptcy is federal law and incorporates some state law, variations between districts within a state that persist over time must be due to local culture.[37] Their examination of chapter choice found tremendous variation between states as well as judicial districts within states. For example, 20% of the filings in the Southern District of Alabama were chapter 13 cases compared to 66% in the Middle District of Alabama.[38] Moreover, the authors found statistically significant persistence in the district rates over time.[39]

Sullivan, Warren, and Westbrook argued that the complex and numerous decisions that went into a bankruptcy case made the consumer bankruptcy system particularly susceptible to the development of local legal cultures.[40] They also argued that influential individuals in a legal community changed over time and thus were an unlikely source for their findings about patterns that had held up over twenty years.[41]

Braucher studied four bankruptcy divisions[42] from two pairs of cities that shared a federal judicial district.[43] The two pairs of cities

---

[35] *Id.* at 74.

[36] See *id.* at 41–42 (studying districts of Northern Ohio, Northern Alabama, Maine, Northern Illinois, Oregon, Western Texas, Southern California, and Southern New York).

[37] Sullivan et al., supra note 7, at 812.

[38] *Id.* at 828.

[39] *Id.* at 829–30 (basing this finding on data from the Administrative Office of the U.S. Courts covering 1970, 1980, and 1990).

[40] *Id.* at 836–39.

[41] *Id.* at 839.

[42] A division is a subunit within a judicial district. See, e.g., 28 U.S.C. § 124 (2000) (dividing the Northern District of Texas into seven divisions).

[43] Braucher, supra note 6, at 515.

were in two parts of the country—Ohio and Texas—that had distinct chapter 13 rates.[44] Braucher demonstrated the existence of local legal culture through in-depth qualitative interviews with legal professionals.[45] She showed how judges and especially trustees shaped local legal culture by imposing requirements not in the Bankruptcy Code and incentivizing attorneys to use chapter 7 or chapter 13.[46] She also analyzed the complex interactions among the incentives of attorneys and their clients that led to the use of one bankruptcy chapter or another.[47]

Taken together, the Sullivan, Warren, and Westbrook and Braucher studies left little doubt that many local legal cultures existed in the bankruptcy system. Using different research methods, two sets of scholars had come to the same fundamental conclusions about the existence and nature of the local legal cultures. The idea was on the scholarly map, and many scholars both replicated and expanded their findings.

Using data from the AO, Whitford showed wide variation in chapter 13 rates among judicial districts in 1990, 1992, and 1993.[48] Whitford later updated these findings using 1993, 2002, 2009, and 2010 data, suggesting that the percentage of chapter 13 cases in each district had remained relatively consistent across these four years.[49] Bermant, Flynn, and Bakewell drilled down to divisions as the unit of locality. They used 2001 AO data to demonstrate that state chapter 13 rates masked variations among districts and that district

---

[44] *Id.*

[45] *Id.* at 512–13.

[46] See, e.g., *id.* at 546–47 (finding that, while consumer attorneys earned higher fees for chapter 13 cases than chapter 7s in all four divisions, the divisions with higher chapter 13 rates featured larger differences in the amount by which the attorney fees for a chapter 13 exceeded those for a chapter 7 case).

[47] *Id.* at 562–63.

[48] William C. Whitford, The Ideal of Individualized Justice: Consumer Bankruptcy as Consumer Protection, and Consumer Protection in Consumer Bankruptcy, 68 Am. Bankr. L.J. 397, 411–14 (1994).

[49] William C. Whitford, Small Ball, 90 Texas L. Rev. See Also 9 app. A (2011).

chapter 13 rates masked variation among divisions.[50] Norberg and Schreiber Compo found widespread disparities in chapter 13 rates among seven judicial districts in the South and mid-Atlantic regions and that the high chapter 13 districts tended to have fewer chapter 13 debtors with mortgages than the other districts, suggesting that debtors without mortgages were filing under chapter 13 in the former districts due to local legal culture.[51] Ondersma replicated Sullivan, Warren, and Westbrook's analysis of the persistence of local legal culture with an expanded data set that included data on exemption laws, poverty and unemployment rates, and foreclosure rates, none of which could explain the variation of chapter 13 choice across localities.[52]

B. Race and Ethnicity

The concept of "local legal culture" was at the same time both path-breaking and incomplete. As one of this chapter's authors put it:

> "Local" is a problem because it is generally taken to mean areas defined by political boundaries . . . rather than boundaries that are psychologically meaningful to people. "Legal" is a problem because the cultural values we discuss may be a product of broad community sentiment, rather than ones unique to the local legal community. "Culture" is a problem because . . . we have no measures of the attitudes, values, and beliefs of professionals in the legal system. On the other hand, the advantage of the present definition is that it fits with a common conception of the term that many people have—local legal culture is what the people in a local legal community "do"; it is their practices that define them.[53]

---

[50] Gordon Bermant, Ed Flynn & Karen Bakewell, Bankruptcy by the Numbers: Thoughts on the "Local Legal Culture," Am. Bankr. Inst. J., Feb. 2002, at 24, 24.

[51] Scott F. Norberg & Nadja Schreiber Compo, Report on an Empirical Study of District Variations, and the Roles of Judges, Trustees and Debtors' Attorneys in chapter 13 Bankruptcy Cases, 81 Am. Bankr. L.J. 431, 436–37 (2007).

[52] Ondersma, supra note 17, at 303–05.

[53] Cohen & Lawless, supra note 12, at 180.

Thus, scholars needed to and did start to unpack the constituent parts of what made for a "culture" that was both "local" and "legal." The most widely known of these efforts have focused on racial and ethnic differences in who files chapter 13. In her original study, Braucher noted that Ohio standing trustees were concerned that black debtors were overrepresented in chapter 13, with one stating that black debtors were possibly "being taken advantage of."[54]

The earliest efforts appeared either as byproducts of research with other goals or based on nonrandom samples that limited statistical inference. In a paper about the rise of filings after the 1978 implementation of the Bankruptcy Code, White found that the percentage of African-American debtors in a county's population was associated with a statistically significant increase in the proportion of chapter 13 cases.[55] Interestingly, she found no statistically significant relationship between African-Americans and chapter 7 filings, but the proportion of Spanish-speaking debtors in a county was significantly negatively associated with chapter 7 filings.[56]

Using data from the 1991 CBP, Chapman found that although African-Americans appeared to be overrepresented in consumer bankruptcy, they were not overrepresented in chapter 7, which implied that they were overrepresented in chapter 13.[57] Specifically, his data analysis found that non-Hispanic whites were statistically significantly more likely to file under chapter 7 than other racial and ethnic groups.[58] Chapman found that this effect was uniform in all but one of the studied districts that yielded data appropriate for his analysis.[59] Van Loo used data from the 2001 CBP to find 61.8% of black debtors used chapter 13 compared to 29.4% of Hispanic and 20.5% of

---

[54] Braucher, supra note 6, at 559–60.

[55] Michelle J. White, Personal Bankruptcy under the 1978 Bankruptcy Code: An Economic Analysis, 63 Ind. L.J. 1, 48 (1987).

[56] Id. at 47.

[57] Robert B. Chapman, Missing Persons: Social Science and Accounting for Race, Gender, Class, and Marriage in Bankruptcy, 76 Am. Bankr. L.J. 347, 387 n.226 (2002).

[58] Id.

[59] Id.

white debtors.[60] After controlling for the influence of income, education, and employment, he found that only 19.8% of blacks and 19.4% of Hispanics in chapter 13 obtained a discharge compared to 28.3% of non-Hispanic whites.[61] Van Loo attributed the lower discharge rates to more aggressive uses of motions to dismiss in the chapter 13s of black debtors as compared to debtors of other races.[62] Although doing more extensive data analysis than the previous articles, the Chapman and Van Loo studies relied on earlier iterations of the CBP that were not national random samples, limiting the statistical inferences that could be drawn.

Using CBP data from 2007 that was collected from a national random sample, Braucher, Cohen, and Lawless found that blacks were disproportionately likely to file under chapter 13.[63] This effect held even when controlling for twenty variables that theoretically should determine a filing under chapter 13 including homeownership, pending foreclosure, legal representation, monthly income, asset levels, total debt, priority debt, the percentage of debt that was secured or credit card debt, and demographic variables such as marital status and education. The study also developed a control variable that effectively isolated the effects of geography from those of race, and yet race was still a statistically significant determinant in chapter choice.[64] Even after controlling for the variables that should determine chapter choice, blacks were roughly twice as likely to file chapter 13 as debtors of other races. The authors also found that blacks did not receive more favorable treatment in chapter 13 and were indeed slightly more likely to have their cases dismissed. In articles

---

[60.] Rory Van Loo, A Tale of Two Debtors: Bankruptcy Disparities by Race, 72 Alb. L. Rev. 231, 234 (2009).

[61.] Id.

[62.] Id. at 237. He was not able to analyze Hispanic debtors because the sample of those receiving a discharge was too small. He limited this analysis to discharged debtors because almost all of the debtors with dismissed cases were subject to motions to dismiss. Id. at n.28.

[63.] Braucher et al., supra note 33, at 400–04.

[64.] Id. at 403; see also Cohen & Lawless, supra note 12, at 186–87 (reporting an earlier version of the study).

for a symposium discussing this paper, Doherty[65] and Eisenberg[66] reanalyzed the authors' data and confirmed their findings.

The same Braucher, Cohen, and Lawless paper also included an experimental vignette that asked consumer bankruptcy attorneys to select a bankruptcy chapter for a hypothetical couple with a mix of financial characteristics that could suggest chapter 7 or chapter 13.[67] The only variations were the race of the couple (white, black, no race identified) and the couple's expressed chapter preference (chapter 7, chapter 13, no preference).[68] Attorneys who thought they were counseling a black couple were about twice as likely to recommend chapter 13 as attorneys who thought they were counseling a white couple.[69] Attorneys were less likely to say that a black couple who wanted chapter 7 were persons of "good values" or were "competent" but had directly the opposite reaction to a white couple who wanted chapter 7.[70]

Greene, Patel, and Porter found that the debtor's race had a major impact on chapter 13 plan completion.[71] Using data from the 2007 CBP, they found black debtors were 17% less likely to receive a discharge than their non-black counterparts when controlling for all the other statistically significant variables in the study.[72] The authors concluded: "More than amount of debt, prior bankruptcies, trying

---

[65.] Joseph W. Doherty, One Client, Different Races: Estimating Racial Disparity in chapter Choice Using Matched Pairs of Debtors, 20 Am. Bankr. Inst. L. Rev. 651, 678 (2012).

[66.] Theodore Eisenberg, The CBP Race Study: A Pathbreaking Civil Justice Study and Its Sensitivity to Debtor Income, Prior Bankruptcy, and Foreclosure, 20 Am. Bankr. Inst. L. Rev. 683, 700 (2012).

[67.] Braucher et al., supra note 33, at 405.

[68.] Id. at 406–07.

[69.] Id. at 411–12.

[70.] Id. at 413–15.

[71.] Greene et al., supra note 26, at 1086. Race appeared to be the second most important factor. Slightly edging out race, the variable with the largest impact (a 19% difference) was amount of unsecured debt. Id. The greater the amount of non-priority unsecured debt, the more likely the debtor was to receive a discharge. Id. at 1051. The authors argue that debtors with high levels of unsecured debt have increased incentives to complete their plans. Id. at 1089.

[72.] Id. at 1060, 1086.

to save a home from foreclosure, or having a job—all features that are imbedded in chapter 13 of the Bankruptcy Code—race matters."[73]

Using a sample from Cook County, Illinois, Morrison, and Uettwiller found many of the same racial pathologies that other researchers have documented.[74] But they provided a new possible explanation for the high chapter 13 rates and poor chapter 13 outcomes among black debtors—parking tickets and related government fines, which are dischargeable in chapter 13 but not chapter 7.[75] Blacks were overrepresented among bankrupt debtors with more than $500 in fines, the group of filers that had the highest termination rates. Within this group, blacks and debtors of other races had similar chances of having their cases terminated.[76] Moreover, when the authors excluded the "fines" group from the population of bankruptcy filers, blacks remained disproportionately represented but at smaller rates.[77] Morrison and Uettwiller suggest that government fines may be driving the chapter 13 racial disparities in Cook County because African-Americans appear to be particularly vulnerable to receiving these fines, and debtors within the "fines" group have low incomes that make it challenging to complete chapter 13 plans.[78]

Foohey, Lawless, Porter, and Thorne have found blacks disproportionately represented among so-called "no money down" chapter 13s, where the entire attorney's fee is funded through the chapter 13 plan. Indeed, the largest determinants of a no-money-down chapter 13 are the judicial district where the case is filed and the race of the debtor. Using data from the 2007 and 2013–2015 CBPs, they found that the

---

[73] *Id.* at 1086.

[74] Edward R. Morrison & Antoine Uettwiller, Consumer Bankruptcy Pathologies, 173 J. Institutional & Theoretical Econ. 174, 176 (2017).

[75] See 11 U.S.C. § 523(a)(7) (2012) (prohibiting discharge of government fines); *id.* section 1328(a)(2) (incorporating several nondischargeability provisions from section 523(a) into the chapter 13 discharge but excluding section 523(a)(7)). In addition, bankruptcy's automatic stay prevents creditor collection activity while a debtor is in bankruptcy and lasts for the duration of a chapter 13 case. *Id.* section 362(a), 1301.

[76] Morrison & Uettwiller, supra note 74, at 187 fig.1.

[77] *Id.* at 185 tbl.4, 186.

[78] *Id.* at 194.

financial characteristics of debtors filing no-money-down chapter 13 cases resembled those of chapter 7 debtors more than those of debtors filing "traditional chapter 13s."[79] They tied these findings to local legal culture by demonstrating that, when controlling for other relevant factors, the higher the chapter 13 rate in a district, the higher the use of no-money-down plans and the higher the racial difference in chapter use.[80] In fact, much of the racial disparity in chapter use in high chapter 13 districts may be accounted for by no-money-down cases.

In an article for *ProPublica*, Kiel and Fresques used AO data supplemented by demographic data via zip codes to find that nationally the odds of filing under chapter 13 were twice as high for debtors living in a mostly black area.[81] Compared to black debtors who filed under chapter 7, the black chapter 13 debtors had less income, fewer assets, lower secured debts, and dramatically lower unsecured debts.[82] The authors did an in-depth study on two districts with especially troubling disparities—the Northern District of Illinois and the Western District of Tennessee.[83] In both districts, Kiel and Fresques found that a handful of law firms accounted for a significant number of all chapter 13 filings, and, at least in Tennessee, the practice "nearly always" was to file with no money down. Like Morrison and Uettwiller, Kiel and Fresques found many black debtors were filing under chapter 13 to avoid suspension of their driver's licenses.[84]

Most recently, Cohen, Lawless, and Shin replicated the 2007 CBP findings about racial disparities in chapter use with 2013–2015 data from the current CBP.[85] Further, the authors surveyed a national

---

[79] 9. Foohey et al., supra note 2, at 1077–80.

[80] *Id.* at 1089 fig.4. It is important to note that, even in low-chapter 13 districts, African-Americans are approximately 10% less likely to file chapter 7 as debtors of other races in the presence of controls. *Id.*

[81] Paul Kiel & Hannah Fresques, Data Analysis: Bankruptcy and Race in America, ProPublica (Sept. 27, 2017), https://projects.propublica.org/graphics/bankruptcy-data-analysis [https://perma.cc/KK6C-K75X].

[82] *Id.*

[83] *Id.*

[84] *Id.*

[85] Dov Cohen, Robert M. Lawless & Faith Shin, Opposite of Correct: Inverted Insider Perceptions of Race and Bankruptcy, 91 Am. Bankr. L.J. 623, 630–32 (2017).

random sample of consumer bankruptcy attorneys and found that their beliefs about the percentage of African-Americans and whites who filed under chapter 13 was exactly reversed from the real-world percentages.[86] On average, attorneys believed that whites were more than twice as likely to file under chapter 13 as African-Americans when in fact the opposite is true.[87]

III. Data and Analysis

A. Methodology

Our theory conceptualizes the chapter choice decision as being the result of three different dynamics: (1) the individual debtor's circumstances; (2) the community from where the debtor comes; and (3) the legal norms and rules of the debtor's judicial district. The first idea captures traditional explanations for chapter choice, such as the idea that homeowners will be more likely to file chapter 13 because it offers greater protections to homeowners than chapter 7. Because these determinants are individual to the debtor, they would not represent a "local culture." The second idea is that certain communities may offer financially distressed debtors fewer options or constrain debtors' bankruptcy choices. Given the previous findings, the racial composition of a community may be a particularly important factor. The third idea is that the legal professionals—lawyers, trustees, and judges—implement formal rules or have informal norms that direct bankruptcy debtors to a particular chapter choice.

Our data came from the Integrated Database assembled by the AO and made available through the Federal Judicial Center.[88] Specifically, we used the "Bankruptcy Snapshot 5-year File" for the

---

[86.] *Id.* at 638. The authors surveyed these attorneys before publishing the results of their original work on race and chapter 13 in Less Forgiven: Race and chapter 13 Bankruptcy. Cohen & Lawless, supra note 12, at 175.

[87.] Cohen et al., supra note 85, at 638.

[88.] Integrated Database, Fed. Judicial Ctr., www.fjc.gov/research/idb [https://perma.cc/ZSF6-PR4S].

governmental fiscal years 2012–2016.[89] This file contains all bankruptcy cases filed, pending, or terminated at any point from October 1, 2011, to September 30, 2017; although, we only used cases filed on January 1, 2012, and after. The database contains (1) much of the information found in the bankruptcy petition—such as chapter choice, legal representation, method of paying filing fees, debtor's zip code, and case status (pending/dismissed)—and (2) the information found in the summary of schedules on asset, debt, income, and expense levels.[90]

It is possible for a case to appear more than once in the database if it is pending for more than one year. The full database contains 12,502,973 records of 6,675,597 unique bankruptcy cases. Because we are interested in the filing decision for chapter 7 and chapter 13, we used the case record from the year of filing. We further eliminated (1) cases filed outside the fifty states and the District of Columbia; (2) records representing a reopened case; (3) cases where the debtor's bankruptcy petition identified the debts as predominately business in nature; (4) cases filed by nonindividuals; and (5) cases filed by persons who were not U.S. residents. Our final database had 4,343,794 unique bankruptcy cases filed from fiscal year 2012–2016.

We then downloaded zip-code-level data using the U.S. Census Bureau's American FactFinder website.[91] The American Community Survey (ACS)[92] provided data on population by race, Hispanic/Latino origin, owner- versus renter-occupied housing units, and income. We used ACS five-year estimates for the years 2012–2016, exactly overlapping with our bankruptcy data.

---

[89] IDB Bankruptcy 2008–Present, Fed. Judicial Ctr., www.fjc.gov/research/idb/interactive/IDB-bankruptcy [https://perma.cc/88VF-VV4W].

[90] *Id.*

[91] American FactFinder, U.S. Census Bureau, https://factfinder.census.gov [https://perma.cc/6VAN-WRLW].

[92] American Community Survey, U.S. Census Bureau, www.census.gov/programs-surveys/acs/ [https://perma.cc/WEV6-9D4D].

The U.S. Census Bureau's County Business Patterns[93] series provided zip-code-level data on consumer-lending storefronts as a measure of constrained financial advice and lending within a community. We used the 2014 data from this series because that year is the midpoint of our bankruptcy database. Consistent with Bhutta,[94] we downloaded the count of establishments identified in two North American Industry Classification System (NAICS) codes:[95]

- 522390 Other Activities Related to Credit Intermediation: This code provides information on services such as "Check cashing services, Money order issuance services, Loan servicing, Travelers' check issuance services, Money transmission services, Payday lending services."
- 522291 Consumer Lending: This code provides information on "establishments primarily engaged in making unsecured cash loans to consumers. *Illustrative Examples:* Finance companies (i.e., unsecured cash loans), Personal credit institutions (i.e., unsecured cash loans), Loan companies (i.e., consumer, personal, student, small), Student loan companies."

For a shorthand reference, we call the sum of these counts "fringe lending," although the term is overinclusive. We used the zip-code-level population counts from the ACS to construct a measure of fringe lending storefronts per 1,000 residents in the zip code.

We merged the zip-code-level data from the U.S. Census with the bankruptcy database using the zip code for the first debtor listed in the bankruptcy petition. This method has two complications. First, the ACS uses zip-code tabulation areas (ZCTAs),

---

[93] County Business Patterns, U.S. Census Bureau, www.census.gov/programs-surveys/cbp.html [https://perma.cc/G5KQ-XEUD].

[94] Neil Bhutta, Payday Loans and Consumer Financial Health, J. Banking & Fin., Oct. 2014, at 230, 235.

[95] Office of Mgmt. & Budget, Exec. Office of the President, North American Industry Classification System (2017), www.census.gov/eos/www/naics/ [https://perma.cc/99S2-W2NQ].

which in most instances are identical to the corresponding zip code, but ZCTAs can sometimes diverge from exact contiguity with a zip code depending on where census tract boundaries fall. Second, in 2.9% of the joint cases, the second debtor listed a zip code different from the first debtor. As a robustness check, we reran our regressions omitting these cases, and the results did not change.

B. Results

To test our theories, we constructed a series of regressions on the determinants of the bankruptcy chapter choice between chapter 7 and chapter 13. Because the outcome is a binary variable, we ran a logistic regression, and for ease of interpretation we report odds ratios. The odds ratio can be interpreted as the effect of the variable on the probability of filing chapter 13. Table 8.1 reports the regression results with an expanded table of the odds ratios for the fixed effects of each judicial district appearing in the appendix.

The first regression captures case characteristics. The second regression adds zip-code-level data as our measure of the debtor's community. The final regression then adds fixed effects for each judicial district. Our measures are not perfectly mutually exclusive. For example, the racial composition of a neighborhood tells us something both about the probability of the debtor's race and perhaps the socioeconomic status of the neighborhood.

Finally, we created a map (Figure 8.1) grouping the judicial districts into six clusters based on the final regression. The map reports the odds ratio and thus can be interpreted as the probability of observing a chapter 13 filing in each district as compared to the median district, the Middle District of Florida, after controlling for the variables in the regression. The map provides a visual overview of the wide variation in chapter 13 use across the country and within many states as well as the regional clustering of many of the high chapter 13 districts.

Table 8.1 Logistic Regression on Probability of Filing chapter 13.
Odds Ratios

	(1)	(2)	(3)
Case Characteristics			
Real Property (ln)	1.02*	1.03*	1.03*
Personal Property (ln)	1.01	1.03	1.05*
Secured Debts (ln)	1.10*	1.09*	1.08*
Priority Debts (ln)	1.11*	1.11*	1.10*
Unsecured Debts (ln)	0.58*	0.59*	0.60*
Income (ln)			
Filing Fee (Reference Category: Installments Completed)	1.72*	1.78*	1.88*
Installments in Progress	2.05*	1.95*	1.76*
Full at Filing	0.47*	0,53*	0.55*
Fee Not Paid	0.31	0.33	0.31
Waived (IFP)	0.002*	0,002*	0.002*
Prior Bankruptcy	5.20*	4.81*	4.68*
Joint Filing	0.87*	0.95	0.95
Pro Se Filer			
Filing Year (Reference Category: 2012)	0.21*	0,26*	0.37*
2013	1.03*	1.02	1.01
2014	1.13*	1.10*	1.10*
2015	1.22*	1.18*	1.18*
2016	1.24*	1.20*	1.21*
Zip Code Characteristics			
Black Percent in Zip Code		5.00*	3.06*
Latino Percent in Zip Code		1.01	1.09
Mean Income ($ 1,000s)		0.99*	1.00
Mean Income Squared ($ 1,000s)		1.00*	1,00
"Fringe Lending" (per 1,000)		2.29*	1.05
Renter-occupied Property Percent		0.40*	0.96
Judicial District Fixed Effects			Yes

NOTES: The table reports odds ratios for the probability of filing a chapter 13 out of a database composed of all chapter 7 and chapter 13 cases filed from FY 2012 to 2016. Standard errors are clustered at the judicial district level in all three regressions. For the case characteristic and zip-code characteristic variables, an asterisk indicates statistical significance where $p < .05$. Full results for the district fixed effects are presented in the Appendix.

IV. Discussion

The most striking finding is that, at the zip-code level, the only variable that matters consistently is the zip code's racial composition. At the case level, the characteristics that one would expect to drive chapter 13 filings are in fact associated with chapter 13 cases. Chapter 13 is more likely with higher amounts of real property, secured debts, priority debts, unsecured debts, and income, as well as paying the filing fee in installments, prior bankruptcy, and retaining an attorney. Higher amounts of real property, secured debt, and priority debt are likely to make chapter 13 attractive to debtors because that chapter provides tools for managing real estate and those debts.[96] A higher income increases a debtor's ability to propose and complete a feasible chapter 13 plan.[97] Chapter 13 is associated with debtors paying legal fees in installments,[98] so the chapter's correlation with debtors paying filing fees in installments is not surprising. Prior bankruptcy is strongly associated with chapter 13, partly because debtors face longer waiting periods after an earlier discharge to file again under chapter 7 than under chapter 13.[99] In addition, chapter 13 debtors

---

[96.] See 11 U.S.C. § 1322(a)(2) (2012) (stating that, unless the creditor consents, all priority debts must be paid in full, although without interest); *id.* section 1322(b)(5) (providing an option to cure mortgage in default).

[97.] Although the requirement that debtors pay all of their disposable income in chapter 13 would appear to lessen the relevance of income level to plan success, a debtor's income also must be high enough to pay the required thresholds of secured and priority debt. *Id.* section 1325(b); see *id.* section 506(a)(2) (valuing collateral on secured debts); *id.* section 1322(a)(2) (requiring full payment of priority debts, although without interest); *id.* section 1322(b)(2) (prohibiting modification of mortgages on primary residences); *id.* section 1325(a)(5) (prohibiting modification of many secured debts in personal property). In addition, some districts require a certain percentage payment to the general unsecured creditors beyond the disposable income requirement. Morrison & Uettwiller, supra note 74, at 189.

[98.] Foohey et al., supra note 2, at 1074.

[99.] Compare 11 U.S.C. § 727(a)(8) (2012) (listing an eight-year waiting period if prior discharge was in a chapter 7 case), and *id.* section 727(a)(9) (prescribing a six-year waiting period if prior discharge was in a chapter 12 or chapter 13 case), with *id.* section 1328(f) (requiring a two-year waiting period if prior discharge was in a chapter 13 case and a four-year waiting period if discharge was obtained via any other bankruptcy chapter).

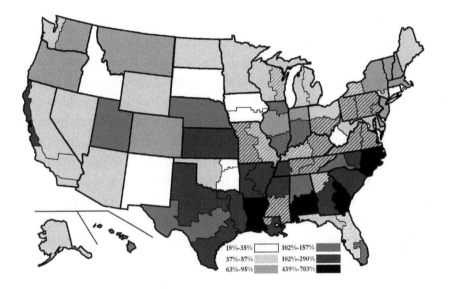

18%-35%		102%-157%	
37%-57%		182%-290%	
63%-95%		439%-703%	

who drop out prior to discharge because they cannot afford the payments often try again later.[100] Finally, given the greater complexity of chapter 13 and the dismal track record of pro se filers in confirming chapter 13 plans,[101] it makes sense that being represented is positively associated with filing chapter 13.

But once we move to the zip-code level, the logical connection between chapter 13 and factors associated with it becomes more complex. We tested zip-code income, Latino percentage of the zip code, black percentage of the zip code, fringe lending, and percentage of zip-code housing that is rental units. The fringe-lending variable examines the effects of living in lower-quality neighborhoods. Because we used racial percentages in zip codes as a proxy for race, we needed to consider the possibility that black neighborhoods

---

[100.] Sara Sternberg Greene, The Failed Reform: Congressional Crackdown on Repeat chapter 13 Bankruptcy Filers, 89 Am. Bankr. L.J. 241, 252 (2015).

[101.] See Angela Littwin, The Do-It-Yourself Mirage: Complexity in the Bankruptcy System, in BROKE: How Debt Bankrupts the Middle Class 157, 160 tbl.9 (Katherine Porter ed., 2012) (finding that represented debtors were approximately 45 times more likely to confirm chapter 13 plans than their pro se counterparts when controlling for demographic and bankruptcy variables).

were associated with chapter 13 rather than black debtors. African-Americans tend to live in poorer-quality neighborhoods due to decades of housing discrimination during and after the Jim Crow Era.[102] Zip-code percentage of housing that is rented was another proxy for neighborhood quality, but this variable's inclusion also reflects our thinking that homeowners are more likely to file under chapter 13. At the zip-code level, both of these variables were significant. Fringe lending was positively associated with chapter 13. When interpreting that result, it is important to note that most zip codes have zero or one fringe lender per thousand residents, with more than half of zip codes having no fringe lenders. So the odds ratio of 2.21 means that the difference between having zero and one fringe lender per thousand people in a zip code is a 221% increase in the likelihood of a debtor in that zip code filing under chapter 13. Percentage of property in a zip code that was renter-occupied is negatively correlated with chapter 13, supporting the classic association of chapter 13 with homeowners. Income was negatively correlated with chapter 13, which is surprising because it was positively correlated with chapter 13 at the case level. Reconciling the findings suggests that, all else equal, an increase in an individual debtor's income is an indicator of chapter 13, while a decrease in zip-code income is an indicator of chapter 13. The latter result supports Kiel and Fresques' counterintuitive finding that, in high chapter 13 districts, lower incomes were associated with chapter 13.[103]

The only variable that was not significant at the zip-code level was Latino percentage. On the one hand, this result is surprising. Like African-Americans, Latinos experience lending discrimination,[104] so we might expect them to be steered into chapter 13 the

---

[102.] Mehrsa Baradaran, The Color of Money: Black Banks and the Racial Wealth Gap 141–42 (2017).

[103.] Kiel & Fresques, supra note 81.

[104.] Ethan Cohen-Cole, Credit Card Redlining, 93 Rev. Econ. & Stat. 700, 700 (2011); Simon Firestone, Race, Ethnicity, and Credit Card Marketing, 46 J. Money, Credit & Banking 1205, 1206 (2014).

way that black debtors appear to be.[105] And the analyses of data from early CBPs identified Latino as well as black disparities in chapter use[106] and case outcomes.[107] In addition, Puerto Rico has a long-standing history as a high chapter 13 district,[108] which may result from some of the same implicit racial associations found with respect to blacks in the attorney-vignette study.[109] On the other hand, neither of the two most recent CBP studies found a Latino effect,[110] and this study's lack of Latino findings supports those results.

More interesting than the significance of income, fringe lending, and rental housing at the zip-code level is the fact that none of these variables retain their significance once we control for judicial district by adding fixed effects in the third regression. Our database contained the universe of over 4.3 million bankruptcy filings in the study period. Although we are cautious to interpret from a null result, we believe our finding suggests that the geographic pattern of chapter use is being determined by legal boundaries rather than neighborhood boundaries.

The one variable that remains significant even when controlling for district fixed effects is the black percentage in a zip code. It is positively correlated with the chapter 13 rate, and the effect is strong. The difference between a debtor living in a zip code that is 0% black and 100% black is a 306% increase in likelihood of that debtor filing under chapter 13.[111] Of course, we cannot rule out the possibility that debtors of other races living in predominantly black zip codes also have high odds of filing under chapter 13. There could be unobserved characteristics of black neighborhoods that are associated with chapter 13. Our attempts to control for neighborhood quality

---

[105] Braucher et al., supra note 33, at 417–18.

[106] Chapman, supra note 57, at 387 n.226.

[107] Van Loo, supra note 60, at 234.

[108] Bermant et al., supra note 50, at 24; Whitford, supra note 48, at 406–07.

[109] Braucher et al., supra note 33, at 415–16.

[110] Id. at 400; Foohey et al., supra note 2, at 1081.

[111] We also ran the same regressions with a binary variable for whether the zip code was majority black. We get a similar result: a 170% increase in the probability of filing under chapter 13 for persons living in majority-black districts.

provide some evidence that neighborhoods are not the issue but cannot fully address this concern.

Prior studies also give us more confidence that our racial finding is hardly spurious. The 1991, 2001, 2007, and current iterations of the CBP all found racial disparities in chapter use,[112] and this study provides important support for these findings. However, all of these CBPs were surveys and are thus subject to the critique of nonresponse bias.[113] A major contribution of this study is to provide support for the racial disparities found by the CBP using data that did not require voluntary participation by respondents.

While the most important characteristic of the results of adding the district fixed effects is the effect that the addition has on other variables, the distribution of chapter 13 filings among judicial districts also sheds light on the relationship between chapter 13 and the South. The South has been viewed as the chapter 13 belt since at least 2002.[114] As Figure 8.1 shows, our results support this finding in interesting ways. First, the South appears to be committed to chapter 13. With the exception of Kansas, all of the states that have a majority of districts in the top two chapter 13 clusters were part of the Confederacy during the U.S. Civil War.[115] Conversely, Florida is the only former Confederate state that does not have a majority of districts with greater-than-median chapter 13 filing rates, although several Southern districts have chapter 13 rates that are not significantly different from that of the reference, median district, the Middle District of Florida. On the other hand, there are several high chapter 13 districts in other parts of the country, such as the Northern District of California, the District of Kansas, and the District of Utah. However, most

---

[112] Braucher et al., supra note 33, at 404; Chapman, supra note 57, at 389; Foohey et al., supra note 2, at 1086; Van Loo, supra note 60, at 234.

[113] Braucher et al., supra note 33, at 423–24.

[114] See Bermant et al., supra note 50, at 24 (noting an "intensive chapter 13 practice runs in a broad band across the South and includes Puerto Rico").

[115] Alabama, Arkansas, Florida, Georgia, Louisiana, Mississippi, North Carolina, South Carolina, Tennessee, Texas, and Virginia. See, e.g., G. Edward White, Recovering the Legal History of the Confederacy, 68 Wash. & Lee L. Rev. 467, 482, 495 (2011).

of the non-Southern states with high chapter 13 rates have districts that fall in the third-highest cluster, meaning that their chapter 13 percentages are 102% to 157% greater than the reference district. And none of these states have any districts in the highest cluster, with chapter 13 rates that are 439% to 703% greater than those in the Middle District of Florida.

This map also sheds interesting light on Sullivan, Warren, and Westbrook's original findings. The 1981 CBP covered three states: Illinois, Pennsylvania, and Texas.[116] Illinois and Pennsylvania have turned out to be two of the non-Southern states that contain above-median chapter 13 districts. This may have made it more difficult to notice the concentration of the chapter 13 belt in the South until relatively recently.

V. Conclusion

Our research builds on and extends prior studies. We confirmed CBP findings on race and chapter choice with a non-survey database. Specifically, we found that race and judicial district appear to be the key factors in chapter choice beyond the economic profile of a bankruptcy case. We began to address the question of whether the "local" in "local legal culture" is shaped by legal geography or general geography. Our findings suggest that legal boundaries are playing a more important role.

This study also points to directions for future research. We obtained one finding on the meaning of "local" in "local legal culture." Additional research would make the relationship between "local" and "legal" clearer. For example, it could examine places where zip codes span more than one judicial district to see if the changes in chapter 13 rate are occurring at the zip-code or district boundaries. Already, our finding on the meaning of "local" suggests the need to explore the roles of professionals more deeply. One possibility is to

---

[116.] Sullivan et al., supra note 7, at 834 n.105.

examine law-firm patterns in districts with varying chapter 13 rates. Kiel and Fresques's study of Tennessee suggests that law-firm concentration may be playing a role in the relationship between race and chapter 13.[117] Finally, this study points in the direction of returning to the methods of Sullivan, Warren, and Westbrook and Braucher's original scholarship on local legal culture by supplementing big data with in-depth qualitative research with judges, lawyers, trustees, and other bankruptcy actors.

[117.] Kiel & Fresques, supra note 81.

APPENDIX

Table 8A.1 Judicial District Level Fixed Effects from Logistic Regression (Reference District = Middle District of Florida, Median District)

DC Circuit	Odds Ratio	Sixth Circuit (continued)	Odds Ratio
District of Columbia	0.21*	Michigan, Eastern	0.53*
First Circuit		Michigan, Western	0.49*
Maine	0.48*	Ohio, Northern	0.45*
Massachusetts	0.63*	Ohio, Southern	1.02
New Hampshire	0.69*	Tennessee, Eastern	1.40
Rhode Island	0.35*	Tennessee, Middle	1.22
Second Circuit		Tennessee, Western	2.87*
Connecticut	0.24*	*Seventh Circuit*	
New York, Eastern	0.18*	Illinois, Central	0.63*
New York, Northern	0.63*	Illinois, Northern	1.35*
New York, Southern	0.52*	Illinois, Southern	1.32*
New York, Western	0.91	Indiana, Northern	0.83*
Vermont	0.68*	Indiana, Southern	1.21*
Third Circuit		Wisconsin, Eastern	0.92
Delaware	0.75*	Wisconsin, Western	0.47*
New Jersey	0.70*	*Eighth Circuit*	
Pennsylvania, Eastern	1.13	Arkansas, Eastern	2.01*
Pennsylvania, Middle	1.10	Arkansas, Western	1.84*

(Continued)

261

Table 8A.1 (continued)

DC Circuit	Odds Ratio	Sixth Circuit (continued)	Odds Ratio
Pennsylvania, Western	1.13	Iowa, Northern	0.21*
Fourth Circuit		Iowa, Southern	0.33*
Maryland	0.37*	Minnesota	0.53*
North Carolina, Eastern	4.39*	Missouri, Eastern	0.83
North Carolina, Middle	2.36*	Missouri, Western	1.05
North Carolina, Western	1.41*	Nebraska	1.35*
South Carolina	2.38*	North Dakota	0.44*
Virginia, Eastern	1.17	South Dakota	0.32*
Virginia, Western	1.04	*Ninth Circuit*	
West Virginia, Northern	0.42*	Alaska	0.53*
West Virginia, Southern	0.32*	Arizona	0.46*
Fifth Circuit		California, Central	0.44*
Louisiana, Eastern	1.94*	California, Eastern	0.43*
Louisiana, Middle	1.16	California, Northern	2.01*
Louisiana, Western	7.01*	California, Southern	0.46*
Mississippi, Northern	2.07*	Hawaii	1.16*
Mississippi, Southern	1.23	Idaho	0.23*
Texas, Eastern	1.92*	Montana	0.67*
Texas, Northern	2.47*	Nevada	0.49*
Texas, Southern	2.44*	Oregon	0.70*
Texas, Western	1.57*	Washington, Eastern	0.81*
Sixth Circuit		Washington, Western	0.50*
Kentucky, Eastern	1.10	*Eleventh Circuit*	
Kentucky, Western	0.95	Alabama, Middle	5.86*
Tenth Circuit		Alabama, Northern	1.43*
Colorado	0.71*	Alabama, Southern	4.85*
Kansas	1.82*	Florida, Northern	0.44*
New Mexico	0.22*	Florida, Middle	*omitted*
Oklahoma, Eastern	0.25*	Florida, Southern	1.40*

(Continued)

Table 8A.1 (continued)

DC Circuit	Odds Ratio	Sixth Circuit (continued)	Odds Ratio
Oklahoma, Northern	0.30*	Georgia, Middle	2.90*
Oklahoma, Western	0.57*	Georgia, Northern	0.92
Utah	1.34*	Georgia, Southern	4.53*
Wyoming	0.42*		

NOTES: Odds ratios are reported for each judicial district's fixed effect on the probability of filing chapter 13. as compared to the median district, the Middle District of Florida. Standard errors are clustered at the judicial district level in the regressions. The table is an expansion of Regression (3) from Table 8.1. For the district fixed effects, an asterisk indicates statistical significant where $p < .0006$, using a Bonferroni adjustment from the standard statistical significance threshold of $p < .05$ for the 90 districts.

Bankruptcy's Lorelei

The Dangerous Allure of Financial Institution Bankruptcy

*Adam J. Levitin**

T he idea of a bankruptcy procedure for large, systemically important financial institutions exercises an irresistible draw for some
policymakers and academics. Financial institution bankruptcy (FIB)
promises to be a transparent, law-based process in which resolution
of failed financial institutions is navigated in the courts. FIB presents itself as the antithesis of an arbitrary and discretionary bailout
regime. It promises to eliminate the moral hazard of too big to fail
by ensuring that creditors will incur losses, rather than being bailed
out. FIB holds out the possibility of market discipline instead of an
extensive bureaucratic regulatory system.

* Agnes N. Williams Research Professor of Law, Georgetown University Law
Center. This chapter draws on congressional testimony I gave in July 2015 before
the House Financial Services Committee regarding the CHOICE Act, which
would amend the Bankruptcy Code to include a financial institutions bankruptcy
subchapter. The chapter has also benefitted from comments from Don Bernstein,
Anna Gelpern, Edward Janger, Richard Levin, and the participants at the 2018 Jay
Westbrook Symposium. Thank you to Julia Dimitriadis and David Frey for research
assistance and to the North Carolina Law Review Association for republication permission. Copyright © Adam J. Levitin. This work was originally published in 97:2 N.
Carolina L. Rev. 243–92 (2019). Reproduced with permission.

This chapter argues that FIB is a dangerous siren song that lures with false promises. Instead of instilling market discipline and avoiding the favoritism of bailouts, FIB would likely simply result in bailouts in bankruptcy garb. It would encourage bank deregulation without the elimination of moral hazard that produces financial crises. In particular, it would undermine the federal regulators' single most powerful tool for managing systemic risk, the living wills power, even while imposing a resolution process that is doomed to failure.

A successful bankruptcy is not possible for a large financial institution absent massive financing for operations while in bankruptcy, and that financing can only reliably be obtained on short notice and in distressed credit markets from one source: the U.S. government. Government financing of a bankruptcy would inevitably come with strings attached, including favorable treatment for certain creditor groups. This would result in bankruptcies that resemble those of Chrysler and GM, which are much decried by proponents of FIB as having been disguised bailouts.

The central flaw with the idea of FIB is that it fails to address the political nature of systemic risk. What makes a financial crisis systemically important is whether its social costs are politically acceptable. When they are not, bailouts will occur in some form because crisis containment inevitably trumps rule of law. Resolution of systemic risk is a political question, and its weight would warp the judicial process. FIB will merely produce bailouts in the guise of bankruptcy while undermining judicial legitimacy and the rule of law.

I. Introduction

"Financial institution bankruptcy" (FIB) is the Lorelei of the restructuring world.[1] The idea of FIB calls out in a golden voice, singing

---

[1] Heinrich Heine, Die Lorelei (1824) (poem naming the siren who, from her perch atop a mountain overlooking the River Rhine, draws the gazes of sailors upwards and away from the treacherous rocks in their course).

"I am Law, I am Law. I brook no favoritism or cronyism, I permit no bailout. My rules are neutral, predictable, and generally applicable. I answer not to the whim of unaccountable bureaucrats, but am Law." With this siren song of false promises, the tempting concept of FIB—the use of federal bankruptcy courts as a forum for resolving large, failed financial institutions—lures unwitting policymakers to the rocky shoals of a financial crisis, for FIB is not workable as a restructuring system. Ultimately, the real work a FIB procedure would do would be to undermine the "living wills" process that gives federal regulators substantial discretion to impose additional regulatory requirements on or even break up the largest banks. FIB thus threatens to weaken financial regulation while providing an unworkable process for dealing with the consequences, a formula that all but guarantees bailouts.

The lure of the FIB Lorelei comes not from her inherent beauty, but from her apparent comparative attractiveness relative to the alternative method of dealing with the failure of large financial institutions—bailouts. Nobody likes a bailout. Bailouts are messy by nature. They do not follow rules or law. Instead, they are ad hoc, improvised, and unpredictable responses to crises that are readily open to abuse. Bailouts are messy mainly because they have a singular goal to which all other concerns, including rule of law, are temporarily subordinated—containing financial crises so they do not wreak broader havoc on the economy. Implicit in bailouts is the idea that the rule of law is a means to social welfare, not an end in itself. In a bailout, if rule of law impedes social welfare, the law will be stretched, changed, ignored, or jettisoned, at least temporarily.[2]

Revulsion toward bailouts is not just a function of their lawlessness. It is also because bailouts create opportunities for government favoritism, as some have alleged regarding the GM and Chrysler

---

[2] Anna Gelpern, Financial Crisis Containment, 41 Conn. L. Rev. 1051, 1057 (2009) ("[C]ontainment may call for measures ... that are legally and politically fraught."); Adam J. Levitin, The Politics of Financial Regulation and the Regulation of Financial Politics: A Review Essay, 127 Harv. L. Rev. 1991, 2017 (2014) (book review).

bankruptcies.[3] By deciding whom to bail out and on what terms, the government is not just picking winners and losers in the economy but also potentially enriching particular parties at taxpayer expense.[4] Given that bailouts are often undertaken through independent regulatory agencies that are not directly answerable at the ballot box, this cronyism is all the more distressing because there is not even an ex post disciplinary mechanism.

Moreover, to the extent creditors of large financial institutions believe ex ante they will be bailed out if a large financial institution fails, they will be more reckless in their lending to large financial institutions and extend too much underpriced credit.[5] The expectation of bailouts not only creates a moral hazard for lenders, but it also incentivizes financial institutions to grow to be too big to fail—that is, to grow to a size and importance where their creditors are likely to be bailed out if they fail because the social costs and

---

[3] See, e.g., Todd J. Zywicki, Economic Uncertainty, the Courts, and the Rule of Law, 35 Harv. J.L. & Pub. Pol'y 195, 200 (2012) ("When politicians are not constrained they take advantage of that freedom of opportunity to benefit themselves. The General Motors and Chrysler bailouts might be the most obvious and egregious examples of this dynamic from the financial crisis."); Paul Roderick Gregory, American Airlines Shows the Corruption of Obama's GM Bailout, Forbes (Feb. 6, 2012, 2:16 PM), www.forbes.com/sites/paulroderickgregory/2012/02/06/american-airlines-shows-the-corruption-of-obamas-gm-bailout/#48a8730d5eb8 [https://perma.cc/MTD3-UCP7] (arguing that the Obama Administration's bailout of GM was the result of political favoritism toward the United Auto Workers labor union).

[4] See Zywicki, supra note 3, at 200 ("With Chrysler, the government intervened to take money from the company's creditors—which included the pension funds for teachers and policemen—and give it to the retirement and health care funds of the politically powerful United Auto Workers, who had an unsecured claim in the case.").

[5] See, e.g., Financial Institution Bankruptcy Act of 2017: Hearing on H.R. 1667 Before the Subcomm. on Regulatory Reform, Commercial and Antitrust Law of the H. Comm. on the Judiciary, 115th Cong. 9 (2017) (statement of John B. Taylor) (arguing that the expectation of bailouts reduces creditor incentive to monitor loans). The concern about creditors expecting bailouts sits in tension with another frequent criticism of bailouts—namely, their unpredictability. See, e.g., David A. Skeel Jr., Single Point of Entry and the Bankruptcy Alternative, in Across the Great Divide: New Perspectives on the Financial Crisis 311, 320 (Martin Neil Baily & John B. Taylor eds., 2014) (noting the problem of unpredictability for bailouts).

disruption from not doing so would be politically unacceptable.[6] The result of anticipated bailouts is a downward spiral of reckless lending and bailouts.

FIB is conceived of as a totally private regime, but such a totally private resolution system for large financial institutions is an ideological pipe dream that has become an unhealthy distraction in financial regulatory policy debates. This chapter argues that the idea of FIB functioning without extensive government involvement is a pernicious market fantasy, a siren song that is not workable. FIB poses a number of insurmountable practical obstacles and irreconcilable policy goals, most notably the inability of a large failed financial institution to obtain the "debtor-in-possession" (DIP) financing required to preserve the value of its assets during bankruptcy. Attempting to resolve a large systemically important financial institution's (SIFI's) failure through a FIB process without DIP lending would result in a value-destroying disaster that would exacerbate the spillover effects from the institution's failure. Thus, while FIB holds out the promise of being an alternative to bailouts, any viable FIB process would inevitably be little more than a bailout masquerading as a bankruptcy. Nonetheless, all FIB legislation to date has all been for wholly private FIB processes.

The first of these obstacles is that failed financial institutions would require enormous liquidity support while in bankruptcy— tens if not hundreds of billions of dollars. To be sure, it is possible to construct a bankruptcy based on a high-speed sale process. But a curtailment of the failed firm's time in bankruptcy prior to an expedited sale is no solution to the liquidity problem. Instead, it merely shifts the liquidity problem to the asset purchaser, which lacks the protection of the automatic stay because it is not a debtor subject to bankruptcy court jurisdiction. If the purchaser is insufficiently liquid, it will be subject to a creditor run, in which case the FIB process will have accomplished nothing in terms of financial stability.

[6.] Adam J. Levitin, In Defense of Bailouts, 99 Geo. L.J. 435, 439–40 (2011) [hereinafter Levitin, In Defense of Bailouts].

The enormous level of liquidity support required to ensure a smooth FIB process would have to be obtained on extremely short notice in distressed financial markets. Realistically, it could come from one source and one source only: the U.S. government. As DIP lender (or as the lender to the asset purchaser in the event of a high-speed sale), the U.S. government would get to call the shots in the bankruptcy—that is what DIP lenders do. For example, DIP lenders routinely dictate detailed timelines for asset sales with bidding procedures to their liking and impose corporate officers of their choosing on debtors.[7] The U.S. government as DIP lender would be able to dictate which assets would be transferred to and which liabilities would be assumed by the solvent purchaser and therefore effectively paid in full. In other words, the executive branch of the U.S. government would be determining the effective distributional consequences of the bankruptcy, which would not necessarily be in accord with formal statutory distributional requirements.

This scenario is exactly what occurred in the Chrysler and GM bankruptcies. In both cases, the U.S. government, as DIP lender, required fast asset sales that complied with the terms on which it insisted,[8] and the assets were sold to entities partially owned by the U.S. government. Moreover, in both cases, the asset sales were conditioned upon the buyer assuming certain favored liabilities of the debtor, particularly obligations owed to the firms' unionized employees and retirees who would have received nothing in a liquidation. Ironically, proponents of FIB have been among the leading critics of those bankruptcies, but Chrysler and GM are the template for what can be expected with a FIB process. FIB will result in precisely what its proponents despise—a bailout that rewards some favored creditors (here, the unionized employees)—albeit in the form of bankruptcy.

---

[7] Adam J. Levitin, Business Bankruptcy: Financial Restructuring and Modern Commercial Markets 376, 408–09 (2nd ed. 2018) [hereinafter Levitin, Business Bankruptcy].

[8] See, e.g., Douglas G. Baird, Lessons from the Automobile Reorganizations, 4 J. Legal Analysis 271, 288–89 (2012).

Because of financial institutions' massive liquidity needs, the only way FIB could realistically function is with government involvement. Such government involvement would warp the bankruptcy process to produce results that are indistinguishable from bailouts. And it would do so with the added harm of being done under color of law, thereby undermining the very rule of law virtue that makes bankruptcy attractive in the first place.

None of this may matter to some FIB proponents, however. For some FIB supporters, the ultimate goal may be bank deregulation. Generally, the existence of a FIB process would facilitate the argument that private market discipline can substitute for public regulation. The operational problems with FIB would not become manifest until a large financial institution fails. In the interim, however, the availability of a FIB process would serve as a cudgel to push for bank deregulation based on claims of adequate market discipline through bankruptcy.

More specifically, however, FIB legislation undermines the single most powerful tool regulators have for policing systemic risk: the "living wills" provisions of the Dodd-Frank Wall Street Reform and Consumer Protection Act.[9] The living wills power requires the largest financial institutions to present plans for their resolution in bankruptcy to federal regulators. If regulators do not deem a resolution plan credible, then regulators have substantial discretion to impose additional regulatory requirements on the financial institution or even to break it up.[10] But enacting a special FIB procedure would mean that Congress believes it possible for these large institutions to resolve themselves in bankruptcy, making it all but impossible for regulators not to deem credible these institutions' living wills.

Thus, FIB proposals would simultaneously tie regulators' hands in terms of preventing crises ex ante while imposing an unworkable process for managing crises ex post. This means FIB is ironically a

---

[9.] Dodd–Frank Wall Street Reform and Consumer Protection Act, Pub. L. No. III-203, section 165(a), (d), 124 Stat. 1423, 1423–24, 1426 (2010) (codified at 12 U.S.C. § 5365(a), (d) (2012)).

[10.] 12 U.S.C. § 5365(d)(5) (2012).

recipe for a bailout, for that will be the only response possible in the wake of a failed FIB.

FIB proponents also fail to grapple with the inappropriateness of the courts as a venue for dealing with systemic risk. The failure of a SIFI is materially different from that of most nonfinancial businesses. The failure of a nonfinancial business is a private matter between the business and its creditors. The spillover effects from such non-financial bankruptcies are likely to be more limited in most situations. While there can be domino effects up and down supply chains and across an industry due to single-sourced suppliers,[11] the failure of nonfinancial firms do not pose a threat to the credit market and payment system that are the lifeblood and arteries of the economy.

SIFIs are another matter. Their failure threatens disruption to the entire global financial system. It is, then, not simply a private matter but a matter of public policy concern, both because of its broad-ranging economic effects and its likelihood of triggering federal government involvement in the form of financial support. Put another way, the public is affected by the distribution in the bankruptcy of a SIFI, even though it is not a "creditor." Resolution of SIFIs is thus a political question because it implicates the public fisc and general distributional questions, not simply firm-specific ones.[12]

The courts, however, are a poor venue for resolving political problems—as the political question doctrine recognizes—because political pressures can corrupt the judicial process and generally undermine its legitimacy.[13] FIB would turn bankruptcy into a political process for which it is wholly unsuited.[14]

---

[11] Levitin, In Defense of Bailouts, supra note 6, at 453–61 (explaining how nonfinancial firms can pose systemic risk).

[12] Adam J. Levitin, Safe Banking: Finance and Democracy, 83 U. Chi. L. Rev. 357, 443 (2016).

[13] See *Baker v. Carr*, 369 U.S. 186, 267 (1962) (Frankfurter, J., dissenting); Alexander M. Bickel, The Least Dangerous Branch: The Supreme Court at the Bar of Politics 69 (2nd ed. 1986).

[14] Given the dysfunction of the formal legislative process in Congress, one might reasonably argue that the courts are a preferable forum for addressing political issues, insofar as they are a forum that will in fact address issues, even if the process is less than democratic.

Bankruptcy is a process suited for addressing the microconcerns of individual firms, not macropolicy concerns. It is not a transparent, participatory forum capable of giving effective voice to noncreditor constituencies who may nevertheless be significantly affected by the bankruptcy.[15] Furthermore, bankruptcy is not a democratic forum. Many key issues are decided solely by a non–Article III judge and are, as with many issues, effectively unreviewable on appeal.[16] To the extent there is a vote, it is a vote only of classes of impaired creditors and shareholders, not affected third parties.[17] If the government were involved in the process, it would participate by contract through a court order approving a non-appealable DIP financing agreement.[18] The terms of such an agreement are not subject to the normal procedural safeguards of Administrative Procedures Act rulemaking or to any constraints beyond some minimal requirements in the Bankruptcy Code.[19] Bankruptcy is thus a particularly nontransparent, nonparticipatory form of policymaking.[20]

[15.] See, e.g., In re Alpha Nat. Res. Inc., 544 B.R. 848, 856 (Bankr. E.D. Va. 2016) (denying standing to environmental groups to object to court approval of a settlement agreement between the debtor coal company and the state of West Virginia).

[16.] Some issues are effectively unreviewable because of statutory limitations on appellate remedies. See, e.g., 11 U.S.C. § 363(m) (2012) (prohibiting review of consummated sale orders on appeal); id. section 364(e) (prohibiting review of consummated financing orders on appeal). But see id. section 1144 (allowing revocation of confirmation orders if procured by fraud). Other issues become functionally moot because they are not appealable—absent leave of the bankruptcy court—until the issuance of a final order. Id. section 158(a). Additionally, most circuits recognize some form of the doctrine of equitable mootness, which limits the appellate review. See, e.g., In re Nica Holdings, Inc., 810 F.3d 781, 788–90 (11th Cir. 2015); In re Charter Commc'ns, Inc., 691 F.3d 476, 481–82 (2d Cir. 2012); In re Cont'l Airlines, 91 F.3d 553, 559 (3d Cir. 1996). Further, critical questions such as valuation are appealed on a clear error basis, which means that the bankruptcy court receives deference for its valuation determination. See Levitin, Business Bankruptcy, supra note 7, at 325.

[17.] 11 U.S.C. § 1126(a), (f) (2012) (providing the holders of claims and equity interests the right to vote on a bankruptcy plan, but conclusively deeming unimpaired classes of claims and interests to have voted to support the plan).

[18.] See id. section 364(a)–(e).

[19.] See id.

[20.] See Steven M. Davidoff & David Zaring, Regulation by Deal: The Government's Response to the Financial Crisis, 61 Admin. L. Rev. 463, 468 (2009).

This does not mean that the politics disappear from bankruptcy, only that they function differently outside the legislative process. The distributional concerns that are so intense when dealing with systemic financial crises mean that political pressures will inevitably corrupt the FIB process and turn FIB into nothing more than a bailout in judicial garb.

This chapter proceeds in five parts. Part I lays out the background against which FIB proposals have emerged: the inadequacy of chapter II for resolving SIFIs; discontent with the bailouts following the 2008 financial crisis; and unease with the post-2008 legislative response, the "Orderly Liquidation Authority" regime created by the Dodd-Frank Wall Street Reform and Consumer Protection Act. Part I also explains how FIB proposals would function to undermine the living wills process that provides the most potent tool in the arsenal of the existing financial regulatory regime. Part II explains the basic form that FIB would likely take before addressing the fundamental tension between trying to reduce both moral hazard and systemic disruption through bankruptcy. Part III then turns to a discussion of the practical obstacles to using bankruptcy to restructure financial institutions: lack of DIP financing; international coordination difficulties; problems concerning derivatives and other financial contracts; and the lack of a mechanism for addressing the valuation uncertainty that would chill the market for buyers of the failed institution's assets. The only way to overcome these obstacles is through federal government intervention in a bankruptcy, turning bankruptcy into a bailout. Part IV demonstrates how the resolution of SIFIs is a political question and therefore best avoided by the courts. Accordingly, the chapter concludes by suggesting that rather than follow FIB's siren song onto jagged rocks, we would do better to devote our energies to crafting a procedural mechanism for bailouts that imposes transparency, basic procedural checks, and ex post accountability on government and bailout recipients.

II. The Siren Song of Bankruptcy

The government's response to the 2008 financial crisis was varied, but can largely be characterized as an ad hoc series of bailouts of a wide range of financial institutions and markets. Some of these bailouts were marred by a sense of cronyism or deliberate action to protect favored financial institutions. Aversion to the capricious and cronyistic nature of the bailouts has prompted calls to revise the Bankruptcy Code to provide an effective mechanism for the resolution of large financial institutions in bankruptcy.

A. The Inadequacy of chapter 11 for Resolving Financial Institutions

Bankruptcy has always been available as a forum for resolving *certain* failed financial institutions, but only in the sense of a well-ordered liquidation. Restructuring such institutions, however, whether through a plan of reorganization or through a going-concern asset sale, is not currently practically possible in bankruptcy.

As a preliminary matter, some financial institutions are not eligible for bankruptcy in the first place. Banks and insurance companies cannot file for bankruptcy[21] and are instead resolved under the "Federal Deposit Insurance Corporation" (FDIC) bank receivership or applicable state insurance insolvency regime. These resolutions are facilitated by the availability of funding from the FDIC's Deposit Insurance Fund and state insurance insolvency funds.

In addition, banks and insurance companies are rarely stand-alone corporations. They are usually part of larger corporate conglomerates. In such conglomerates, while the bank or insurance company subsidiary is not eligible for bankruptcy, the holding company and other affiliates are able to file. Holding companies,

---

[21] 11 U.S.C. § 109(b)(2), (d) (2012).

however, typically liquidate in chapter 11 bankruptcy. Liquidation is often the only option since there is generally no business left to restructure after the subsidiary bank or insurance company has been taken into receivership in which it is either wound-down or sold. Likewise, securities and commodities broker-dealers are eligible for bankruptcy, but only for chapter 7 liquidation,[22] although this can be transformed into a liquidation run by the "Securities Investor Protection Corporation" (SIPC).[23] Reorganization in bankruptcy is not allowed for securities and commodities brokerages.

Thus, if a financial conglomerate were to fail, its various pieces would be resolved under several different regimes: chapter 11 for the holding company, chapter 7 and possibly SIPC liquidation for the broker-dealer subsidiary, FDIC receivership for the bank subsidiary, and a state insurance receivership for the insurance company receivership. (This assumes an entirely domestic firm; foreign subsidiaries would further complicate the picture.) The result of this piecemeal resolution regime is the loss of any synergies that exist within the conglomerate. In addition, depending on the details of the firms' structuring, there could be serious operational disruptions.[24]

In theory, then, one might attempt to resolve the firm in a single chapter 11 proceeding at the holding company level. If the holding company were to guarantee the obligations of its subsidiaries, then structural priority would subordinate the holding companies' creditors to those of its subsidiaries. With all losses concentrated on holding company creditors, there would be no need to put any subsidiaries into a receivership. The holding company could then attempt to use the chapter 11 process to arrange a going-concern sale of its various subsidiaries, which, if successful, would preserve any synergies within the affiliate constellation and also prevent any operations disruptions.

[22.] *Id.* section 109(d).

[23.] 15 U.S.C. § 78eee (2012).

[24.] For example, disruptions might result if there were centralized cash or IT management or intercompany licensing or leasing arrangements.

It is unlikely, however, that such a resolution could work under the existing chapter 11 bankruptcy process. Chapter 11 is inadequate for resolution of a financial conglomerate through a going concern sale of all of the operating subsidiaries because of the exception to the automatic stay for certain financial contracts. The filing of a bankruptcy petition triggers the "automatic stay," a federal injunction against most collection activities outside of the bankruptcy claims process.[25] The stay only applies to the actual debtor, not to its nondebtor affiliates, so it would not protect the subsidiaries in the event of the parent holding company's bankruptcy.

There are also numerous exceptions to the automatic stay, most notably a set of exceptions that allow the debtor's counterparties on various types of financial contracts—swaps, repos, forward contracts, securities contracts, commodities contracts, and master netting agreements—to accelerate, terminate, and liquidate these agreements and any collateral posted by the debtor to guarantee their performance.[26] Even in the best circumstances, a sale would not be instantaneous upon the bankruptcy filing. As a result, the debtor's counterparties could always accelerate and terminate their contracts and then liquidate any collateral the debtor posted, if they are in the money. Thus, the counterparties could deprive the debtor of critical assets that would be necessary to continue to operate as a going concern and thereby frustrate any sale. Instead, there would be a disorderly piecemeal liquidation of the debtor that might impair its operations and result in its subsidiaries being taken into receivership themselves.

To the extent that a financial firm is not systemically important, the disruptions caused by its failure and piecemeal resolution are no more concerning than any other market inefficiency. In this regard, chapter 11's shortcomings as a process for one-stop shopping for quotidian financial institution resolution are unfortunate, but not a critical policy concern. But for systemically important firms, avoidance

---

[25] 11 U.S.C. § 362(a) (2012).

[26] *Id.* section 362(b)(6), (7), (17), (27); *id.* section 555, 559–61.

of disruptions and spillover effects from the resolution process is of paramount importance as a financial regulatory policy matter.

B. Calls for a FIB Process

In light of the shortcomings of existing bankruptcy law as a method for resolving systemically important failed financial institutions, there has been considerable interest in revising the Bankruptcy Code to facilitate financial institution resolution, although to date bankruptcy law remains unchanged in this regard. The Dodd–Frank Wall Street Reform and Consumer Protection Act, the major legislative response to the 2008 crisis, called for a study of bankruptcy alternatives for resolving large financial institution failures.[27] The House of Representatives has since thrice passed a version of a "Financial Institutions Bankruptcy Act."[28] A FIB procedure has also appeared in both versions of the CHOICE Act,[29] the Republican Dodd-Frank Act alternative, the second iteration of which passed the House.[30] Another financial institutions bankruptcy bill has been repeatedly introduced in various versions in the Senate.[31] Likewise, various academics and the Hoover Institution have called for the creation of a "chapter 14" in the Bankruptcy Code for a FIB procedure.[32] These

---

[27] Dodd–Frank Wall Street Reform and Consumer Protection Act, Pub. L. No. 111–203, section 216, 124 Stat. 1376, 1519 (2010).

[28] Financial Institutions Bankruptcy Act of 2014, H.R. 5421, 113th Cong. (2014) (passed House); Financial Institutions Bankruptcy Act of 2016, H.R. 2947, 114th Cong. (2016) (passed House); Financial Institutions Bankruptcy Act of 2017, H.R. 1667, 115th Cong. (2017) (passed House).

[29] Financial CHOICE Act of 2016, H.R. 5983, 114th Cong. section 231–32 (2016); Financial CHOICE Act of 2017, H.R. 10, 115th Cong. section 121–23 (2017) (passed House).

[30] H.R. 10.

[31] Taxpayer Protection and Responsible Resolution Act, S.1841, 114th Cong.; Taxpayer Protection and Responsible Resolution Act, S. 1861, 113th Cong. A third version of the legislation was discussed at a Senate Judiciary Committee hearing in November 2018, but had not yet been formally introduced by the time this work went to press. Senate Judiciary Committee, Hearing, Big Bank Bankruptcy: 10 Years after Lehman Brothers, Nov. 13, 2018

[32] See, e.g., Skeel, supra note 5, at 329–33; Thomas H. Jackson, Bankruptcy Code chapter 14: A Proposal, in Bankruptcy Not Bailout 25, 26 (Kenneth E. Scott & John B. Taylor eds., 2012); Thomas H. Jackson, Resolving Financial Institution: A Proposed

proposals would cover all bank and financial holding companies, not just systemically important ones (however measured). But the policy impetus for these proposals is driven by concerns about large, systemically important institutions.

Bankruptcy, according to the logic behind FIB proposals, ensures the rule of law.[33] It is a transparent, judicially supervised process, with public court filings and hearings in open court. In bankruptcy, all transactions outside of the ordinary course of business require judicial approval,[34] and bankruptcy law gives all parties in interest a general right to be heard and to challenge proposed transactions in court.[35] Furthermore, any sort of FIB regime would draw on well-established rules from corporate bankruptcy.[36]

Bankruptcy, FIB backers argue, would prevent discretionary, cronyistic intervention by government and would allow for the restructuring of failed financial institutions without disruptions to the wider economy.[37] Any resolution of a failed financial institution

---

Bankruptcy Code Alternative, Banking Perspectives (2014), www.theclearinghouse. org/banking-perspectives/2014/2014-q1-banking-perspectives/articles/resolving-financial-institutions [https://perma.cc/4CCR-37SR] [hereinafter Jackson, Resolving Financial Institutions]; see generally Hoover Inst., Making Failure Feasible: How Bankruptcy Reform Can End "Too Big to Fail" (Kenneth E. Scott, Thomas H. Jackson & John B. Taylor eds., 2015) (proposing a version of chapter 14 that responds to criticisms of FIB).

[33.] See, e.g., Financial Institution Bankruptcy Act of 2015: Hearing on H.R. 2947 Before the Subcomm. on Regulatory Reform, Commercial and Antitrust Law, 114th Cong. 2 (opening remarks of Tom Marino, Chairman, Subcomm. on Regulatory Reform, Commercial and Antitrust Law) ("The bankruptcy process has long been favored as the primary mechanism for dealing with distressed and failing companies. This is due to its impartial nature, adherence to established precedent, judiciary oversight, and grounding in the principles of due process and the rule of law."); Jackson, Resolving Financial Institutions, supra note 32.

[34.] 11 U.S.C. §§ 363(c), 364(b)–(d), 365(a) (2012).

[35.] Id. section 1109(b).

[36.] See, e.g., Financial CHOICE Act of 2016, H.R. 5983, 114th Cong. section 231–32 (2016); Financial CHOICE Act of 2017, H.R. 10, 115th Cong. section 121–23 (2017) (passed House) (incorporating chapter 11 bankruptcy provisions for a FIB procedure).

[37.] See, e.g., Financial Institution Bankruptcy Act of 2017: Hearing on H.R. 1667 Before the Subcomm. on Regulatory Reform, Commercial and Antitrust Law of the H. Comm. on the Judiciary, 115th Cong. 3 (2017) (statement of John B. Taylor), https://judiciary.house.gov/wp-content/uploads/2017/03/Taylor-Testimony.pdf

would be determined efficiently by private ordering in the context of bankruptcy, not by government fiat.[38] At the same time, FIB proponents believe that bankruptcy would ensure that a failed financial institution's creditors would internalize their losses, and the credible threat of this loss internalization would incentivize creditors to demand that financial institutions assume less risk.[39]

C. The Orderly Liquidation Authority as a Response to the 2008 Bailouts

Despite these supposed virtues of bankruptcy, Congress has so far declined to pursue it as the venue for resolving systemically important failed financing institutions. Congress instead opted to leave in place the hodgepodge combination of chapter 7, chapter 11, SIPC liquidation, FDIC bank receivership, and state insurance receiverships as the venues for resolving the various pieces of non-SIFIs. For systemically important institutions, Congress instead adapted the FDIC bank receivership process into a broader financial conglomerate resolution procedure known as the title II "Orderly Liquidation Authority" (OLA).[40]

[https://perma.cc/7BJU-2NMW] ("The goal of these provisions is to let a failing financial firm go into bankruptcy in a predictable, rules-based manner without causing disruptive spillovers in the economy while permitting people to continue to use its financial services without running.").

[38] See, e.g., Jackson, Resolving Financial Institutions, supra note 32 ("In bankruptcy, it is market-discipline first and foremost; in Title II, there inevitably is a heavier layer of regulatory overlay and control."); John B. Taylor, It's Time to Pass the Financial Institutions Bankruptcy Act, Econ. One (Mar. 23, 2017), https://economicsone.com/2017/03/23/its-time-to-pass-the-financial-institutions-bankruptcy-act/ [http://perma.cc/N6PM-PGD9] (noting that, in contrast to government decision-making in an OLA resolution, "under bankruptcy reorganization, private parties, motivated and incentivized by profit and loss considerations, make key decisions about the direction of the new firm").

[39] See, e.g., Hearing on H.R. 1667, supra note 37, at 2 (statement of John B. Taylor) ("chapter 11 ensures that creditors bear losses and this reduces moral hazard and excessive risk-taking.").

[40] See 12 U.S.C. §§ 5381-94 (2012).

The OLA gives federal regulators broad powers to place failing "financial companies"—not just insured depositories—that pose systemic risk into a receivership administered by the FDIC. The OLA, which has not been used to date, has numerous statutory limitations upon it,[41] but it would also give federal regulators substantial discretion in whether to trigger the authority. Triggering the OLA would require the turning of "three keys" by various regulators: (1) the Treasury Secretary, in consultation with the President, must determine that the firm is in default or in danger of default, that its resolution outside of OLA would have "serious adverse effects on the financial stability of the United States," and the effect on creditors is "appropriate" given the threat to financial stability; (2) two-thirds of the Federal Reserve Board must approve the receivership; and (3) two-thirds of the FDIC Board (or two-thirds of the Securities and Exchange Commission for broker-dealers or the Director of the Federal Insurance Office for insurance companies) must approve the receivership.[42] The requirement of the three keys ensures that OLA would not be triggered without broad buy-in from both a politically accountable party and politically insulated independent agencies. In other words, OLA is designed to be a consensus-based procedure.

Once OLA is triggered, the FDIC would have substantial discretion in implementing a receivership.[43] For example, while the FDIC is directed to "ensure that unsecured creditors bear losses in accordance with" a statutory order of priority that is substantially similar to that of chapter 7 bankruptcy,[44] the FDIC is also authorized to sell some or all the assets of the failed financial institution.[45] Such a

---

[41.] See, e.g., *id.* section 5386 (imposing mandatory terms on all orderly liquidation actions, including a priority of distributions).

[42.] *Id.* section 5383(a)(1).

[43.] *Id.* section 5384, 5386, 5390.

[44.] *Id.* section 5386(3). The order of priority for creditor claims is set out in section 5390(b).

[45.] *Id.* section 5390(a)(1)(A) (giving FDIC as receiver all powers of failed financial institution); *id.* section 5390(a)(1)(G) (authorizing the transfer of any asset or liability or merger of the failed financial institution); *id.* section 5390(a)(9)(E) (providing directions for the disposition of assets of failed financial institutions); *id.* section

sale may be to a third-party buyer or to a "bridge" financial institution formed by the FDIC, the stock of which could then be sold to a third-party purchaser, thereby enabling a stock sale rather than an asset sale.[46]

An asset sale may be accompanied by an assumption of select liabilities as a form of consideration from the buyer.[47] Greater assumption of liabilities would reduce the purchase price paid in other forms of consideration. To illustrate, a purchaser might pay $50 billion in cash and stock for the assets of a failed financial institution, or it could pay only $40 billion in cash and stock and assume liabilities of $10 billion. A creditor whose obligation is assumed by a buyer or by the bridge financial institution will get paid in full by the buyer or bridge institution (unless it too fails) and no longer has a claim in the receivership. That creditor, therefore, would not be subject to the distributional priority limitation on the FDIC in the receivership.[48]

The only generally applicable material limitation on the FDIC's ability to transfer liabilities of the failed financial institution to a bridge company is that "similarly situated creditors"—an undefined phrase with several statutory exceptions—must be treated the same in most situations.[49] However one interprets the phrase "similarly

---

5390(h)(5) (authorizing a bridge company to acquire assets or assume liabilities of the failed financial institution).

[46.] *Id.* section 5390(a)(1)(F) (authorizing FDIC to create a "bridge company"); *id.* section 5390(h)(3)(A) (permitting a bridge financial company to assume or acquire assets and liabilities of failed financial institution); *id.* section 5390(h)(5)(A) (authorizing the FDIC as receiver to merge the failed financial institution with another company or "transfer any assets and liabilities" of the failed financial institutions). A stock sale is a simpler and cheaper transaction because the only asset that needs to be transferred is ownership of the stock. In contrast, an asset sale might require separate formal deed recordings and transfer taxes to be paid on individual assets, particularly in the case of real estate transfers.

[47.] *Id.* section 5390(h)(3)(A).

[48.] *Id.* section 5390(a)(1)(G) (authorizing a merger or transfer of any asset or liability of the failed financial institution); *id.* section 5390(b) (setting forth priority of claims).

[49.] *Id.* section 5390(b)(4) (requiring claims of similarly situated creditors to be treated similarly); *id.* section 5390(h)(5)(E) (requiring similarly situated creditors to be treated in a similar manner when assets or liabilities are transferred to a bridge company). Other limitations apply to particular types of asset transfers. See, e.g.,

situated creditors," no such limitation applies to assumption of liabilities in sales to third-party buyers.

The federal government is also authorized to provide financing to continue operating the failed financial institution in OLA.[50] This financing, which would ultimately be recouped from other large financial institutions, facilitates the entire resolution process and ensures that value is not lost because of illiquidity. Notably, OLA does not provide statutory restrictions on the terms of financing beyond a provision detailing the priority of the government's funding claim on the failed firm's assets.[51] This means that the government could set the terms of its financing simply as a matter of contract, not statute.

Indeed, given that the enormous situational leverage the government will have over a failed firm in an OLA proceeding, the government would get whatever terms it wants—the government's offer is one that the failed firm cannot refuse. As such, the terms of government financing in an OLA would likely be at least as onerous as DIP financing agreements in chapter 11 bankruptcy. Government-provided financing in OLA, therefore, would therefore come with various contractually negotiated provisions that both determine the shape of any restructuring and which could effectively benefit certain creditor constituencies at the expense of others.[52] Not surprisingly, the discretion vested in federal regulators has led to criticisms that the OLA is nothing more than a codified bailout regime.[53]

---

id. section 5390(c)(9) (requiring qualified financial contracts with a counterparty, if transferred at all, to be transferred as a complete book of business).

[50.] Id. section 5384(d) (authorizing funding for OLA); id. section 5390(b)(2) (providing priority for DIP financing); id. section 5390(n) (creating an "Orderly Liquidation Fund"); id. section 5390(o) (providing for assessments on financial institutions to fund an Orderly Liquidation Fund).

[51.] Id. section 5384(d).

[52.] Levitin, Business Bankruptcy, supra note 7, at 409–12.

[53.] See, e.g., Examining How the Dodd–Frank Act Could Result in More Taxpayer-Funded Bailouts: Hearing on H.R. 34 Before the H. Comm. on Fin. Servs., 113th Cong. 2 (2013) (opening remarks of Jeb Hensarling, Chairman, H. Comm. on Financial Services) ("Regrettably, Dodd–Frank not only fails to end too-big-to-fail and its attendant taxpayer bailouts; it actually codifies them into law. . . . Title II, Section 210, notwithstanding its ex post funding language, clearly creates a taxpayer-funded

D. FIB's Relationship to OLA and Living Wills

The relationship between FIB proposals and OLA varies depending on the version of legislation proposed. In some bills, FIB proponents have paired FIB legislation with a repeal of OLA and various prudential regulatory safeguards.[54] Other FIB bills would leave OLA intact. But even FIB bills that preserve OLA still effectuate a significant regulatory rollback, however, because the creation of a FIB procedure would allow banks to satisfy the Dodd-Frank Act's living wills requirement[55] and thereby allows financial institutions to avoid the imposition of additional, discretionary derisking regulation.

Indeed, the political attraction of FIB may be less in its inherent benefits as a resolution mechanism than in its collateral effect of undermining the case for ex ante prudential bank regulation. Advocates of FIB never explicitly tie FIB to bank deregulation, but the connection may be seen in the inclusion of a FIB proposal as part of the first title in the major House Republican-sponsored bank deregulation bill, which would have repealed OLA along with various prudential regulatory tools.[56] FIB may in fact be a deregulatory Trojan Horse.

Indeed, there has always been an important subtext to all FIB proposals, namely the claim that a proper bankruptcy system vitiates the need for prudential regulation of financial institutions. The thinking is that the threat of ex post losses for creditors in bankruptcy creates adequate ex ante incentives for them to lend prudently and thereby reduces risk within the financial system in general. In other words, FIB is ultimately premised on the conviction that market discipline can substitute for government regulation as a mode of reducing systemic risk.[57]

---

bailout system that the CBO estimates will cost taxpayers over $20 billion."); see also Evan Weinberger, Trump Orders Review of 2 Key Dodd–Frank Powers, Law360 (Apr. 21, 2017, 1:31 PM), www.law360.com/articles/915818/trump-orders-review-of-2-key-dodd-frank-powers [https://perma.cc/7DJS-2BP6 (staff-uploaded archive)].

[54] See, e.g., Financial CHOICE Act of 2017, H.R. 10, 115th Cong. section 111 (2017) (passed House) (repealing OLA); id. section 131–52 (repealing various prudential regulatory tools provided by the Dodd–Frank Wall Street Reform and Consumer Protection Act of 2011).

[55] 12 U.S.C. section 5365(d) (2012).

[56] See H.R. 10; id. section 131–52 (repealing various prudential regulatory tools provided by the Dodd–Frank Wall Street Reform and Consumer Protection Act of 2011).

[57] Ironically, this market discipline is imposed through government regulation in the form of bankruptcy law.

More recent FIB legislation has not included a repeal of OLA, and OLA includes a provision allowing the FDIC as OLA receiver to dismiss other insolvency proceedings.[58] This raises the question of what FIB accomplishes if it co-exists with OLA. It is hard to imagine regulators preferring the FIB process in which they have less control than OLA, not least because they will take the political blame for any problems that occur in either mode of resolution. If regulators have the choice, they would likely either trigger OLA at the outset or take over a FIB and convert it to OLA. The point-lessness of having OLA and FIB co-exist suggests that eschewing the repeal of OLA is a tactical move by FIB advocates. Enacting FIB will get the camel's nose under the tent, and those advocates can separately repeal OLA after passage because FIB would render it superfluous.

At the very least, however, the presence of a FIB procedure would undermine the Dodd-Frank Act requirement that the cer-tain very large financial institutions prepare living wills that must be approved by regulators. These living wills require financial institu-tions to demonstrate that the financial institution could be resolved in a case under title 11 (the Bankruptcy Code).[59] Failure to do so can result in more stringent capital, leverage, and liquidity requirements, restrictions on growth, activities, and operations, or even divestiture orders.[60]

The point of living wills is not to be actual resolution plans. As dis-cussed earlier, it is not credible to resolve a large financial institution under title 11, including in chapter 11 thereunder.[61] (Indeed, if it were possible, then there would be no need for FIB proposals.[62]) Instead, living wills are a tool that allows federal regulators discretion to force

---

[58.] 12 U.S.C. section 5388 (2012).

[59.] *Id.* section 5365(a), (d).

[60.] *Id.* section 5365(d)(5).

[61.] See supra Part I.B.

[62.] The persistence of FIB proposals should cast doubt on the findings of credi-bility of living wills by the Federal Reserve and FDIC. The fact that regulators have found living wills that would utilize chapter 11 credible, however, suggests that they are unlikely to suddenly find the backbone to insist that a special FIB process would not work for an institution that could not demonstrate the availability of commit-ted liquidity.

the very largest financial institutions to simplify their structures and operations or to impose greater regulatory requirements on these institutions. From the perspective of such big banks, living wills are potentially the most threatening tool in the regulatory arsenal. While regulators have not yet exercised the full extent of the living wills power to break up big banks, the ability of regulators to order divestment without additional legislative authorization is the single greatest threat to the banks' business model of being too big to fail.

As things currently stand, any proposal to resolve a complex financial institution in bankruptcy is a questionable proposition. There is no public law that prevents the debtor's "qualified financial contract" (QFC) counterparties from running on the debtor and its subsidiaries upon the parent company's bankruptcy filing. Rather, there is only a set of contractual provisions in the QFCs of the largest financial institutions that create a very limited stay.[63] The stay is likely too short to enable a successful restructuring in most cases, and it is uncertain if it would even be specifically enforceable. It is even less certain whether the ability to enforce the contractual stay would prevent disruptive runs in the first place. Thus, it is easy to imagine foreign counterparties in particular simply grabbing collateral and forcing the debtor to attempt to recover it later through the slow engine of litigation, by which point it might be too late.

The obstacles to resolving complex financial institutions under title II mean that regulators currently have significant ability to claim that *any* proposed resolution plan under title II is not credible, and thereby have the authority to impose additional discretionary

---

[63.] Since 2017, federal regulations have required that all globally significantly important bank holding companies and their depository subsidiaries to conform their QFCs to certain mandatory terms. 12 C.F.R. section 47.3 (national bank subsidiaries), 252.82 (GSIBs and member bank subsidiaries), 382.2 (state insured bank subsidiaries). Those terms include a stay until the later of 48 hours or 5 p.m. the next business day and the applicability of U.S. resolution law 12 C.F.R. section 47.5(g) (national bank subsidiaries), 252.84(g) (GSIBs and member bank subsidiaries), 382.4(g) (state insured bank subsidiaries). No equivalent requirement exists for QFCs that do not involve globally significantly important bank holding companies and their depository subsidiaries.

regulatory requirements by exercising the living wills power. Having a specific FIB process, however, would enable the largest financial institutions to argue that they necessarily satisfy the living wills requirement because by definition any financial institution eligible for FIB could resolve itself using that process under title 11. The creation of any FIB procedure would therefore deprive federal regulators both of a key regulatory tool for derisking the largest financial institutions as well as of the possibility of ultimately breaking up the biggest banks. And this may be precisely what some FIB proponents want.

III. Imagining FIB

A. The Good Bank/Bad Bank Transaction

A FIB process could take many forms, but any FIB process is likely to include certain features, and these are the focus of this chapter. The key feature of any FIB process would likely be an asset sale that partitions the assets of the failed financial institution between a new "good bank" and the old, failed "bad bank." In recent years, sale-based reorganization has frequently replaced the traditional form of chapter 11 bankruptcy reorganization, in which the reorganization is undertaken pursuant to a plan subject to a creditor vote and various statutory requirements.[64] In the sale-based reorganization, some or all of the failed firm's assets are sold, moving them into a new capital structure, with any remaining assets then liquidated in bankruptcy.[65] Unlike a plan, a sale is not subject to a creditor vote or to the other statutory requirements for plan confirmation.[66]

The sale-based reorganization method in bankruptcy is essentially the same as a long-standing bank resolution technique, known as a "good bank/bad bank" (GB/BB) structure. Although the terminology

---

[64.] Levitin, Business Bankruptcy, supra note 7, at 825–27.

[65.] Id.

[66.] Id.; see also 11 U.S.C. section 363 (2012).

originated in the bank resolution context,[67] the transaction structure is in no way specific to banks. Understanding the GB/BB structure is essential for understanding the practical difficulties with FIB as well as the policy tensions that lie within it.

Financial institutions often run into trouble with a particular type of debt overhang problem: uncertain asset valuation. If a financial institution has assets, such as a book of mortgages or mortgage-backed securities, whose value declined by an uncertain although material amount, the effect is a solvency problem for the institution. The valuation uncertainty means that the institution might be insolvent, and that will make it difficult for the institution to continue contracting—no one wants to assume the risk of trading with an insolvent financial institution.[68]

A common solution for the valuation uncertainty problem is to divide the failed firm's good assets from its bad ones using a GB/BB structure. While a GB/BB structure can be used even when there is no valuation uncertainty, a GB/BB structure can address valuation uncertainty by partitioning the assets of the financial institution through a sale that separates the assets of uncertain value from those of certain value: the "good" assets (those of certain value) are sold to a new entity, the "Good Bank" that serves as the acquisition vehicle for new equityholders.[69] The Good Bank will also assume certain favored liabilities of the financial institution. These liabilities might be favored for any of the following reasons: they are necessary for the Good Bank to maintain the ongoing good will of certain creditors, such as suppliers and employees; the creditors on the favored

---

[67.] See Edward D. Herlihy & Craig M. Wasserman, Making the Good Bank/Bad Bank Structure Work, Int'l Fin. L. Rev., Apr. 1992, at 34, 34–37.

[68.] For example, a firm that used asbestos products in its manufacturing might have significant contingent liabilities. The extent and timing of the firm's liability is currently unknown, but any potential liability diminishes the firm's ability to obtain unsecured debt because of the possibility of large competing tort claims.

[69.] See Morrison & Foerster, Good Bank-Bad Bank: A Clean Break and a Fresh Start 1–5 (2009), https://media2.mofo.com/documents/20090218goodbankbadbank.pdf [https://perma.cc/7U3X-3YXP] (describing variations of GB/BB structures).

liabilities are simply preferred for personal reasons, such as insiders; or because of the favored creditors' political connections.

The failed financial institution thus becomes the "Bad Bank," as it is left with the "bad" assets of uncertain or negative value plus the proceeds of the sale transaction. The Bad Bank also remains obligated on the disfavored liabilities. The Bad Bank is still of uncertain solvency because of the uncertain valuation of the bad assets (and possibly of the disfavored liabilities), but the Good Bank is not, and that is critical. The assets of the Good Bank can be productively deployed because the Good Bank will not suffer from the debt overhang problem, so counterparties will not eschew doing business with it. Thus, the GB/BB format liberates the good assets from the bad assets and from disfavored liabilities.[70]

A GB/BB structure can be implemented in a variety of ways, including in bankruptcy. In bankruptcy, a GB/BB structure is implemented through a sale of the Good Bank assets under section 363(b) and (f) of the Bankruptcy Code,[71] presumably prior to the confirmation of a bankruptcy plan. The Bad Bank assets are then subsequently liquidated pursuant to a plan of liquidation. Such a format capitalizes on the speed of bankruptcy sales, which must be held "after notice and a hearing," a phrase defined to mean only such notice and hearing as is appropriate under the circumstances, and which may mean that no notice or hearing is required if time is of the essence.[72] Thus, if the Good Bank assets are flighty customer relationships—the financial institution equivalent of melting ice cream—they are preserved

---

[70.] The "single-point-of-entry" (SPOE) mechanism that is frequently used in the resolution plans (living wills) required of certain large financial institutions, 12 U.S.C. § 5365(d)(4) (2012), is a GB/BB structure. In SPOE the equity and certain debt obligations of the debtor holding company are left behind with any undesirable assets, while the good assets are transferred to a new holding company, along with other (favored) liabilities. While SPOE often focuses on the equity and long-term debt of the debtor holding company getting "bailed-in"—that is, left behind—the key to SPOE is really in the selective transfer of favored assets and liabilities to a new firm, which is just the GB/BB structure.

[71.] *Id.* section 363(b), (f).

[72.] See *id.* section 102(1).

through a fast sale.[73] Moreover, the ultimate liquidation of the Bad Bank is largely done automatically by adherence to the liquidation priorities in chapter 7 bankruptcy, even if the liquidation is carried out in chapter 11.[74] Creditors have few grounds and even less reason to attempt to hold up the post-sale liquidation, because they cannot use it to unwind the prior asset sale.[75]

For the GB/BB structure to work, however, two conditions must hold. First, creditors must be prevented from undertaking collection actions while the asset sale is pending, or else the sale may fall apart as key assets might no longer be available for creditors. In bankruptcy, the automatic stay generally prevents such creditor actions, except in the case of certain financial contracts; swaps, repos, securities and commodities futures contracts, forward contracts, and master netting agreements may all be terminated, accelerated, and liquidated without running afoul of the automatic stay.[76] This presents little obstacle for most debtors, but is an issue for financial institution debtors as discussed next.

Second, the asset purchaser—the Good Bank—must have confidence in the valuation of the assets it purchases. If the assets' value is too uncertain, a buyer would be unlikely to step forward. One way around this problem is by enabling prospective buyers to have sufficient time to conduct due diligence on the assets, such that they can come up with a valuation on which to base a bid. But if time is of the essence with the GB/BB transaction—the ice cream is melting—then such diligence will not be possible. In such a case, either the purchase price would be severely depressed or the transaction would not happen, unless a third-party would be willing to guaranty the purchased

---

[73] Melissa B. Jacoby & Edward J. Janger, Ice Cube Bonds: Allocating the Price of Process in chapter 11 Bankruptcy, 123 Yale L.J. 862, 866–67 (2014).

[74] 11 U.S.C. § 725–26 (2012) (chapter 7 distribution baseline); *id.* section 1129(a)(7) (requiring adherence to a chapter 7 distribution baseline in chapter 11).

[75] See *id.* section 363(m) (providing that the "reversal or modification on appeal" of a sale order "does not affect the validity of a sale . . . to an entity that purchased . . . in good faith").

[76] *Id.* section 362(b)(6), (7), (17), (27); *id.* section 555, 559–61.

assets. The automatic stay generally provides the breathing room for the necessary diligence to occur. But, as noted earlier, the stay does much less work for financial institution debtors.

The result of a GB/BB structure is that the holders of the favored liabilities assumed by the Good Bank would be paid in full, so long as the Good Bank remains solvent. The holders of the disfavored liabilities, however, recover in bankruptcy only from the bad assets and the sale proceeds from the good assets. This means that the risk of loss on the bad assets, as well as the risk of underpricing the good assets, lies with the creditors who hold the disfavored liabilities. A GB/BB structure thus operates as a type of priority system that ensures 100% repayment for favored liabilities and does not guarantee any particular repayment for disfavored liabilities.

For example, suppose that a bankrupt company has $150 of assets and $300 in total liabilities as follows: $100 to a class of unsecured bondholders, $100 to a class of tort claimants, and $100 to a class of employees. These three classes of claims are all general unsecured claims of equal priority and should be paid out pro rata in a bankruptcy liquidation, with all three classes receiving 50¢ on the dollar.[77]

Suppose then that the assets were purchased by a third party. If the third party paid fair market value in cash for the assets—$150—there would be no effect on the distribution to the creditors. The old assets would simply have been transformed into cash from other forms of property. The plain asset sale does not change the distribution. The creditors would assume the risk, however, that the sale is underpriced. If the assets are really worth $200, then they should receive a 66.7% dividend. Of course, if the assets are really worth $200, then one would expect another buyer—perhaps a creditor—to bid more than $150 for them, but this presupposes no limitations on bidding procedures and other transactional and informational frictions.

Now, however, suppose that the purchaser wants to keep the existing workforce and wants to ensure labor peace. The purchaser

---

[77.] See *id.* section 726(b).

therefore reduces its offer from $150 in cash to an offer of only $50 in cash and the assumption of the $100 in employee claims. If the purchase is approved, the debtor would be left with $50 in assets and $200 in claims, so the bondholders and tort claimants are paid 25¢ on the dollar. In contrast, the employees' claims would be assumed by a solvent third party purchaser, so they would be paid in full, 100¢ on the dollar. The assumption of liabilities in the asset purchase effectively gives the employees priority over the bondholders and tort claimants despite all parties formally having the same priority.

Finally, assume that there is some uncertainty about the valuation of some of the assets. The buyer might be willing to assume the valuation risk on those assets, but if the buyer purchases only the good assets, then the remaining assets—and the valuation uncertainty— remain with the creditors whose claims were not assumed in the sale. In other words, the valuation risk not just of the sale price but also the valuation risk of the remaining assets is concentrated on the bondholders and tort claimants. The employees, whose claims the buyer assumed, have escaped the risk of an underpriced sale as well as the valuation risk of the assets left behind.

The GB/BB structure is already the preferred transactional form for many large, nonfinancial business bankruptcies. Many large bankruptcies now use an asset sale, rather than a plan, as their primary means of effectuating a reorganization.[78] Some version of a GB/BB structure would likely be used in a FIB for two reasons.

First, the GB/BB structure allows for the quick redeployment of the good assets, which is important to minimize disruptive spillover effects. A GB/BB transaction has both a sale and a subsequent liquidating plan, but the key part of the transaction is the sale; it is not critical that the liquidating plan be achieved with particular alacrity. Indeed, the GB/BB approach effectively divides the bankruptcy process into two parts: an asset sale process that supposedly maximizes the value of the debtor's assets, followed by a separate,

---

[78.] Levitin, Business Bankruptcy, supra note 7, at 825–27.

subsequent process for evaluating claims and distributing value to allowed claims. The former is a process that has little role for a judge, while the latter is an adjudicative process in terms of claims evaluation. Distribution, however, may then be done robotically according to a statutory cash flow waterfall.

The alternative to a sale followed by a plan-based liquidation is a plan-based reorganization. The timeline for a plan in a FIB need not follow the current Federal Rules of Bankruptcy Procedure. Nonetheless, any sort of plan-based reorganization would necessarily be slower than the sale component of a GB/BB transaction because a plan-based reorganization must provide some time for dissemination and consideration of a disclosure statement,[79] as well as for voting (meaning dissemination of ballots and counting of ballots cast), a confirmation hearing, and a post-confirmation appellate period.[80]

Second, in contrast to a bankruptcy plan, a sale is not a procedure that is vulnerable to holdouts, at least under current bankruptcy law. Consensual confirmation of a bankruptcy plan requires obtaining consent of the majorities of all impaired classes of claims and interests,[81] as well as satisfaction of a number of other statutory requirements.[82] A bankruptcy plan may also be confirmed via the "cramdown" procedure with consent of only a single impaired class (excluding insiders).[83] Neither type of confirmation, however, may happen as quickly as needed. In contrast, the standards for a preplan asset sale are much looser; no creditor consent whatsoever is required, and the debtor merely has to show an "articulated business justification."[84]

[79.] See Fed. R. Bankr. P. 3017(a) (requiring twenty-eight days' notice before a disclosure statement hearing).

[80.] See Fed. R. Bankr. P. 3020(e) (requiring a fourteen-day delay after a plan is confirmed before it is effective, which matches the fourteen-day window for filing an appeal under Federal Rule of Bankruptcy Procedure 8002(a)(1)).

[81.] 11 U.S.C. § 1126(c), 1129(a)(7) (2012).

[82.] *Id.* section 1129(a).

[83.] *Id.* section 1129(b).

[84.] See In re Lionel Corp., 722 F.2d 1063, 1070–71 (2d Cir. 1983).

B. The Resolution Dilemma: Reducing Moral Hazard or Reducing Systemic Spillovers

FIB proposals seek to simultaneously achieve two irreconcilable goals. On the one hand, FIB proposals seek to reduce moral hazard by forcing creditor loss internalization.[85] If creditors incur losses as a result of poor lending decisions, they will be incentivized to take more care in the future. Conversely, if creditors are bailed out of their bad deals, they have no incentive to take care, as they are left with a "heads I win, tails you lose" bargain. Thus, to reduce moral hazard, it is imperative that creditors (or at least adjusting ones) bear losses in a FIB (or at least that they credibly believe that they will bear losses). The whole point of the moral hazard reduction is to encourage better ex ante behavior by creditors; it is not meant to be punitive. In a GB/BB transaction, loss internalization can be achieved by leaving creditors' obligations behind in the Bad Bank.

At the same time, however, FIB seeks to ensure a "smooth landing" for the economy by minimizing the spillovers from the failure of a large financial institution.[86] The failure of a large financial institution can result in a domino chain of failures as questions of solvency metastasize throughout the financial system. A GB/BB transaction can be used to achieve such a smooth landing and head off spillovers by having the Good Bank assume creditors' obligations.

If the goal is to eliminate moral hazard, it is necessary for bankruptcy *to impose losses* on creditors that can adjust ex ante. Yet the most certain way to prevent such spillovers is to ensure that creditors *do not incur losses* in a bankruptcy. This means it is not possible to simultaneously prevent moral hazard and prevent spillovers in

---

[85] See, e.g., Hearing on H.R. 1667, supra note 37, at 2 (statement of John B. Taylor) ("chapter 11 ensures that creditors bear losses and this reduces moral hazard and excessive risk-taking.").

[86] See, e.g., *id.* ("The goal of these provisions is to let a failing financial firm go into bankruptcy in a predictable, rules-based manner without causing disruptive spillovers in the economy while permitting people to continue to use its financial services without running.").

regard to the same creditor. Either the creditor will bear losses or it will not in a bankruptcy.

One way around this conundrum is to differentiate between types of creditors—some creditors will bear losses and provide the market discipline that will limit future bank risk-taking, while others will not bear losses and will be effectively bailed out because the Good Bank will assume their obligations. Such a differentiation of creditors is politically problematic. It means picking winners and losers, an issue FIB supporters avoid discussing entirely, because the moral hazard problem they seek to eliminate will persist if *any* creditors have their obligations assumed (or even think that they will have their obligations assumed).

Consumers, tax authorities, tort creditors, and vendors are basically nonadjusting creditors, so it makes no sense to place losses on them because they do not present a moral hazard problem. That leaves as the adjusting creditors only the financial creditors, such as unsecured bond debt, any secured debt, and repo and derivatives counterparties. Yet these financial creditors are exactly whom we are most worried about being the channel for a domino effect of failures throughout the economy. Protecting these financial creditors, or a subset of them, is exactly the type of crony capitalism problem that bailout critics raise. There is no way to both create market discipline and prevent domino effects that cascade throughout the economy. Ultimately, a choice must be made. This is the "resolution dilemma."

The choice should be easy: reduce the economic dislocation caused by the failure of a financial institution. Market discipline is a wonderful thing, but it should not become a fetish. It is not an end in and of itself but rather a means toward achieving greater economic stability. There are other tools available for reducing excessive risk-taking by financial institutions—namely, prudential regulation. Prudential regulatory regimes are not fail-safe, and particular features may impose costs that outweigh their benefits. But given the difficulty in credibly committing ex ante to impose losses on creditors no matter the economic consequences, prudential regulation is the only realistic alternative. No matter how many laws proclaim "no bailouts," no one believes that government will follow through when doing so becomes an economic suicide pact.

Once we recognize the resolution dilemma, however, one has to ask: Why bother with the bankruptcy? To the extent that a bankruptcy system protects creditors from incurring losses, it is just another form of a bailout, hiding in bankruptcy's clothing. If the reluctant choice is to go with bailouts, why try to disguise them in the garb of bankruptcy? Let the wolf come as a wolf, not in sheep's garb.

One could make a more sophisticated argument that using a bankruptcy procedure will create the impression or at least uncertainty about the likelihood that there will be loss internalization even if there ultimately will not be, and this deke will improve market discipline. While this is not an argument actually made by FIB proponents, it has some virtue. The uncertainty would reduce moral hazard without having to surrender the smooth landing when a financial institution actually fails. Yet such an argument relies on sophisticated financial institutions being snookered by the system's design, and if they are not fooled, they will double down on reckless lending. Moreover, it is an argument for completely cynical legislation—for creating a FIB regime not intended for actual use but instead to scare bank counterparties that it could be used. This argument also runs against the concern about lack of transparency in bailouts: What is less transparent than disguising a bailout as a bankruptcy? The tension between reducing moral hazard and reducing spillover effects points to the pointlessness of FIB.

IV. The Impracticability of Financial Institution Bankruptcy

Beyond the conceptual problem inherent in a GB/BB framework for restructuring a financial institution in bankruptcy, there are also four core practical obstacles: the inability to obtain adequate financing for a restructuring; problems with international coordination; the difficulty of dealing with derivatives and other financial contracts; and the lack of a mechanism for addressing valuation uncertainty for potential Good Bank purchasers. Any one of these obstacles alone should throw cold water on dreams of FIB. Together, however, they show that a private FIB process is a fantasy. FIB can only possibly work with massive government involvement, at which point its supposed virtues dissipate, and it compares less favorably to bailouts whether executed ad hoc or through a previously authorized administrative device like the OLA.

A. DIP Financing Is Not Feasible for Large Financial Institutions

1. Normal Sources of DIP Financing Will Not Be Available

For a debtor to have any chance of successfully restructuring itself in bankruptcy, it must have adequate liquidity to pay its operating costs. The debtor needs to have the cash to keep the lights on, retain employees, maintain insurance coverage, pay taxes, and more.

For a financial institution, such liquidity demands are even greater. Financial institutions trade on trust and confidence. Counterparties will enter into contracts with these institutions only if they feel reasonably confident that the financial institution will meet its obligations. For a financial institution to operate, it must constantly be able to access the market. For example, if a bank were to make a fixed rate loan, it also would have to be able to access interest rate swap markets to hedge its interest rate risk. But if swap counterparties do not think the bank will be able to honor its commitment on the swap, they will not contract with it.

This means that, for a financial institution to continue operating in bankruptcy, it must have essentially the level of liquidity that it would have if it were not financially distressed. Anything less will result in a self-fulfilling prophecy of a run, as creditors will raise prices, demand more collateral, or refuse to rollover debts because of a lack of confidence in the survival of the debtor. This is precisely what occurred with Lehman Brothers in 2008—its clearing bank, JPMorgan, demanded that Lehman post more collateral.[87] And, as the 2008 crisis clearly demonstrated, the liquidity demands on a financial institution in bankruptcy will be extraordinary.[88]

Yet the nature of most debtor firms is that they lack liquidity when they file for bankruptcy. Most firms do not file for bankruptcy until they absolutely have to do so. They will only file when there is an acute liquidity crisis pending, such that they will not be able to make a debt payment or meet payroll.

There is every reason to think the same would be true with financial institutions. As long as a financial institution is liquid, it can keep operating even if insolvent. Indeed, the financial institution's management would be strongly incentivized to do so, as management loses nothing by "gambling on resurrection."[89] If the company's fortunes turn around, everything would return to normal, the firm's equity retains value, and the managers are heroes for fixing the company. If the firm still fails, the managers have not lost shareholder funds but value that would otherwise go to creditors.[90] It is possible, of course, to conceive of a FIB regime that permits for the filing of

---

[87.] See, e.g., Jonathan Stempel, JPMorgan to Pay $1.42 Billion Cash to Settle Most Lehman Claims, Reuters (Jan. 25, 2016, 9:00 PM), www.reuters.com/article/us-jpmorgan-lehman-idUSKCN0V4049 [http://perma.cc/SNU5-ZMXS].

[88.] Large financial institutions are already subject to a "liquidity coverage ratio" intended to ensure that they will not find themselves pressed for liquidity. 12 C.F.R. section 50.10 (2018) (covering national banks); id. section 329.10 (covering state member banks); id. section 249.10 (covering insured state banks). But if the liquidity coverage ratio is simply the financial regulatory equivalent of building a higher levy, it is always vulnerable to being wiped out by a strong enough hurricane, or here, financial crisis. See Adam J. Levitin, Prioritization and Mutualization: Clearinghouses and the Redundancy of the Bankruptcy Safe Harbors, 10 Brook. J. Corp. Fin. & Com. L. 129, 139 (2015) [hereinafter Levitin, Prioritization and Mutualization].

[89.] See Levitin, Business Bankruptcy, supra note 7, at 315.

[90.] Notably, corporate law in most states imposes no liability on corporate directors and officers for gambling on resurrection. Directors do not bear fiduciary duties to creditors, see N. Am. Catholic Educ. Programming Found., Inc. v. Gheewalla, 930 A.2d 92, 99 (Del. 2007), and Delaware does not recognize the tort of "deepening insolvency," Trenwick Am. Litig. Tr. v. Ernst & Young, L.L.P., 906 A.2d 168, 174 (Del. Ch. 2006), aff'd sub nom. Trenwick Am. Litig. Tr. v. Billett, 931 A.2d 438 (Del. 2007).

an involuntary petition, perhaps triggered by regulatory action. But there is a real possibility that regulators will be reluctant to pull the trigger lest they do so prematurely, with the result that they pull it too late and face a worse crisis than otherwise.

Thus, by the time a financial institution ends up in bankruptcy, it would likely have very little liquidity, probably not enough to keep operating. To the extent it still has enough liquidity to operate, it would assuredly evaporate as creditors (particularly those funding repo lines of credit) demand payment on existing obligations and refuse to extend new credit out of fear that the debtor would lack the liquid funds to pay on its obligations as they come due.

The liquidity crisis a financial institution is likely to face when it files for bankruptcy necessitates a fresh source of liquidity. In this regard, a FIB is not materially different from any other business bankruptcy. In a typical business bankruptcy, the debtor will address the liquidity problem by obtaining DIP financing—a new, post-petition financing facility that will provide the debtor with the funds to continue operations.[91]

Adequate DIP financing, however, is not possible for a financial institution of any size.[92] An enormous DIP financing facility would be required for a financial institution, far more than for a Main Street company such as a manufacturer. Moreover, particularly for a financial institution whose ability to do business depends on customers' confidence in its ability to honor its commitments, a DIP financing facility would need to be in place immediately, on day one of the case. Without a DIP facility in place at the time of filing, counterparties would flee a financial institution, resulting in a self-fulfilling collapse. Both requirements present insurmountable problems.

[91.] See Levitin, Business Bankruptcy, supra note 7, at 389–90, 396–98.

[92.] This fact alone should call into question the credibility of all resolution plans filed under the Dodd–Frank Act's living wills provision, 12 U.S.C. § 5365(d) (2012). As noted above, however, the purpose of the living wills requirement may be less about ensuring that living wills are actually credible than about giving regulators extra discretion to impose additional regulatory requirements on the largest financial institutions, including the option of breaking up these institutions. See supra Part I.D.

A large financial institution would require a DIP facility of tens if not hundreds of billions of dollars. JPMorgan Chase, for example, has around $560 billion in high-quality liquid assets that cover peak short-term cash outflows.[93] To maintain counterparty confidence to continue operations and not cause a creditor run, a firm like JPMorgan would need to maintain its nondistressed level of liquidity, in this case around $560 billion. Similarly, Bank of America and Citibank would each require around $425 billion in liquidity to maintain its nondistressed financial profile,[94] while Goldman Sachs would require $210 billion.[95] While a financial institution would not enter bankruptcy with zero liquidity, it is not likely to enter into bankruptcy until its liquidity position is dire, so it would likely still need a liquidity source for a substantial portion of its predistressed liquidity level, likely in the tens of billions of dollars if not more.

Private lending markets are not capable of providing such large amounts of liquidity to a bankrupt firm, even for a very short period of time. The largest private syndicated loan in history, $75 billion, was raised in November 2015 for AB InBev's takeover bid for SAB-Miller, but that syndicate took weeks to assemble for a solvent firm.[96] A failed megabank does not have the luxury of that time.

[93.] JPMorgan Chase & Co., Liquidity Coverage Ratio Disclosure: For the Quarterly Period Ended December 31, 2017, at 1, http://files.shareholder.com/downloads/ONE/6370549969x0x972718/FE4E3462-AFE3-4342-8BD6-D0B039E84EA5/4Q17_Liquidity_Coverage_Ratio_Report_Final.pdf [http://perma.cc/P9A7-GE8H (staff-uploaded archive)].

[94.] Bank of Am., Pillar 3 U.S. Liquidity Coverage Ratio (LCR) Disclosures: For The Quarter Ended June 30, 2017, at 4, http://phx.corporate-ir.net/External.File?item=UGFyZW50SUQ9Mzg3MTUifENoaWxkSUQ9LTF8VHlwZToz&t=1&cb=63639114355719331 [http://perma.cc/85XV-PQ3K]; Citigroup, Inc., U.S. LCR Disclosure: For the Quarterly Period Ending 6/30/17, at 2, www.citigroup.com/citi/investor/data/lcr170630.pdf?ieNocache=165https://bit.ly/2Ms5Lra [http://perma.cc/X69Q-TG64].

[95.] The Goldman Sachs Grp., Inc., Liquidity Coverage Ratio Disclosure: For the Quarter Ended June 30, 2017, at 2, www.goldmansachs.com/investor-relations/financials/archived/other-information/2q-2017-liquidity-coverage-ratio.pdf [http://perma.cc/R3BM-4CHT].

[96.] Alasdair Reilly & Tessa Walsh, AB InBev Backs SABMiller Buy with Record $75 Billion Loan, Reuters (Nov. 11, 2015, 6:42 AM), www.reuters.com/article/

Perhaps the best yardstick is past DIP lending. The largest private DIP financing ever assembled was a mere $9 billion loan for Energy Future Holdings in 2014.[97] Even the U.S. government's DIP loan to GM, the largest DIP loan ever, was only $33 billion.[98] None of these past DIP loans come close to approaching the level of DIP financing a large financial institution would require to continue operating in bankruptcy. Furthermore, the emergency nature of DIP liquidity provision would preclude syndication because of the time needed to market the loan (here, in secrecy) to potential syndicate members, each of which would have to conduct its own diligence.

DIP loans are also almost always first lien, superpriority loans. No DIP lender wants to lend on an unsecured basis because the borrower is, by definition, bankrupt and a serious credit risk. A bankrupt financial institution would be hard-pressed to offer a new DIP-lending consortium for unencumbered collateral, as most valuable assets would likely already be pledged.

Bankruptcy law contemplates the possibility of priming liens for DIP loans,[99] meaning that the DIP loans would get a lien with priority over existing liens. Such priming liens, however, would likely be bitterly contested. At the very least, approval of priming liens would require a lengthy valuation hearing, delaying the financing, as well as evidence that the debtor had tried and failed to find financing on other terms.[100]

Further complicating DIP financing for complex bankruptcies is that it must be arranged in advance to be available at the start of

---

us-abinbev-loans/ab-inbev-backs-sabmiller-buy-with-record-75-billion-loan-idUSKCN0T019E20151111 [http://perma.cc/8BZW-CJGE].

[97] Billy Cheung, Energy Future Holdings Lining Up $9 Billion Bankruptcy Financing, Reuters (Mar. 27, 2014, 9:35 AM), www.reuters.com/article/us-energy-future-hd-loans/energy-future-holdings-lining-up-9-billion-bankruptcy-financing-idUSBREA2Q13020140327 [http://perma.cc/M7CN-RA6R].

[98] Id.; Christine Caufield, GM Gets OK to Tap $33.3B in DIP Financing, Law360 (June 25, 2009, 12:00 AM), https://lawlibproxy2.unc.edu:2147/articles/108332/gm-gets-ok-to-tap-33-3b-in-dip-financing [http://perma.cc/AE69-DAHV (staff-uploaded archive)].

[99] 11 U.S.C. § 364(d)(1) (2012).

[100] See id.

a case. Large, multibillion-dollar loans are never made by single institutions. Instead, they are syndicated facilities in which numerous financial institutions each provide the funding for a part of the facility.[101] Lining up a syndicate, much less one so large, takes time. The $75 billion loan for AB InBev took weeks to arrange for a solvent firm.[102]

A financial institution, however, does not have the luxury of time. First, it might be in trouble in part because of market-wide problems. If markets have frozen, DIP financing will not be available. And the failure of a large financial institution is itself likely to result in a market freeze. Second, DIP financing would likely come from other financial institutions—the failed institution's current counterparties because nearly all large financial institutions trade with each other. As soon as a firm began to attempt securing DIP financing, it would be advertising to its creditors that it will be filing for bankruptcy, which would precipitate a run on the firm, resulting in a premature bankruptcy.

Private capital markets are simply incapable of coming up with enormous liquidity for a potentially insolvent company, much less overnight and when markets are in turmoil. Now consider the possibility that multiple financial institutions fail simultaneously, as occurred in 2008. There's simply no chance of adequate DIP financing from the private sector.

2. Alternative Sources of DIP Financing Are Problematic

The federal government could, in theory, provide the massive DIP financing required with the necessary limited notice to creditors, but the whole point of FIB proposals is to keep the government out of the process and let the restructuring be a private ordering. Once the government is involved, it will assuredly flex its muscles and insist on favorable terms for its loan or for favorable treatment for particular,

---

[101.] Levitin, Business Bankruptcy, supra note 7, at 71–75.

[102.] Reilly & Walsh, supra note 96.

politically favored creditors. If OLA is any guide, none of this would be restricted by statute, not least because no one wants to constrain the flexibility of a response ex ante without knowing the particular circumstances involved. Even if there were statutory restrictions, however, there would be strong pressure to figure out a way around them in the FIB procedure or else FIB simply would not be used for resolution. Instead, the terms of the DIP loan would be contractually determined and presented to the court for approval on a take-it-or-leave-it basis. The court's only option when faced with such terms is to approve them because denying the DIP loan means triggering a serious financial crisis, something no judge wants to do.[103] It is hard to see a FIB operating without government DIP lending, which undermines the entire point of FIB.

It is true that a FIB with a GB/BB structure could take the form of a very quick asset sale (and liability assumption) from the failed financial institution to some buyer, and that buyer might agree to supply liquidity during the interim before the sale's closing. But consider who the buyers might be. To swallow up the good assets of a large financial institution—an institution that might have tens of billions if not hundreds of billions or even trillions of dollars in assets—a buyer would need to be of similar or greater size. For example, as of the end of 2017, JPMorgan Chase Bank, N.A. reported assets of just more than $2.5 trillion,[104] while Citigroup, N.A. reported assets of around $1.8 trillion.[105] There are few such buyers around to begin with, and in a global financial crisis, the potential buyers would themselves possibly be in financial difficulty or reluctant to assume additional risk, much less without the opportunity for serious diligence. Thus, in the 2008 crisis, Lehman Brothers was unable

---

[103.] See, e.g., Baird, supra note 8, at 290.

[104.] JPMorgan Chase & Co., 2017 Annual Report 38 (2018), www.jpmorganchase.com/corporate/investor-relations/document/annualreport-2017.pdf [http://perma.cc/TCC8-2B94].

[105.] Citigroup, Inc., 2017 Annual Report 1 (2018), www.citigroup.com/citi/investor/quarterly/2018/ar17_en.pdf [https://perma.cc/P3SU-7HXZ].

to find a buyer.[106] The shotgun marriages between Bank of America and Merrill Lynch, JPMorgan and Washington Mutual, JPMorgan and Bear Stearns, and Wells Fargo and Wachovia were all done with a heavy (and sometimes heavy-handed) dose of governmental involvement.[107] And those deals sometimes included government loss-sharing agreements,[108] which is presumably anathema to FIB proponents because of its supposed private-ordering virtues and lack of involvement of the public fisc.

Another possibility would be a standby DIP facility for financial institutions. No financial institution would willingly pay for such a facility in part because the lack of a DIP lending facility and thus the unavailability of a viable bankruptcy process increases the likelihood of a bailout, so it would have to be required by regulation. Conceptually such a facility is possible with a credit-linked note structure.[109]

[106.] Robert J. Samuelson, Opinion, Lehman Brothers Collapsed 10 Years Ago. Whose Fault Was It? Wash. Post (Aug. 26, 2018), www.washingtonpost.com/opinions/lehman-brothers-collapsed-10-years-ago-whose-fault-was-it/2018/08/26/79137b2e-a7dd-11e8-a656-943eefab5daf_story.html?utm_term=.1d4386b06a93 [https://perma.cc/39P6-7LXC].

[107.] William D. Cohan, The Final Days of Merrill Lynch, The Atlantic (Sept. 2009), www.theatlantic.com/magazine/archive/2009/09/the-final-days-of-merrill-lynch/307621/ [https://perma.cc/43C4-ZRKJ]; David Ellis & Jeanne Sahadi, JPMorgan Buys WaMu, CNN: Money (Sept. 26, 2008, 12:18 PM), https://money.cnn.com/2008/09/25/news/companies/JPM_WaMu/ [https://perma.cc/Q7ZM-VAMD]; Sara Lepro & Jennifer Malloy Zonnas, Wells Fargo Buys Wachovia for $15.1 Billion, ABC News (Oct. 3, 2008), https://abcnews.go.com/Business/SmartHome/story?id=5946486&page=1 [https://perma.cc/MU5K-VQVC]; Liz Moyer, A Decade after Its Fire-Sale Deal for Bear, a Look at What JP Morgan Got in the Bargain, CNBC (Mar. 16, 2018, 7:13 AM), www.cnbc.com/2018/03/14/a-decade-after-its-fire-sale-deal-for-bear-a-look-at-what-jp-morgan-got-in-the-bargain.html [https://perma.cc/AC62-G3VS].

[108.] See, e.g., Press Release, JPMorgan Chase & Co., JPMorgan Chase and Bear Stearns Announce Amended Merger Agreement and Agreement for JPMorgan Chase to Purchase 39.5% of Bear Stearns (Mar. 24, 2008), www.sec.gov/Archives/edgar/data/19617/000089882208000320/pressrelease.htm [http://perma.cc/F4C9-NVXE] (noting that the Federal Reserve Bank of New York was assuming any losses on the $30 billion purchase beyond the first $1 billion of losses).

[109.] For a description of credit-linked notes, see William W. Bratton & Adam J. Levitin, A Transactional Genealogy of Scandal: From Michael Milken to Enron to Goldman Sachs, 86 S. Cal. L. Rev. 783, 852 (2013).

First, a financial institution sponsor could create a "special-purpose entity" (SPE). The SPE would then issue notes and escrow the investment proceeds from the note, investing the proceeds in liquid, safe assets like Treasury securities. The SPE would also enter into a swap with the financial institution that would be triggered by the financial institution's bankruptcy filing. Until the financial institution filed for bankruptcy, it would make periodic payments to the SPE. The SPE would in turn pay the noteholders, who would also receive the investment earnings on the escrowed funds. Upon a bankruptcy filing, however, the flow of funds would reverse: the SPE would pay out the escrowed funds to the financial institution in the form of a pre-negotiated DIP facility.

While credit-linked notes are a common financing structure, they have never before been used for a DIP lending facility, and such a facility would not be cheap. Credit-linked notes would function as a type of insurance for a financial institution to ensure that it would have funding in the event that it failed. If the financial institution filed for bankruptcy, then the DIP facility would be funded automatically, like an insurance payment triggered by a loss. The periodic payments to the SPE are essentially insurance premiums for DIP lending insurance. If this process were workable, it would add substantial costs to running a financial institution simply by virtue of the volume of credit-linked notes that would have to be issued. Such cost might in fact be desirable, if the credit-linked note requirement were triggered only upon a certain size or complexity threshold. A regulatory requirement of a standby DIP facility through credit-linked notes would serve as a type of tax on SIFIs, which would create an incentive for those firms to reduce their size and complexity. But all this presupposes that there would even be a market for such credit-linked notes.

One can get some sense of market appetite for this sort of credit risk by looking at the market for catastrophe bonds. Catastrophe bonds are a type of security that provides a capital-market-funded type of insurance for firms concerned about exposure to natural disasters such as hurricanes and earthquakes.[110] The bonds work similarly to credit-linked notes, where a transaction sponsor forms an SPE with no assets or noncontractual liabilities. The SPE then issues catastrophe bonds; the investors in the bonds have no recourse against the sponsor, only against the SPE. The funds used by investors to pay for the bonds are held in escrow by the SPE. If a specified catastrophe event does not occur, the funds remain in escrow, and the investors receive periodic interest payments from the transaction sponsor plus the investment earnings on the escrowed funds. The escrowed funds are ultimately returned when principal payments are due on the bonds. If a specified catastrophe does occur, however, the escrowed funds are released by the SPE to the transaction's sponsor. Because the bonds are nonrecourse against the sponsor, the effect of the release of the escrowed funds to the sponsor is that the catastrophe bond investors will incur a loss; the SPE has no other assets to repay the bondholders. Thus, the catastrophe bond investors assume the risk of the catastrophe up to the level of their investment.

Catastrophe bonds tend to be issued by reinsurance companies as a way using capital markets to reinsure the risks they have assumed.[111] The total global catastrophe bond market has never had more than $31 billion of bonds outstanding, and issuance has never exceeded $12.5 billion per year in a market where there is unlikely to be substantial correlations between catastrophes. For example, a hurricane in the Caribbean is not correlated with an earthquake in California.[112]

Another measure of market appetite for this type of risk is the market for "contingent convertible" (co-co) bonds. Co-cos are a

---

[110.] For a general description of catastrophe bonds, see Thomas Berghman, Note, A Market Under(writing) the Weather: A Recommendation to Increase Insurer Capacity, 2013 U. Ill. L. Rev. 221, 250–51 (2013).

[111.] See James Ming Chen, Correlation, Coverage, and Catastrophe: The Contours of Financial Preparedness for Disaster, 26 Fordham Envtl. L. Rev. 56, 70 (2014).

[112.] Catastrophe Bonds and ILS Issued and Outstanding by Year, Artemis, www.artemis.bm/deal_directory/cat_bonds_ils_issued_outstanding.html [http://perma.cc/2UMC-395U].

type of "bail-in-able" capital—debt that converts to equity upon the occurrence of a specified trigger event. The conversion de-levers the debtor, immediately increasing its solvency. It also helps the debtor's liquidity as the conversion reduces its debt service. Such co-co bonds are fairly popular among European banks, but the total amount outstanding has never exceeded $140 billion.[113] Critically, co-cos do not themselves provide liquidity to the debtor upon conversion. They simply change where they sit in the debtor's capital structure. Nonetheless, they provide a measure for the appetite among investors for assuming credit risk on large financial institutions.

The largest financial institutions in the United States would require a couple magnitudes more of credit-linked notes than the entire catastrophe bond market or co-co bond market to finance a bankruptcy. JPMorgan alone, for example, would need up to $560 billion of liquidity support.[114] Given the high correlation risk between credit-linked notes for large financial institution, it's doubtful that there would be sufficient demand from global credit markets for such credit-linked notes to be sellable at a nonprohibitive rate.

Ultimately if a firm is too big to finance in bankruptcy or "too big to DIP," it's also too big to fail. If the private market cannot provide the DIP financing, that is a strong indicator that the firm is systemically important.[115]

There is only one source in the world capable of credibly providing a DIP loan of tens or hundreds of billions of dollars with minimal

---

[113.] Justin Yang, Co-Co Bond Market Pulls through Recent Setbacks, Wall St. J., (June 25, 2017), www.wsj.com/articles/coco-bond-market-pulls-through-recent-setbacks-1498477962 [http://perma.cc/VU7M-SWYS]. That total is likely inflated in part because it reflects the relatively high yields on co-cos in a low interest rate environment. When rates rise, investors seeking to achieve certain return hurdles will have more options for higher-yielding investments and thus less interest in co-cos.

[114.] See supra text accompanying note 93.

[115.] Indeed, this suggests that perhaps bankruptcy could be used as a systemic risk shibboleth: if a firm is capable of prearranging standing DIP financing on a level that regulators believe is sufficient (presumably its maximum liquidity needs over the past several years), then bankruptcy might be a reasonable regime for the firm. But if the firm is too big to DIP, then it is also too big to fail and should be dealt with outside a bankruptcy regime.

notice. That is the U.S. government. No other entity in the world has this sort of financial strength. Yet it is inconceivable to imagine the federal government acting as a DIP lender without attaching strings to the extension of credit, such as demanding particular treatments for favored creditor constituencies.[116] And that takes us right back to the bailout situation, which has simply been moved into the bankruptcy system.

B. Lack of International Coordination Will Frustrate Financial Institution Bankruptcy

A second problem a FIB would face is international coordination, most critically because of a lack of agreement about loss distribution.[117] Large financial firms often operate internationally and have cross-border assets that may be a critical component of a financial firm's value. Chapter 15 of the Bankruptcy Code provides a voluntary mechanism for international coordination between U.S. and foreign insolvency proceedings.[118] The coordination at issue in a U.S. FIB may well be with other foreign regulatory processes rather than with bankruptcy, and foreign financial regulators are hardly guaranteed to cooperate with a U.S. bankruptcy court.

[116.] In theory, conditions for DIP lending could be legislated, but it is difficult to do ex ante, and any such legislation would likely have a hydraulic effect on contractual terms—to the extent that one term is forbidden, it will likely be recreated synthetically through other terms.

[117.] See Anna Gelpern, Common Capital: A Thought Experiment in Cross-Border Resolution, 49 Tex. Int'l L.J. 355, 372 (2014); Jay Lawrence Westbrook, SIFIs and States, 49 Tex. Int'l L.J. 327, 347–48 (2014).

[118.] 11 U.S.C. § 1501(a) (2012). Chapter 15 authorizes the filing of an "ancillary case" by a foreign representative—such as a foreign trustee or court—to seek U.S. recognition of a "foreign proceeding." Id. section 1504. If granted, the U.S. automatic stay immediately comes into effect, and the foreign representative is authorized to operate the U.S. debtor's business in the ordinary course. Id. section 1520(a), 362(a). Additionally, chapter 15 enables U.S. bankruptcy trustees to be authorized "to act in a foreign country on behalf of a [U.S. bankruptcy] estate." Id. section 1505. This mechanism enables coordination between U.S. and foreign insolvency proceedings, but it is not self-executing, nor does it guaranty any particular result. It simply creates a mechanism for U.S. judicial recognition of foreign proceedings, but it does not bind U.S. courts to cooperation with foreign proceedings.

Foreign regulators are likely to face domestic political pressure to ringfence the assets of the debtor firm's foreign affiliates, meaning that they would not make these assets available to support U.S. creditors' claims.[119] In such a case, substantial going concern value could be lost as foreign creditors dismantle the financial institution's foreign assets.

C. Financial Contract Safe Harbors Will Frustrate Financial Institution Bankruptcy

Large financial institutions have substantial books of QFCs. All of these financial instruments are potentially valuable assets. As noted previously,[120] under current bankruptcy law, nondebtor QFC counterparties may accelerate, terminate, and liquidate their positions without violating the automatic stay that otherwise stops creditor collection efforts upon the filing of a bankruptcy.[121] This means that if at any point post-petition the counterparty is in the money, the counterparty can terminate the contract and seize any collateral that has been posted for the transaction.[122] Thus, as soon as a financial institution is in trouble, QFC counterparties can run. The rationale for this treatment of QFCs is to limit systemic risk by ensuring that a firm's failure does not lock counterparties into a bankruptcy, thus resulting in a domino effect of failures as the counterparties are left illiquid and ultimately insolvent.[123]

[119.] Westbrook, supra note 117, at 346–47.

[120.] See supra Part I.B.

[121.] 11 U.S.C. § 362(b)(6), (b)(7), (b)(17), (b)(27) (2012); id. section 555, 556, 559, 561.

[122.] Levitin, Business Bankruptcy, supra note 7, at 301.

[123.] H.R. Rep. No. 97-420, at 1 (1982), as reproduced with permission in 1982 U.S.C.C.A.N. 583, 583 (noting that "certain protections are necessary to prevent the insolvency of one commodity or security firm from spreading to other firms and possibly threatening the collapse of the affected market"). The report goes on to note that "[t]he prompt liquidation of an insolvent's position is generally desirable to minimize the potentially massive losses and chain reaction of insolvencies that could occur if the market were to move sharply in the wrong direction." Id. at 4, 1982 U.S.C.C.A.N. at 585.

A FIB system need not keep with current law, of course. Every version of FIB legislation has proposed a stay of the longer of forty-eight hours or until 5 p.m. the next business day for QFCs, in keeping with the International Swaps and Derivatives Association's forty-eight-hour Universal Resolution Stay Protocol. This term is required to be incorporated into the contractual terms of most swaps contracts, as well as in the other QFCs for globally systemically important bank holding companies and their depository subsidiaries,[124] but it is not in all QFCs.[125] The goal of the forty-eight-hour stay is to facilitate a transfer of the failed institutions' derivatives book to a solvent institution through a "weekend" bankruptcy that will not disrupt global financial markets.[126]

But what if a buyer cannot be found on such short notice? If all large financial institutions are distressed, there might not be any buyers capable of assimilating a large QFC book. In such a case, a temporary stay, no matter what the length, merely would delay the start of a run. Unless the stay were to last beyond the time of the sale in a GB/BB transaction, it would not be adequate to protect

---

Whether the safe harbors continue to limit systemic risk post-Dodd–Frank Act is another matter. In other work, I have observed that the Dodd–Frank Act's requirement that most swaps clear through clearinghouses eliminates the financial contagion concern for cleared swaps, while most other QFCs, other than repos, are already cleared through clearinghouses. Levitin, Prioritization and Mutualization, supra note 88, at 132, 146, 154. The use of clearinghouses prevents domino effects and renders the safe harbors duplicative. *Id.*

[124] See supra note 63.

[125] Financial Institutions Bankruptcy Act of 2014, H.R. 5421, 113th Cong. section 3 (2014) (creating proposed 11 U.S.C. § 1187(a)(3)); Financial Institutions Bankruptcy Act of 2016, H.R. 2947, 114th Cong. section 3 (same); The Financial CHOICE Act of 2016, H.R. 5983, 114th Cong. section 232 (same); Financial Institutions Bankruptcy Act of 2017, H.R. 1667, 115th Cong. section 3 (same); Financial CHOICE Act of 2017, H.R. 10, 115th Cong. section 122 (same); Int'l Swaps & Derivatives Ass'n, Inc., ISDA 2015 Universal Resolution Stay Protocol 41 (2015), https://online.ercep.com/media/attachments/httpassetsis daorgmediaa-en-94349.pdf [http://perma.cc/2DNM-ZGZ8]. OLA has a stay until 5 p.m. on the business day following the appointment of the FDIC as a receiver. 12 U.S.C. § 5390(b)(10)(B) (2012).

[126] H.R. Rep. No. 114-477, at 14–15 (2016).

the debtor's QFC book. The longer the stay, however, the less work the QFC exceptions would do to prevent systemic risk.[127]

The bigger problem with QFCs, however, is that the value of a debtor's individual QFC positions, much less the value of its total QFC book or segments thereof, is often not immediately known. This is especially true when some of the QFCs are hedges of various loans and others are simply freestanding gambles. JPMorgan Chase Bank, N.A. had, as of March 31, 2018, over $56 trillion in derivative exposures in what are surely thousands of contracts.[128] Citibank, N.A. had over $55 trillion in derivative exposures at the same time.[129]

It would take substantial time to responsibly sort through those positions, particularly at a time when the firm is in disarray and key personnel in the debtor's organization may be looking for or have already taken other employment opportunities. This means that there would be substantial valuation uncertainty about the QFC book of the financial institution, even if its problems do not stem from that book of business.[130] Because of that valuation uncertainty, a potential buyer in a GB/BB structure would either not purchase the QFC book or would insist on a steep discount because of the valuation uncertainty. Either situation would likely magnify the losses

---

[127.] The solution utilized in some FIB bills, as well as in OLA, is to have a "bridge institution" assume the qualified financial contracts, including derivatives. A bridge institution, however, is not a permanent solution. It is a holding pen for assets until the assets or the equity of the bridge institution can be sold to a purchaser. All the creation of the bridge institution does is impose an intermediate step in moving the failed firm's valuable assets to new ownership. Yet just as with a DIP, a bridge institution itself requires financing to maintain its liquidity, and to the extent that a buyer or other source of financing cannot be found before the stay on the qualified financial contracts expires, there will be a run on the bridge institution.

[128.] Statistics on Depository Institutions, FDIC, https://www5.fdic.gov/sdi/main.asp?formname=compare [http://perma.cc/4NXA-KT9H (staff-uploaded archive)].

[129.] Id.

[130.] The all-or-nothing assumption requirements that require the transfer as a block of all or no QFCs with any given counterparty only add to the valuation uncertainty problem. While these provisions are designed to prevent cherry-picking and create pressure for the transfer of all QFCs, they also mean that the transferee has no idea what it is taking. Notably, such an all-or-nothing assumption is also required in OLA. 12 U.S.C. § 5390(c)(9)(A) (2012).

in bankruptcy and thus would increase the likelihood of a domino effect as impaired creditors themselves fail.

D. Financial Institution Bankruptcy Lacks a Mechanism for Addressing Valuation Uncertainty Like the Orderly Liquidation Fund

The valuation uncertainty problem is particularly acute for QFCs, but it is hardly limited to them. The failed financial institution might have a large book of residential or commercial mortgages of uncertain value, and the need for speed created by the automatic stay exceptions for QFCs also creates a valuation uncertainty problem for non-QFC assets.

In FDIC receiverships, including under OLA, the valuation uncertainty problem for QFCs and other types of assets can be addressed through an FDIC shared loss agreement. A common form of FDIC bank resolution is through a Purchase and Assumption agreement in which a solvent bank agrees to take over certain assets of a failed bank. Sometimes the FDIC guarantees the performance of some of the purchased assets under such agreements.[131] The result is that the purchased assets are on the books of the purchaser, but the valuation risk, at least to the extent that it is due to the credit performance on the purchased assets, lies at least in part with the FDIC. Nothing, however, prevents the FDIC from expanding loss-sharing agreements to cover risks beyond credit performance.

The FDIC uses such shared loss agreements in part because of the need for speed in the FDIC resolution process. The FDIC likes, when possible, to maintain the operations of a failed bank without interruption. That means finding a buyer between the time when

---

[131.] See, e.g., Thomas P. Vartanian & Gordon L. Miller, A Review of the FDIC's Latest Tools for Resolving Problem Banks, A.B.A. Banking L. Committee J., Mar. 2009, at 1, 8, www.americanbar.org/content/dam/aba/administrative/business_law/news letters/CL130000/full-issue-200903.pdf [https://perma.cc/U428-ZTRL]; Loss-Share Questions and Answers, FDIC (Oct. 11, 2018), www.fdic.gov/bank/individual/failed/lossshare/index.html [https://perma.cc/9YSS-KQZR].

the FDIC takes over a bank (often at the close of business on Friday) and when the bank is next scheduled to open for business. Such a speedy turnaround precludes meaningful diligence of the assets—and hence a precise valuation—by the purchaser. The use of shared loss agreements enables the transaction to close quickly by shifting valuation risk onto the FDIC.

The limited stay for QFCs generates a similar need for speed in FIB proposals. There is no provision for FDIC shared loss agreements in FIB proposals, however, because this sort of use of government funds (even if they are only of a mutual insurance fund adminis-tered by the government) is anathema to the whole "private" FIB concept. In contrast, OLA expressly provides for an Orderly Liqui-dation Fund that could be used to address the valuation uncertainty in quick-turnaround GB/BB transactions that preclude careful buyer diligence of assets.[132]

Thus, not only does FIB lack a credible mechanism for financ-ing a bankruptcy, even a very fast one, but it also lacks a mecha-nism to overcome the valuation uncertainty problem that the GB/BB transaction structure is meant to overcome. A GB/BB problem is supposed to address valuation uncertainty by separating good assets from a debt overhang. But if the assets to be transferred to the Good Bank are of uncertain value, it is unlikely that there will be a pur-chaser readily available within forty-eight hours absent a regulatory shotgun to the back.

V. Systemic Financial Risk as a Political Question

A. The Political Nature of Systemic Risk

The failure of a large financial institution is not merely a pri-vate matter between the debtor and its creditors. It is a matter of

---

[132]   12 U.S.C. § 5390(n) (2012).

public concern because of the possibility of a systemic financial risk externality—that the failure of a financial institution would impose costs throughout the financial system, potentially resulting in a domino effect of financial institution failures and ultimately a contraction of economic activity in the real economy because of a lack of liquidity from financial markets. As I have argued elsewhere, there is no meaningful economic definition of "systemic risk."[133] It is not a measurable concept. Instead, the term is only sensible as a label for the *political* importance of a firm's financial failure in terms of political unwillingness to allow the social consequences from the institution's failure to materialize without intervention. Systemic risk is a political question, but the bankruptcy court system is not built to handle political questions.

American courts have a long-standing political question doctrine—the courts will not insert themselves into political questions properly committed to another branch of government.[134] There are two related reasons underlying this prudential doctrine. First, if the courts insert themselves into political issues, they might simply be disregarded, thereby eroding the standing of the courts. Second, the political question doctrine protects the legitimacy of the courts for when they rule on nonpolitical questions.

We should see systemic financial problems as political questions. The failure of large financial institutions creates a high likelihood of spillover effects into the broader economy and a response that involves the public fisc. Thus, systemic financial crises are ultimately distributional matters writ large and affect the general public, not just disputes between private parties. Such policy questions are not appropriate for the courts, much less for non–Article III courts. The courts are designed for conducting an adversarial process to resolve cases and controversies among litigants, not for determining broader questions of economic distribution in society that may affect third

---

[133.] See Levitin, In Defense of Bailouts, supra note 6, at 439–40.

[134.] *Nixon v. United States*, 506 U.S. 224, 228–29 (1993); *Baker v. Carr*, 369 U.S. 186, 210–11 (1962).

parties. Those parties have no voice in the court whether because of lack of legal standing, lack of knowledge of the case, or lack of wherewithal to participate in the case. Such broader distributional policy questions are therefore best left to the political branches of government.

It is true that courts regularly adjudicate matters involving the public fisc—all tax cases, for example[135]—but these are adjudicated within a statutory framework that deals with the liability of individual entities to the government or vice versa. It is never in the context of general distributional questions, such as which groups of creditors should be paid and which should not be. That sort of distributional decision should be reserved for the legislature, which may delegate the ultimate decision to an administrative agency, as with OLA. The combination of the use of the public fisc outside normal government spending processes with distributional decisions about who should benefit directly or indirectly from the use of those public funds is a fundamentally different matter than courts are used to addressing.

B. The New Bankruptcy: Bankruptcy as a Public Policy Forum

Since 2008, however, bankruptcy has changed. It has ceased to simply be a forum for readjusting financial obligations of private firms and individuals and has also become a forum for resolving thorny political problems. The Chrysler and GM bankruptcies were the first and most explicit instance of this. The auto manufacturers' bankruptcies provided an avenue for the federal government to intervene to support the industrial economy throughout the Rust Belt. Likewise, post-2008 bankruptcy has been used as a way to provide a lifeline to the struggling domestic coal industry by enabling coal producers

---

[135.] See, e.g., *Fredericks v. Comm'r*, 126 F.3d 433, 435, 449 (3d Cir. 1997) (adjudicating dispute between appellant and the Internal Revenue Service about whether appellant's tax deficiency assessment resulting from disallowance of tax-shelter deduction was valid and analyzing the impact of the doctrine of estoppel on the public fisc).

to shed their environmental liabilities and continue production.[136] To be sure, bankruptcy law always played a role in addressing public policy questions, such as how to allocate the risk of mass toxic torts or how to deal with the volatile finances of the airline industry. But post-2008 bankruptcy has been used more explicitly and deliberately by the executive branch as a forum for implementing policy.

Also starting in 2008, the use of chapter 9 municipal bankruptcy began to change. Prior to 2008, there were only two hundred non-erroneous chapter 9 filings, only thirty four of which were by general-purpose municipalities.[137] Most were by special-purpose hospitals,[138] water or sanitary districts,[139] or other specialized local governments with discrete financial problems. The only general-purpose government of any size to file prior to 2008 was Orange County, California, which governs the unincorporated areas of the county; most other general-purpose municipalities had fewer than one thousand residents.[140]

[136.] See Joshua Macey, Bankruptcy as Bailout: Coal, chapter 11, and the Erosion of Federal Law, 71 Stan. L. Rev. (forthcoming 2019) (on file with author).

[137.] Author's analysis of PACER data; see generally Omer Kimhi, chapter 9 of the Bankruptcy Code: A Solution in Search of a Problem, 27 Yale J. on Reg. 351 (2010) (expressing doubts about bankruptcy's utility in the municipal context).

[138.] See, e.g., In re Green Cty. Hosp., 59 B.R. 388, 391 (S.D. Miss. 1986).

[139.] See, e.g., In re Sullivan Cty. Reg'l Refuse Disposal Dist., 165 B.R. 60, 63 (Bankr. D. N.H. 1994).

[140.] For example, Moffett, Oklahoma, population 128 in the 2000 census, filed for bankruptcy after it lost its revenue from operating an illegal speed trap on the interstate highway. Tony Thornton & Sheila Stogsdill, Moffett Seeks Bankruptcy Protection: Town Bears Toll of Designation as a Speed Trap and Debts Incurred by the Late Mayor, NewsOK (Feb. 2, 2007, 12:00 AM), https://newsok.com/article/3007448/moffett-seeks-bankruptcy-protectionbrspan-classhl2town-bears-toll-of-designation-as-a-speed-trap-and-debts-incurred-by-the-late-mayorspan? [http://perma.cc/TC64-PTZZ]. Likewise, the city of Washington Park, Illinois, population 5,345 in the 2000 census, filed for chapter 9 unsuccessfully twice, once after a town employee embezzled the town's funds and another after a successful challenge to the town's topless dancer license fee. Nicholas J. C. Pistor, Washington Park Files for Bankruptcy Protection, St. Louis Post-Dispatch (July 31, 2009), www.stltoday.com/news/washington-park-files-for-bankruptcy-protection/article_b2a68ed0-91a3-53c7-87bc-d157c6aa181a.html [https://perma.cc/4RF5-VHK5 (staff-uploaded archive)] (describing Washington Park, IL's repeated bankruptcy filings following successful challenges to topless dancer license fee). While these examples are colorful, they are

Since 2008, however, chapter 9 has been used by large, general-purpose municipalities: Detroit, Michigan; San Bernardino, Stockton, and Vallejo, California; and Jefferson County, Alabama, have all gone through chapter 9.[141] Navigating these cities' insolvencies was not just a matter of financial decisionmaking but also political decisions. All bankruptcies involve distributional choices between creditor constituencies: Will money go to bondholders, vendors, or tort creditors for their prepetition claims? But with municipal bankruptcies there are also taxpayers who are not creditors, yet whose interests are very much implicated by any sort of payment plan: What level of municipal services will be offered going forward? What will municipal tax rates be? Will prized municipal assets that add substantially to quality of life, such as the artwork in the Detroit Institute of Arts, be sold to pay creditors or retained? Chapter 9 cases require navigating the politics of failed cities.

Bankruptcy scholarship has only just started grappling with the increased use of bankruptcy to manage political problems. Melissa Jacoby and Edward Janger have both recently written about how bankruptcy can manage the politics of decisions in chapter 9.[142] In earlier work regarding proposals to allow states to file for bankruptcy, I have suggested that bankruptcy is generally an inherently political process because of its distributional nature, but when bankruptcy affects more than creditors, its politics become

---

also typical of the size of general-purpose municipalities that have historically filed for chapter 9 bankruptcy.

[141] See Voluntary Petition, In re City of Detroit, No. 13-53846 (Bankr. E.D. Mich. July 18, 2013); Chapter 9 Voluntary Petition, In re City of San Bernadino, No. 6:12-bk-28006 (Bankr. C.D. Cal. Aug. 1, 2012); Voluntary Petition, In re City of Stockton, No. 12-32118 (Bankr. E.D. Cal. June 28, 2012); Voluntary Petition, In re City of Vallejo, No. 2008-26813 (Bankr. E.D. Cal. May 23, 2008); Voluntary Petition, In re Jefferson County, Alabama, No. 11-05736-TBB9 (Bankr. N.D. Ala. Nov. 9, 2011).

[142] See Melissa B. Jacoby, Federalism Form and Function in the Detroit Bankruptcy, 33 Yale J. on Reg. 55, 70-71 (2016); Melissa B. Jacoby, Presiding over Municipal Bankruptcies: Then, Now, and Puerto Rico, 91 Am. Bankr. L.J. 375, 385-88 (2017); Edward J. Janger, Towards a Jurisprudence of Public Law Bankruptcy Judging, 12 Brook. J. Corp. Fin. & Com. L. 39, 46-48 (2017).

unmanageable.[143] Likewise, in other work with Aurelia Chaud-hury and David Schleicher, I consider this problem in the context of simultaneous financial crises for overlapping municipal governments.[144]

All of this work recognizes the fundamental difficulty of managing politics in the bankruptcy process. While bankruptcy judges have figured out creative ways to do this in chapter 9, it is far from an ideal process because it gives an unelected judge tremendous discretion and is ultimately not at all a democratic process. This observation does not commend the expansion of bankruptcy to political cases like those of too-big-to-fail financial institutions.

Ironically, some of those who support the idea of FIB, such as Professors David A. Skeel, Jr. and Mark J. Roe, were sharp critics of the Chrysler and GM bankruptcies.[145] The Chrysler and GM bankruptcies both used a GB/BB format with the firms' good assets and certain politically favored liabilities—such as obligations to the firms' unionized workforces—assumed by the "Good Chrysler" and "Good GM," and the bad assets and disfavored liabilities left behind in "Bad Chrysler" and "Bad GM" for liquidation.[146] The Chrysler and GM

[143.] Adam J. Levitin, Bankrupt Politics and the Politics of Bankruptcy, 97 Cornell L. Rev. 1399, 1451–55 (2012) (arguing that bankruptcy problems need to be addressed in political rather than financial terms).

[144.] Aurelia Chaudhury, Adam J. Levitin & David Schleicher, Junk Cities: Resolving Insolvency Crises in Overlapping Municipalities, 107 Cal. L. Rev. (forthcoming 2019).

[145.] See Mark J. Roe & David Skeel, Assessing the Chrysler Bankruptcy, 108 Mich. L. Rev. 727, 729–31 (2010) (criticizing the Chrysler bankruptcy for failing to adhere to bankruptcy priorities). While Professor Skeel has strongly endorsed financial institutions bankruptcy, see, e.g., Skeel, supra note 3, at 329, Professor Roe rightly recognizes the problems with FIB, but argues it should exist as an option alongside a regulatory resolution scheme. See Mark J. Roe, Why Regulators Are Needed to Handle Failed Banks, N.Y. Times (June 6, 2017), www.nytimes.com/2017/06/06/busi ness/dealbook/why-regulators-are-needed-to-handle-failed-banks.html [https://perma.cc/S5MY-5A55].

[146.] See Jeffrey McCracken, John D. Stoll & Neil King Jr., U.S. Threatens Bankruptcy for GM, Chrysler, Wall St. J. (Mar. 31, 2009, 12:01 AM), www.wsj.com/articles/SB123845591244871499 [https://perma.cc/6QL5-8UDE] (describing use of bankruptcy for implementing good bank/bad bank plan).

bankruptcies were harshly criticized as having violated bankruptcy rules of priority and for being sub rosa reorganization plans.[147]

While these criticisms are arguably incorrect,[148] they underscore a more fundamental point: the bankruptcy system is not designed for dealing with systemic financial crises. When the bankruptcy system is used to handle systemically important firms, it is very likely to be warped by the weight of political concerns and cease to be the neutral, fair process that FIB advocates imagine it to be.[149] This will be all the more true if DIP financing comes from the only realistic source, the U.S. government.

Contemporary bankruptcy practice often follows the "golden rule"—he who has the gold makes the rules.[150] This means that it is often the DIP lender calling the shots on things such as whether there will be an asset sale, what assets will be sold, and what the bidding procedures will be.[151] Sometimes these issues have to be decided at the very beginning of a case before creditors have managed to organize themselves.

In such a situation, the only party capable of staring down an overreaching DIP lender is the bankruptcy judge, but bankruptcy judges

---

[147.] See Roe & Skeel, supra note 145, at 741; see also Barry E. Adler, A Reassessment of Bankruptcy Reorganization after Chrysler and General Motors, 18 Am. Bankr. Inst. L. Rev. 305, 308 (2010); Ralph Brubaker & Charles Jordan Tabb, Bankruptcy Reorganizations and the Troubling Legacy of Chrysler and GM, 2010 U. Ill. L. Rev. 1375, 1377–79 (2010).

[148.] The absolute priority rule applies only in a cramdown confirmation, and then only to nonconsenting classes of unsecured claimants and equity interests. 11 U.S.C. § 1129(b)(2)(B)—(C) (2012). By its own terms, it does not apply to asset sales or to consensual plans. The objecting creditors in Chrysler were part of a consenting class of secured creditors. In re Chrysler LLC, 405 B.R. 84, 104 (Bankr. S.D.N.Y. 2009), aff'd, 576 F.3d 108 (2d Cir. 2009), appellate decision vacated as moot sub nom. Ind. State Pension Tr. v. Chrysler LLC, 558 U.S. 1087 (2009). For a convincing argument that there was nothing particularly unusual or illegal about the transaction structures used in the GM and Chrysler bankruptcies, see generally Stephen J. Lubben, No Big Deal: The GM and Chrysler Cases in Context, 83 Am. Bankr. L.J. 531 (2009).

[149.] See, e.g., Brubaker & Tabb, supra note 147, at 1405.

[150.] See, e.g., Adler, supra note 147, at 308, 313–14. This alone should call into question the desirability of bankruptcy as a mechanism for dealing with any problem.

[151.] See id.

are not well suited for this role. Bankruptcy judges are not Article III judges with life tenure. When a non–Article III judge who likely has no expertise regarding the particular debtor firm or financial markets generally is presented with a situation in which he is told that he must immediately approve a transaction or else the global economy will collapse, the judge is put in an untenable position. The judge is likely to approve the transaction, whether or not it complies with the law. The judge might make some noise, but will ultimately be rolled.[152]

The rule-of-law virtues of the bankruptcy system will inevitably become warped if the system is dragooned to handle systemic risks that trump any law. Put differently, it is bad for bankruptcy courts to deal with systemic risk, and it is bad for systemic risk to have bankruptcy courts managing the resolution process. Political questions like resolution of systemic financial distress should be resolved in the political forum, not the courts.

VI. Conclusion

What would happen if we go down the FIB rabbit hole? One of three things. First, the bankruptcy process would be abused, as alleged to have occurred in the GM and Chrysler bailouts, to achieve the financial stability end sought by whatever administration is in office. In other words, a bailout would occur through bankruptcy. Second, there would be a questionably illegal, ad hoc bailout, with lots of finger-wagging, clucking, and tsk-tsking after the fact, as occurred with the use of the Exchange Stabilization Fund to aid Mexico in 1995,[153] or the Federal Reserve's Maiden Lane structures in 2008,[154]

---

[152] See, e.g., Baird, supra note 8, at 290.

[153] See Russell Dean Covey, Note, Adventures in the Zone of Twilight: Separation of Powers and National Economic Security in the Mexican Bailout, 105 Yale L.J. 1311, 1313–14 (1996) (arguing that the Clinton administration's use of the Exchange Stabilization Fund in 1995 to bail out Mexico was illegal).

[154] See, e.g., Alexandra Mehra, Legal Authority in Unusual and Exigent Circumstances: The Federal Reserve and the Financial Crisis, 13 U. Pa. J. Bus. L. 221, 238–41

or the use of the Exchange Stabilization Fund in 2008 to bailout money market mutual funds.[155] Or third, Congress would rapidly pass bailout-authorization legislation, much as it did with the Emergency Economic Stabilization Act in 2008.[156]

None of these are desirable outcomes. Nobody likes bailouts. But realistically they are inevitable when things get bad enough because no one wants to deal with the political consequences of a true economic meltdown.[157] The realistic goal is not avoiding bailouts altogether but finding a predictable legal framework for the bailouts that distributes as much of the cost as possible to the beneficiaries of the bailout at a time when it will not cause systemic disruption. Insisting on bankruptcy as a bailout alternative is ideologically driven self-deception. The pursuit of the Fool's Gold of FIB will ultimately result in bailouts whether in the guise of bankruptcy or otherwise.

Furthermore, it does no favor to the rule of law to saddle legal procedures like bankruptcy with political questions like bailouts. No end is served by pretending that bailouts are creatures of law; a wolf in sheep's clothing is still a wolf. Yet that is precisely what the pipe dream of FIB would do. We need to accept that as distasteful as bailouts may be, as long as there are SIFIs the resolution dilemma will always be resolved with a bailout.

We do not want to be comfortable with bailouts, and we should not be. The best way to avoid bailouts is through better ex ante regulation. If risk is adequately managed on the front end, there will be no need to deal with the consequences on the back end. Yet markets change and innovate, and there is constant political pressure for deregulation. Even without these pressures, no system of regulation is foolproof, so bailouts may be unavoidable in some circumstances.

(2011); Eric A. Posner, What Legal Authority Does the Fed Need During a Financial Crisis? 101 Minn. L. Rev. 1529, 1548–49 (2017).

[155.] See, e.g., Phillip A. Wallach, To the Edge: Legality, Legitimacy, and Responses to the 2008 Financial Crisis 75–77 (2015).

[156.] Emergency Economic Stabilization Act of 2008, Pub. L. No. 110-343, section 101-02, 122 Stat. 3765, 3767–70 (2008).

[157.] Levitin, In Defense of Bailouts, supra note 6, at 439–40.

Avoiding the resolution dilemma and its inevitable outcome means ensuring a robust prudential regulatory regime that can reduce systemic risk and prevent crises in the first place. Regulators' single most potent tool for managing risk is the living wills process, including the authority for regulators to break up the biggest banks before they break the economy. A FIB process would neutralize the living wills power, thereby both preventing regulators from managing systemic risk and saddling them with a resolution process that is doomed to fail. Most importantly, FIB would require regulators to step in with a bailout to contain the resulting crisis—simply put, FIB all but guarantees bailouts rather than being an antidote. We should plug our ears to the bankruptcy Lorelei's louche song before it lures us onto the financial rocks and call out FIB for the fib it is.

Controlling Creditor Control

Jevic and the End(?) of *LifeCare*

*Jonathan C. Lipson**

A ll good things must come to an end. For debates about the kind of priority rules we want in chapter 11 bankruptcy, that day was March 22, 2017, when the Supreme Court reminded us in *Czyzewski v. Jevic Holding Corp.* (*In re Jevic*) that "absolute," not "relative," priority should govern final distributions of a debtor's assets.[1] Absolute priority means that, absent an agreed alternative, senior creditor *A* must be

---

* Harold E. Kohn Professor of Law, Temple University-Beasley School of Law. This was written as part of a Festschrift in honor of the remarkable career of Jay L. Westbrook, whose work inspired this chapter. Pamela Foohey provided helpful comments and Dina Bleckman excellent research support. Reproduced with permission from Norton Journal of Bankruptcy Law and Practice, Vol. 27 No. 5 (Oct. 2018), with permission of Thomson Reuters. Copyright © 2018. Further use without the permission of Thomson Reuters is prohibited. For further information about this publication, please visit https://legal.thomsonreuters.com/en/products/lawbooks or call 800.328.9352.

[1]. *Czyzewski v. Jevic Holding Corp.*, 137 S. Ct. 973, 979, 197 L. Ed. 2d 398, 63 Bankr. Ct. Dec. (CRR) 242, 77 Collier Bankr. Cas. 2d (MB) 596, 41 I.E.R. Cas. (BNA) 1613, Bankr. L. Rep. (CCH) P 83082 (2017), rev'g, 787 F.3d 173, 61 Bankr. Ct. Dec. (CRR) 21, 2015 I.E.R. Cas. (BNA) 160363, Bankr. L. Rep. (CCH) P 82826, 165 Lab. Cas. (CCH) P 10774 (3d Cir. 2015). See also In re Jevic Holding Corp., 688 Fed. Appx. 166 (3d Cir. 2017) (vacating and remanding Third Circuit opinion). I use the term "relative" priority in the loose sense that it is an alternative to "absolute" priority embraced by the Supreme Court in Jevic. Sticklers may point out that the lower courts in Jevic blessed neither absolute nor relative priority, but instead merely skipped one group of creditors to favor another.

paid before mid-priority creditor *B*, who must be paid before junior claimant (e.g., general unsecured creditor) *C*, and so on. "Relative" priority, by contrast, means that a court may permit junior claimants who might be out of the money under absolute priority to recover something because the court believes that doing so serves some greater good: *A* first, then *C*, then *B;* or, *A* first, then *B* and *C* share, etc.

In *Jevic*, the lower courts approved a kind of relative priority (*A* first, then *C*, with nothing to *B*) believing that the greater good was closure: resolving a case that appeared hopeless because the debtor had no assets to fund a plan or trustee-supervised liquidation.[2] The Supreme Court reversed, holding that "[a] distribution scheme ordered in connection with the dismissal of a [c]hapter 11 case cannot, without the consent of the affected parties, deviate from the basic priority rules that apply under the primary mechanisms the Code establishes for final distributions of estate value in business bankruptcies."[3] Those "basic priority rules" were, for all practical purposes, the "absolute" priority contemplated by the Bankruptcy Code.

At one level, this was not news: The Court has backed absolute priority for over one hundred years.[4] Yet, observers say that *Jevic*

---

[2] *Czyzewski v. Jevic Holding Corp.*, 137 S. Ct. 973, 982, 197 L. Ed. 2d 398, 63 Bankr. Ct. Dec. (CRR) 242, 77 Collier Bankr. Cas. 2d (MB) 596, 41 I.E.R. Cas. (BNA) 1613, Bankr. L. Rep. (CCH) P 83082 (2017) (lower court approved priority-skipping distribution because it found that "there would be no funds to operate, investigate, or litigate were the case converted to a proceeding in [c]hapter 7.").

[3] *Czyzewski v. Jevic Holding Corp.*, 137 S. Ct. 973, 983, 197 L. Ed. 2d 398, 63 Bankr. Ct. Dec. (CRR) 242, 77 Collier Bankr. Cas. 2d (MB) 596, 41 I.E.R. Cas. (BNA) 1613, Bankr. L. Rep. (CCH) P 83082 (2017). See also *Czyzewski v. Jevic Holding Corp.*, 137 S. Ct. 973, 978, 197 L. Ed. 2d 398, 63 Bankr. Ct. Dec. (CRR) 242, 77 Collier Bankr. Cas. 2d (MB) 596, 41 I.E.R. Cas. (BNA) 1613, Bankr. L. Rep. (CCH) P 83082 (2017)

[4] The absolute priority rule (APR) is generally associated with the Supreme Court's Boyd opinion, *N. Pac. Ry. Co. v. Boyd*, 228 U.S. 482, 492 (1913), although its Louisville opinion made an earlier, important contribution. See *Louisville Trust Co. v. Louisville, N.A. & C. Ry. Co.*, 174 U.S. 674, 684, 19 S. Ct. 827, 43 L. Ed. 1130 (1899) ("[T]he stockholder's interest in the property is subordinate to the rights of creditors. First, of secured, and then of unsecured, creditors."). Since then, the Court has reiterated its commitment to absolute priority in *Case v. Los Angeles Lumber Products Co.*, 308 U.S. 106, 60 S. Ct. 1, 84 L. Ed. 110 (1939), *Norwest Bank Worthington v. Ahlers*, 485 U.S. 197, 202, 108 S. Ct. 963, 99 L. Ed. 2d 169, 17 Bankr. Ct. Dec. (CRR) 201, 18 Collier

is one of the Court's more important opinions on chapter 11 reorganization in many years.[5] Why the fuss? Because *Jevic* was as much about the procedural mechanism used as it was about its distributive consequences.

That mechanism was a so-called "structured dismissal," a procedural concoction under which senior and junior claimants (*A* and *C*) sought to split the very limited assets of the debtor, a trucking company, while paying nothing on account of the "mid-priority" wage claims held by the petitioners, the debtor's terminated drivers (*B*).[6]

Although *Jevic* does not forbid structured dismissals,[7] it does establish guardrails for their use. As articulated in *Jevic*, these guardrails have implications beyond end-of-case decisions. They seek

---

Bankr. Cas. 2d (MB) 262, Bankr. L. Rep. (CCH) P 72186 (1988), and, to a lesser extent, *Bank of America Nat. Trust and Sav. Ass'n v. 203 North LaSalle Street Partnership*, 526 U.S. 434, 441, 119 S. Ct. 1411, 143 L. Ed. 2d 607, 34 Bankr. Ct. Dec. (CRR) 329, 41 Collier Bankr. Cas. 2d (MB) 526, Bankr. L. Rep. (CCH) P 77924 (1999). Perhaps the closest the Court has come to relative priority was in recognizing the possibility of the "equitable adjustment" of contract claims in order to effectuate a reorganization under prior law—a position surely untenable today. Compare *Otis & Co. v. Securities and Exchange Commission*, 323 U.S. 624, 634, n.14, 65 S. Ct. 483, 89 L. Ed. 511 (1945) ("Creditors' contracts also have been declared subject to equitable adjustment in corporate reorganizations so long as they receive 'full compensatory treatment' whether the reorganization is in bankruptcy . . . or in compliance with regulatory statutes").

5. See Ralph Brubaker, Taking Bankruptcy's Distribution Rules Seriously: How The Supreme Court Saved Bankruptcy from Self-Destruction, 37 Bankr. L. Letter NL 1, Apr. 2017 ("The Supreme Court's recent decision in *Czyzewski v. Jevic Holding Corp.* has the potential to be one of the most consequential events for bankruptcy reorganization law and practice since the famous 1913 absolute-priority decision in *Northern Pacific Railway v. Boyd*.").

6. In re Jevic Holding Corp., 787 F.3d 173, 188, 61 Bankr. Ct. Dec. (CRR) 21, 2015 I.E.R. Cas. (BNA) 160363, Bankr. L. Rep. (CCH) P 82826, 165 Lab. Cas. (CCH) P 10774 (3d Cir. 2015), as amended, (Aug. 18, 2015) and cert. granted, 136 S. Ct. 2541, 195, 195 L. Ed. 2d 867 (2016) and rev'd and remanded, 137 S. Ct. 973, 197 L. Ed. 2d 398, 63 Bankr. Ct. Dec. (CRR) 242, 77 Collier Bankr. Cas. 2d (MB) 596, 41 I.E.R. Cas. (BNA) 1613, Bankr. L. Rep. (CCH) P 83082 (2017). A portion of the drivers' claims was "mid-priority" because they were entitled to a statutorily created fourth priority over general unsecured creditors. 11 U.S.C. § 507(a)(4).

7. *Czyzewski v. Jevic Holding Corp.*, 137 S. Ct. 973, 985, 197 L. Ed. 2d 398, 63 Bankr. Ct. Dec. (CRR) 242, 77 Collier Bankr. Cas. 2d (MB) 596, 41 I.E.R. Cas. (BNA) 1613, Bankr. L. Rep. (CCH) P 83082 (2017) (the Court "express[ed] no view about the legality of structured dismissals in general").

to preserve broad-based stakeholder participation in chapter II, the predictability of its outcomes, and the integrity of the process. These, in turn, protect the legitimacy of a system that seeks to manage the disappointment of expectations on a sometimes massive scale. Bankruptcy is the place where broken contracts, unremedied torts, and unpaid taxes go to die.[8] Knowing how the endgame will be played—the process by which those claims will be treated by a debtor that cannot pay them all—affects all that comes before.

That the Court has long embraced absolute priority, and reaffirmed it in *Jevic*, has not stopped academics from debating its merits.[9] Those who question its rigidity do so on the reasonable grounds that there will be cases where some other order creates greater wealth (or better reduces losses) than absolute priority.[10] Those who defend it do so on the equally reasonable grounds that in most (maybe all) cases, the efficiency gains of absolute priority outweigh those of any alternative.[11]

[8.] As Warren and Westbrook put it: "Bankruptcy is the forum in which our society makes its final decisions about the life and death of a business and who gets what. To that forum come bank lenders and pensioners, tort victims and trade creditors, unpaid doctors and disappointed bondholders, each with a different economic role in society and each with a different economic relationship with the debtor." Elizabeth Warren & Jay Lawrence Westbrook, Contracting Out of Bankruptcy: An Empirical Intervention, 118 Harv. L. Rev. 1197, 1254 (2005).

[9.] See John D. Ayer, Rethinking Absolute Priority after Ahlers, 87 Mich. L. Rev. 963, 974–76 (1989) ("Fifteen years after [1913's] Boyd, two scholars were able to argue that corporate practice recognized two priority rules—a rule of absolute priority, à la Boyd, and a rule of 'relative' priority, functioning in practice much like the informal 'share' scheme that obtained before Boyd."). I tersely and selectively summarize these debates in Part I in the following.

[10.] See, e.g., Douglas G. Baird, Priority Matters: Absolute Priority, Relative Priority, and the Costs of Bankruptcy, 165 U. Pa. L. Rev. 785, 792 (2017) (providing examples of relative priority); Anthony J. Casey, The Creditors' Bargain and Option-Preservation Priority in chapter II, 78 U. Chi. L. Rev. 759, 807 (2011) ("The focus of Option-Preservation Priority is the relationship between classes of creditors and the decisions that affect the maximization of assets in chapter II.").

[11.] See, e.g., Mark J. Roe & Frederick Tung, Breaking Bankruptcy Priority: How Rent-Seeking Upends the Creditors' Bargain, 99 Va. L. Rev. 1235, 1236 (2013) ("The absolute priority rule provides the fixed framework within which the players negotiate the plan of reorganization and within which the judge evaluates it").

Professor Jay Westbrook, the subject of the Festschrift for which this chapter was written, recognized the underlying problem here, and so wisely (and mercifully) excused himself from these debates.[12] He saw that priority rights were not merely about the order of distributions, but also creditor control.[13] Being at the front of the line—first in priority—might do more than just increase your take: It might, Westbrook saw, also give you the power to write the rules for everyone behind you. This, I want to suggest, is ultimately what was at stake in *Jevic*—who controls the reorganization process?—and has become the focal point of much of our best recent bankruptcy scholarship.[14]

In this brief chapter, I connect Westbrook's insights about creditor control to the process-oriented reasoning of *Jevic* and its doppelganger, *In re ICL Holding Co* (a.k.a. *"LifeCare"*), a case decided at the appellate level the same day, and the same way, as *Jevic*.[15] Both

---

[12.] See Jay Lawrence Westbrook, The Control of Wealth in Bankruptcy, 82 Tex. L. Rev. 795, 801, 805 (2004) [hereinafter, Westbrook, Control] ("This Article does not join the debate as to the efficiency of secured credit"). The debate was often cast in terms of "contractualist" versus mandatory rules. Warren and Westbrook, supra note 8, 118 Harv. L. Rev. at 1254 ("The contractualists have given us an entertaining debate, but it is time to move on.").

[13.] Westbrook, Control, supra note 12, 82 Tex. L. Rev. at 806 ("The key requirement is to understand control of the recovery process as a valuable element of a security interest distinct from priority in distribution, a point virtually unexamined in the secured-credit literature."). See also Elizabeth Warren & Jay L. Westbrook, Secured Party in Possession, 22 Am. Bankr. Inst. J., 12, 12 (2003).

[14.] See, e.g., Melissa B. Jacoby & Edward J. Janger, Tracing Equity: Realizing and Allocating Value in chapter 11, 96 Tex. L. Rev. 673, 677 (2017) ("Distributional rights determine who has decision-making power in a chapter 11 bankruptcy case.").

[15.] In re ICL Holding Co., Inc., 802 F.3d 547, 551–52, 61 Bankr. Ct. Dec. (CRR) 155, 74 Collier Bankr. Cas. 2d (MB) 607, Bankr. L. Rep. (CCH) P 82867 (3d Cir. 2015). The LifeCare debtors had previously been known as "Lifecare." LifeCare Holdings, Inc. was at one time a leading operator of long-term acute care hospitals. See In re ICL Holding Co., Inc., 802 F.3d 547, 549–50, 61 Bankr. Ct. Dec. (CRR) 155, 74 Collier Bankr. Cas. 2d (MB) 607, Bankr. L. Rep. (CCH) P 82867 (3d Cir. 2015). While in chapter 11, Lifecare was referred to as "LCI." According to Judge Ambro, "Per its plan of reorganization it became 'ICL.'" 802 F.3d at 547 n. 1. It is not entirely clear what this means. A search of the docket reveals no evidence that a plan was ever confirmed. Dkt. No. 14-2709 (3d Cir. 2015). Instead, the case appears to have been resolved by a structured dismissal similar in certain respects to that involved in Jevic—except that the "final" distributions were not made pursuant to that court order, but instead earlier in the case.

Jevic and *LifeCare* were controlled foreclosures that made priority-skipping distributions; both originated in the important and controversial Delaware bankruptcy court; the secured creditors in both sought to resolve the cases through structured dismissals; their appeals in the Third Circuit were argued the same day before different panels, each of which affirmed.[16]

There, however, the similarity ends. Although the Supreme Court reversed in *Jevic*, it was not asked to opine on *LifeCare*, and so did not. Whether, or to what extent, *LifeCare* remains good law is unclear. Some believe that both cases committed the same priority sin, and so perhaps *Jevic* signals the end of *LifeCare*,[17] or at least its precedential debility.[18] Others, however, view *LifeCare* as answering a different question—what constitutes property of the debtor's estate?[19] If, as in *LifeCare*, a bankruptcy court concludes that property belongs to a secured creditor and not the estate, then the secured creditor—not the court—controls the distribution of that property. Controlling that property can, in turn, lead to control of the bankruptcy process, itself.

Jevic and *LifeCare* are difficult to reconcile.[20] They present a choice not only about doctrine but also deeper questions that have

---

[16.] Both were argued on January 14, 2015. See In re ICL Holding Co., Inc., 802 F.3d 547, 61 Bankr. Ct. Dec. (CRR) 155, 74 Collier Bankr. Cas. 2d (MB) 607, Bankr. L. Rep. (CCH) P 82867 (3d Cir. 2015); In re Jevic Holding Corp., 787 F.3d 173, 61 Bankr. Ct. Dec. (CRR) 21, 2015 I.E.R. Cas. (BNA) 160363, Bankr. L. Rep. (CCH) P 82826, 165 Lab. Cas. (CCH) P 10774 (3d Cir. 2015), as amended, (Aug. 18, 2015).

[17.] In an unpublished decision in Constellation Enterprises, for example, the Delaware Bankruptcy Court apparently struck a proposed priority-skipping distribution on grounds that it offended Jevic. See Dan Rafferty et al., How Will Jevic Change chapter 11 Practice? 082317 ABI-CLE 343 (discussing unpublished decision in In re Constellation Enterprises, LLC, et al., case no. 16-11213 (CSS), docket nos. 944–48, 955 & 956)).

[18.] See Rafferty et al., supra, 082317 ABI-CLE 343 ("it is unclear whether LifeCare remains good law after Jevic.").

[19.] See In re Nuverra Environmental Solutions, Inc., 2017 WL 3326453, at *3 (D. Del. 2017) (citing LifeCare for proposition that a "gift from senior lenders to certain, but not all, classes of general unsecured creditors" is permissible). See also In re Short Bark Industries, Inc. et al., Case No. 17-11502(KG) (Bankr. D. Del. 2017) (approving escrow set-aside for general unsecured creditors at beginning of case even though no provision was made for priority unsecured claims).

[20.] Because they rest on different doctrinal foundations, the mere fact that Jevic comes from the Supreme Court is not dispositive.

animated much of Westbrook's work: what sort of chapter II system do we want, and for whose benefit should it work? Cases like *LifeCare* would, if unchecked by *Jevic*, spell the end of chapter II as a negotiated process for reorganizing troubled companies because it would strip unsecured creditors of leverage Congress intended to give them, instead vesting case control in secured creditors. Hence, the question in the title of this chapter: Does *Jevic* end *LifeCare*—or is it the other way around?

This chapter has three parts. First, one summarize the priority debates, and how Westbrook's focus on creditor control transformed them, anticipating cases like *Jevic* and *LifeCare*. Part 2 uses *Jevic* and *LifeCare* to show how secured creditors exert control at three key moments in chapter II cases: (i) case financing; (ii) asset disposition (i.e., the decision to sell or reorganize the debtor); and (iii) the distribution of proceeds from that disposition. Part 3 then develops *Jevic*'s procedural framework, pointing out tensions with *LifeCare*.

I. The Priority Debates and Westbrook's Contribution

A. The Priority Debates

Academics have debated the merits of various approaches to priority for about a century.[21] In the modern era, these debates took one of

---

[21] Who, for example, can forget the infamous Billyou-Blum Smackdown of 1954? Compare De Forest Billyou, "New Directions": A Further Comment, 67 Harv. L. Rev. 1379, 1380–81 (1954) (arguing that "[i]t is indisputable that the term "absolute" priority was unknown in legal literature until 1928, when it was adopted in a now classic paper published by Professor Bonbright and Mr. Bergerman to describe a standard of priority that they felt was desirable in, but not typical of, equity receivership reorganization.") (citing James C. Bonbright and Milton M. Bergerman, Two Rival Theories of Priority Rights of Security Holders in a Corporate Reorganization, 28 Colum. L. Rev. 127, 130 (1928)) with Walter J. Blum, The "New Directions" for Priority Rights in Bankruptcy Reorganizations, 67 Harv. L. Rev. 1367, 1375 (1954) ("On the practical level, Billyou's main argument for applying the investment value theory to the second aspect of priority is at once the most interesting and the most baffling portion of his article.").

two principal forms: (i) as disputes over absolute or relative priority[22] and (ii) as disputes over whether debtors should be permitted to fully encumber their assets or, instead, be required to reserve ("carve out") some unencumbered value for unsecured claimants.[23] Permeating these debates were garden-variety—and irreconcilable—differences of opinion about the merits of public versus private ordering, command versus contract.[24]

One point of agreement, however, was the end that priority rules served: wealth maximization was the "consensus position," Westbrook observed.[25] There were, however, four problems with these debates and their distributive focus.

First, and somewhat technically, it is not entirely clear what "priority" actually is as a doctrinal matter, or how it affects distributions in reorganization. The Bankruptcy Code recognizes three sets of "ordinary" priority rules: (1) those provided by state law, with respect to secured claims, which confer priority rights (liens) in a debtor's property, such as those under Article 9 of the Uniform Commercial Code;[26] (2) statutory priority rights under Bankruptcy Code section 507, such as the one at issue in *Jevic*, giving the drivers' wage claims fourth ("mid") priority as unsecured claims;[27] and (3) the common law "absolute priority rule" (APR), which applies to plans of reorganization and (now we know) structured dismissals,

---

[22.] See sources in notes 10–11.

[23.] See Edward J. Janger, Predicting When the Uniform Law Process Will Fail: Article 9, Capture, and the Race to the Bottom, 83 Iowa L. Rev. 569, 573–74 (1998) (comparing, among others, Steven L. Harris & Charles W. Mooney, Jr., A Property-Based Theory of Security Interests: Taking Debtors' Choices Seriously, 80 Va. L. Rev. 2021, 2021 (1994) and Elizabeth Warren, Article 9 Set Aside for Unsecured Creditors, UCC Bulletin, Oct. 1996, at 1).

[24.] See Jonathan C. Lipson, Bargaining Bankrupt: A Relational Theory of Contract in Bankruptcy, 6 Harv. Bus. L. Rev. 239, 241 (2016) (observing that the debate is "enduring because it is often conceptualized as one of finding balance between permissive and mandatory rules—drawing lines between contract and command.").

[25.] Westbrook, Control, supra note 12, 82 Tex. L. Rev. at 821.

[26.] Article 9 of the Uniform Commercial Code governs security interests in personal property, and has been enacted in all fifty states.

[27.] 11 U.S.C.A. § 507(a).

and more generally contemplates that creditors have priority over owners (e.g., shareholders).[28]

These priority rules sit at the junction of other, deeper doctrines, including contract, property, and Congress' bankruptcy power. To assert that a particular priority rule will have this or that distributive effect would seem to gloss over a great deal of underlying doctrinal complexity. Indeed, the idea that any particular rule choice will determine a legal outcome has long irritated legal realists and their fellow travelers, even in simple disputes, such as alleged breach of contract.[29] If we cannot agree about the predictive force of simple doctrines in simple cases, there will be limits to the ability of any choice of priority rule to produce particular distributive outcomes in complex cases. While the rules clearly matter, it is easy to exaggerate their force.

Second, even if we could draw a straight line from doctrine to outcome, legal professionals are not especially well-equipped methodologically to make claims about the resulting value. True, this may not be hard in simple liquidations. But the whole point of reorganization under chapter 11 is to save going concerns if possible.[30] Estimating that future value—e.g., for distribution to creditors as shares of stock of the reorganized company—is perhaps the most difficult problem that bankruptcy judges routinely face, and is one for which lawyers,

---

[28.] 11 U.S.C.A. § 1129(b). The Bankruptcy Code also recognizes contractual subordination, which is the creation of priority by agreement. 11 U.S.C.A. § 510(a).

[29.] See, e.g., Stewart Macaulay, The Reliance Interest and the World outside the Law Schools' Doors, 1991 Wis. L. Rev. 247, 288 (1991) ("Imagining that rules of law create a high degree of predictability, and that, as a result, we gain freedom, is a rich fantasy."). See also Duncan Kennedy, Form and Substance in Private Law Adjudication, 89 Harv. L. Rev. 1685, 1700 (1976) (characterizing as indeterminate situations in which "a 'rule' that appears to dispose cleanly of a fact situation is nullified by a counterrule whose scope of application seems to be almost identical").

[30.] H.R. Rep. No. 95-595, at 220 (1977) ("The purpose of a business reorganization case, unlike a liquidation case, is to restructure a business's finances so that it may continue to operate, provide its employees with jobs, pay its creditors, and produce a return for its stockholders . . . It is more economically efficient to reorganize than to liquidate, because it preserves jobs and assets.").

judges, and law professors are typically not well trained.[31] Not surprisingly, those who made the most forceful claims for the distributive virtues of one approach or the other tended to rely on *a priori* theoretical or normative arguments, rather than empirical ones.[32] This is a persistent problem. As Westbrook recently observed, dryly: "More research is needed."[33]

Third, in many cases, the priority debates conflated two questions, one harder than the other. The "easy" question involved distributive welfare, meaning: How can we make the pie bigger (or shrink it less)? Because no one seriously argues that bankruptcy should produce smaller recoveries, this question is difficult only in the respects noted earlier (i.e., it is hard to predict payouts from rule choices). But at least some disputants in these debates recognized that the much tougher questions involved allocative equity, meaning: How do we decide the size of the slices, and does the answer to that question in turn affect the overall size of the pie? Contractualist writers tended either to ignore the question, or to assume that the former would solve for the latter. This is theoretically correct: If the pie is big enough to feed everyone, then we care less about relative shares of it.[34] But, because bankruptcy is a collective process where the pie can almost never feed everyone, rules about metering the portions may matter.[35]

---

[31] See Kenneth Ayotte & Edward R. Morrison, Valuation Disputes in Corporate Bankruptcy, U. Pa. L. Rev. (forthcoming 2018) (describing common valuation errors) (manuscript on file with author).

[32] See, e.g., Thomas H. Jackson & Anthony T. Kronman, Secured Financing and Priorities Among Creditors, 88 Yale L.J. 1143 (1979); Saul Levmore, Monitors and Freeriders in Commercial and Corporate Settings, 92 Yale L.J. 49 (1982).

[33] See Jay Lawrence Westbrook, Secured Creditor Control and Bankruptcy Sales: An Empirical View, 2015 U. Ill. L. Rev. 831, 835 (2015) [hereinafter, Westbrook, Empirical].

[34] See, e.g., Douglas G. Baird & Robert K. Rasmussen, chapter 11 at Twilight, 56 Stan L. Rev. 673 (2003).

[35] See Elizabeth Warren, Bankruptcy Policy, 54 U. Chi. L. Rev. 775 (1987) ("In bankruptcy, with an inadequate pie to divide and the looming discharge of unpaid debts, the disputes center on who is entitled to shares of the debtor's assets and how these shares are to be divided.").

Fourth, these debates largely ignored the procedural implications of the positions at issue, which is where Westbrook's contribution comes in, via a 2004 paper, *The Control of Wealth in Bankruptcy*.[36] Here, Westbrook recognized that the priority debates failed because the disputants "proposed mechanisms for establishing priorities in distribution without explaining just how or by whom the recovery process would be managed."[37] Focusing only on the distributive question—"how much"—without also asking the procedural question—"how"—would produce a fruitless discussion.[38]

B. Westbrook on Secured Creditor Control

It is in hindsight difficult to overstate the importance of Westbrook's contribution on this front.[39] While he is perhaps better known for other things (e.g., his pathbreaking empirical work[40] and bankruptcy pedagogy;[41] his scholarship on transnational insolvency[42] and executory contracts),[43] the insight that priority affects both distribution and control has enormous implications for how we evaluate and manage the chapter 11 system.

[36.] See generally Westbrook, Control, supra note 12, 82 Tex. L. Rev. 795.

[37.] 82 Tex. L. Rev. at 798.

[38.] 82 Tex. L. Rev. at 797 (arguing that "control of the bankruptcy process, rather than formal rules of security and priority, is the key to understanding both secured-credit and bankruptcy law: Control is the function of bankruptcy; priority is the end for which it is employed.").

[39.] The idea that senior creditors can assert control rights was not, itself, new. See, e.g., George G. Triantis, Debt Financing, Corporate Decision Making, and Security Design, 26 Canadian Bus. L.J. 93, 100–02 (1996). What was new, as explained in this chapter, is the extent to which senior creditors have come to use priority to capture control of the chapter 11 reorganization process. Controlling a borrower is related to, but different from, controlling its bankruptcy case.

[40.] See, e.g., Elizabeth Warren & Jay L. Westbrook, Financial Characteristics of Businesses in Bankruptcy, 73 Am. Bankr. L. J. 499 (1999).

[41.] See Lynn M. LoPucki, Bringing Realism to the Classroom—A Review of Warren and Westbrook's The Law of Debtors and Creditors, 1987 Wis. L. Rev. 641.

[42.] See, e.g., Jay L. Westbrook, A Global Solution to Multinational Default, 98 Mich. L. Rev. 2276 (2000).

[43.] See Jay L. Westbrook, A Functional Analysis of Executory Contracts, 74 Minn. L. Rev. 227 (1989).

Perhaps because Westbrook is at heart an empiricist, his work on priority suggests a certain ambivalence about these issues, which pivots around procedural context. Outside of bankruptcy, having a single, dominant secured party (DSP) might well produce efficiency gains through a lower rate of interest, higher borrowing limit, and so on.[44] In that context, the secured creditor's priority would entitle it, after default, to control the assets on which it has a lien under generally applicable law, e.g., Article 9 of the Uniform Commercial Code.[45]

But, Westbrook recognized, there was really no point to having a bankruptcy process if DSPs could maintain—much less enhance—that control in bankruptcy. Thus, he argued that chapter 11 was meant "largely [to] negate[] the control aspect of secured credit, while leaving intact the priority [distributive] function."[46] He acknowledged that, even in 2004, a DSP could use its priority rights to "veto" the reorganization process, thus indirectly controlling it.[47] But, he observed, "The only thing that is essential to bankruptcy is that the bankruptcy regime gets control of the debtor's assets and be able to dispose definitively of its liabilities, so the assets can be safely sold or recapitalized and the value distributed to the chosen beneficiaries."[48]

This, then, focuses the question: Who gets to control the bankruptcy regime? Congress designed chapter 11 to allow management of the corporate debtor or a trustee to do so, for the benefit of unsecured creditors.[49] That, however, is not how the system has

---

[44.] See Westbrook, Control, supra note 12, 82 Tex. L. Rev. at 816 ("the enterprise control given to the dominant secured party has the potential to be substantially more valuable to the parties than the mere collateral control granted to the ordinary secured party.").

[45.] See, e.g., UCC § 9-601, 9-609 & 9-610.

[46.] See Westbrook, Control, supra note 12, 82 Tex. L. Rev. at 806.

[47.] 82 Tex. L. Rev. at 831 ("Even under present law, a dominant secured party will often be able to veto a bankruptcy. There is little more that any contractualist could ask of a legal regime.").

[48.] 82 Tex. L. Rev. at 825.

[49.] 11 U.S.C.A. § 1101, 1107 (defining debtor in possession (DIP) and its rights, powers, and duties). See Westbrook, Empirical, supra note 33, 2015 U. Ill. L. Rev.

developed. Today, secured creditors exert significant control of the debtors on whose assets they have liens—and the reorganization process, itself.

II. Secured Creditor Control of the Bankruptcy Regime: *Jevic* and *LifeCare*

How much control secured creditors wield and how they wield it are difficult questions to answer precisely. In part, this is because secured creditors may take control well before bankruptcy, through workout negotiations.[50] For example, they may "encourage" the appointment of a "chief restructuring officer" or "turnaround manager" for the debtor.[51] While it is unlikely that a secured creditor would demand the appointment of a specific turnaround expert,[52] secured creditors with any sophistication will have a list of preferred workout experts, and may share that list with distressed debtors as "recommendations." The powers and incentives of these restructuring professionals are beyond the scope of this chapter, but there is legitimate concern that the relationships amongst them and secured creditors enhance the latters' control of the process.[53]

---

at 833 ("Traditionally, the various institutions of modern chapter 11 bankruptcy produced a certain balance among the debtor and various creditor constituencies.").

[50.] See, e.g., Thomas H. Jackson, On the Nature of Bankruptcy: An Essay on Bankruptcy Sharing and the Creditors' Bargain, 75 Va. L. Rev. 155, 170 (1989) ("A more subtle form of self-interested behavior will occur among certain classes of secured creditors. These creditors, by contract, may have significant control over the decisionmaking apparatus of a firm teetering on insolvency.").

[51.] See In re Ampal-American Israel Corp., 57 Bankr. Ct. Dec. (CRR) 227, 2013 WL 1400346, at *6 (Bankr. S.D. N.Y. 2013) ("A debtor will frequently retain a CRO, subject to court order, at the insistence and with the approval of creditors, usually a secured creditor").

[52.] But it is not unheard of. See In re Lyons Equipment Co., Inc., 436 B.R. 281, 283, 53 Bankr. Ct. Dec. (CRR) 192 (Bankr. W.D. N.Y. 2010) ("in this case, a secured creditor caused the appointment of a chief restructuring officer to operate the business of the debtor.").

[53.] See, e.g., A. Mechele Dickerson, Privatizing Ethics in Corporate Reorganizations, 93 Minn. L. Rev. 875, 919 (2009) (turnaround experts "are predisposed to favor

336 JONATHAN C. LIPSON

However it happens, secured creditors often seek to control three key moments in a chapter 11 case: (i) financing at the beginning; (ii) asset disposition (the decision whether to sell the assets or reorganize); and (iii) how to make distributions at the end. The dynamics of the *Jevic* and *LifeCare* cases illustrate.

A. Case Financing

In order to operate in chapter 11, debtors usually need cash. While the Bankruptcy Code provides that assets (e.g., earnings) that a debtor acquires after commencement of the case are supposed to be free of prebankruptcy liens,[54] it also permits a debtor to borrow more money during the case secured by post-petition-acquired property, on a "super-priority" basis.[55] Super-priority lending on this basis was meant to be exceptional, and in theory prepetition lenders were not supposed to make the new loans in bankruptcy, lest they use the new loans (and new assets the debtor acquires post-petition) to top off a prebankruptcy deficiency.[56]

Secured creditors have, however, learned how to obtain so-called "roll-ups" which do just this. Indeed, that is how *Jevic* started, and the roll-up there rendered the problematic structured dismissal a virtual fait accompli.

Jevic was a New Jersey trucking company that had laid off most of its drivers on the eve of bankruptcy. Because the bankruptcy was

---

only one entity involved in the debtor's chapter 11 reorganization: the creditor who was responsible for getting them hired").

[54] Such liens might otherwise attach pursuant to an after-acquired property clause, permissible under UCC section 9-204, but constrained by Bankruptcy Code section 552(a). Compare UCC 9-204(a) with 11 U.S.C.A. § 552(a). A prepetition security interest will attach to postpetition property that is "proceeds" of prepetition collateral. 11 U.S.C.A. § 552(b).

[55] 11 U.S.C.A. § 364.

[56] See In re Texlon Corp., 596 F.2d 1092, 5 Bankr. Ct. Dec. (CRR) 109, 20 C.B.C. 621, Bankr. L. Rep. (CCH) P 67109, 27 Fed. R. Serv. 2d 460 (2d Cir. 1979) (disapproving cross-collateralization in that case, but declining to forbid it per se). See also Charles J. Tabb, A Critical Reappraisal of Cross-Collateralization in Bankruptcy, 60 S. Cal. L. Rev. 109, 115 (1986).

a controlled liquidation, the debtor needed only a modest amount of operating cash. Nevertheless, it borrowed about $55 million on a super-priority basis from its prebankruptcy secured creditor, CIT Group, Inc. (CIT), mostly, it appears, to repay CIT's prepetition loan.[57]

The details of the *Jevic* debtor in possession (DIP) loan are beyond the scope of this chapter, but it gave CIT significant control of Jevic's reorganization. First, like most DIP lenders, the DIP loan gave CIT a "veto" over any major actions in the case.[58] For example, the loan agreement limited the debtors' ability to make non-ordinary course payments,[59] incur any indebtedness equal or senior in priority to the DIP financing,[60] or to make any disbursements materially outside the budget incorporated into the DIP financing.[61] Moreover, many events that might occur in the case would be defaults under the loan agreement, permitting CIT immediately to foreclose. These included conversion of the case to a chapter 7 liquidation, or the appointment of a trustee or examiner[62] filing a plan or disclosure statement which did not provide for the full payment of the DIP loan or to which CIT

[57.] See Final Order (I) Authorizing Debtors-in-Possession to Obtain Senior Debtor-in-Possession Financing; (II) Granting Liens, Security Interests, and Superpriority Status; (III) Authorizing Use of Cash Collateral; and (IV) Affording Adequate Protection Lenders, at 6, 9, In re Jevic Holding Corp. et al., No. 08-01106 (Bankr. D. Del. June 20, 2008) [hereinafter, Jevic DIP Order].

[58.] Jevic DIP Order, supra note 57, at 50.

[59.] Exhibit A: Senior DIP Credit Agreement at 37, section 7.11, In re Jevic Holding Corp., No. 08-11006 (BLS) (Bankr. D. Del. May 20, 2008) [hereinafter DIP Loan Agreement]. The form of DIP Loan Agreement was attached to motion for the Jevic DIP Order, but the final, executed agreement does not appear to be available. See Emergency Motion for Interim & Final Orders (I) Authorizing Debtors-In-Possession to Enter into Senior Debtor-in-Possession Credit Agreement & Obtain Postpetition Financing Pursuant to Sections 363 & 364 of the Bankruptcy Code; (II) Granting Liens, Security Interests & Superpriority Claims; (III) Authorizing the Use of Cash Collateral; (IV) Affording Adequate Protection to Prepetition Lenders; & (V) Providing for the Payment of Secured Prepetition Indebtedness at para 8, In re Jevic Holding Corp., No. 08-11006 (BLS) (Bankr. D. Del. May 20, 2008). This discussion assumes that the executed version was the same as that presented to the Bankruptcy Court.

[60.] DIP Loan Agreement at 37, section 7.12.

[61.] DIP Loan Agreement at 38, section 7.15.

[62.] DIP Loan Agreement at 39, section 8.7(a).

did not agree;[63] making any challenge to CIT's prepetition claims[64] or liens;[65] the entry of an order granting relief from the stay permitting other creditors to foreclose on any of the debtor's assets in excess of \$50,000;[66] or any change in senior management of the debtor.[67]

Second, it required the debtors to waive any prepetition claims that they may have had against CIT.[68] While the creditors' committee had authority to investigate CIT's prebankruptcy actions, it had only 75 days to do so,[69] and any lawsuit that succeeded was an automatic default under the DIP financing.[70] This was a problem because the debtors had been the subject of a prebankruptcy leveraged buyout by Sun Capital, a private equity firm, which was financed by CIT. There was good reason to think that that deal was vulnerable to a fraudulent transfer attack.[71] While the creditors' committee ultimately sued Sun and CIT on behalf of the estate, the *Jevic* DIP loan limited their time to do so.[72] It also limited their budget to investigate,[73] and borrowings under it could not be used to pay counsel for this work.[74]

---

[63] DIP Loan Agreement at 39, section 8.7(c).

[64] DIP Loan Agreement at 39, section 8.7(e).

[65] DIP Loan Agreement at 40, section 8.7(l).

[66] DIP Loan Agreement at 40, section 8.7(i).

[67] DIP Loan Agreement at 40, section 8.8.

[68] As noted below, some of the debtors' prebankruptcy transactions may have been avoidable as, e.g., preferential or fraudulent transfers. 11 U.S.C. § 544, 547–548.

[69] Jevic DIP Order, supra note 57, at 39.

[70] Jevic DIP Order, supra note 57, at 39 ("The entry of an order of the Bankruptcy Court, which results in the impairment of the [prepetition loan and security interest] shall constitute an immediate Event of Default under this Final Order and the Senior DIP Financing Documents.").

[71] See *Czyzewski v. Jevic Holding Corp.*, 137 S. Ct. 973, 980, 197 L. Ed. 2d 398, 63 Bankr. Ct. Dec. (CRR) 242, 77 Collier Bankr. Cas. 2d (MB) 596, 41 I.E.R. Cas. (BNA) 1613, Bankr. L. Rep. (CCH) P 83082 (2017) (discussing leveraged buyout and fraudulent transfer challenge) (citation omitted).

[72] Jevic DIP Order supra note 57, at 24, 39.

[73] The Jevic DIP Order approved a "carveout" for professional fees of \$1.3 million for estate professionals, and the lenders' professionals. Jevic DIP Order supra note 57, at 19, 34. For a discussion of carveouts, see Charles W. Mooney, Jr., The (Il)Legitimacy of Bankruptcies for the Benefit of Secured Creditors, 2015 U. Ill. L. Rev. 735, 750 (noting that "[i]t is not unusual for a secured creditor to carve out from proceeds of its collateral funds to cover professional fees and other administrative expenses").

[74] See Jevic DIP Order, supra note 57, at 27, 41.

Despite this, the committee navigated the fraudulent transfer claim past motions to dismiss, at which point they, Sun, and CIT settled.[75] The settlement, embodied in the ill-fated structured dismissal, would have paid committee counsel and other first-priority expenses of administering the estate, and made a very small payment to general unsecured creditors. It would have skipped the fourth-priority wage claims of the drivers, however, because Sun was litigating with them separately over Sun's potential liability under employment law.[76] Sun did not want to fund its adversary's litigation against it. Moreover, it would have precluded the drivers from asserting these fraudulent transfer claims against Sun and CIT in state court after dismissal—even though they had objected, and even though they were not being paid for their priority claims.[77]

Because the debtors were in a controlled liquidation of fully encumbered assets, the fraudulent transfer claim was one of the key assets of the estate. Whoever controlled that controlled much of

---

[75] See In re Jevic Holding Corp., 2011 WL 4345204 (Bankr. D. Del. 2011)

[76] See *Czyzewski v. Jevic Holding Corp.*, 137 S. Ct. 973, 981, 197 L. Ed. 2d 398, 63 Bankr. Ct. Dec. (CRR) 242, 77 Collier Bankr. Cas. 2d (MB) 596, 41 I.E.R. Cas. (BNA) 1613, Bankr. L. Rep. (CCH) P 83082 (2017) (citing 787 F.3d, at 177–78, n. 4). (Sun's counsel acknowledged before the Bankruptcy Court that "Sun probably does care where the money goes because you can take judicial notice that there's a pending WARN action against Sun by the WARN plaintiffs. And if the money goes to the WARN plaintiffs, then you're funding someone who is suing you who otherwise doesn't have funds and is doing it on a contingent fee basis.")

[77] The settlement agreement approved by the Bankruptcy Court in the Jevic structured dismissal would have released Sun and CIT from "third party actions or proceedings relating in any way to, or arising from any transaction with or in connection to, the Debtors or their estates of whatever kind or nature . . . including, without limitation, any and all claims asserted in or which could have been asserted in, or which related to the subject matter of the Adversary Proceeding. . . . " See Joint Motion of the Debtors, CIT, Sun Capital, and the Official Committee of Unsecured Creditors Pursuant to 11 U.S.C. § 105(a), 349 and 1112(b) and Fed. R. Bankr. P. 9019 for Entry of an Order: (I) Approving Settlement Agreement and Releasing Claims; (II) Dismissing the Debtors' Cases Upon Implementation of Settlement; and (III) Granting Related Relief Filed, 2(c)(i), (ii), at 4–6 (emphasis supplied), In re Jevic Holding Corp., No. 08-11006 (Bankr. D. Del., June 27, 2012). Among other things, this apparently would have enjoined the drivers from suing under New Jersey's fraudulent transfer act. See, e.g., N.J. Stat. Ann. section 25:2-20 (2015).

the chapter II case. The DIP loan sought to vest that control in CIT, although it ultimately overplayed its hand.

B. Asset Disposition

The second point at which secured creditors may control a case is the decision whether and (if so) how to sell the debtor's assets or, instead, to reorganize "in place." Traditionally, these were expected to be decisions that management made in conjunction with unsecured creditors, represented by a committee. Secured creditors had limited say, unless their collateral was declining precipitously in value, in which case there was a good chance they could lift the stay to take it, thereby negating the question.[78] Today, however, cases like *LifeCare* show that secured creditors can structure "sales" of collateral to control the reorganization process.

The *LifeCare* debtors operated twenty seven long-term acute care hospitals in 10 states and had about 4,500 employees.[79] Prior to the sale, the debtors were apparently marketed to various suitors, none of whom was willing to pay more than about 80% of the outstanding secured debt. The secured creditors, however, were willing to credit bid about 90% of what they were owed, and to pay the costs of professionals, including a creditors' committee.[80] One day before going into bankruptcy, the debtors entered into an asset purchase agreement with the secured creditors with a view toward consummating the transaction in bankruptcy.[81]

The key litigated question involved the distribution of two pots of money: (i) an escrow funded by the secured creditors prior to bankruptcy to cover the sale's costs ("Prepetition Escrow");[82] and (ii) a trust created during bankruptcy to hold $3.5 million paid by the secured

---

[78]. 11 U.S.C. § 362(d).

[79]. In re ICL Holding Co., Inc., 802 F.3d 547, 550, 61 Bankr. Ct. Dec. (CRR) 155, 74 Collier Bankr. Cas. 2d (MB) 607, Bankr. L. Rep. (CCH) P 82867 (3d Cir. 2015).

[80]. 802 F.3d at 550.

[81]. 802 F.3d at 550.

[82]. 802 F.3d at 550.

creditors to settle objections to the sale made in the bankruptcy ("Postpetition Trust").[83] The Postpetition Trust held funds for the benefit of general unsecured creditors, and, like *Jevic*, would skip over "mid-priority" claims, here of the government for unpaid capital gains taxes associated with the sale.[84] The government objected, arguing that making a distribution to junior unsecured creditors violated absolute priority, which the Bankruptcy Court overruled.[85]

On appeal, Third Circuit Judge Ambro affirmed the Bankruptcy Court, reasoning that neither the Postpetition Trust nor the Prepetition Escrow contained property of the estate. He acknowledged that the secured creditors had funded the Postpetition Trust to settle objections to the sale. But, he wrote, "that money never made it into the estate. Nor was it paid at LifeCare's direction. In this context, we cannot conclude here that when the secured lender group, using that group's own funds, made payments to unsecured creditors, the monies paid qualified as estate property."[86]

Although the Prepetition Escrow presented "a more difficult question,"[87] the "economic reality," Judge Ambro reasoned, was that the secured creditors purchased all of the debtors' assets, including their cash. While some of that cash was to be used to consummate the transaction, it was not generally available to the debtors, and any residual was to revert to the purchasers.[88] In any case, because the secured creditors were undersecured credit bidders, "once the sale closed, there technically was no more estate property."[89]

---

[83] 802 F.3d at 550–51.

[84] 802 F.3d at 550–51 ("The Government, for its part, argued that the sale would result in capital-gains tax liability estimated at $24 million, giving it an administrative claim that would go unpaid.").

[85] 802 F.3d at 552 (the government argued that "the settlement money was property of the estate" and that "bypassing it and paying the unsecured creditors disturbed the Code's priority scheme for the payment of creditors.").

[86] 802 F.3d at 556.

[87] 802 F.3d at 556.

[88] 802 F.3d at 556.

[89] 802 F.3d at 556.

Control of the sale process in *LifeCare* led to control of the debtors' chapter II cases. Because the secured creditors refused to support a plan of reorganization, and there were no higher bids for the
debtors' assets, the secured creditors' "purchase" was apparently
the only option. Because the disputed funds were provided by the
secured creditors, rather than the debtors, the secured creditors controlled their use.[90] While it is not clear how often secured creditors
go to the lengths seen in *LifeCare*,[91] it would appear that their priority rights, and the fact that they were undersecured, gave them control of the decision whether, and how, to sell or reorganize, and thus
of this key moment in the case.

C. Final Distributions

The secured creditors in both *Jevic* and *LifeCare* sought to control final distributions. The focus of both cases has been on the
"priority-skipping" nature of these distributions, because that clearly
challenges conventional notions of "absolute" priority. But at a sub-
tler level, it also challenges control over who decides how and to
whom final distributions should be made.

This is often framed as a problem of "gifting," the idea that a
senior creditor may, under some circumstances, share its recovery
with junior claimants, in order to induce them to support the senior creditors' larger goals. Until the rise of structured dismissals,
this often arose in connection with plan voting, where the plan
might pay more to creditors who voted for the plan than if it were

---

[90] See Debtors' Motion for Entry of an Order Pursuant to II U.S.C. § 105(a), 305(a),
349 and 1112(b) and Fed. R. Bankr. P. 1017(a) (A) Dismissing the Debtors' chapter II
Cases and (B) Granting Related Relief, In re ICL Holding Co., Inc. Case No. 12-13319
(KG) (Bankr. D. Del. Dec. 24, 2013) [dkt no. 1103] ("The Debtors' existing secured
lender group . . . would not consent to or finance a plan, but provided a counter-
proposal in the form of a term sheet for the sale of substantially all of the Debtors'
assets.") [hereinafter LifeCare Dismissal Order].

[91] See Westbrook, Empirical, supra note 33, at 833 ("Our data strongly suggest
that secured creditor control is less pervasive than has been asserted, that section 363 sales are by no means universal, and that secured credit dominance is not
closely related to 363 sales.").

approved over their dissent. This was controversial for fear that it may taint the vote.[92]

At least in theory, nothing in the Bankruptcy Code prohibits gifting via structured dismissal, so long as "affected creditors" "consent," a point the *Jevic* majority took pains to note.[93] What constitutes "consent" is beyond the scope of this chapter,[94] but there is little doubt about the absence of consent in either *Jevic* or *LifeCare*: the "skipped" mid-priority creditors objected vigorously in both cases. In *Jevic*, the objection ultimately succeeded; in *LifeCare*, it did not. The next Part seeks to explain the difference, and some of its implications.

III. Jevic as a Proceduralist Opinion—The End of LifeCare?

Jevic and *LifeCare* illustrate how the DSP identified by Westbrook nearly fifteen years ago can use priority to control chapter 11 cases. Yet, the cases take two different doctrinal and conceptual approaches. *Jevic* takes what may be characterized as a "proceduralist" path; *LifeCare*, by contrast, follows what may be characterized as a "property"

[92.] Compare In re Armstrong World Industries, Inc., 432 F.3d 507, 509, 45 Bankr. Ct. Dec. (CRR) 222, 55 Collier Bankr. Cas. 2d (MB) 789, Bankr. L. Rep. (CCH) P 80434 (3d Cir. 2005) and In re DBSD North America, Inc., 634 F.3d 79, 97, 65 Collier Bankr. Cas. 2d (MB) 201, Bankr. L. Rep. (CCH) P 81933 (2d Cir. 2011) with In re SPM Mfg. Corp., 984 F.2d 1305, 23 Bankr. Ct. Dec. (CRR) 1529, 28 Collier Bankr. Cas. 2d (MB) 451, Bankr. L. Rep. (CCH) P 75090 (1st Cir. 1993) (permitting gifting in a chapter 7 liquidation).

[93.] *Czyzewski v. Jevic Holding Corp.*, 137 S. Ct. 973, 983, 197 L. Ed. 2d 398, 63 Bankr. Ct. Dec. (CRR) 242, 77 Collier Bankr. Cas. 2d (MB) 596, 41 I.E.R. Cas. (BNA) 1613, Bankr. L. Rep. (CCH) P 83082 (2017). See also *Czyzewski v. Jevic Holding Corp.*, 137 S. Ct. 973, 978, 197 L. Ed. 2d 398, 63 Bankr. Ct. Dec. (CRR) 242, 77 Collier Bankr. Cas. 2d (MB) 596, 41 I.E.R. Cas. (BNA) 1613, Bankr. L. Rep. (CCH) P 83082 (2017) ("A distribution scheme ordered in connection with the dismissal of a chapter 11 case cannot, without the consent of the affected parties, deviate from the basic priority rules that apply under the primary mechanisms the Code establishes for final distributions of estate value in business bankruptcies.").

[94.] See Jonathan C. Lipson, The Secret Life of Priority: Corporate Reorganization after Jevic, 93 Wash. L. Rev. 631 (2018).

approach. Taken seriously and on their own terms, these are incompatible. Only one can dominate, and the one that we prefer will affect the sustainability and legitimacy of the chapter 11 system. At this point, Delaware's influential bankruptcy court seems uncertain about this, so there may be a chance to guide the analysis in the right direction.[95]

A. Jevic as Proceduralism

"Proceduralism" might be a dirty word to some bankruptcy scholars. The term has sometimes been used to describe writers with a view that bankruptcy is (or should be) largely "procedural," rather than "substantive." There are two main cites for this position, and neither tells us much about what that would actually mean.[96] But, there is a wide world of "proceduralism" that the bankruptcy literature largely ignores.[97]

While space constraints preclude fuller discussion, *Jevic*'s reasoning provides important guidance about procedural concerns central to chapter 11: stakeholder participation, predictability of outcomes, and procedural integrity. All, ultimately, are in service of assuring the legitimacy of the reorganization process. And, all conflict with the property-based reasoning of cases like *LifeCare*. Thus, the important question courts will face is whether *Jevic* spells the end of *LifeCare*—or vice versa?

[95.] See discussion in notes 17–19, supra.

[96.] Douglas G. Baird, Bankruptcy's Uncontested Axioms, 108 Yale L.J. 573, 576–77 (1998) (dividing bankruptcy law scholars into "traditionalists" and "proceduralists"); Charles W. Mooney, Jr., A Normative Theory of Bankruptcy Law: Bankruptcy As (Is) Civil Procedure, 61 Wash. & Lee L. Rev. 931, 931 (2004) (defending "proceduralism" as an account of U.S. bankruptcy law).

[97.] The base cite is Henry M. Hart, Jr. & Albert M. Sacks, The Legal Process (1958 tentative edition) (William N. Eskridge, Jr. & Philip P. Frickey eds, 1994). But there is much more. Indeed, just within the sub-genre of the study of federal courts, it is possible to develop a bibliography of a couple hundred pages. See Thomas E. Baker, Federal Court Practice and Procedure: A Third Branch Bibliography, 30 Tex. Tech L. Rev. 909 (1999). See also William N. Eskridge, Jr., Metaprocedure, 98 Yale L.J. 945, 947 (1989) (reviewing Robert M. Cover, Owen M. Fiss & Judith Resnik, Procedure (1988)).

1. Participation

Although *Jevic*'s holding was about the priority of distributions, its reasoning reflected concerns about stakeholder participation in the reorganization process, for two reasons.

First, Justice Breyer well understood what was at stake in *Jevic*: the survival of plans of reorganization as the procedural heart of chapter 11. "[T]he distributions at issue" in *Jevic*, he observed, were forbidden because they "more closely resemble proposed transactions that lower courts have refused to allow on the ground that they circumvent the Code's procedural safeguards."[98] The "proposed transactions" he had in mind were all-assets sales that older courts had rejected as disguised plans under the "sub rosa plan" doctrine.[99] A plan sub rosa can be problematic because it would "enable[] a debtor to restructure its debt while bypassing many of the Bankruptcy Code's fundamental creditor protections."[100]

[98.] *Czyzewski v. Jevic Holding Corp.*, 137 S. Ct. 973, 986, 197 L. Ed. 2d 398, 63 Bankr. Ct. Dec. (CRR) 242, 77 Collier Bankr. Cas. 2d (MB) 596, 41 I.E.R. Cas. (BNA) 1613, Bankr. L. Rep. (CCH) P 83082 (2017). The majority opinion opens not with a statement about priority, but instead plans: "Bankruptcy Code chapter 11 allows debtors and their creditors to negotiate a plan for dividing an estate's value. See 11 U.S.C. § 1123, 1129, 1141. But sometimes the parties cannot agree on a plan . . ." *Czyzewski v. Jevic Holding Corp.*, 137 S. Ct. 973, 978, 197 L. Ed. 2d 398, 63 Bankr. Ct. Dec. (CRR) 242, 77 Collier Bankr. Cas. 2d (MB) 596, 41 I.E.R. Cas. (BNA) 1613, Bankr. L. Rep. (CCH) P 83082 (2017).

[99.] *Czyzewski v. Jevic Holding Corp.*, 137 S. Ct. 973, 986, 197 L. Ed. 2d 398, 63 Bankr. Ct. Dec. (CRR) 242, 77 Collier Bankr. Cas. 2d (MB) 596, 41 I.E.R. Cas. (BNA) 1613, Bankr. L. Rep. (CCH) P 83082 (2017) (citing In re Braniff Airways, Inc., 700 F.2d 935, 940, 10 Bankr. Ct. Dec. (CRR) 933, 8 Collier Bankr. Cas. 2d (MB) 522 (5th Cir. 1983) (prohibiting an attempt to "short circuit the requirements of chapter 11 for confirmation of a reorganization plan by establishing the terms of the plan sub rosa in connection with a sale of assets") and In re Lionel Corp., 722 F.2d 1063, 1069, 11 Bankr. Ct. Dec. (CRR) 553, 9 Collier Bankr. Cas. 2d (MB) 941, Bankr. L. Rep. (CCH) P 69510 (2d Cir. 1983) (reversing a bankruptcy court's approval of an asset sale after holding that section 363 does not "gran[t] the bankruptcy judge carte blanche" or "swallo[w] up chapter 11's safeguards")).

[100.] In re Energy Future Holding Corp., 527 B.R. 157, 168, 60 Bankr. Ct. Dec. (CRR) 177, Bankr. L. Rep. (CCH) P 82774 (D. Del. 2015), aff'd, 648 Fed. Appx. 277 (3d Cir. 2016), cert. denied, 137 S. Ct. 447, 196 L. Ed. 2d 336 (2016).

These protections are about participation. They include the right to information about the plan and the right to vote for or against it.[101] None of that happens in a structured dismissal, which is governed instead by the amorphous standards cobbled together by lower courts like those in *Jevic*.[102] To have affirmed those courts, therefore, would have threatened the procedural foundation of the reorganization process, participation through chapter 11 plans.[103] If doing this was illicit in *Jevic*, then perhaps it was in *LifeCare*, as well.

Second, the structured dismissal may chill participation in the form of litigation to challenge harmful prebankruptcy transactions. The *Jevic* structured dismissal sought to eliminate the drivers' ability to sue Sun and CIT in state court, even though they (the drivers) should have been entitled to do so after dismissal.[104] Although not the basis for reversal, this feature of the structured dismissal was highly problematic.

LifeCare may have involved a similar problem. For example, any transfers of LifeCare property to its secured creditors within 90 days of bankruptcy should have been scrutinized as preferential transfers, potentially voidable under Bankruptcy Code section 547.[105] Similarly, the asset purchase agreement entered into immediately before bankruptcy should have been scrutinized on fraudulent transfer grounds,

---

[101] 11 U.S.C.A. § 1125, 1126 & 1129.

[102] Structured dismissals are apparently approved if the proponent can show "cause" under, among others, Bankruptcy Code section 1112, 363, 349 and Federal Rule of Bankruptcy Procedure 9019. These offer judges and participants little guidance. I further develop this point in Lipson, supra note 94, at 647–50.

[103] There are, to be sure, many other ways in which creditors and other stakeholders may "participate" in chapter 11 cases, including by market behavior and bargaining. These are important, but beyond the scope of this brief paper. For a further discussion, see Lipson, supra note 94.

[104] Section 349, governing dismissals, is generally designed to restore the prebankruptcy status quo. 11 U.S.C. section 349(a).

[105] Payments to undersecured creditors during this period are usually avoidable on preference grounds. In re Norwalk Furniture Corp., 428 B.R. 419, 426 (Bankr. N.D. Ohio 2009) ("Prepetition transfers made to creditors holding secured claims, but whose claims are undersecured, may be preferential.").

since it was apparently intended to hinder and delay the collection efforts of the U.S. government.[106]

Litigation is an important form of participation in chapter 11. *Jevic* implies that secured creditors cannot take this form of participation from other stakeholders (i.e., the objecting drivers). *LifeCare* suggests otherwise.

2. Predictability

Jevic's proceduralist majority was also concerned about predictability in at least two ways that conflict with *LifeCare*'s property-based approach. First, whatever its other limits, absolute priority is inherently more predictable than other ways of ordering distributions ex post. Absent an explicit agreement otherwise, distributions go *A* then *B* then *C*. While there will always be marginal cases where it is not clear whether a particular claimant qualifies as *B* or *C*, the baseline rules are fixed. Limiting judicial discretion to alter this order increases predictability.

Second, the *Jevic* majority was suspicious of the claim that the case was "rare," warranting an exception. The Third Circuit had reasoned that priority-skipping final distributions may be approved "in a rare case," if the bankruptcy court has "'specific and credible grounds to justify [the] deviation.'"[107] Justice Breyer rejected this, noting that it was "difficult to give precise content to the concept 'sufficient reasons'" to justify a priority deviation at the end of a case.[108] Given the Court's long-standing preference

---

[106.] The Bankruptcy Code empowers the estate to avoid transfers intended to hinder or delay creditors. 11 U.S.C. section 548, 549 & 544.

[107.] *Czyzewski v. Jevic Holding Corp.*, 787 F.3d at [21a] (quoting Iridium, 478 F.3d at 466) (alteration in original). Judge Scirica's dissent at the Third Circuit was also appropriately skeptical. "It is not unusual for a debtor to enter bankruptcy with liens on all assets, nor is it unusual for a debtor to enter chapter 11 proceedings . . . with the goal of liquidating . . . It is not difficult to imagine another secured creditor who wants to avoid providing funds to priority creditors." See 787 F.3d at 189–90.

[108.] *Czyzewski v. Jevic Holding Corp.*, 137 S. Ct. 973, 986, 197 L. Ed. 2d 398, 63 Bankr. Ct. Dec. (CRR) 242, 77 Collier Bankr. Cas. 2d (MB) 596, 41 I.E.R. Cas. (BNA) 1613, Bankr. L. Rep. (CCH) P 83082 (2017).

for absolute priority in final distributions, it would appear to tolerate no judicially created exceptions.

LifeCare conflicts with *Jevic's* predictability concerns. Aside from the obvious distributive unpredictability of making payments outside the Bankruptcy Code's priority structure, *LifeCare's* reasoning is destabilizing in two ways.

First, *LifeCare's* property analysis is problematic. Under Article 9 of the Uniform Commercial Code, the Postpetition Trust and Prepetition Escrow may not have been the property solely of the secured creditors, but also the bankruptcy estate. Uniform Commercial Code (UCC) Article 9 defines proceeds to include "whatever is acquired upon the sale, lease, license, exchange, or other disposition of collateral" and "rights arising out of collateral."[109] LifeCare's secured creditors had no reason other than purchasing the debtors' assets to make those payments; the funds would have been "acquired upon the sale" or "arisen out" of the debtors' assets.[110] Moreover, *Whiting Pools* holds that a chapter 11 debtor's estate retains a property interest in collateral even if it was seized prior to bankruptcy by an undersecured creditor.[111] *Whiting Pools* may not be popular with secured creditors, but it has not been overruled by the Third Circuit. As noted earlier, prepetition transfers by LifeCare to its dominant (but undersecured) creditors may also have been avoidable and recoverable by the estate.

LifeCare would seem to mean that DSPs can structure a prepetition deal to exclude property from a debtor's estate in order to "facilitate . . .

---

[109] *Czyzewski v. Jevic Holding Corp.*, 137 S. Ct. 973, 986, 197 L. Ed. 2d 398, 63 Bankr. Ct. Dec. (CRR) 242, 77 Collier Bankr. Cas. 2d (MB) 596, 41 I.E.R. Cas. (BNA) 1613, Bankr. L. Rep. (CCH) P 83082 (2017).

[110] For a discussion of the breadth of the UCC's definition of proceeds, see Jonathan C. Lipson, Remote Control: Revised Article 9 and the Negotiability of Information, 63 Ohio St. L.J. 1327, 1332 (2002) (observing that "[t]he proceeds security interest is not limited to collateral in the hands of the debtor.").

[111] *U.S. v. Whiting Pools, Inc.*, 1983-2 C.B. 239, 462 U.S. 198, 209, 103 S. Ct. 2309, 2315, 76 L. Ed. 2d 515, 10 Bankr. Ct. Dec. (CRR) 705, 8 Collier Bankr. Cas. 2d (MB) 710, Bankr. L. Rep. (CCH) P 69207, 83-1 U.S. Tax Cas. (CCH) P 9394, 52 A.F.T.R.2d 83-5121 (1983) ("[T]he reorganization estate includes property of the debtor that has been seized by a creditor prior to the filing of a petition for reorganization.").

a smooth . . . transfer" to themselves.[112] But transferees usually want to "facilitate" smooth transfers of others' property to themselves, so it is not clear that this is much of a standard. Vesting this power in the secured creditor—rather than the court—destabilizes ordinary property analyses, threatening doctrinal predictability.

Second, it gives the DSP control of the valuation process. Where a DSP is marginally over- or under-secured, it may have an incentive to manipulate the value of collateral in order to assure that it controls the option to acquire it through a credit bid. It will likely know more about the value of the debtors' assets than outside bidders, and this may also chill bidding, the very thing that might otherwise produce better information about asset values.[113]

While there seems little doubt that the *LifeCare* DSPs were undersecured, its reasoning may encourage future secured creditors to tinker with "economic reality" in order to control collateral valuation. Whether, or to what extent, they may do so injects needless uncertainty into the already-murky valuation process.

3. Procedural Integrity

Perhaps the most acute conflict between *Jevic* and *LifeCare* concerns the risk of collusion. Here, collusion could take two distinct forms. First, the *Jevic* Court worried about "senior secured creditors and general unsecured creditors teaming up to squeeze out priority unsecured creditors."[114] Both *Jevic* and *LifeCare* involved "mid-priority"

[112.] In re ICL Holding Co., Inc., 802 F.3d 547, 557, 61 Bankr. Ct. Dec. (CRR) 155, 74 Collier Bankr. Cas. 2d (MB) 607, Bankr. L. Rep. (CCH) P 82867 (3d Cir. 2015) (quoting June 11, 2013 Hr'g Tr. 23:9–13).

[113.] In re Philadelphia Newspapers, LLC, 599 F.3d 298, 316, 52 Bankr. Ct. Dec. (CRR) 255, Bankr. L. Rep. (CCH) P 81719 (3d Cir. 2010), as amended, (May 7, 2010); In re Fisker Automotive Holdings, Inc., 510 B.R. 55, 56, 70 Collier Bankr. Cas. 2d (MB) 1525 (Bankr. D. Del. 2014); In re The Free Lance-Star Publishing Co. of Fredericksburg, VA, 512 B.R. 798 (Bankr. E.D. Va. 2014).

[114.] *Czyzewski v. Jevic Holding Corp.*, 137 S. Ct. 973, 986–87, 197 L. Ed. 2d 398, 63 Bankr. Ct. Dec. (CRR) 242, 77 Collier Bankr. Cas. 2d (MB) 596, 41 I.E.R. Cas. (BNA) 1613, Bankr. L. Rep. (CCH) P 83082 (2017) (citing *Bank of America Nat. Trust and Sav. Ass'n v. 203 North LaSalle Street Partnership*, 526 U.S. 434, 444, 119 S. Ct. 1411, 143 L. Ed.

350 JONATHAN C. LIPSON

squeeze-outs. Unless you accept *LifeCare*'s property analysis, this should have been forbidden in *LifeCare* for the same reason it was forbidden in *Jevic*. In both cases, junior and senior claimants agreed to a deal seeking to eliminate the rights of those in the middle.

Second, as noted earlier, the *Jevic* structured dismissal would have released CIT and Sun from fraudulent transfer liability in connection with Jevic's LBO, precluding the drivers from their only recourse outside of bankruptcy following dismissal. Although the *Jevic* Court did not focus on this, it is hard to overstate the danger the release created.

Fraudulent transfer law may be one of the last checks on excessive lending in the acquisition context. It leads investors such as Sun and lenders such as CIT to worry that they may be liable for an over-leveraged acquisition that harms a debtor and its other creditors. If, however, a structured dismissal provides a ready escape hatch when everything falls apart, they will have less reason to exercise restraint in those deals.

The *LifeCare* structured dismissal also provided releases to its DSPs.[115] Although it is not clear whether anyone even assessed claims against LifeCare's secured creditors,[116] as discussed earlier there is reason to think that they may have had exposure to avoidance actions.

B. The End of *LifeCare*?

Although *LifeCare* conflicts with *Jevic*'s process values, it is in certain respects a more difficult case. Unlike *Jevic*, which was a controlled liquidation, *LifeCare* apparently sought to maintain the viability of

---

2d 607, 34 Bankr. Ct. Dec. (CRR) 329, 41 Collier Bankr. Cas. 2d (MB) 526, Bankr. L. Rep. (CCH) P 77924 (1999)).

[115] See LifeCare Dismissal Order supra note 90, at 2–3, 2.

[116] A review of the docket reveals no evidence that there were any efforts to investigate, prosecute, or settle avoidance actions in that case. This may be because counsel to the creditors' committee may have assessed them and concluded that there was no merit. Or, because the same firm (the Pachulski firm) was also counsel to the creditors' committee in Jevic, it may have concluded that the escrow and trust created by the secured creditors were sufficient to buy peace.

a healthcare company with 4,500 employees as well as patients and other stakeholders. Even a controlled liquidation may have seemed potentially disastrous. And, because LifeCare's assets were owned by many affiliates in ten states, foreclosure using state-law procedures would have been problematic.

So, the outcome in *LifeCare* may compensate for its procedural infirmities. In that case it—not *Jevic*—was the "rare case" that required procedural exceptionalism. Its property-based analysis was the product of the exigencies of the case, and it should be limited to its facts.

IV. Conclusion

At this point, the question is open. We do know, however, that its approach conflicts with *Jevic's* proceduralist orientation because of the creditor control that it permitted. *Jevic* creates a response, a way to control controlling creditors, but there is no guarantee that courts will view it that way. While we do not know whether we have reached the end of *LifeCare*, we do know that Jay Westbrook was among the first to warn us about the problems of creditor control it reflects.

A Functional Analysis of SIFI Insolvency

*Stephen J. Lubben**

In a 1989 article that remains one of the clearest, most sensible explications of an especially tricky point of bankruptcy law, Jay Westbrook announced a forthright methodology: "1 call my approach 'functional,' because it proceeds by working through the problem from first principles."[1] The same basic technique can tell us a lot about how banks—and other bank-like creatures or SIFIs,[2] to use the industry lingo—should fail.

Since the disgrace of Lehman, the question of how to handle failing SIFIs has been quite vexed.[3] On the one hand, governmental rescue of shareholders and other investors is beyond annoying, and there is some intuitive sense that if management does a poor job, they and their

---

* Harvey Washington Wiley Chair in Corporate Governance & Business Ethics, Seton Hall University School of Law. 1 am grateful for Dan Awrey and Art Wilmarth's comments on an earlier version of this work. Copyright © 96 Tex. L. Rev. 1377–1402 (2018). Reproduced here with permission.

[1.] Jay Lawrence Westbrook, A Functional Analysis of Executory Contracts, 74 Minn. L. Rev. 227, 230 (1989). In a recent article, Professor Westbrook abandoned the phrase "Functional Analysis" in favor of the alternative "Modern Contract Analysis," but 1 take that change to be limited to the specific context of section 365 of the Bankruptcy Code. Jay Lawrence Westbrook & Kelsi Stayart White, The Demystification of Contracts in Bankruptcy, 91 Am. Bankr. L.J. 481, 484 n.16 (2017).

[2.] Systemically Important Financial Institutions.

[3.] Kathryn Judge, The First Year: The Role of a Modern Lender of Last Resort, 116 Colum. L. Rev. 843, 849 (2016).

investor backers should face the consequences just like any other firm.[4] That bank managers would have the temerity to pay themselves large bonuses shortly after a taxpayer rescue only emphasizes the point.[5]

On the other hand, there is a widespread understanding that a large bank, or a sufficiently interconnected one, is not quite like Kmart, Enron, or even American Airlines, in that when the bank fails, it tends to take a large chunk of the economy along with it.[6] Pre-failure regulation can mitigate some of the effects,[7] but by the time we get to insolvency—or "financial distress," if we want to acknowledge that here we are talking as much about liquidity as balance sheets[8]—the regulatory string has pretty much played out.[9] And in the end, we have trouble deciding if we really mean to treat large financial institutions like normal failed firms.[10]

Thus, the 2010 legislative response to Lehman, and AIG, and Bank of America, and Citibank, and every other large financial institution that almost failed (or did, in the case of Lehman) was notably

---

[4] See Arthur E. Wilmarth, Jr., Turning a Blind Eye: Why Washington Keeps Giving In to Wall Street, 81 U. Cin. L. Rev. 1283, 1379–81 (2013) (noting that major banks have entered relatively modest settlements with the SEC without admitting liability—a practice that one judge criticized as "half-baked justice at best" because it fails to impose sanctions on specific individuals).

[5] Saule T. Omarova, Wall Street as Community of Fate: Toward Financial Industry Self-Regulation, 159 U. Pa. L. Rev. 411, 415 (2011).

[6] Kathryn Judge, Interbank Discipline, 60 UCLA L. Rev. 1262, 1272 (2013); see also Henry T. C. Hu, Swaps, the Modern Process of Financial Innovation and the Vulnerability of a Regulatory Paradigm, 138 U. Pa. L. Rev. 333, 367–70 (1989) (contending that there is widespread belief that the collapse of a financial institution "could cause the money supply to drop unexpectedly, thereby causing unemployment to rise and output to fall").

[7] See Martin Wolf, Banking Remains Far Too Undercapitalised for Comfort, Fin. Times, Sept. 21, 2017, at 9 ("Banking remains less safe than it could reasonably be. That is a deliberate decision.").

[8] See Adam J. Levitin, In Defense of Bailouts, 99 Geo. L.J. 435, 455–56 (2011) (explaining how a "domino effect" can exist among financial firms, expanding financial distress beyond insolvency and into liquidity).

[9] See Peter Conti-Brown, Elective Shareholder Liability, 64 Stan. L. Rev. 409, 419 (2012) (highlighting the fact that Dodd–Frank is a preventative regulatory measure that seeks to prevent financial crises and taxpayer-funded bailouts).

[10] Anat R. Admati, Financial Regulation Reform: Politics, Implementation, and Alternatives, 18 N.C. Banking Inst. 71, 74–75 (2013).

wobbly on the question of "how will a big bank fail?" Dodd-Frank created a new, Federal Deposit Insurance Corporation (FDIC)-focused "orderly liquidation authority" (OLA) to handle these cases but then made it incredibly difficult to actually use OLA.[11] Instead, banks are told to plan for failure under the Bankruptcy Code, and this time they should not expect any of the help that Lehman got.[12]

When, if ever, the new system will be used is left uncertain, particularly given that the ability to invoke the process is left in the hands of a politically appointed Treasury Secretary after consultation with the President.[13] In past administrations, we might have assumed that, when push came to shove, the Secretary would do the right thing. Present-day developments might leave us a bit more circumspect on this point.[14]

Ultimately, after nearly a decade of waffling between "special" and "normal" bankruptcy for banks, I believe we are now ready to build upon what we have learned and to take the necessary further step: stop feigning that bank insolvency can or should happen in bankruptcy court.

I reach this conclusion through application of Professor Westbrook's functional analysis. Namely, we need to consider what it is that we are trying to achieve in a bank insolvency case and how that compares with bankruptcy law in general. Bank insolvency, I submit, is all about special priorities: both ordinal and temporal.

---

[11] See David A. Skeel, Jr. & Thomas H. Jackson, Transaction Consistency and the New Finance in Bankruptcy, 112 Colum. L. Rev. 152, 196 (2012) (explaining that the trigger for using the OLA is "more complex—calling for U.S. Treasury initiation with the concurrence of the Federal Reserve and FDIC . . .").

[12] Stephen J. Lubben, Transaction Simplicity, 112 Colum. L. Rev. Sidebar 194, 203 (2012).

[13] 12 U.S.C. section 5383(b) (2012).

[14] Cf. Barry Schwartz, George Washington and the Whig Conception of Heroic Leadership, 48 Am. Soc. Rev. 18, 26 (1983). Schwartz observes:

At a time when most Americans take for granted their government's ability to outlive its unscrupulous leaders and protect individual liberties, it is difficult to appreciate the whiggish obsession about abuse of power, or to take seriously the conviction that government stands or falls on the virtues of its leaders.
                                                                        Id.

The Bankruptcy Code, on the other hand, takes an "equality is equity" approach to priorities as a baseline, mostly using state law to draw the claim—asset border.[15] Bargaining for results within the general "equality" framework is another key feature of traditional insolvency law.[16]

Financial institution insolvency law expressly rejects this model; it instead is all about protecting some favored group from the effects of insolvency.[17] There is no equality here, and it was never intended that there would be equality.[18] And thus it is time to stop pretending SIFI insolvency is "normal" corporate insolvency—it is bigger.

I. The Problem

Large American financial institutions are typically made up of a holding company and several additional key pieces.[19] Each piece of

---

[15] See, e.g., Westbrook, supra note 1, at 252 (characterizing the principle that "all creditors be treated equally" as the "most universal of all insolvency principles throughout the world"). For more on the stated goals of chapter 11, see Sarah Pei Woo, Regulatory Bankruptcy: How Bank Regulation Causes Fire Sales, 99 Geo. L.J. 1615, 1621–22 (2011).

[16] Thomas S. Green, Comment, An Analysis of the Advantages of Non-Market Based Approaches for Determining chapter 11 Cramdown Rates: A Legal and Financial Perspective, 46 Seton Hall L. Rev. 1151, 1155 (2016).

[17] See Daniel R. Fischel et al., The Regulation of Banks and Bank Holding Companies, 73 Va. L. Rev. 301, 318 (1987) ("The primary difference is that the thrust of bankruptcy laws is to ensure that creditors of the same class are treated equally, whereas federal deposit insurance ensures that certain classes of creditors are paid in full."). The authors of the foregoing argue that "the economic functions of bankruptcy laws and federal deposit insurance are very similar." Id. In this chapter, I argue otherwise.

[18] In an earlier era, the bank and bankruptcy systems may have had similar goals, but that was before the advent of deposit insurance and the general move away from creditor equality in the financial context. See Davis v. Elmira Sav. Bank, 161 U.S. 275, 284 (1896) ("[O]ne of the objects of the national bank system was to secure, in the event of insolvency, a just and equal distribution of the assets of national banks among all unsecured creditors, and to prevent such banks from creating preferences in contemplation of insolvency.").

[19] This part of the chapter draws heavily on my forthcoming book: Stephen J. Lubben, The Law of Failure: A Tour through the Wilds of American Business Insolvency Law (forthcoming 2018).

the financial institution, including the holding company, is subject to a different regulatory and insolvency regime.[20]

For example, in a June 2017 report to the Federal Reserve and the FDIC, JPMorgan Chase & Co. noted that it is "supervised by multiple regulators."[21] The Report describes the domestic front as follows:

- The Federal Reserve acts as an umbrella regulator. . . .
- The firm's national bank subsidiaries, JPMCB and CUSA, are subject to supervision and regulation by the OCC and, with respect to certain matters, by the Federal Reserve and the FDIC.
- Nonbank subsidiaries, such as JPMS LLC, are subject to supervision and regulation by the SEC and, with respect to certain futures-related and swaps-related activities, by the CFTC.
- The firm conducts securities underwriting, dealing[,] and brokerage activities in the United States through JPMS LLC and other broker-dealer subsidiaries, all of which are subject to SEC regulations, the Financial Industry Regulatory Authority[,] and the New York Stock Exchange, among others.
- Certain of the firm's subsidiaries are registered with, and subject to oversight by, the SEC as investment advisers.
- In the United States, one subsidiary is registered as a futures commission merchant, and other subsidiaries are either registered with the CFTC as commodity pool operators and commodity trading advisors or exempt from such registration. These CFTC-registered subsidiaries are also members of the National Futures Association.
- JPMCB, J.P. Morgan Securities LLC, J.P. Morgan Securities, PLC[,] and J.P. Morgan Ventures Energy Corporation have registered with the CFTC as swap dealers.

[20.] See John C. Coffee, Jr. & Hillary A. Sale, Redesigning the SEC: Does the Treasury Have a Better Idea? 95 Va. L. Rev. 707, 719–20 (2009) (describing the United States' unique approach to regulation: three different agencies oversee banks, while another agency oversees securities and yet another oversees futures); Patricia A. McCoy et al., Systemic Risk through Securitization: The Result of Deregulation and Regulatory Failure, 41 Conn. L. Rev. 1327, 1343 (2009).

[21.] JPMorgan Chase & Co., Resolution Plan Public Filing 134 (2017).

- The firm's commodities business is also subject to regulation by the Chicago Mercantile Exchange, London Metals Exchange[,] and the Federal Energy Regulatory Commission.[22]

Other large American financial institutions would also be subject to insurance regulators, typically at the state level. Most, of course, are also subject to foreign regulation.[23]

There are historical reasons for this fragmentation, mostly tied to the tendency to develop American financial law in times of crisis, beginning with the Civil War, with new laws being added piecemeal to address then-recent events.[24] As with most American legislation, particularly at the federal level, there has never been a single reform law enacted to consolidate the whole. The result is that both pre-failure regulation and post-failure "resolution" of a large financial institution is typically achieved piece by piece, with one regulator taking an arm while another takes a leg. As discussed in the following passages, Dodd-Frank only partially improves on this situation.

A. The Fundamentals of Financial Institution Insolvency

A prototypical large American financial institution or SIFI is comprised of four basic regulated pieces: a holding company, one or more

---

[22.] *Id.*

[23.] JPMorgan Chase specifically mentions regulators in England, Japan, and Hong Kong. *Id.*

[24.] See Mark J. Roe, Some Differences in Corporate Structure in Germany, Japan, and the United States, 102 Yale L.J. 1927, 1948–49 (1993) (introducing the development of American banking regulation); Arthur E. Wilmarth, Jr., The Transformation of the U.S. Financial Services Industry, 1975–2000: Competition, Consolidation, and Increased Risks, 2002 U. Ill. L. Rev. 215, 225–27, 313–14 (2002) (summarizing the restructuring of the banking industry, including the passage of the FDICIA in 1991 in response to banking failures); see also Kenneth E. Scott, The Dual Banking System: A Model of Competition in Regulation, 30 Stan. L. Rev. 1, 9 (1977) (stating that "the national banking system was created during the Civil War"); Edward L. Symons, Jr., The "Business of Banking" in Historical Perspective, 51 Geo. Wash. L. Rev. 676, 698–99 (1983) (discussing the National Bank Act).

depository banks, a broker-dealer, and insurance companies.[25] Interspersed between is the "dark matter" of global banks: unregulated subsidiaries. These allow banks to do financy stuff outside the regulatory architecture of the core parts of the bank, although in theory they remain subject to the umbrella regulation of the Federal Reserve.[26]

In a world before Dodd-Frank, or in a world where OLA is not invoked, the holding company is subject to the normal Bankruptcy Code process, presumably chapter 11.[27] While the Federal Reserve has regulatory powers over the holding company under the Bank Holding Company Act of 1956,[28] that Act contains no insolvency provisions.[29] Thus, we fall back on the business insolvency system of general applicability. Recent examples have included the notorious September 15, 2008, chapter 11 filing of Lehman Brothers Holdings, Inc. and the chapter 11 filing of Washington Mutual's parent company.[30]

Most depository banks are insured by the FDIC.[31] Whenever the Comptroller of the Currency appoints a receiver for an insured

---

[25] Howell E. Jackson, The Expanding Obligations of Financial Holding Companies, 107 Harv. L. Rev. 507, 509 (1994).

[26] Michael S. Barr, The Financial Crisis and the Path of Reform, 29 Yale J. on Reg. 91, 99 (2012).

[27] See Cassandra Jones Havard, Reconciling the Dormant Conflict: Crafting a Banking Exception to the Fraudulent Conveyance Provision of the Bankruptcy Code for Bank Holding Company Asset Transfers, 75 Denv. U. L. Rev. 81, 81–82, 89–92 (1997) (clarifying that the "Bankruptcy Code . . . governs the insolvency proceedings of the bank holding company" and providing examples of holding companies filing under chapter 11).

[28] 12 U.S.C. section 1841 (2012).

[29] Cf. Henry N. Butler & Jonathan R. Macey, The Myth of Competition in the Dual Banking System, 73 Cornell L. Rev. 677, 697–98 (1988) (noting that "[t]he Bank Holding Company Act regulates the activities of any company that controls a bank" without mention of insolvency proceedings).

[30] See Diane Lourdes Dick, The chapter 11 Efficiency Fallacy, 2013 BYU L. Rev. 759, 790 (2013) (describing the Washington Mutual bankruptcy); see also Stephen J. Lubben & Sarah Pei Woo, Reconceptualizing Lehman, 49 Tex. Int'l L.J. 297, 303 (2014) (describing the Lehman bankruptcy).

[31] Key exceptions include certain financial technology companies (at this point, more potential than real) and trust companies, both of which might operate under a national bank charter without deposit insurance. See, e.g., 12 U.S.C. section 27(a) (2012) (outlining when the comptroller may authorize an association to commence banking).

national bank, the Comptroller must appoint the FDIC receiver.[32] As the exclusive statutory receiver of any insolvent insured national bank, the FDIC cannot be removed as receiver, and the courts have no ability to interfere with the process.[33] Likewise, even under the old pre-New Deal rules, and those still applicable to uninsured national banks (mostly trust companies), the Comptroller has the ability to appoint the receiver without ever going to court.[34]

Recent examples of the modern FDIC approach include the aforementioned Washington Mutual primary operating subsidiary and the banks shown on the following table, which includes all the FDIC receiverships in 2017.[35] Note the inevitable resolution of these banks by transferring the deposits to a healthy institution;[36] the FDIC pursued a similar strategy with Washington Mutual, where Chase took over its branches and deposits.[37]

Bank Name	City	State	Acquiring Bank	Closing Date
Washington Federal Bank for Savings	Chicago	IL	Royal Savings Bank	Dec. 15, 2017
The Farmers and Merchants State Bank of Argonia	Argonia	KS	Conway Bank	Oct 13, 2017
Fayette County Bank	Saint Elmo	IL	United Fidelity Bank, fsb	May 26, 2017
Guaranty Bank	Milwaukee	WI	First-Citizens Bank & Trust Company	May 5, 2017
First NBC Bank	New Orleans	LA	Whitney Bank	Apr. 28, 2017

[32.] 12 U.S.C. section 1821(c)(2)(A)(ii) (2012); see also Edward H. Klees, How Safe Are Institutional Assets in a Custodial Bank's Insolvency? 68 Bus. Law. 103, 108–09 (2012) (explaining that the FDIC acts as receiver for insolvent national banks).

[33.] 12 U.S.C. section 1821(j) (2012).

[34.] Hirsch Braver, Liquidation of Financial Institutions: A Treatise on the Law of Voluntary and Involuntary Liquidation of Banks, Trust Companies, and Building and Loan Associations section 1015, at 1182 (1936).

[35.] Fed. Deposit Ins. Corp., Failed Bank List, www.fdic.gov/bank/individual / failed/banklist.html [https://perma.cc/AU5F-9LVM].

[36.] Cheryl D. Block, A Continuum Approach to Systemic Risk and Too-Big-to-Fail, 6 Brook. J. Corp. Fin. & Com. L. 289, 334–35 (2012).

[37.] Dick, supra note 30, at 793–94.

Bank Name	City	State	Acquiring Bank	Closing Date
Proficio Bank	Cottonwood Heights	UT	Cache Valley Bank	Mar. 3, 2017
Seaway Bank and Trust Company	Chicago	IL	State Bank of Texas	Jan. 27, 2017
Harvest Community Bank	Pennsville	NJ	First-Citizens Bank & Trust Company	Jan. 13, 2017

Normally broker-dealers are handled under SIPA—the Securities Investor Protection Act. SIPA created SIPC—the Securities Investor Protection Corporation—a quasi-private company that oversees an insurance fund for customers.[38] Although SIPC is an independent body, the Securities and Exchange Commission (SEC) has oversight power over its bylaws and rules and may compel SIPC to promulgate regulations to effectuate the purposes of SIPA.[39] The insurance in this case, unlike the more familiar FDIC deposit insurance, protects only against securities or cash that are missing at the point of insolvency; there is no guarantee of value.[40]

The law provides that SIPC or the SEC may file an application for a protective decree with a federal district court if SIPC determines that any member has failed or is in danger of failing to meet obligations to customers and meets one of four worrisome conditions.[41] Upon filing, the case is quickly referred to the bankruptcy court.[42] The powers of the trustee in a SIPA case are essentially the same as those vested in a chapter 7 trustee appointed under the Bankruptcy

---

[38] Onnig H. Dombalagian, Substance and Semblance in Investor Protection, 40 J. Corp. L. 599, 600 (2015).

[39] 15 U.S.C. § 78ccc(e) (2012).

[40] See Jeanne L. Schroeder, Is Article 8 Finally Ready This Time? The Radical Reform of Secured Lending on Wall Street, 1994 Colum. Bus. L. Rev. 291, 463–64 ("SIPC buys [unsatisfied customer] claims . . . up to the statutory maximum amount . . . and is subrogated to the customers' general credit claims against the debtor.").

[41] 15 U.S.C. § 78eee(a)(3)(A), 78eee(b)(1), 78ggg(b) (2012). The institution of a case under the SIPA brings any pending bankruptcy case to a halt. Irrespective of the automatic stay, the SIPC may file an application for a protective decree under SIPA. 11 U.S.C. § 742 (2012).

[42] 15 U.S.C. § 78eee(b)(4) (2012).

Code, but the SIPA trustee operates with somewhat less judicial oversight.[43] Before the case even gets underway before the court, customers will have their accounts transferred to a healthy broker.[44]

While the holding company is in chapter 11, the depository bank is handled by the FDIC, the broker-dealer is liquidated by a SIPA trustee, and the insurance companies will be subject to state court receiverships under the oversight of the state insurance commissioner.[45] Insurance companies, no matter what size, are regulated by the states, and thus their insolvencies are also a question of state law.[46]

The basic structure of insurance failure is fairly uniform across the states: the insurance regulator goes to court and gets a receiver appointed, often the regulator itself,[47] to take control of the insurance company.[48] State guaranty funds, set up and paid for by solvent insurance companies operating within the jurisdiction, pay covered policyholder claims up to certain limits, which are often rather low.[49]

[43.] 15 U.S.C. § 78fff-1(a) (2012); see also *id.* section 78fff-1(b)(2) (describing trustee's conditional authority to guarantee all or part of the indebtedness of the debtor to a lender).

[44.] Dombalagian, supra note 38, at 605.

[45.] Stephen J. Lubben, Financial Institutions in Bankruptcy, 34 Seattle U. L. Rev. 1259, 1274 (2011).

[46.] See generally, e.g., Cal. Ins. Code, section 1064.1–1064.13 (West 2012) (giving examples of insolvency under California State law).

[47.] Iowa Code Ann. section 505.9 (West 2015). In New York, the regulator acting as receiver has a separate, dedicated staff, collectively known as the New York Liquidation Bureau. See also *State ex rel. ISC Financial Corp. v. Kinder*, 684 S.W.2d 910, 913 (Mo. Ct. App. W.D. 1985) ("The director of insurance is to be the receiver and he is to conduct the affairs of the receivership under the supervision of the court, in accordance with the statutory system.").

[48.] See Ala. Code section 27-34-50 (2007) (fraternal benefit societies); Del. Code Ann. tit. 18, section 5906 (West 2015) (domestic insurers); Haw. Rev. Stat. Ann. section 432:2-606 (LexisNexis 2014) (domestic societies); Iowa Code Ann. section 508.22 (West 2015) (life insurance companies); Nev. Rev. Stat. Ann. section 696B.220 (West 2015) (domestic insurers); N.Y. Ins. Law section 7405 (McKinney 2016) (domestic insurers); Utah Code Ann. section 31A-27a-401 (LexisNexis 2017) (domestic insurers); W. Va. Code Ann. section 33-10-6 (LexisNexis 2017) (domestic insurers).

[49.] See, e.g., Ala. Code section 27-44-8 (2007) (capping liability at $100,000 in cash values per insured); Cal. Ins. Code section 1063.2 (West 2014) (describing the mechanics of compensating insured persons in case of an insurance company's insolvency); Ky. Rev. Stat. Ann. section 304.36-020 (LexisNexis 2011) (establishing funding for insured persons

And then the unregulated bits of a big financial institution bring us back to chapter 11 of the Bankruptcy Code. At least the holding company and the "extra" bits of the financial institution end up in the same process; the other pieces are in a variety of forums—some in courts, some not.

B. Dodd-Frank's OLA Solution

Recognizing that this overall system was somewhat less than ideal, the drafters of Dodd-Frank created a new super bankruptcy system, OLA. But OLA only partially solves the problem of an integrated financial institution being pulled apart by regulatory (and insolvency) balkanization.[50] And it does nothing to address the issue of cross-border SIFls, which is rather important, considering that every SIFl is, almost by definition, a cross-border SIFl.[51]

First, Dodd-Frank's drafters had no stomach for a fight with state insurance regulators, and thus insurance company insolvency remains outside the new order.[52] Broker-dealers are swept up in the

---

in cases of insurers' insolvency); Mass. Gen. Laws Ann. ch. 175D, section 5 (West 2007) (same); 27 R.I. Gen. Laws Ann. section 27-34.3-8 (West 2017) (discussing the association's ability to pay the impaired insurer's contractual obligations); Wyo. Stat. Ann. section 26-42-106 (2018) (same); see also *de la Fuente v. Fla. Ins. Guar. Ass'n*, 202 So. 3d 396, 401 (Fla. 2016) (describing and applying Florida's statutory fund for claims against insolvent insurance companies). In New York, there are three distinct, statutory security funds, known as the Property/Casualty Insurance Security Fund, the Public Motor Vehicle Security Fund and the Workers' Compensation Security Fund. In addition, life insurance policy holders are protected by the Life Insurance Company Guaranty Corporation of New York, created under Article 77 of the State's insurance law. See *Ky. Ins. Guar. Ass'n v. Nat. Res. & Envtl. Prot. Cabinet*, 885 S.W.2d 315, 316, 318 (Ky. Ct. App. 1994) (construing broadly Kentucky's statutory fund for claims against insolvent insurance companies).

[50.] Lubben, supra note 45, at 1268.

[51.] Edward F. Greene & Joshua L. Boehm, The Limits of "Name-and-Shame" in International Financial Regulation, 97 Cornell L. Rev. 1083, 1106 (2012); see also Oscar Couwenberg & Stephen J. Lubben, Corporate Bankruptcy Tourists, 70 Bus. Law. 719, 722 (2015) (stating that "most large corporate groups have at least some international operations").

[52.] See Stavros Gadinis, From Independence to Politics in Financial Regulation, 101 Cal. L. Rev. 327, 371 (2013) ("Because insurance companies are state-regulated, the Act does not change states' insolvency regimes but establishes a mechanism that allows the federal government to trigger the insolvency process at the state level.");

process, but in an opaque way: the OLA receiver can take whatever assets it wants, leaving the residue behind. And the entire process is extremely difficult to commence and operates only as a backstop to the normal rules.[53]

In particular, to invoke OLA, the FDIC needs the agreement of the Federal Reserve Board of Governors (by a two-thirds majority) and the Treasury Secretary, who is required to consult with the President.[54] If the SIFI in question is more broker-dealer than depository bank—Goldman Sachs might be an example here—the SEC takes over the FDIC's role in initiation, but the FDIC will, nonetheless, become the receiver if the process goes forward.[55] The statute expressly provides that the regulators must consider the effect of default on financial stability, on low income, minority, or underserved communities, and on creditors, shareholders, and counterparties.[56]

The Treasury Secretary is separately charged with evaluating the use of OLA under a two-part test.[57] First, the Secretary looks at whether the SIFI is in default or in danger of default.[58] A bank is in default when it is likely to file for bankruptcy, has incurred debts that will deplete all or most of its capital, has more debts than assets, or will likely be unable to pay its debts in the normal course of business.[59] In essence, a bank is insolvent if it is insolvent under any reasonable definition of the term.

---

see also Matthew C. Turk, The Convergence of Insurance with Banking and Securities Industries, and the Limits of Regulatory Arbitrage in Finance, 2015 Colum. Bus. L. Rev. 967, 1007 (2015) (explaining how Dodd–Frank maintains a "decentralized state-led system").

[53.] See David Zaring, A Lack of Resolution, 60 Emory L.J. 97, 124 (2010) (detailing the complexity of commencing the resolution-powers process).

[54.] 12 U.S.C. § 5383(a)(1)(A) (2012).

[55.] See id. section 5383(a)(1)(B). The statute provides:

In the case of a broker or dealer, or in which the largest United States subsidiary (as measured by total assets as of the end of the previous calendar quarter) of a financial company is a broker or dealer, the Commission and the Board of Governors, at the request of the Secretary, or on their own initiative, shall consider whether to make the written recommendation. . . .

[56.] Id. section 5383(a)(2)(A)–(C), (G).

[57.] Id. section 5383(b).

[58.] Id. section 5383(b)(1).

[59.] Id. section 5383(c)(4).

Second, the Secretary must evaluate the systemic risk involved in the potential default of the SIFI in question.[60] The Secretary also must find that "no viable private sector alternative is available to prevent the default of the financial company."[61]

If the SIFI clears these hurdles, the company's board is presented with a choice: consent (and be exculpated from any potential liability to shareholders) or we, the regulators, will go to court.[62] Presumably, the board consents in most cases, and the FDIC is appointed as a receiver for the company.

As a receiver, the FDIC takes on the duties of transferring or selling assets, creating bridge financial organizations that can help assume assets or liabilities during the liquidation process, and approving valid claims against the company that will need to be paid.[63] The Orderly Liquidation Fund acts as a government-run DIP loan[64] throughout the process.[65] The Treasury lends the FDIC money to resolve the institution.[66] If there is a net cost, the FDIC then recoups the money spent by imposing a fee on surviving large, complex financial institutions.[67]

OLA provides a set of basic rules for all proceedings.[68] All action under OLA must be taken to preserve the financial stability of the economy as a whole, not merely to preserve the specific company in question.[69] Shareholders cannot receive payment until all other claims

---

[60.] *Id.* section 5383(b)(2).

[61.] *Id.* section 5383(b)(3).

[62.] *Id.* section 5387, 5382(a)(1)(A)(i).

[63.] See generally *id.* section 5390 (outlining the powers and duties of the FDIC once appointed as receiver).

[64.] Companies that enter chapter 11 continue to be run by their existing management in almost all cases. The ongoing entity is known as the debtor in possession (DIP). DIP loans are typically asset-based, revolving working-capital facilities agreed to at the start of a chapter 11 case to provide both immediate cash as well as ongoing working capital during the process.

[65.] *Id.* section 5390(n).

[66.] *Id.* section 5390(n)(1).

[67.] *Id.* section 5390(o).

[68.] *Id.* section 5386.

[69.] *Id.* section 5386(1).

are paid—that is, the normal priority rules apply.[70] Management "responsible" for the SIFI's failure must be "removed."[71] Presumably, that means they must be fired—and not banished, or transported to Australia, or something like that. The FDIC is also prohibited from providing equity financing to the SIFI, which makes sense, given that other parts of Title II also call for liquidation of the defaulting SIFI.[72]

C. SPOE and "chapter 14"

Because the application of OLA to an entire financial institution would appear to be unwieldly and would not cover the international aspects of the corporate group, a new approach was needed.[73] Single point of entry (SPOE) was that new strategy.

The SPOE idea benefits from a simple elegance: insolvency should only involve the holding company and no other part of the institution.[74] All problems would be solved at the holding-company level by having the holding company take on the burdens of financing the entire operation.[75] Other subsidiaries might interact with the outside world as part of their normal trading operations— the swaps subsidiary would continue to engage in trading, for example—but the holding company would be in charge of all general finance.[76]

---

[70] *Id.* section 5386(2)–(3).

[71] *Id.* section 5386(4).

[72] *Id.* section 5384(a).

[73] See generally Stephen J. Lubben, Resolution, Orderly and Otherwise: B of A in OLA, 81 U. Cin. L. Rev. 485 (2012) (examining the complexity of resolving Bank of America under OLA and accompanying issues).

[74] For a critical review of SPOE, see Stephen J. Lubben & Arthur Wilmarth, Jr., Too Big and Unable to Fail, 69 Fla. L. Rev. 1205 (2017).

[75] Kwon-Yong Jin, How to Eat an Elephant: Corporate Group Structure of Systemically Important Financial Institutions, Orderly Liquidation Authority, and Single Point of Entry Resolution, 124 Yale L.J. 1746, 1751–52 (2015).

[76] Jeffrey N. Gordon & Wolf-Georg Ringe, Bank Resolution in the European Banking Union: A Transatlantic Perspective on What It Would Take, 115 Colum. L. Rev. 1297, 1325 fig.3 (2015).

Thus, if the financial institution were to encounter financial distress, its equity interests in its subsidiaries would quickly move to a new "bridge bank," while its bondholders would look to the equity of that new holding company for their recovery.[77] Shareholders in the old institution—"to use an expression more forcible and familiar than elegant"[78]—would be wiped out. At the same time, the subsidiaries would benefit from forgiveness of their liabilities to the parent company, providing a source of relief for strained balance sheets.

SPOE itself addresses the problems of using OLA, but there remains the issue of Dodd-Frank's stated preference for normal bankruptcy procedures. To meet this challenge, a variety of parties have come forth with proposals to amend the Bankruptcy Code to facilitate a SPOE-style bankruptcy proceeding.[79] Lumped under the general heading of "chapter 14," after one of the early Hoover Institute proposals,[80] these plans would allow a quick holding-company-only bankruptcy case for a financial institution. In some cases, the new chapter 14 would replace OLA entirely, while in others it would simply make the Bankruptcy Code a more attractive alternative to OLA.[81]

[77.] Catherine Gallagher Fauver, The Long Journey to "Adequate": Wells Fargo's Resolution Plan, 36 Rev. Banking & Fin. L. 647, 658 (2017).

[78.] Adrian H. Joline, Railway Reorganizations, 8 Am. Law. 507, 508 (1900) (referring to shareholders in railroad foreclosure cases).

[79.] Edward J. Janger & John A.E. Pottow, Implementing Symmetric Treatment of Financial Contracts in Bankruptcy and Bank Resolution, 10 Brook. J. Corp. Fin. & Com. L. 155, 180 (2015); Jodie A. Kirshner, The Bankruptcy Safe Harbor in Light of Government Bailouts: Reifying the Significance of Bankruptcy as a Backstop to Financial Risk, 18 N.Y.U. J. Legis. & Pub. Pol'y 795, 831 (2015).

[80.] Stephen J. Lubben, What's Wrong with the chapter 14 Proposal, Deal Book, N.Y. Times (Apr. 10, 2013), https://dealbook.nytimes.com/2013/04/10/whats-wrong-with-the-chapter-14-proposal/?mcubz=3 [https://perma.cc/D97Z-U5SW].

[81.] Stephanie P. Massman, Developing a New Resolution Regime for Failed Systemically Important Financial Institutions: An Assessment of the Orderly Liquidation Authority, 89 Am. Bankr. L.J. 625, 637 (2015). One early version, which would have replaced Title II entirely, is reviewed in Bruce Grohsgal, Case in Brief against "chapter 14," Am. Bankr. Inst. J., May 2014, at 44, 113. Instead of creating a new chapter 14 of the Code to deal with large financial institutions that seek bankruptcy

Most of the recent versions of chapter 14 have been designed to use SPOE within a procedure that at least resembles chapter 11. The debtor holding company would file a petition and would initiate a near immediate 363 sale of its assets to a buyer—trust.[82] The debtor would then move toward confirmation of a liquidating plan that would distribute interests in the trust as payment to creditors.[83]

Chapter 14 thus tethers the Bankruptcy Code to the SPOE approach to bank resolution. The vital question then is whether SPOE will work, or, more aptly, whether it will work most of the time.[84] Undoubtedly, there is something odd about fixing a short-coming in a financial institution through the holding company when the holding company itself is probably the least likely place for such a flaw to develop.[85] Almost like doing a root canal by way of orthoscopic surgery on the knee—it could work, but it seems terribly indirect.

And the notion that all the operating subsidiaries throughout the world will continue business as usual in the days after the parent company has failed assumes a high degree of rationality in the midst of financial collapse. It is almost as if the proponents of SPOE have already forgotten what happened in 2008. At the very least, they

---

protection, the Financial Institution Bankruptcy Act of 2014, passed by the House but never acted upon by the Senate, sought to create a new Subchapter V of the Code to deal with such entities. Compare H.R. 5421, 113th Cong. (2014) (enacted) with Financial Institution Bankruptcy Act of 2014, H.R. REP. NO. 113-630, at 11 (2014). The pending CHOICE Act, discussed later in this chapter, would combine the latter approach with a full repeal of Title 11 of Dodd–Frank. Financial CHOICE Act of 2017, H.R. 10 section 111 (as passed by House, June 18, 2017), www.congress.gov/bill/115th-congress/house-bill/10/text#tocHF34EA86F881447208D253C613F969973 [https://perma.cc/TRC2-32M9].

[82] For more on the 363 sale process, evaluated from a comparative perspective, see Stephanie Ben-Ishai & Stephen J. Lubben, Involuntary Creditors and Corporate Bankruptcy, 45 U.B.C. L. Rev. 253, 256, 272 (2012).

[83] Id. at 272.

[84] Lubben & Wilmarth, supra note 74.

[85] John Crawford, "Single Point of Entry": The Promise and Limits of the Latest Cure for Bailouts, 109 Nw. U. L. Rev. Online 103, 107 (2014); Nizan Geslevich Packin, Supersize Them? Large Banks, Taxpayers and the Subsidies That Lay Between, 35 Nw. J. Int'l L. & Bus. 229, 276 (2015).

assume that the presence of Dodd-Frank will provide the assurance and calm that was rather obviously lacking before.

And while U.S. regulators seem to be in favor of SPOE for domestic SIFIs, they seem quite happy to force "multiple points of entry" on international banks operating in the United States through mechanisms such as the Fed's foreign bank (intermediate) holding company rules.[86] This has the predictable effect of undermining resolution planning at the international level as regulators jockey for position in anticipation of the next Lehman Brothers Europe.[87]

Overall, SPOE has something of the character of a parlor trick or one of those 1980s law review articles that suggested that chapter 11 could be replaced with a few simple contracts. One is left with the nagging feeling that it's all a bit too crafty to actually work outside the parlor or the slide deck.

D. The Fundamental Problem

Chapter 14, SPOE, and OLA contain a stated preference for the Bankruptcy Code that papers over the reality that this country does not typically address bank insolvency under the Code. Rather, a receiver, appointed by a regulator, runs the show when a bank fails.

And while broker-dealers, insurance companies, and SIFIs more generally may not be "banks" in the narrow, legalistic sense, they are banks in the economic sense.[88] They take in funds with the promise of liquidity and invest those funds in longer-term assets, like loans,

---

[86.] Press Release, Board of Governors of the Federal Reserve System, Fed. Reserve, Federal Reserve Board Approves Final Rule Strengthening Supervision and Regulation of Large U.S. Bank Holding Companies and Foreign Banking Organizations (Feb. 18, 2014), https://www.federalreserve.gov/newsevents/pressreleases/bcreg20140218a.htm [https://perma.cc/BZD5-CAWP].

[87.] See Lubben & Woo, supra note 30, at 326–27 (predicting international regulators' responses to banking regulations in the United States and the United Kingdom).

[88.] Karl S. Okamoto, After the Bailout: Regulating Systemic Moral Hazard, 57 UCLA L. Rev. 183, 195 (2009); Morgan Ricks, Regulating Money Creation after the Crisis, 1 Harv. Bus. L. Rev. 75, 97 (2011).

mortgage-backed securities, and the like.[89] And "when short-term debt funds longer-term liabilities, a defining characteristic of banks and much of the shadow banking system, the institutions that result are inherently fragile."[90]

The fundamental problem, then, is what to make of the conflicting approach to bank insolvency. I address that issue in the next part of this chapter and argue that at heart this represents a confusion of bank insolvency and bankruptcy.

II. Functional Analysis

"Whenever an area of law has become conceptually and doctrinally confused, it is always helpful to return to first principles."[91] With regard to bank or SIFI failure, such a return to core principles is long overdue.

"Equality of distribution among creditors is a central policy of the Bankruptcy Code. According to that policy, creditors of equal priority should receive pro rata shares of the debtor's property."[92] That is, traditional business bankruptcy is focused on questions of creditor rank and equality within ranks.[93]

Rank questions have both temporal and ordinal components. For a variety of practical reasons, some creditors get paid before others.[94]

---

[89] Jeffrey N. Gordon & Christopher Muller, Confronting Financial Crisis: Dodd–Frank's Dangers and the Case for a Systemic Emergency Insurance Fund, 28 Yale J. on Reg. 151, 158, 162 (2011).

[90] Kathryn Judge, The Importance of "Money," 130 Harv. L. Rev. 1148, 1150 (2017) (reviewing Morgan Ricks, The Money Problem: Rethinking Financial Regulation (2016)).

[91] Westbrook, supra note 1, at 243.

[92] *Begier v. IRS*, 496 U.S. 53, 58 (1990).

[93] See Chrystin Ondersma, Shadow Banking and Financial Distress: The Treatment of "Money-Claims" in Bankruptcy, 2013 Colum. Bus. L. Rev. 79, 106 ("[Not] all creditors have always been treated equally without exception; secured creditors are protected up to the value of their collateral. . . .").

[94] See Stephen J. Lubben, The Overstated Absolute Priority Rule, 21 Fordham J. Corp. & Fin. L. 581, 605 (2016) ("Operating companies pay creditors according to business needs, without regard for actual priority.").

And negotiations over a chapter 11 plan hinge on who gets paid what within those classes that have yet to be paid when it comes time to formulate a plan.[95] What counts as a "claim" and what counts as an "asset" for purposes of bankruptcy is determined by reference to underlying state law, sometimes with a federal Bankruptcy Code overlay.

While the Code provides the framework of rank, the precise treatment of creditors within those ranks is a matter of negotiation. In a traditional chapter 11 case, this negotiation results in a reorganization plan that provides an outline of the reorganized debtor.[96] The plan can radically alter the debtor's management, its ownership, its tax profile, its relationship with employees and future claimants, and perhaps even the type of business the debtor performs.[97] In place of a reorganization plan, the debtor might file a liquidation plan or a plan containing features of both.

Consider a recent example. Teen-apparel specialty chain rue21, Inc. emerged from bankruptcy on September 22, 2017.[98] Under the confirmed plan, prepetition holders of the $538.5 million term loan received about two-thirds of the equity in the reorganized company.[99] Holders of the $250 million 9.0% senior unsecured

---

[95.] See Maxx M. Johnson, The Not-So-Settled Absolute Priority Rule: The Continued Threat of Priority-Deviation through Interim Distributions of Assets in chapter 11 Bankruptcy, 13 Seton Hall Cir. Rev. 291, 294 (2017) ("Priority for creditors could mean the difference between getting paid in full and not getting paid at all.").

[96.] See Michelle M. Harner, The Search for an Unbiased Fiduciary in Corporate Reorganizations, 86 Notre Dame L. Rev. 469, 494 (2011) ("The creditor's objective and pursuit of control . . . might conflict with the debtor's restructuring plan or the efforts of other creditors or shareholders to influence the process.").

[97.] See Chrystin Ondersma, Employment Patterns in Relation to Bankruptcy, 83 Am. Bankr. L.J. 237, 247 (2009) (finding that companies lose around 50% of employees in the years near bankruptcy filing).

[98.] Rue21, Inc., rue21 Completes Financial Restructuring Process, PR Newswire (Sept. 22, 2017), www.prnewswire.com/news-releases/rue21-completes-financial-restructuring-process-300524488.html [https://perma.cc/JQA3-5Q66].

[99.] First Amended Debtors' Disclosure Statement for the Debtors' First Amended Joint Plan of Reorganization Pursuant to chapter 11 of the Bankruptcy Code at 10, 25, In re rue21, Inc., 575 B.R. 90 (Bankr. W.D. Pa. 2017) (No. 17-22045).

notes due in 2021, and all other unsecured claims, received a 4% equity stake.[100] The remainder of the new equity went to a DIP lender.[101]

In all cases, the distribution of the new equity was the product of negotiation between the various creditor groups, each trying to get as much as possible. Those negotiations happen within the equality framework established by the Bankruptcy Code.[102]

That stands in direct contrast to financial institution insolvency, where the key decisions about who gets what have already been made before the case commences.[103] In particular, financial institution insolvency mechanisms decide in advance that certain favored creditors will receive priority at the expense of the remaining creditors. Indeed, what happens after those favored creditors are taken out of the insolvency process is typically of lesser concern.

We see this most directly in broker-dealer liquidations where customers are made whole—through a segregated fund of customer property and a gap-filling insurance scheme—before any other creditor is even considered.[104] To the same effect are insurance receiverships, where policyholders are expressly elevated under the law of every state to an elite status that precedes all others.

[100.] *Id.* at 12, 26.

[101.] *Id.* at 16–17.

[102.] On the general construction of corporate bankruptcy systems, see Oscar Couwenberg & Stephen J. Lubben, Essential Corporate Bankruptcy Law, 16 Eur. Bus. Org. L. Rev. 39, 42–44 (2015).

[103.] Richard M. Hynes & Steven D. Walt, Why Banks Are Not Allowed in Bankruptcy, 67 Wash. & Lee L. Rev. 985, 989 (2010).

[104.] See In re Bernard L. Madoff Inv. Sec. LLC, 654 F.3d 229, 240 (2d Cir. 2011) (noting that the "SIPC provides advances on customer property"). To be sure, if we view broker-dealers as holding assets in custody on behalf of their clients, they are somewhat different from the other financial institutions because it is not that clients receive preferential treatment vis-à-vis other creditors. Rather, it is that their assets never formed part of the bankrupt broker-dealer's estate in the first instance. Of course, we also backstop that segregation from the estate with a special insurance fund, which then pushes broker-dealers a bit closer to the traditional financial institutions. Perhaps it is best to admit that they operate under a somewhat mixed model.

Depository banks operate under a similar regime, through a combination of deposit insurance and, more recently, a federal depositor preference statute. More practically, the frequent use of purchase and assumption—or "P and A"—transactions, where depositors are transferred over to an acquiring bank, represents an even more obvious means of excluding a special class from an insolvency process.[105]

The "safe harbors" in the Bankruptcy Code provide a similar status for repo and derivatives trades, excepting them from all of the key provisions of the Bankruptcy Code.[106] To be sure, the safe harbors are far sloppier in providing their priority—in that they extend far beyond what is needed to protect the financial institutions engaged in these trades.[107] But whatever we think about the merits, they represent a policy decision by Congress to ditch the normal insolvency rules in favor of a system in which a certain preferred group prevails over the default rule of creditor equality.[108]

What, then, are the first principles of business insolvency at play here? At heart, business bankruptcy, and most of business insolvency, is aimed at recognizing a standard set of creditor priorities and ensuring creditor equality within those priorities. Creditors are urged to bargain for their specific treatment.

Bank insolvency, on the other hand, is about advancing legislatively defined policy goals that have been set in advance of

---

[105] Paul Lund, The Decline of Federal Common Law, 76 B.U. L. Rev. 895, 950–51 (1996).

[106] Stephen J. Lubben, Failure of the Clearinghouse: Dodd–Frank's Fatal Flaw? 10 Va. L. & Bus. Rev. 127, 152 (2015); Rizwaan J. Mokal, Liquidity, Systemic Risk, and the Bankruptcy Treatment of Financial Contracts, 10 Brook. J. Corp. Fin. & Com. L. 15, 43 n.21 (2015).

[107] Edward J. Janger, Response, Arbitraging Systemic Risk: System Definition, Risk Definition, Systemic Interaction, and the Problem of Asymmetric Treatment, 92 Texas L. Rev. See Also 217, 228–29 (2013).

[108] John J. Chung, From Feudal Land Contracts to Financial Derivatives: The Treatment of Status through Specific Performance, 29 Rev. Banking & Fin. L. 107, 136, 138–39 (2009). For a general critique of the policymaking behind the safe harbors, see Stephen J. Lubben, Subsidizing Liquidity or Subsidizing Markets? Safe Harbors, Derivatives, and Finance, 91 Am. Bankr. L.J. 463, 472–77 (2017).

insolvency.[109] We may disagree about the wisdom of certain of those goals, but they are set through a legislative process and not within the framework of creditor bargaining so familiar to bankruptcy attorneys.[110]

On the surface, bank insolvency thus looks like normal insolvency, but it is really quite different.[111] The next part of this chapter, thus, looks at the implications of that conclusion for one key aspect of insolvency law: the role of bankruptcy courts.

III. The Problem of Courts

In one of their myriad attempts to replace Dodd-Frank's OLA with a new chapter of the Bankruptcy Code, House Republicans argued that

> the bankruptcy process is administered through the judicial system, by impartial bankruptcy judges charged by the Constitution to guarantee due process in public proceedings under well-settled rules and procedures. It is a process that is faithful to this country's belief in the Rule of Law.[112]

[109.] Helen A. Garten, A Political Analysis of Bank Failure Resolution, 74 B.U. L. Rev. 429, 445 (1994).

[110.] For key insights into the tensions that naturally exist between the bank and bankruptcy frameworks, see Sarah Pei Woo, Simultaneous Distress of Residential Developers and Their Secured Lenders: An Analysis of Bankruptcy & Bank Regulation, 15 Fordham J. Corp. & Fin. L. 617, 664–76 (2010).

[111.] See Thomas W. Joo, Who Watches the Watchers? The Securities Investor Protection Act, Investor Confidence, and the Subsidization of Failure, 72 S. Cal. L. Rev. 1071, 1105 (1999) ("SIPA's goals are very different. It is concerned primarily with the health of the securities industry. SIPA does not attempt to maximize the debtor's estate . . . but only liquidation procedures.").

[112.] Staff of H. Comm. on Fin. Servs., 114th Cong., The Financial CHOICE Act: A Republican Proposal to Reform the Financial Regulatory System 26 (Comm. Print 2016), http://financialservices.house.gov/uploadedfiles/financial_choice_act_comprehensiveoutline.pdf [https://perma.cc/3HU3-Y4F8].

It is hard to quarrel with the rule of law, capitalized or not. Nonetheless, I use this part of the chapter to explain why courts are an uneasy fit in the case of a SIFI insolvency.

As a starting point, "corporate bankruptcy scholars tend to characterize bankruptcy as an extension of the private transactional realm, with judges external to that world."[113] This conception of business bankruptcy, although clearly overstated and even wrong, presents a problem for efforts to apply the "normal rules" to SIFI insolvency. In short, given the broad public effects and regulatory considerations tied to a SIFI's failure, the notion that a system of private bargaining could or should address the matter is nonsensical.[114]

Financial institutions create debt instruments that are something more than debt, and indeed become valuable social products.[115] More broadly,

> financial markets are integral to the production of commercial goods, public goods, and social services. Many businesses and individuals regularly rely upon financial institutions to provide short-term loans when the individual or business experiences temporary cash management difficulties.[116]

---

[113] Melissa B. Jacoby, Federalism Form and Function in the Detroit Bankruptcy, 33 Yale J. on Reg. 55, 69 (2016).

[114] See Anna Gelpern, Common Capital: A Thought Experiment in Cross-Border Resolution, 49 Tex. Int'l L.J. 355, 356 (2014) ("Like the public-policy functions, government commitments permeate the bank balance sheet. Central-bank liquidity support, deposit insurance, regulatory valuation of assets and liabilities, and resolution procedures all represent government commitments that shape the way in which a bank does business.").

[115] See Donald F. Turner, The Scope of Antitrust and Other Economic Regulatory Policies, 82 Harv. L. Rev. 1207, 1233 (1969) ("In short, if banking is peculiar in that bank failures pose a particularly serious problem, it is also peculiar in that competition in lending performs a uniquely valuable function.").

[116] Kristin N. Johnson, Things Fall Apart: Regulating the Credit Default Swap Commons, 82 U. Colo. L. Rev. 167, 185 (2011).

In addition, financial institutions play key roles in the creation of money.[117] About 70% of the U.S. money supply is in the form of deposits.[118] For deposits to perform this function—and more broadly for banks to function as the institutional backbone of the payment system—depositors need to be reasonably confident that (1) there will not be a significant delay in transferring or withdrawing deposited funds (illiquidity) and (2) these funds will not be written down or converted into equity in the context of any bankruptcy proceeding (loss of value).[119]

All would tend to argue against some sort of closed insolvency system where the public interest is shut out in favor of bilateral or even multiparty private negotiation.

And indeed the entire notion of systemic importance undermines the basis for private bargaining.[120] That the failure of a SIFI affects not only the bank itself or its investors, but also other companies and individuals, inherently takes it out of the realm of private bargain and into a more general, public sphere.[121]

Turning to a more sensible conception of corporate bankruptcy, we have to acknowledge that modern bankruptcy courts play an active role in moving the case to confirmation of a plan.[122]

[117.] See Adam J. Levitin, Safe Banking: Finance and Democracy, 83 U. Chi. L. Rev. 357, 361 (2016) (discussing ways in which banks' lending practices aid in wealth creation).

[118.] Money Stock & Debt Measures-H.6 Release, Fed. Res. Sys., www.federalreserve.gov/releases/h6/current/default.htm [https://perma.cc/FL8L-EBFM].

[119.] See Dan Awre & Kristin van Zwieten, The Shadow Payment System, 43 J. Corp. L. (forthcoming 2018) (manuscript at 31–32), http://dx.doi.org/10.2139/ssrn.2843772 [https://perma.cc/7LUQ-3XBA] (making this argument with regard to shadow payment systems).

[120.] See Steven L. Schwarcz, Systemic Risk, 97 Geo. L.J. 193, 198 (2008) (explaining the wide-ranging economic consequences of failed financial institutions and the resultant need to account for systemic risk).

[121.] See Saule T. Omarova, Bankers, Bureaucrats, and Guardians: Toward Tripartism in Financial Services Regulation, 37 J. Corp. L. 621, 627 (2012) ("Thus, financial crises directly implicate virtually every area of public concern, including housing, education, health care, labor markets, and environmental protection.").

[122.] See Melissa B. Jacoby, What Should Judges Do in chapter 11? 2015 U. Ill. L. Rev. 571, 580–81 (chronicling the widespread nature of "active case management" by judges in chapter 11 proceedings).

Thus, chapter II is a multifaceted competition between various stakeholder groups and the debtor, with the court pushing the entire thing forward within a framework that we shorthand by reference to the *"pari passu* principle."[123]

A full theoretical conception of judging within chapter II is beyond the scope of this chapter. But the aim here is to contrast any reasonable conception of chapter II with the aims of financial institution insolvency. In short, we have to consider chapter II, a multiparty negotiation conducted within the structure of creditor equality, with the policy aims of bank insolvency, broadly defined. A bankruptcy proceeding

> is a specialized process for dispute resolution in connection with firms and individuals in financial or economic distress, but it is hardly narrow, technical, or specialized in substance. Bankruptcy cases frequently raise a broad range of legal issues beyond the intricacies of bankruptcy-specific doctrine. They routinely implicate non-bankruptcy-specific rules of decision and have done so throughout the modern history of federal bankruptcy law. Both as a matter of doctrine and theory, bankruptcy law aims to honor to the greatest extent possible the parties' non-bankruptcy entitlements. Typically, state common law or statutory rights make up those non-bankruptcy entitlements, and bankruptcy courts therefore must decide matters that require application of non-bankruptcy-specific common law or statutory provisions.[124]

In contrast, financial institution insolvency advances the policy goals of the legislature and financial regulators. Specifically, it

---

[123.] Cf. Samuel L. Bufford, Coordination of Insolvency Cases for International Enterprise Groups: A Proposal, 86 Am. Bankr. L.J. 685, 692 (2012) (discussing the application of the pari passu principle to international insolvency cases); Christoph G. Paulus, The Interrelationship of Sovereign Debt and Distressed Banks: A European Perspective, 49 Tex. Int'l L.J. 201, 205 (2014) (highlighting the negative consequences of failing to follow the pari passu principle in international bankruptcy proceedings).

[124.] Troy A. McKenzie, Judicial Independence, Autonomy, and the Bankruptcy Courts, 62 Stan. L. Rev. 747, 773–74 (2010).

advances the policy of regulators—including the legislature—at the point of financial distress.[125] Its primary aim is not adjudicatory, but rather regulatory.

The fact that bank insolvency has specific policy aims itself suggests an immediate point of difference with chapter 11. Whereas normal corporate insolvency provides a framework for negotiation, SIFI insolvency aims to preordain the outcome of the process.

A bankruptcy judge is an uneasy fit in such a process, inasmuch as the judge is left with little to do when the key decisions have all been made in advance by statute or regulation. An example is seen in OLA itself, where the court's sole role is to determine whether the Treasury Secretary's determination on two points—"that the covered financial company is in default or in danger of default and satisfies the definition of a financial company under section 5381(a)(11)"—was arbitrary and capricious.[126] After that the court is essentially told to "go away."[127]

The still-pending Financial CHOICE Act, a sweeping chapter 14–style bill that the House passed in June 2017,[128] follows a more extreme path. Although it purportedly replaces OLA with normal bankruptcy procedures, one of the first things to happen in a bank bankruptcy under the Act is the removal of all of the debtor's assets from the bankruptcy estate.[129] Essentially, the bankruptcy court is left to sort out a fight over the residue, while the bulk of the action happens off stage.

Indeed, after the initial transfer, everything will apparently be resolved under state trust law, presumably New York State's law. The bill provides that "[a]fter a transfer to the special trustee under

---

[125.] See Jonathan C. Lipson, Against Regulatory Displacement: An Institutional Analysis of Financial Crises, 17 U. Pa. J. Bus. L. 673, 710 (2015) (arguing that financial institution insolvencies are regulated to achieve the policy goals of legislative bodies and regulatory agencies).

[126.] 12 U.S.C. § 5382(a)(1)(A)(iv) (2012).

[127.] For example, *id.* section 5382(a)(1)(B), 5388, 5390(a)(9)(D).

[128.] Financial CHOICE Act of 2017, H.R. 10, 115th Cong. Sec. 122, section 1181–92 (2017) (as passed by the House June 8, 2017), www.congress.gov/bill/115th-congress/house-bill/10/text/eh? [https://perma.cc/Y6EN-YU5H].

[129.] *Id.* section 1186.

this section, the special trustee shall be subject only to applicable non-bankruptcy law, and the actions and conduct of the special trustee shall no longer be subject to approval by the [bankruptcy] court in the case under this subchapter."[130]

The CHOICE Act provides that the trust

> shall be a newly formed trust governed by a trust agreement approved by the court as in the best interests of the estate, and shall exist for the sole purpose of holding and administering, and shall be permitted to dispose of, the equity securities of the bridge company in accordance with the trust agreement.[131]

Thus, the bankruptcy court has some fleeting power before approval of the trust, but that must be exercised under extreme time limits—perhaps as little as one day.[132]

The terms of the trust are only subject to a few vague rules, and the pronouncement that "the trustee shall confirm to the court that the [Federal Reserve] Board has been consulted regarding the identity of the proposed special trustee and advise the court of the results of such consultation."[133] The latter leaves open at least the theoretical possibility that a trustee could be appointed in the face of Fed objections—so long as the bankruptcy court is willing to sign the order.

The only other express role for regulators is a requirement that the trustee consult with the FDIC and the Fed before selling the shares of the debtor, and, again, the trustee must disclose the results of those discussions to the bankruptcy court.[134] The court, however, has no actual power over the trustee at this point.

[130.] *Id.* section 1186(d).

[131.] *Id.* section 1186(a)(1).

[132.] *Id.* section 1185.

[133.] *Id.* section 1186(a)(2).

[134.] The regulators are given general standing to appear before the bankruptcy court. *Id.* section 1184.

Thus, an elected New York Supreme Court judge and (perhaps) the state attorney general will exercise some loose oversight over the process, but otherwise, the assets will largely disappear from the public eye. If that looks too menacing to management, the trust could be formed under the law of some other jurisdiction—indeed, there appears to be no express requirement that the trust be formed under domestic law. Thus, the bankruptcy court might have twenty-four hours to approve a trust governed by Manx law, to take one possible example.

The trust might even avoid application of the Bank Holding Company Act if it were established with a term of less than twenty-five years.[135] The underlying holding company that the trust owns would be subject to regulation, but the trust has the potential to be entirely opaque. This from legislation that is sold as increasing transparency.

In short, while a modern chapter 11 case features "hands on" judicial involvement, and that is a key feature of chapter 11 as practiced, such a role is inconsistent with the policy goals of a financial institution insolvency case. The CHOICE Act, the most prominent of the recent chapter 14 proposals, is at best a pretend bankruptcy case for financial institutions.

IV. Facing Facts

At a broad level, the global financial system is designed to fail.[136] The very structure of SIFIs and the nature of the explicit and implicit governmental backstops baked into the system will always encourage

---

[135] 12 U.S.C. § 1841(b) (2012) (excluding any trust with terms of less than twenty-five years from the definition of "company," resulting in such trusts not being subject to BHCA regulation). Presumably the bankruptcy court, particularly if asked by regulators, could order compliance with the BHCA when transferring estate assets to the trust.

[136] See generally Anat Admati & Martin Hellwig, The Bankers' New Clothes: What's Wrong with Banking and What to Do about It (2013) (arguing that despite superficial reforms in the wake of the recent recession, the banking industry still practices risky financial behaviors that reflect a fragile banking system).

banks to take ever-larger risks.[137] But this is inextricably linked to my earlier observation that banks supply social goods; as a nation, we like money and credit, but using the same institutions to provide both presents us with some important and awkward policy trade-offs.

Regulators inevitably find it impossible to keep up, since bankers will always beat them in resources and influence.[138] Nevertheless, because we worry about a world without big banks, and what it would look like, we tolerate this death-defying condition.[139]

In this context, the insolvency system for SIFIs matters quite a bit.[140] A bank near insolvency must not be allowed to operate, since shareholders have nothing left to lose from taking ever riskier bets, and have every incentive to leave taxpayers "holding the bag." The credibility of the threat to take the SIFI away from its owners—the shareholders and managers—and run it in the public interest is vital if this downward spiral is to be avoided.

One fundamental aspect of a credible SIFI insolvency system is that, upon activation, the outlines of "what will happen" are both clear and credible.[141] One part of that certainty traditionally

---

[137.] See Arthur E. Wilmarth, Jr., The Dodd–Frank Act: A Flawed and Inadequate Response to the Too-Big-to-Fail Problem, 89 Or. L. Rev. 951, 1023–24 (2011) (arguing that Dodd–Frank fails to eliminate the incentive for large banks to rely on federal bailout programs when considering risky activities).

[138.] Henry T.C. Hu, Misunderstood Derivatives: The Causes of Informational Failure and the Promise of Regulatory Incrementalism, 102 Yale L.J. 1457, 1463 (1993); cf. Frank Pasquale, Law's Acceleration of Finance: Redefining the Problem of High-Frequency Trading, 36 Cardozo L. Rev. 2085, 2114 (2015) (describing "the bleak realities at resource-starved agencies").

[139.] See Helen A. Garten, Regulatory Growing Pains: A Perspective on Bank Regulation in a Deregulatory Age, 57 Fordham L. Rev. 501, 536–37 (1989) (describing different capital-regulation approaches aimed at motivating banks to avoid risk-taking behavior).

[140.] But see Jonathan R. Macey & Geoffrey P. Miller, Bank Failures, Risk Monitoring, and the Market for Bank Control, 88 Colum. L. Rev. 1153, 1157 (1988) ("Despite the surface plausibility of this theory, it is unlikely that a generalized bank panic like that which occurred during the Depression would occur today.").

[141.] See Edward J. Janger, Treatment of Financial Contracts in Bankruptcy and Bank Resolution, 10 Brook. J. Corp. Fin. & Com. L. 1, 4–5 (2015) (highlighting the disorderly outcome of non-FDIC-administered resolutions in comparison to the predictable and prompt process of bank insolvency proceedings).

comes from the complete protection of certain favored classes of creditors—that is, in bank insolvency, priority dominates over equality.

Another aspect of the clarity that SIFI resolution requires is an understanding at the outset of the process of how the resolution case will proceed.[142] Bank, broker-dealer, and insurance company resolutions all follow formally distinct insolvency models in this country, yet any such entity works through its insolvency with similar goals. For example, when a broker-dealer fails, customer accounts are moved to a healthy broker, any gap in customer assets is made up by SIPC, and the typical customer ceases to concern itself with the insolvency process.[143] Stockbrokers from the local Main Street broker to Lehman Brothers have followed this model.

Chapter 11 offers no similar certainty at inception. First, the parties might dispute and litigate the question of what "equality" looks like in any particular chapter 11 case. Next, the precise form of the reorganization plan is up for grabs in every case. Plans in one case are often modeled on what "worked" in a prior case, but the precise contours of the plan are largely unknown at the commencement of the case.

This uncertainty does not work in the context of financial institution insolvency.[144] And thus, banks are resolved without court involvement, and broker-dealers and insurance companies are resolved with

---

[142.] See Robert R. Bliss & George G. Kaufman, U.S. Corporate and Bank Insolvency Regimes: A Comparison and Evaluation, 2 Va. L. & Bus. Rev. 143, 176–77 (2007) (concluding that "[r]educing uncertainties surrounding the bank-insolvency-resolution process would further reduce the adverse externalities from bank insolvencies" and "may also reduce the incentives for banks to engage in excessive risk taking and moral hazard").

[143.] Kenneth J. Caputo, Customer Claims in SIPA Liquidations: Claims Filing and the Impact of Ordinary Bankruptcy Standards on Post-Bar Date Claim Amendments in SIPA Proceedings, 20 Am. Bankr. Inst. L. Rev. 235, 243 n.48 (2012).

[144.] Cf. Andrea M. Corcoran, Markets' Self-Assessment and Improvement of Default Strategies after the Collapse of Barings, 2 Stan. J.L. Bus. & Fin. 265, 291 (1996) (asserting that flexibility in financial emergencies should not be compromised).

court involvement only in the later stages of the process, when the issue becomes reconciling claims more than stabilizing the institution. These are fundamentally different processes from chapter 11.[145]

OLA tries to hide this reality by providing a thin veneer of judicial oversight at the outset of the case before quickly dispensing with the judge.[146] The CHOICE Act is in many respects even more disingenuous in that it pretends to be a normal bankruptcy process.[147] But the court loses control over the debtor's assets at the outset of the case, and the public agencies—the FDIC and the Fed—are not granted any meaningful participation in the process. Even the regulatory status of the post-transfer trust—which clearly should be considered "a financial holding company" under the Bank Holding Company Act, but might evade even that basic regulation—is left rather vague under the proposed Act.

The entire chapter 14 project is based on this same basic misunderstanding of the goals of bankruptcy, as contrasted with the goals of SIFI resolution.[148] In theory, a SIFI could be resolved in a bankruptcy process, but policymakers have generally believed that the societal costs would be too high. And indeed, if we think back to the pre-FDIC bank receiverships—where depositors were mere unsecured creditors[149]—that supposition is likely correct.

[145.] Irit Mevorach, Beyond the Search for Certainty: Addressing the Cross-Border Resolution Gap, 10 Brook. J. Corp. Fin. & Com. L. 183, 213 (2015).

[146.] Stephen J. Lubben, A New Understanding of the Bankruptcy Clause, 64 Case W. Res. L. Rev. 319, 409 (2013).

[147.] See John Crawford, Lesson Unlearned?: Regulatory Reform and Financial Stability in the Trump Administration, 117 Colum. L. Rev. Online 127, 140 (2017) ("The CHOICE Act would repeal Title II of the Dodd–Frank Act and replace it with a new subchapter of the Bankruptcy Code, chapter 11, subchapter V.").

[148.] See Anna Gelpern, Financial Crisis Containment, 41 Conn. L. Rev. 1051, 1102–06 (2009) (reviewing the policies, procedures, and decisions evaluated in bankruptcy considerations).

[149.] Hirsch Braver, Liquidation of Financial Institutions: A Treatise on the Law of Voluntary and Involuntary Liquidation of Banks, Trust Companies, and Building and Loan Associations section 501 (1936).

Chapter 14 advocates point to the transparency of chapter 11 as a virtue to be lauded over normal bank insolvency procedures.[150] The latter, in their view, are too apt to become mechanisms of bailout and favoritism, whereas chapter 11 looks like a more virtuous market system. The question is whether realizing due process "up front"—as opposed to after the fact, in the form of a lawsuit against the FDIC or other regulators—really works in conjunction with the policy goals that motivate bank-resolution mechanisms.

Arguably, the CHOICE Act itself tells us that the answer to this question is "no," since the actual in-court part of the process is so slight under the proposed law. If that is the best that the advocates of "bankruptcy for banks" can do, we might suspect that true bankruptcy will never actually work.

V. Conclusion

Bank insolvency uses much of the language of "normal" insolvency. But bank resolution is not the same as chapter 11 or any other business insolvency process. Bank insolvency is about special priorities, whereas corporate bankruptcy is about creditor equality and bargaining. Too often, we let the similar language confound the analysis.

In an idealized world, bank insolvency is a purely technical project with fixed distributional consequences. In reality, particularly when the insolvency has systemic consequences, it takes on a political dimension as well. That is, while certain policy choices are made ex ante, through the choice of resolution mechanism, other policy choices will have to be made ex post, when failure actually happens.

[150.] See Hester Pierce, Eliminating Dodd–Frank's Overrated Escape Hatch, Real-Clear Markets (May 25, 2017), www.realclearmarkets.com/articles/2017/05/25/eliminatingdodd-franksoverratedescapehatch102707.html [https://perma.cc/BN5V-W4AG] (calling bankruptcy "a predictable, time-tested, transparent mechanism"); see also Chadwick Welch, Dodd–Frank's Title II Authority: A Disorderly Liquidation of Experience, Logic, and Due Process, 21 Wm. & Mary Bill Rts. J. 989, 992 (2013) (arguing that bank insolvency procedures "muddl[e] what should be a framework of transparent rules").

All of the "super chapter 11" or "chapter 11 for banks" proposals—including the actually enacted OLA—attempt to put a judicial gloss on the policy and political process that is bank insolvency. Some, like the CHOICE Act, appear aimed at moving policy choices away from regulators by pretending to give power to judges, while actually moving policy choices to private actors.[151]

It is thought that this judicial veneer will provide a kind of legitimacy to bank insolvency that proponents believe was lacking in the rescue efforts in 2008. But, if taken seriously, the judicial role is entirely incompatible with efforts to contain a systemic crisis. Moreover, the veneer is quite apt to crack in any event: consider the broad role played by the U.S. and Canadian governments in the automotive bankruptcy cases, which involved at best marginally systemic debtors.[152] Somewhat confusingly, many of the critics of those cases nonetheless support some form of chapter 14.

If we do not take the judicial role in bankruptcy for banks seriously and see it as instead a smokescreen, the conclusions are even more disturbing. At best, the CHOICE Act—and proposals like it—are little more than disguised power grabs by insiders designed to use rule of law concerns as a cover for a deregulatory agenda. When an actual systemic crisis comes, it seems inevitable that the need for governmental assistance will arise yet again, and we will be right back where we were in 2008.[153]

My goal has been to draw attention to the confused thinking involved in many current approaches to bank insolvency. Bank and business insolvency use similar language to describe fundamentally different mechanisms. Only by a return to first principles can we reach sensible policy analysis.

[151.] See Arthur E. Wilmarth, Jr., The Financial Industry's Plan for Resolving Failed Megabanks Will Ensure Future Bailouts for Wall Street, 50 Ga. L. Rev. 43, 57–58, 58 n.57 (2015) (discussing the benefits of a Wall Street proposal to private actors).

[152.] See Stephen J. Lubben, No Big Deal: The GM and Chrysler Cases in Context, 83 Am. Bankr. L.J. 531, 531, 536 (2009) (discussing governmental involvement in the Chrysler and General Motors chapter 11 bankruptcies).

[153.] See Recent Case, State Nat'l Bank of Big Spring v. Lew, 795 F.3d 48 (D.C. Cir. 2015), 129 Harv. L. Rev. 835, 839 (2016) (describing future OLA litigation concerns).

Cross-Border Insolvency

Recognition of Insolvency-Related Judgments and Choice of Law Characterization

Rosalind Mason[*]

I. Introduction

In recent decades, national economies have been characterized by accelerated growth in international trade and investment and by globalized production and distribution of goods and services. Yet whether within a domestic or a global marketplace, a proportion of businesses will inevitably be unable to meet their financial obligations, for a range of internal or external reasons. The internationalization of national economies has however increased the likelihood that the effects of an insolvency will not be confined to the one state. In such instances, a state's private international law becomes relevant

[*] Adjunct Professor, Faculty of Law, Queensland University of Technology. Professor Mason retired as Professor of Insolvency and Restructuring Law at QUT in 2019.
This chapter is based on a presentation at the Symposium to honour Professor Jay Westbrook held at the University of Texas, Austin, in February 2018. Reproduced with updated information from Norton Journal of Bankruptcy Law and Practice, Vol. 27 No. 5 (Oct. 2018), with permission of Thomson Reuters. Copyright © 2018.

in determining how it resolves a foreign element in any legal dispute arising out of the insolvency.

To increase the certainty for stakeholders in managing such cross-border insolvencies, symmetry is advocated between the issues addressed by private international law. In order to achieve the predictability, certainty, and transparency of regulation so important for dealing with a debtor in general default with the least possible delay and expense, not only is it necessary to achieve symmetry between international jurisdiction and multistate effects, it is also necessary to address the law to be applied by the courts when exercising jurisdiction locally or giving effect to a foreign order.

This chapter asks the question of how best to align the elements of private international law as they intersect with insolvency to improve consistency and reduce conflict in cross-border insolvencies. This question continues to be relevant in global discussions and this chapter asks whether a recent United Nations Commission on International Trade Law (UNCITRAL) project may assist, in an incremental way,[1] to achieving international consensus on the element of choice of law in international insolvency.

The first part of this chapter provides a high-level overview of private international law and its theories as relevant to cross-border insolvency. The second opens with a discussion of the UNCITRAL Working Group V (WGV) project on Recognition and Enforcement of Insolvency-Related Judgments. It then compares the issues which have been identified as related to insolvency with those for which the applicable law has been addressed in multistate instruments and initiatives. The chapter concludes that, in the context of growing consensus through the lens of recognition and enforcement under the 1997 Model Law on Cross-Border Insolvency regarding an acceptable exercise of jurisdiction to open insolvency proceedings, the 2018 Model Law on Recognition and Enforcement of Insolvency-Related

---

[1.] Jenny Clift, Choice of Law and the UNCITRAL Harmonisation Process, 9 Brook. J. Corp. Fin. & Com. L. 29 (2014).

Judgments may likewise contribute to consensus on the applicable law on issues related to multistate insolvencies.

II. Private International Law and Cross-border Insolvency Law

The approach of insolvency law theories to analyzing multistate insolvency has been essentially about which states have jurisdiction to adjudicate on the insolvency or restructuring of a debtor, using concepts of "unity" and "plurality" of proceedings.[2] This question of jurisdiction though is often then linked with the concomitant question as to multistate effects, whether other states will recognize and give effect to such adjudication, using descriptors of "universality" and "territoriality."[3] During the span of Professor Westbrook's scholarship, the debate on these extremes has become more nuanced with the addition of approaches such as "cooperative territoriality"[4] and "modified universalism."[5]

This universality/territoriality spectrum does not adequately address the third element of a comprehensive private international law analysis[6]—the applicable law in the proceedings. Domestic

---

[2] Ian F. Fletcher, Insolvency in Private International Law, section 1.12 (2nd ed. 2005). Under the principle of "unity," there is one set of insolvency proceedings in respect of the one debtor, while "plurality" has more than one set of proceedings in progress concurrently in different states.

[3] Ian F. Fletcher, Insolvency in Private International Law, section 1.13 (2nd ed. 2005). "Universality" refers to the extraterritorial effect of one set of proceedings in every other jurisdiction, while "territoriality" refers to the limitation of the effects of a set of proceedings to its place of origin.

[4] Lynn M. LoPucki, The Case for Cooperative Territoriality in International Bankruptcy, 98 Mich. L. R. 2216 (2000).

[5] Jay L. Westbrook, A Global Solution to Multinational Default, 98 Mich. L. R. 2276 (2000).

[6] The three elements are (i) choice of forum—whether a court can and will hear and determine the matter; (ii) the recognition and effect accorded foreign insolvency proceedings; and (iii) choice of law: Eugene F. Scoles et al., Conflict of Laws (3rd ed., 2000, West Publishing, St Paul) section 1.2.

legislation, for example, in common law countries whose insolvency statutes derive from England and Wales, typically leave questions of the applicable law to judge-made private international law. Some regional multilateral conventions, such as the Nordic Convention[7] and the European Insolvency Regulation[8] address applicable law. By comparison, the influential UNCITRAL Model Law on Cross-Border Insolvency ("the MLCBI") focuses on local access of foreign representatives; recognition of foreign orders; relief to assist foreign proceedings; and cooperation between courts and coordination of concurrent proceedings.[9]

As argued in John Martin's and my paper at UNCITRAL's 50th Anniversary Congress, "in order to achieve a consistent outcome in cross-border insolvencies, a uniform choice of law approach is inextricably linked with uniformity in choice of forum, that is agreement upon the allocation of jurisdiction to a primary or other insolvency proceeding."[10] While the MLCBI does not allocate jurisdiction, it does base its recognition and automatic relief provisions upon the place of the debtor's "center of main interests" (COMI).[11]

On the issue of the applicable law, there is an obvious argument that the law of the COMI should govern the insolvency proceedings and be applied in other recognizing states. Nevertheless

---

[7] Nordic Convention on Bankruptcy between Norway, Denmark, Finland, Iceland and Sweden, Article 1 (1933). See Ian F. Fletcher, Insolvency in Private International Law, Appendix VI (2nd ed. 2005).

[8] Regulation (EU) 2015/848 of the European Parliament and of the Council of May 20, 2015 on Insolvency Proceedings (Recast), Article 7 ff: http://eur-lex.europa.eu/legal-content/EN/TXT/?uri=CELEX%3A32015R0848.

[9] UNCITRAL Model Law on Cross-Border Insolvency Guide to Enactment and Interpretation (2013), section 24. (Guide to Enactment and Interpretation).

[10] Rosalind Mason & John Martin, "Conflict and Consistency in Cross Border Insolvency Judgments," paper presented at the UNCITRAL 50th Anniversary Congress (2017): www.uncitral.org/pdf/english/congress/Papers_for_Programme/46-MASON_and_MARTIN-Conflict_and_Consistency_in_Cross_border_Insolvency_Judgments.pdf

[11] Article 20, MLCBI. Proceedings commenced in a jurisdiction with which the debtor has a lesser connection ("establishment"—see below) may also be recognized and granted local discretionary relief.

the pragmatic drafters of the MLCBI recognizing the difficulties in achieving domestic adoption of a cross-border insolvency instrument were careful not to import the consequences of the foreign insolvency law into the local system.[12]

If consensus can be achieved regarding choice of law rules, followed by their international adoption, it is suggested that the risk of inconsistent judgments will largely be avoided. Such rules, if binding in the relevant states, should produce decisional harmony through a unique identification of the law to govern the adjudication of the dispute.

Some multilateral instruments in cross-border insolvency have already reached agreement on the law of the "home state" or COMI jurisdiction applying to many issues arising in a cross-border insolvency. It is, perhaps, the identification of the issues for which the choice of law is a different jurisdiction for which an attempt ought to be made to achieve consensus within the international commercial and legal community.[13]

A gradual increase in cooperative jurisprudence in cross-border insolvency matters[14] was dealt a blow in 2013 by the decision of the United Kingdom Supreme Court in *Rubin v. Eurofinance SA; New Cap Reinsurance Corp (in liquidation) v. Grant*[15] ("*Rubin/New Cap*" decision).

[12.] For example, the Article 20 mandatory stay following automatic recognition of the foreign insolvency proceeding and the related appointment of the foreign insolvency representative in the debtor's COMI refers to local relief in terms of the enacting state's insolvency laws: Article 20(2).

[13.] For recent scholarly discussions on choice of law in multistate insolvency, see Edward J Janger, Virtual Territoriality 48 Colum. J. Transnat'l L. 401 (2009–2010); Charles W Mooney Jr, Harmonising Choice-Of-Law Rules for International Insolvency Cases: Virtual Territoriality, Virtual Universalism, and the Problem of Local Interests, 9 Brook. J. Corp. Fin. & Com. L. 131 (2014–2015); John A. E. Pottow, Beyond Carve-outs and toward Reliance: A Normative Framework for Cross-Border Insolvency Choice of Law 9 Brook. J. Corp. Fin. & Com. L. 197 (2014–2015).

[14.] See Lord Hoffmann's judgments in *Cambridge Gas Transport Corp v. Official Committee of Unsecured Creditors of Navigator Holdings PLC* [2006] UKPC 26 and *In re HIH Casualty and General Insurance Ltd* [2008] UKHL 21.

[15.] *Rubin v. Eurofinance SA; New Cap Reinsurance Corp (in liquidation) v. Grant*, [2013] 1 AC 236.

The court declined recognition of a foreign judgment that arose in an insolvency context and prompted the WGV project on the Recognition and Enforcement of Insolvency-Related Judgments.

This chapter will later discuss the WGV deliberations on identifying which judgments are "insolvency-related" for recognition and enforcement purposes to see whether they may provide any insights to assist consensus on characterizing aspects of insolvency when selecting the applicable law.

Before doing so, this chapter provides a brief context and examines private international law's three dimensions of jurisdiction; recognition and enforcement; and choice of law—the theories underpinning each and their relevance to insolvency.

A. Jurisdiction: Theory and Application to Insolvency

A state's[16] participation in international trade in goods and services can be affected by its response to issues of jurisdiction and recognition and enforcement of foreign judgments. This can provide a favorable setting for trade because of the potential to deliver "legal certainty, in the general sense that the application of a law to a particular relationship is reasonably predictable regardless of where . . . that relationship is considered."[17] If one judgment purporting to be universally enforceable is recognized in other states as *res judicata*, it sets the one legal relationship at one defined value for every state granting that recognition. Even though certainty is only created once the judgment has been rendered, this can be increased when it is possible to know beforehand which states are likely to have jurisdiction to determine the dispute. Even more certainty is achieved where the states agree on common rules of jurisdiction for particular multistate disputes, which thus determine which particular state's courts render the universally definitive judgment and so which laws will be applied.[18]

[16.] The term "state" is used in this chapter for a legal area, instead of, e.g., "country."
[17.] Reid Mortensen, Judgments Extension under CER, N. Z. L. Rev. 237, 240 (1999).
[18.] Reid Mortensen, Judgments Extension under CER, N.Z. L. Rev. 237, 240 (1999).

1. General Theories of Jurisdiction

The term "jurisdiction" carries a number of connotations, two of which are of fundamental importance. The first is geographical jurisdiction, that is, the physical area of a court's competence. The second is subject matter jurisdiction, which is a court's authority to deal with disputes. The scholar von Mehren justified the exercise of subject matter jurisdiction based on power theory and fairness theory.[19]

Power theory justifies the exercise of jurisdiction "if the legal order has, directly or indirectly, an effective hold over the defendant."[20] This theory focuses on the object (the person or thing) over which power is exercised.[21] It largely ignores litigational fairness or convenience, although such factors may become relevant to declining jurisdiction under the doctrine of *forum non conveniens*. In addition, it ignores any interest of the state in the parties or in the underlying dispute.

By comparison, fairness theory explains and justifies the exercise of adjudicatory authority by reference to the criteria of convenience, fairness, and justice. In order to assess the propriety of asserting jurisdiction under fairness theory, the court examines either the parties' or the dispute's relationship with the forum. It does not focus on the object over which authority is exercised.

Von Mehren argued that, in the United States, power theory has been replaced by fairness theory.[22] Relevantly, the U.S. discussion of adjudicatory jurisdiction is influenced by the Due Process Clause of the Fourteenth Amendment to the American Constitution: no State shall "deprive any person of life, liberty, or property, without due process of law."

[19.] This discussion is largely drawn from Arthur T. von Mehren, Adjudicatory Jurisdiction: General Theories Compared and Evaluated, 63 B. U. L. Rev. 279 (1983).

[20.] Arthur T. von Mehren, Adjudicatory Jurisdiction: General Theories Compared and Evaluated, 63 B. U. L. Rev. 279, 285 (1983).

[21.] These coincide with distinctions between jurisdiction *in personam* and jurisdiction *in rem*.

[22.] Arthur T. von Mehren, Adjudicatory Jurisdiction: General Theories Compared and Evaluated, 63 B. U. L. Rev. 279 (1983). Also see Eugene F. Scoles et al., Conflict of Laws, section 5-5 (3rd ed. 2000).

However, in countries with an English legal heritage, such as Australia, the predominant paradigm for civil and commercial matters remains that of power over the defendant. This reflects its basis in procedural considerations and the concern in actions *in personam* with parties rather than the cause of action. Jurisdiction to adjudicate in a particular action *in personam* requires valid service of the originating process on the defendant, typically within the jurisdiction although service may in limited circumstances be permitted outside the jurisdiction. Jurisdiction to adjudicate in an action *in rem* is based on the presence of the *res* (such as a ship) within the court's geographical jurisdiction.

This focus upon power is clearly evident in the *Rubin/New Cap* decision. Lord Collins noted "if the judgments in issue on the appeals are regarded as judgments *in personam* within the Dicey Rule [43],[23] then they will only be enforced in England at common law if the judgment debtors were present . . . in the foreign country when the proceedings were commenced, or if they submitted to its jurisdiction."[24]

2. Jurisdictional Theories and Insolvency

Although power theory may be a predominant paradigm in matters of jurisdiction generally, does it provide the better explanation for jurisdiction to make an order in matters of insolvency? While Lord Collins did not accept the arguments that there was "a sui generis category of insolvency orders or judgments subject to special rules,"[25] considerations of fairness assist more in explaining when such jurisdiction is and should be exercised.

The liquidation or reorganization of a debtor's property to meet its obligations is a complex procedure with an inherent integrity

---

[23.] Dicey, Morris & Collins, Conflict of Laws (15th ed. 2012) at para 14R-054.

[24.] *Rubin v. Eurofinance SA*; *New Cap Reinsurance Corp (in liquidation) v. Grant* [2013] 1 AC 236 at [10].

[25.] *Rubin v. Eurofinance SA*; *New Cap Reinsurance Corp (in liquidation) v. Grant* [2013] 1 AC 236 at [102] ff.

through the unity of the estate being realized and distributed or restructured. The administration is complex and integrated, with interconnecting aspects of insolvency law.[26] The diverse interests in the administration of a debtor's estate in insolvency mean that it is more than a procedural matter enforcing a creditor's remedy. It goes to the rights and interests not only of the parties directly involved, but also the collective body of creditors, third parties and the state.

Since the time of the first English bankruptcy statute in 1542,[27] it has been acknowledged that the exercise of natural person insolvency jurisdiction does not require the physical presence of the debtor within the jurisdiction; for example, it referred to collective distribution of the estates of debtors who had absconded to foreign realms and countries to defraud creditors. Also, there are problems associated with explaining jurisdiction over legal persons in terms of concepts of power and personal service. Corporations' "presence" has been interpreted in terms of activities being done on the company's behalf.[28]

Fairness theory explains more adequately than power theory when jurisdiction is or should be exercised to commence and administer insolvency proceedings. Fairness theory justifies the exercise of general jurisdiction[29] based on the parties' relationship with the forum, independent of the underlying dispute.[30] It looks to a juridical relation based on the parties' close or strong ties to the state rather than the object over which authority is exercised. While residence and incorporation have been relevant to personal and corporate

---

[26.] See, for example, the notion of collectivism in a liquidation that links a state's voidable transaction provisions with its distribution rules.

[27.] 34 and 35 Henry VIII c 4 (1542).

[28.] Arthur T. von Mehren, Adjudicatory Jurisdiction: General Theories Compared and Evaluated, 63 B. U. L. Rev. 279, 299 (1983).

[29.] General jurisdiction is "the authority of a court to adjudicate any claim (or any but a limited class of claims) without any requirement of a link between the claim and the forum state": Andreas F. Lowenfeld, International Litigation and the Quest for Reasonableness (1996) at 48.

[30.] The underlying dispute resulting in an insolvency administration is typically the general default by the debtor in meeting debts as they fall due.

insolvency jurisdiction, they have been more significant as jurisdictional grounds that justify a local court's recognition and enforcement of foreign orders.

Thus under fairness theory, the history of insolvency jurisdiction is better explained in terms of specific[31] rather than general jurisdiction. In common law and civil law traditions for insolvency and related matters, connections typically comprise nationality, domicile, residence, personal presence, presence of assets or (economic and non-economic) activity, or submission/consent. Thus it is more helpful to examine the dispute's rather than the parties' relationship with the state, to determine whether it is fair to exercise jurisdiction.

Fairness theory justifies the exercise of specific jurisdiction based on the underlying dispute's litigational or substantive relationship with the state. This relationship encompasses fairness considerations such as questions of convenience, impartiality and expense to the parties if the forum were to exercise authority over the dispute. Insolvency proceedings, being collective administrations, squarely raise the issue of multiple or indeterminate parties.[32] Factors of convenience and expense to the parties have also influenced the exercise of concurrent jurisdiction to make an ancillary order where a debtor has been carrying on business within the state. The other criterion for specific jurisdiction under fairness theory is the dispute's substantive relation to the state—that is, the forum's interest in applying its law to the dispute. This has influenced the exercise of jurisdiction to commence local ancillary insolvency proceedings to ensure that local policies are implemented.

---

[31] Specific jurisdiction is where the court's authority to adjudicate is "with respect to issues deriving from, or connected with, the very controversy that establishes the jurisdiction to adjudicate": Arthur T. von Mehren & Donald T. Trautman, Jurisdiction to Adjudicate: A Suggested Analysis 79 Harv. L. Rev. 1121, 1136 (1966).

[32] Arthur T. von Mehren & Donald T. Trautman, Jurisdiction to Adjudicate: A Suggested Analysis, 79 Harv. L. Rev. 1121, 1153 (1966). They refer to disputes which involve persons not bound together voluntarily but who otherwise have some unity of interests, such as creditors of a decedent leaving assets in several states.

A court's jurisdiction to adjudicate on disputes during the course of the insolvency administration may be explained by power theory, for example, the presence of local assets. However, the substantive relation of the dispute with the forum may equally justify proceedings on the basis of fairness. For example, a liquidator may issue proceedings against a creditor who is not in the jurisdiction to recover a pre-liquidation payment made by the company in circumstances which establish the payment is a voidable transaction. The liquidator may seek to effect service outside the jurisdiction on the basis of the relation between the dispute and the forum, in particular the latter's rules on the collective distribution of the debtor's estate.

Such an insolvency-related issue was central to the *Rubin/New Cap* case which concerned recognition and enforcement of an approximately US$10m judgment against third parties under State and Federal law in respect of fraudulent conveyances and transfers.[33] Adversary proceedings were issued in the U.S. Bankruptcy Court and resulted in a default summary judgment. The court's exercise of jurisdiction was based on the defendants' choice of the U.S. as the place to carry on their business.[34] However when recognition and enforcement of the default judgment was sought in the United Kingdom, this was held to be an insufficient basis for recognition of the judgment. Such recognition under private international law required the judgment to be based on presence in or submission to the jurisdiction of the foreign state in which the proceedings were commenced.[35]

Next, the chapter deals with theories underpinning recognition and enforcement of judgments and how these relate to insolvency.

[33.] *Rubin v. Eurofinance SA* [2009] EWHC 2129 (Ch).

[34.] *Rubin v Eurofinance SA* [2009] EWHC 2129 (Ch) at [17].

[35.] *Rubin v. Eurofinance SA*; *New Cap Reinsurance Corp (in liquidation) v. Grant* [2013] 1 AC 236; [2012] UKSC 236 at [10]. See Dicey, Morris and Collins, Conflict of Laws (15th ed. 2012) Rule 43. Statutes sometimes apply to reciprocal recognition and enforcement of judgments in general civil and commercial matters (not insolvency), e.g., Australia's Foreign Judgments Act 1991 (Cth).

B. Recognition and Enforcement of Judgments: Theory and Application to Insolvency

1. Recognition and Enforcement Theories

Various theories have been proposed to justify recognition[36] and enforcement[37] of foreign judgments: the theory of obligation;[38] the principle of *res judicata*;[39] the doctrines of comity and reciprocity; and the notion of sufficient connection. These latter three provide most assistance to understanding the dynamics of local responses to foreign insolvency orders.

The doctrine of comity is an enduring leitmotif in private international law.[40] It has been described by the U.S. Supreme Court in *Hilton v. Guyot*[41] as follows:

> "Comity" in the legal sense, is neither a matter of absolute obligation on the one hand, nor of mere courtesy and good will, on the other. But it is the recognition which one nation allows within its territory to the legislative, executive or judicial acts of another nation, having due regard both to international duty and convenience, and to the rights of its own citizens or of other persons who are under the protection of its law.

Thus, not being a binding rule of law, the extension of comity through recognition of a foreign judgment is a matter of discretion to be exercised in light of the facts of the particular case.

[36.] That is, the conclusive or *res judicata* effect of a judgment.

[37.] That is, the execution of a judgment—compliance with its terms by the defendant.

[38.] The common law approach to recognition and enforcement of money judgments as a private transaction: Hessel E. Yntema, The Enforcement of Foreign Judgments in Anglo-American Law, 33 Mich. L. Rev. 1129 (1935). However, insolvency orders also affect third parties.

[39.] This reflects considerations of "justice, legal order, simplicity and economy in the administration of justice": Niv Tadmore, Recognition of Foreign in Personam Money Judgments in Australia, 2(2) Deakin L. Rev. 129, 139 (1995). However concurrent administrations are common in multistate insolvency.

[40.] D.J. Llewellyn Davies, The Influence of Huber's De Conflictu Legum on English Private International Law, 18 B.Y.I.L. 49 (1937) 66.

[41.] *Hilton v. Guyot*, 159 U.S. 113, 163–64, 16 S. Ct. 139, 40 L. Ed. 95, 2007 A.M.C. 2028 (1895).

Linked to the concept of comity is that of reciprocity.[42] That is, if the facts exist in the foreign state which, if occurring locally, would justify the local court exercising jurisdiction and indeed the foreign court does exercise jurisdiction (whether or not on the same grounds as local jurisdictional rules), then the foreign court's order is recognized locally.

Recognition has also been based upon a theory of "sufficient" connection. In the English case of *Schemmer v. Property Resources Ltd*[43] regarding a foreign order appointing a receiver, Goulding J stated that the court must be satisfied of "a sufficient connection between the defendant and the jurisdiction in which the foreign receiver was appointed" to justify recognition of the foreign court's order as having effect outside its jurisdiction. In the Canadian case of *Re Cavell Insurance Co*,[44] the Ontario Court of Appeal stated that "the real and substantial connection principle is now clearly applicable both to the recognition of foreign judgments and interprovincial judgments."

2. Recognition and Enforcement Theories and Insolvency

First, to address comity, writing prior to *Rubin/New Cap*, Fletcher stated, "There is an established tradition among judges within the common law 'family' of extending international cooperation to each other in the name of the doctrine of 'comity.'"[45] Considerations of comity have been cited in support of a number of decisions

---

[42.] This is not to be confused with "reciprocal" action that if a foreign jurisdiction recognizes local orders, then local courts will recognize corresponding foreign orders, as occurs in statutes on recognition of foreign judgments such as Australia's Foreign Judgments Act 1991 (Cth).

[43.] 1975] Ch 273 at 287.

[44.] *Re Cavell Insurance Co* (2006) 269 DLR (4th) 679; [2006] CanLII 16529 (ON CA) at [39].

[45.] Ian F Fletcher, Insolvency in Private International Law: National and International Approaches (2nd ed. 2005) at 17. In addition, prior to the adoption of the UNCITRAL MLCBI in chapter 15, one of the factors that U.S. courts had to consider in exercising their discretion to assist foreign insolvency administrators without the need for local formal insolvency proceedings was comity: Bankruptcy Code s 304(c)(5).

rendering assistance to foreign insolvency representatives under statutory provisions.[46]

While comity is not obligatory, having been described as a "doctrine of pragmatism,"[47] a pragmatic approach to multistate insolvencies nevertheless has much to recommend itself. As Professor Westbrook wrote in 1991, "Pragmatism dominates the worldwide effort to find a solution to the problem of transnational business bankruptcy."[48] Subsequent development of the MLCBI and its adoption and application in many countries bears out the importance of pragmatism.

Statutory aid and auxiliary provisions in insolvency statutes, such as those that exist between states that share a common English heritage, also afford an opportunity for recognition and enforcement of foreign insolvency orders where the MLCBI does not apply.[49] Courts have referred to comity as a factor in proceedings brought under these provisions.[50] In the 2017 Federal Court of Australia case of *Cooksley*,[51] Justice Logan, commented "[t]he long recognised importance of affording assistance, of 'comity', is, if anything, even greater in modern times . . ." It is implicit in the Nordic Convention, in the European Insolvency Regulation, and in the MLCBI that states are extending comity in the area of insolvency.

---

[46] For example, *Turners & Growers Exporters Ltd v. The Ship "Cornelis Verolme"* [1997] 2 NZLR 110 at 126 and *Re Chow Cho Poon (Pte) Ltd* [2011] NSWSC 300 at [78] in which Barrett J referred in passing to "notions of comity."

[47] That is, a means to certain ends "rather than a coherent doctrine underpinning the area of private international law." Its "ultimate purposes are convenience and utility . . . driven by local interests which happen to be common among nations": Niv Tadmore, Recognition of Foreign in Personam Money Judgments in Australia, 2(2) Deakin L. Rev. 129 (1995) at 136.

[48] Jay L. Westbrook, Theory and Pragmatism in Global Insolvencies: Choice of Law and Choice of Forum, 65 Am. Bankr. L. J. 456 (1991).

[49] *Williams v. Simpson* [2010] NZHC 1631 and 1786 (Heath J); *Re Gainsford* [2012] FCA 904 (Logan J).

[50] *Re Doyle* (1993) 41 FCR 40 at 48, 52, 53 and 56; *Taylor v. Dow Corning Australia Pty Ltd* [1999] 1 VR 235.

[51] *Re Official Assignee in Bankruptcy of Property of Cooksley* [2017] FCA 1193 (Logan J) at [12].

Secondly on the relevance of reciprocity, states are engaging in reciprocal action in the case of the direct conventions,[52] in the Nordic Convention and in the European Insolvency Regulation. Further, in the common law tradition, aspects of local (subject matter) jurisdiction to deal with a dispute are inextricably linked with the question whether an equivalent foreign determination will be recognized and enforced in the local (geographical) jurisdiction.[53] This is because of the emphasis placed on whether the foreign (rendering) court exercised international jurisdiction[54] as a criterion for recognition and enforcement of the foreign order by the local (enforcing) court.[55]

Thirdly, recognition of foreign insolvency orders has also been extended on the basis of a debtor's sufficient connection with the foreign jurisdiction. In English and Australian cases prior to these states' adoption of the MLCBI, recognition of a bankruptcy adjudication had occurred, for example, where the debtor has submitted to the jurisdiction[56] and of a foreign liquidation order where the order was pronounced in the place of incorporation of the foreign company.[57]

Under the MLCBI, the effects and relief available following recognition of foreign insolvency proceedings depend upon whether the foreign proceeding is categorized as either (a) a "foreign main proceeding'; or (b) a "foreign non-main proceeding."

[52.] In a direct convention, the states agree on the allocation of jurisdiction in specific matters where a foreign element is involved.

[53.] This may be by action estoppel or issue estoppel. See *Carl Zeiss Stiftung v. Rayner and Keeler Ltd* (No 2) [1967] AC 853.

[54.] That is, proper jurisdiction in terms of local private international law rules. See, for example, The American Law Institute and The International Insolvency Institute Report by Ian Fletcher and Bob Wessels, Transnational Insolvency: Global Principles for Cooperation in International Insolvency Cases, (2012) Global Principle 13 International Jurisdiction on which forum will have jurisdiction to open an insolvency case for a debtor.

[55.] Jan H. Dalhuisen, Dalhuisen on International Insolvency & Bankruptcy, (1984) vol I, Part III, section 1.08. (loose-leaf updated to 1984).

[56.] *Re Anderson* [1911] 1 KB 896.

[57.] *Re Alfred Shaw & Co Ltd* (1897) 8 QLJ 93.

The foreign main proceeding relies upon the debtor's connection with the foreign adjudicating state, that it is their COMI. In "the absence of proof to the contrary" the presumption is that it is the debtor's registered office (or habitual residence in the case of an individual).[58] Recognition of a foreign non-main proceeding requires proof that the debtor's connection with the foreign adjudicating state amounted to having an "establishment" which is defined as "any place of operations where the debtor carries out a non-transitory economic activity with human means and goods or services."[59]

We now discuss the question of the applicable law to be applied by a court exercising jurisdiction in a multistate insolvency, the third essential element of a comprehensive private international law analysis.

C. Choice of Law: Theory and Application to Insolvency

1. The Substantive Law Approach to Multistate Insolvency

The substantive law approach seeks "the creation of rules of decision that directly govern multistate transactions."[60] Harmonized substantive insolvency laws remains an elusive "perfect" solution in light of the diversity of states' insolvency laws and the way in which insolvency laws are integrated with so many other areas of local law and legal culture.

A modest attempt was made, unsuccessfully, through a Uniform Law annexed to the 1970 draft European Bankruptcy Convention to achieve uniform insolvency laws and thus resolve some multistate issues. More recently, UNCITRAL and the World Bank endorsed general advisory principles applicable to insolvency.[61] Nevertheless,

---

[58.] Article 16(3) MLCBI.

[59.] Article 2(f) MLCBI.

[60.] Friedrich K. Juenger, Choice of Law and Multistate Justice (1993) at 45.

[61.] The UNCITRAL Legislative Guide on Insolvency Law (2004) and the World Bank Principles for Effective Insolvency and Creditor Rights Systems (2011).

an incrementally closer alignment of substantive insolvency laws is contributing to convergence in this field.[62]

More "harmonization" success has been achieved through consensus on uniform laws on the recognition of foreign insolvency proceedings and insolvency representatives. Significantly the MLCBI has been adopted by 44 states around the globe, even though the text has been modified by many states in the process of adoption.

A slightly different approach to "harmonization" has been the development of a common practice in managing multistate insolvencies, such as court approval of governance protocols for concurrent administrations known as protocols or cross-border insolvency agreements.[63] This practice to coordinate administrations has been adopted by courts from a range of states, a high-profile North American example being the Nortel Networks, Inc. case.

While states may be moving toward common principles informing their insolvency regulation, this is far removed from the position where states agree on the drafting of the legislation itself and on its integration with their existing local legislative schemes and legal culture. As a collective regime, insolvency laws involve more than balancing the interests of the immediate private parties and differences can extend beyond substantive principles to procedural systems affecting local parties' expectations.

It is important to distinguish attempts to achieve uniform substantive laws directly governing multistate transactions from those seeking a predictable outcome through uniform choice of law rules. A substantive law approach to the applicable law creates uniform rules of decision to govern multistate issues directly. Under the unilateral and multilateral approaches to achieve a similar degree of harmonization, uniform choice of law rules are needed to identify an applicable local or foreign law.

[62.] For example, reforms to improve corporate restructuring options in the European Union and in Singapore.

[63.] See examples cited in the UNCITRAL Practice Guide on Cross-Border Insolvency Cooperation (2009)

2. The Unilateral Approach to Choice of Law
in Multistate Insolvency

Where a court exercises jurisdiction in a dispute then, if the choice of applicable law is raised as an issue, the court's approach may be to define the circumstances in which relevant local substantive laws will apply. This unilateral approach examines "the scope of application of substantive rules of decision."[64] It applies local laws unless they are limited through the presence of foreign contacts.[65] To this extent, it reflects a "territorial" approach to cross-border insolvency. Whether through consideration only of the local law or through conscious selection of it as the applicable law from among local and foreign laws, many multistate insolvency disputes are resolved by referring only to the law of the forum.

The impact of insolvency as a statute-based area of commercial law is also clear.[66] When insolvency disputes have arisen with foreign elements, courts have not necessarily considered whether the law of the forum is the applicable rule of decision. Instead they have assumed that local legislation applies and interpreted that legislation, despite municipal insolvency laws typically addressing foreign elements to a limited extent. It is often only where there is no local statute on point (in a substantive and territorial sense) and no local statute directs which law is to apply, that the court determines the choice of law governing the point in issue.

3. The Multilateral Approach to Choice of Law in Multistate
Insolvency

Alternatively, if the choice of applicable law is raised as an issue in a dispute containing foreign elements, the court's approach may be to select from among the potentially applicable local and foreign laws.

---

[64] Friedrich K. Juenger, Choice of Law and Multistate Justice (1993) at 13.

[65] A.A. Ehrenzweig, The Lex Fori—Basic Rules in the Conflict of Laws 58 Mich. L. Rev. 637, 686 (1960).

[66] P.St.J. Smart, Cross-Border Insolvency, (2nd ed. 1998) at 3.

Under this multilateral choice of law, a court may determine that both local and foreign rules or sets of rules are potentially applicable and select one from among them.[67]

This multilateral approach bears more similarities to insolvency's universalism on recognition and enforcement, in that one outcome may be the local application of a foreign state's law. Two methods have evolved for such a multilateral approach. They are jurisdiction-selection and rule-selection.[68] The typical common law tradition has been a jurisdiction selecting approach, under which the court chooses a legal system to apply to the transaction, which system then determines the dispute.[69]

The multilateral choice of law rules look to "connect the dispute with one jurisdiction or another."[70] The initial step of characterization of a conflicts problem is not without its difficulties. Differences between jurisdictions may arise in characterization of the dispute, such as whether it concerns an issue of property law or insolvency law.[71] They may also arise in respect of the connecting factor, for example if the "home state" of a company is its place of incorporation or the place of its principal place of business. Such differences can affect the goal of decisional harmony.[72]

---

[67] D. H. Bliesener, Fairness and Choice of Law: A Critique of the Political Rights-Based Approach to Conflict of Laws 42 Am. J. Comp. L. 687 (1994) at 706.

[68] Rule selection requires the court to examine legal rules and select from among local or relevant foreign rules to determine the dispute: D. H. Bliesener, Fairness and Choice of Law: A Critique of the Political Rights-Based Approach to Conflict of Laws 42 Am. J. Comp. L. 687, 694 (1994).

[69] *Banco Atlantico SA v. The British Bank of the Middle East* [1990] 2 Lloyd's Rep 504 at 506.

[70] M. Davies, S. Ricketson & G. Lindell, Conflict of Laws: Commentary and Materials, (1997) at 369.

[71] J.L. Westbrook & D. T. Trautman, "Conflict of laws issues in international insolvencies" in J. S. Ziegel (ed.) Current Developments in International and Comparative Corporate Insolvency Law, (Oxford, 1994) at 662–63.

[72] Friedrich K. Juenger, Choice of Law and Multistate Justice (1993), at 51 on characterization.

The threshold categorization of an issue is as substantive or procedural.[73] If it is a matter of substance, then the law of the cause of action applies. If it is a procedural matter, then the connecting factor is the law of the forum. However, distinguishing between substantive and procedural laws is often an ambiguous exercise.[74] And while the jurisdiction-selection approach is the current practice,[75] theoretical issues arise as to what exactly is being characterized. Likewise connecting factors can be equivocal, for example, if it is a legal concept such as the proper law of the contract.

This openness to application of a foreign rule also raises questions of sovereignty;[76] however a multilateral choice of law may be at least partially explained by the doctrine of comity. Juenger proposed "that conflicts rules should be evaluated in the light of their suitability for inclusion in an international choice-of-law convention acceptable to all nations."[77]

From a choice of law perspective, in insolvency matters, courts have often focused on the local insolvency legislation and its territorial scope. Also a number of multilateral choice of law cases in insolvency matters disclose a general forum bias.[78] Accordingly, the development of a multilateral approach which aligns well with the twenty-first-century increase in coordination and cooperation in international insolvencies has been lagging. Until recently, there has been less attention given to choice of law issues in a multistate

---

[73] Richard Garnett, Substance and Procedure in Private International Law (2012).

[74] Edward J Janger, Virtual Territoriality 48 Colum. J. Transnat'l L. 401 (2009–2010).

[75] See the Global Rules annexed to the ALI-III Report, Transnational Insolvency: Global Principles for Cooperation in International Insolvency Cases and the applicable law rules in the European Insolvency Regulation (Recast).

[76] F.C. von Savigny (trans W. Guthrie), A Treatise on the Conflict of Laws (2nd ed. rev. 1880) at section 2, 18–21.

[77] Friedrich K. Juenger, Choice of Law and Multistate Justice (1993), at 39.

[78] *Re Suidair International Airways Ltd* [1951] 1 Ch 165; *Re BCCI (No 10)* [1997] 2 WLR 172. However, see *In re Condor*, 601 F.3d 319 (5th Cir. 2010) on the application of a foreign avoidance law in a chapter 15 case concerning a non-U.S. insurance company.

insolvency scholarship[79] and it has received rather limited attention in global forums.[80]

The chapter now turns to whether the UNCITRAL WGV project on Recognition of Insolvency-Related Judgments may supplement this limited attention and assist in achieving incremental international consensus on the element of choice of law in international insolvency.

III. Characterization of Insolvency-Related Judgments and Issues

A. UNCITRAL WGV Project: Model Law on Recognition and Enforcement of Insolvency-Related Judgments (MLIJ)

Recognition of insolvency-related judgments (originally described as "insolvency-derived judgments") was listed as a possible topic for future work for the Working Group in a Background Paper for the December 2013 WGV session. It stated: "Thought might be given as to whether the UNCITRAL Model Law [on Cross-Border Insolvency] should specifically cover the enforcement of insolvency-derived judgements as part of the heads of discretionary relief available under article 21."[81] The topic received support in subsequent Sessions and in July 2014, UNCITRAL granted WGV a mandate "to develop a

---

[79.] Notable exceptions include Hannah Buxbaum, Rethinking International Insolvency: The Neglected Role of Choice-of-Law Rules and Theory, 36 Stan. J. Int'l L. 23 (2000); Edward J. Janger, Virtual Territoriality 48 Colum. J. Transnat'l L. 401 (2009–2010); Charles W Mooney Jr, Harmonising Choice-Of-Law Rules for international insolvency Cases: Virtual Territoriality, Virtual Universalism, and the Problem of Local Interests, 9 Brook. J. Corp. Fin. & Com. L. 131 (2014–2015); John A.E. Pottow, Beyond Carve-outs and Toward Reliance: A Normative Framework for Cross-border Insolvency Choice of Law 9 Brook. J. Corp. Fin. & Com. L. 197 (2014–2015).

[80.] Jenny Clift, Choice of Law and the UNCITRAL Harmonisation Process 9 Brook. J. Corp. Fin. & Com. L. 29 (2014).

[81.] A/CN.9/WG.V/WP.117 at [43].

model law or model legislative provisions to provide for the recognition and enforcement of insolvency-derived judgements."[82]

The Secretariat prepared a Note[83] for the December 2014 WGV session that addressed a list of issues including the definition of "'Insolvency-[derived] [related]' judgements"[84] and then outlined two possible approaches. One approach was to list certain categories of judgements that would be covered, some of which might be monetary judgements (such as preference actions) and others non-monetary judgments (such as recognition of the discharge of a debtor). A second approach was "to adopt a definition identifying general characteristics to be possessed by an insolvency-related judgement."[85] Over the life of this project, WGV moved to the second approach.

The Note also listed possible characteristics relevant to defining the appropriate connection between the judgement and insolvency proceedings: "that the judgement is related to the core of the insolvency proceeding concerning the debtor, that the judgement affects the debtor or its insolvency estate, and that the aim of the action leading to the judgement could not be achieved without the commencement of insolvency proceedings."[86] A range of proposals were put forward on the question of defining an "insolvency-related judgment."[87] These provide useful insights into the complexities surrounding the ambit and far-reaching effects of an "insolvency."

At the December 2014 session, "there was some agreement that, for the purposes of recognition and enforcement, judgements could be divided into three general categories: (a) those that were part of insolvency proceedings; (b) those that might be part of insolvency proceedings, but involved third parties, for example, judgements

---

[82] A/69/17, para 155.

[83] A/CN.9/WG.V/WP.126.

[84] A/CN.9/WG.V/WP.126, at [16] ff.

[85] A/CN.9/WG.V/WP.126, at [19].

[86] A/CN.9/WG.V/WP.126, at [23] (footnotes omitted).

[87] A/CN.9/829, at [55]—[57].

relating to avoidance of transactions and determination of property of the estate; and (c) other judgements."[88]

Since the May 2015 Session, the agreed approach has been to draft a new Model Law.[89] For that Session, an initial draft Model Law contained a definition for "insolvency-related judgment" which began with a general definition of "a judgement that is closely related to a foreign proceeding and was issued after the commencement of that proceeding" followed by an inclusive list of judgments (including variants in drafting).[90] Draft Article 2(d)'s opening paragraph stated,

> A judgement is presumed to be "closely related to a foreign proceeding" if it has an effect upon the insolvency estate of the debtor and either: (i) is based on a law relating to insolvency; or (ii) due to the nature and legal basis of its underlying claims, would not have been issued without the commencement of the foreign proceeding.

That draft definition has been refined in subsequent WGV sessions[91] and the list of judgments has evolved, appearing in a Guide to Enactment to accompany the Draft Model Law. This list as refined arguably provides some insights into the issue of characterization of issues that typically fall within the ambit of "insolvency." If a more comprehensive view is taken than that by Lord Collins who did not accept that insolvency orders or judgments are subject to special rules, then this broader appreciation of the issues that are involved in the administration of an insolvency may contribute to an international consensus on applicable law.

[88.] A/CN.9/829, at [62].

[89.] A/CN.9/WG.V/WP.130.

[90.] Draft Article 2(d).

[91.] A/CN.9/864 (Report) and A/CN.9/WG.V/WP.135 (Draft MLIJ) (Dec. 2015); A/CN.9/870 (Report) and A/CN.9/WG.V/WP.138 (Draft MLIJ) (May 2016); A/CN.9/898 and A/CN.9/WG.V/WP.143 (Draft MLIJ) and A/CN.9/WG.V/WP.143.1 (Commentary and Notes) (Dec. 2016); A/CN.9/903 A/CN.9/WG.V/WP.145 (Draft MLIJ) (May 2017); A/CN.9/931 and A/CN.9/WG.V/WP.150 (Draft MLIJ) and A/CN.9/WG.V/WP.151 (Draft Guide to Enactment) (Dec. 2017); A/CN.9/WG.V/WP.156 (Draft MLIJ) and A/CN.9/WG.V/WP.157 (Draft Guide to Enactment) (May 2018).

Importantly, since the Symposium in February 2018, WGV has approved, subject to a limited number of amendments, the substance of a Draft Model Law on Recognition and Enforcement of Insolvency-Related Judgments (MLIJ) and of a Draft Guide to Enactment of the MLIJ ("MLIJ Guide") to go forward to UNCITRAL.[92] Subsequently, at its 51st Session in mid-2018, UNCITRAL has adopted the version of the MLIJ and MLIJ Guide annexed to its Report and recommended favorable consideration by states when revising or adopting legislation relevant to insolvency.[93]

Under Article 2(d) as adopted by UNCITRAL, "insolvency-related judgment":

i. A[m]eans a judgment that

    a. [a]rises *as a consequence of or is materially associated with an insolvency proceeding,* whether or not that insolvency proceeding has closed; and

    b. [w]as issued on or after the commencement of that insolvency proceeding; and

ii. [d]oes not include a judgment commencing an insolvency proceeding.[94]

The Guide to Enactment contains general comments at [57–59] on the types of judgment covered and at [60] contains a non-exhaustive list of examples of the types of judgment that might be considered insolvency-related foreign judgments:

(a).   A judgment dealing with *constitution and disposal of assets of the insolvency estate,* such as whether an asset is part of, should be turned over to, or was properly (or improperly) disposed of by the insolvency estate;

(b).   A judgment determining *whether a transaction involving the debtor or assets of its insolvency estate should be avoided* because it

---

[92.] Working Group V 53rd session, May 7–11, 2018, New York.

[93.] A/73/17 (Report) (Fifty-first session) and Annex III (MLIJ and Guide to Enactment) (June–July 2018).

[94.] UNCITRAL Model Law on Recognition and Enforcement of Insolvency-Related Judgments (2018), § 2(d) (emphasis added).

upset the principle of equitable treatment of creditors (preferential transactions) or improperly reduced the value of the estate (transactions at an undervalue);

(c).   A judgment determining that *a representative or director of the debtor is liable for action taken when the debtor was insolvent* or in the period approaching insolvency, and the cause of action relating to that liability was one that could be pursued by or on behalf of the debtor's insolvency estate under the law relating to insolvency, in line with part four of the Legislative Guide;

(d).   A judgment determining *whether the debtor owes or is owed a sum or any other performance not covered by subparagraph (a) or (b)*. Enacting states will need to determine whether this category should extend to all such judgments regardless of when the cause of action arose. While it might be considered that a cause of action that arose prior to the commencement of the insolvency proceedings was sufficiently linked to the insolvency proceeding, as it was being pursued in the context of, and could have an impact on, that proceeding, it might also be considered that a judgment on such a cause of action could have been obtained by or against the debtor prior to the commencement of the insolvency proceeding and, thus, lacked a sufficiently material association with the insolvency proceedings. Enacting states may also wish to have regarding the treatment of such judgments under other international instruments;

(e).   A judgment (i) *confirming a plan* of reorganization or liquidation, (ii) *granting a dischssssarge* of the debtor or of a debt, or (iii) *approving a voluntary or out-of-court restructuring agreement*. The types of agreement referred to in subparagraph (iii) are typically not regulated by the insolvency law and may be reached through informal negotiation to address a consensual modification of the claims of all participating creditors. In this Model Law, the reference is to such agreements that are ultimately referred to the court for approval in formal proceedings, such as an expedited proceeding of the type addressed in the Legislative Guide; and

(f).   A judgment for the *examination of a director* of the debtor, where that director is located in a third jurisdiction.[95]

---

[95] UNCITRAL Model Law on Recognition and Enforcement of Insolvency-Related Judgments Guide to Enactment (2018) at [60] (emphases added).

B. Choice of Law Rules on Insolvency Matters in Multilateral Agreements

So, does the MLIJ definition and the MLIJ Guide's examples of insolvency-related judgments align with the characterization of insolvency matters found in existing choice of law rules in multilateral instruments? As the discussion in the following passages shows, identification of issues within the broad ambit of "insolvency" issues is only part of the story. There is no international consensus as yet on the selection of the jurisdiction whose laws are to apply, if it is not to be the law of the state of the opening of proceedings.

This discussion is limited to the rules in the *European Insolvency Regulation (Recast)* (2015) as well as the recommendations in the *UNCITRAL Legislative Guide on Insolvency Law* (2004) and the *Global Rules on Conflict-of-Laws Matters in International Insolvency Cases* (the Global Rules) proposed in the Annex to the ALI-III Report on *Transnational Insolvency: Global Principles for Cooperation in International Insolvency Cases* (2012).

The *UNCITRAL Legislative Guide on Insolvency Law* (2004)[96] includes recommendations on applicable law in insolvency proceedings. These were drafted by UNCITRAL in close cooperation with the Hague Conference on International Law and in consultation with WGVI which was addressing secured transactions.[97] This Guide on legislative provisions recommends that "[t]he insolvency law of the State in which insolvency proceedings are commenced (*lex fori concursus*) should apply to all aspects of the commencement, conduct, administration and conclusion of those insolvency proceedings and their effects."[98] These provisions are certainly broad enough to

---

[96.] UNCITRAL Legislative Guide on Insolvency Law (2004) Pt 2 at 68. (Legislative Guide) Recommendations 30–34 address the law applicable to the validity and effectiveness of rights and claims, the law applicable in insolvency proceedings and exceptions thereto.

[97.] Jenny Clift, Choice of Law and the UNCITRAL Harmonisation Process 9 Brook. J. Corp. Fin. & Com. L. 29 (2014) at 47.

[98.] Legislative Guide, Recommendation 31. Examples include "(c) [c]onstitution and scope of the insolvency estate; (d) [p]rotection and preservation of the

fall within the MLIJ Article 2(d) definition of an "insolvency-related judgment."[99] The Legislative Guide however notes certain exceptions to the application of the law of the insolvency proceedings in respect of issues dealing with "payment or settlement system; regulated financial market; employment."[100]

The *ALI-III Global Rules on Conflict-of-Laws Matters in International Insolvency Cases* (2012), in the context of international jurisdiction principles to identify "the state of the opening of proceedings," nominate in Rule 12 that "[s]ave as otherwise provided [herein], the law applicable to insolvency proceedings and their effect shall be that of. . . 'the state of the opening of proceedings'. [Its law] shall determine the conditions for the opening of those proceedings, their conduct, administration, conversion, and their closure." There are modifications to this in Rules 13–14 dealing with cross-border movement of assets and exceptions in Rules 15–23 addressing, for example, secured creditors; set off; employment; and detrimental acts.

Likewise the *European Insolvency Regulation (recast)* (2015) in Article 7.1 states that "[s]ave as otherwise provided in this Regulation, the law applicable to insolvency proceedings and their effects shall be that of . . . the 'State of the opening of proceedings'." Article 7.2 provides that the law of the state in which the proceedings were opened shall "determine the conditions for the opening of those proceedings, their conduct and their closure." It then lists 13 specific examples including aspects that the MLIJ Guide would consider

---

insolvency estate; . . . (f) [p]roposal, approval, confirmation, and implementation of a plan of reorganization; (g) [a]voidance of certain transactions that could be prejudicial to certain parties; (h) [t]reatment of contracts; and. . . (s) [d]ischarge."

[99.] Note however that "commencement" is addressed by the MLCBI rather than the MLIJ.

[100.] Legislative Guide, Recommendation 32 exempts "the effects of insolvency proceedings on the rights and obligations of the participants in a payment or settlement system or in a regulated financial market" and recommends that these be governed solely by the law applicable to that system or market." Legislative Guide, Recommendation 32 recommends that "the effects of insolvency proceedings on rejection, continuation and modification of labour contracts . . . be governed by the law applicable to the contract."

"insolvency-related" such as "(b) the assets which form part of the insolvency estate and the treatment of assets acquired by or devolving on the debtor after the opening of the insolvency proceedings."[101] The following Articles 8–18 contain provisions on the law to apply in respect of matters such as rights *in rem*; set-off; reservation of title; immoveable property; payment systems and financial markets; employment; and detrimental acts.

To the extent that the matters which are the subject of a judgment arise "as a consequence of or is materially associated with an insolvency proceeding" and follow the commencement of that proceeding; then many of the matters listed in these multilateral initiatives or instruments align with the MLIJ definition of an "insolvency-related judgment."

IV. Conclusion

This chapter has canvassed various theories underpinning the three dimensions of private international law, that is, whether a court can and will hear and determine a matter; whether it will recognize and give effect to a foreign order or judgment in such a matter; and what law it will apply in determining the matter. It has also discussed those theories as they may apply in an insolvency context.

On whether a court should exercise specific jurisdiction to hear an insolvency matter, there is merit in considering issues of fairness such as convenience, impartiality and expense to the parties. Insolvencies are "real-time" litigation, not forensic, and it is critical to bring order to bear for the collective interests concerned. Thus the commencement of proceedings and the appointment of

---

[101.] Compare, for example, European Insolvency Regulation (recast) Article 7.2 (b), (j), (k), and (m) with the Guide's list of judgments on the assets comprising the insolvency estate; third-party voidable transactions; directors or officers' liability for insolvent trading; confirming a plan of reorganization or liquidation; granting a discharge of the debtor or of a debt; approving a voluntary or out-of-court restructuring agreement.

an insolvency representative are key. However these are intrinsically linked to a subsequent fair and efficient administration to protect the interests of all interested persons and to protect and maximize the value of the insolvent estate. In multistate insolvencies where the location of a debtor's COMI is difficult to identify, it may well be that the appointment of an insolvency representative in the place of the debtor's registered office, even if a "letter box" jurisdiction specializing in corporate governance and related specialist professional services, is the most effective way of bringing order to bear and thereby achieving a critical COMI going forward.

One test of the efficacy of such exercise of jurisdiction is arguably the recognition and relief granted to such proceedings in other jurisdictions—based on the pragmatic notion of comity, which may well encourage mutual trust.[102] The recognition of and relief to foreign orders that have been granted by many jurisdictions following the adoption of the Model Law concerning foreign proceedings and foreign representatives may grow further following adoption of the new Model Law on insolvency-related judgments.[103]

The comprehensive view of insolvency that may now gather momentum would augur well for a growing consensus on the applicable law that courts may apply, in particular the application of the laws of the state of the opening of proceedings. Those disputes, for which the characterization of the issue and the selection of the jurisdiction whose laws apply, point elsewhere may become starker. Consequently, consensus may be reached on the issues for which the choice of law is a different jurisdiction to the state of opening of insolvency proceedings. Such rules, if binding in the relevant states, should produce decisional harmony through a unique identification of the law to govern the adjudication of disputes.

[102.] On the importance of which, see Irit Mevorach, The Future of Cross-Border Insolvency: Overcoming Biases and Closing Gaps (2018) at 183–84.

[103.] The Preamble to the MLIJ includes in its purpose "to promote comity and cooperation between jurisdictions regarding insolvency-related judgments."

This chapter's broad sweep through private international law theory as relevant to insolvency has been made to encourage consideration of how best to align the elements of private international law as they intersect with insolvency. This is in light of an overall goal to improve consistency and reduce conflict in cross-border insolvencies. To support the growing international consensus on the importance of cooperation and coordination, the UNCITRAL project on recognition of insolvency-related judgments may assist incrementally in addressing not only recognition and enforcement, but also have a consequential beneficial effect on consensus regarding the exercise of jurisdiction and importantly the choice of applicable law.

Triggering the Insolvency Proceeding

Luis Manuel C. Méjan[*]

Depending of the specific insolvency regime applying in each country, usually an insolvency proceeding is commenced (a) by the debtor himself, which is called a "voluntary" proceeding, or (b), by one or more creditors, by order of some authority regulating companies, or compulsory by the debtor when it reaches some point in the development of the business. Those are called "involuntary" proceedings. There is some basis about the quality of the debtor: a merchant, a natural person, a farmer, a financial institution, etc., that determines whether the insolvency proceeding may start. All these situations refer to what is called the subjective element for the commencement. In this chapter, we are going to focus on the objective element: what conditions are required to commence an insolvency proceeding, either voluntary or involuntary.

If we are going to talk about what generates the initiation of an insolvency proceeding, it is necessary to understand two things

---

[*] PhD, Professor at ITAM (Instituto Tecnológico Autónomo de México). Written in occasion of the Conference honoring Jay Westbrook.

first: one, what is insolvency and, two, what is pursued with a proceeding that treats insolvency.

I. What Is Insolvency

Insolvency is, to start with, an extraordinary situation. It is normal for people to comply with the commitments they have acquired and to satisfy the obligations they incur. They may even face an eventual breach in which the law assigns creditors ordinary ways that allow them to be able to satisfy their credit even by forced means.

In an insolvency situation, the ordinary ways that a person has to negotiate and to make financial structures are insufficient to the size of the problem. It is no longer possible to address only the legal status of one or a few stakeholders, but it is essential to extend the treatment to the universality of the debtor's legal relations.

This state of things has been defined with different expressions throughout history and across geography.

A. Many Definitions

The name of "bankruptcy" (attributed by various authors to various sources in history (Italy, Catalonia) refers to the site where the merchant practiced his operations (a bench) that was broken in symbolic form to represent the exit and the end of the business. Such denomination refers to the breaking of a common order with a certain definitiveness.

Later on, Salgado de Somoza wrote his famous treatise (the first) on the situation of insolvency and gave him the name "Labyrinthus creditorum *concurrentium* ad litem per debitorem communem inter illos causatam"[1] referring to the maze in which the creditors *concurred* because of their common debtor. Amatore

---

[1] Salgado de Somoza, Francisci, "Labyrinthus creditorum concurrentium ad litem per debitorem communem inter illos causatum," Lugduni, Sumptibus Laurentii Anisson, MDCLIV.

Rodriguez made his book "Tractatus de Concursu[2] some years after comes the term "concurso" that is used in Spanish-speaking countries.

In other languages, the term equivalent to *failure* has been wildly used: faillite (French), fallimento (Italian), falência (Portuguese), and quiebra (Spanish, meaning "broken"). Nevertheless, France has found other terms to designate the phenomenon as it calls the part of the Code of Commerce that deals with the topic "Des entreprises en difficulté (on the enterprises in difficulty)"[3] and its first title "De la Sauvegarde (on the Safeguard)." The scholars refer now to the subject as the "Droit des entreprises en difficulté (law of the companies in difficulties)" to what they used to call "Droit de faillites (Bankruptcy Law)."[4] This is a path that several countries have followed so that in the title of their laws the emphasis is placed on the rescue and salvation of the companies that dominate the matter at present.[5]

B. The Term "Insolvency"

"Insolvency" is the most commonly used term to refer to the situation in question. Many legislations carry the term of insolvency in its title,[6] and in general the legal discipline that deals with the phenomenon has been called Insolvency Law.

Black's Law Dictionary defines insolvency as ". . . inability or lack of means to pay debts."[7]

---

[2] Rodriquez, Amatore, "Tractatus de Concursu et Privilegiis Creditorum," Venetiis, Apud Turrinum, MDLXIV

[3] Péérochon, Franççoise et Bonhomme, Regine, "Entreprises en Difficultéé. Instruments de Créédit et de Paiement" 8eme éédition. Librairie géénéérale de droit et de jurisprudence. Lextenso ééditions. Paris 2009

[4] Saint-Alary-Houin, Corinne, Droit des Entreprises en Difficultéé" 6e éédition. Montchrestien, Lextenso ééditions. Pariz, 2009. P. 1

[5] The Chilean Law is called "Law of Reorganization and Liquidation of Companies and Persons."

[6] It is the case of Germany's law: "Insolvenzordnung."

[7] Black, Henry C. Black's Law Dictionary. West Publishing Co. 6th ed. St Paul. 1990, p. 797.

In Spain, we find this definition: "State of insolvency: patrimonial structure of the debtor that makes the regular fulfillment of its obligations impossible."[8]

In France: "State of the one who is not in a position to pay what he owes."[9]

The jurisprudence in Italy has come to make this definition: "to define the state of insolvency, it is necessary to take into account not only the simple materiality of the breach, but its meaning that indicates a state of patrimonial impotence of the debtor, of the generalized or permanent crisis of the entrepreneur and the deterioration of his credit."[10]

Finally, United Nations Commission on International Trade Law (UNCITRAL) defines it as follows: "'Insolvency': when a debtor is generally unable to pay its debts as they mature or when its liabilities exceed the value of its assets."[11]

From all these definitions and considerations, it can be deduced that the problem that insolvency deals with, lies in the fact that the economic–financial situation that a person is going through, jeopardizes the possibility of operating ordinarily. This, for a natural person, is serious enough because it limits its performance in the society and the solution of the most urgent needs. In the case of a company, it is so serious that it implies subsisting or not and this implies an impact on the sources of work force, the generation of gross domestic product and the movement and circulation of capital.

[8.] "état de celui qui n'est pas en mesure de payer ce qu'il doit) Suárez Llamas, Luis. Las Claves de la Ley Concursal. Thomson Aranzadi. Navarra. 2005, p. 35.

[9.] IFPPC. Petit Dictionnaire de la Faillite. La Documentation Franççaise. p. 130.

[10.] Per definire lo stato d'insolvenza, occorre tener conto non della semplice materialitàà delle inadempienze, ma del loro significato, che riveli uno stato d'impotenza patrimoniale del debitore, del dissesto generale o permanente dell'imprenditore commerciale e della distruzione del suo credito. Cited in Caputo, Eduardo, La Legge fallimentare. Repertorio completo di dottrina e giurisprudenza dal 1942 al 1968. p. 55. (free translation by the author) Trib.Roma, 22 giugno 1967, in Dir. fall., 1967, II, 674. Conf. App. Firenze, 21 giugno 1963, in Giur. tosc., 1963, 739.

[11.] UNCITRAL Legislative Guide on Insolvency Law. Glossary, p. 5

As Vallens puts it: "The concrete content of this notion differs less than the various definitions it receives in the various laws."[12] In general terms, it can be established that the basis for the occurrence of the insolvency phenomenon may be the following:

1. Patrimonial insufficiency. The value of the liabilities is higher than the value of the assets.
2. The debtor does not generate sufficient flow to fulfill the obligations that are due.
3. The cessation or dismissal of payments in general form.
4. Combinations of these elements.

II. Criteria Used in Practice

Countries use one or more of these constants in practice to define when the insolvency legal situation is triggered and the consequent process. Several examples from different countries of the world are presented without the intention of making a complete sample, but only to show examples of detonating criteria of the insolvency proceeding.

A. Latin America

In **Argentina**, the fact of cessation of payments is sufficient regardless of the cause that originates it. That is, it does not take into account whether or not there are sufficient assets, liquid or not, the fact of the breach of payment obligations is sufficient. The cessation must be widespread and not sporadic, because what it asks for is a "state" of cessation, that is, a generalized and prolonged situation in a more or less definitive manner.[13]

[12.] Vallens, Jean-Luc, L'insolvabilitéé des entreprises en droit comparéé. Joly éédi-tions. Lextenso ééditions. Paris, 2011, p. 23. "Le contenu concret de cette notion dif-fèère moins que les dééfinitions variéées qu'elles reççoit dans les diverses lois."

[13.] Artíículo 1°° de la Ley 24522. http://servicios.infoleg.gob.ar/infoleglnternet/anexos/25000-29999/25379/texact.htm

Brazil requires a lack of payment of a certain and liquid obligation materialized in an executive title higher than a certain figure (40 minimum wages). The mere breach is sufficient without the need to prove the insolvency.[14]

In **Chile,** there are different procedures depending on whether a reorganization or liquidation is desired. For the reorganization, a standard of debts is not requested but only a list of liabilities and the assets. For liquidation: to have ceased in the payment of an executive obligation or have initiated at least two enforcement proceedings against him.[15]

The **Colombian** case is based on a situation of cessation of payments and this entails a definition that refers to the time in which the breach has been made, the number of creditors affected and the proportional relationship that exists between the amount of the unpaid with the total of your liabilities. Colombia includes the possibility of imminent insolvency.[16]

Mexican law requires the state of default and defines it with a formula of proportion in the assets and liabilities of the merchant.[17]

Paraguayan legislation establishes that insolvency is manifested by "one or more breaches" or "other external facts at the discretion of the judge's" that manifest the powerlessness of fulfilling debts.[18]

In the case of **Peru**, it is requested that the amount of unpaid obligations have a certain expiration time and that it keeps a percentage

---

[14] Artículo 94, Nova Lei Concursal Brasileira. Colombo Arnoldi, Paulo Roberto, A nova Lei Concursal Brasileira, Lemos&Cruz Publicaççoes Juridicas, Franca, p. 124 "Falta de pagamento de obrigaççao lííquida e certa, materializado em um tíítulo executivo, devidamente protestado e superior a 40 salários míínimos. Portante deve ser tíítulo lííquido, cierto, exigíível e comprobado Para a lei de falêência basta a mera impontualidade do devedor, nao se exigindo a prova da insolvencia."

[15] Artículos 56 y 117 de la Ley de Reorganización y Liquidación de Empresas y Personas. www.leychile.cl/Navegar?idNorma=1058072&buscar=Ley+20.720

[16] Artículo 9 de la Ley 1116 de 2006 www.supersociedades.gov.co/delegatura_insolvencia/Documents/Normatividad/Ley_1116_de_2006.pdf.

[17] Artículos 9 y 10 Ley de Concursos Mercantiles.

[18] Ley N°° 154/69. Ley de Quiebras, artículo 1°°. www.cej.org.py/games/Leyes_por_Materia_juridica/CIVIL/LEY%20No154.pdf.

relationship with the paid capital or other concepts (UIT Tax units— an indexation formula).[19]

B. Europe

Spanish law states that the declaration of insolvency will proceed in the case of insolvency of the common debtor and that the debtor is in a state of insolvency when he cannot fulfill his obligations on a regular basis. In other words, it defines insolvency as illiquidity and also requires the plurality of creditors (common debtor). Admits the case of imminence[20]

In the case of **Germany,** it is required the existence of a reason that will generally be the illiquidity understood as the impossibility to pay its overdue obligations which is presumed when the debtor on a regular basis has ceased in his payments. Overindebtedness (that occurs if the assets no longer cover their obligations) is also a cause for the insolvency proceeding. The imminence is also admitted.[21]

Italy requires that the employer is in a state of insolvency, meaning that he cannot meet his obligations regularly.[22] In introducing the reform to the figure of the preventive agreement (concordato preventivo), Italy changed the requirement of the entrepreneur "in a state of insolvency" to be "in a state of crisis,"[23] i.e., Italy aligns with those who depart from the basis of both the

---

[19] Artículos 24 y 26 Ley General del Sistema Concursal (Ley N° 27809) del 08/08/2002 y sus reformas posteriores. www.indecopi.gob.pe/documents/51767/203503/04+ley27809.pdf/4f23b875-a030-4ad1-959c-e5a69125fcec.

[20] Artículo 2 de la Ley 22/2003, de 9 de julio, Concursal. Edit. Lefebvre El Derecho. Madrid, 2015, p. 40.

[21] Secciones 16 a 19 de la Insolvenzordnung www.gesetze-im-internet.de/englisch_inso/.

[22] Legge Fallimentare. Art. 5. 1. L'imprenditore che si trova in stato d'insolvenza èè dichiarato fallito. 2. Lo stato d'insolvenza si manifesta con inadempimenti od altri fatti esteriori, i quali dimostrino che il debitore non èè più in grado di soddisfare regolarmente le proprie obbligazioni. www.fallco.it/legge_fallimentare.php.

[23] Legge Fallimentare. "Art 160. 1. L'imprenditore che si trova in stato di crisi può proporre ai creditori un concordato preventivo." www.fallco.it/legge_fallimentare.php.

situation of insolvency as well as the financial crisis, although it does not have a legal definition.[24]

France opens the process of Safeguarding (Sauvegarde), Judicial Recovery (Redressement judiciaire), and Judicial Liquidation (Liquidation Judiciaire) to the debtor who is in default due to not being able to meet his required liability with his available assets.[25]

C. Common Law Countries

In the legislation of the United States of America, the term insolvency applies to physical or mercantile entities according to the traditional accounting equation: assets less than liabilities; however, when it refers to a public entity (municipality) takes the concept of inability to pay their debts when they are due.[26] In general, to enter in a case of insolvency proceedings the subject must be able to be "debtor" according to the provisions of the corresponding chapters. The generic rule is that everyone can be a debtor and an extensive regulation of exceptions is made.[27] This leads to the general situation of accepting that the one who can go to the proceeding is who needs a reorganization in its financial structure, being the reason

---

[24] The Magistrato Luciano Panzani writes in a paper for a lecture in the International Insolvency Institute in March 2008: "The entrepreneur may file a petition to the Court to be admitted when he is insolvent, but also when there is only a crisis situation and technically insolvency not yet. The law doesn't say when there is a crisis situation, but generally we can say that this situation occurs when there are financial or economic difficulties in the enterprise managing which have not yet reached insolvency. It has been said by first commentators that crisis implies the insolvency's danger, but insolvency is not reached."

[25] I Code de Comerce. Article L631-1 Il est instituée une procéédure de redressement judiciaire ouverte àà tout déébiteur mentionnéé aux articles L. 631-2 ou L. 631-3 qui, dans l'impossibilitéé de faire face au passif exigible avec son actif disponible, est en cessation des paiements. See also L621-1. Y L.641-1. www.legifrance.gouv.fr/affichCode.do?cidTexte=LEGITEXT000005634379.

[26] Artículo 101, numeral 32 (C), Artículo 109 (c), USA Code, Title 11 Bankruptcy, chapter 1. www.law.cornell.edu/uscode/text/11.

[27] Artículo 109, USA Code, Title 11 Bankruptcy, chapter 1. www.law.cornell.edu/uscode/text/11

for it to have a problem of insolvency or of illiquidity, although its demonstration is not required by law.[28]

Curiously, **Australia** does not define who is insolvent but who is solvent: "it is solvent if, and only if, the person is able to pay their debts, while they become enforceable."[29]

In the United Kingdom, an individual or a company may make a "voluntary arrangements" proposal "for a composition in satisfaction of its debts or a scheme of arrangement of its affaires" (Section 1 of its Insolvency Act); there may be a voluntary liquidation (Winding-up) because it cannot by reason of its liabilities continue its business, (Section 84) and can be liquidated, among many other causes, because "it is unable to pay its debts" (Section 122) and, the following Section 123 defines a series of objective criteria of inability to repay debts.[30]

D. Other Countries

Canada, for its part, stipulates that a person is insolvent when he is unable to meet his obligations or has ceased paying his current obligations in the ordinary course of business as they generally become due, or all of his property is insufficient to cover all their obligations.[31]

The Russian Federation provides as a basis for the proceeding the inability to satisfy claims of creditors when they are three months overdue and, in the case of a natural person, their debts are higher than the value of their assets.[32]

[28.] "There is no requirement that the debtor be insolvent either on a balance sheet basis (fair value of assets less liabilities) or on some equity insolvency basis (unable to or failing to pay debts as they generally become due)" Samet, Joseph and Reid, Ira A. Basics of chapter 11. Baker and McKenzie, New Cork, 2008.

[29.] Vaatstra, Justin, writing in Fonseca Lobo, Otto Eduardo. World Insolvency Systems: a comparative study. Carswell. Toronto. 2009. P. 1.

[30.] www.legislation.gov.uk/ukpga/1986/45/contents.

[31.] Article2, Bankruptcy and Insolvency Act, http://laws-lois.justice.gc.ca/eng/acts/B-3/.

[32.] Art. 3 Federal Law on Insolvency, Russian Federation, October 24, 2005.

Some countries, such as Mauritius, request that the amount owed be greater than a certain amount (Mauritian Insolvency Act requires at least 50,000 rupees).[33]

In South Africa, a company can initiate a rescue procedure if it is "financially distressed," that is, it does not seem possible to be able to repay all of its debts or be insolvent within the next six months.[34]

E. The International Scope

OHADA (L'Organisation pour l'Harmonisation en Afrique du Droit des affaires, an international organization that pursues legal integration work among its member countries in the African region The OHADA now has 17 states) has enacted, among other Uniform Acts, the Uniform Act on Bankruptcy Proceedings. This Act contemplates three procedures related to the subject of insolvency, for each of which indicates different initial requirements: Conciliation is open to individuals and legal entities experiencing difficulties, which are proved or predictable, but who have not yet reached insolvency; preventive settlement shall be open to the debtor who, without being insolvent, shall confirm financial or serious economic problems; and reorganization and judicial assets liquidation shall be opened for any debtor who finds himself in a insolvency, meaning that the debtor is unable to pay its due claims out of its available assets except in situations where credit reserves or payment deadline extensions consented by creditors enable the debtor to deal with current debts.[35]

---

[33] Insolvency Act 2009 4. (3) www.fscmauritius.org/media/1155/insolvency-act-2009-130114.pdf.

[34] Companies Act: 128. (f) "financially distressed," in reference to a particular company at any particular time, means that—(i) it appears to be reasonably unlikely that the company will be able to pay all of its debts as they fall due and payable within the immediately ensuing six months; or (ii) it appears to be reasonably likely that the company will become insolvent within the immediately ensuing six months; 129. (1) Subject to subsection (2)(a), the board of a company may resolve that the company voluntarily begin business rescue proceedings and place the company under supervision, if the board has reasonable grounds to believe that—(a) the company is financially distressed; and (b) there appears to be a reasonable prospect of rescuing the company. www.gov.za/documents/companies-act.

[35] OHADA's Uniform Act on Bankruptcy Proceedings, Articles 5-1, 6 and 25. www.ohada.com/actes-uniformes/1668/uniform-act-on-bankruptcy-proceedings.html.

The **UNCITRAL** Legislative Guide analyzes the totality of possibilities in the world of insolvency and recommends considering, to detonate the process, the inability to pay debts when due (i.e., admits the case of imminence) or, the accounting criterion of liabilities higher than assets.[36]

Similarly, the **World Bank** pronounces the most adequate test to commence an insolvency proceeding should be the debtor's inability to pay debts as they mature, although insolvency may also exist where the debtor's liabilities exceed the value of its assets.[37]

In his book "L'insolvabilité des entreprises en droit comparé," **Jean Luc Vallens** addresses the issue after analyzing various jurisdictions to conclude that most states have opted for a financial test (Cash Flow) based on the debtor's inability to honor their overdue debts as well as the accounting criterion (balance sheet test) that is based on an inadequacy of the asset vis à vis the liabilities.[38]

To similar conclusions, **Vallens** himself arrives, who jointly with **Giulio Cesare Giorgini,** carried out a comparative study of the insolvency proceedings of thirty one countries from a questionnaire that was prepared by them and responded by professionals and academics in these jurisdictions. The study offers an interesting list of other criteria to trigger the insolvency proceedings (see the topic on pages 29 to 31) and also shows the relevance that this topic may have for creditors, especially in cases where a country contemplates more than one possibility in its insolvency proceedings.[39]

A similar study, prepared by Jay Westbrook, Charles D. Booth, Christoph G. Paulus, and Harry Rajak under the name "A Global View of Business Insolvency Systems" reviews the criteria found in

---

[36.] Recommendations 16 and 17. UNCITRAL Legislative Guide on Insolvency Law.

[37.] Principle C 4.2, Leroy, Anne-Marie; Grandolini, Gloria M. 2016. Principles for effective insolvency and creditor and debtor regimes. Washington, D.C.: World Bank Group. http://documents.worldbank.org/curated/en/518861467086038847/Principles-for-effective-insolvency-and-creditor-and-debtor-regimes. P. 21.

[38.] Vallens, Jean-Luc, Lìnsolvabilitéé des entreprises en droit comparéé. Joly ééditions. Lextenso ééditions. Paris, 2011, p. 24.

[39.] Vallens, Jean-Luc et Giorgine, Giulio CESARE, "étude Comparative des Procéédures d'Insolvabilitéé" Sociéétéé de Léégislation Comparéée. Volume 18, Paris, 2015, Partie I.

the world to reach the conclusion that while with these criteria are intended to make the proceeding simple and economical, sometimes they are ambiguous, restrictive or full of difficulties, which often leads to unnecessary litigation at the very moment of the start of the proceedings that results in inefficient systems.[40]

III. Two Components: An Economic Ingredient and a Legal One

The analysis of the examples mentioned in the preceding paragraph leads to the conclusion that the state of insolvency carries both an economic and a legal ingredient.

The economic ingredient consists, in terms of accounting, that there is an imbalance in the patrimonial situation of the person who consists of not counting in his assets with sufficient assets to face the lines of the liability. Either in a form of totality (totality of assets less than total liabilities) either in an operational form of flows (totality of liquid resources generated less than the liabilities that are becoming due). Some regimes add to this situation some formulas of accounting proportion, amounts or times of issues which, by the variables, should be considered as mere accidents.

The legal ingredient is given when the debtor is placed in the situation of not fulfilling his obligations. This breach must not be, momentary, transient or reduced to a single case, but must be a material incapacity leading to a state of widespread default.

Can the first one be given without the second? No.

There may be cases in which a person has very few assets or few flows of resources, but is finding ways to fulfill their obligations: to resort to family or friends who are willing to provide free resources or to assume their obligations; the realization of personal assets of the partners of a company or goods not being part of the company

---

[40.] Westbrook, Jay, Booth, Charles D., Paulus, Christoph G. and Rajak, Harry "A Global View of Business Insolvency Systems," The World Bank, Washington, 2010, p. 66.

to comply with the commitments. In these cases, even when there is insolvency in the strict sense of the word (liabilities greater than the assets) or illiquidity (absence of flows to cover the obligations that are becoming enforceable), the alleged detonating of the bankruptcy is not given, since there are no creditors who are dissatisfied.

Can the second be given without the first? Yes.

Indeed, a person may systematically fail to comply with his obligations, not because he does not have the resources to do so, but for some other reason (for example, in a supervening disability or in case of death, or absence, a period of time may elapse in which the guardian or the executor have not yet been appointed and meanwhile the person has consistently failed to comply with their obligations; either as a result of bad faith or criminal conduct, for example, abandoning business, abruptly closing operation without attending to the same in the future, disappear without leaving trace, etc.).

This observation leads to the dismissal of accounting approaches as the essential basis of the insolvency situation.

The term "state of insolvency" should be understood then by the fact of real or imminent breach of economic obligations. The situation is a purely legal situation of breach of obligations regardless of the reason that motivates it.

However, it is a fact that when the economic ingredient exists, companies need the remedy offered by the insolvency law. The debtor and the creditors will look for what and how many assets there are in the estate, what is the state of the business and which financial engineering may be convenient. It is possible that sufficient realizable assets or operating decisions of the company can be found to liquidate even in full all the debts (although ordinarily when there are liquidation situations, the creditors will receive less than what they are ordinarily entitled to) and this will occur within an insolvency procedure.

On this situation will come the procedural constructions of how to prove either the economic ingredient, or the legal one. It may suffice that the debtor merely decrees it satisfied; it may require more formal proof; it may be guided by presumptions, and so forth. The situations will vary if it is a voluntary proceeding or if it is a forced one demanded by creditors or ordered by the authority.

IV. The Imminence

There is a third important ingredient to define the time to trigger the start of an insolvency proceeding: imminence. The concept of imminence has come to revolutionize the vision of insolvency proceedings as it leaves behind the idea that it is only a remedy of last necessity and in extreme circumstances.

Basically, the situation of imminence refers to the possibility of initiating insolvency proceedings even before the circumstances that ordinarily trigger it be present.

When for a business all the factual and economic indicators point out that the time will inevitably come when the two ingredients: the economic and the legal, will be presented, will it be healthy to have to wait for the accounting and financial imbalance to occur in order to be able to start a voluntary insolvency procedure? The most elementary logic makes answer "no" to this question and the reason for this is the purpose pursued by an insolvency procedure (this is the second thing important to understand as announced in the first paragraph of this chapter).

An insolvency proceeding seeks, of course, to take care of the creditors and to solve their situation, it can also pursue the punishment of clumsy or malevolent traders, but, above all, it must pursue the search for a solution and redefinition of the universe of legal relationships of the merchant, taking into account the fact that a company is a vital element in society: it generates gross domestic product, generates jobs, generates taxes, generates economic activity in the production chains. It is no longer about the interests of the creditors, the debtor trader or its shareholders only, it is about their interests plus those of the community where they operate.

The Black's Law Dictionary defines imminent (imminent) as "Near at hand; mediate rather than immediate; close rather than touching; impending; on the point of happening; threatening; menacing; perilous. Something which is threatening to happen at once."[41] The concept entails three elements: immediacy, inexorability and threat, that is, it is something that will happen soon, which is going to happen unfailingly and which is a risk for the recipient.[42]

Time is a crucial element in the insolvency process. It is in these processes where the phrase "Time is money" has its full meaning, the more you defer looking for a solution, the longer and bureaucratic the procedures, the more the tangible and intangible assets of a company will deteriorate. "Both for voluntary and involuntary cases, delays often destroy the value to the debtor and its creditors and make it more likely that the proposed bailout results in a liquidation."[43]

This is where the concept of imminence comes in as a possible trigger for the insolvency proceedings: if this will be the one that serves to reorganize the company or to liquidate it in an orderly manner, it should not be expected that the objective condition of the insolvency occurs when it is evident that if the things continue like this, it will inevitably arrive. In this way, an insolvency proceeding must be able to start not only when the economic and legal circumstances that trigger the insolvency have occurred, but when it is unavoidable that they will occur. The value of the assets is at stake either to reorganize the company with a conciliation that achieves an agreement between debtor and creditors, either to liquidate it in the best possible way.

---

[41] Black, Henry Campbell, Black's Law Dictionary, 6th ed., St Paul Minn, West Publishing Co., 1990, p. 750

[42] It is necessary to consider that in the common language the term "imminent" is used only for something that has to happen soon without exception although it does not involve a risk: "the arrival of the travelers is imminent." In the case of insolvency all the elements are given.

[43] Westbrook, Jay, Booth, Charles, Paulus, Christoph & Rajak Harry, A Global View of Business Insolvency Systems. Washington DC, The World Bank.

On the other hand, imminent insolvency is not a special procedure nor does it produce different consequences, neither in the insolvent nor in its creditors, it is simply one more way of how the debtor can start with the proceeding in a timely manner. Creditors should not ordinarily be assigned the possibility of initiating an involuntary proceeding, this must be, logically, only in the cases of a voluntary one.

Normally, a list of the obligations pending maturity accompanied by the expectations of collection (sales, etc.) should be sufficient to demonstrate the imbalance between income and discharge flows. ". . . the proof of imminent insolvency," says Ángel Rojo, referring to the provision in the Spanish bankruptcy law, "rests on the objectivity of probability reasoning, that is, on the objective nature of the self-foresight of real insolvency."[44]

Finally, the use of the concept as a trigger for the insolvency proceedings will bring with it some consequences that must be considered: the impact on the suspect period, the directors' accountability in the suspect period (twilight zone), and so on.

V. Conclusions

Insolvency proceedings appear when the phenomenon of insolvency occurs.

Insolvency occurs ordinarily as a result of two components: an economic one, consisting of the inability to fulfill the obligations as they are become due or in the situation that the assets that are owned have a value lower than the total of liabilities, the other legal, consisting in the fact of incurring in the breach of the obligations in a generalized manner.

The different jurisdictions in the world use various criteria to measure the presence of these two components and thus base the initiation of insolvency proceedings.

---

[44] Rojo, ÁÁngel, "Presupuesto objetivo" (art. 2) en Rojo-Beltrán, Comentario de la Ley Concursal, Madrid, 2004, pág. 177.

A component that has been added in many insolvency regimes is that the procedure can be initiated not only when the components have appeared, but when it is imminent that they will appear, thus improving the chances that the proceeding achieve the goal of maximizing the value of business either to reach its reorganization, whether for liquidation.

Modified Universalism as Customary International Law

*Irit Mevorach**

I. Introduction

"**M**odified universalism" is to date the dominant approach for addressing cross-border insolvency.[1] Heavily influenced by the scholarship and advocacy of Professor Jay Westbrook,[2] it has evolved into a set of norms that can guide parties in actual cases. Adapted to the reality of a world divided into different legal systems and myriad business structures and insolvency scenarios, modified

---

* Professor of International Commercial Law, School of Law, Faculty of Social Sciences, University of Nottingham, United Kingdom. I would like to thank Ian Fletcher, John Pottow, Janis Sarra, Adrian Walters, Dino Krisiotis, Marko Milanovic, Sandesh Sivakumaran, and Tomer Broude for reading and providing invaluable comments on drafts of my 2018 book, The Future of Cross-Border Insolvency: Overcoming Biases and Closing Gaps 80–126 (Oxford University Press: 2018), which forms the basis for this chapter that was published previously by the Texas Law Review with permission. Copyright © 96 Tex. L. Rev. 1402 (2018). Reproduced with permission.

[1.] "Cross-border insolvency" (or international insolvency) means here any form of process or solution, including liquidation, reorganization, or restructuring processes, concerning commercial entities or financial institutions that have cross-border presence (e.g., assets, creditors, branches, or subsidiaries).

[2.] See generally Jay L. Westbrook, A Global Solution to Multinational Default, 98 Mich. L. Rev. 2276 (2000) (recognizing modified universalism as the best interim solution to addressing multinational insolvencies before movement to a "true universalism" approach).

universalism seeks to achieve global collective processes with efficient levels of centralization of insolvency proceedings. It thus requires the identification of a home country where proceedings would be centralized, except where it is efficient to open additional proceedings elsewhere.[3] This outbound aspect of modified universalism is complemented by a choice-of-law norm that, in principle, refers to the *lex fori concursus* (the law of the forum) with limited exceptions.[4] Norms concerning recognition, cooperation, and relief ensure that the global collective proceedings are given worldwide effect,[5] subject to specific safeguards where recognition or relief may

---

[3.] See, e.g., Reinhard Bork, Principles of Cross-Border Insolvency Law 23 (2017) (discussing the circumstances under which it may be reasonable to permit the commencement of additional proceedings); Ian F. Fletcher, Insolvency in Private International Law 16–17 (2nd ed. 2005); Roy Goode, Principles of Corporate Insolvency Law 786 (4th ed. 2011) ("But some leeway is also given to the concept of territoriality to accommodate the legitimate expectations of local creditors in relation to local assets. Thus the opening of territorial proceedings is permitted in a State where the debtor has an establishment or assets. . . ."); Jay L. Westbrook, SIFIs and States, 49 Tex. Int'l L.J. 329, 332 (2014) (advocating for the assignment of one jurisdiction as the primer inter pares to most effectively coordinate international financial crises).

[4.] See, e.g., Bork, supra note 3, at 31 ("Second, the proceedings follow the law of the opening state (lex fori concursus), which not only boosts efficiency but also constitutes an aspect of universalism.") (citation omitted); Leif M. Clark & Karen Goldstein, Sacred Cows: How to Care for Secured Creditors' Rights in Cross-Border Bankruptcies, 46 Tex. Int'l L.J. 513, 515 & n.7 (2011) ("The focus on which country would act as the home court was done in anticipation of that country applying its own laws, including choice of law rules."); Jay L. Westbrook, Universalism and Choice of Law, 23 Pa. St. Int'l L. Rev. 625, 634 (2005). Professor Westbrook observes:

The emerging international rule in multinational bankruptcy cases focuses on the center of the debtor's main interests. Up to now, that standard has been adopted primarily as a choice-of-forum rule rather than a choice-of-law rule, but it is necessary to use it for both purposes to achieve the goals of universalism.

Id.

[5.] See, e.g., Bork, supra note 3, at 32 (explaining that, for universalism to function, states must cooperate and offer their assistance, especially by recognizing and enforcing foreign proceedings); Goode, supra note 3, at 786 (describing the key universalist elements, including recognition in other countries of the forum state's judgments and assistance by local courts in asset recovery); Westbrook, supra note 3, at 345 (noting the necessity of international coordination and cooperation in the management of distressed financial institutions).

be denied if universal standards of fairness, nondiscrimination, and due process are not respected.[6] Modified universalism has been quite prevalent in practice, including where key international instruments such as the United Nations Commission on International Trade Law (UNCITRAL) Model Law on Cross-Border Insolvency (Model Law)[7] and the EU Insolvency Regulation (EIR)[8] seem to generally follow its approach.[9] There are, however, still gaps in the cross-border insolvency system and in the available frameworks (even where instruments seem to generally embrace modified universalism), including in terms of the entities covered and the participating countries.[10] Generally, the status of modified universalism is

---

[6.] Such circumstances can be grouped under the notion of "public policy."

[7.] See generally U.N. Comm'n on Int'l Trade L., UNCITRAL Model Law on Cross-Border Insolvency with Guide to Enactment and Interpretation, U.N. Sales No. E.14.V.2 (2014) (identifying as its four main features access to local courts for representatives of foreign proceedings; recognition of foreign proceedings; relief to assist foreign proceedings; and cooperation among courts and other competent authorities of the various states).

[8.] See generally Regulation 2015/848, of the European Parliament and of the Council of May 20, 2015, on Insolvency Proceedings, 2015 O.J. (L 141) 19, 19, 59 (EU) (repealing and recasting Council Regulation 1346/2000); Council Regulation 1346/2000 of May 29, 2000, on Insolvency Proceedings, 2000 O.J. (L 160) 1 (EC). The Council Regulation observes:

The proper functioning of the internal market requires that cross-border insolvency proceedings should operate efficiently and effectively and this Regulation needs to be adopted in order to achieve this objective. . . . [T]here is a need for a Community act requiring coordination of the measures to be taken regarding an insolvent debtor's assets.

Id. The Recast EIR entered into force on June 26, 2017. Id. at 56. The regime applies directly to all EU member states except Denmark, which opted out. Id. at 29.

[9.] See Goode, supra note 3, at 785–86 ("The current trend, as exemplified by the UNCITRAL Model Law on Cross-Border Insolvency and the EC Insolvency Regulation . . . is clearly in favour of a modified universalist approach. . . .").

[10.] For example, the Model Law has been adopted by only 45 jurisdictions. U.N. Comm'n on Int'l Trade Law, Status: UNCITRAL Model Law on Cross-Border Insolvency (1997), www.uncitral.org/uncitral/en/uncitral_texts/insolvency/1997Model_status.html [https://perma.cc/N7SN-V8UT]. It does not fully cover the cross-border insolvency and resolution of financial institutions—indeed, the absence of a uniform framework for cross-border insolvency of such institutions is a major gap in the international system for cross-border insolvency and resolution, Irit Mevorach,

somewhat amorphous, and its norms are often perceived as broad principles or aspects of a general trend.[11]

This chapter considers how modified universalism may be elevated from a broad approach to a recognized, international legal source that can be invoked and applied in a more concrete and consistent manner across legal systems in circumstances of international insolvencies alongside the application of written instruments where such instruments exist.[12] It draws from sources of international law, specifically the concept of customary international law (CIL), and shows that CIL is a key legal source that can fill gaps in international instruments, influence existing instruments, and regulate in areas not covered by instruments or regarding countries that are not parties to them. CIL is also useful in taking into account certain biases and territorial inclinations that can influence countries and implementing institutions' decisions and that can, therefore, impede movement toward the universal application of modified universalism.[13] CIL is a "debiasing" measure where its

---

Beyond the Search for Certainty: Addressing the Cross-Border Resolution Gap, 10 Brook. J. Corp. Fin. & Com. L. 183, 184, 218 n.160 (2015), and it does not fully or expressly cover all aspects of cross-border insolvency (for example, it does not provide specific rules concerning choice of law).

[11.] See, for example, the references of the U.K. court in In re HIH Cas. & Gen. Ins. Ltd. [2008] UKHL 21, [2008] 1 WLR 852 (appeal taken from Eng.), to a "principle rather than a rule," an "aspiration," and a "thread" or the reference of the U.S. court in In re Nortel Networks, Inc., 532 B.R. 494, 558 (Bankr. D. Del. 2015), to "terms such as 'universalism.'"

[12.] I address the question of instrument choice, particularly the choice between a treaty regime or a regime based on a model law for cross-border insolvency, in Irit Mevorach, The Future of Cross-Border Insolvency: Overcoming Biases and Closing Gaps 127–68 (2018).

[13.] See generally Daniel Kahneman & Amos Tversky, Prospect Theory: An Analysis of Decision Under Risk, 47 Econometrica 263 (1979) (developing the "prospect theory" in decision-making scholarship); Amos Tversky & Daniel Kahneman, Judgment Under Uncertainty: Heuristics and Biases, 185 Science (n.s.) 1124 (1974) (showing how choices and decisions are strongly biased and often deviate in predictable ways from economically optimal behavior). "Behavioral international law" provides

application does not require active action by all participants, such as entry into a treaty or enactment of model laws, as it operates as a default (opt-out) rule. It can thus overcome certain robust biases such as status quo and loss aversion.[14]

The normative implication is a policy push toward the transformation of modified universalism into CIL so that it can become part of the international insolvency legal order. This chapter thus explores to what extent CIL can be utilized in the field of cross-border insolvency and considers possible obstacles in this regard. It proceeds as follows. Part I overviews the notion of CIL, including how it is formed and applied, its limitations, and its continued significance. Part II considers the advantages of CIL from a behavioral perspective as a debiasing mechanism. Part III explores the obstacles that might be in the way of formalizing modified universalism as CIL in view of possible narrow perceptions of private international law and cross-border insolvency, as well as the way modified universalism has been conceptualized as an interim approach. Part IV argues that such perceptions are no longer merited. Cross-border insolvency law has a significant international role, and modified universalism has the characteristics of a stand-alone norm. Part V suggests steps to transition modified universalism from a general trend to CIL and demonstrates the benefits of such development for future international insolvencies.

---

further theoretical grounds and indicative studies regarding the application of recognized biases in international law contexts. See generally Anne van Aaken, Behavioral International Law and Economics, 55 Harv. Int'l L.J. 421 (2014); Tomer Broude, Behavioral International Law, 163 U. Pa. L. Rev. 1099 (2015) (showing that bounds on decision-making may operate when actors in international law make decisions concerning international law issues).

[14] See generally Christine Jolls & Cass R. Sunstein, Debiasing through Law, 35 J. Legal Stud. 199 (2006) (analyzing how "debiasing" through law could work to address a variety of legal questions). In the context of international law, see generally van Aaken, supra note 13, at 449. See also infra Part II.

II. CIL as a Key International Legal Source

A. Establishing CIL

CIL is one of the key sources of international law,[15] widely acknowledged and applicable in different legal traditions.[16] It has a privileged position in the international law system and forms the backbone of many areas of international law.[17] CIL arises from the general and consistent practice of states, where that practice is based on a belief in the conformity of the practice with international law.[18] This is the classical understanding of CIL, consistent with its description in the Statute of the International Court of Justice as "evidence of a general practice accepted as law."[19] It encompasses objective and subjective elements, which are complementary and intertwined.[20] The objective

---

[15] Statute of the International Court of Justice, art. 38 (San Francisco, June 26, 1945), 3 Bevans 1179, 59 Stat. 1055, T.S. No. 993, entered into force 24 Oct. 1945. CIL is considered one of the three primary sources of international law, the other two being treaties and general principles of law. See Brigitte Stern, Custom at the Heart of International Law, 11 Duke J. Comp. & Int'l L. 89, 89 (2011) (noting the centrality to the international order of both custom and treaty). "General principles of law" is a source close to CIL but one that refers to fundamental principles concerning substantive justice and procedural fairness and by which states are bound because of the universal understanding of basic legal concepts by all legal systems. Charles T. Kotuby Jr., General Principles of Law, International Due Process, and the Modern Role of Private International Law, 23 Duke J. Comp. & Int'l L. 411, 412, 422 (2013).

[16] Alan Watson, The Evolution of Law 43–44 (1985).

[17] Andrew T. Guzman, Saving Customary International Law, 27 Mich. J. Int'l L. 115, 116 (2005).

[18] See J. L. Brierly, The Law of Nations: An Introduction to the International Law of Peace 59–60 (Sir Humphrey Waldock ed., 6th ed. 1963) ("Evidence that a custom in this sense exists in the international sphere can be found only by examining the practice of states . . . whether they recognize an obligation to adopt a certain course. . . [that] shows 'a general practice accepted as law.'"); Vaughan Lowe, International Law 38 (2007) (describing the two essential components of customary international law: a general practice of states and a belief in the conformity of the practice with international law); Hugh Thirlway, The Sources of International Law 53–91 (2014) ("It is in fact the consistency and repetition rather than the duration of the practice that carries the most weight.").

[19] Statute of the International Court of Justice, art. 38(1)(b) (San Francisco, June 26, 1945), 3 Bevans 1179, 59 Stat. 1055, T.S. No. 993, entered into force 24 Oct. 1945.

[20] Thirlway, supra note 18, at 62.

element of CIL requires sufficient evidence of state practice that follows the potential CIL.[21] Such evidence should show consistency and practice by various relevant actors, although not necessarily by all countries.[22] Additionally, the required recurrence of the practice may depend on the frequency of circumstances that require action pursuant to the CIL.[23] The subjective (psychological) element is what countries have accepted as law (*opinio juris*). Thus, evidence of state practice should be complemented by evidence that the practice is regarded as an expression of a rule of international law, a conviction that there was an obligation to follow the norm.

The primary and most direct evidence of the existence of CIL would be the actions of countries through the acts of their organs. Thus, when a country acts in a legally significant way or refrains from acting, it contributes to the development of state practice accepted as law. Countries' actions may be discerned, for example, from decisions to adopt certain legislation and from the decisions of national courts.[24] Additionally, treaties and conventions may point to the existence of CIL.[25] Various instruments that may be considered soft law may also provide evidence of an established CIL or contribute to the evolution of new CIL, being determinative of the *opinio juris* or of state practice.[26] Thus, a nonbinding instrument can have a legal effect on customary law. The wording in such an instrument

---

[21] Hugh Thirlway, The Sources of International Law, in International Law 91, 100–05 (Malcolm D. Evans ed., 2014).

[22] See Curtis A. Bradley & Mitu Gulati, Withdrawing from International Custom, 120 Yale L.J. 202, 210 (2011) ("It is not clear how much state practice is required in order to generate a rule of CIL, although most commentators agree that [it] must be 'extensive' or 'widespread' . . . .") (citations omitted).

[23] Thirlway, supra note 18, at 65, 67.

[24] Jurisdictional Immunities of the State (*Ger. v. It.: Greece intervening*), Judgment, 2012 I.C.J. Rep. 99, 55 (Feb. 3).

[25] Continental Shelf (Libya/Malta), Judgment, 1985 I.C.J. Rep. 13, 27 (June 3); see Thirlway, supra note 18, at 58–59 (describing the significance of the International Law Association's Report on the Formation of Customary International Law in studying the relationship between state practice and opinio juris).

[26] Alan E. Boyle, Some Reflections on the Relationship of Treaties and Soft Law, 48 Int'l & Comp. L.Q. 901, 904 (1999).

is important because it must be "of a fundamentally norm-creating character such as could be regarded as forming the basis of a general rule of law."[27] It would also be important to consider the level of support given to the instrument by countries and any statements accompanying such instrument that may be relevant to the assessment of countries' beliefs about the conformity of the practice with international law.[28]

B. Effect of CIL

Once CIL has become pervasive enough, countries are bound by it regardless of whether they have codified the laws domestically or through treaties. Unanimity among all countries is not required for it to have a universal effect. Likewise, if an obligation is included in a treaty but also amounts to CIL, it will also bind countries that are not parties to the treaty.[29] Countries in some cases, however, may be exempted from CIL. Under the doctrine of the "persistent objector,"[30] countries can consistently object to CIL (opt-out) in its formative stages.[31] The threshold for being regarded a persistent objector is, however, very high, and the objection should be made widely known.[32] Persistent objections should also be made while the rule is still accumulating and before it becomes CIL. Thereafter, in principle, once the CIL is established, it is no longer possible

---

[27] North Sea Continental Shelf (Ger./Den.; Ger./Neth.), Judgment, 1969 I.C.J. Rep. 3, 72 (Feb. 20); see Alan Boyle, Soft Law in International Law-Making, in International Law 118, 130–33 (Malcolm D. Evans ed., 2014) (describing the importance of wording in nonbinding instruments that may create customary law).

[28] Boyle, supra note 27, at 130–31.

[29] Thirlway, supra note 18, at 35–36.

[30] See id. at 86–88 (providing an overview of the persistent objector doctrine).

[31] Bradley & Gulati, supra note 22, at 211; Guzman, supra note 17, at 164–65.

[32] Dino Kritsiotis, On the Possibilities of and for Persistent Objection, 21 Duke J. Comp. & Int'l L. 121, 129 (2010) (noting, for example, the circumstances in Fisheries (U.K. v. Nor.), Judgment, 1951 I.C.J. Rep. 116, 131 (Dec. 18), where it was ruled that "the ten-mile rule for the closing lines of bays 'would appear to be inapplicable as against Norway inasmuch as she has always opposed any attempt to apply it to the Norwegian coast'").

to opt out of the rule except through specific bilateral agreements that establish a different rule.[33]

CIL may be invoked in domestic or international tribunals, yet the application of CIL does not depend on establishing international enforcement mechanisms. Application heavily relies on domestic enforcement structures. Thus, all nations seem to accept that CIL forms an integral part of national law[34] and that courts should take judicial notice of CIL.[35] When ascertaining the existence and nature of an alleged CIL, domestic courts may have recourse to various types of sources and authoritative material, including "international treaties and conventions, authoritative textbooks, practice and judicial decisions."[36] The actual implementation of CIL in national laws differs, however, to some extent, among jurisdictions.[37] In civil law jurisdictions, the general rule is that CIL takes precedence over inconsistent ordinary national legislation and directly creates rights and duties within the territory.[38] In common law jurisdictions, CIL is recognized as part and parcel of the legal system, and legislation is presumptively construed in a manner that would avoid a conflict with international law.[39]

[33.] Thirlway, supra note 18, at 88.

[34.] Eileen Denza, The Relationship Between International and National Law, in Inter-national Law 412, 426 (Malcolm D. Evans ed., 2014).

[35.] See Malcolm N. Shaw, International Law 99–100 (7th ed. 2014) (describing the doctrine of incorporation, which holds that customary international law is automatically part of the local law without any need for constitutional ratification).

[36.] The Cristina [1938] AC 485 (HL) 497 (appeal taken from Austl.).

[37.] See Shaw, supra note 35, at 99–127 (providing an overview of the implementation of CIL in national laws).

[38.] See, e.g., Hans-Peter Folz, Germany, in International Law and Domestic Legal Systems 240, 245 (Dinah Shelton ed., 2011) (describing CIL's precedence over German statutes and its creation of rights and duties for Germans); Giuseppe Cataldi, Italy, in International Law and Domestic Legal Systems 328, 342–44 (Dinah Shelton ed., 2011) (describing Italy's practice of automatically incorporating CIL into its domestic legal system such that CIL assumes the force of constitutional law).

[39.] For example, CIL is part of the public policy of the U.K. and part of the domestic law and does not necessitate the interposition of a constitutional ratification procedure. Shaw, supra note 35, at 99–100.

C. Limitations and Critique

CIL tends to be vague, and the way it emerges is rather unclear.[40] Furthermore, because CIL is based on an evolving experience, it is evidently problematic to ascertain when rules have reached the stage where they can be applied as CIL.[41] There is also a circularity problem. For a rule to qualify as CIL, countries should feel obligated to follow it, but how would countries feel such legal obligation before the rule becomes customary?[42] This uncertainty, as well as CIL's reliance on domestic enforcement mechanisms, also makes CIL prone to nonobservance, especially when it attempts to address difficult cross-border conflicts.[43] There have also been challenges to CIL for lacking a coherent theory and doctrine.[44] It is arguably impossible to observe the universe of countries' practices to be able to ascertain whether references to CIL are made out of obligation.[45] It has also been argued that CIL does not actually affect country behavior and has little impact in view of the lack of enforcement mechanisms on the international level.[46] Another uncertainty revolves around the question of whose practice and opinion should be considered when attempting to identify the existence of CIL, including the extent to which non-state actors' actions should be taken into account, which countries' actions or omissions should be considered, and whether

---

[40.] *Id.* at 102.

[41.] Thirlway, supra note 18, at 54–55.

[42.] Anthony D'Amato, The Concept of Custom in International Law 53, 66 (1971).

[43.] See Barbara C. Matthews, Emerging Public International Banking Law? Lessons from the Law of the Sea Experience, 10 Chi. J. Int'l L. 539, 556–57 (2010) (describing the questionable level of domestic enforcement of CIL and detailing the difficulties of codifying the Law of the Sea).

[44.] See Thirlway, supra note 18, at 231 (noting that CIL is one of international law's "intellectual puzzles"); Karol Wolfke, Custom in Present International Law, at xiii (2nd ed. 1993) (describing the ambiguity of the term "custom" with regard to international law).

[45.] See Guzman, supra note 17, at 150–53 (highlighting the numerous interpretations of state practice in discussions of CIL).

[46.] Jack L. Goldsmith & Eric A. Posner, The Limits of International Law 39 (2005); see also Guzman, supra note 17, at 128 (discussing the argument that because CIL lacks an enforcement mechanism, CIL does not affect state behavior).

only the actions of countries that are affected or that are capable of taking action regarding a certain matter are relevant.[47] There is also a risk that CIL is too sticky and fails to allow for developments to meet changing circumstances and new needs of countries and of the international business and financial community.[48]

D. CIL's Continued Significance

Notwithstanding the difficulties that CIL presents, it continues to hold a privileged position in the international legal system.[49] Furthermore, over time there has been some shift from relying only on induction from national practice in identifying CIL to deducing its emergence from broader data sets, including international pronouncements and activities of non-state actors.[50] Some scholars have also theorized CIL in functional terms, suggesting that CIL may be effective when countries interact repeatedly over time, and it may influence country behavior through reputational and direct sanctions.[51] It has also been considered that although the development of CIL might be a slow process, with technological changes, the rise of international institutions, and other developments, CIL

---

[47] Thirlway, supra note 18, at 59–61; see also Till Müller, Customary Transnational Law: Attacking the Last Resort of State Sovereignty, 15 Ind. J. Global Legal Stud. 19, 28–30 (2008) (reviewing scholarship regarding non-state actors' influence on the formation of CIL).

[48] Thirlway, supra note 18, at 68.

[49] Niels Petersen, Customary Law Without Custom? Rules, Principles, and the Role of State Practice in International Norm Creation, 23 Am. U. Int'l L. Rev. 275, 309 (2007) (arguing that such unwritten international law not only counts but "may even gain importance").

[50] See, e.g., Roozbeh B. Baker, Customary International Law: A Reconceptualization, 41 Brook. J. Int'l L. 439, 446 (2016) (discussing the debate concerning "modern custom" and "traditional custom" viewpoints on customary international norms); Anthea Elizabeth Roberts, Traditional and Modern Approaches to Customary International Law: A Reconciliation, 95 Am. J. Int'l L. 757, 758 (2001) (describing the difference between traditional inductive and modern deductive methods of identifying custom).

[51] See, e.g., Guzman, supra note 17, at 134, 139 (noting the role that reputational and direct sanctions play in compliance with CIL).

may emerge more quickly than in the past.[52] The works of influential international committees of recent times provide further guidance regarding the manner of CIL formation and identification.[53] Importantly, regarding the subjective acceptance of CIL, it is explained that it should be "distinguished from mere usage or habit"[54] and may be negated where it can be shown that participants, when acting in a particular way, were motivated by considerations such as courtesy, convenience, or tradition rather than by a conviction that their acts amounted to CIL.[55]

It is recognized that CIL is binding on all countries whether or not they participated in the relevant practice. Any country in theory can affect CIL, and the position of countries may be considered even where they could not in fact take or refrain from taking an

---

[52.] See, e.g., Bin Cheng, Custom: The Future of General State Practice in a Divided World, in The Structure and Process of International Law 513, 532 (Ronald MacDonald & Douglas M. Johnston eds., 1983) ("[C]ustomary international law, instead of being sluggish and backward as a source of international law, is in fact dynamic, living, and ever-changing. . . .").

[53.] See generally Int'l Law Ass'n, Statement of Principles Applicable to the Formation of General Customary International Law, Final Report of the Committee, London Conference (2000) [hereinafter Statement of Principles] (attempting to create a practical guide with concise and clear guidelines for the application of customary international law principles); Int'l Law Comm'n, Rep. on the Identification of Customary International Law: Text of the Draft Conclusions Provisionally Adopted by the Drafting Committee, U.N. Doc. A/CN.4/L.872 (May 30, 2016) [hereinafter Draft Conclusions] (describing the way in which the rules of customary international law are determined).

[54.] Draft Conclusions, supra note 53, at 3.

[55.] See Statement of Principles, supra note 53, at 35 (describing the practice of sending condolences on the death of a head of state as an example of a practice that, although frequently observed as a matter of comity, does not give rise to a legal obligation); see also North Sea Continental Shelf (Ger./Den.; Ger./Neth.), Judgment, 1969 I.C.J. Rep. 3, 77 (Feb. 20). The court noted:

The frequency, or even habitual character of the acts is not in itself enough. There are many international acts, e.g., in the field of ceremonial and protocol, which are performed almost invariably, but which are motivated only by considerations of courtesy, convenience or tradition, and not by any sense of legal duty.

Id.

action.[56] Surely, where countries do possess the capacity to engage and interact with other parties, such countries would be more influential and thus privileged regarding the formation and shaping of CIL. However, the reliance of international law on the practice of the more powerful countries can ensure fewer deviations from and violations of CIL where such countries formed the rules. Constraining violations by powerful countries is crucial for the stability of the system, as the impact of breach could be much more pronounced and widespread when committed by such jurisdictions. In addition, because powerful countries are less affected by CIL violations (as they are more resilient to the implications of a breach), they may be less deterred by them. Therefore, it is another advantage if these countries play an important role in shaping the rules.[57]

Today, treaty law covers many areas of international law. There are also various other ways for countries to cooperate through soft-law instruments.[58] However, CIL remains binding on countries even outside the treaty framework. The two sources operate in parallel, and the codification of CIL in a treaty does not abrogate the rule as CIL.[59] CIL still plays an important role "regulating both within the gaps of treaties as well as the conduct of non-parties

---

[56.] See Thirlway, supra note 18, at 59–60 (noting, as to the question of whether customary international law existed with respect to the use of nuclear weapons, the fact that a majority of states did not possess nuclear weapons and could therefore neither choose to use them nor refrain from using them).

[57.] Guzman, supra note 17, at 151.

[58.] See Kal Raustiala, Form and Substance in International Agreement, 99 Am. J. Int'l L. 581, 614 (2005) (concluding that there has been a dramatic increase in international cooperation through contracts, unwritten understandings, and pledges).

[59.] See Military and Paramilitary Activities in and against Nicaragua (Nicar. v. United States), Judgment, 1986 I.C.J. Rep. 14, 177 (June 27). The Court held:

[E]ven if the customary norm and the treaty norm were to have exactly the same content, this would not be a reason for the Court to hold that the incorporation of the customary norm into treaty-law must deprive the customary norm of its applicability as distinct from that of the treaty norm.

Id.

to the treaties"[60] because countries are bound by CIL even if they have not expressed explicit consent. The effect of CIL is also important regarding matters that are not regulated by treaties or by other instruments and for newly emerging issues not yet covered by a treaty.[61] In addition, CIL can serve to influence treaty regimes and may be important and relevant for treaty interpretation where, for example, the treaty refers to rules of CIL.[62] Thus, important areas of international law, including the law of state responsibility, foreign direct investment, diplomatic immunity, human rights, and state immunity,[63] are governed wholly or partially by CIL where treaties are not universal, where a treaty is absent, or where the treaty does not cover all issues. CIL is in use, for example, in international investment law where certain aspects of regulating foreign investment have become settled international law[64] and where CIL remains of fundamental importance despite the proliferation of bilateral investment agreements in this field.[65]

[60.] Bradley & Gulati, supra note 22, at 209.

[61.] Where both a treaty and CIL regulate the same situation, normally the treaty is the prevailing lex specialis, at least regarding rules that existed at the time of the conclusion of the treaty. See Thirlway, supra note 21, at 108–09 (observing that even in a situation where customary law exists alongside treaty law, no problem of theory is raised, since the latter is free to modify customary entitlements).

[62.] Guzman, supra note 17, at 120 & n.18 (noting the example of the United States Model Bilateral Investment Treaty art. II (Apr. 1994), which refers to "treatment less favorable than that required by [customary] international law").

[63.] Id. at 116 n.1.

[64.] See Patrick Dumberry, Are BITs Representing the "New" Customary International Law in International Investments Law? 28 Pa. St. Int'l L. Rev. 675, 676–78 (2010) (describing the role of custom as a source of international law in the regulation of foreign investment).

[65.] CIL in this field includes, inter alia, the requirement of nondiscrimination, the fair and equitable treatment of foreign investors, the entitlement of foreign investors to national treatment once admitted into the country, and the requirement regarding nondiscriminatory regulatory measures and obligations to respect human rights by multinational companies. For more detail, see Surya P. Subedi, International Investment Law, in International Law 727, 740–41 (Malcolm D. Evans ed., 2014). These rules may apply in the absence of a bilateral agreement, where agreements make reference to CIL, or to fill gaps in treaties when treaties are silent on certain issues.

E. CIL's Relevance to the Cross-Border Insolvency System

The nature and characteristics of CIL make it an important legal source for a cross-border insolvency system based on modified universalism and a useful method to shape the international interactions in this subsystem of international law. CIL is responsive to emerging trends in practice. It is based on experience, and it can arise whether written instruments are applicable or not. It applies to all countries, whereby treaties or other instruments apply only to signatories or countries that adopted the instruments. Thus, if modified universalism is recognized as CIL, gaps in the cross-border insolvency system can be filled. Modified universalism is also sufficiently flexible—its emerging norms accommodate different types of business structures and different degrees of global or regional integration, and it can also adapt to changing conditions. Thus, it is akin to CIL, which as a legal source tends to be supple and adaptable. CIL is also not too rigid as a legal source, notwithstanding its universal application through general experience. It can develop gradually over time, and it is possible to change or create new CIL to meet the developing needs of nations.[66] Thus, conduct inconsistent with CIL may in relevant circumstances be a way to create new rules.[67] At the same time, where CIL represents an emerging, widespread, and normatively desirable practice, its tendency to stick is an important advantage.[68]

---

[66] Thirlway, supra note 18, at 69; cf. *id.* at 102 (noting the permanent nature of general principles of law).

[67] The ICJ explained in this regard that "[r]eliance by a State on a novel right or an unprecedented exception to the principle might, if shared in principle by other States, tend towards a modification of customary international law." Military and Paramilitary Activities in and Against Nicaragua (*Nicar. v. U.S.*), Judgment, 1986 I.C.J. Rep. 14, 207 (June 27).

[68] Rachel Brewster, Withdrawing from Custom: Choosing between Default Rules, 21 Duke J. Comp. & Int'l L. 47, 55 (2010) ("If customary international law already incorporates rules that are net welfare increasing for the international community, then a shift towards the [provision of more opt-out rights, including after formation,] may be welfare decreasing.").

III. The Behavioral Force of CIL

A. CIL as a Debiasing Mechanism

CIL can also assist in overcoming territorial inclinations and biases.[69] Decision-makers, including actors making choices regarding issues of international law, may be inclined to avoid changes and cling to the status quo, especially where choices of certain options are perceived as resulting in a loss (e.g., loss of sovereignty or control over locally situated assets or entities), and more so if the choice requires active action.[70] Additionally, the way options are framed matter to people's choices. Specifically, cognitive psychology studies have shown the effect of legislative framing and the use of default options on choices between alternative options.[71] It has been shown, for example, that people favor agreements that are consistent with legal default rules or terms of trade that are conventional for the type of bargain at issue.[72] This may be due to the stress or

---

[69.] For more detail on the possible operation of biases and bounds on decision-making in international law, and specifically in cross-border insolvency, see Mevorach, supra note 12, at 49–79.

[70.] The existence of loss aversion, whereby losses are exaggerated and given greater weight than gains, and its link to a status quo bias and the endowment effect, has been observed in a wealth of empirical research, including neurobiological experiments, which showed that this pattern of behavior (responding differently to perceived losses as opposed to perceived gains, measured against a perceived status quo position) is tied to the brain's greater sensitivity to potential losses than to gains; experimental studies have also shown that loss aversion has a specific effect when considering avoiding an option verses actively approaching an option. See generally Nicholas D. Wright et al., Approach-Avoidance Processes Contribute to Dissociable Impacts of Risk and Loss on Choice, 32 J. Neuroscience 7009 (2012); Nicholas D. Wright et al., Manipulating the Contribution of Approach-Avoidance to the Perturbation of Economic Choice by Valence, 7 Frontiers in Neuroscience 1 (2013).

[71.] See Daniel Kahneman et al., Anomalies: The Endowment Effect, Loss Aversion, and Status Quo Bias, 5 J. Econ. Persp. 193, 199 (1991) (pointing to studies showing the effect of such manipulation on a choice between alternative automobile insurance policies).

[72.] See, e.g., Omri Ben-Shahar & John A.E. Pottow, On the Stickiness of Default Rules, 33 Fla. St. U. L. Rev. 651, 662 (2006) (explaining that a deviation from default terms can raise suspicion among parties); Daniel Kahneman et al., Experimental Tests of the Endowment Effect and the Coase Theorem, 98 J. Pol. Econ. 1325, 1343–44 (1990) (concluding that participants' preferences were dependent upon their

sometimes physical effort involved in making changes, but it is also likely because defaults tend to be perceived as representing the existing status quo and the recommended, endorsed option.[73] Furthermore, switching from a default option may be perceived as a risk and a loss; thus, it may be weighed more heavily than the possible gains because of loss aversion.[74] Empirical research in international law concerning adherence to options in treaties has also shown the significant impact of default rules, which were likely perceived as the endorsed status quo position, on countries' (and their implementing institutions') choices.[75] More generally, behavioral international law studies have noted the importance of default mechanisms in choice architecture in international law.[76] Thus, a rule can be set up as an opt-out rule or an opt-in rule. An opt-in rule means that the default is nonadherence to the rule. In an opt-out scheme, the default is adherence. If people tend not to deviate from default rules, there is an advantage in setting up opt-out rules, especially where universality of the application of the rule is critical. Thus, if sources of international law that provide an opt-out system are used, higher participation can be expected in comparison to opt-in systems.

---

reference positions); Russell Korobkin, The Status Quo Bias and Contract Default Rules, 83 Cornell L. Rev. 608, 646–47 (1998) (stating that participants of the experiment preferred whichever contract term was the default term given).

[73.] See, e.g., John Beshears et al., The Importance of Default Options for Retirement Savings Outcomes: Evidence from the United States, in Nat'l Bureau of Econ. Res., Social Security Policy in a Changing Environment 167, 184–87 (Jeffrey R. Brown et al. eds., 2009) (describing this phenomenon in the context of experiments studying individuals' investment decisions regarding their savings plans).

[74.] Eric J. Johnson & Daniel Goldstein, Do Defaults Save Lives? 302 Science 1338, 1338 (2003).

[75.] Jean Galbraith, Treaty Options: Towards a Behavioral Understanding of Treaty Design, 53 Va. J. Int'l L. 309, 352 (2013).

[76.] See Broude, supra note 13, at 1140–41 (noting how individuals have a tendency to adopt default rules even when they are inefficient); van Aaken, supra note 13, at 450–52 (explaining how choice architecture, through default rules' opt-in/opt-out mechanisms, provides a framework through which to view international law). Choice architecture is the study of how the ways in which options are presented affect decision-making. See Richard H. Thaler & Cass Sunstein, Nudge: Improving Decisions about Health, Wealth, and Happiness 3 (2009) (defining a choice architect as someone responsible for organizing the context of decision-making).

CIL can be particularly advantageous as a debiasing mechanism of international law because CIL is an opt-out system where countries are bound by such CIL that has developed through the general practice of nations. Although CIL emerges from the consistent practice of countries, it is not a consensual mechanism. It does not require that countries agree to or enact the rule and as such does not represent a deviation from the status quo. The existence of CIL is based on an understanding that it is a norm of the international community. This does not necessarily mean, though, that a given country consents to the norm. Rather, the acceptance of the binding rule must be felt by countries generally.[77] Critically, to not be bound by the rule, a country needs to actively object to it.[78] As such, CIL is a mechanism of international cooperation that can promote universal application of the norm because opt-out rules are expected to increase participation, particularly on the global level, in the absence of mechanisms to impose regulation directly on countries' legal systems. It might be harder to ensure universal application through, for example, treaties, as treaties require an active opt-in. The fact that CIL requires adherence (or objection) to the rule in its entirety also promotes integrity in its application.[79] Thus, with no room for cherry-picking, it is more likely that the norm will remain uniform and coherent.

B. CIL: Shifting the Reference Point

Outcomes are perceived as gains or losses usually relative to a reference point that people denote during the decision-making process, "rather than as final states of wealth or welfare."[80] The reference point usually corresponds to the current asset position (status quo)

[77.] Andrew T. Guzman, Against Consent, 52 Va. J. Int'l L. 747, 776 (2012).

[78.] The emergence of the persistent objector doctrine, see supra note 30 and accompanying text, may have been part of an effort to make international law less consensual. Bradley & Gulati, supra note 22, at 240.

[79.] Van Aaken, supra note 13, at 452.

[80.] Kahneman & Tversky, supra note 13, at 274. Values are attached to changes rather than to final states, and the perception of changes is also affected by past and present context of experience. Id. at 274, 277.

whereby gains/losses are deviations from the reference point.[81] Thus, a negative perception of modified universalism outcomes is expected particularly where the country's reference point is a regime generally based on territorialism, namely if the country does not have an established internationalist approach in its domestic methods for addressing cross-border insolvency. A modified universalist CIL can, in addition to applying directly in areas not covered by treaties or other instruments, also indirectly promote the adoption of instruments (such as the Model Law) where these instruments reflect modified universalism. A strong leading norm, elevated from a trend to CIL, may gradually affect the reference points of countries and implementing institutions and level the playing field. When recognized as CIL, countries may feel more obliged to follow modified universalism and, over time, assimilate it into the legal system. Thus, adherence to instruments that are premised on modified universalism would less likely be perceived as a change and as a loss.

IV. Conceptual Impediments

A. Public and Private International Law as Distinct Disciplines

Notwithstanding the rather widespread adherence to modified universalism, it has not been invoked or applied as CIL. Modified universalism is not explicitly embraced in the global instruments for cross-border insolvency. Courts in common law jurisdictions often apply common law notions akin to a universalist/cooperative approach, noting that modified universalism is recognized as a broad principle under common law, or they apply the notion of comity. Yet, comity entails different interpretations and is not universal.[82]

[81.] *Id.* at 274.

[82.] It generally refers to the tradition among judges within the common law camp to cooperate and assist foreign jurisdictions. See Fletcher, supra note 3, at 17 (contrasting comity with insularity). But its precise meaning is quite elusive.

Modified universalism that could be applied as a universal and uniform norm has usually been considered a broad concept within the constraints of domestic, private international law to the extent that if we were to try identifying it now as CIL, it would be difficult to show consistent practice that is based on belief in the conformity of the practice with international law, and therefore CIL might be disproved. The problem could lie in a narrow perception of cross-border insolvency law as a legal field addressing procedures and technicalities. Because cross-border insolvency law primarily regulates the private international law of insolvency, it can be understood as a field disconnected from public international law and public international law sources. As such, cross-border insolvency law might not be sufficiently influenced by international laws and might not engage in creating CIL.

The relation between private and public international law has been a subject of much debate and considerable theoretical development.[83] In the early nineteenth century, private international law was perceived as a category and an integral part of public international law pursuant to the idea of a unitary international law based on the traditions of *Roman jus gentium*, the *Statutists*, and the natural law; in the latter half of that century, it evolved and crystallized as a separate field with a distinct role.[84] Pursuant to this (modern) traditional separation of roles, public international law governs the

---

[83.] See, e.g., K. Lipstein, Principles of the Conflict of Laws, National and International 63–64 (1981) (examining the influence of public international law on its private counterpart); Kotuby, supra note 15, at 411–12, 433 (2013) (noting the increasingly global discourse surrounding private international law); Ralf Michaels, Public and Private International Law: German Views on Global Issues, 4 J. Priv. Int'l L. 121, 121–22 (2008) (describing scholars' different perspectives on public and private international law depending on their geographical and historical context); Ole Spiermann, Twentieth Century Internationalism in Law, 18 Eur. J. Int'l L. 785, 788–89, 792 (2007) (providing an historical overview of public and private international law); John R. Stevenson, The Relationship of Private International Law to Public International Law, 52 Colum. L. Rev. 561, 564–67 (1952) (analyzing the diverse views of scholars regarding the proper relationship between public and private international law).

[84.] See generally Stevenson, supra note 83 (describing the historical relationship between private and public international law).

relations between nations, provides a legal framework for organized international relations, and addresses the rights and obligations of countries with respect to other countries or individuals. Private international law, on the other hand, deals with the domestic laws of countries that govern conflicts between private persons. Against this backdrop, it has been doubted that rules that are fundamental to private international law (e.g., the rule that rights in rem as applied to immovable and movable property are governed by the *lex situs*, or that form is governed by the *lex loci actus*) could and have generated customary (public) international law.[85]

Generally, the traditional division between private and public international law and the evolution of private international law as a domestic legal order regulating in the domain of private interests contributed to the gradual isolation of private international law from public international law and the general exclusion of a role for international sources.[86] This model has resulted in a private international law system that does not contribute much to the ordering of international private relations but instead often adds to the complexity of international transactions—as private international laws of different systems often conflict or operate with broad exceptions, creating uncertainty and costs.[87] This division of roles between private and public international law also arguably constrains the ability to regulate the important domain of private international interaction in view of the operation of private power in the global economy.[88]

---

[85] Pavel Kalensky, Trends of Private International Law 17–18 (1971); Lipstein, supra note 83, at 64–65.

[86] See Alex Mills, The Private History of International Law, 55 Int'l & Comp. L.Q. 1, 44–45 (2006) ("By defining private international law as part of domestic law, it defines private international lawyers as domestic, not international; it emphasizes their attachment to a sovereign territory.").

[87] Id. at 45–46.

[88] A. Claire Cutler, Artifice, Ideology and Paradox: The Public/Private Distinction in International Law, 4 Rev. Int'l Pol. Econ. 261, 279 (1997); Mills, supra note 86, at 46.

B. Cross-Border Insolvency as a System of Procedural Private International Law

That cross-border insolvency is a body of specific and narrow rules concerning insolvency procedures has been a common understanding and description of this area of the law.[89] Often, international insolvency does not exist as a "systematically elaborated legal framework" and the domestic private international laws apply.[90] Cross-border insolvency has been generally regarded as "an arcane and rarified area of specialization."[91] Narrow assumptions concerning the role of cross-border insolvency have been notable in the practice and observed in the 1980s and early the 1980s. It has been noted that countries have generally presumed that international insolvency is an aspect of private law.[92] Such views resulted in limited interest of countries in the field of cross-border insolvency where countries have confined their role to the regulation of procedure concerning international insolvency. This peripheral interest of governments has also arguably constrained negotiations on insolvency treaties and could explain the general failure in concluding treaties in this field.[93]

The approach to cross-border insolvency has evolved over time, and importantly, there has been growing recognition of the difficulty to control cross-border insolvencies efficiently by relying on the domestic private international laws of national systems. It has been acknowledged that domestic private international laws related to insolvency have preserved the problem of diversity and

---

[89] Bob Wessels, International Insolvency Law 1 (4th ed. 2015).

[90] *Id.* at 4.

[91] Fletcher, supra note 3, at 6–7.

[92] *Id.* at 5.

[93] Thomas M. Gaa, Harmonization of International Bankruptcy Law and Practice: Is It Necessary? Is It Possible? 27 Int'l Law. 881, 897 (1993); John Honsberger, The Negotiation of a Bankruptcy Treaty (1985), reproduced with permission in Meredith Memorial Lectures: Bankruptcy—Present Problems and Future Perspectives 287, 291 (1986).

conflicts between national laws.[94] Consequently, hugely influential uniform frameworks have emerged, notably the Model Law. Yet, as international instruments that attempt to regulate the specialized field of cross-border insolvency, they, too, can be understood as merely providing certain tools to address private international procedures more efficiently but not as creating general norms that intend to influence substantive results.[95] The important framework for cross-border insolvency applicable in Europe (the EIR) has also evolved as an aspect of the European Community private international law system.[96] It has been observed that the European insolvency framework has not provided a uniform and comprehensive legal framework.[97] In all, the important advance of cross-border insolvency regimes has been tempered by a modest approach concerning the role of cross-border insolvency law and of the frameworks that are being devised to govern cross-border insolvency cases.

C. Modified Universalism as a Transitory Approach

A tendency to underrate the role of cross-border insolvency is exacerbated where modified universalism is perceived as an interim solution, inextricably linked to the aspiration to achieve pure universalism.[98] At least in theory, pure universalism is often considered the ultimate ideal for regulating cross-border insolvency and modified universalism the best solution pending movement to true universalism.[99] Modified universalism is thought to provide a pragmatic

---

[94] Fletcher, supra note 3, at 6–7.

[95] See, e.g., *Bank of W. Austl. v. David Stewart Henderson* [No. 3] [2011] FMCA 840, 43 (Austl.) ("[The Model Law] was promoted as having a procedural effect as opposed to a substantive effect that might have included automatic recognition and enforcement or effects.").

[96] Wessels, supra note 89, at 6.

[97] *Id.* at 7.

[98] For discussion of the proposition that cross-border insolvencies should always be unitary and universal, see Bork, supra note 3, at 28–29; Fletcher, supra note 3, at 11.

[99] Westbrook, supra note 2, at 2277.

transitory approach whilst country laws still differ and could foster the smoothest transition to true universalism.[100]

It is inevitable, however, that whilst modified universalism remains conceptually transitory, its ability to solidify and become CIL is undermined. CIL must represent settled obligatory practice;[101] therefore, a transitory doctrine would be an oxymoron. True, rules or principles of a temporary character may stay in such an interim state for a long time and until a new regime develops. CIL can change, and new CIL can emerge when conduct inconsistent with it may in relevant circumstances show the appearance of new rules. CIL does not have to stay still. Yet, for CIL to emerge in the first place, it should be demonstrated that it is followed consistently based on the belief about the conformity of the practice with international law. It may be difficult to form such a type of law, however, where modified universalism is in this midpoint between an interim solution and a fundamental norm and is conceptually linked to another presumably better approach, thus representing a transitory stage in the development of more ideal rules.

V. Reconceptualization: The International Role of Cross-Border Insolvency

A. Internationalization of Private International Law

Gradually since the twentieth century, and more so in recent decades, the division between private and public international law has become uncertain and blurred.[102] The traditional separation of roles of the two

---

100. *Id.*

101. See supra subpart I(A).

102. See, e.g., Michaels, supra note 83, at 121–22 (discussing the recent trend toward merging the fields of private and public international law); Spiermann, supra note 83, at 793–94 ("The 'internationalist' school according to which private international law was part and parcel of public international law still claimed many followers in early 20th century theory."). See generally Alex Mills, The Confluence of Public and Private International Law (2009) (challenging the distinction normally drawn between public and private international law by exploring the ways in which the former shapes, and is given effect by, the latter).

fields no longer fits with the current state of globalization or with modern intervention by countries in terms of regulating private market activities, adding a public component or public-interest component to private business law.[103] The conceptualization of the relationship between private and public international law and of the role of private international law is in a state of evolution, too, because of these changes in world realities. It is becoming clear that private international law of a narrow character cannot properly address modern challenges in an increasingly interconnected world.[104] It has been noted that while international disputes in the past were largely limited to regional relations among close legal systems, the discourse has become truly global in recent decades.[105] Therefore, private international law should not be perceived as a mere system of technical rules regarding the proper forum, law, and the facilitation of recognition and enforcement of foreign judgments.[106] Furthermore, private international law should not insulate itself and attempt to regulate private interactions separately from the broader international order, as such isolation obscures the operation of private power in the global political economy.[107]

There are also growing overlaps and intersections of the roles of each field in practice. Thus, public international law shows a rising interest in economic relations, and multinational corporations and individuals are no longer outside its remit.[108] It has also been noted that public international law is becoming domesticated and more technical.[109] Importantly, the result of increasing intersections and

---

[103.] See, e.g., Michaels, supra note 83, at 122–23 (discussing how the distinction between private and public international law has become less clear).

[104.] Kotuby, supra note 15, at 411–12.

[105.] Id.

[106.] See id. at 412 (arguing that private international law should have an interest and a meaningful role to play in identifying and ensuring compliance with general international principles regarding the way transnational disputes are resolved).

[107.] See Cutler, supra note 88, at 279 ("[T]he public/private distinction operates ideologically to obscure the operation of private power in the global political economy.").

[108.] See, e.g., Andrew T. Guzman, A Compliance-Based Theory of International Law, 90 Calif. L. Rev. 1823, 1826 (2002) (discussing the need for a coherent theory of compliance given international law's increased pertinence to global economic and business relations).

[109.] Anne-Marie Slaughter & William Burke-White, The Future of International Law Is Domestic (or, the European Way of Law), 47 Harv. Int'l L.J. 327, 327 (2006).

overlaps between private and public international law has been a gradual expansion of the role and scope of private international law.[110] Thus, many of the tasks of private international law, for example, its dealing with recent problems of sovereign state insolvency, might have previously been viewed as belonging to public international law.[111]

Movement toward the internationalization of private international law has been apparent for some time with the conclusion of treaties and other international instruments in recent years on matters of jurisdiction, choice of law, and recognition and enforcement of foreign judgments.[112] This trend has coincided with the internationalization of national economies and their increased interdependence. Internationalization can also be seen in the rise of international commercial law and its development from the early stages of the Merchant Law to modern legal orders on a transnational scale.[113] International organizations have been playing a significant part. For example, UNCITRAL has been charged with the task of coordinating global law reform to support international trade.[114] In this gradual reunification of private and public international law,

---

[110.] Michaels, supra note 83, at 123.

[111.] *Id.* at 137.

[112.] See generally Regulation 2015/848, 2015 O.J. (L 141) 19 (EU) (recognizing that an international agreement is necessary to effectuate cross-border insolvency proceedings); Council Regulation 1215/2012, 2012 O.J. (L 351) 1, 3 (EU) (promulgating rules and principles for jurisdictional issues and for the recognition and enforcement of judgments in international civil and commercial matters); U.N. Comm'n on Int'l Trade Law, UNCITRAL Model Law on Cross-Border Insolvency with Guide to Enactment and Interpretation, U.N. Sales No. E.14.V.2 (2014) (identifying as its purpose the provision of "effective mechanisms for dealing with cases of cross-border insolvency"); The Hague Conference on Private International Law, www.hcch.net/ [https://perma.cc/7RG9-42PS].

[113.] Harold J. Berman, The Law of International Commercial Transactions, 2 Emory J. Int'l Disp. Resol. 235, 243 (1988). For a summary of these developments, see Rosalind Mason, Cross-Border Insolvency and Legal Transnationalisation, 21 Int'l Insolv. Rev. 105, 108–12 (2012).

[114.] See G.A. Res. 2205 (XXI), at 8 (Dec. 16, 1966) (directing UNCITRAL to engage in a variety of tasks to "further the progressive harmonization and unification of the law of international trade").

private international law is not swallowed by or fully merged with public international law. Rather, its role and scope are augmented.[115]

B. Substantive and International Impact of Cross-Border Insolvency

The increased role of private international law and the relevance of public-international-law sources to the mission of private international law should be highlighted more in the context of cross-border insolvency. A broad internationalist approach assigned to private international law is particularly justified in the field of insolvency where private and public interests intersect: insolvency law is considered "meta-law."[116] Insolvency principles are closely linked to fundamental public policy and social goals, and insolvency outcomes can impact the economy and the wider public.[117] Cross-border insolvency law is not merely procedural but also affects substantive rights, even where it is mainly confined to the harmonization of private international laws pertaining to insolvency.[118] Through a cross-border insolvency framework, it is possible to enforce a collective insolvency process on the global level, including by requiring the transfer of assets to the central proceedings and imposing additional duties and requirements regarding the conduct of such proceedings with

---

[115.] Michaels, supra note 83, at 137–38; see also Robert Wai, Transnational Liftoff and Juridical Touchdown: The Regulatory Function of Private International Law in an Era of Globalization, 40 Colum. J. Transnat'l L. 209, 219–20 (2002) (describing the doctrinal reforms in private international law).

[116.] Manfred Balz, The European Union Convention on Insolvency Proceedings, 70 Am. Bankr. L.J. 485, 486 (1996).

[117.] The claim that insolvency law's role is merely procedural and should be confined to the respect of pre-acquired rights through orderly distribution of the estate has been strongly rejected by proponents of the "traditionalist" approach. See generally Elizabeth Warren, Bankruptcy Policy, 54 U. Chi. L. Rev. 775 (1987). Cf. Thomas H. Jackson, Translating Assets and Liabilities to the Bankruptcy Forum, 14 J. Legal Stud. 73, 75 (1985) (contending that the traditional approach to bankruptcy distributes assets in a suboptimal way that is different from how a sole owner would have them distributed).

[118.] See Bork, supra note 3, at 17–18, 113–14 (setting out the various procedural and substantive aspects of insolvency law).

the important substantive result of equitable treatment of creditors wherever located. Cross-border insolvency can also do more than connect national legal systems. It can engage in the identification of best practices and in the formulation of international standards, and it can prevent financial collapse.[119]

Cross-border insolvency is of a true international nature, as many cases of general default involve multinational enterprises with branches and subsidiaries spanning multiple countries. The way a court or authority in one country handles international insolvency cases often has significant implications across borders in numerous jurisdictions, affecting a broad range of stakeholders. As aforementioned, the administration of cross-border insolvencies can also have an impact on the public and the economy at large.[120] Indeed, international insolvencies and, to an even larger extent, multinational defaults of financial institutions often not only affect the private business community but might influence wider public interests and even threaten the economic and political stability of nation-states.[121] The collapse of Lehman Brothers and other institutions during the global financial crisis are notable examples.[122] The insolvency of Hanjin Shipping in 2016, as well, is an example of how the filing of bankruptcy in one jurisdiction can present paramount global challenges. There, it was a matter of public interest that the South Korean proceedings be swiftly recognized so that cargo worth millions of dollars could resume moving to its various destinations.[123]

[119.] Wessels, supra note 89, at 2–3.

[120.] See Douglass G. Boshkoff, Some Gloomy Thoughts Concerning Cross-Border Insolvencies, 72 Wash. U. L.Q. 931, 935 (1994) (commenting that "[b]ankruptcy law has become so important to the national economy that reform no longer can be left to a few academics and insolvency practitioners").

[121.] Gaa, supra note 93, at 909.

[122.] The collapse of Lehman Brothers nearly brought down the world's financial system in 2008. Mevorach, supra note 10, at 194.

[123.] The former General Counsel for Hanjin Shipping America noted:

When Hanjin Shipping, once the seventh largest container carrier in the world and the fourth largest container carriers in the transpacific (Asia—U.S. & Canada) trade, filed for bankruptcy, few believed that a "too big to fail" organization like Hanjin would not be given a government bail-out. So, naturally, no one really

The international insolvency regime is a critical component of the international economic framework. The effective resolution of cross-border insolvency contributes to international trade and investment, as the United Nations General Assembly acknowledged when initiating the work in this field.[124] Cross-border insolvency of banks and other financial institutions is also an integral aspect of the global financial system and the architecture of international financial law.[125] Already, and for several decades now, transnational actors have been engaged in the creation of standards in insolvency and the development of frameworks for cross-border insolvency. Against the backdrop of the general evolution of private international law, such work on international frameworks for insolvency should continue to develop within their broader international context.

C. Separation of Modified Universalism from the Pure Theory of Universalism

In accordance with its international role, the cross-border insolvency system should strive to transform modified universalism to an established, binding CIL. Conceptually, this requires that modified universalism is no longer regarded as a transitory doctrine linked to pure universalism but rather a stand-alone norm. Such conceptual

---

appreciated the kind of disruption and losses that would subsequently affect the global supply chain.

Wook Chung, Hanjin Shipping: From the Eye of the Storm and Back, Marine Log (Mar. 8, 2017), www.marinelog.com/index.php?option=com_k2&view=item&id=25323:hanjin-shipping-from-the-eye-of-the-storm-and-back&Itemid=230 [https://perma.cc/5J2F-S46U].

[124] See G.A. Res. 52/158, 6 (Dec. 15, 1997) (resolving that the UN is "convinced that fair and internationally harmonized legislation on cross-border insolvency that respects the national procedural and judicial systems and is acceptable to States with different legal, social and economic systems would contribute to the development of international trade and investment").

[125] See Chris Brummer, Soft Law and the Global Financial System: Rule Making in the 21st Century 233–34, 319–24 (2015) ("Cross-Border bankruptcy has been largely operationalized as an outgrowth of domestic (national policy) .... [and] authorities have begun to coordinate . . . how cooperation would arise between jurisdictions should a multinational bank or firm fail.").

separation is also justified where it is *modified* universalism that provides concrete rules fitting with business and legal realities, thus guiding parties in actual cases. Pure universalism offers the most viable theoretical model for cross-border insolvency when it envisages a collective process on the global level encompassing all stakeholders whose interests are implicated and all assets wherever located. Yet modified universalism translates the model to a practical approach.[126]

Would such conceptual separation risk, however, the further spread and application of universalism? Arguably, formalizing modified universalism might make participants more reluctant to follow it. It might be that it is this humility and modesty attached to modified universalism that allowed it to grow through "incrementalism."[127] It may be conceived that rather than making explicit proclamations about the intentions of frameworks and pointing to concrete international laws, it is better to provide tools that achieve the same intentions without "scaring off" countries from participating in the regime.

Yet if modified universalism is eventually transformed to CIL, it can benefit from the additional advantage that it can operate as a debiasing mechanism: namely, it can, at least to some extent, address countries' aversions and reluctance to adhere to modified universalist instruments. Furthermore, by concealing the justificatory basis (the source) of certain solutions and focusing on technical results, there is a risk that both the frameworks' design and the application of the rules they prescribe would be inconsistent. It is also more difficult to fill in gaps in the system in the absence of a general, settled norm. Finally, it was perhaps the case in the earlier stages of development of the cross-border insolvency system that some obscurity regarding

---

126. See Mevorach, supra note 12, at 1–48, for a discussion of the evolution of modified universalism from the theory of pure universalism.

127. John A.E. Pottow, Beyond Carve-Outs and Toward Reliance: A Normative Framework for Cross-Border Insolvency Choice of Law, 9 Brook. J. Corp. Fin. & Com. L. 197, 198 (2014) (suggesting, however, an independent normative theory for choice of law based on modified universalism); John A.E. Pottow, Procedural Incrementalism: A Model for International Bankruptcy, 45 Va. J. Int'l L. 935, 939 (2005).

its norms was merited so that frameworks could gain the initial traction and expand. Yet the cross-border insolvency system has gone through significant development, and the main cross-border insolvency instrument (the Model Law) has been adopted in a significant number of countries. It is now, therefore, time to stabilize the system further, including through greater clarity about its underlying norms and their legal status.

Such separation and the use of CIL as a source for cross-border insolvency, while requiring that modified universalism is understood and used as a stand-alone norm, should not cause concern to proponents of incremental developments in this field. The use of CIL does not preclude developments. Because it is a source that is flexible and changeable, it can evolve over time, and it is possible to change or create new CIL to meet the developing needs of nations.

VI. Transformation: Modified Universalism Becoming CIL

A. Evidence of a General Practice Accepted as Law

Modified universalist approaches are already widespread in practice. Modified universalism seems to have generally guided the key existing frameworks for cross-border insolvency. These frameworks, in particular the Model Law, have been applied quite successfully by participating countries.[128] This practice is also not confined to a few specific jurisdictions, although it is undoubtedly more paramount in certain countries and regions. It is also not limited to specific entities, though a modified universalist practice is less established

---

[128.] See Irit Mevorach, On the Road to Universalism: A Comparative and Empirical Study of the UNCITRAL Model Law on Cross-Border Insolvency, 12 Eur. Bus. Org. L. Rev. 517, 550 (2011) (showing that the Model Law has been implemented and applied by countries in quite a universalist manner); see also Jay L. Westbrook, An Empirical Study of the Implementation in the United States of the Model Law on Cross Border Insolvency, 87 Am. Bankr. L.J. 247, 268 (2013) (showing the success of the Model Law's application in the United States).

with regard to multinational enterprise groups and financial institutions.[129] The usage of cross-border insolvency protocols and the increased cooperation between courts and between insolvency representatives in cross-border insolvencies are also demonstrations of a modified universalist practice.[130]

Yet for modified universalism to finally transform from an emerging to an established CIL, it is crucial that its application by relevant actors is generally pervasive and consistent. Hesitancy, contradiction, or fluctuation in invoking and applying the norm can undermine and ultimately negate the identification of CIL. Furthermore, the norm should be accepted as law. Thus, CIL might be disproved where it can be shown that participants who followed modified universalism were not motivated by a legal duty and acted in the belief that their acts amount to customary law. It has been argued, for example, regarding the concept of international comity, that "[a]t best, it is only incidental that some civil-law systems arrive at results comparable to the decisions of U.S. courts."[131] Regarding cross-border insolvency, it can be argued that because decisions

---

[129.] See, e.g., Mevorach, supra note 10, at 184 (noting that the Model Law does not specifically address international financial institutions); see also Barbara C. Matthews, Prospects for Coordination and Competition in Global Finance, 104 Am. Soc'y Int'l L. Proc. 289, 291–92 (2010) (identifying some convergence of key rules pertaining to the resolution of banks that may amount to CIL but also noting the gap in the cross-border resolution system).

[130.] It was already suggested in the 1990s that cross-border insolvency Concordats and cross-border insolvency agreements, which aim to create close cooperation and the centralization of the process in a lead forum, are likely to become evidence of an international customary norm. David H. Culmer, The Cross-Border Insolvency Concordat and Customary International Law: Is It Ripe Yet? 14 Conn. J. Int'l L. 563, 564 (1999); see also Gaa, supra note 93, at 882 (asking whether developments in the area should continue by way of the evolving international common law of bankruptcy or whether states should take the initiative to negotiate treaties identifying the applicable law).

[131.] Joel R. Paul, Comity in International Law, 32 Harv. Int'l L.J. 1, 35 (1991). Comity may be described as "the deference of one nation to the legislative, executive, and judicial acts of another—not as an obligation, but as a courtesy serving international duty and convenience." David Farmer, chapter 15: Ancillary and Other Cross-Border Cases, 18 Haw. Bar J., Oct. 2015, at 14, 16.

or actions taken in this field are often either not explicitly based on modified universalism or are based on modified universalism as a broad approach linked to independent domestic common law developments,[132] its usage is in fact a demonstration of a tradition— but not of CIL.

To establish modified universalism as autonomous CIL and make the identification of CIL more plausible, clear pronouncements are needed that can show a consistent acceptance of modified universalism and the application of the norm in accordance with international law. Of primary importance is how countries address cross-border insolvency, especially influential countries (including emerging cross-border insolvency "hubs"[133]) that are more often affected by the norm and have the chance to interact with other state-actors and shape the norm in the process. State-actors' actions matter also when they proclaim intentions and act in international fora, including when deliberating on international instruments or other mechanisms in the form of hard or soft law, as such actions can demonstrate a crystallization of CIL. Existing international frameworks for cross-border insolvency have been somewhat obscure regarding the approach they are following,[134] and thus there is room

---

[132.] See, for example, the restrictive application of modified universalism by the U.K. Supreme Court in *Rubin v. Eurofinance SA* [2012] UKSC 46 [16], [2013] 1 AC 236 (appeal taken from Eng.) ("[T]here has been a trend, but only a trend, to what is called universalism. . . ."), and the Court's narrow interpretation in *Hooley Ltd. v. Victoria Jute Co.* [2016] CSOH 141 [36] (Scot.) (holding that the Scottish court would refuse to defer to India's insolvency process).

[133.] Notably, Singapore is "a key hub for cross-border restructuring and insolvency." Kannan Ramesh, Jud. Comm'r, Sup. Ct. of Sing., Speech at the INSOL International Group of 36 Meeting: The Cross-Border Project—A "Dual-Track" Approach 10 (Nov. 30, 2015), www.supremecourt.gov.sg/Data/Editor/Documents/In-sol%2036_Speech_khb_upload%20 version.pdf [https://perma.cc/ZZL4-KCT9].

[134.] For example, the preamble to the Model Law states that its purpose is to "provide effective mechanisms for dealing with cases of cross-border insolvency," but there is no specific reference to modified universalism, namely to a regime that aims to provide a global approach to multinational default, modified to fit business structures. U.N. Comm'n on Int'l Trade Law, UNCITRAL Model Law on Cross-Border Insolvency with Guide to Enactment and Interpretation, U.N. Sales No. E.14.V.2 (2014).

for clearer pronunciations in instruments of the universal application of modified universalism, intended for general adherence.

How the key players of cross-border insolvency (bankruptcy courts and other implementing institutions, especially in countries most influential in this field) refer to and apply norms of modified universalism is also crucial and could matter beyond the creation of precedent within the jurisdiction, as it can influence and form CIL. Such actors when reaching decisions in line with modified universalism could proclaim the intention of following its prescribed solutions more explicitly and as a matter of obligation. Especially where provisions in instruments are insufficient to address all aspects of a given issue or where the country is not a party to an international framework, modified universalism norms become most relevant. In such cases, instead of, for example, solely relying on inherent discretionary powers in the legal system to assist foreign courts, or grounding decisions on notions such as comity that are often vague and confined to specific countries,[135] courts could explicitly refer to modified universalism as the guiding international law and, in the process, establish the acceptance of modified universalism as CIL.

At various times, American courts have reached universalist decisions based primarily on the Model Law, but also on the principle of international comity enshrined in chapter 15 of the Bankruptcy Code (the American version of the Model Law). In the case of *In re Daebo*,[136] for example, the bankruptcy judge, referring also to *In re Atlas Shipping A/S*,[137] noted that "chapter 15 'contemplates that the court should be guided by principles of comity and cooperation with foreign courts in deciding whether to grant the foreign

---

[135.] See Kevin J. Beckering, United States Cross-Border Corporate Insolvency: The Impact of chapter 15 on Comity and the New Legal Environment, 14 Law & Bus. Rev. Am. 281, 281 (2008) (describing comity as an "impediment" to attaining unification in the area of cross-border insolvency); John J. Chung, In re Qimonda AG: The Conflict Between Comity and the Public Policy Exception in chapter 15 of the Bankruptcy Code, 32 B.U. Int'l L.J. 89, 96, 104 (2014) (describing comity as an "amorphous concept" that courts have struggled to define).

[136.] In re Daebo Int'l Shipping Co., 543 B.R. 47 (Bankr. S.D.N.Y. 2015).

[137.] 404 B.R. 726 (Bankr. S.D.N.Y. 2009).

representative additional post-recognition relief.'"[138] Relying on the comity principle, the court then granted certain relief to the foreign Korean rehabilitation proceedings and vacated attachments pursuant to the Korean stay of actions concerning the company's assets. This decision was in line with modified universalism norms regarding recognition, cooperation, and relief, yet modified universalism was not mentioned explicitly as the applicable norm.

In future cases of this kind, judges could, in addition to applying domestic concepts of international comity, and especially where technical statutory rules require reinforcement or a separate justificatory force, refer explicitly to modified universalist norms that require uniform adherence, thus contributing to the transformation of them into CIL. The fact that powerful nations such as the United States have adopted international instruments, especially the Model Law, should not be a factor working against modified universalism becoming CIL; rather, this development should be a catalyst for making the norms that such instruments pursue more widespread. The inclination could be to just rely on provisions of instruments as adopted locally and refrain from considering norms beyond the instruments,[139] thus impeding the use of modified universalism as an international norm. Yet by appreciating the role of key actors as creators of international law and the potential of modified universalism to become universal, international law that transcends local differences can help overcome such tendencies.

Decisions of international tribunals could contribute to entrenching modified universalism as CIL as well, if they pronounce modified universalism norms more explicitly. In a case that reached the Court of Justice of the European Union (CJEU), *MG Probud Gdynia*,[140] for example, it was not clear whether the German authorities could order

---

[138.] In re Daebo, 543 B.R. at 53 (quoting In re Atlas, 404 B.R. at 738). Chapter 15 of the U.S. Bankruptcy Code refers to the principle of comity in section 1507(b) and 1509.

[139.] See, e.g., In re Bear Stearns High-Grade Structured Credit, 374 B.R. 122, 132 (Bankr. S.D.N.Y. 2007), aff'd, 389 B.R. 325 (S.D.N.Y. 2008) (holding that there is no residual common law discretion under chapter 15).

[140.] Case C-444/07, 2010 E.C.R. I-0417.

enforcement measures regarding assets of the company situated in Germany (where a Polish company had a branch), in circumstances where the main proceedings were taking place in Poland.[141] The CJEU concluded that the German authorities erred in their attempt to impose such local enforcement measures.[142] The court noted the universality of the main Polish proceedings based on the provisions of the EIR.[143] It further stated, also citing *Eurofood*,[144] that pursuant to the EIR provisions and recitals, proceedings opened in a member state must be recognized and be given effect in all other member states.[145] This rule, the court explained, "is based on the principle of mutual trust."[146] Mutual trust is certainly a core notion that facilitated the establishment of the compulsory cross-border insolvency system within the EU.[147] The premise of mutual trust in the administration of justice in the EU requires giving full faith and credit to courts of other member states.[148] Like comity, however, mutual trust is a vague concept,[149] and its justificatory force is limited.[150] It is also confined in the EIR context to relationships between states within the region.[151] Conversely, a reference to modified universalism could

---

[141.] *Id.* at 16–20.

[142.] *Id.* at 44.

[143.] *Id.* at 43.

[144.] Case C-341/04, 2006 E.C.R. I-3813.

[145.] Case C-444/07, MG Probud Gdynia, 2010 E.C.R. I-0417, 27 (citing Case C-341/04, Eurofood IFSC Ltd., 2006 E.C.R. I-3813).

[146.] *Id.*

[147.] Regulation 2015/848, of the European Parliament and of the Council of May 20, 2015, on Insolvency Proceedings, 2015 O.J. (L 141) 19, 26 (EU) ("The recognition of judgments delivered by the courts of the Member States should be based on the principle of mutual trust."); Case C-444/07, MG Probud Gdynia, 2010 E.C.R. I-0417, 28; Case C-341/04, Eurofood IFSC Ltd., 2006 E.C.R. I-3813, 39.

[148.] See also Matthias Weller, Mutual Trust: In Search of the Future of European Union Private International Law, 11 J. of Priv. Int'l L. 64, 68 (2015) (referring to mutual trust as a "rather opaque, yet almost omnipresent buzzword . . .").

[149.] Wessels, supra note 89, at 46.

[150.] Weller, supra note 148, at 101 ("The justificatory force of mutual trust is limited. Using mutual trust as legal fiction does not work, at least not beyond the point reached in the system.").

[151.] See Christoph G. Paulus, The ECJ's Understanding of the Universality Principle, 27 Insolvency Intelligence 70, 71 (2014) ("[T]he European legislator's power

both provide concrete justification for the decision to require that full effect be given to the foreign main proceedings and contribute to the transformation of modified universalism to CIL.

The transformation of modified universalism to CIL may not take too long in view of the already existing widespread practice in this direction and the extensive traction that norms of modified universalism have gained in recent years. What is required is not taking a big leap to pure universalism but settling on the norms of modified universalism. Certainly, to develop the norms into CIL requires that countries and implementing institutions have opportunities to interact. Yet cross-border insolvency cases are not a rare phenomenon. Changes in political powers and shifts of economic centers also mean that country interaction is likely to spread more, creating a critical mass and concentration of activity conducive to CIL. It is important to note, however, the evolutionary nature of CIL and hence the fact that the work on its transformation and further development is a process: "The customary process is in fact a continuous one, which does not stop when the rule has emerged. . . . Even after the rule has 'emerged,' every act of compliance will strengthen it, and every violation, if acquiesced in, will help to undermine it."[152] Furthermore, the notion of elevating modified universalism to the status of CIL should not be understood as a replacement of international negotiations and deliberations that attempt to improve the written instruments.[153] To the contrary, creating and guarding modified uni-

---

to regulate issues of insolvency is confined to membership relationships within the EU. . . .").

[152] Maurice H. Mendelson, The Formation of Customary International Law, in 272 Recueil des Cours: Collected Courses of The Hague Academy of International Law 155, 175 (1998).

[153] For example, see the ongoing deliberations of UNCITRAL Working Group V on the design of model laws on recognition and enforcement of insolvency-related judgments and on the cross-border insolvency of multinational enterprise groups. U.N. Comm'n on Int'l Trade Law, Rep. of Working Group V (Insolvency Law) on the Work of Its Fifty-Second Session, U.N. Doc. A/CN.9/931 (Jan. 15, 2018), www.uncitral.org/uncitral/en/commission/working_groups/5Insolvency.html [https://perma.cc/B43H-K2VZ].

versalism as an international custom should facilitate such negotiations because of the behavioral force of CIL and its ability to shift the reference point of actors regarding universalism. Vice versa, the development of regional and international frameworks can further define and develop the CIL rules.

B. Use of CIL in Future Cross-Border Insolvencies

Modified universalism established as CIL can promote a wider coverage and a more consistent application of the norms. As noted earlier, there are still important gaps in the cross-border insolvency system, including participation in the main international framework for cross-border insolvency (the Model Law) and the entities and issues covered by international instruments.[154] Modified universalism, standing on its own two feet, emerging as CIL, can assist in closing such gaps in the complex international system.[155] The pervasiveness of CIL as an international legal source is an important advantage where modified universalism requires universality and full coverage of the market (market symmetry[156]). Once CIL has become prevalent, countries are bound by it regardless of whether they have codified the laws domestically or through treaties unless they have actively objected to it. Thus, while more action through the recognition of the international role of cross-border insolvency is important, it is enough that modified universalism is practiced generally and especially by influential economies and transnational actors. Countries (and their implementing institutions) that are more averse to change will still become party to a system based on modified universalism.

[154.] See supra note 10 and accompanying text.

[155.] Cf. Guzman, supra note 17, at 119 n.17 (explaining that, even though bilateral treaties dominate the foreign investments legal regime, many investments are not covered by these treaties, yet the legal rules included in the treaties seem to have become CIL and, therefore, are generally more universally binding).

[156.] See Westbrook, supra note 2, at 2283 (explaining the importance of market symmetry—the idea that bankruptcy systems in a legal regime cover all transactions and stakeholders within that market—to cross-border insolvency).

In practical terms, this means, for example, that in future cases involving countries that have not (1) taken action to adopt the Model Law, (2) ensured that the Model Law, where enacted, actually becomes effective in the jurisdiction, (3) become a party to any other international instrument that follow modified universalism, or (4) enacted rules that otherwise facilitate global collective insolvencies, such countries will still be expected to follow modified universalism. It will also be possible to rely on uniform norms of cross-border insolvency rather than invoke domestic mechanisms when, for example, recognition, relief, or assistance is sought in a foreign jurisdiction. Such norms may be invoked by foreign actors[157] in the court or other body presiding over the process. If the norms are rejected by the relevant institution, the rejection may be regarded as a breach of international law. Provisions in international instruments, too, would apply to countries not party to the framework to the extent that the framework reflects the rules of CIL. Thus, even where a framework does not bind certain countries, its provisions may form part of the global legal order of insolvency.

The use of CIL can overcome outdated notions of comity and reciprocity and equalize the treatment of foreign proceedings and the approach to foreign requests—for example, in a country such as South Africa, which has adopted the Model Law but has not given effect to its provisions.[158] CIL can also assist when taking actions in

---

[157] Foreign actors may be state as well as non-state actors. Indeed, both may be subject to the rights and obligations of international law as the scope of international law has been expanded. Specifically, CIL is increasingly invoked by non-state actors. For a discussion of the increasing role of non-state actors in the realm of international law, see Anthea Roberts & Sandesh Sivakumaran, Lawmaking by Non-state Actors: Engaging Armed Groups in the Creation of International Humanitarian Law, 37 Yale J. Int'l L. 107, 112–25 (2012).

[158] South Africa included a reciprocity condition requiring it to designate relevant countries that could invoke the Model Law's provisions, yet such designation never took place. Cross-Border Insolvency Act 42 of 2000 section 2 (S. Afr.); see also R. H. Zulman, Cross-Border Insolvency in South African Law, 21 S. Afr. Mercantile L.J. 804, 816–17 (2009) (noting that comity and reciprocity enshrined in the South African version of the Model Law are outmoded and not in conformity with modern thinking on the subject).

cross-border insolvencies in countries such as China, which has not adopted the Model Law. Recognition and enforcement in China of foreign insolvency proceedings are conditioned on the existence of a relevant international treaty, in addition to other requirements such as that the insolvency proceeding shall not jeopardize the sovereignty and security of the state or public interests.[159] This specific domestic cross-border insolvency regime that was introduced in China in 2006 was still an obstacle to the smooth administration of cross-border insolvencies. For example, in litigation in the context of the cross-border insolvency of Lehman Brothers, a Chinese court considered that proceedings opened in the UK should not be given effect in China (with regard to property situated in China) because of a lack of reciprocity, as China did not have a relevant arrangement with the UK.[160] Going forward, where modified universalism is applied as CIL, foreign insolvency representatives should be able to invoke it and attempt recognition and enforcement to promote a collective global approach in the foreign main forum, including in such circumstances where the relevant country is not a party to uniform frameworks and so long as it is not a persistent objector to the CIL regime.

As aforementioned, CIL also plays a role regulating within the gaps of treaties or other instruments. For example, based on modified universalism's norm of cooperation, courts and other authorities would have the authority and the duty to cooperate and communicate, including where the debtor is an entity that is not explicitly

---

[159] Zhong hua ren min gong he guo qi ye po chan fa (中华人民共和国企业破产法) [Enterprise Bankruptcy Law of the People's Republic of China] (promulgated by the Standing Comm. Nat'l People's Cong., Aug. 27, 2006, effective June 1, 2007), art. 5.

[160] Xinyi Gong, To Recognise or Not To Recognise? Comparative Study of Lehman Brothers Cases in Mainland China and Taiwan, 10 Int'l Corp. Rescue 240, 241 (2013). The court reached this conclusion even though the U.K. has adopted the Model Law and therefore would be required to recognize foreign insolvencies pursuant to the terms of the instrument. See id. at 242 (asserting that Article 5 of the Enterprise Bankruptcy Law grants outbound universal effect to insolvency proceedings initiated in China and that this might be recognized in the U.K. pursuant to the Model Law, which does not condition recognition by reciprocity).

covered under existing instruments. The case of *Lehman Brothers*[161] is illustrative. In this case, cooperation was achieved because of the participants' initiative and voluntary will, yet this cooperation was constrained.[162] The enterprise type and structure (i.e., the fact that Lehman Brothers was a multinational financial institution/enterprise group) resulted in aspects of the case falling outside the scope of existing instruments.[163] Where modified universalism is recognized as CIL, cooperation would become a universal legal requirement, including for the purpose of reaching efficient centralized solutions for more complicated enterprise structures.[164]

As modified universalism established as CIL is flexible enough to accommodate changing conditions, it can also be invoked regarding newer types of processes and procedures that may not be covered in written instruments. The shift in the focus of insolvency procedures from formal liquidations to rescue-oriented and various informal processes, including in the time approaching insolvency where there is likelihood of insolvency or financial difficulties, is an example of such changes in the practice of insolvency that instruments

---

[161.] In re Lehman Bros. Int'l (Eur.) [2011] EWHC (Ch) 2022, [2011] All ER 273 (Eng.).

[162.] See Paul L. Davies, Resolution of Cross-Border Groups, in Research Handbook on Crisis Management in the Banking Sector 261, 263–64 (Matthias Haentjens & Bob Wessels eds., 2015) (discussing how both the U.S. and the U.K. took unilateral action in the bailouts of non-national entities, including Lehman Brothers, in order to protect national interests); James M. Peck, Cross-Border Observations Derived from My Lehman Judicial Experience, 30 Butterworths J. Int'l Banking & Fin. L. 131, 132 (2015) (explaining that cross-border conflicts and self-interested behaviors in the context of the Lehman insolvencies were unavoidable).

[163.] Mevorach, supra note 10, at 191 (explaining that the general cross-border Model Law for insolvency lacked sufficient measures to address the Lehman insolvency and that no specific cross-border framework exists for international financial institutions).

[164.] Since the fall of Lehman Brothers, UNCITRAL has been developing model provisions concerning enterprise groups (deliberations were ongoing at the time this chapter went to print). U.N. Comm'n on Int'l Trade Law, Working Group V (Insolvency Law), Facilitating the Cross-Border Insolvency of Multinational Enterprise Groups: Draft Legislative Provisions, U.N. Doc. A/CN.9/WG/V/WP.158 (Feb. 26, 2018). Thus, going forward, CIL may address gaps in the new regime including in terms of its universal application pending wide enactment by countries.

may be slow to capture.[165] However, modified universalism norms can be invoked regarding interim, out-of-court, or pre-insolvency procedures even where they are not covered within the scope of cross-border domestic laws or international instruments. An example of such an approach is the decision of the Singapore court in the *Gulf Pacific Shipping* case.[166] In this case, the court, based on "internationalist concerns," decided to recognize the appointment of liquidators over Hong Kong shipping company Gulf Pacific and grant the requested assistance, despite the debtor being in out-of-court proceedings regarding which the domestic powers of assistance were constrained.[167]

Furthermore, to the extent that CIL does not contradict special treaty law, it can override conflicting laws in civil law countries and will be considered part and parcel of the public policy in common law jurisdictions where legislation is to be construed in a manner that would avoid a conflict with the international norm. Thus, modified universalism understood as CIL can provide the separate, *sui generis* basis and justification for the uniform private international laws based on global collectivity. Any ordinary domestic private international laws could sit alongside the cross-border insolvency CIL regime rather than be considered in conflict with it in the given circumstances. Thus, in future cases with circumstances of the type arising, for example, in *Rubin*—where the existing cross-border insolvency instrument might not provide a clear answer (in that case, regarding the question of enforcement of insolvency-related

---

[165.] See, e.g., Proposal for a Directive of the European Parliament and of the Council on Preventive Restructuring Frameworks, Second Chance and Measures to Increase the Efficiency of Restructuring, Insolvency and Discharge Procedures and Amending Directive 2012/30/EU, at 28, COM (2016) 723 final (Nov. 22, 2016) (attempting to harmonize aspects related to preventive restructuring proceedings in EU member states).

[166.] [2016] SGHC 287 at [6] [(HC, S'pore)] (unreported) (recognizing the foreign proceedings and allowing the liquidators to obtain information regarding a closed bank account of the company).

[167.] *Id.* at [10].

judgments of the main insolvency forum)[168]—the foreign insolvency representative would be able to rely on modified universalism as an international norm.[169] Such an outcome was unattainable in the *Rubin* case, and the request to enforce the judgment of the central foreign court was denied because modified universalism was applied as a general principle of common law subject to the domestic private international law regime.[170] In other circumstances, courts may be asked, for example, to give full effect to a foreign stay on actions concerning the assets of the enterprise, instead of (as happened in *Pan Ocean*[171]) apply domestic *ipso facto* rules that allow them to terminate contracts, thus undermining the collectivity of the cross-border insolvency process.[172] Similarly, courts could be asked to recognize transactions already approved by foreign main reorganization proceedings, instead of (as happened, e.g., in *Elpida*[173]) applying the domestic rules concerning asset sales.[174] The application of the domestic rule can undeniably delay the process, as well as provide local creditors an unjustified chance to challenge the sale, undermining the norm of a global, nondiscriminatory approach prescribed by modified universalism.

[168.] *Rubin v. Eurofinance SA* [2012] UKSC 46 [91], [2013] 1 AC 236 (appeal taken from Eng.).

[169.] Since Rubin, UNCITRAL has been developing a model law on the enforcement of insolvency-related judgments (deliberations were ongoing at the time this chapter went to print). U.N. Comm'n on Int'l Trade Law, Rep. on the Work of Working Group V (Insolvency Law) on its Fifty-Second Session, U.N. Doc. A/CN.9/931, Annex, Draft Model Law on Cross-Border Recognition and Enforcement of Insolvency-Related Judgments at 16 (Jan. 15, 2018); U.N. Comm'n on Int'l Trade Law, Working Group V (Insolvency Law), Recognition and Enforcement of Insolvency-Related Judgments: Draft Model Law, U.N. Doc. A/CN.9/WG/V/WP.156 (Feb. 19, 2018). Thus, going forward, CIL may assist in closing gaps in the new regime, including in terms of its universal application pending wide enactment by countries.

[170.] *Rubin v. Eurofinance SA* [2012] UKSC 46 [177], [2013] 1 AC 236 (appeal taken from Eng.).

[171.] *Pan Ocean Co. v. Fibria Celulose S/A* [2014] EWHC (Civ) 2124, [2014] All ER 03 (Eng.).

[172.] *Id.*

[173.] In re Elpida Memory, Inc., No. 12-10947, 2012 WL 6090194 (Bankr. D. Del. Nov. 16, 2012).

[174.] *Id.* at *8-9.

Modified universalism based on CIL could also serve to influence international instruments. It could reinforce technical rules where the instrument refers to the rules of CIL. Currently, requirements in cross-border insolvency frameworks, for example, cooperation "to the maximum extent possible,"[175] could be understood in different ways. They could be interpreted in a universalist manner, suggesting obligatory cooperation to achieve universality within the parameters of modified universalism. Yet they could also be understood as suggesting cooperative territorialism, namely self-serving cooperation, that promotes local interests in the case at hand while still allowing, for example, ring-fencing of assets if that appears to be in the interests of national stakeholders. The lack of clear statements concerning the level of universalism that should be followed also renders proclamations of objectives—such as effectiveness, efficiency, or fairness, stated as the aims of cross-border insolvency systems[176]—open to interpretation and variation in the cross-border context. Thus, fairness and efficiency may be viewed from a vested-rights, territorial perspective or from a global, universalist perspective. Going forward, CIL can be used to ensure a consistent application of objectives and requirements enshrined in frameworks in line with modified universalism. Modified universalism based on CIL can also provide specific substance to requirements to interpret instruments by having regard to their "international origin."[177]

[175.] U.N. Comm'n on Int'l Trade L., UNCITRAL Model Law on Cross-Border Insolvency with Guide to Enactment and Interpretation 13, U.N. Sales No. E.14.V.2 (2014).

[176.] *Id.* at 3. The Model Law on Cross-Border Insolvency promotes several objectives:
Cooperation between the courts and other competent authorities of this State and foreign States involved in cases of cross-border insolvency; [g]reater legal certainty for trade and investment; [f]air and efficient administration of cross-border insolvencies that protects the interests of all creditors and other interested persons, including the debtor; [p]rotection and maximization of the value of the debtor's assets; and [f]acilitation of the rescue of financially troubled businesses, thereby protecting investment and preserving employment.
Id.

[177.] See, e.g., *id.* at 5 ("[R]egard is to be had to [this law's] international origin and to the need to promote uniformity in its application and the observance of good faith."); see also Jay L. Westbrook, Interpretation Internationale, 87 Temp. L. Rev. 739, 750–51 (2015) (arguing that "system" texts that establish an international framework require an international rather than an insular interpretation).

VII. Conclusion

Lessons from international law, as well as insights from cognitive psychology of decision-making, highlight the advantages that can be gained from modified universalism conceptualized and formed as CIL. Modified universalism recognized as CIL could fill gaps and promote consistency in the application of regional and international frameworks. Furthermore, a modified universalist CIL can assist in the areas where biases impede movement to more optimal solutions. If the rules of modified universalism are generally conceived as CIL, modified universalism will be the default universal rule, embraced as an opt-out regime, and adherence to it would not require positive action from all participants. Such use of legislative framing can affect the consequences of inaction and can result in higher participation, with greater universality and integrity, in the application of modified universalism. In this respect, it is important that the role of cross-border insolvency is reinforced. Indeed, as a private international law system, it has international objectives to pursue. Private international law generally is increasingly being reunited with the international law system, and its role is augmenting. The international nature of cross-border insolvency and the fact that insolvency addresses both private and public interests further justify the solidification of its international role. Thus, cross-border insolvency law should engage in international norm creation and, in that regard, could rely on modified universalism where it provides concrete and practical rules that can be followed consistently. Key actors, importantly courts and other authorities presiding over cross-border insolvency cases—as well as regulators, policymakers, and international organizations engaged in international insolvency lawmaking—should be less context-dependent and should perceive their roles more broadly, considering public international law sources and mechanisms for creating and enhancing international obligations.

Insolvency Law as Credit Enhancement and Enforcement Mechanism

A Closer Look at Global Modernization of Secured Transactions Laws

Charles W. Mooney Jr.[*]

I. Introduction and Background

In a 2004 article[1] (*Credit Enhancement*) I explained how the insolvency-related provisions of the Cape Town Convention (CTC) and its Protocol on aircraft equipment (Aircraft Protocol)[2] could provide important and effective credit enhancement

[*] Charles A. Heimbold, Jr. Professor of Law, University of Pennsylvania Law School. Thanks to Marek Dubovec for valuable comments on an earlier draft of this work. Reproduced with permission from Norton Journal of Bankruptcy Law and Practice, Vol. 27 No. 5 (Oct. 2018), with permission of Thomson Reuters. Copyright © 2018. Further use without the permission of Thomson Reuters is prohibited. For further information about this publication, please visit https://legal.thomsonreuters.com/en/products/law-books or call 800.328.9352.

[1] Charles W. Mooney, Jr., Insolvency Law as Credit Enhancement: Insolvency-Related Provisions of the Cape Town Convention and the Aircraft Equipment Protocol, 13 Int'l Insolvency Rev. 27, 34–39 (2004) [hereinafter, Mooney, Credit Enhancement].

[2] Convention on International Interests in Mobile Equipment 2001, 2307 UNTS 285 (CTC); Protocol to the Convention on International Interests in Mobile Equipment on Matters Specific to Aircraft Equipment 2001, 2367 UNTS 517 (Aircraft Protocol).

for secured financing of commercial aircraft. The article argued that the principal effects of these provisions would occur *outside* bankruptcy as a result of the facilitation of otherwise unavailable financing or reductions in the costs of financing and *not* through their operation in actual insolvency proceedings.[3] In the years since publication of that article much water has flowed under the proverbial bridge in the important and related domains of global reforms of insolvency laws and secured transactions laws.[4] This brief chapter revisits the relationship between insolvency law and secured credit. Taking into account earlier work—my own and that of others—relating to secured transactions law reforms and the role and social benefits of secured credit, it suggests that more nuanced and complex relationships mandate a more holistic approach toward law reforms in the areas of secured transactions and insolvency laws. An overarching theme is that in any given jurisdiction merely enacting modern, sensible secured

---

[3.] Mooney, Credit Enhancement, 13 Int'l Insolvency Rev. at 39–42. For a consideration of more general ex ante effects, see Robert K. Rasumssen, The Ex Ante Effects of Bankruptcy Reform on Investment Incentives, 72 Wash. U. L.Q. 1159, 1163 ("Ex post efficiency involving the relatively few firms that file for bankruptcy should not come at the expense of ex ante inefficiency for all firms in the economy.").

[4.] For example, a substantial literature has emerged that is highly critical of the so-called "safe-harbors" for financial contracts. See, e.g., Stephen J. Lubben, Derivatives and Bankruptcy: The Flawed Case for Special Treatment, 12 U. Pa. J. Bus. L. 61 (2009); Mark J. Roe, The Derivatives Market's Payment Priorities as Financial Crisis Accelerator, 63 Stan. L. Rev. 539 (2011); David A. Skeel, Jr. & Thomas H. Jackson, Transaction Consistency and the New Finance in Bankruptcy, 112 Colum. L. Rev. 152 (2012); Richard Squire, Shareholder Opportunism in a World of Risky Debt, 123 Harv. L. Rev. 1151 (2010); Michael H. Weiss, Using Derivatives to Create Bankruptcy Proof Loans, 30 Cal. Bankr. J. 207 (2010). I have been critical as well of the overbreadth of the United States safe harbors, while recognizing the utility of safe harbors of an appropriate scope. Charles W. Mooney, Jr., The Bankruptcy Code's Safe Harbors for Settlement Payments and Securities Contracts: When is Safe Too Safe? 49 Texas Int'l L.J. 245 (2014). Yet most of the critiques emphasize the detrimental role of the safe harbors in the run-up to insolvency proceedings or in a financial crisis environment. For an evaluation that focuses on their global operation and laudable effects on liquidity, see Philipp Paech, The Value of Financial Market Insolvency Safe Harbours, 36 Oxford J. L. Stud. 855 (2016). For a rebuttal of Paech, see Riz Mokal, Liquidity, Systemic Risk, and the Bankruptcy Treatment of Financial Contracts, 10 Brook. J. Corp., Fin. & Com. L. 15, 58–68 (2015).

transactions laws and insolvency laws may be insufficient to produce the intended benefits from either set of laws.[5]

The chapter's focus is particularly appropriate for honoring Jay Westbrook in recognition of his many contributions to scholarship and law reform[6] and as an acknowledgement his catholic interests and pursuits. Among many other contributions, Jay has provided insight and wisdom for contemplation of the central role of priorities (including avoidance powers) in insolvency law, a sphere in which secured transactions law plays a central role.[7] Over his distinguished career he has devoted much effort and applied his enormous skills toward teaching and scholarship in the areas of insolvency law and secured transactions law. The cohort of legal scholars to which Jay and I belong were taught and inspired by a generation of professionals for whom these two bodies of law were inextricably tied. For these scholars, practitioners, and reformers a central, even dominant, issue in the United States during the mid-twentieth century was the treatment of nonpossessory security interests in insolvency proceedings—principally under the Bankruptcy Act and later the Bankruptcy Code. Uniform Commercial Code (UCC) Article 9 was conceived, created, and implemented under this background

---

[5.] In another project now in progress, I build further on this theme by considering secured transactions law reforms through the lens of Alan Watson's pathbreaking book, Legal Transplants. See Charles W. Mooney, Jr, Lost in Transplantation? UCC Article 9 Principles As Legal Transplants, in Secured Transactions Law in Asia (Louise Gullifer & Dora Neo eds., Hart Publishing, Oxford) (forthcoming 2019) (on file with author) (discussing, inter alia, Alan Watson, Legal Transplants: An Approach to Comparative Law (2nd ed. 1993) (1974)).

[6.] For example, Jay served as the United States Reporter for the American Law Institute's Transnational Insolvency Project and as co-chair of the United States delegation to the United Nations Commission on International Trade Law (UNCITRAL) for international insolvency projects.

[7.] See Jay L. Westbrook, Breaking Away: Local Priorities And Global Assets, 46 Tex. Int'l L.J. 601 (2011); Jay L. Westbrook, Introduction, University of Texas International Insolvency Symposium: The Priority Dilemma, 46 Tex. Int'l L.J. 437 (2011); Jay L. Westbrook, Priority Conflicts as a Barrier to Cooperation in Multinational Insolvencies, 27 Penn. St. Int. L. Rev. 869 (2009); Jay L. Westbrook, Avoidance Of Pre-Bankruptcy Transactions In Multinational Bankruptcy Cases, 42 Tex. Int'l L.J. 899 (2007) [hereinafter, Westbrook, Avoidance].

of bankruptcy law. The work of luminaries such as Grant Gilmore, Homer Kripke, and Peter Coogan, among others, readily comes to mind.[8] Interestingly, this close relationship between the two areas and the corresponding focus in particular of academics is largely a phenomenon centered in North America, where it is commonplace for law teachers to teach both secured transactions law and bankruptcy/debtor-creditor law. In most of the world academics specializing in insolvency law are more likely also to be specialists in civil procedure (which to my mind, of course, also makes much sense[9]).

My observations in these pages also are inspired and informed in part by an ongoing research project consisting of a qualitative empirical study of business credit in Japan—the Japanese Business Credit Project (or JBCP)—involving interviews of representatives of Japanese financial institutions, governmental bodies, and businesses as well as legal professionals such as practitioners and academics.[10] The chapter draws additional inspiration and insight from an invitational conference on the coordination of global reforms of secured transactions laws held in February 2017 (2017 Coordination Conference).[11] That conference brought together individuals representing many of the most important organizations that toil "on the ground" for reforms of secured transactions laws and insolvency laws. Unfortunately, too little of their experience and too few of their insights have found their way into the relevant literature. Given Jay's prominence in the field of empirical legal studies and his important contributions to law

---

[8] See 1 Grant Gilmore, Security Interests in Personal Property at xi (1965) (referring to the important roles played by Kripke and Coogan).

[9] See Charles W. Mooney, Jr., A Normative Theory of Bankruptcy Law: Bankruptcy As (Is) Civil Procedure, 61 Washington & Lee Law Review 931 (2004).

[10] See Part III infra.

[11] The 2017 Coordination Conference was held on February 9–10, 2017, at the University of Pennsylvania Law School, Philadelphia, PA. It was co-sponsored by the International Insolvency Institute (III), the National Law Center for Inter-American Free Trade (NLC), and the Organization for the Harmonization of Business Law in Africa. See Part III infra. A follow-up coordination conference was held in Madrid, October 16–17, 2018, co-sponsored by the III, the NLC, and Universidad Carlos III de Madrid.

reforms, the value of connecting these experiences with the literature is especially appropriate to note in this well-deserved tribute for Jay.

Following this Introduction, Part II of the chapter outlines what I refer to as the "modern principles of secured transactions law" (Modern Principles) that underlie recent and ongoing law reform efforts. It summarizes these reform initiatives and the principal theses and perspectives of both the advocates and critics of the Modern Principles. Part III proceeds on the assumption that the Modern Principles reflect in general a global consensus on the optimal features of secured transactions laws. It provides a synopsis of the discussions at the 2017 Coordination Conference. It also offers an overview of the JBCP and the principal relevant insights that the study has yielded thus far, albeit in tentative fashion given the current stage of the research and analysis. It concludes that the various obstacles and challenges to the implementation of Modern Principles-based secured transactions law reforms are under-studied and under-theorized. It reaches the same conclusion with respect to the relationship between secured transactions law and the relevant influences on a given State's business credit market. It calls for more rigorous investigation and analysis. Part IV considers links between both insolvency law and private international law (i.e., conflict of laws or choice-of-law rules) and secured transactions law. It argues that both bodies of law play roles that are vital to the operation of secured transactions in the business credit markets and that each should feature prominently in the processes of adoption and implementation of secured transactions law reforms. Part VI concludes the chapter.

II. Modern Principles of Secured Transactions Law and Current Reform Efforts

There has emerged a global consensus as to the set of Modern Principles that reflect general principles to which secured transactions law should adhere. The 2016 United Nations Commission on International Trade Law (UNCITRAL) Model Law on Secured Transactions

(Model Law)[12] is the epitome of the Modern Principles. It is a relatively direct descendant of UCC Article 9[13] and the various personal property security acts (PPSAs) adopted by Canadian Provinces[14] (together, sometimes referred to here as North American law). The Modern Principles also are reflected in other model laws,[15] in other secured transactions laws enacted by several States during recent years,[16] and in laws that are currently being considered by other States.[17] While some disagreement

---

[12.] United Nations Commission on International Trade Law (UNCITRAL) Model Law on Secured Transactions (July 1, 2016) [hereinafter, Model Law], www.uncitral. org/pdf/english/texts/security/ML_ST_E_ebook.pdf. The Model Law was inspired by its predecessor, UNCITRAL Legislative Guide on Secured Transactions (2007), www.uncitral.org/pdf/english/texts/security-lg/e/09-82670_Ebook-Guide_09-04-10English.pdf [hereinafter, Legislative Guide]. In July 2017 UNCITRAL approved the Guide to Enactment of the UNCITRAL Model Law on Secured Transactions. UNCITRAL Model Law on Secured Transactions: Guide to Enactment (2017) [hereinafter, GTE], https://uncitral.un.org/sites/uncitral.un.org/files/media-documents/uncitral/en/mlst_guide_to_enactment_e.pdf.

See A/CN.9/914 & Add. 1–6, www.uncitral.org/uncitral/commission/sessions/50th.html.

[13.] Unif. Commercial Code (U.C.C.) Article 9 (Secured Transactions) (Am. Law Inst. & Unif. Law Comm'n 2017).

[14.] See, e.g., Ontario Personal Property Security Act, R.S.O. 1990, c. P. 10 (OPPSA).

[15.] See, e.g., European Bank for Reconstruction and Development, Model Law on Secured Transactions (2004), available at www.ebrd.com/news/publications/guides/model-law-on-secured-transactions.html; Organization of American States, Model Inter-American Law on Secured Transactions, available at www.oas.org/dil/Model_Law_on_Secured_Transactions.pdf.

[16.] For example, Colombia, Ley No.1676 del 20 de Agosto de 2014, Por la Cual se Promueve el Acceso al Créédito y se Dictan Normas sobre Garantíías Mobiliarias; See Mayer Brown, 'Colombia's New Law on Security Interest over Movable Assets Comes into Effect (April 28, 2014) available at www.mayerbrown.com/files/Publication/4868229b-de56-4b53-8669-a55fcfdd728a/Presentation/PublicationAttachment/56e374b9-fab3-467f-b3b1-aa1d67beafbb/Update_New_Regulations_Moveable_Assets_Colombia_0414.pdf; Jordan, Pakistan; E-Mail from Murat Sultanov, Secured Transactions Specialist, World Bank Group, to Charles W. Mooney Jr. (June 18, 2018, 03:01 EDT) (on file with author).

[17.] These states currently include, e.g., Bahrain, Bangladesh, Chile, Paraguay, Sri Lanka, St. Lucia, and Tunisia. E-Mail from Andres F. Martinez, Senior Financial Sector Specialist, World Bank Group, to Charles W. Mooney Jr. (July 1, 2017, 08:34 EDT) (on file with author); E-Mail from Murat Sultanov, Secured Transactions Specialist, World Bank Group, to Charles W. Mooney Jr. (July 1, 2017, 07:41 EDT) (on file with author); E-Mail from Murat Sultanov, Secured Transactions Specialist, World Bank Group, to Charles W. Mooney Jr. (June 18, 2018, 03:01 EDT) (on file with author).

might exist at the margin, I would include in the Modern Principles the following features: (i) public notice as a general condition for third-party effectiveness (perfection), including (x) a grantor identifier-based registry for registration of notices of security interests and (y) recognition of the historical effectiveness of possession of tangible assets; (ii) clear and predictable priority rules to enhance certainty; (iii) provision for effective enforcement of security interests following a debtor-assignor's default; (iv) availability of all types of personal property as collateral, including future assets, securing future obligations; (v) free assignability of receivables; (vi) comprehensive coverage of all forms of security devices; (vii) extension of security interests to the proceeds of collateral; (viii) the general acceptance of freedom of contract for inter-party relations; and (ix) clear private international law (choice-of-law) rules. Other important principles embraced by the Model Law and other modern iterations of secured transactions laws are implicit in and follow as a part of the policy penumbra of these features. The Modern Principles also are embodied in the enormously successful CTC[18] and Aircraft Protocol[19] as well as the other CTC Protocols,[20] although these instruments adopt an object-based registry rather than a grantor identifier-based registry, as contemplated by the Modern Principles.[21]

[18.] CTC, supra note 2.

[19.] Aircraft Protocol, supra note 2.

[20.] Since entering into force on Mar. 1, 2006, the CTC and Aircraft Protocol have been adopted by 73 contracting States and one regional economic integration organization (European Union). UNIDROIT, Status of the Convention on International Interests in Mobile Equipment, www.unidroit.org/status-2001capetown, accessed Jan. 5, 2018). The Protocols covering railway rolling stock and space assets are not yet in force. Luxembourg Protocol to the Convention on International Interests in Mobile Equipment on Matters Specific to Railway Rolling Stock, 2007, 46 ILM 662; Protocol to the Convention on International Interests in Mobile Equipment on Matters Specific to Space Assets (adopted Mar. 9, 2012). A fourth Protocol covering mining, agricultural, and construction equipment is in progress. See UNIDROIT, Report (Nov. 2017), www.unidroit.org/english/documents/2017/study72k/cge02/s-72k-cge02-report-e.pdf.

[21.] CTC, supra note 2, art. 18 (registration requirements).

The "overall objective" of the Model Law and related UNCITRAL texts "is to increase the availability and decrease the cost of credit by providing for an effective and efficient secured transactions law."[22] The same can be said of the CTC and its Protocols.[23] Several studies and overwhelming empirical evidence confirm that the CTC and Aircraft Protocol have fulfilled this objective.[24] While the Aircraft Protocol may be *sui generis* in its strikingly demonstrable effects, the adoption of the UNCITRAL texts under the continued influence of North American law and the ongoing Modern Principles-influenced global reforms demonstrate that at least an important segment of expert opinion subscribes to the general effectiveness of the Modern Principles-based laws. Moreover, the adoption of the Modern principles would offer benefits of a coherent, accessible, and easily understandable legal regime for secured transactions even if it might not result in measurable increases in availability and reductions of costs in a given market.[25]

The apparent credit-enhancing attribute of Modern Principles-based laws does not alone, of course, prove that these laws *generally* promote social welfare. Indeed, for the past several decades an academic debate has ensued in the United States over the merits of affording security interests full priority in the bankruptcy proceeding of a debtor.[26] Critics of priority afforded under modern secured transactions laws and insolvency laws typically have focused on the "efficiency" (or not) of secured credit, with emphasis on the

---

[22.] GTE, supra note 12, ll., para 4.

[23.] Roy Goode, Official Commentary to the Convention on International Interests in Mobile Equipment and Protocol Thereto on Matters Specific to Aircraft Equipment, 2.1, at 13 (3rd ed. 2013).

[24.] Charles W. Mooney, Jr., The Cape Town Convention's Improbable-but-Possible Progeny Part Two: Bilateral Investment Treaty-Like Enforcement Mechanism, 55 Va. J. Int'l L. 451, 454–58 (2015) (summarizing economic studies and CTC Discount, under which debtors located in CTC/Aircraft Protocols can receive substantial discounts on costs of financing).

[25.] See Section IV of this chapter, infra.

[26.] See Thomas H. Jackson & Anthony T. Kronman, Secured Financing and Priorities Among Creditors, 88 Yale L.J. 1143 (1979).

distributional effects of priority afforded security interests over unsecured creditors of debtors that actually become insolvent as well as the inability of some classes of creditors (such as tort creditors and taxing authorities) to adjust to the debtor's creation of senior security interests.[27] The academic debate continues.[28]

This chapter need not review and rehash these debates. Instead, it proceeds on the basis that in the setting of global secured transactions law reforms the Modern Principles reflect the current coin of the realm. Given that, a principal goal here is to draw attention to the challenges and obstacles faced in the adoption and implementation of Modern Principles-based secured transactions laws. Related to that aspiration, it also examines relationships between secured transactions law and the attributes of and influences on markets for business credit. Part III next turns to these tasks by drawing on the 2017 Coordination Conference and the JBCP.

[27.] See, e.g., Lucian Arye Bebchuk & Jesse M. Fried, The Uneasy Case for the Priority of Secured Claims in Bankruptcy, 105 Yale L.J. 857 (1996). For a survey of much of the early literature and a rebuttal, see Steven L. Harris & Charles W. Mooney, Jr., A Property-Based Theory of Security Interests: Taking Debtors' Choices Seriously, 80 Va. L. Rev. 2021 (1994); Steven L. Harris & Charles W. Mooney, Jr., Measuring the Social Costs and Benefits and Identifying the Victims of Subordinating Security Interests in Bankruptcy, 82 Cornell L. Rev. 1349 (1997).

[28.] See, e.g., Barry E. Adler & George Triantis, Debt Priority And Options In Bankruptcy: A Policy Intervention, 91 Am. Bankr. L.J. 563 (2017); Wei Zhang, The Paradoxes of Secured Lending: Is There a Less Uneasy Case for the Priority of Secured Claims in Bankruptcy? 16 U. Pa. J. Bus. L. 789 (2014). Currently work is underway to develop a formal methodology for assessing the economic benefits of commercial law reforms more generally under the auspices of the Commercial Law Center, Harris Manchester College, University of Oxford, and the International Institute for the Unification of Private Law (UNIDROIT) Foundation. See Jenifer Varzaly, The Economic Assessment of International Commercial Law Reform: Best Practice Guidelines (on file with author); see generally Economic Assessment of International Commercial Law Reform, www.law.ox.ac.uk/research-subject-groups/economic-assessment-international-commercial-law-reform. A cost-benefit analysis also is being conducted in connection with the draft MAC Protocol to the CTC. Warwick Economics and Associates, Preliminary Report to UNIDROIT, An Economic Assessment of the Fourth Protocol to the Convention on International Interests on Mobile Equipment on Matters Specific to Agricultural, Construction and Mining Equipment (Oct. 2, 2017), www.unidroit.org/english/documents/2017/study72k/cge02/warwick-economic.pdf.

III. Secured Transactions Laws and Markets for Business Credit: Insights from the 2017 Coordination Conference and the Japanese Business Credit Project

Many of the challenges to adoption and implementation of Modern Principles-based secured transactions laws were considered at the 2017 Coordination Conference, during which several themes emerged.[29] One overarching theme was that enactment by a State of statutory reforms is insufficient of itself for successful implementation of a modern secured transactions law. Another was that global reform efforts would benefit greatly from increased coordination among the various organizations involved with that work. Examples of coordination failures abounded.

In many States modern reforms are resisted by entrenched interests, such as banks with dominant market shares of financing in the business credit markets.[30] It was generally acknowledged that the inability of banks to obtain favorable regulatory capital treatment for loans secured by personal property was a serious impediment to reforms. Resistance also is commonly asserted by legal academics and lawyers who may be troubled, for example, by apparent conflicts between the Modern Principles and existing legal traditions or by perceived potential disruptions of established practices and transactional patterns. Such resistance is typical in the case of many potential law reforms. Of particular interest here, however, are circumstances

---

[29] See note 11, supra. The 2017 Coordination Conference was conducted under the Chatham House Rule: "When a meeting, or part thereof, is held under the Chatham House Rule, participants are free to use the information received, but neither the identity nor the affiliation of the speaker(s), nor that of any other participant, may be revealed." Chatham House, www.chathamhouse.org/about/chatham-house-rule. The brief discussion here is based on my notes taken during the conference.

[30] See, e.g., Summary of Thai Banker Association.. Opinions regarding the Business Security Act in connection with the World Bank's 29 Recommendations and DB Legal Rights Index (summarizing objections to World Bank's recommendations for reforms of secured transactions laws of Thailand) (on file with author).

in which modern reforms may be enacted but are nonetheless ineffective, mentioned next.

Apparently many states have undertaken reforms with the primary goal of improving their rankings in the World Bank Doing Business Survey,[31] even though achieving that goal has not translated into actual improvements in access to credit through secured financings. New laws on the books sometimes sit on shelves, largely unused, because prospective users and beneficiaries lack sufficient understanding. Moreover, the generally poor state of insolvency laws around the world jeopardizes secured transactions law reforms. In some States modern, sophisticated registries have been inadequately utilized because of inadequate training of the registry staff as well as the user base. Difficulties in valuing collateral, especially movables, reflect another typical problem that was discussed. Judicial hostility to enforcement of secured transactions also was identified as a recurring problem.

Several problems associated with implementation of reforms were discussed. For example, some States have received conflicting advice and have enacted secured transactions laws that are not sufficiently compatible with newly adopted insolvency laws. Some advisors present States with very simple, streamlined versions of secured transactions laws that others consider hopelessly incomplete. Other advisors favor more complete statutory approaches that some consider hopelessly complex.

A clear consensus emerged that an important but enormously challenging obstacle to reform is the need for capacity building— stimulation of the capacities of prospective debtors and creditors to usefully and profitably employ secured transactions law reforms. This would include steps such as consultations with and education of the various stakeholders affected by secured transactions laws as well

---

[31] The World Bank, Doing Business, www.doingbusiness.org. States may benefit in general from the perception that a higher ranking indicates an investment friendly economy. A State's leaders also may reap internal political benefits from higher rankings as well.

as cultural shifts in relevant attitudes and social norms.[32] Of course, the foregoing offers only a taste of the discussions. But a common thread appears to be that capacity building in various forms, including fundamental and structural changes in characteristics of credit markets and cultural and legal traditions and norms, are necessary conditions for successful implementation of modern secured transactions laws. Enactment of statutory text, alone, often may be a necessary but insufficient step.

The Legislative Guide, the Model Law, and the Guide to Enactment (GTE) do not adequately address these concerns. Instead, they are devoted almost exclusively to the development and enactment of *statutory text*. One might have thought that the GTE, at least, would take a broader approach, understanding that the nature of the Legislative Guide and Model Law necessarily are statutory-text-oriented. But the GTE also declares a relatively narrow purpose—"to explain briefly the thrust of each provision of the . . . Model Law . . . and its relationship with the corresponding recommendation(s) of the . . . Legislative Guide . . . and other UNCITRAL texts on secured transactions."[33] Although the GTE does state that it "is designed to assist States in implementing the recommendations of" these texts, it limits its assistance largely to the explanatory purpose just mentioned.[34] Currently UNCITRAL's Working Group VI (Security Interests) has begun work on a new text—a "practice guide" for the Model Law (Practice Guide).[35] Like its UNCITRAL forebears, the Practice Guide appears to be directed primarily to users of statutory text based on the Model Law and not toward structural reforms addressing issues unrelated to statutory text. But the Practice Guide project

---

[32] See, e.g., Neil B. Cohen, Capacity Building as a Key Determinant of Success in Secured Transactions Reform, www.uncitral.org/pdf/english/colloquia/4thSec Trans/Presentations/2ContGonST2/COHEN_Colloquium_Presentation.pdf.

[33] GTE, supra note 12, I., para I.

[34] Id., para 4.

[35] Draft Practice Guide to the UNCITRAL Model Law on Secured Transactions: Annotated List of Contents, https://documents-dds-ny.un.org/doc/UNDOC/LTD/V17/071/55/PDF/V1707155.pdf?OpenElement [hereinafter, Practice Guide].

has only just begun and it is encouraging that it contemplates a section devoted to financing micro-business.[36] One hopes that that the
attention to micro-business will extend beyond the mere adoption
and use of statutory text.

The foregoing is not so much a criticism of these UNCITRAL
texts as it is a recognition that the Working Group and UNCITRAL
generally may not be well suited to undertake projects beyond the
more technical, statutory-text-oriented work to date. A more holistic examination of business credit markets and the proper domain of
Modern Principles-based statutory reforms would be welcome. The
JBCP aspires to such an examination.

The JBCP is a research project that I am currently undertaking
with two Japanese scholars.[37] Our goal is an assessment of Japanese markets for private business credit, including the Japanese
laws that govern secured transactions in tangible movables (such
as a firm's inventory or business equipment) and claims (such as a
firm's accounts receivable) to secure extensions of business credit.[38]
Among other aspects of the Japanese business credit market, the
study investigates underlying causes of Japan's failure to embrace
the Modern Principles in its legal framework. It examines Japan's law
on perfection by registration of assignments of movables and claims
(PRAMC)[39] and hypothetical revisions of that Act which would provide a first-to-register priority rule. The JBCP was inspired by some

---

[36.] *Id.*, Part IV.D., at 14–15.

[37.] My co-investigators are Megumi Hara (Professor of Law, Gakushuin University Law School) and Kumiko Koens (Professor, Yamagata University Faculty of
Literature and Social Sciences, Department of Public Policy and Social Studies). Professor Koens and I undertook preliminary work on the project during the summer
of 2016. During this same time-frame Dr. Dubovec and I were organizing the 2017
Coordination Conference.

[38.] See Research Outline, Nov. 24, 2016 (on file with author) [hereinafter, Research
Outline].

[39.] Dōsan oyobi Saiken no Jōto no Taikō Yōken
ni kansuru Minpō no tokurei tō ni kansuru Hōritsu [Act
on Special Provisions, etc., of the Civil Code Concerning the Perfection Requirements for the Assignment of Movables and Claims], Law No. 104 of 1998 as amended
and renamed by Law No. 148 of 2004 (Japan) [hereinafter PRAMC].

puzzling features of the Japanese market and related aspects of Japanese law. Consider that Japan possesses the third largest economy in the world (based on 2017 GDP),[40] is the home of sophisticated financial institutions as well as commercial and industrial firms of every type and size, and has a highly experienced and learned legal profession. Moreover Japan has an excellent track record of modernizing its insolvency laws, reflecting a propensity to learn and borrow from experiences in other States.[41] This background presents some puzzles. For example, why does Japan retain a relatively primitive legal regime for secured transactions and why has it failed to adopt the Modern Principles?[42] Notwithstanding this ostensibly unfriendly legal regime, why is business credit nonetheless apparently readily available in Japan?[43] And why are financings secured by movables (equipment and inventory), claims (receivables), and other personal property collateral such a small fraction of business credit in Japan when compared to the United States?[44]

---

[40] Statistic Times, List of Countries by Projected GDP (April 23, 2017), http://statisticstimes.com/economy/countries-by-projected-gdp.php.

[41] See, e.g., Minji Saisei Hōō [Civil Rehabilitation Act], Law No. 225 of 1999 (Japan) [hereinafter, Civil Rehabilitation Act].

[42] See infra (discussing PRAMC and its interaction with Japanese Civil Code (Minpō)).

[43] See, e.g., Bank of Japan, Financial System Report, Financial Activity Indexes, 30–33 (Oct. 2017), https://nao1.safelinks.protection.outlook.com/?url=http%3A%2F%2Fwww.boj.or.jp%2Fen%2Fresearch%2Fbrp%2Fsr%2Fdata%2Ffsr171023a.pdf&data=01%7C01%7Ccmooney%40law.upenn.edu%7Ccef92b7479b3460e208d08d5574b0b3c%7C6cf568beb84a4e319df6359907586b27%7C1&sdata=Xgnl4m36mm6VwkxD3zhnyw807HA5JGEAYcdOmJae8Xg%3D&reserved=0) (demonstrating "financial institutions' active lending attitude").

[44] For convenience, such asset-based secured financing is referred to here as "ABL." See Ministry of Economy, Trade and Industry, Dōsan/Saiken Jōtotanpo no Genjō to Torikumi no Hōkōōsei, [Current Status and Direction of Efforts on Transfer of Movable Assets/Claims as Collateral] (June 21, 2016) (on file with author) (unsecured credit, 46.6%; personal guaranty supported credit, 34.8%; real property secured credit, 15.6%; shares, bonds promissory notes secured credit, .7%; other property secured credit, 2.5%). While strictly comparable data for the Unites States is not available, the volume of ABL in the United States indicates that it represents a much larger share of business loans. See ABL Advisor, the ABL Advisor Deal Tables, www.abladvisor.com/loan-volume-report ($60 billion of ABL in the United States in 2015); Federal Reserve Bank of

Consider Japan's PRAMC. That law provides for a *sui generis* public-notice registration system for assignments (both outright and for purposes of security) of interests in movables and claims.[45] But this system co-exists with methods of assignment that are effective against third parties under the Japanese Civil Code *without* registration or any other form of effective public notice.[46] For example, an effective title-transfer assignment (jōto tanpo) of a movable may be made effective by the assignor's declaration without any actual delivery of possession of the movable (a so-called "fictitious delivery.")[47] It follows that the interest of a creditor that searches the registry, finds no conflicting registration of an assignment, and registers its own assignment as the first-to-register assignee, would nevertheless be subordinate to an earlier-in-time "secret" assignment made effective under the Civil Code.[48]

Substantial data exists with respect to the characteristics of the sources of business credit in Japan and the business debtors to which

---

St. Louis, Total Value of Loans for All Commercial and Industry Loans, Domestic Banks, spreadsheets available from https://fred.stlouisfed.org/series/EVAXDBNQ ($282.32 billion commercial and industrial loans in 2015).

[45] By providing a national registration system for the assignments of movables and claims, PRAMC is a step in the right direction toward the Modern Principles and an improvement over pre-PRAMC law. But it fails to conform to the Modern Principles in several respects, including with respect to searches of the registry and indications of the property covered by a registration.

[46] Minpōō [Civil Code] art. 183 ("If an agent manifests an intention that The thing possessed by it shall thenceforward be possessed on behalf of its principal, the principal shall thereby acquire possessory rights.")

[47] *Id.*; Souichirou Kozuka & Naoe Fujisawa, Old Ideas Die Hard?: An Analysis of the 2004 Reformation of Secured Transactions Law in Japan and its Impact on Banking Practices, 31 T. Jefferson L. Rev. 293, 306–07 (2009) (discussing predecessor of PRAMC to the same effect).

[48] *Id.* Given these attributes of the Japanese legal framework, it is not surprising that Japan scores only 5 out of 12 on the 2018 World Bank Doing Business Survey (hereinafter, WB DB Survey) "strength of legal rights index under the "Getting Credit" topic. The World Bank, Doing Business, Japan, www.doingbusiness.org/data/exploreeconomies/japan#getting-credit#tokyo. While there is much to criticize about the WB DB Survey, such a critique is beyond the scope of this essay. Japan ranks only 77th out of 190 under "Getting Credit" in the 2018 WB DB Survey. *Id.* However, other evidence indicates that business credit is readily available in Japan. See note 43, supra.

the credit is extended.[49] But these data do not adequately address or explain the puzzle of why the landscape of Japanese business credit and the relevant legal regime has evolved and persists. The JBCP is investigating why the patterns and characteristics of Japanese business credit markets exist, how they have developed, and what are the underlying cultural, political, and legal influences. While we have developed a set of hypotheses to be tested through our research,[50] we approach the project from the perspective of basic research without taking any positions as to the nature of any potential modifications of the Japanese legal regime. The methodology for the JBCP is based on semi-structured interviews supported by analyses of published and unpublished commentary and reports of judicial decisions, empirical analyses of data on business credit markets in Japan and other markets. To date we have conducted more than thirty interviews of commercial bankers, staff of government ministries and regulators, and academics. Although our formal analysis of interview data is only beginning, some preliminary data from our research to date are illustrative.

One preliminary indicative result is that it is likely that ABL in Japan would be quite limited even if the Modern Principles were incorporated into Japanese private law, all other factors being equal. This is consistent with several of our initial hypotheses on which the research has been structured.[51] Reasons for this potential ineffectiveness of secured transactions reforms include lenders' concerns about the reliability of ex ante valuations of recoveries from movables collateral. The relative unlikelihood that a Japanese business firm in financial distress will become subject to a formal insolvency proceeding

---

[49.] See, e.g., Ono, Arito, et al., A New Look at Bank-Firm Relationships and the Use of Collateral in Japan: Evidence from Teikoku Databank Data, in The Economics of Interfirm Networks (T. Watanabe, I. Uesugi &A. Ono eds.) 191–214 (2015).

[50.] See Research Outline, supra note 38, 6–7. Note that consideration of hypothetical revisions of the PRAMC that would provide a first-to-register priority rule provide an analytical medium for exploring in interviews the normative case for modernization of Japanese secured transactions law.

[51.] Id.

in which collateral might be valued and dealt with contributes to these concerns.[52] Another explanation for such potential ineffectiveness is the stigma commonly associated with public registration of assignments. All of these considerations find some support in our preliminary data. One implication of this potential futility of Modern Principles-based reforms it that changes in the structure of the business credit market would be essential for the effectiveness of such reforms. Such changes might be beneficial (development of a robust secondary market for movables, for example) or not (increased incidence of priority conflicts). This reaffirms a theme that emerged from the 2017 Coordination Conference, discussed earlier—merely enacting Modern Principles-based secured transactions laws in any given market may not yield the intended benefits of increased availability of credit at a lower cost. The JBCP seeks to increase understanding of how and under what circumstances Modern Principles-based secured transactions laws could be most effective and to identify the underlying social, cultural, legal, and economic prerequisites for successful implementation of effective secured transactions laws.

Another explanation as to why adoption of the Modern Principles in Japan might not produce beneficial reductions in the cost of credit or increases in the availability of credit is the already existing availability of low-cost credit even in the absence of Modern Principles.[53] For example, preliminary indications are that the observance of business norms in Japan makes conflicting claims to the same

---

[52.] This phenomenon is discussed in Part IV, infra. There are, of course, other reasons for concerns about recoveries that we hypothesize, such as thin secondary markets and wrongful dispositions or removals by debtor firms. *Id.*

[53.] In an extremely low interest rate environment, such as exists in Japan, a material reduction of financing costs is not realistic. See Bank of Japan, Average Contract Interest Rates on Loans and Discounts (Nov. 2017) (Short-term loans: 0.325%, City banks; 1.002%, Regional banks; 1.298%, Regional banks II; 1.955%, Shinkin banks. Long-term loans: 0.965%, City banks; 0.888%, Regional banks; 0.988%, Regional banks II; 1.674%, Shinkin banks.), www.boj.or.jp/en/statistics/dl/loan/yaku/yaku 1711.pdf. But the potential for increasing the availability of business credit in such an environment should remain an important goal. On availability of credit, see notes 43 & 48, supra.

collateral rare, which would potentially mute the effects of adopting a Modern Principles-based first-to-register priority scheme. Even more significant, the prevalence of government guarantees for loans to small and medium sized businesses substantially reduces incentives for lenders to rely on collateral when such guarantees are available.[54]

The foregoing notwithstanding, even if adoption of a Modern Principles-based secured transactions regime would not offer optimal benefits, on balance such adoption would likely provide substantial benefits for the Japanese market (and for other markets). The Modern Principles offer a coherent, user-friendly legal framework for parties wishing to utilize personal property as collateral. There is little to commend legal regimes that are costly, cumbersome, and uncertain, moreover, and irrespective of the magnitude of potential benefits of the adoption of the Modern Principles in Japan, there is value in achieving a better understanding of the potential effects (or lack thereof) of reforming secured transactions laws in Japan and in other markets.

In sum, reform processes would benefit from more rigorous studies of approaches to secured transactions law reforms beyond the mere adoption of statutes and guidance from closely related texts. In addition to academic research projects such as the JBCP, reform efforts also would benefit greatly from a more systematic approach to the use—and memorialization in the literature—of experiences and lessons learned from work of individuals and organizations "on the ground" in the process of implementing reforms.

---

[54] For example, in the sample of borrowers that were the subject of one important study, of the borrowers that provided non-real property collateral or guarantees, 44.6% had loans covered by public guarantees and only 14.2% had loans covered by other collateral or private guarantees. If bank deposit collateral (essentially just a compensating balance compensation arrangement rather than credit enhancement) and private guarantees are not considered, non-real property collateral was provided by only 2.4% of the borrowing firms. Ono, Arito, et al., A New Look at Bank-Firm Relationships and the Use of Collateral in Japan: Evidence from Teikoku Databank Data, in The Economics of Interfirm Networks (T. Watanabe, I. Uesugi & A. Ono eds., 2015).

IV. Insolvency Law and Private International Law as Instruments of Secured Transactions Law Reform

This part considers the roles and significance of insolvency law and the rules of private international law (choice-of-law) for the operation and effectiveness of secured transactions laws. First, consider insolvency law. It is widely accepted and not controversial that an effective secured transaction legal regime necessarily requires the existence of an insolvency law framework that generally respects and recognizes the effectiveness of security interests in insolvency proceedings. As mentioned earlier, the Secured Transactions Legislative Guide, the Insolvency Legislative Guide, and the Model Law on Secured Transactions contemplate the existence and importance of this baseline.[55] Of course, the devil is in the details and controversy exists as to treatment in specific circumstances.[56] But in some jurisdictions the role of insolvency proceedings is not merely benign in its recognition and respect for security but may play a crucial, even indispensible, role in the effectiveness of secured transactions law. The contrast between the U.S. and Japanese environments is especially striking in this context.

Secured creditors in the domestic United States setting may reliably predict that in the case of a debtor's financial distress the firm typically will end up in a chapter 11 proceeding if a consensual out-of-court workout arrangement cannot be achieved.[57] This being the case, these creditors normally would have confidence as well that judicial supervision accompanying a chapter 11 case will typically result in collateral being identified and available. Moreover, the valuation and treatment of secured claims in a chapter 11 case

---

[55.] See Legislative Guide, XII.A.3., para 13, at 425; Model Law, art. 35 (security rights retain priorities in insolvency proceedings); GTE, III., para 8.

[56.] See Legislative Guide, XII.A.5., paras 18–36, at 427–31.

[57.] Of course, a corporate debtor whose financial condition is essentially hopeless may simply be abandoned or liquidated.

provide an important means of enforcing security interests as a viable alternative to nonjudicial dispositions or collections of collateral or judicial enforcement outside on an insolvency proceeding. Under the Bankruptcy Code a claim is a secured claim to the extent of the amount of the secured debt, if the collateral value exceeds the debt, or the value of the collateral, in the case of an undersecured claim (i.e., if the debt exceeds the collateral value).[58] In general a secured creditor is entitled to receive the value of its secured claim even if the collateral is not disposed of and the reorganized debtor continues to own and use the collateral after confirmation of a plan of reorganization.[59] Moreover, chapter 11 may be especially beneficial to a secured creditor's recovery when a chapter 11 debtor's assets (including the secured creditor's collateral) are sold as a going business in a "363 sale."[60] Of course, recoveries of value from of collateral—whether inside or outside of an insolvency proceeding—contribute to (and benefit from) the existence of a robust, thick secondary market for collateral such as inventory and equipment. This would be the case whether a disposition occurs as a part of a going business disposition or, instead, in piecemeal transactions (including in a liquidation proceeding under chapter 7). But it also stands to reason that the ready availability and typical use of chapter 11 as a medium for disposition supports such a secondary market by providing a relatively user-friendly, transparent, and reliable platform for the disposition of assets.

Contrast the situation in the United States with that in Japan, where the incidence of formal insolvency proceedings for distressed

---

[58.] See 11 U.S.C. § 506(a) (determination of secured status).

[59.] For example, a secured claim may be dealt with by issuing securities providing for a payment stream the present value of which equals the amount of the secured claim. See 7 Collier On Bankruptcy 1129.04[2][a] (Alan N. Resnick & Henry J. Sommer eds., 16th ed., 2016).

[60.] For a discussion of sales of substantially all of a chapter 11 debtor's assets under Bankruptcy Code section 363, see Charles W. Mooney, Jr., The (Il)Legitimacy of Bankruptcies for the Benefit of Secured Creditors, 2015 U. Ill. L. Rev. 735, 738–41 [hereinafter, Mooney, Secured Creditors].

debtors is quite small by comparison.[61] Secured creditors in Japan accordingly lack the confidence and assurance with respect to collateral that the likely prospect of a chapter 11 proceeding provides in the United States. Note that this is not the result of adverse treatment of secured claims under Japanese insolvency law. Even when insolvency proceedings ensue, the failure of Japan's Civil Rehabilitation Law routinely to stay enforcement of and administer secured claims may well contribute to the absence of a predictable framework for handling secured claims against distressed debtors.[62] But the principal problem in this context appears to be the underutilization of insolvency proceedings for distressed business debtors, not the substance of Japanese insolvency laws.[63] This is not so much a product of inadequate laws on the books but one of local legal culture.[64] It is this underutilization, combined with the absence of a robust secondary market for movables, that seems to make reliance on inventory and equipment as collateral much less appealing in Japan than in the United States. Insolvency law can provide an hospitable environment for recognition and enforcement that encourages

---

[61] During the January-September 2017 period the number of court filings of business insolvency proceedings in Japan (an average of 700 filings per month) were less than 1% of the number of filings in the United States (an average of 7,905 per month). Trading Economics, Japan Bankruptcies, https://tradingeconomics.com/japan/bankruptcies; Trading Economics, United States Bankruptcies, https://tradingeconomics.com/united-states/bankruptcies. Compare the relative size of each country's GDP for 2017, which (in billions of US$) was 19,417.114 for the United States and $4,841.221 for Japan (about 25% of the United States GDP).

[62] See Civil Rehabilitation Act, supra note 41, art. 53 (right of separate satisfaction of security interest); International Law Office, Civil Rehabilitation Procedure, 2 (2006), www.internationallawoffice.com/Newsletters/Insolvency-Restructuring/Japan/Asahi-Koma-Law-Offices/Civil-Rehabilitation-Procedure ("As a general rule, secured creditors may foreclose on their collateral outside the proceedings under the civil rehabilitation procedure.").

[63] Of course, it is plausible that the underutilization of insolvency proceedings may result from the substance of the relevant insolvency laws in ways that may be unrelated to the treatment of secured claims.

[64] See, e.g., Teresa A. Sullivan, Elizabeth Warren, & Jay Lawrence Westbrook, The Persistence of Local Legal Culture: Twenty Years of Evidence from the Federal Bankruptcy Courts, 17 Harv. J. L. & Pub. Pol. 801 (1994).

the use of secured transactions and thereby facilitates the availability of business credit.[65] But the central point here is that the substance of insolvency law may matter little if the law is underutilized (or if the relevant insolvency law does not adequately deal with secured claims). This is consistent with the thesis of Credit Enhancement that a principal role of insolvency law is the effect of its long shadow on the primary behavior of market participants outside of and unrelated to any actual or anticipated insolvency proceeding. In this case it is not only possible flaws in the applicable insolvency law but the underutilization of insolvency law that casts the shadow.

The rules of private international law, like insolvency law, play an important role in the operation and effectiveness of secured transactions laws. For example, at the outset of a secured financing a prospective creditor must take account of the applicable law in order to ensure that a prospective security interest is effectively created and perfected (third-party effectiveness) and will achieve the desired priority (vis-a vis third parties such as a debtor's creditors, potential insolvency representative, and buyers). Accordingly, global efforts toward modernization and harmonization of secured transactions laws, discussed earlier,[66] have included harmonized secured transactions choice-or-law rules (STCOL rules) as a core feature.[67]

A secured creditor also must take account of which State's insolvency laws might apply. For example, under which State's law governing avoidance of preferences and fraudulent transfers would the

---

[65] Such a hospitable environment contemplates that the applicable insolvency law would provide a regularized and coherent structure for the recognition and administration of secured claims. It does not necessarily contemplate that secured creditors would have a controlling influence over the proceeding. See, Mooney, Secured Creditors, supra note 60, at 751–63. For an empirical analysis of the so-called "secured creditor control" phenomenon, see Jay L. Westbrook, Secured Creditor Control and Bankruptcy Sales: An Empirical View, 2015 U. Ill. L. Rev. 831.

[66] See Part II, supra.

[67] See Model Law, arts. 84–100; Charles W. Mooney, Jr., Choice-of-Law Rules for Secured Transactions: An Interest-Based and Modern Principles-Based Framework for Assessment, 22 Unif. L. Rev. 638 (2018) (advocating a framework for evaluating STCOL rules that takes account of the various stakeholders' interests and the substance of the Modern Principles).

security interest and payments of secured obligations be tested?[68] The applicable insolvency law, including the applicable avoidance law, might or might not be the law of the forum in which an insolvency proceeding might be opened.[69] While a consensus on the need for and characteristics of harmonized STCOL rules may be emerging,[70] it may be that less consensus exists as to the need for and the content of harmonized insolvency choice-of-law rules (HICOL rules).[71] However, unless an international governmental organization (such as UNCITRAL or the Hague Conference on Private International Law) or a non-governmental organization (such as the American Law Institute or the International Insolvency Institute) seriously explores the prospect for the adoption of HICOL rules, the prospects will remain uncertain and the merits will remain untested. Hopefully an appropriate organization will undertake a project on HICOL rules in the near future.[72]

[68.] See Westbrook, Avoidance, supra note 7, at 901–04 (arguing that the insolvency law of the "home country" (i.e., the State of the debtors "center of main interests"), which should govern the distribution of the proceeds of an avoidance recovery, also should govern avoidance actions).

[69.] See, Id.; Charles W. Mooney, Jr., Harmonizing Choice of Law Rules For International Insolvency Cases: Virtual Territoriality, Virtual Universalism, and the Problem of Local Interests, 9 Brook. J. Corp., Fin. & Com. L. 120, 128 (2014) [hereinafter, Mooney, Harmonizing] (discussing a "synthetic" proceeding in State A in which the State A court applies the insolvency law of State B for the benefit of State B creditors).

[70.] See note 12, supra. That is not to say, however, that a consensus exists on all aspects of a STCOL regime. For example, disagreement remains as to whether perfection and priority of assignments of claims (receivables) should be governed by the law of the assignor's (debtor's) location (the better approach) or another law, such as the law governing the claim. For an utterly convincing analysis and argument supporting a location-of-assignor STCOL rule, see Catherine Walsh, The Law Applicable to the Third Party Property Effects and Priority of an Assignment: Whither the EU? 22 Unif. L. Rev. 721 (2018). For another, generally favorable assessment of the location-of-assignor STCOL rule, see Yuko Nishitani, Cross-border Assignment of Receivables: Conflict of Laws in Secured Transactions, 22 Unif. L. Rev. 826 (2017).

[71.] See Mooney, Harmonizing, supra note 69 (exploring prospects for and benefits of implementing HICOL rules).

[72.] To date UNCITRAL has not given priority to a consideration of HICOL rules. There is precedent lending support for NGOs to embark on such a project. See American Law Institute & International Insolvency Institute, ALI-III Global Principles for Cooperation in International Insolvency Cases 2012, www.iiiglobal.org/sites/default/files/ALI-III%20Global%20Principles%20booklet_0.pdf.

V. Conclusions and Some Paths Forward

Several conclusions may be drawn from this discussion.

The Model Law and related UNCITRAL texts, together with the CTC and the Aircraft Protocol, have established and solidified a global consensus in support of the Modern Principles of secured transactions law. But a State's enactment of a Modern Principles-based statutory text may not be sufficient to achieve the desired goals of increasing the availability and decreasing the cost of business credit. A corollary emerging from the JBCP is that these goals may be achieved (or may already exist) in some markets even in the absence of a modern secured transactions law. This suggests the potential benefits of more rigorous studies of secured transactions law reform processes and business credit markets. In particular, studies should more systematically incorporate and memorialize the experiences of individuals and organizations pursuing reforms "on the ground." An intergovernmental organization such as UNCITRAL or UNIDROIT may not be the best sponsor for such investigations. Non-governmental organizations, perhaps in support of conventional academic studies (such as the JBCP), may present better alternatives.

The discussion also reaffirms the conclusion in Credit Enhancement that insolvency law has major instrumental effects on primary behavior of market participants unrelated to actual or anticipated insolvency proceedings. Preliminary indications from the JBCP suggest that the relatively remote possibility in Japan that a firm will resort to formal insolvency proceedings or that secured claims will be effectively dealt with in insolvency proceedings negatively affect the reliable ex ante valuation of recoveries from movables collateral in the Japanese market. This clearly indicates that if insolvency proceedings dealing effectively with secured claims were the norm for financially distressed firms it could enhance the reliability of such ex ante valuations.

Private international law rules also are crucially important to the implementation and effectiveness of the Modern Principles, as discussed earlier. It is well established (and confirmed by the text of the Model Law) that STCOL rules perform an essential function for the operation of secured transactions laws. But an exploration of HICOL rules, including their potential impact on the application and operation of secured transactions laws is needed and overdue. Hopefully an appropriate organization will take up this project in the not too distant future.

Fine-Weather Insolvency Law and Bad-Weather Insolvency Law—On the Extrinsic Framework of Insolvency Law

Christoph G. Paulus[*]

I. Some Background

Jay once described cross-border insolvency law in practice as working like "a team of surgeons, each of whom is able to treat only one part of the patient."[1] Needless to point out that this is one of those seemingly simplistic insights which only can be achieved after years and years of expertise gained by hard work in the realm of this kind of surgery. It takes the depth and the width of Jay's knowledge to fully grasp the implications of this metaphor. Given this, I take the liberty to look in this chapter a bit closer to those various parts of the patient and to attempt to determine some of their differences.

Thereby, it will become visible that some of the differences are just rooted in different approaches toward insolvency law and that these variations alone do not justify to negate the fine weather badge for those jurisdictions. The bad weather, in contrast, comes into play

---

[*] Professor of Law *Emeritus* at the Humboldt-Universität zu Berlin. A version of this chapter was published in German at 35 Zeitschrift für Wirtschaftsrecht (ZIP) 1657 ff. (2016). Reproduced with permission.

[1] Westbrook, Priority Conflicts as a Barrier to Cooperation in Multinational Insolvencies, 27 Penn St. Intl.L.R. 869 (2009).

only when and if one (or, even worse, several) of the self-assumed or self-set premises of our hospital system fall apart.

With this weather imagery, I pick up earlier deliberations which I have published elsewhere[2] and which I still deem to be quite helpful (or, at least, illuminating) for understanding potential and limits of any insolvency law. It not only clarifies the economic dependencies of this field of law but also a number of other factors determining its success or failure. I trust in Jay's magnanimity that he will forgive me when I use for the purpose of demonstration primarily German or European examples; but I have to bow to my limitations as one of those aforementioned surgeons.

What follows will be structured by beginning with a description of the fine-weather insolvency law followed by identifying several pillars of the insolvency law's extrinsic structure, before then ideas about needs and shape of a bad-weather insolvency law are to be submitted.

II. Fine-Weather Insolvency Law

The fine-weather version is well known and needs no long description. There is a debtor confronted with the common pool problem, i.e., this person cannot fulfill the entirety of his or her obligations as they fall due.[3] In order to prevent in such a situation the creditors' race to the highly attractive position of full satisfaction of their claims insolvency law replaces the so far applicable priority principle (first come, first serve) by the principle of equal treatment by which the

---

[2] Paulus, Die Insolvenzrechtsreform und der Schutz gesicherter Gläubiger, Zeitschrift für Wirtschaftsrecht (ZIP) 1985, pp. 1449, 1451; idem, Gedanken über Wetter, das Insolvenzrecht und andere Misshelligkeiten, in Bruns / Kern / Münch / Piekenbrock / Stadler / Tsikrikas (eds.), Festschrift für Rolf Stürner zum 70. Geburtstag Bd. I, 2013, p. 797 ff.; idem, Gutwetter-Insolvenzrecht und Schlechtwetter-Insolvenzrecht: Über die ökonomischen Grundbedingungen des Insolvenzrechts, ZIP 2016, 1657 ff.

[3] For an overview of the differences of what insolvency means compare Méjan, in this volume.

creditors, generally speaking, are put on the same level (*par condicio creditorum* or *pari passu*) by becoming satisfied pro rata and proportionally on what is owed to them. To be sure, the equal treatment is usually not more than the idealistic starting point from which many deviations are admitted, usually called privileges. In their classification system of such privileges, legislatures express their understanding of economic, social, and other political needs.

The differences here are enormous as, for instance, the comparison between the German and the Italian law demonstrates. Whereas the latter has more than 40 privileges on offer, the written German law has none. They do exist nevertheless but are somewhat hidden.[4] But this does not mean that one of those two laws would be a bad-weather insolvency law—despite the fact that such differences do create problems, for instance with regard to the banking union. As indicated supra, it is neither a sign of fine or bad-weather insolvency law when other differences exist with a potentially massif influence on a case's final outcome. Whereas the German insolvency law sees it (at least allegedly) as its overarching purpose to provide for the best satisfaction of the creditors, does its French counterpart see as its primary focus the salvation of as many as possible working places. In a German–French case, thus, enormous irritations arise when the debtor company is sold either to the highest bidder (when the German administrator is in charge) or to the guarantor of rescuing most working places (when the French side is in charge). And in the U.S., insolvency law is designed to help the debtor. The contrasts between those approaches could not be bigger but this has nothing to do with my weather metaphoric; they are just expression of different philosophies.[5] The question of which purpose an insolvency law is

---

[4.] Needless to point out that, for instance, the financial industry has managed to receive its, by now, globally wide spread safe harbor in Germany as well, sec. 104 Insolvenzordnung (InsO, Insolvency Ordinance); on this Paulus, Multinational Enterprises and National Insolvency Laws (or: Lobbying for Special Privileges), available at https://papers.ssrn.com/sol3/papers.cfm?abstract_id=3029567.

[5.] For a summary of different philosophies of insolvency law, see Flessner, Philosophies of Business Bankruptcy Law: An International Overview, in: Ziegel (ed.),

designed for can be answered in many different ways—the IMF adds to the multiplicity of variations the one according to which an insolvency mechanism is needed for overcoming hold-out creditors.[6]

But apart from such differences as to the angle from which the common pool problem is approached, commonalities exist in most insolvency laws about negotiation procedures for both the debtor and her creditors as to the drawing up and voting on a plan when and if the debtor's reorganization is intended; similarly, further commonalities exist with regard to the liquidation mechanism which, in the end of the day, consists of a formalized sales procedure whereby the economic outcome of this procedure depends on various factors. Accordingly, depending on the path chosen in a particular insolvency proceeding does the debtor continue its business after the proceeding when and if successfully reorganized or, alternatively, its assets have been sold either piecemeal or as a whole. The economic purpose of this redistribution process is to allocate unproductive assets as promptly as possible to a place of their optimal productivity.[7]

This entire mechanism is based on a rather ingenious feature which in German scholarship is called enforced community (Zwangsgemeinschaft).[8] It means that debtor and creditors are, as it were, put into the same boat which they are allowed to leave, generally speaking, only when and if the proceeding is closed. Tools such

---

Current Developments in International and Comparative Corporate Insolvency Law (1994) 19.

[6.] Compare Sovereign Debt Restructuring—Recent Developments and Implications for the Fund's Legal and Policy Framework, April 26, 2013, available at www.imf.org/external/np/pp/eng/2013/042613.pdf.

[7.] Vgl. Paulus, Über die volkswirtschaftliche Bedeutsamkeit effektiver Insolvenzsysteme, in: Paulus (ed.), Restrukturierung in Krisenzeiten, 2014, p. 11; idem/ Potamitis/Rokas/Tirado, Insolvency Law as a Main Pillar of Market Economy—A Critical Assessment of the Greek Insolvency Law, 24 International Insolvency Review 2015, 1 ff.

[8.] On this enforced community see, e.g., Neumann, Die Gläubigerautonomie in einem künftigen Insolvenzverfahren, 1995, p. 55 ff.; Hänel, Gläubigerautonomie und das Insolvenzplanverfahren, 2000, p. 63 ff.; Paulus, Insolvenzrecht, 3rd ed., 2017, p. 5 marg. no. 11; in an international context compare also Westbrook / Booth / Paulus / Rajak, A Global View of Business Insolvency Systems, 2010, p. 158.

as the automatic stay, the debtor's replacement by an administrator, the replacement of the unanimity requirement by the majority vote, or the judicial control make sure that the boat can steer into the right direction and is not torn into other directions because of diverging interests of the "boat people." The fundamentality of the enforced community for any functioning insolvency mechanism is best recognized when it is not foreseen by law—the best example for this is when it comes to a sovereign's inability to fulfill its obligations.[9]

III. Pillars of the Structure

Probably all insolvency statues and rules as well as the relevant guidelines[10] or principles[11] are built on the basic assumption that certain economic conditions are fulfilled. This is true at least as far reaching back into history as the initial idea of revenge became replaced by the distribution of the debtor's assets.

To begin with, there is the supposition that there exists a credit-based economy at all. Since in a pure barter economy it is to be assumed that there is no need for a solution of a common pool problem; since trade is generally performed there on a concurrent exchange of products or assets. Accordingly, the time factor is essential for the emergence of insolvency law. A German judge once has phrased this as "The spring of insolvency is credit."[12] By transforming transactions from point in time exchanges into space of time transactions the risk of non-performance is created and law has to step

---

[9.] Just compare Paulus, Geordnete Staateninsolvenz—eine Lösung mit Hilfe des Vertragsrechts, ZIP 2011, 2433; idem (ed.), A Debt Restructuring Mechanis for Sovereigns—Do We Need a Legal Procedure? 2012, p. 191 ff.

[10.] UNCITRAL, Legislative Guide on Insolvency Law, 2005; available at www. UNCITRAL.org/english/texts/insolven/insoguide.pdf.

[11.] World Bank compare http://pubdocs.worldbank.org/pubdocs/publicdoc/ 2016/5/998191463585986043/ICR-Principles-Insolvency-Creditor-Debtor-Regimes-2015.pdf; International Monetary Fund compare www.imf.org/external/pubs/ft/ orderly.

[12.] Leopold Levy, Lehrbuch zum Konkursrecht, 1926, 2nd ed., Berlin, p. 2.

in to mitigate that risk. A striking example for this transformation is the ordinary purchase by which the object of purchase is given for the payment of the price at the same time. By inventing and introducing retention of title arrangements, the purchase contract turns into a credit business.

A further basic assumption of insolvency law is the availability of credit. As the term "dip-financing" makes sufficiently clear any reorganization—but also in many cases the liquidation—is performed (better: is to be performed) with the support of money lent from outside; this outside includes shareholders as well as banks or any other third party.

Speaking of liquidation, this option of literally each and every insolvency law on this globe insinuates the existence of a market on which the respective assets are demanded; plus, there must be sufficient money around that those assets can be paid. In short, the requirements for a fair market price formation must be given. When, in contrast, the debtor's reorganization is at stake insolvency law assumes the marketability of its products and the respective economic capabilities of the debtor's management.

There are, of course, dozens of further assumptions which need not be listed here. They reach from the existence of a social security net that is stable enough to cope with so and so many additional unemployed to an institutional framework (courts, judges, administrators, etc.) which manages the tasks imposed on them by the law.

In contrast, the (absolute) priority rule for the distributional process within an insolvency proceeding which is so dearly and intensively discussed by so many insolvency scholars and practitioners[13] does not belong here. Since it deals just with a means to an end to reach a fair and just result but does not constitute an implicit assumption of economic pre-existing facts.

[13.] S. etwa Marinc/Vlahu, The Economics of Bank Bankruptcy Law, 2012, p. 11; Baird/Bernstein, Absolute Priority, Valuation Uncertainty, and the Reorganization Bargain, John M. Olin Law & Economics Working Paper No. 259, 2005; Bebchuk, The ex ante costs of violating absolute priority in bankruptcy, 57 Journal of Finance, 2002, 445 ff.

IV. Bad-Weather Insolvency Law

A. Simple Solutions

The namesakes for the title "bad-weather insolvency law" has been for me a tremendously rainy season a couple of years ago in Germany. The water caused such a flooding that tiny creeks turned into torrential rivers, entire villages had to be evacuated, the first and often the second floor, too, of houses of an entire region were underwater for days if not weeks. The German legislator reacted quickly by prolonging the notorious three-week term in sec. 15 InsO[14] which applies to the entrepreneurial duty to file for insolvency once an opening reason is given. A similar quick reaction of the legislator took place in Germany at the outset of the financial crisis in 2008. Within weeks the definition of what constitutes overindebtedness in s. 19 par. 2 InsO was changed into the form which had been abolished only a few years before.[15] It became clear that the previously renewed definition was based on an overly optimistic economic assumption which in the crisis scenario would have caused the insolvency related collapse of a massif amount of companies all over Germany. Even before those two incidents, the German re-unification, too, had led to a (temporary) change of insolvency law.[16] The companies and businesses of the former East had so many employees that the rule according to which each and every employment contract transfers to the buyer of the company or business—even when done in the course of an

---

[14.] Just compare Nolting, Insolvenzrechtliche Fragen im Zusammenhang mit der Flutkatastrophe, Neue Zeitschrift für Insolvenzrecht (NZI) 2003, 82 ff.; Seibert, Unterbrechung der Insolvenzantragspflichten für Flutopfer bis 31. März 2003, ZIP 2003, 91 f. Regarding the heavy rain fall in spring 2016 and its implications on the filing duty compare www.mechthild-heil.de/2016/06/24/mechthild-heil-mdb-cdu-insolvenzantragspflicht-fuer-hochwasser-opfer-wird-voruebergehend-ausgesetzt.

[15.] Compare Art. 5 and 6 of the Code of Stabilisation of the Financial Market (Finanzmarktstabilisierungsgesetz—FMStG) from Oct. 17, 2008, BGBl I 2008, 1982. On this see A. Rokas, Die „neue" Legaldifinition der Überschuldung, Zeitschrift für das gesamte Insolvenz- und Sanierungsrecht (ZInsO) 2009, 18 ff.

[16.] On art. 32 par. 2 of the Introductory Code for the Insolvency Ordinance (EGInsO) Müller-Glöge in: Münchener Kommentar-BGB, section 613a marg. no. 2.

insolvency proceeding—would have made the latter unsellable. Accordingly, this very rule, sec. 613a BGB (Civil Law Code), was suspended for sales in the new Bundesländer until the introduction of the new insolvency statute in 1999.

It is rather obvious that the bad weather in such cases as the described ones[17] is quite easily manageable. Little changes within the law or the suspension of one rule (or just a few) do the job to keep the fine-weather insolvency law afloat. Graver difficulties arise when the market has collapsed as it has been (and, irrespective of the public announcements, as it is still) the case in a country like Greece. Accordingly, the following deliberations look for ways how to surrogate the market mechanisms with traditional legal instruments (infra II and III) and what else can be done (IV ff.).

B. Too Big to Fail

A different—or better: a metaphorical—bad-weather zone is at stake when and if the debtor is too big, too complex, too interconnected to become subject to the general insolvency law. Despite the fact that the term "too big to fail" seems nowadays to be reserved for financial institutions[18] it is, as a matter of fact, a rather widespread phenomenon: depending on the unemployment rate in a particular region even smaller companies might achieve the status of too big to fail when and if social politics there cannot cope with an increase of that rate. Moreover, allegedly there are still cities in Russia of a million or more inhabitants which are dependent on the continuation of a single factory.

---

[17] It should be noted that J. Payne, for instance, in her article on "The Role of the Court in Debt Restructuring" is addressing the possibility of fluctuations of market prices with regard to valuation issues; available at https://papers.ssrn.com/sol3/papers.cfm?abstract_id=2902528.

[18] Compare Parry (Hg.), Too Big to Fail? Large National and International Failures under the Spotlight, Papers from the INSOL Europe Academic Forum Conference in Nottingham, June 2012; Kenadjian (ed.), Too Big to Fail—Brauchen wir ein Sonderinsolvenzrecht für Banken? 2012.

Like those notorious financial institutions, these companies, too, have escaped from the realm of the fine-weather insolvency law and are, thus, beyond the economic reach of the general market mechanisms. It is well known that legislators have tried to abolish—more realistically: to mitigate—the traditional remedy in those cases, namely the respective state's bailout by means of the tax payers' money. However, at least with regard to the European Bank Recovery and Resolution Directive (BRRD) it is to be said that its rules on the new bail-in instrument is so complicated and so complex that serious doubts are inevitable as to its general applicability.[19]

C. Debt-Equity-Swap, Credit Bidding

In cases of a debt-equity swap (des), things are a bit more complicated but have in common with the aforementioned too-big-to-fail phenomenon the elimination of the standard market mechanism of a mutual contract. Leaving aside the danger of abuse (suffice it to mention the loan to own-strategy[20]) such a swap effects an exchange of a claim with equity in the debtor company. Instead of paying the "purchase price" at the time of the business transfer, it is treated as if it had already been paid much earlier under the flag of, for instance, a loan agreement. It makes the market superfluous at the later time. A similar mechanism applies in case of the so-called contingent convertible bonds that, in the end of the day, are something like stocking up with a debt-equity swap.[21]

---

[19] Compare Wojcik, Bail-in in the Banking Union, CMLR 2016, 91 ff.; Triantaphyllakis, Italienische Banken: Wenn nicht alle Wege zum Bail-in führen, Wertpapier-Mitteilungen (WM) 2016, 2248 ff.

[20] On this just see Palenker, Loan-to-own—Schuldenbasierte Übernahmen in Zeiten moderner Restrukturierungen und mangelnder Gläubigertransparenz, Baden-Baden 2019.

[21] On this Möhlenkamp / Harder, Die umgekehrte Wandelschuldverschreibung (CoCo-Bonds)—ein neues Sanierungsinstrument? ZIP 2016, 1093, 1095; Nodoushani, Contingent Convertible Bonds, WM 2016, 589 ff.

A further version of the elimination of the immediate need for a market appears under the name of "credit bidding." To the degree of its legal admissibility the secured creditor is not only permitted to participate in the bidding process but is also freed from a payment obligation up to the amount of what this creditor has previously lent to the debtor. Under German law, such credit bidding is permitted, s. 168 par. 3 InsO, and is technically construed as a set-off of the secured creditor's loan repayment claim with the bidding price.[22] The example teaches that set-off is an additional remedy to bypass the market mechanism of immediate exchange.

As plausible and as smart these tools appear with regard to their economic results, they are not free from dangers. With a view on China, it is only recently that the IMF has pointed in this direction:[23] (1) The take-over of a company—or parts of it—by a creditor might lead to the creation of "zombie companies," i.e., market participants which have actually no survival chances there and which actually should be liquidated and, thus, expelled from that very market. (2) Moreover, a creditor (most prominent example: a bank) rarely commands the necessary and adequate expertise to run the company, let alone to carry it back to profitability. The primary economic purpose of any fine-weather insolvency law to transfer as rapidly as possible unproductive assets back to their best possible productivity[24] gets thereby typically distorted. After all, it is quite unlikely that a bank has expertise (or just knowledge) in the market conditions for a sausage stand, an air carrier, or a screw manufacturer. (3) And finally, there is the particular danger in jurisdictions such as Germany that a "normal" loan turns into a

---

[22.] Special rules might apply in certain circumstances, e.g., under sec. 114a Statute on real estate foreclosures (Zwangsversteigerungsgesetz = ZVG).

[23.] Compare https://blog-imfdirect.imf.org/2016/04/26/tackling-chinas-debt-problem-can-debt-equity-conversions-help; additionally Daniel / Garrido / Moretti, Debt Equity Conversions and NPL Securitization in China: Some Initial Considerations, IMF Technical Notes and Manuals, 2016.

[24.] In addition to fn. 7 Paulus, section 1 InsO und sein Insolvenzmodell, NZI 2015, 1001, 1003.

subordinated claim in insolvency because the loan is treated then as a shareholder loan.

D. NPL Securitization

In the aforementioned paper, the IMF addresses also the non performing loans (NPL) securitization as an emergency measure; even though its primary addressee is China, the NPL issue is cause of serious head ache not only there. Finance ministries all over the European Union are struggling right now with an estimated amount of €950 bln.[25] and the European Systemic Risk Board has come up not too long ago (in July 2017) with some ideas as to strategies how to cope with this issue.[26] According to the aforementioned IMF paper, what has to be kept in mind is not only the existence of a respective market; it is also necessary to design the securitization in a way that cluster risks are avoided to the highest degree possible and, in order to avoid any moral hazard strategies from the banks, they should keep their skin in the game. And finally, what is indispensable for the underlying market is the existence of a legal and economic framework that offers the buyers of NPLs the realistic chance to enforce the debtor's restructuring.

The chapter also warns us to use securitization as an isolated measure. To become successful, it must be embedded in a whole range of additional measures such as a sufficiently resilient social security system that cushions the increased unemployment rate, or the need for expertise to differentiate between viable companies and those which are bound to become liquidated—as it is throughout indispensable to have at hand the adequate legal tools for restructuring and liquidating companies.

[25.] Compare www.manager-magazin.de/unternehmen/banken/faule-kredite-banken-in-eu-sitzen-auf-950-milliarden-euro-fauler-kredite-a-1188564.html.

[26.] Compare www.esrb.europa.eu/pub/pdf/reports/20170711_resolving_npl_report.en.pdf. See additionally, Aiyar/Bergthaler/Garrido, Illyina/Jobst/ Kang/ Kovtun/ Liu/Monaghan/ Moretti, A Strategy for Resolving Europe's Problem Loans, IMF Staff Discussion note from September 2015.

E. No Properly Functioning Market

An even worse bad-weather front is approaching when the regular market conditions are not given since there is not enough economic power. Needless to point out that, particularly for an European, it is Greece that comes to mind when addressing this storm. Liquidation, being statistically the predominant proceeding, is based on a sales mechanism—be it by way of auction or be it otherwise. The price achieved thereby is deemed to be fair and the sales process is generally attributed to the debtor's default resulting from some kind of economic failure (such as miscalculation, excessive risk-taking, mismanagement, etc.). This assumption of causation, however, loses much of its credibility when the market is (more or less) collapsed. Here, the default—more precisely: its consequences—might become unwarranted and unfair not least because of the interconnectedness of the economy. Moreover, the auction (or other liquidation sale) might turn out to be under such circumstances an inadequate price-finding tool because of the unfairly low prices—with the consequence that the entire mechanism becomes detrimental for both the debtor and her creditors (or at least some of them).

When creditors are bound to suffer under such economic conditions of an illiquid market they will be less inclined to use auctions etc. The consequence thereof seems to be in Greece that it is less costly for debtors to default which, in turn, creates the moral hazard of strategic defaulting. A rough estimation from Greece[27] is that 20% of defaulters are doing this for strategic reasons. Almost a decade after the outbreak of the crisis, Greece is still struggling with this bad weather and it is hard to see which remedy could serve as a cure.

F. Compensation of Lacking Liquidity

A German proverb has it that "emergency makes inventive" (*Not macht erfinderisch*). Presently, the country plagued with one of the

---

[27.] Personal mail from Stathis Potamitis to the present author from Jan. 19, 2018.

highest emergency indicators seems to be Venezuela. The economy is very much down and the situation for the population is close to (if not even right within) disastrous; the inflation is extremely frightening and futures are given as securities not only since this year. In short, illiquidity is—maybe even more so than in Greece—a burning issue. In this situation, Venezuela's president presented in late 2017 the idea to the general public to introduce a new currency called Petro.[28] Its economy rescuing property shall be that this currency is a virtual one like Bitcoin (whose success story might have lead the president to think that a similar success could be gained by the Petro) and that it shall be backed by the still existing oil reserves as well as mineral and diamond mines in that country.

The idea resembles a bit of the German storyteller who refers to Baron von Münchhausen who had once rescued himself and his horse by dragging himself out of a swamp on his own hair. Even though the idea of a digital currency as a rescue measure appears appealing on first sight it is hard to imagine that the tradability of the Petro will be better than the one of the present Bolívar currency. After all, the blockchain based currency—there are right now more than 1.000—might overcome the dependency from governments and central banks, but it is more likely than not still dependent on trust. The trust into the backing oil reserves, however, will probably dwindle away to the degree that those reserves have already been used as collateral. Under such circumstances, it is to be feared that digital currencies will not solve the bad-weather insolvency problem in any country.

G. Foreign Investors

What comes to mind in sight of such massif liquidity problems is that if there is no (or not sufficient) liquidity on the internal market it would be helpful to look abroad where the liquidity exists. What is

---

[28.] Compare www.zeit.de/wirtschaft/2017-12/venezuela-nicolas-maduro-digital waehrung-kryptowaehrung-petro.

needed, therefore, are foreign investors that are willing to bring their money into that particular country. An investor's readiness to do so depends, as a matter of fact, on a number of factors of which not all—like political stability of that country—are legal in their nature.

To the degree, though, to which the legal environment is concerned a high priority is likely to rest on the level of protection and the efficiency of law enforcement.[29] The latter includes not only a modern and effective procedural, enforcement, and insolvency law but also the infrastructure to transform the written text of the law into a living and practical reality. The degree to which an increased efficiency of the law in this context is seen as quintessential within Europe can be derived from the Action Plan on Building a Capital Markets Union;[30] it points explicitly to the elimination of all respective obstacles.[31]

Deficiencies in this area[32] are directly reflected in the costs and the prices which foreign investors will be ready to incur. How intensely the economic principles dominate in such a surrounding became very visible in Germany in the beginning of the re-unification under the "governance" of the Treuhandanstalt (i.e., Trust Agency in charge of the privatization of previous GDR companies[33]). The economic conditions dumped the prices.

---

[29] On this Dolzer / Bloch, Der rechtliche Schutz ausländischer Investitionen, in: Kronke / Melis / Schnyder (eds.), Handbuch Internationales Wirtschaftsrecht, 2005, p. 1044 ff.; Krajewski, Wirtschaftsvölkerrecht, 2006, p. 167 ff. compare. Additionally the World Bank's examination list for their ROSCs (=Reports on the Observation of Standards and Codes: Insolvency and creditor rights systems, compare www.world bank.org/ifa/FINAL-ICRPrinciples-March2009.pdf

[30] Available at: http://eur-lex.europa.eu/legal-content/EN/TXT/PDF/?uri=CELEX:52015DC0468&from=EN.

[31] *Ibid.*, particularly at 6.2, p. 27 f.

[32] The remedy of arbitration, e.g., Internatinal Centre for the Settlement of Investment Disputes (ICSID), which is quite frequently offered through Bilateral Investment Agreements (BIT), might not always be sufficiently compensating (the 46 BITs of Greece are listed at http://investmentpolicyhub.unctad.org/IIA/CountryBits/81#iiaInnerMenu).

[33] On this, see Paulus, The Reunification of Germany, in: Burdette (Hg.), INSOL International, The Implications of Brexit for the Restructuring and the Insolvency Industry—A Collection of Essays, 2017, S. 29 ff.

H. Barter

Thus, when and if the institutional and legal framework does not comply with the foreign investors' expectations and when and if the domestic market does not have sufficient financial means to perform a fine-weather liquidation, a potential alternative is barter—including the use of pseudo-currencies such as cigarettes or variations of Maduro's Petro or promises of future incomes. Apart from this present-day example, the Dawes Plan from August 16, 1924, demonstrates that the combination of payment in kind plus promises for the future are an attractive remedy in times of crises. That Plan provided for Germany relief from the pressing reparation obligations after World War 1: not only that the payment was reduced to 55% of the annual nominal amount; it was also foreseen that this reduced sum was supposed to be fine-tuned with the respective economic situation.[34]

I. Nationalization

It is to be assumed that the remedy of last resort is the nationalization of enterprises or some kind of bailout. The consequence thereof, however, is likely to be an increased level of indebtedness which in turn might lead to a deterioration of the living conditions due to increased borrowing costs plus increased inflation. At the end of such a vicious circle the insolvency of the sovereign possibly lurks around so that finally it will be the sovereign's creditors who, by means of the notorious haircuts will have to bear the costs.

The bailout can be done openly or hidden. An example for the latter is the sovereign which acquires (all or parts of the) shares of the troubled company and provides then, as owner or shareholder, fresh money; this was roughly the strategy of Cyprus in case of her

---

[34] In this context highly informative Buxbaum, Sovereign Debtors Before Greece: The Case of Germany, 65 U.Kan.L.R. 59 ff. (2016).

Central Cooperative Bank.[35] With regard to the European situation, an open bailout has always to cope with the intricacies of the general prohibition of state-aid; compare art. 107 TFEU.[36]

The aforementioned state insolvency scenario is the worst—nevertheless rather realistic—case as the examples from Argentina, Greece and the many other—less attention from the general public receiving—countries demonstrate which, like most of the island states in the South Sea or in the Caribbean are suffering from the Global Warming. That part of the population that is not part of the happy few which can save their goods through capital flight or the like is the one which usually suffers most from the downfall.

The fact that in sight of such wide-spread, collective misery politicians in the entire world still have not yet found a common ground for establishing fixed, reliable, and transparent legal rules for a resolvency proceeding[37] is first of all embarrassing and has probably many reasons. One of them will be that rulers always did[38] and still do appreciate their power positions so that they, by means of ad hoc solutions can adjust to the circumstances of the individual case; this path-dependency is true also for the European Stability Mechanism.[39] Another reason rests in the massive secondary market for non-performing loans. The possibility to

---

[35.] On this Triantaphyllakis (as in fn. 19) with allusions to other country's interest in circumventing the bail-in mechanism.

[36.] On this see Guidelines on State aid for rescuing and restructuring non-financial undertakings in difficulty, 2014/C 249/01.

[37.] Compare Paulus (ed.), A Debt Restructuring Mechanism for Sovereigns—Do We Need a Legal Procedure? München 2014; Paulus, How could the general principles of national insolvency law contribute to the development of a state insolvency regime? ESCB Legal Conference 2016, 6–7 October, January 2017, S. 64 ff. (available at www.ecb.europa.eu/pub/pdf/other/escblegalconference2016_201702. en.pdf?e2dea3a78485afe4c70d5d5010f368be).

[38.] Informative Heimbeck, Die Abwicklung von Staatsbankrotten im Völkerrecht—Verrechtlichung und Rechtsvermeidung zwischen 1824 und 1907, 2013; additionally Waibel, Echoes of History: The International Financial Commission in Greece in: Paulus (as in fn. 9), p. 3 ff.

[39.] Compare Paulus/Tirado, Sweet and Lowdown: A Resolvency Process and the Eurozone's Crisis Management Framework, Law and Economics Yearly Review 2013, 504 ff. (= http://papers.ssrn.com/sol3/papers.cfm?abstract_id=2330423.

purchase on this market receivables at a reduced price ignites the gigantic market[40] and—that is one of the often-used arguments in favor—alleviates thus the debt restructuring of sovereigns by means of negotiations. Since when a buyer acquires, e.g., bonds at a tenth of the nominal value (suffice it to refer here to the notorious case *NML Capital v. Argentina*[41]), it will be prepared to receive something like fifty or sixty percent of the nominal value because this still likely means a considerable profit. Usually, this is described as a win-win situation which, however, completely ignores the misery of the individual citizen's situation in such circumstances.[42] In order to overcome such cynics, it appears to be indispensable to establish a predictable and transparent legal procedure such as a resolvency procedure.[43]

V. Ideas about Alternatives

A. Discharge Function

An alternative to the weather dichotomy would be to untie insolvency law from its traditional concentration on the debtor-creditor relationship. This is very dominant in a jurisdiction like the German one which has in its introductory section of the

---

[40] In the European Union alone the total of NPLs adds up to 950 Bln. €; www.manager-magazin.de/unternehmen/banken/faule-kredite-banken-in-eu-sitzen-auf-950-milliarden-euro-fauler-kredite-a-1188564.html. See also European Central Bank, Guidance to banks on non-performing loans, Mar. 2017, available at www.bankingsupervision.europa.eu/ecb/pub/pdf/guidance_on_npl.en.pdf.

[41] Compare Sandrock, Recht der Internationalen Wirtschaft (RIW) 2015, 93; Paulus, WM 2015, 953 with further references; Samples, Rogue Trends in Sovereign Debt: Argentina, Vulture Funds, and Pari Passu under New York Law, 35 Northwestern J of Intl Law & Business (2014) S. 49 ff.; Muse-Fisher, Starving the Vultures: *NML Capital v. Republic of Argentina* and Solutions to the Problem of Distressed-Debt Funds, 102 Cal. L. Rev. (2014), S. 1671 ff.

[42] Belgium tries to tackle this discrepancy with an interesting law that was enacted a few years ago, compare Paulus, Geierfonds vor Gericht ausbremsen? Zeitschrift für Rechtspolitik (ZRP) 2016, 146 ff.

[43] For references, compare fn. 37.

Insolvency Ordinance, sec. 1, explicitly stated that the law's goal is to satisfy the creditors:[44]

> The insolvency proceedings shall serve the purpose of collective sat-isfaction of a debtor's creditors by liquidation of the debtor's assets and by distribution of the proceeds, or by reaching an arrangement in an insolvency plan, particularly in order to maintain the enter-prise. Honest debtors shall be given the opportunity to achieve dis-charge of residual debt.

But even if an insolvency law's goal is to rescue as many working places as possible, to rescue the enterprise as such, to foster entrepre-neurialship, or to provide the debtor with a fresh start, the creditors always do have their role in the proceeding in that, at least, their partial satisfaction is said to be at stake.[45]

By this creditor orientation, however, only one part of the insolvency laws' tasks is covered. In economic terms, it is similarly important that this law's efficiency serves the purpose of market con-solidation plus—and this is nowhere else as radically pursued than in the United States (thereby standing in stark contrast to most parts of the globe, particularly to Germany)—the empowerment of the debtor to a fresh start.[46] The debtor's financial situation gets cut back by means of an insolvency proceeding to a level of sustainability.[47]

---

[44] There is a lot of misunderstanding around this norm, compare Flessner, Insol-venzverfahren ohne Insolvenz? Vorteile und Nachteile eines vorinsolvenzlichen Reorganisationsverfahrens nach französischem Vorbild, Zeitschrift für Insolvenzre-cht (KTS) 2010, 127, 142 f.; Paulus (fn. 22), 1001 ff.

[45] Just compare Jackson, The Logic and Limits of Bankruptcy Law, 1986, p. 3.

[46] Compare Madaus, Schulden, Entschuldung, Jubeljahre—vom Wandel der Funktionen des Insolvenzrechts, Juristenzeitung (JZ) 2016, 548 ff.

[47] Just see World Bank, Report on the Treatment of the Insolvency of Natural Persons, S. 115: Tz. 359. One of the principal purposes of an insolvency system for natural persons is to re-establish the debtor's economic capability, in other words, economic rehabilitation. Rehabilitation can be said to include three elements. First, the debtor has to be freed from excessive debt. The benefits of the discharge have been extensively discussed from the point of view of the debtors, creditors and the society in section I.9, above. Second, the debtor should be treated on an equal basis with non-debtors after receiving relief (the principle of non-discrimination).

This is true insofar as the discharge is granted within a reasonable, i.e., limited period. Usually, this period is determined in a plan on which debtor and creditors have agreed upon in the course of the proceeding or it is prescribed by law (e.g., when and if the debtor is a natural person). Outside the United States, this period is increasingly cut down to three years, even though Germany indulges the "luxury" of a six years period.[48] It should be noted, though, that even the three years period implicitly bears the creditors' interests in mind which is often explained and justified by a reference to the fundamental rule of *pacta sunt servanda*.

This justification becomes dubitable, though, when looking at sec. 90 no. 2, 96, 99 of the Restructuring and Resolution Code[49] which is the German transformation legislation of the European Directive on Banking Resolution and Restructuring.[50] In the context of the resolution mechanism for a financial institution, sec. 62 ff. SAG, the said rules provide that the resolution authority is permitted to reduce or to write down ("reduce to zero"[51]) the principal amount and that this regulatory act is to understood as a satisfaction of the claim! In contrast, the normal way of a claim's satisfaction is regulated in sec. 362 BGB; accordingly, a liability is extinguished when and if the debtor has done everything necessary for the fulfillment of its obligation. It is only in the banking sector that a claim's extinction can be effected by means of a command of the resolution authority!

Third, the debtor should be able to avoid becoming excessively indebted again in the future, which may require some attempt to change debtors' attitudes concerning proper credit use. Abrufbar unter: http://siteresources.worldbank.org/INTGILD/ Resources/WBInsolvencyOfNaturalPersonsReport_01_11_13.pdf.

[48.] Note that the EU Directive on Preventive Restructuring Frameworks, on Discharge of Debt and Disqualifications, and oon Measures to increase the Efficiency of Procedures Concerning Restructuring, Insolvency and Discharge od Debt from May 15, 2019, provides for a 3-years period max.

[49.] Gesetz zur Sanierung und Abwicklung von Instituten und Finanzgruppen (SAG) from Dec. 10, 2014, BGBl. I, p. 2091.

[50.] http://eur-lex.europa.eu/legal-content/DE/TXT/PDF/?uri=CELEX: 32014L0059&from=de.

[51.] Compare Art. 53 par. 3 BRRD.

B. Models

It has possibly been ancient Roman law that pushed aside a previously existent and (in some parts of the old world) practiced tradition, according to which social peace and the individual's liberty to operate was fostered by granting a general discharge in certain intervals. The probably most renown example is the biblical jubilee year[52] which provided for a debt relief among Jews every seven years. It should be noted that this Jewish and Mesopotamic tradition was incorporated into Christianity, when Pope Bonifaz VIII. declared this in the year 1300; moreover, Pope John Paul II. tried to re-activate this mechanism in his annual speech "urbi et orbi" on January 1, 2000, by asking the lending countries to cancel the debts of the developing countries in toto.

To be sure, such a bad-weather insolvency law would be rather radical;[53] however, as the example of the banking regulation amplifies, it would not be an anomaly—and it cannot be otherwise in sight of gigantic and ever-growing debt mountains.[54] It is to be feared that the sheer amount of debts has already left the realm of law and entered that of symbolism. Accordingly, the roughly $18 billion of

---

[52] Compare Levitikus (3. Mose), 25 8–15. On the Jubilee Year and its introduction into Christianity by Pope Bonifatius VIII. In 1300 (Bulle: Antiquorum habet fida relatio) compare Thurston, Holy Year of the Jubilee, in: Herbermann (ed.), The Catholic Encyclopedia (1907–1912), Vol. 7, available at http://oce.catholic.com/index.php?-title=Holy_Year_of_Jubilee. Its historical roots reach far back into Mesopotamia, compare Scheuermann (ed.), Das Jobeljahr im Wandel (2000); Bergsma, The Jubilee from Leviticus to Qumran (2007); A.Michel (ed.), Èthique du Jubilé—vers une réparation du monde? 2005. See also Paulus, Historische Betrachtungen zur Restschuldbefreiung des Schuldners, ZInsO 2019, 1153 ff.

[53] This is written by someone from the European continent; for someone from the U.S. where the purpose of insolvency law is to offer a fresh start to the debtor, this is far less radical (if radical at all).

[54] For a first impression of the amount just of the global public debt, compare https://debtclock.s3.amazonaws.com/index.html. Note, however, that this already incomprehensible figure is probably to be doubled (if not tripled) because of the hidden debts! The hiding spots can be quite effective: in 2013/2014 Mozambique managed to hide the amount of $2 bln. from IMF and World Bank, just see the Staff Report for the 2017 Article IV Consultation for the Republic of Mozambique from Feb. 15, 2018.

debts seem to represent the global dominance and economic power of the United States whereas much smaller debt amounts in politically and economically weak countries express economic needs and emergency. A satisfaction pursuant rules such as the aforementioned sec. 362 BGB are illusory if not utopian.

Given this, it appears to be permissible or even necessary to think about and develop unorthodox ideas. Two of them shall be presented whereby it is to be clarified right from the outset that they offer (regrettably) only limited solutions. A comprehensive solution such as a resolvency proceeding for sovereigns will not be discussed here.[55]

The first idea is a simple change of existing contractual rules. Sec. 367 par. 1 BGB determines a ranking of payment calculations: When a debtor repays to its creditor an amount insufficient for the extinction of the entire liability, then this amount is credited first to the costs, then to the interests, and only finally to the principal debt.[56] This is meant to impede an increase of the interests but, at the same time, this rule prevents the principal debt from shrinking and thereby reducing the interests. One is tempted to see this rule as a quite rational and harmless norm with, on first sight, no implications for the problems to be addressed in the present context. The contrary is true, however; this becomes evident when looking at sec. 497 par. 3 BGB which addresses almost the same situation but comes to a slightly different determination, namely that the ranking order is not costs, interests, principal, but rather costs, principal, interests. The fact that this rule was introduced in a package of consumer protection legislation is a clear indicator that this rule is more debtor-friendly than sec. 367 BGB.[57] It is this context which

---

[55.] On this, just compare the contributions—among them that from Jay—in: Paulus (ed.), A Debt Restructuring Mechanism for Sovereigns—Do We Need a Legal Procedure? 2014.

[56.] Interests first and then principal debt is a time-honored solution, compare Iustinian's Digests 36.4.5.21 (Ulpian). The German Supreme Court for Civil Law Matters decided that this rule is to be applied also in an insolvency proceeding, dec. from 17.2.2011—IX ZR 83/10, NZI 2011, 247.

[57.] Schürnbrand in: Münchener Kommentar-BGB, section 497 marg. no. 25; Paulus, Ein drittes Plädoyer für unscheinbare Normen, Juristische Schulung (JuS) 2017, 103, 105.

makes respective deliberations[58] plausible whether or not rules on consumer protection should and could be instrumentalised for inter-state business as well.

Whereas this ranking order is probably not more than just a tiny little piece in a necessarily much broader mosaic of supportive measures, is the second idea to be presented here much more radical. The argument behind it is based on the lawyers' strange adherence to and belief in symbolic acts. One anecdote and one case (heavily discussed among ancient Roman jurists) shall demonstrate what is meant with this:

As to the anecdote:[59] "Times are hard, everyone has debts and everybody lives on tick. A tourist travels through the town and stops at a little hotel. He tells the hotelier that he would want to have a look into the rooms available as he considers to stay here overnight. As a bail for the keys, he leaves a 100 € bill on the counter. The hotelier hands him over the keys, picks up, as soon as the tourist is upstairs, the money bill and runs to the town's butcher and pays his debt there. The butcher takes the bill and runs down the street to the farmer to pay his debt. So it goes from the farmer to the cooperative director, from there to the inn keeper, and from there to the prostitute. Since she has an open invoice at the hotel, the bill finally comes back to the counter from which the 100 € bill's round trip began. And in just this moment the tourist comes down the stairs, returns the keys to the hotelier, and picks up the bill. He decided not to stay in this hotel."

The Roman law case dwells more or less on the same mechanism of an actually symbolic form of debt reduction or extinction, respectively: D owes C 100 and pays, as a first installment, ten. C accepts the 10 and, in return, hands them back to D as a gift. D thanks him and repeats the scene by offering the just-received 10 as a second installment. C accepts it and repeats the ritual, again and again. After eight more repetitions of such exchange, the question arises whether or

---

[58.] Compare Kaden (in this volume).
[59.] On this, compare Misik, Inflation, Polar 17, 2014, p. 15, 17.

not the original debt of 100 is satisfied and, therefore, extinguished, when this back and forth has happened ten times. The republican jurists were initially divided in their answers but after quite some time they decided to answer the question to the positive. So, the debt of 100 was finally understood as having been served by those 10 installment payments. Most legal historians see this discussion as evidence for the Roman jurists' interest also in theoretical questions. It is only David Daube who realized that this scenario has not been an intellectual gimmick but served the very practical need of rescuing upper-class peers from the bankruptcy stigma and at the same time allowing them to save their faces.[60]

Now, what is to be learned from these two somewhat irritating stories? Firstly, they both disclose the law's belief and trust in formalities quite nicely. Certain rituals—shifting the money ten times back and forth[61] or transferring a banknote in a way that the recipient acquires full disponibility of it—need to be performed in order to achieve a certain result. To be sure, the formalism could be reduced in both cases to an agreement between the parties involved with the same result: in the Roman law example the agreement would be about the haircut of 90%, i.e., reduction of the amount due to 10% combined with a waiver of the rest; in the "circulating bill" story, the parties would have to agree to a sort of netting. The second lesson of both stories is that a debt reduction can be achieved without burdening the debtor. Like in the case of the aforementioned legislative order of sec. 99 SAG or the cram-down rule of sec. 245 InsO in a plan proceeding[62] a benevolent creditor can help the debtor without violating the latter's pride. One should just imagine what happens if

---

[60.] Daube, Roman Law—Linguistic, Social and Philosophical Aspects,1969, p. 93 ff. on Dig. 46.3.67, Marcellus XIII dig.

[61.] It is a somewhat "entertaining" aperçu that, in the beginning of the Greek crisis, the payment streams mostly came from Frankfurt/M. and Paris and were sent back right away. However, this back and forth was done only once!

[62.] Sec. 245 InsO (taken from: www.gesetze-im-internet.de/englisch_inso/englisch_inso.html#p0983):

(1) Even if the necessary majorities have not been achieved, a voting group shall be deemed to have consented if

the European Central Bank would give the amount of €1 billion to a
Greek entity and asking it to let it circulate around like in the example and insisting that the €1 billion. has to be returned after five days.
Like a tornado which leaves an aisle in the forest the money would
leave behind an aisle of debt reduction.

VI. Résumé

It is obvious that the bad-weather insolvency law cannot offer
golden solutions. There are legal mechanisms, though, which could
be used as a compensation for a non-existing market; they reach
from promises of future performances to debt-equity-swaps and to
set-offs. However, even when ignoring for the moment that these
mechanisms barely manage the main task of any functioning fine-
weather insolvency law—namely to allocate unproductive assets as
quickly as possible to their best possible productivity—it is hard to
see that they could sustain an entire economy for a longer period of
time. This could be done through foreign investments, which, for

---

1. the members of such a group are likely not to be placed at a disadvantage by the
insolvency plan compared with their situation without such plan,

2. the members of such a group participate to a reasonable extent in the economic value devolving on the parties under the plan, and

3. the majority of the voting groups have backed the plan with the necessary
majorities.

(2) A reasonable participation of a group of creditors for the purpose of subsection (1) no. 2 shall exist if under the plan

1. no other creditor will receive economic values exceeding the full amount of
his claim;

2. neither a creditor with a lower-ranking claim to satisfaction without a plan,
compared with the creditors forming his group, nor the debtor nor a person holding
the debtor's shares receives an economic value; and

3. no creditor to be satisfied on an equal footing with the creditors forming his
group without a plan receives an advantage with respect to such creditors.

(3) A reasonable participation of a group of shareholders for the purpose of subsection (1) no. 2 shall exist if under the plan

1. no creditor receives economic benefits exceeding the full amount of his claim and

2. no shareholder who would be equal in rank to the shareholders in the group if
no plan were drawn up is better placed than they are.

obvious reasons, presupposes realistic chances for profit. In the end, a nationalization appears to be inevitable; but this option is more often than not burdened with the inherent danger of prolonging the inescapable exit of the companies and thereby increasing the ultimate damage for not only the creditors but also the country itself. If a country enters the so far still legally unregulated sphere of insolvency we have learned from the Argentinian, Greek and many other examples what the costs are. In the end it is this country's unsecured creditors who have to pay for the damage (thereby leaving aside the innumerable personal tragedies of that country's population).

Alternatively, the traditional insolvency law could be replaced—at least temporarily—by a model that had been applied every now and then in history: just a discharge of overindebted debtors. This can be achieved either by statutory regulation (such as sec. 90, 96, 99 SAG or the U.S. insolvency discharge rules) or by applying acts which, in the eyes of lawyers, carry the meaning of extinguishing debts. These bad-weather protection examples prove that the space "behind" the regular insolvency proceeding is not necessarily a law-free zone; the preceding thoughts are meant to incentivize further deliberations as to how to cope with such situations. They should not be left to illegal practices where the strongest takes it all.

A New Approach to Executory Contracts

John A. E. Pottow[*]

I. Introduction and Summary

Few topics have bedeviled the bankruptcy community as much as the proper treatment of executory contracts under section 365 of the Bankruptcy Code.[1] The case law is "hopelessly convoluted" and a "bramble-filled thicket."[2] While many have struggled in the bootless task of providing coherence to the unwieldy corpus of case law and commentary, all would agree Jay Westbrook has been at the modern vanguard of this Sisyphean task.[3] (I assign Westbrook to the "modern" forefront, thereby relegating Vern Countryman, whose legacy in this domain rightly persists, to the annals of history, choosing as my perhaps arbitrary dividing line the adoption of the 1978 Bankruptcy Code.)[4]

[*] John Philip Dawson Collegiate Professor of Law at the University of Michigan Law School. The author thanks Conor McNamara, Michigan JD class of 2018, for research assistance. He also thanks Asher Steinberg, as well as all participants in the symposium (too many of whom to list here generously gave me comments). Copyright © 96 Tex. L. Rev. 1437–82 (2018). Reproduced here with permission.

[1] 11 U.S.C. § 365 (2012).

[2] *Cohen v. Drexel Burnham Lambert Grp., Inc. (In re Drexel Burnham Lambert Grp., Inc.)*, 138 B.R. 687, 690 (Bankr. S.D.N.Y. 1992) (citations omitted).

[3] See, e.g., Jay Lawrence Westbrook, A Functional Analysis of Executory Contracts, 74 Minn. L. Rev. 227, 239 (1989).

[4] 11 U.S.C. § 101 (2012). See generally Vern Countryman, Executory Contracts in Bankruptcy: Part I, 57 Minn. L. Rev. 439, 442–44 (1973) [hereinafter Countryman I] (propounding a seminal test).

Why have executory contracts proved so nettlesome? Under the Code, a large part of the damage is self-inflicted, resulting from unfortunate drafting that begat an ever-accumulating snowball of confused jurisprudence.[5] But there is also a salience bias (vividness bias, really) at work of disproportionate focus on the striking plight of the contractual counterparty who is aggrieved when a debtor deploys executory-contract rights under section 365—rights that accord the debtor certain powers in dealing with executory contracts otherwise unavailable at state law. (This bias underestimates the baseline unhappiness that bankruptcy inflicts upon all creditors equally and fairly.) Westbrook has relatedly noted that courts in their struggle to do equity under the Code sometimes resist these executory-contract powers.[6] In doing so, they gravitate to the textual restriction of section 365 to "executory" contracts.[7] Skeptical courts frequently conclude that a contract is not "executory"—and therefore cannot fall under section 365—to deny relief that strikes these courts as unseemly. Indeed, a judicial cottage industry in bankruptcy has developed on the definition of "executoriness" and concomitant scope of access to section 365.[8]

Countryman gets first credit for tackling the definitional challenge of what it means for a contract to be "executory" under the prior Bankruptcy Act. His eponymous test for executoriness is well cited in many opinions and is otherwise known as the "material breach" test.[9] Westbrook, albeit with characteristic gentility, upended that doctrinal framework by advocating an abolition of the concept of executoriness from the Code altogether and replacing it by (or subsuming it within) a "functional" analysis focused on debtor

---

[5.] See infra note 21 and accompanying text.

[6.] Jay Lawrence Westbrook & Kelsi Stayart White, The Demystification of Contracts in Bankruptcy, 91 Am. Bankr. L.J. 481, 510–11 (2017) ("The problem with wild cards is that chance—sometimes found under the mask of equity—can favor either player.").

[7.] 11 U.S.C. § 365(a) (2012) (referencing "executory" contracts).

[8.] See, e.g., Am. Bankr. Inst., Commission to Study the Reform of chapter 11, 112 (2014) [hereinafter ABI Report] ("[C]ourt[s] on a case-by-case basis determine[] whether a particular contract is executory."); Westbrook & White, supra note 6, at 494–95 (noting that "courts continued to expand the application" of multiple executoriness tests "to more and more kinds of contracts").

[9.] Countryman I, supra note 4, at 460.

economic benefit.[10] His executoriness discussion, started three decades ago, and especially his back-and-forth on the topic with Michael Andrew, is canonical bankruptcy scholarship.[11]

The challenges of defining executoriness persist through today. The recent American Bankruptcy Institute's Commission on the Reform of chapter 11 tasked a specific Expert Group to examine the Code's treatment of executory contracts.[12] The Group's first recommendation was to abolish the requirement of executoriness as a restriction on section 365.[13] (Yes, Westbrook was front and center on the group.) The Commission, however, stunned the insolvency community by not only rejecting the Group's recommendation, albeit in an apparently divided decision, but doubling down on executoriness: it advocated its *retention* in the Code and the *codification* of the Countryman material breach test for definition.[14] In doing so, the Commission noted— without an apparent whiff of irony—that this decision would allow reliance on "well developed" case law.[15] To describe the executory-contracts precedents in bankruptcy as "well developed" (or even "vaguely helpful") skirts credulity.[16] Were the Commission's recommendations

---

[10.] Westbrook, *supra* note 3, at 230.

[11.] See generally Michael T. Andrew, Executory Contracts in Bankruptcy: Understanding "Rejection," 59 U. Colo. L. Rev. 845, 849 (1988) [hereinafter Andrew, Rejection] (characterizing "the election to 'assume or reject' [as] the election to assume or not assume"); Michael T. Andrew, Executory Contracts Revisited: A Reply to Professor Westbrook, 62 U. Colo. L. Rev. 1, 3 (1991) [hereinafter Andrew, Reply to Westbrook] (noting "contrary views on specific elements of Westbrook's analysis").

[12.] See generally ABI Report, *supra* note 8 (outlining "Recommended Principles" for the treatment of executory contracts in bankruptcy).

[13.] Advisory Comm. on Executory Contracts and Leases, ABI Commission to Study the Reform of chapter 11: Executive Summary Regarding Section 365 Issues 1 (2013) [hereinafter ABI Advisory Committee] ("The Advisory Committee recommends eliminating the term 'executory' in favor of adopting the Functional Test which allows the trustee or debtor in possession . . . to keep beneficial contracts and reject burdensome ones based solely upon benefit/harm to the estate."), http://commission.abi.org/sites/default/files/ABI-365-Comm-Overview-Summary_(WEST_34307609_3).DOCX [https://perma.cc/2PH7-GCHJ].

[14.] ABI Report, *supra* note 8, at 112.

[15.] *Id.* at 112, 115 (describing case law as a "valuable resource").

[16.] See Westbrook & White, *supra* note 6, at 497 ("[T]here was no thorough explanation of the majority recommendation or how it addresses the courts' frustration with executoriness analysis and their divergent conclusions.").

in any danger of attracting congressional attention, this linguistic leg-erdemain might be worrisome, but thankfully the dysfunction of our modern Congress has ridden to the rescue. Thus, the debate over the role (and very definition) of "executoriness" in bankruptcy law has not only been rekindled, but appears to be here to stay.

Acknowledging that the thrust of commentary heeds Westbrook's call to abolish executoriness as a gatekeeper to the section 365 pow-ers,[17] I want to offer a novel approach and argue against that grain. Specifically, in this Article I will suggest not only that the fight should be called off, but that defeat should be conceded. Executoriness, for better or worse (mostly worse), is here to stay in the Code. My resig-nation may seem like Westbrook heresy, but there is a method to my madness. Here is my key contention: the impulse behind the resist-ance to the abolition of executoriness, reflected most recently by the American Bankruptcy Institute (ABI) Commission's intransigence, is at root a reluctance (perhaps conscious, perhaps not) by elite lawyers to relinquish what they feel is a legal arbitrage opportunity to com-bat debtor power.[18] Namely, counterparties believe that the doctrinal fluidity of the concept of executoriness allows them wide latitude to argue a contract is executory when such a classification will accord them legal advantage over the debtor but in the next case argue that a similar contract is not executory when that contrary label will accord the leg up.[19] As such, executoriness's confusion and uncertainty is a feature rather than a bug.

Principled commentators like Westbrook decry this sneaki-ness, bemoaning the deadweight litigation loss. A clear, sensible

---

[17.] As far back as 1997, The National Bankruptcy Review Commission recom-mended deleting "executory" from section 365 to end the executoriness debates. Nat'l Bankr. Review Comm'n, Bankruptcy: The Next Twenty Years 454 (1997).

[18.] Economically, the ambiguity creates more of an option value than an arbitrage because there are not, of course, two separate markets, but I use arbitrage because I think it better captures the two-facedness of the evil presented.

[19.] Beyond the scope of this chapter is a formal model of the role of risk aversion addressing why lawyers do not equally foresee enjoying the benefits of being the debtor's counsel with the offsetting section 365 power they so fear. Loss aversion is likely interacting with the vividness bias.

rule defining executoriness should be established with a defensible normative foundation. Countryman offered one; Westbrook had another.[20] My approach sidesteps this skirmish. Rather than fight on what the definition of executoriness should be in an effort to wipe out the grey zone, my tack is to blunt the arbitrage impulse *ab initio*. The way to do so is by taking seriously how the Code should treat a *non-executory contract*, the presumable residual category of a contract flunking the executoriness test (whatever test is selected). The treatment of non-executory contracts is woefully undertheorized in bankruptcy literature, and so I try to fill this unwelcome void.[21] Indeed, cases where executoriness is litigated simply end after a declaration of non-executoriness without any rigorous working-through of the consequences.[22] This is regrettable. Treating the structure and policies of the Bankruptcy Code holistically, I will try to show what should happen to a non-executory contract in bankruptcy, entirely outside the domain of section 365. My conclusion is that while non-executory contracts may be treated as formally distinct from executory contracts, *their functional outcomes will mimic those of executory contracts by synthetic replication through other Code provisions*. If my analysis holds and non-executory contracts, while different, garner largely similar treatment to executory contracts, then the pernicious opportunity for arbitrage from the executoriness game will collapse.

This chapter will proceed as follows. First, it will offer an abbreviated explanation of the treatment of executory contracts under the Code, chronicling the development of the concept of executoriness

---

[20.] Compare infra note 63 and accompanying text (Countryman), with infra note 73 and accompanying text (Westbrook).

[21.] "[O]ne rule that could be considered 'well-settled' is that once a contract has been determined to be 'non-executory,' there are no rules." Westbrook & White, *supra* note 6, at 498. Even Countryman, whose treatment of executory contracts is encyclopedic, at most indirectly intimated at the proper treatment of non-executory contracts. See *id.* at 519 (characterizing charitably Countryman's treatment of the issue as "implicit").

[22.] See, e.g., In re Drake, 136 B.R. 325, 328 (Bankr. D. Mass. 1992) ("[T]he [a]greement cannot be deemed executory."); see also Westbrook & White, *supra* note 6, at 499 (collecting cases).

and the subsequent challenges of its effects. Second, it will explain a new approach that embraces and makes its peace with executoriness by focusing on the proper treatment of non-executory contracts. Third, it will address some of the anticipated counterarguments to the new approach. Finally, it will offer a quick road test to demonstrate how the new approach would have more easily resolved a major litigated precedent in this field.

II. The Problem of Executoriness and the Traditional Approach(es)

A. The Genesis of Executoriness and Section 365

1. The Historical Problem of Provability

Insolvency systems have been wrestling with executory-contract rights for quite some time. For example, the 1898 Bankruptcy Act sometimes respected so-called *ipso facto* clauses that terminate contracts automatically (*ipso facto*) upon the insolvency of a party,[23] an outcome now banned under section 365.[24] But the origin of the problems of modern executory contracts has to do with statutory drafting that addressed a different issue—the now-abolished concept of *provability*. Under the Act, only some financial grievances against an insolvent debtor were

---

[23.] See, e.g., *Irving Tr. Co. v. A.W. Perry, Inc.*, 293 U.S. 307, 311 (1934) (holding enforceable a provision that provided the "filing of the petition in bankruptcy was . . . a breach of the lease"). Even the old cases bristled at this doctrine and so cabined its reach at every turn. See, e.g., *Gazlay v. Williams*, 210 U.S. 41, 48–49 (1908) (holding the *ipso facto* provision ineffective); see also Vern Countryman, Executory Contracts in Bankruptcy: Part II, 58 Minn. L. Rev. 479, 522 (1974) [hereinafter Countryman II] (noting the old Act's "forfeiture provisions . . . are by their terms confined to leases"). I am leaving aside in this historical discussion the bizarre, now largely buried doctrine of "anticipatory breach" by bankruptcy. See *Cent. Tr. Co. v. Chi. Auditorium Ass'n*, 240 U.S. 581, 592 (1916) ("We conclude that proceedings, whether voluntary or involuntary, resulting in an adjudication of bankruptcy, are the equivalent of an anticipatory breach of an executory agreement.").

[24.] 11 U.S.C. § 365(e) (2012).

"provable,"[25] which functioned as a sort of bankruptcy version of ripeness. Consider, for example, a debtor who ran over someone's foot. The victim might claim money is owing; the debtor—driver might deny liability. If no lawsuit had yet been commenced, let alone concluded with a monetary judgment of a debt owing, then the claim was not *provable* in the debtor's bankruptcy proceeding.[26] This could be a mixed blessing. It was initially bad for the creditors, because they could not participate in the division of the debtor's assets, but it was sometimes good as well, because if the debtor survived after bankruptcy (e.g., the debtor was an individual or a reorganized corporation), then the unprovable claim survived as well, continuing to haunt the debtor post-discharge.[27] But if the debtor were a corporation in liquidation, the provability bar was all bad news for the creditor.

What about contracts? To understand the impact of provability, we first need to understand what trustees did with contracts, and to understand that, we need to understand what they did with leases. As remains the case today, trustees were entitled to all the debtor's property (some would say, "vest in title," some would say, "control as a mere custodian"),[28] but they were also free to abandon uneconomical assets.[29] The abandonment doctrine applied to leases of real property as well.[30] If the debtor had an ongoing ("unexpired")

[25.] See, e.g., *Zavelo v. Reeves*, 227 U.S. 625, 632 (1913) ("[O]nly provable debts are discharged.").

[26.] See, e.g., *Brown & Adams v. United Button Co.*, 149 F. 48, 53 (3d Cir. 1906) (holding that a claim for unliquidated damages that results from the injured property of another is not provable in bankruptcy).

[27.] See Countryman I, *supra* note 4, at 443 ("[U]nder section 17a of the Bankruptcy Act only provable debts are discharged.").

[28.] 11 U.S.C. § 541(a) (2012). While assignees under the Acts vested in the debtor's property outright, equity receivers (who preceded modern reorganizations) merely controlled debtor property as custodians. *Quincy, Mo. & Pac. R.R. Co. v. Humphreys*, 145 U.S. 82, 97 (1892) ("[The equity receivers] were ministerial officers, . . . mere custodians.").

[29.] See *Am. File Co. v. Garrett*, 110 U.S. 288, 295 (1884) (recognizing the principle based on historical English practice).

[30.] See, e.g., *Quincy, Mo.*, 145 U.S. at 102 (applying the abandonment doctrine to a long-term lease).

lease that was financially burdensome, the trustee could abandon it. Now, that raised a provability problem, especially when traditional real-property remedies are considered.[31] Under many states' property law, the rent covenant stemmed from the realty itself, and so dispossession terminated the prospective obligation to pay rent.[32] (The separate contractual promise to pay the rent prospectively, which the trustee might have breached by rejecting the lease, was a separate problem.)[33] In other words, while the bankruptcy system could get its head around a claim for unpaid back rent quite well (a debt owing to the creditor/landlord), it struggled with whether a claim for unpaid future rent triggered by the trustee's abandonment of an uneconomical long-term lease was provable, especially when the landlord had possession of the land returned by the debtor's vacating the premises.

Related uncertainty befell contracts. If the debtor were current on any invoices, would abandonment ("rejection") of the contract trigger a provable claim for breach of future expectation loss?[34] Case law initially struggled, much wanting to find that it should.[35] Congress tried to clarify the matter, beginning in 1933, to allow for more widespread provability. Starting with railroad receivership cases in section 77 of the Act (amended two years later), it allowed for a rejection counterparty to be "deemed . . . a creditor . . . to the extent of the

---

[31] The provability problem extended to leases of personalty as well. See Countryman I, *supra* note 4, at 449–50 n.50 (collecting cases).

[32] For example, *William Filene's Sons Co. v. Weed*, 245 U.S. 597, 601 (1918) ("Rent issues from the land.").

[33] See *Miller v. Irving Tr. Co.*, 296 U.S. 256, 258 (1935) ("Under the clause in question, it was, at the time the petition in bankruptcy was filed, uncertain, a mere matter of speculation, whether any liability ever would arise under it.").

[34] The older Acts were more forgiving of contract provability than "pure tort." For example., section 63a(8) allowed for provability of "contingent contractual liabilities," but not tort claims, *Schall v. Comers*, 251 U.S. 239, 248–49, 253 (1920), absent reduction to judgment (or implied assumpsit), *Davis v. Aetna Acceptance Co.*, 293 U.S. 328, 331 (1934).

[35] See, e.g., *Irving Tr. Co. v. A.W. Perry, Inc.*, 293 U.S. 307, 310–11 (1934) (holding an *ipso facto* clause effective to terminate a lease and trigger a provable claim).

actual damage or injury."[36] Section 77 begat 77B (extending the application beyond railroad reorganizations to corporations), which in turn begat chapter X in 1938's Chandler Act's more general corporate reorganization "chapter" provisions.[37]

Similarly, in the liquidation context, 1934 amendments to the Act's section 63a(7) allowed for "claims for damages respecting *executory contracts* including future rents," which was rewritten in the Chandler Act for "claims for anticipatory breach of contracts, *executory in whole or in part*, including unexpired leases of real or personal property."[38] These amendments also resolved what was implicit from the abandonment doctrine: that the trustee could never be forced to take unwanted property; it was the trustee's election whether to assume or reject an unexpired lease,[39] and so Congress provided that *affirmative acknowledgment* was required to assume a lease, with the default in liquidation being deemed rejection after a period of time. Specifically, "[w]ithin sixty days after the adjudication, the trustee shall assume or reject any executory contract, including unexpired leases of real property. . . . Any such contract or lease not assumed or rejected within such time . . . shall be deemed to be rejected."[40]

[36.] Bankruptcy Act, ch. 774, section 77, 49 Stat. 911, 914 (1935); see also Bankruptcy Act, ch. 204, section 77, 47 Stat. 1467, 1474 (1933) (allowing creditors of a railroad to file a petition).

[37.] Bankruptcy Act, ch. 424, section 77B, 48 Stat. 911, 915 (1934) (including "claims under executory contracts, whether or not such claims would otherwise constitute provable claims under this Act").

[38.] Bankruptcy Act, ch. 424, section 63a(7), 48 Stat. 911, 924 (1934) (emphasis added); Bankruptcy Act, ch. 575, section 63a(9), 52 Stat. 840, 873 (1938) (emphasis added).

[39.] See *United States Tr. Co. v. Wabash W. Ry. Co.*, 150 U.S. 287, 299–300 (1893) ("The general rule . . . is undisputed that an assignee or receiver is not bound to adopt the contracts, accept the leases, or otherwise step into the shoes of his assignor, if in his opinion it would be unprofitable or undesirable to do so; and he is entitled to a reasonable time to elect whether to adopt or repudiate such contracts.").

[40.] Bankruptcy Act, ch. 575, section 70b, 52 Stat. 840, 880–81 (1938). Countryman chronicles how the judicially created doctrine of abandonment carried forth the English practice that "[i]t has long been a recognized principle of the bankrupt [sic] laws that the assignees were not bound to accept property of an onerous or unprofitable character." Countryman I, *supra* note 4, at 440 (quoting *Am. File Co. v. Garrett*, 110 U.S. 288, 295 (1884)).

This explicit treatment of lease claims under section 63a(7) and contract claims under section 63a(9), albeit with slightly different language, solved the provability conundrum of postpetition repudiation ("rejection") damages for these unfinished transactions; they were henceforth all provable claims. This statutory introduction of the term "executory" made sense, of course, because only if a contract is *executory* (i.e., not completely "executed") can there be a claim for anticipatory repudiation upon the trustee's disclamation.[41] If the contract is fully performed, by contrast, there are no future obligations over which to fight about provability, only unpaid matured debts to be filed as claims.[42] Similarly, a lease needs to be *unexpired* for there to be a potential breach claim for unpaid future rents. An expired lease may have some back rent owing but again raises no provability issues; fully concluded transactions are unremarkable for provability. Thus, "executory" entered the U.S. bankruptcy statutory lexicon through these Depression-era provisions that were designed to clarify the provability status of claims for unfulfilled future obligations triggered by a bankruptcy trustee's abandonment of financial detritus.

2. *Provability's Solution and the Introduction of Executoriness (and Section 365)*

As part of Congress's bankruptcy overhaul resulting in the 1978 Code, the concept of provability was finally abolished with a wide definition of "claim" that covered all conceivable monetary obligations, such as contingent, unmatured, and unliquidated claims, like the tort cause of action discussed previously.[43] Everything was now a "claim" and hence both provable and dischargeable in a bankruptcy proceeding (no more haunting the discharged debtor with the financial sins of

---

[41] See Andrew, Reply to Westbrook, *supra* note 11, at 34 n.155 (noting that under the equivalent U.K. Insolvency Act, a trustee may "disclaim" "any unprofitable contract," which has the effect of its exclusion from the estate) (citations omitted).

[42] 11 U.S.C. § 502 (2012).

[43] *Id.* section 101(5); H.R. Rep. No. 95-595, at 180 (1977) ("H.R. 8200[, the Bankruptcy Code,] abolishes the concept of provability in bankruptcy cases."). (Source text is entirely capitalized.).

the past). With everything becoming provable, the very need for that term was eliminated.[44] Congress's intent in so doing was to corral every possible financial beef with a debtor into one forum and compel resolution with comprehensive finality.[45] This neater solution was widely praised and, had Congress just thought of it back in 1938, would have obviated the requirement for section 63a and the language of "executory" contracts.[46] Congress also consolidated the prior Chandler Act provisions into section 365, which now covers the estate's treatment of executory contracts and unexpired leases.[47] Section 365(a) provides: "[T]he trustee, subject to the court's approval, may assume or reject any *executory contract* or unexpired lease of the debtor."[48]

Note that section 365(a) codified the court's oversight role in the assumption or rejection of contracts, too, which in turn spawned jurisprudence over the standard by which the court ought to assess the debtor's decision (with a majority approach settling on a business

---

[44.] Well, nearly everything. A painful strand of cases has emerged finding that executory contracts (usually leases) neither assumed nor rejected in a chapter 11 simply "ride through," saddling the debtor with an ongoing lease and the counterparty with an unprovable claim. For example, In re Bos. Post Rd. Ltd. P'ship, 21 F.3d 477, 484 (2d Cir. 1994) ("A debtor in chapter 11 must either assume or reject its leases with third parties. . . . If the debtor does neither, the leases continue in effect and the lessees have no provable claim against the bankruptcy estate.").

[45.] See H.R. Rep. No. 95-595, at 309 ("By this broadest possible definition [of claim] . . . the Bill contemplates that all legal obligations of the debtor, no matter how remote or contingent, will be able to be dealt with in the bankruptcy case.") (Source text is entirely capitalized.); S. Rep. No. 95-989, at 21–22 (1978) (using the same language); H.R. Doc. No. 93-137, pt. 2, at 154–55 nn.1–5 (1973) (containing the proposed text).

[46.] See, e.g., Westbrook & White, *supra* note 6, at 494 (describing the "Code['s] eliminat[ion of] the concept of 'provability'" as an "important change"); see also In re M.A.S. Realty Corp., 318 B.R. 234, 237 (Bankr. D. Mass. 2004) (describing the revision that eliminated provability as "a distinction of critical importance"); *Cohen v. Drexel Burnham Lambert Grp., Inc.* (*In re Drexel Burnham Lambert Grp., Inc.*), 138 B.R. 687, 706–07 (Bankr. S.D.N.Y. 1992) (describing the Code's abolishment of provability as a "structural innovation[]").

[47.] See Westbrook & White, *supra* note 6, at 492 ("These [statutory] origins are important because they reveal that Congress intended the statutory predecessor to section 365 to ensure that counterparties holding rejected contracts, including leases, would be paid and discharged.").

[48.] 11 U.S.C. § 365(a) (2012) (emphasis added).

judgment rule level of deference).[49] But even more important than section 365(a) was the power conferred on trustees and debtors under section 365(b). Unhelpfully phrased as a *restriction* on assumption, section 365(b)'s true import is to confer a *power* upon the debtor to cure contractual defaults.

If there has been a default in an executory contract or unexpired lease of the debtor, the trustee may not assume such contract or lease unless, at the time of assumption of such contract or lease, the trustee—(A) cures, or provides adequate assurance that the trustee will promptly cure, such default.[50]

This flex of preemptive federal law trumps general state contract law, because a material breach of contract ordinarily allows the aggrieved counterparty the self-help remedy of termination.[51] Section 365(b) overrides this and says notwithstanding the (material) breach of an executory contract, if the breach is cured pursuant to section 365(b), the debtor in federal bankruptcy may assume the contract and carry on under its benefits. The counterparty's self-help remedy of termination is scuttled.[52] This cure-and-assume power irritates contractual counterparties tremendously, of course, because the contracts those parties most want to terminate are bad deals that they made, which are by zero-sum game reasoning precisely the sorts of good deals that the debtor/trustee is anxious to assume. But for section 365(b), the debtor would be unable to do this in the face of a material breach at common law. Counterparties equally hate a debtor's rejection of an executory contract containing a good deal for the counterparty by the same logic.

[49.] *Lubrizol Enters., Inc. v. Richmond Metal Finishers, Inc. (In re Richmond Metal Finishers, Inc.)*, 756 F.2d 1043, 1046 (4th Cir. 1985) ("[The] question [of acceptance or rejection] must start with . . . deference mandated by the sound business judgment rule. . . .").

[50.] 11 U.S.C. § 365(b)(1) (2012).

[51.] 1 Restatement (Second) of Contracts section 237 (Am. Law Inst. 1981).

[52.] See, e.g., In re Circle K Corp., 190 B.R. 370, 376 (B.A.P. 9th Cir. 1995) (noting how section 365(b) overruled such pre-Code cases as In re Schokbeton Indus., Inc., 466 F.2d 171 (5th Cir. 1972), which held that breach precludes assumption and bankruptcy accords no power to cure).

Section 365's power is even worse for the counterparty, because it cannot even be "contracted around." For example, the parties' decision to say that a filing for bankruptcy *ipso facto* terminates the contract is explicitly invalidated.[53] And even seemingly *impossible-to-cure* breaches are, in some contexts, excused under section 365.[54] In sum, section 365 provides a powerful arrow in the debtor's quiver, according the debtor the option to "reshape" the bankruptcy estate with an option to assume valuable contractual rights,[55] either for performance by the debtor itself or for assignment to a third party for a price, notwithstanding the existence of a breach.[56]

B. Executoriness as a Restraint on Section 365: The Creation of New Problems

Counterparty hostility to section 365 drives the annals of case law of litigants seeking to avoid its reach. And the key to their stratagem is textual seizure upon the statutory qualifier that only "executory" contracts are subject to section 365 and all her debtor powers. Aggrieved counterparties often insist that the debtor's contract is not an executory contract and hence cannot "enter" section 365. Important for explaining the chaotic case law in this area, the litigious counterparties are what might be called "equal opportunity executoriness critics." When the debtor had a good contract (and hence a bad one for the counterparty) it sought to assume, the counterparty would claim the contract was not executory and, therefore, could not avail itself of the cure and assumption powers of section 365.[57]

---

[53] 11 U.S.C. § 365(e)(1) (2012).

[54] *Id.* section 365(b)(1)(A) (rescuing certain lease defaults).

[55] Elizabeth Warren, Jay Lawrence Westbrook, Katherine Porter & John A.E. Pottow, The Law of Debtors and Creditors 453–54 (7th ed. 2014).

[56] Lest the uninitiated reader worry Congress went wild with section 365, she should be assuaged by the provisions that incorporate common law bars on assignment, such as an inability to assign "personal" contracts. See 11 U.S.C. § 365(c)(1) (2012).

[57] *Post v. Sigel & Co., Ltd. (In re Sigel & Co., Ltd.)*, 923 F.2d 142, 145–46 (9th Cir. 1991) (rejecting counterparty's argument that contract's non-executoriness precluded debtor assumption under section 365).

But in cases in which the contract was burdensome for the debtor (and hence good for the counterparty), the counterparty would then argue that the contract was not executory and, therefore, could not be rejected.[58] Note the bizarre logic under this reasoning, as some courts blithely pronounced: if "the contract is not executory, . . . [it is] neither assumable nor capable of rejection."[59] A contract that neither can be assumed nor rejected creates an existential legal crisis, which some have described as "zombie" contracts that leave the debtor in a "legal limbo."[60] Many a court caught in the middle of an executoriness fight would make the initial decision, whether the contract was indeed executory or not, and then simply hide from the consequence of a finding of non-executoriness, presumably hoping the parties would just sort out amongst themselves what to do next in this limbo.[61] Court after court, right up to the circuit level, has continued to struggle.[62] And debtors, too, flounder over just what they can do in a world of uncertain executoriness.[63]

---

[58] For example, *Lycoming Engines v. Superior Air Parts, Inc. (In re Superior Air Parts)*, 486 B.R. 728, 738 (Bankr. N.D. Tex. 2012) ("[W]hen a contract is non-executory, the debtor remains bound to its obligations."); In re Spectrum Info. Techs., Inc., 193 B.R. 400, 403 (Bankr. E.D.N.Y. 1996) (noting creditor's objection that the "[a]greement is not an 'executory contract' . . . and, therefore, not subject to rejection").

[59] In re Hawker Beechcraft, Inc., 486 B.R. 264, 276 (Bankr. S.D.N.Y. 2013). These cases are legion: "This Court has already ruled that the Settlement Agreement is not executory, and therefore the Debtor could not reject it. Likewise, since it is not an executory contract, the Debtor cannot assume it." In re Airwest Int'l, Inc., No. 86-00145, 1988 WL 113101, at *3 (Bankr. D. Haw. Oct. 12, 1988).

[60] See Westbrook & White, *supra* note 6, at 482 ("We propose an end to zombie contracts and the obsolete notions that keep them upright by abolishing the 'material breach' rule."); Westbrook, *supra* note 3, at 239.

[61] For example, In re Interstate Bakeries Corp., 751 F.3d 955, 964 (8th Cir. 2014) (limiting itself to declaration of non-executoriness); In re S.A. Holding Co., LLC, 357 B.R. 51, 59 (Bankr. D.N.J. 2006) (same).

[62] "Because section 365 applies only to executory contracts, a debtor-in-possession does not have the option of rejecting or assuming non-executory contracts and remains bound by the debtor's obligations under those contracts after the bankruptcy filing." *Stewart Foods, Inc. v. Broecker (In re Stewart Foods, Inc.)*, 64 F.3d 141, 145 (4th Cir. 1995) (noting elsewhere in its opinion that the consequence of deemed continuation is the same as assumption).

[63] For example, In re Sudbury, Inc., 153 B.R. 776, 776 (Bankr. N.D. Ohio 1993) (seeking to avoid unwelcome contract by arguing in the alternative either it was

"Executoriness," a little textual throwaway from the Chandler Act era's amendments clarifying archaic provability issues, has now become the hook of one of bankruptcy law's most intractable (and pointless) sources of jurisprudential confusion—What is an "executory" contract in bankruptcy that the debtor can subject to section 365?[64]

C. Traditional Responses to Executoriness's Problems

1. Defining Executoriness: Countryman and the Material Breach Test

This brings us back to Vern Countryman. Neither the Act nor the Code defined "executory," perhaps thinking it too obvious.[65] An important academic figure in the development of the 1978 Bankruptcy Code, Countryman propounded a widespread test that now bears his name for whether a contract is executory. Under Countryman's definition, a contract is executory if both parties have sufficient unperformed obligations so that either's discontinuance would constitute a material breach, hence the label "material breach" test.[66] Courts loved the test's seeming simplicity, although only a few openly recognized that it just pushed litigation onto the "materiality" prong.[67]

---

executory and would be rejected or it was non-executory and therefore incapable of assumption).

[64] An interesting, but ultimately unhelpful, Supreme Court foray into this riddle is *Central Tablet Mfg. Co. v. United States*, 417 U.S. 673 (1974), which attempted to distinguish "executory" from "executed." *Id.* at 684–85, n.7.

[65] In the adoption of the Code in 1978, Congress candidly admitted it had no definition of "executory." H.R. Rep. No. 95-595, at 347 (1977) ("Though there is no precise definition of what contracts are executory, it generally includes contracts on which performance remains due to some extent on both sides.") (Source text is entirely capitalized.).

[66] Countryman I, *supra* note 4, at 460.

[67] See *Chattanooga Mem'l Park v. Still (In re Jolly)*, 547 F.2d 349, 350–51 (6th Cir. 1978) (noting that material breach test does "not resolve this [executoriness] problem"). The zenith of confusion over "materiality" of remaining obligations—and hence the make-or-break point on executoriness—likely arises in the intellectual property cases with licensing agreements. Westbrook and White assemble a

The material breach test does indeed work well for many simple contracts, but problems arise with more nuanced arrangements. Take, for example, option contracts, where the debtor merely holds a valuable option to purchase Blackacre for a favorable price. Lacking an obligation ever to exercise the option, the debtor could scarcely be said to commit a "material breach" (or any breach) should she decline to exercise it. Under the Countryman test, this option contract would not be executory and hence could not fall under section 365 with its power to assume.[68] Counterparty—optioners who made bad deals were quick to make this argument in their debtor's bankruptcy cases, convincing courts accepting the Countryman test that the debtor simply *could not assume the option* as it could not fall under section 365(a).[69] Other problematic examples abound, including the chimerical rights hanging over a departed employee with a noncompete clause in her (erstwhile) employment contract. Clearly the employer had no remaining obligations that could be materially breached, even though the employee clearly did. The Countryman test said the noncompete was no longer an executory contract, and thus the debtor *could not reject it* under section 365, meaning the debtor—employee remained somehow permanently saddled with a de facto nondischargeable obligation.[70] And so on. Indeed, courts often resorted to "analytical gymnast[ics]" to find contracts executory (or not) in order to bring them under (or outside) section 365's scope to achieve just results.[71]

---

considerable footnote showing the demoralizing conflict in case law over materiality in this domain. See Westbrook & White, *supra* note 6, at 508 n.141, 504 n.125.

[68] For example, *Travelodge Int'l, Inc. v. Cont'l Props., Inc. (In re Cont'l Props., Inc.)*, 15 B.R. 732, 736 (Bankr. D. Haw. 1981) ("Since the Agreement is an option contract and not an executory contract, it cannot be assumed.").

[69] For example, *Intermet Realty P'ship v. First Pa. Bank (In re Intermet Realty P'ship)*, 26 B.R. 383, 388 (Bankr. E.D. Pa. 1983) ("There is no interest which could be termed an executory contract and assumed by the debtor.").

[70] See, e.g., In re Spooner, No. 11-31525, 2012 WL 909515, at *3 (Bankr. N.D. Ohio Mar. 16, 2012) (finding a noncompete contract not executory and hence un-rejectable).

[71] *Bronner v. Chenoweth-Massie P'ship (In re Nat'l Fin. Realty Tr.)*, 226 B.R. 586, 589 (Bankr. W.D. Ky. 1998). Compare In re Ichiban, Case No. 06-10316-RGM,

2. Backlash: Westbrook's Call for Abolition

The seminal scholar to confront the problems of the executoriness doctrine and the Countryman test was Westbrook, who advocated the simplest solution: abolishing the executoriness requirement altogether and refocusing attention on the section 365(a) question whether the debtor's business decision to assume or reject a contract should survive judicial scrutiny.[72] For what one assumes was branding purposes, Westbrook felt compelled to style his abolition- ist argument a "functionalist" approach to defining executoriness, even going so far as suggesting courts could fit his approach into existing case law.[73] More specifically, Westbrook initially said the test of whether a contract is executory is whether there is an economic benefit to assuming or rejecting it for the estate.[74] He then clarified in subsequent writing that the assumed precondition of the defi- nition of executory is the historical common law definition—i.e., whether there was literally any performance, by any party, any- where, left under the contract that still had to be done.[75] Stripped bare, Westbrook's position was not really an *interpretation* of execu- toriness at all; it was a compelling normative argument to purge the

---

2014 WL 2937088, at *1–2 (Bankr. E.D. Va. June 30, 2014) (finding that seemingly trivial notice and appraisal provisions, while contingent, are sufficiently mate- rial for remaining ongoing obligations to render LLC agreement executory), with In re Knowles, No. 6:11-bk-11717-KSJ, 2013 WL 152434, at *4 (Bankr. M.D. Fla. Jan. 15, 2013) (contending that similar provisions are too remote to be mate- rial remaining obligations and so contract is non-executory). In In re Drake, 136 B.R. 325, 325 (Bankr. D. Mass. 1992), the trustee argued in the alternative that the employee—debtor's noncompete agreement was either non-executory and, therefore, could not be rejected or executory and, therefore, could be assumed and assigned!

[72.] Westbrook, *supra* note 3, at 230 (advocating "abolishing the requirement of executoriness altogether").

[73.] See *id.* at 327 ("[T]he functional approach fits neatly within the existing struc- ture and the detailed provisions of the Code.").

[74.] *Id.* at 253 (delineating "Net Value" calculus in bankruptcy).

[75.] 1 Samuel Williston, A Treatise on the Law of Contracts section 1:19 (4th ed. 2007) (observing that courts identify an executory contract as "a contract, the obli- gation of which relates to the future, or a contract under which the parties have bound themselves to future activity that is not yet completed or performed.").

executoriness requirement.[76] Some courts bit,[77] but for many, it was a bridge too far.[78]

3. Doubling Down: The ABI Commission's Retrenchment

Despite some enthusiastic takers, Westbrook's alternative never gained the traction of the Countryman test. True, the recent ABI Commission's Expert Group right out of the gates took Westbrook's abolitionist argument as its first recommendation for improvements to the Code on the topic of executory contracts.[79] The Commission, however, rejected this suggestion, preferring instead the "well-developed" case law on executoriness, because it provides guidance to parties and courts.[80] In fact, the Commission recommended codifying the Countryman test into law, cheerfully burying the vexing questions of options, noncompetes, and other difficult contract cases into an encyclopedic footnote to its report,[81] vying for the 2014 Understatement of the Year Award in admitting that courts "struggled" and the test produced inconsistencies.[82] But the decision was not just motivated by pedigree. Lying just beneath, or even at the surface, was a naked distributive concern: that section 365 accords too much power to the debtor, and so the executoriness wrinkle serves a "gating feature" function that allows some counterparties to win arguments on executoriness grounds that prevent a debtor from gaining access to section 365 and taking action that the counterparty dreads.[83]

---

[76] He eventually came clean. Westbrook & White, *supra* note 6, at 484 n.16 ("Functional Analysis was not an approach to determining executoriness, but a proposal to abandon executoriness all together as a threshold test.").

[77] See, e.g., In re Bayou Shores SNF, LLC, 525 B.R. 160, 168 (Bankr. M.D. Fla. 2014) (finding the contract executory under the functional approach and Countryman test).

[78] See, e.g., *Butler v. Resident Care Innovation Corp.*, 241 B.R. 37, 44 (D.R.I. 1999) (criticizing functional analysis as "ignor[ing] the statutory mandate that the contract be executory").

[79] See ABI Advisory Committee, *supra* note 13.

[80] See ABI Report, *supra* note 8.

[81] *Id.* at 113 n.416.

[82] *Id.*

[83] *Id.* at 115 (bemoaning the "unfair[ness]" abolition of executoriness would visit on counterparties).

Even leaving aside the vividness bias of the Commission's concern—focusing on the highly visible plight of the counterparty succumbing to the debtor's power under section 365 to the ignorance of the more diffuse benefit to all other stakeholders of the estate aided by that debtor's adroit treatment of a contract—the primary objection to the retention of executoriness as a "gating" valve is that the concept lacks normative coherence or principle. (Westbrook himself witheringly agrees.)[84] Similar gatekeeping could arise by saying the judge gets to flip a coin and each time it's heads the debtor can't use section 365. That, too, would reduce the power of the debtor, but not in a way that any well-designed legal system would consider tolerable. A principled way to reduce debtor leverage would be to accord greater discretion to the judge under section 365(a), perhaps tacking on an ability to deny rejection or assumption if it would be inequitable under the circumstances, but that's a topic for another day.[85] Nonetheless, the Commission has doubled down on executoriness, suggesting it should stay in the Code as a beacon for litigious contractual counterparties.[86]

III. A Better Approach to Executoriness: Taking Non-Executoriness Seriously

A. Sharpening the Debate

To find a way out of this mess, we need a new approach. Let us consider the two archetypal contracts for which the debtor is likely to face an executoriness challenge. As mnemonic, we can use aviary labels: first, the unwanted "albatross" that the debtor wants to drop

---

[84.] The Commission retained executoriness as a safety valve on debtor abuse "at the sacrifice of logic and, more importantly, predictable commercial results." Westbrook & White, *supra* note 6, at 486–87.

[85.] Westbrook and White would seem to agree. *Id.* at 486.

[86.] ABI Report, *supra* note 8, at 114 (noting litigation experience of some ABI Commissioners).

like a hot potato but the counterparty seeks to cast as non-executory, hoping that doing so will stymie the debtor's rejection efforts by barring access to section 365 (and its rejection powers); and second, the coveted "golden goose" that the debtor is desperate to keep but the counterparty also seeks to cast as non-executory to similarly stymie the debtor's assumption by foreclosing section 365 (and its assumption powers). Think of a hot realty option to scoop up Blackacre for a song: it's a golden goose for the option holder; it's an albatross for the option granter.

1. The Easy Case: The Non-Executory Golden Goose (Without Default)

Let's start with the golden goose contract that the debtor wishes to keep, which, for even further simplicity, we'll assume is not in default. Suppose the counterparty challenges executoriness. If the debtor wins on the executoriness argument, the contract is assumed under section 365. If the debtor loses, the contract cannot be assumed under section 365. But what does that mean? The non-executory contract is still property—best thought of as a chose in action to sue for the debtor's rights under the contract.[87] More accurately, it is hybrid property conjoining the debtor's right to enforce the contract benefits with the deleterious obligations to perform that the counterparty can translate into a claim if breached under section 502.[88] Thus, formally, the contract-qua-hybrid property passes to the estate under section 541's capacious reach to "all legal or equitable interests of the debtor in property."[89] This allows the debtor to enjoy its economic

---

[87.] The Act provided for "rights of action arising upon contracts," 30 Stat. 565 (1898), amended by 66 Stat. 429 (1952), 11 U.S.C. § 110(a)(5) (1958), and "property, including rights of action," id., as property of the estate.

[88.] Technically, the acceleration of all claims, 11 U.S.C. § 101(5) (2012), means that the liabilities crystallize as well so as to permit comprehensive discharge. But that is of no moment when the debtor wishes to assume.

[89.] Id. section 541(a)(1).

benefit as property of the estate.[90] All this is done irrespective of section 365. Thus, at least in the absence of default, whether the contract is executory or not has no effect on the debtor's exploitation of the economic rights; section 365, and *a fortiori* "executoriness," is irrelevant.[91]

2. The Harder Case: The Non-Executory Albatross

The albatross is where things start to get complicated. If the debtor wants to reject an unwanted contract, but the counterparty launches an executoriness challenge, the debtor faces more of a hurdle. Again, if the debtor wins, no problem and the contract is rejected under section 365(a). But if the counterparty succeeds in arguing the contract is non-executory and hence cannot be rejected under section 365, what happens? In a thoughtful historical discussion, Michael Andrew noted that under prior American and English practice, the undesirable contract never entered into the bankruptcy estate in the first place—it was "excluded," because unless and until a receiver or an assignee accepted debtor property under the Act, the historical abandonment doctrine left the estate unscathed.[92] Whatever the historical accuracy of his argument (and it does appear accurate),[93] Andrew's "exclusionary" approach now seems outdated given the 1978 Code's intentional inclusivity through the expanded definition of claim, where *everything* is included in the estate to enable comprehensive resolution of financial distress.

[90.] Countryman indirectly accepted this reasoning. Countryman I, *supra* note 4, at 458–59.

[91.] See, e.g., *Warner v. Warner (In re Warner)*, 480 B.R. 641, 652, 655 (Bankr. N.D.W. Va. 2012) (LLC agreement that was not executory still entered the bankruptcy estate under section 541); *Ehmann v. Fiesta Inv., LLC (In re Ehmann)*, 319 B.R. 200, 206 (Bankr. D. Ariz. 2005) (same).

[92.] See Andrew, Rejection, *supra* note 11, at 881 (noting that courts "excluded 'executory' contract and lease assets from the bankruptcy estate . . . absent an election by the trustee to accept them").

[93.] For example, *Copeland v. Stephens* (1818), 106 Eng. Rep. 218, 222 (KB) (holding title to leases and contracts does not pass to estate unless "accepted").

Many courts struggle with the non-executory albatross, assuming that it nevertheless persists if it is unable to be rejected under section 365(a).[94] Yet a contract is still a contract, and even if it cannot be rejected under section 365, it can still be repudiated. Moreover, bankruptcy courts do not generally order specific performance against the trustee (due to the innocence of the other creditors from the debtor's prior acts).[95] Thus, for most contracts, the only real remedy for the counterparty from debtor repudiation is a breach claim for damages.[96]

Now, under formal rejection of an executory contract via section 365, the Code specifies that the counterparty has a provable unsecured damages claim relating back to the petition date.[97] But if the contract is non-executory and the debtor wants to repudiate, courts become flummoxed, most apparently implying (hoping?) that the debtor has to perform.[98] Andrew, of course, solves this problem by having the albatross never enter the estate in the first place and so not be a problem for the trustee (but then presumably also being not provable, taking us back to the unhappy, old days). Yet, there is

---

[94] For example, In re Capital Acquisitions & Mgmt. Corp., 341 B.R. 632, 637 (Bankr. N.D. Ill. 2006) (finding LLC operating agreement non-executory and thus "enforceable" in bankruptcy).

[95] See, e.g., In re Pina, 363 B.R. 314, 333–35 (Bankr. D. Mass. 2007) (refusing to enforce prepetition injunctive judgment where it would harm unsecured creditors by diminishing size of bankruptcy estate); ABI Report, *supra* note 8, at 119 ("[R]ejection of an executory contract or unexpired lease should not . . . entitle the non-breaching, nondebtor party to a right of specific performance.").

[96] For simplicity, this chapter will assume all breach claims are reducible to damages to avoid the sidebar of can-be-compelled-to-accept-monetary-judgment issues. 11 U.S.C. § 101(5)(B) (2012). Critically for bankruptcy, these damages will never be compensatory for the counterparty if paid with the general unsecured dividend. Thus, in an idealized contract world of frictionless damages awards, a counterparty would be economically indifferent to performance or breach-remedied-by-full-expectation damages. Not so in bankruptcy, where any damage award (absent priority) will be paid out for pennies on the dollar. Westbrook, *supra* note 3, at 253 (labeling, one feels gleefully, the discounted bankruptcy dividend as "little tiny Bankruptcy Dollars").

[97] 11 U.S.C. § 365(g)(1) (2012).

[98] For example, In re KBAR, Inc., 96 B.R. 158, 159–60 (Bankr. C.D. Ill. 1988) (holding Hardee's franchise agreement to be no longer executory and hence its covenants could not be rejected in bankruptcy but rather remained in full force).

a plausible argument that cannot be ignored: if the debtor demurs performance of such a contract, the breach claim becomes an administrative charge against the estate *entitled to priority repayment*.[99]

The argument for priority status of a non-executory contract's abandonment damages goes something like this. Everyone agrees that if the debtor assumes an executory contract under section 365 and then subsequently breaches, the breach damages are administrative expenses of running the estate; that's in the Code.[100] Just as the trustee has to pay utility bills postpetition, if the trustee enters into a contract postpetition, so too does that business expense become a cost of running the estate that is entitled to administrative priority.[101] An assumed executory contract is no different from a new contract entered into postpetition: it's a cost of running the show that the trustee willingly incurs on the calculus that the benefits outweigh the burdens (the same way most trustees find paying the electric bill worth it to keep the lights on).

Following my formalism on the golden goose discussed previously, however, if the contract is somehow non-executory, it still has to go somewhere, under the doctrine of Conservation of Contractual Mass. It must, therefore, enter the estate under section 541 automatically. Thus, the trustee must dispose of it as *estate property* to get rid of it (in this case, repudiate the contract and give rise to a concomitant breach claim). Since this abandonment occurs postpetition, it must be another cost of running the estate (think of it as paying the garbage collector to haul off unwanted debris). Ergo, the breach damages are also an administrative expense, just as with an executory contract the trustee assumes but later breaches.[102] The only difference

---

[99.] See 11 U.S.C. § 507(a)(2) (2012) (priority repayment status for administrative claims); *id.* section 365(g)(2) (conferring administrative status on post-assumption breach claims).

[100.] *Id.* section 365(g)(2).

[101.] *Id.* section 503(b)(1).

[102.] The counterparty tried this tack in In re Airwest Int'l, Inc., No. 86-00145, 1988 WL 113101 (Bankr. D. Haw. Oct. 12, 1988), but the court held it was "premature" to adjudicate the priority claim pending assessment whether postpetition conduct by the debtor was tortious. *Id.* at *3.

here from section 365 is that this de facto assumption prior to rejection is purely involuntary and never approved by the bankruptcy court.[103] This prospect of favored priority helps explain why a counterparty to an albatross seeks a declaration of non-executoriness. The first best position, of course, is to trick the court into thinking that exclusion from section 365 simply ends the discussion and the debtor is just out of luck and must go on performing forever; but the nearly as attractive fallback position is to say that if such a non-executory contract is rejected, the breach damages must be treated as administrative claims entitled to first priority payout.[104]

3. *The Hardest Case: Non-Executory Golden Goose (with Default)*

Finally, let us return to the golden goose, which we discovered is easy for the debtor to retain when we assume the absence of default. But if we relax that assumption and put the debtor in default, then we see the incentive to fight over executoriness. The power to cure defaults effectively neutralizes the state law contract rights of the counterparty to respond to a material breach with the self-help remedy of termination by forcing the counterparty to accept the debtor's cure and keep the contract alive.[105] This allows, by federal preemptive power of the Code, a debtor to resurrect a slain golden goose (or more precisely, resuscitate a mortally wounded one). If the contract is

---

[103.] Compare 11 U.S.C. § 541(a)(1) (no approval required for automatic vesting of the estate with all the debtor's property), with *id.* section 365(a) (requiring court approval for assumption).

[104.] Note that absent recognized property rights, they will not prevail in an action against the debtor for specific performance in a bankruptcy court. For a good property rights analysis case, see In re Walter Energy, Inc., No. 15–02741–TOM11, 2015 WL 9487718, at *6 (Bankr. N.D. Ala. Dec. 28, 2015). See also In re Plasencia, 354 B.R. 774, 780 (Bankr. E.D. Va. 2006) (holding that a recorded realty option created a non-rejectable property interest).

[105.] The muscular cure power of section 365(b) can be contrasted with the limited cases where cure is allowed at state law. See, e.g., U.C.C. section 2-508 cmt. 2 (Am. Law Inst. & Unif. Law Comm'n 2014) (explaining the limited power to cure in sale-of-goods contracts if "circumstances" justify).

non-executory, however, and simply sitting in the debtor's lap under section 541, then unless we find a power elsewhere in the Code, there is *no cure power of section 365(b)* to preserve that contract's innate value to the debtor. Thus, we can encapsulate the golden goose problem as one of no express power to cure. And indeed, we can fret further by noting an *ipso facto* clause—providing for the contract to terminate automatically upon filing for bankruptcy—would also escape section 365(e)'s invalidation provision if the contract falls outside that subsection's scope as non-executory.

To summarize, there seem to be both primary and secondary counterparty advantages incentivizing executoriness challenges. For albatrosses, which the counterparty says are non-rejectable, the primary advantage is to trick a debtor or court into requiring performance, period, while the secondary advantage is priority status payment for breach damages in the event of non-performance/rejection/abandonment/repudiation—whatever we want to call it. The primary advantage to the counterparty for golden geese in arguing they are non-assumable is tricking the debtor into just giving up on the contract, while the secondary advantage is to block the cure power of section 365(b). I now seek to demonstrate through a proper understanding of the Code's text and structure that these claimed advantages are not just theoretically repugnant to the Code but *doctrinally unsupportable* (or at the very least, are not doctrinally preordained).

B. Entering the Debate: Working Through the Code on Non-Executoriness

We have here identified the three paradigmatic cases of non-executory contracts in ascending order of legal complexity and now turn to what I contend is their proper treatment under the Code if we take the concept of a non-executory contract seriously (i.e., not as a show-stopper whose declaration magically truncates further discussion).

As previously discussed, the first scenario is easy: a golden goose not in default. Consider, for example, a valuable unexpired option held by the debtor that the optioner wishes to evade. The optioner argues that the option cannot possibly be an "executory" contract due to its flunking the Countryman test (as there would be no material breach if the debtor did nothing until the end of time). The optioner then drops the second shoe and argues that because it is not executory, the option cannot fall under section 365 and, therefore, cannot be assumed under section 365(a). Poof! It disappears as a debtor asset. Commentators have struggled to shoehorn the option into the Countryman test,[106] but the simpler solution, *contra* Westbrook, is to concede that it is not an executory contract. As discussed earlier, however, it cannot just vanish. The unexpired option still exists as inchoate "property of the estate" under section 541,[107] just as a lien is an inchoate twig in the bundle of rights. As such, the debtor need do nothing with regards to this property. If the optioner ever asks the debtor whether the option is "assumed," the debtor can just respond she no more needs to assume the option than she needs to assume the drill press in the factory: it's all valuable property of the estate to be deployed in due course.[108]

[106.] Andrew, Reply to Westbrook, *supra* note 11, at 32–34. This is a frequent problem with insurance cases, in which the prepaid premium seems to discharge the insured's obligations, and so when the unexpired policy needs to be assumed, the debtor—insured will point to all the purportedly executory remaining duties to cooperate, i.e., to assure executoriness. See, e.g., *Pester Ref. Co. v. Ins. Co. N. Am.* (*In re Pester Ref. Co.*), 58 B.R. 189, 191 (Bankr. S.D. Iowa 1985) (finding the contract to be executory).

[107.] See, e.g., *BNY, Capital Funding LLC v. U.S. Airways, Inc.*, 345 B.R. 549, 556 (Bankr. E.D. Va. 2006) ("As an unexercised option, the LOI was property of U.S. Airways's bankruptcy estate.").

[108.] Unlike section 365(a), section 541's automatic vesting of the non-executory golden goose will not give the counterparty definitive notice of its legal obligations—a policy some argue is an important bankruptcy one. See, e.g., Westbrook & White, *supra* note 6, at 518 (asserting that notice to counterparties is necessary to promote fairness). But so what? What notice is needed for a happy counterparty whose contract is not in default—that the contract is continuing to be performed uneventfully as it has been all along? Let that tree fall in the forest! Accordingly, I am unsympathetic to the optioner in *Bronner v. Chenoweth–Massie P'ship* (*In re Nat'l Fin. Realty Tr.*), 226 B.R. 586 (Bankr. W.D. Ky. 1998). That optioner was left uncertain whether an option had been assumed or rejected after broken-off negotiations, mistakenly assuming/hoping it was rejected only to be surprised two years later when

1. Abandoning the Albatross

a. The Power

What about the converse situation of a burdensome contract that the debtor wants to run screaming from? Here, we might flip the debtor to be the optioner in the prior example, or consider an erstwhile employee—debtor laboring under a noncompete clause. The counterparty/option holder now argues that the contract flunks Countryman, so it cannot be rejected pursuant to section 365(a), because of course it doesn't fall under section 365's purview. Noncompete cases are notorious for accepting this view (probably because the court thinks the debtor is trying to pull a fast one by weaseling out of a noncompete clause), and so these cases simply say that the clause somehow "remains valid."[109] But the proper answer, doctrinally, lies again in remembering that, formally, the wart-laden contract is the property of the estate under section 541—but that the trustee can *abandon* the property under section 554, which provides that "[a]fter notice and a hearing, the trustee may abandon any property of the estate that is burdensome to the estate."[110] To be sure, a contract is a curious hybrid form of property conjoining an asset (the chose in action to compel the benefit of the bargain) with a liability (a claim for the consideration the debtor owes). Abandonment of the property on the asset side of the ledger does not "vaporize[]" the counterparty's claim on the

---

a third party exercised the option. *Id.* at 588–90. If the clear default rule is that contracts pass to the estate and remain there unless and until rejected under section 365 or abandoned under section 554, then the counterparty has legal certainty and knows it has a duty to pester.

[109.] *Jenson v. Cont'l Fin. Corp.*, 591 F.2d 477, 482 (8th Cir. 1979) (holding that "the security agreement is not executory," and thus it "remains valid"); see also, e.g., *Meiburger v. Endeka Enters. (In re Tsiaoushis)*, 383 B.R. 616, 621 (Bankr. E.D. Va. 2007) (concluding that an operating agreement was not executory and thus its sections remained "valid and fully enforceable"); *Ready Prod., Inc. v. Jarvis (In re Jarvis)*, No. 04-10806-JMD, 2005 WL 758805, at *5 (Bankr. D.N.H. Mar. 28, 2005) (finding the noncompete agreement non-executory and non-rejectable in granting employer—plaintiff injunctive relief against employee—debtor).

[110.] 11 U.S.C. section 554(a) (2012).

liability side,[111] of course, but that truism does not undermine the debtor's absolute power under section 554 to abandon the albatross. Once again, section 365 is never needed.[112] Courts seem to underappreciate the role of section 554 in this context.[113] Even courts that get to the right result do not seem to understand how they are getting there.[114]

b. The Claim

Thus, the debtor can happily abandon a non-executory contract under section 554, without need to address section 365 and its executoriness gate at all. This, of course, is a breach (formally an anticipatory repudiation, but the result is the same). But that conclusion

---

[111.] *Sunbeam Prods. v. Chi. Am. Mfg., LLC*, 686 F.3d 372, 377 (7th Cir. 2012).

[112.] I leave to one side the concern of seasoned practitioners of "inadvertent" assumption. True, automatic vesting under section 541 does not require an overt act, as does section 365, to check mistaken albatross acquisition, but neither does deemed rejection under section 365(d) protect against inadvertent rejection. In other words, there is no intrinsically "safe" default rule. The choice is between a default rule, with the attendant risks of carelessness, see *Ebert v. DeVries Family Farm, LLC (In re DeVries)*, No. 12-04015-DML, 2014 WL 4294540, at *14 (Bankr. N.D. Tex. Aug. 27, 2014) (finding that because trustee never assumed, section 365(d) deemed executory contract rejected), or the ambiguous quagmire of no default specification, see *Phx. Mut. Life Ins. Co. v. Greystone III Joint Venture (In re Greystone III Joint Venture)*, 995 F.2d 1274, 1281 (5th Cir. 1991) (holding that the chapter 11 debtor's leases continue—and the lessees have no provable claim against the bankruptcy estate—when the debtor neither assumes nor rejects its leases with third parties).

[113.] For example, In re FBI Distribution Corp. simply declares that the postpetition breach of a non-executory contract gives rise to an unsecured prepetition claim, a result I find congenial, but with no reference to section 554. *Mason v. Official Comm. of Unsecured Creditors (In re FBI Distrib. Corp.)*, 330 F.3d 36, 48 (1st Cir. 2003).

[114.] Discussion of section 554 is frequently lacking in these cases. See, e.g., In re Majestic Capital, Ltd., 463 B.R. 289, 301-02 (Bankr. S.D.N.Y. 2012) (using non-executoriness to prevent priority treatment of burdensome severance package, yet nonetheless "grant[ing] the motion to reject"); In re Exide Techs., 378 B.R. 762, 766 (Bankr. D. Del. 2007) (using non-executoriness to prevent debtor from having inadvertently assumed expensive retirement agreement). Andrew, in defending his exclusionary approach, embraces the abandonment power. See Andrew, Rejection, *supra* note 11, at 863 (noting that rejection and abandonment both result in "exclusion of an asset from the estate"). And in a footnote, he seems to agree with the core of my analysis. *Id.* at 890 n.165.

avoids the harder question of what befalls the counterparty's claim that is engendered by such a breach.[115] There are three possibilities: the counterparty has no claim; the counterparty has a general unsecured claim; or the counterparty has an administrative priority claim. The first possibility arises from the Swiftian reasoning that if section 365 does not apply, then presumably section 365(g)(1)'s conferral of the unsecured claim upon the aggrieved counterparty cannot kick in. One doubts the executoriness-denying counterparties intend this to be the logical consequence of their executoriness victory. Nor is it a plausible outcome because it would require de-coupling the contract's liabilities from its assets, a result unseemly to bankruptcy jurisprudence and common sense.[116]

Therefore, there must be some form of damages claim filable by the aggrieved counterparty for the rejection breach. But what sort of claim? Recall that if this were an *executory contract* breach claim, the Code's clear text of section 365(g)(1) designates it as a general unsecured one.[117] Why a different result for a *non-executory* contract? Recall further the reasoning discussed previously that deems the

---

[115.] Andrew's "exclusionary" approach led to the cumbersome conclusion that such contracts would revert to the debtor (not estate) and plausibly give a claim against the debtor for breach that might not be discharged by the debtor's bankruptcy. Andrew, Rejection, *supra* note 11, at 863.

[116.] See *Century Indem. Co. v. Nat'l Gypsum Co. Settlement Tr. (In re Nat'l Gypsum)*, 208 F.3d 498, 506 (5th Cir. 2000) ("Where the debtor assumes an executory contract, it must assume the entire contract, cum onere—the debtor accepts both the obligations and the benefits of the executory contract.").

[117.] 11 U.S.C. § 365(g)(1) (2012). What's interesting about section 365(g)(1) is that its retroactive designation of the claim as occurring prepetition, *id.* section 502(g), appears to be textually necessary to render the counterparty an estate "creditor." *Id.* section 101(10)(A). Would the non-executory breach counterparty, unable to rely on these relation-back provisions, not be able to be a "creditor"? Although little seems to ride on it for the debtor (as the counterparty still holds a dischargeable "claim," *id.* section 524(a)(2), 1141(d)(1)(A)), the counterparty may face some grief under section 726. But it appears to be of little moment: courts routinely consider the non-executory breach counterparty to have a claim under section 502 and seem to muddle through just fine. See, e.g., In re FBI Distrib. Corp., *supra* note 113, at 48 (holding the postpetition breach of non-executory contract triggered the prepetition claim as a "contingent claim. . . [even though] the right to payment arises during the reorganization when the contingency occurs"); *Stewart Foods, Inc. v. Broecker (In re Stewart*

breach as if the contract had been *assumed and then rejected by the estate*. Everyone agrees that that is a priority claim (a stance codified in section 365(g)(2)).[118] If, however, we accept the logic from the golden goose scenario discussed earlier that a non-executory contract vests in the estate automatically by section 541 without need to resort to section 365 at all, then we are faced with the necessary sauce for the gander that to abandon it the debtor must abandon property *of the estate*—hybrid property that carries an appurtenant claim for damages. Thus, since the estate is doing the abandoning that gives rise to the breach claim, the breach claim should be a cost of the estate's doing business, and hence entitled to administrative priority.[119] Viewed this way, section 365(g)(1) is not so much the conferral of provability (that it historically was) but a dispensation withdrawing the presumptive administrative priority of an estate breach claim. Closing the textual circle on this reasoning, because section 365(g)(1) demotes the breach claim to "mere" unsecured status for executory contracts, the lack of a similar demotion clause elsewhere in the Code for non-executory contracts means, just as Andrew feared, that the breach claim against the estate could be deemed to trigger administrative expense priority.[120]

Textual checkmate? Hardly. The solution lies in fighting text with text. And here I have the advantage of the Code's actual language, which Countryman did not have in 1973. The incursion of expenses postpetition is a necessary condition for administrative expenses

---

Foods, Inc.), 64 F.3d 141, 143, 145 (4th Cir. 1995) (holding counterparty had prepetition claim for postpetition breach of stipulated non-executory contract).

[118.] Congress either caps this intrinsically beneficial claim or deems it administrative notwithstanding its lack of benefit (depending on one's perspective) for certain leases. 11 U.S.C. § 503(b)(7) (2012).

[119.] Andrew noted that the historic Copeland case may have been animated (wrongly, in his view) by this very concern. Andrew, Rejection, *supra* note 11, at 859–63 ("[The Copeland concept's] premise, that the estate would become liable merely by succeeding to a contract or lease, was not clearly correct.").

[120.] *Id.* at 860 ("The courts in these pre-statutory cases thus identified contracts and leases as assets having the perceived potential of imposing administrative liabilities upon the estate by virtue of its succession to the debtor's ownership.").

under section 503(b) of the Code.[121] But postpetition timing, while necessary, is not sufficient. Rather, we must take cognizance of the Code's insistence of administrative expenses being "actual" and "necessary,"[122] and as textually inclined courts inform us:

The modifiers "actual" and "necessary" must be observed with scrupulous care[,] because [o]ne of the goals of chapter 11 is to keep administrative costs to a minimum in order to preserve the debtor's scarce resources and thus encourage rehabilitation. In keeping with this goal, section 503(b)(1)(A) was not intended to saddle debtors with special postpetition obligations lightly or give preferential treatment to certain select creditors by creating a broad category of administrative expenses.[123]

Here, the trustee/DIP as fiduciary of the estate has no desire for the counterparty's services. They are not an insurance premium that preserves valuable property the estate wishes to realize. Nor are they taxes, that necessary evil levied on that valuable property, which are also explicitly provided for in section 503.[124] Rather, they are the dead hand of the past, clamoring for a leg up on other creditors, offending bankruptcy's policy of equality.[125] But what is even more important

---

[121.] Section 503(b) deals with expenses of the estate, which are given priority under section 507(a)(2). 11 U.S.C. § 503(b), 507(a)(2) (2012).

[122.] *Id.* section (b)(1)(A). See *Ford Motor Credit Co. v. Dobbins*, 35 F.3d 860, 866–68 (4th Cir. 1994) (holding that "actual and necessary" costs must stem from affirmative use, as opposed to mere passive possession, of estate property by the debtor and such use must provide concrete, as opposed to merely potential, benefit to the estate).

[123.] Dobbins, 35 F.3d at 866 (alterations in original) (internal citations and quotations omitted) (quoting *General Amer. Transp. Corp. v. Martin (In re Mid Region Petroleum, Inc.)*, 1 F.3d 1130, 1134 (10th Cir. 1993)).

[124.] 11 U.S.C. § 503(b)(1)(B) (2012).

[125.] See Dobbins, 35 F.3d at 865 (quoting In re James B. Downing & Co., 94 B.R. 515, 519 (Bankr. N.D. Ill. 1988) ("The presumption in bankruptcy cases is that the debtor's limited resources will be equally distributed among the creditors. Thus, statutory priorities must be narrowly construed.")). A strand of jurisprudence has evolved involving environmental liabilities for burdensome property the debtor abandons postpetition under section 554. Some courts have not allowed administrative priority precisely because of the lack of benefit to the estate. See, e.g., In re H.F. Radandt, Inc., 160 B.R. 323, 327 (Bankr. W.D. Wis. 1993) (Section 503 "mandate[s] that [administrative priority] be granted where necessary to 'preserve' the estate," and "preservation [would not] be accomplished by granting [administrative priority to environmental cleanup]"). But many have tagged the debtor with cleanup costs as an

is that the estate *never* receives any benefit from the rejected contract and its related breach claim. This observation is critical to contrast the situation from that where the debtor affirmatively assumes an executory contract (thus enjoying some benefit from it) and then subsequently breaches it. There, the estate has, however fleetingly, enjoyed some "actual" and "necessary" usage of the contract and must pay the piper for its attendant costs in the event of breach.[126] With this non-executory contract, by contrast, the unwanted property automatically vested into the estate over the debtor's howling, and the debtor abandoned it at the first possible moment.[127] Accordingly, the seeming analogy between the assumed-and-subsequently-rejected (executory) contract and the automatically-vested-but-never-wanted-and-quickly-abandoned (non-executory) contract falls apart.[128] The sim-

---

administrative priority. See, e.g., *United States v. LTV Corp. (In re Chateaugay Corp.)*, 944 F.2d 997, 1009–10 (2d Cir. 1991) ("If property on which toxic substances pose a significant hazard to public health cannot be abandoned, it must follow . . . that expenses to remove the threat posed by such substances are necessary to preserve the estate."). The complex issues of federal environmental policy and the interaction between CERCLA and the Code require caution with generalization from these cases.

[126.] *Dobbins*, 35 F.3d at 867 (collecting authority), focuses on the mere possession of creditor property versus affirmative use or conscious exploitation of resources. *Id.* (citations omitted) (noting that "a benefit to the estate results only from use of the . . . property" and "[t]hat which is actually utilized by a Trustee in the operation of a debtor's business is a necessary cost"). *Dobbins* and its ancestors/progeny have enjoyed more citations vigor than the Supreme Court's odd tort case of *Reading Co. v. Brown*, 391 U.S. 471 (1968), which established the proposition, largely on policy grounds, that a postpetition tort damages claim should enjoy administrative priority. *Id.* at 485. Nearly all subsequent cases have cabined Brown to torts. See, e.g., In re Lazar, 207 B.R. 668, 681 (Bankr. C.D. Cal. 1997) ("From Reading arose the general rule that the postpetition tort liabilities of a business that continues to operate in bankruptcy qualify for administrative expense priority as actual and necessary expenses for preservation of the estate.").

[127.] I have no problem with the debtor paying administrative priority expenses for intra-bankruptcy usage under the contract.

[128.] We might also draw indirect support from the Supreme Court's recent musings in *Czyzewski v. Jevic Holding Corp.*, 137 S. Ct. 973, 985 (2017) that priority provisions can be treated more flexibly in the context of reorganization when value is created for all creditors but less so in the context of final liquidation where claimed priority must be scrutinized especially rigorously.

ple conclusion is that because unwanted non-executory contracts never confer any benefit, ever, upon the estate, their breach damages upon rejection cannot find the textual anchor to avail themselves of section 503(b).[129] They are neither an "actual" nor "necessary" cost of "preserving" the estate. As such, the concern of presumed priority status collapses, permitting the debtor to abandon property of a contractual albatross under section 554.[130] Ample case law supports this proposition.[131]

2. Assuming the Golden Goose

Previously, I have contended that a debtor need do nothing to "assume" an advantageous non-executory contract; it automatically vests its way into the estate through section 541. But for simplicity, that prior discussion assumed the contract was not in default. If we relax that assumption, the debtor faces a harder task. Recall both that (1) general state contract law permits a contract party facing material breach to walk away from the contract in self-help and (2) bankruptcy law tries, absent a countervailing federal bankruptcy policy interest, to respect state law entitlements (such as contract

---

[129.] The court in *Mason v. Official Comm. of Unsecured Creditors (In re FBI Distribution Corp.)*, 330 F.3d 36, 48–49 (1st Cir. 2003) embraced this logic. It disagreed that the breach claim on a non-executory contract should get administrative claim priority, because even though the contract was breached postpetition, and even though as a non-executory contract, it apparently was unrejectable and saddled the estate in perpetuity, it nonetheless did not confer any benefit on the debtor postpetition. *Id.* Accordingly, the breach claim was held to be a general unsecured claim (mimicking the outcome of section 365(g)(1) as if the contract had been executory and rejected), following my proposed analysis.

[130.] At least one court has adopted my approach of treating the "rejected" non-executory contract the same as if rejected under section 365. See In re Hawker Beechcraft, Inc., 486 B.R. 264, 277 (Bankr. S.D.N.Y. 2013) (awarding prepetition breach claim for damages for non-executory contract rejected by debtor); see also In re Majestic Capital, Ltd., 463 B.R. 289, 299 (Bankr. S.D.N.Y. 2012) (allowing the debtor to reject COO's employment contract even though "the contract was not executory" and denying administrative priority).

[131.] See, e.g., Dobbins, 35 F.3d at 868 ("[I]t . . . strikes us as inequitable to tax unsecured creditors for a decline in the value of collateral when the decline does not result from a use that actually benefits the estate.").

remedies) to the maximum extent possible.[132] Thus, we start from an orientation that a contract in material default should be cancelable by the counterparty and not subject to any resuscitation in bankruptcy absent some special Code power.

Section 365, however, accords just such special power. Section 365(b)'s condition on assumption that requires cure necessarily implies a power to cure. The precise scope of the section 365 cure power is not free from textual doubt and warrants its own painful statutory exegesis,[133] but it would be absurd to suggest there is no power to cure implicit in section 365(b). Case closed for executory contracts. For non-executory contracts, which by definition cannot avail themselves of section 365(b) and its cure power, the power to cure must come from elsewhere.

a. Reorganization

Fortunately for reorganization cases, the Code expressly confers a power to cure defaults in a plan of reorganization.[134] Thus, statutorily, there is no important difference between the power to cure executory contracts and non-executory contracts in reorganization

---

[132.] *Butner v. United States*, 440 U.S. 48, 55, 57 (1979) (holding that state law should presumptively determine rights and obligations of debtors and creditors absent a countervailing federal bankruptcy policy evidenced by structure, text, and history of the Code).

[133.] Compare In re Claremont Acquisition Corp., Inc., 113 F.3d 1029, 1035 (9th Cir. 1997) (holding debtors may not assume or reject a contract that is impossible to cure), with In re Vitanza, No. 98-19611DWS, 1998 WL 808629, at *20, *24 (Bankr. E.D. Pa. Nov. 13, 1998) (allowing assumption despite impossible-to-cure default). See also In re Bankvest Capital Corp., 270 B.R. 541, 543 (Bankr. D. Mass. 2001) ("[P]enalty rate obligation and a nonmonetary default are two separate types of breaches which a debtor is not required to cure prior to assumption of a contract."). Congress tried to fix these provisions with BAPCPA, but it's unclear if it did. Risa Lynn Wolf-Smith, Bankruptcy Reform and Nonmonetary Defaults—What Have They Done Now? Am. Bankr. Inst. J., Aug. 2005, at 6, 35. ("[C]hanges made in the Bankruptcy Reform Act of 1994 left practitioners unsure about whether debtors' obligations to cure nonmonetary defaults had been eliminated. The Bankruptcy Abuse Prevention and Consumer Protection Act (BAPCPA) has finally answered some of the questions, though the language is murky.").

[134.] 11 U.S.C. § 1123(a)(5)(G), 1322(c)(1) (2012).

cases.[135] The harder problem, then, is in liquidation cases under chapter 7, where the non-executory contract finds no succor analogous to section 365, 1123, or 1322. And, indeed, there might be an inverse textual implication that the absence of these explicit textual cure provisions should be read to forbid it "interstitially" for chapter 7 debtors.

b. Liquidation

The question of the chapter 7 debtor seeking to assume a defaulted non-executory golden goose is admittedly the thorniest for this analysis. I flag at the outset that this subset is a rare one. Most executoriness fights Westbrook and White unearthed in their comprehensive empirical study were in reorganization cases, and of the subset of liquidation cases, not one involved an assumption battle.[136] Nonetheless, abundant caution counsels that we press on to see if such a power can be found. And to tackle this question, we can initially

---

[135.] There are discrepancies at the margin. For example, the general power to cure in section 1123(a)(1)(G) does not excuse penalties of the sort expressly excused from cure for executory contracts under section 365(b)(2)(D), but it is hard to imagine this wrinkle ever becoming a driver of future executoriness litigation. (A strand of case law unnecessary to resolve here struggles to reconcile section 365(b)(2) and 1123(d). See, e.g., In re Sagamore Partners, Ltd., Bankr. Appeals, 512 B.R. 296, 306–13 (S.D. Fla. 2014) (attempting to harmonize section 365(b)(2) with section 1123(d)), aff'd in part, rev'd in part and remanded sub nom. In re Sagamore Partners, Ltd., Fed. Appx. 864 (11th Cir. 2015); In re Phx. Bus. Park Ltd. P'ship, 257 B.R. 517, 520–21 (Bankr. D. Ariz. 2001) (relying on section 365(b)(2) in addressing section 1123(d) and the 1994 amendments).) Of course, not everyone wants to cure in reorganization. In one unusual case, *Meilburger v. Endeka Enterprises LLC (In re Tsiaoushis)*, the reorganizing debtor wanted to *ipso facto* dissolve an LLC agreement and so argued that the LLC agreement was non-executory to avoid section 365(e)'s invalidation clause. 383 B.R. 616, 616–17 (Bankr. E.D. Va. 2007) (noting chapter 11 trustee's opposition to the LLC property manager's motion contending that the operating agreement was executory). This case's odd posture makes it of limited helpfulness, alas, but still fun.

[136.] See Westbrook & White, *supra* note 6, at 536–61 app. (analyzing thirty-three cases in an appendix—only two of which involved liquidations, and none involved a debtor attempting to assume an executory contract where the counterparty objected on non-executoriness grounds).

divide the liquidation universe of contractual defaults into "*Ipso Facto*" Breaches and "Everything Else" Breaches.

i. Ipso Facto

Consider first *ipso facto* defaults, where the sole breach of the contract is the very occurrence of bankruptcy. Does the Code permit the debtor to cure?[137] I think the answer is probably "yes" given section 541(c)(1).[138] That provision of the Code invalidates *ipso facto* clauses that would terminate a contract and thus prevent it from becoming property of the estate. So the federal hostility to *ipso facto* clauses is clearly established.[139]

The Code also invalidates *ipso facto* clauses and excuses them from the cure requirements of section 365(b).[140] Should this be taken as a textual signal that section 541 cannot be relied upon to do all the work of rescue from *ipso facto* clauses? I don't think so. Even leaving aside the permissibility of Congress using some belt and suspenders to avoid negative implications (perhaps having some overlap between section 541(c)(2) and 365(b)(2)), if we really wanted to get down into the textual weeds, we could point to section 365(b)(2)'s nominally broader scope than section 541(c)(1)'s. For example, section 365(b)(2) expands the denigration of *ipso facto* terms to those triggered by postpetition finances.[141]

[137.] Perhaps "ignore" is better than "cure," because what would "cure" even mean in this context—voluntarily dismissing the petition?

[138.] See 11 U.S.C. § 541(c)(1) (2012) ("[A]n interest of the debtor in property becomes property of the estate . . . notwithstanding any provision in an agreement . . . or applicable nonbankruptcy law— . . . (B) that is conditioned on the insolvency or financial condition of the debtor.").

[139.] Note the historical contrast from earlier bankruptcy laws where *ipso facto* clauses were honored; perhaps Congress over time bristled at the destruction of value. Countryman has an excellent historical discussion on courts' reluctance to give effect to *ipso facto* clauses, with fundamental disagreement over (a) whether the Act's respect of them with regard to unexpired leases should be cabined to leases or extended to all executory contracts, and (b) whether they could be respected only in straight bankruptcy (versus chapter reorganization) cases under the Act. Countryman II, *supra* note 23, at 521–27.

[140.] 11 U.S.C. § 365(b)(2) (2012) (excusing *ipso facto* default cure); section 365(e)(1) (invalidating *ipso facto* default clauses).

[141.] *Id.* section 365(b)(2).

More importantly, if we step back from the text to consider the structure and purpose of the Code, it makes little sense to invalidate an *ipso facto* clause in an executory contract for purposes of getting the contract into the bankruptcy estate only to find that, but for section 365(b)(2), the same contract would be unassumable. What would the purpose of its entry into the estate have even been—to await inevitable rejection? But of course, if we take seriously the concept of a non-executory contract, then we immediately recall section 365 is of no moment because such a contract vests into the estate automatically by virtue of section 541, and it is quite clear that section 541(c)(1) invalidates the *ipso facto* clause at the vesting stage.[142] Accordingly, even for the chapter 7 debtor, who is accorded no textually explicit power to cure defaults, it seems uncontentious to claim that defaults on account of *ipso facto* clauses may be ignored and the federal bankruptcy policy of hostility toward them may comfortably preempt the state law contract right of automatic termination.[143]

ii. Everything Else

The harder question, then, is the Everything Else world of defaults. Can they be cured for the chapter 7 debtor? After all, if a non-executory contract is a discrete "thing" that enters the estate irrespective of section 365, then that "thing" is a contract already in default. Assuming no stay violation,[144] presumably the counterparty

---

[142.] This is the approach taken by In re Denman, 513 B.R. 720, 725, 727 (Bankr. W.D. Tenn. 2014) and *Movitz v. Fiesta Inv., LLC (In re Ehmann)*, 319 B.R. 200, 206 (Bankr. D. Ariz. 2005).

[143.] A strand of LLC cases has tried to revivify state laws providing for *ipso facto* termination of contracts through the back door of section 365(c)(1), which bars assumption of contracts if assignment is prohibited by applicable non-bankruptcy law. 11 U.S.C. § 365(c)(1). These cases sneakily say that while the contract is not *ipso facto* terminated (per section 365(e)), it can never be assumed (per section 365(c)(1)), leading to the same result: killing the contract for the debtor. This proposition is contentious. Compare, e.g., *Nw. Wholesale, Inc. v. PAC Organic Fruit, LLC*, 357 P. 3d 650, 662–63 (Wash. 2015) (holding section 365(e)(1)'s prohibition against *ipso facto* clauses to be inapplicable), with, e.g., *Horizons A Far, LLC v. Webber (In re Soderstrom)*, 484 B.R. 874, 880 (Bankr. M.D. Fla. 2013) (holding section 365 applies if the contract is executory).

[144.] It is readily possible that a declaration of breach could be shown as an attempt to punish the debtor for stiffing the counterparty. See, e.g., *Pester Ref. Co. v. Ins. Co.*

has the right to exercise the termination right for self-help. Can the bankruptcy debtor, nonetheless, ram cure down the counterparty's throat? Here, I concede a need to resort to weaker textual footing, but I take solace in the Code's Last Refuge of the Textually Damned, section 105.[145]

Let's consider the situation in which it may arise. A debtor in liquidation is in default on a valuable contract the trustee wishes to assume, say, an LLC operating agreement, but the counterparty has successfully argued the contract is non-executory because remaining performance is only due on one side. The trustee promptly offers to cure, noting that the counterparty has incurred no financial harm on account of the default. Nonetheless, the counterparty recalcitrantly insists on its rights to terminate the contract, seizing upon the technical right of the default as an escape route from the unfavorable bargain. Just to close the loop, state law has no equitable doctrines of excuse that the hapless debtor can point out to stave off this churlish termination.[146] At wit's end, the trustee comes to the bankruptcy court and says, "Look, this contract has value for the creditors, it's no skin off the counterparty's nose because all defaults have been cured, and so I would like an injunction under section 105 preventing him from exercising his self-help remedy of termination." Could the bankruptcy court issue such relief?

This hypothetical presents sympathetic facts for just such a countervailing federal policy—the preservation of value for creditors with no offsetting harm to the counterparty (other than being made to live with the bad deal it made)—that warrants preempting

---

of N. Am. (In re Pester Ref. Co.), 58 B.R. 189, 191 (Bankr. S.D. Iowa 1985) ("Even if the insurance contract was not treated as an executory contract, the unilateral act of INA to cancel the policy would be barred by the automatic stay of 11 U.S.C. § 362(a).").

[145] 11 U.S.C. § 105(a) (2012) ("The court may issue any order, process, or judgment that is necessary or appropriate to carry out the provisions of this title.").

[146] Cf., e.g., 1 Restatement (Second) of Contracts section 229 (Am. Law Inst. 1981) (establishing that a non-occurrence of a condition can be excused if the non-occurrence would result in disproportionate forfeiture).

the counterparty's state law self-termination rights.[147] Well before *Timbers*,[148] the Supreme Court accorded great latitude to bankruptcy courts to enjoin difficult creditors whose actions would imperil a bankruptcy proceeding's success.[149] And, of course, since the contract is being ratified by the estate, any subsequent breach damages would be entitled to administrative priority as a backstop, according the counterparty even more comfort.[150] As a final kicker, the debtor would note that under chapter 11, this surly creditor would be deemed to have supported the plan as unimpaired.[151] Indeed, on these facts, I would think the case for injunctive relief would be presumptively attractive; albeit requiring some hoops to jump through, cure would be allowed, by hook or by section 105 crook. If that is so, then even the hardest case of a non-executory contract—the non-*ipso facto* default of a chapter 7 debtor's contract—still can be cured under a properly purposive reading of the Code. It's not as textually straightforward as section 365(b), but the cure power is still there.

3. Summary

Note what a thorough working through of the Code's application to a non-executory contract reveals: far from relying on section 365, the debtor or trustee has ample opportunity under the Code, perhaps with some creativity but surely on solid textual footing, to cure an attractive contract's default and thereby retain a golden goose. This means,

---

[147.] Westbrook offers some initial insights into what fundamental bankruptcy policies might be (at least with respect to contracts), listing four basic policies. Westbrook & White, *supra* note 6, at 515–17. I accept these at face value and note that maximization of creditor value appears front and center on this policy list.

[148.] See *United Sav. Ass'n of Tex. v. Timbers of Inwood Forest Assocs., Ltd.*, 484 U.S. 365, 372, 377–78 (1988) (upholding the restriction of secured creditors' compensation for lost time value of their collateral).

[149.] The canonical case for this proposition is *Cont'l Ill. Nat'l Bank & Tr. Co. v. Chi. R.I. & P. Ry. Co.*, 294 U.S. 648, 678–79 (1935), although there was some debate over that holding's application to straight bankruptcy liquidation cases. *Id.* at 671–72. See also Countryman II, *supra* note 23, at 517 (discussing case law).

[150.] 11 U.S.C. § 365(g)(2) (2012).

[151.] *Id.* section 1124(2).

crucially, that the power to cure actually requires no recourse to section 365(b) and thus no concomitant need to demonstrate executoriness: executory and non-executory contracts alike can be cured. And if that is correct, then I have succeeded in my underlying mission of eliminating the main functional difference in the treatment of executory versus non-executory contracts under the Code. Indeed, I am too modest. Not only have I collapsed the difference between executory and non-executory contracts under the Code regarding the ability to assume a golden goose, but I have also similarly collapsed the distinction regarding the rejection of an albatross, by dispatching the concern of priority repayment of section 554 abandonment damages. My mission accomplished, the counterparty has lost the primary foundation for the arbitrage opportunity, which means the *ex ante* incentives to litigate executoriness will dry up. Executoriness remains but it has lost all its sting.[152] As such, I no longer care about the definition of executoriness, and, more importantly, nor will anyone else.[153] This is perhaps a radical approach to executory contracts, but its elimination of senseless litigation should make it normatively attractive.

[152.] At worst, I have created a new boilerplate duty to tack on a footnote to every section 365 motion that says, "in the event this contract is found to be non-executory, the debtor retains its rights under section 541 and moves to abandon under section 554." (This is a trivial evil compared to *Stern v. Marshall*, 564 U.S. 462 (2011), this generation's fount of bankruptcy litigation.)

[153.] If pushed for my own definitional preference, I would revert to Williston's: "[A] contract, the obligation of which relates to the future, or a contract under which the parties have bound themselves to future activity that is not yet completed or performed." 1 Samuel Williston, A Treatise on the Law of Contracts section 1:19 (4th ed. 2007). See also 3A William Collier, Collier on Bankruptcy 63.33, at 1935 (14th ed. 1940) ("All contracts to a greater or less extent are executory. When they cease to be so, they cease to be contracts.") (citing Williston). This approach has a pedigree in the legislative history to the Code, see In re Norquist, 43 B.R. 224, 225, 228 (Bankr. E.D. Wash. 1984) (citing Williston and stating "the Supreme Court in citing the legislative history appears to have agreed with the expression of Congress that a precise definition of an executory contract is inadvisable"), and Westbrook, too, finds it congenial. Westbrook & White, *supra* note 6, at 520 (explaining that "executory" should be understood in light of common law). Thus, I do not care about "truly" non-executory contracts in the sense of discussing sunsets after dark, Westbrook, *supra* note 3, at 243, just those contracts that flunk the Countryman test but still have unperformed aspects.

IV. Counterarguments

I anticipate several respectable counterarguments to this new approach, and so I offer this preemptive rebuttal.

A. Reading "Executory" Out of the Code?

This is a trick objection, because many, like Westbrook, *want* to read it out of the Code, so would see this as praise rather than criticism to my approach of taking the idea of a non-executory contract seriously. But I can see a deeply committed textualist bemoaning that I have rendered "executory" redundant, effectively redrafting section 365 as if the word had been deleted.[154]

This critique misses the mark. My treatment of non-executory contracts merely mimics the treatment of executory contracts under section 365, but does so through a distinct doctrinal route that respects the formal categorical difference. Now, whether this synthetic replication upsets the "structure" of the Code's "implicit policies" by creating near-redundancy is a separate attack, but as soon as we move into the structure and policies of the Code, I gain the theoretical high ground by pointing to the absolute absence of justification found anywhere in the Code (or anywhere else) to treat non-executory contracts differently from executory contracts.[155]

B. Evading Section 365's Burdens?

My response to the prior criticism unfortunately runs right into the snare of this correlative complaint: if non-executory contracts

---

[154.] Similar angst enraged the district court in Stewart, which objected to the treatment of a non-executory contract's breach as a claim under section 502, because to do so would treat the contract as rejected under section 365(b), which was not allowed in its view—a holding that was promptly reversed on appeal. See *Stewart Foods, Inc. v. Broecker (In re Stewart Foods, Inc.)*, 64 F.3d 141, 144–45 (4th Cir. 1995).

[155.] See In re ZRM-Oklahoma P'ship, 156 B.R. 67, 70–71 (Bankr. W.D. Okla. 1993) (emphasizing the importance of interpreting the Code in a "coherent and consistent" manner).

merely mimic section 365 treatment, but don't exactly run through the section 365 gauntlet, then that means the burdensome provisions of section 365 (e.g., the adequate assurances of future performance as a precondition to assumption under section 365(b)(1)(C)), are simply excused for non-executory contracts. If so, I've turned executoriness on its head by creating a reverse arbitrage where the *debtors* will now try to argue their contracts aren't executory to evade such requirements![156]

This concern, while logically articulable, is overstated for two interrelated reasons. First, to a considerable extent, the requirements of

---

[156.] This appears to have happened in the cryptic *Bronner v. Chenoweth-Massie P'ship (In re Nat'l Fin. Realty Tr.)*, 226 B.R. 586, 587–88 (Bankr. W.D. Ky. 1998), in which the receiver wrote a sloppy plan forgetting to assume a valuable option in chapter 11. *Id.* When the counterparty caught him and demanded evidence of assumption, he pivoted to say the contract was non-executory and so had not been presumptively rejected (as all executory contracts had been) under the plan. *Id.* The court agreed and the option, deemed non-executory, survived the plan, saving the receiver's bacon. *Id.* The counterparty's unsuccessful argument had sounded in notice, implying that absent such evidence of assumption the counterparty was right to infer deemed rejection and enjoy repose accordingly. *Id.* The counterparty's problem, however, is really in the Code's lack of default rules for executory contracts in non-chapter 7 cases. Westbrook and White imply that the option should have been deemed rejected under section 365(d), but I don't see how that's the case, unless this was a chapter 7 case, which it did not appear to be. See Westbrook & White, *supra* note 6, at 524. Section 365(d)(2) merely sets a deadline for the assumption/rejection decision, but, unlike section 365(d)(1), it does not specify the consequences of the failure to act. This results in a case law quagmire. See, e.g., *Phx. Mut. Life Ins. Co. v. Greystone III Joint Venture (In re Greystone III Joint Venture)*, 995 F.2d 1274, 1281 (5th Cir. 1991) (noting that a lease neither assumed nor rejected before a chapter 11 plan confirmation just rides through with the debtor still bound and with the creditor without a provable claim). Note section 365(p), which does provide a default rule in the case of inaction, interestingly does not textually restrict its application to unexpired leases. 11 U.S.C. § 365(p) (2012). Indeed, this is not the only provision of section 365 that does not apply on its face to executory contracts: section 365(o) would appear to apply only to non-executory contracts—and this is a subsection of section 365! See *id.* section 365(o):

[T]he trustee shall be deemed to have assumed . . . and shall immediately cure any deficit under, any commitment by the debtor to a Federal depository institutions regulatory agency . . . to maintain the capital of an insured depository institution, and any claim for a subsequent breach of the obligations thereunder shall be entitled to priority under section 507.

section 365(b)(1)(C) (and (b)(1)(B) for that matter) are largely redundant to contract rights under state law.[157] Consider by way of example the ubiquitous Uniform Commercial Code's sales provisions in Article 2. There, the insolvency of the buyer is listed as a categorical example of objective grounds for insecurity, and insecurity gives rise to the right to demand adequate assurance of future performance.[158] Second, recall that the foundation of the statutory power to allow nonconsensual cure (outside the reorganization context) is likely injunctive relief through section 105, and so, in fashioning that relief, a bankruptcy court would be loath to give the debtor a "freebie" of not having to provide assurances that her executory-contract-holding peer would, especially when such assurances are likely the required baseline at state law. (There certainly are no countervailing federal policies requiring *Butner* divergence from state law that spring to mind.) In short, I am not denying the risk,[159] but I think it likely the concern

---

[157.] See 11 U.S.C. § 365(b)(1)(B) (2012) (requiring compensation for breach damages before assumption); *id.* section 365(b)(1)(C) (requiring adequate assurance of future performance before assumption).

[158.] U.C.C. § 2-609 cmt. 3 (Am. Law Inst. & Unif. Law Comm'n 2002) ("[A] buyer who falls behind in 'his account' with the seller . . . impairs the seller's expectation of due performance.").

[159.] One case where this has popped up is *BNY, Capital Funding LLC v. U.S. Airways, Inc.*, 345 B.R. 549 (Bankr. E.D. Va. 2006). There, the debtor was able to retain a contract to make a financial accommodation, despite the bar of section 365(c)(2), by successfully persuading the court that the contract was non-executory and hence fell outside section 365 and section 365(c)(2). *Id.* at 553, 555. Westbrook and White see this as an outrage, where U.S. Airways got out of section 365(c)(2) jail free, Westbrook & White, *supra* note 6, at 525, but I'm more ambivalent. Even leaving aside the court's point that the debtor had onerous financial conditions precedent to meet before exercise (not least of which was keeping current on the aircraft leases to the optioner), 345 B.R. at 555, I am not sure how much divergence from state law evasion of section 365(c)(2) would entail. If, as the U.S. Airways court conceded, the option was a contract (albeit a non-executory one), then the traditional contract defenses and excuses spring into action. Certainly it is an open question whether insolvency of the counterparty would discharge performance, either on grounds of material mistake, 1 Restatement (Second) of Contracts section 152 (Am. Law Inst. 1981), or frustration of purpose, *id.* section 265–68, especially if the subject matter of the contract was to make a loan. At a minimum, adequate assurances would be demandable as a condition to continuation. For a good background discussion of Congress' intent behind section 365(c)(2), see In re Teligent, 268 B.R. 723, 737 (Bankr. S.D.N.Y. 2001).

of seeking a declaration of non-executoriness as a bypass around section 365's conditions on assumptions will arise infrequently.

Finally, I should mention the cognate idea of "evading" judicial review under section 365(a).[160] Recall that the assumption—or rejection—of an executory contract requires court approval.[161] If non-executory contracts do not run through section 365, are non-debtor stakeholders stripped of their judicial oversight protection? Again, I think this concern is overstated, even leaving aside the implicitly heroic assumptions about the judicial role in a corporate decision largely governed by the business judgment rule. First, a non-executory contract that is rejected is abandoned under section 554, and that does require a court hearing even if it does not explicitly require "approval."[162] Few debtors will abandon a valuable contract for nefarious reasons, fess up to it in open court, and then sit back and stare a judge in the eyes and coolly sneer, "Nothing you can do about it because it isn't even your decision to approve!" No litigant has that much political capital to squander, and every judge has heard of section 105 and can trot out decisions intoning that bankruptcy courts are courts of equity.[163] Second, a non-executory contract in default that is assumed will require court blessing as well, either through the discretionary power to confirm the plan of reorganization or the discretionary power to order the cure injunctively in liquidation. So all roads lead to court involvement; no wool will be pulled over judicial eyes.

[160.] Section 365(a)'s requirement of court approval stems from a long history of courts inserting themselves into an oversight role under the Act. See Countryman II, *supra* note 23, at 556.

[161.] See *Allegheny Ctr. Assocs. v. Appliance Store, Inc. (In re Appliance Store, Inc.)*, 148 B.R. 226, 232 (Bankr. W.D. Pa. 1992) (holding that section 365(a) superseded prior case law allowing assumption without court approval).

[162.] The section 554 hearing will also give notice to the counterparty definitively clarifying its contractual rights.

[163.] Adam J. Levitin, Toward a Federal Common Law of Bankruptcy: Judicial Lawmaking in a Statutory Regime, 80 Am. Bankr. L.J. 1, 1 (2006) ("A basic tenet of bankruptcy practice is that 'the bankruptcy court is a court of equity.'") (citations omitted).

C. Forfeiting Section 365's Benefits?

Conversely, there is the reverse concern: that, other than the power to cure, there are other benefits to the debtor in section 365 that the non-executory-contract-holding debtor will not be able to access. Does my synthetic replication of section 365 through other provisions of the Code cover these benefits as well? Here, I think I have met my Waterloo and have to concede not. But it is a trivial Waterloo. The principal benefit in section 365, beyond the general power to cure addressed previously, is the excuse of an impossible-to-cure default for some forms of unexpired leases.[164]

Section 365(b)(1)(A)'s text is a mess, but it appears to excuse impossible-to-cure defaults of real-property leases (and add on some extra requirements for what to do if that lease is non-residential).[165] The implication of the most likely reading of the drafting is that a debtor with an impossible-to-cure default on a personal property lease is just out of luck: the impossibility precludes cure, and non-cure precludes assumption. Here, I am forced to concede an apparent benefit unique to section 365; the debtor outside section 365 has no similar salvation. That said, the problem appears trivial when we, for the first time, confront section 365's application both to unexpired leases and to executory contracts. While "executoriness" has generated a litigation minefield, "unexpired" has not. Parties (and courts) are less likely to disagree whether a lease is over or not; one anticipates an

---

[164.] There is the boondoggle damage claim under section 507(a)(2) and 502(b)(7) for certain nonresidential real property leases, 11 U.S.C. section 507(a)(2), 502(b)(7) (2012), but leases interest me less than contracts for the reasons given in the text. If pressed, I could parse the debtor's power to sidestep "cure[]" with "provid[ing] adequate assurance" of "prompt[]" cure as a possible benefit accorded by the Code unavailable at state contract law, but that's too fine a pinhead upon which to dance. *Id.* section 365(b)(1)(A).

[165.] A plausible reading is that section 365(b) does the opposite and declares that impossible-to-cure defaults on real property leases are just lethal, period, for the debtor seeking assumption, but that nonresidential leases are saved from the fire if the specified conditions are met. This interpretation requires ascribing to Congress an intent to render residential leases harder for debtors to assume than nonresidential ones, a reading of section 365(b) that skirts absurdity.

empty set of litigants fighting over whether and how the debtor can cure the defaults of an *expired* lease.[166]

D. Inapplicability of Other Section 365 Provisions?

There are surely other differences that would arise from whether or not a contract falls under section 365, but it is difficult to say *ex ante* which way they cut, let alone predict whether they will birth a new fount of arbitrage. For example, the sixty-day deemed rejection rule is clearly one that would only apply to executory contracts under section 365,[167] but it's hard to say with any confidence whether this will cause many executoriness fights. It surely does sometimes,[168] but it seems likely that whatever incentive effect it has is dwarfed by the status quo's preoccupation with the make-or-break excutoriness question of power to assume/reject *vel non*.[169]

The two most significant wild cards are the special rules within section 365 for real estate contracts and intellectual property agreements.[170] The real estate rules are easier: the special property-like remedy accorded by section 365(i)(2) likely maps many states' real-property rules for vendees in possession.[171] (Somewhat ironically, a vendee who has moved into full possession is likely to have tendered full payment

---

[166.] Although, they do fight the timing of when the defibrillators have to come off. See 11 U.S.C. § 541(b)(2) (2012) (excluding from estate nonresidential real property leases that expire under their own timing provisions).

[167.] *Id.* section 365(d)(1).

[168.] It came up in *Ebert v. DeVries Family Farm, LLC (In re Devries)*, No. 11-43165-DML-7, 2014 WL 4294540, at *4 (Bankr. N.D. Tex. Aug. 27, 2014) (trustee who missed sixty-day deadline to assume tried to argue that the LLC operating agreement was non-executory so it would not be deemed rejected).

[169.] See, e.g., *Foothills Tex., Inc. v. MTGLQ Inv'rs, L.P. (In re Foothills Tex., Inc.)*, 476 B.R. 143, 155 (Bankr. D. Del. 2012) (conceiving the debtor's entire adversary proceeding to turn on whether the contract was executory).

[170.] 11 U.S.C. § 365(i)(2) (2012) (special counterparty remedies for vendees in possession); *id.* section 365(j) (vendees out of possession); *id.* section 365(n)(1) (intellectual property licensees).

[171.] See, e.g., *Nickels Midway Pier, LLC v. Wild Waves, LLC (In re Nickels Midway Pier, LLC)*, 341 B.R. 486, 496–97 (D. N.J. 2006) (relying on state law to determine that section 365(i) was inapplicable).

and may not be in an executory contract at all.) And because it is such a rarely litigated provision of the Code, it is unclear whether section 365(j)'s rules for vendees not-yet-in-possession intend to strip property rights if state law grants an equitable property remedy under a conversion doctrine. Accordingly, it is difficult to assess whether there is a material (or any) inside-versus-outside section 365 difference here, let alone whether executoriness fights will be prevalent as a consequence.[172]

The hardest prediction pertains to the intellectual property rules of section 365(n). It is difficult to score section 365(n)'s ancillary provisions.[173] Even Westbrook throws up his hands and concedes they largely (if not identically) track preexisting non-bankruptcy contract rights.[174] Review of the case law involving section 365(n) where executoriness is disputed shows an unsurprising focus on the rejection *vel non* question (i.e., can the license be rejected or not).[175] There do not appear to be many secondary disputes over attempts to avoid perceived burdens of these ancillary provisions.[176] Moreover, there are a host of other intellectual property disputes (e.g., trademarks) that do not even fall

---

[172.] The closest case I could find to mentioning this issue was In re Nickels Midway Pier, LLC, which mused in dicta on the preemptive scope of section 365 and its interaction with state law specific performance remedies (and more specifically, the separate provision of the Code defining "claim"). *Id.* at 498–99.

[173.] 11 U.S.C. § 365(n)(1)(B) (2012) (allowing some licensees to retain rights to licensed IP or supplementary agreements in return for continued royalty payments).

[174.] Westbrook & White, *supra* note 6, at 532, 533 n.246. Westbrook indeed brands any divergence from state law in section 365(n) (and cognate subsections) "congressional mistakes." Westbrook, *supra* note 3, at 331 n.434.

[175.] See, e.g., *Lewis Bros. Bakeries Inc. v. Interstate Brands Corp. (In re Interstate Bakeries Corp.)*, 751 F.3d 955, 961–64 (8th Cir. 2014) (applying the Countryman test to uphold the objection that the license could not be rejected as it was non-executory). This case presents the wonderful surreality of the debtor's attempt first to reject the contract, and then subsequent withdrawal of that motion and substitution of a motion to assume it. *Id.* at 959. Nonetheless, the counterparty's resistance persisted in both postures! *Id.* at 964.

[176.] One example is *Szilagyi v. Chi. Am. Mfg., LLC (In re Lakewood Eng'g & Mfg. Co.)*, 459 B.R. 306 (Bankr. N.D. Ill. 2011), in which the parties fought over the scope of the waiver provisions of section 365(n)(2)(C). *Id.* at 341. But there was no challenge to executoriness in that case, which was conceded. *Id.* at 342.

under this subsection's scope.[177] In sum, loath as I am to end on an equivocal note, in all honesty I cannot say whether these residual issues will drive ongoing executoriness disputes; I can just share empirical skepticism that they are likely to be meaningful.[178]

V. A (Very Quick) Road Test Case Study

In closing, let us take a brief road test to see how the new approach would have better served a famous bankruptcy case, *Exide*.[179] In *Exide*, the bankruptcy court (affirmed by the district court) held the debtor's burdensome trademark assignment contract to be executory and allowed its rejection as a key step of the reorganization plan.[180] The counterparty appealed all the way up to the Third Circuit, which reversed and said the debtor's contract was not executory under the Countryman test and hence could not be rejected.[181] The poor bankruptcy court was left with a reorganized debtor that was now saddled with a trademark license that it thought had been cancelled but was now apparently binding.[182] Under the functional approach, of course, it could have been rejected. Executoriness's definition was not just fatal, but unclear in its application to the various courts that faced the issue. Under my approach, the debtor would not have cared. What the debtor could have done as soon as it realized it

---

[177.] 11 U.S.C. § 101(35A) (2012).

[178.] Cf. Westbrook & White, *supra* note 6, at 511 (noting that the focus of executoriness fights is whether debtors can assume/reject the contract).

[179.] In re Exide Techs., 607 F.3d 957 (3d Cir. 2010).

[180.] *Id.* at 961.

[181.] *Id.* at 964 ("Because the Agreement is not an executory contract, Exide cannot reject it.").

[182.] The debtor's backup argument that the contract had nonetheless been dealt with under the plan as a claim was rejected by an angry remand court that invoked judicial estoppel, finding the debtor's conduct end-runny. *Exide Techs. v. Enersys Del., Inc.* (*In re Exide Techs.*), Bankr. No. 02-11125 (KJC), Adv. No. 10-52766 (KJC), 2013 WL 85193, at *1, *7–8 (Bankr. D. Del. Jan. 8, 2013) (noting that the complaint was filed "in an attempt to circumvent" the Third Circuit ruling).

was in dodgy executoriness terrain, which it did,[183] was simply tack a footnote onto its section 365 rejection motion saying that in the alternative, the motion was to abandon burdensome property of the estate under section 554 to which it would not accord any damages priority status. As such, either by section 365(g)(1) or by section 502, the debtor would have paid off a monetary claim to the licensee and moved on, as it hoped, with its reorganized life. All this would have been independent of whether the Third Circuit adhered to Country-man, decided to overrule it in favor of Westbrook, or took some new path (of which there is no shortage of options).[184]

VI. Conclusion

The ABI Commission has made clear that executoriness is here to stay. Since it is, we should stifle its arbitrage-inducing tendencies by demonstrating how section 365's key functional outcomes can be replicated by carefully applying other provisions of the Bankruptcy Code to non-executory contracts, the residual category of agreements that flunk whatever test of executoriness is governing circuit law. This new approach will redirect the executoriness litigation energy to more productive fields. This path does not follow West-brook directly. It does better: it honors him for having shown us the right way.

[183.] *Id.* at *4.
[184.] See, e.g., In re Riodizio, Inc., 204 B.R. 417, 424 (Bankr. S.D.N.Y. 1997) (following neither Countryman nor Westbrook).

'Bankruptcy Light'? The English Debt Relief Order, Bankruptcy Simplification and Legal Change

*Iain Ramsay**

The U.S. Code's days as a paragon may be waning. One particular trend of note is the development of special regimes for low-income, no-asset filings, such as the U.K.'s debt relief order.[1]

* Professor of Law, Kent Law School, University of Kent, Canterbury, United Kingdom. This is one part of a larger comparative study 'The New Poor Person's Bankruptcy: A Qualitative Comparative Study'. Thanks to Laura Binger for research assistance, and to Joe Spooner and Toni Williams for comments. This chapter is based on the paper delivered at the Festschrift for Jay Westbrook at the University of Texas, February 2, 2018. Among Jay's many accomplishments was his pioneering work in promoting the comparative study of consumer bankruptcy in the late 1990s and his enthusiastic encouragement of younger scholars in this field. His empirical research with Elizabeth Warren and Teresa Sullivan provided the starting point for European research on individual bankruptcy. My empirical studies in Canada were inspired by As We Forgive Our Debtors, their seminal empirical analysis of U.S. consumer bankrupts. Reproduced with permission from Norton Journal of Bankruptcy Law and Practice, Vol. 27 No. 5 (Oct. 2018), with permission of Thomson Reuters. Copyright © 2018. Further use without the permission of Thomson Reuters is prohibited. For further information about this publication, please visit https://legal.thomsonreuters.com/en/products/law-books or call 800.328.9352.
[1.] E Warren, J Westbrook, K Porter, J Pottow, The Law of Debtors and Creditors, Text, Cases and Problems (7th ed.) 320.

I. Introduction

Many overindebted individuals have few assets, no repayment capacity, and may be unable to afford access to bankruptcy in those jurisdictions which require individuals to pay for access.[2] These are the 'No Income: No Asset' debtors or 'Low Income, Low Asset Debtors'.[3] The World Bank identifies the treatment of this group as a pressing international policy problem[4] and the IMF has recommended the introduction of simplified procedures for this group in its structural adjustment work in Europe.[5] Bankruptcy simplification is also a significant policy issue in the U.S. where bankruptcy costs have increased substantially since the enactment of the BAPCPA in 2005. Ronald Mann and Katherine Porter propose a 'streamlined

---

[2] See, e.g., R Mann, 'Making Sense of Nation-Level Bankruptcy Filing Rates' in J Niemi, I Ramsay & W Whitford (eds) Consumer Credit Debt and Bankruptcy; Comparative and International Perspectives (Oxford, Hart, 2009) 243–44. German studies suggest that perhaps 80 percent of individual bankrupts are nullinsolvenz (J Heuer, 2016), incapable of making any payments under the six-year waiting period for discharge, while in Sweden approximately 40 percent of debtors on five-year restructuring plans have no repayment capacity but must wait for five years for a discharge I Ramsay, Personal Insolvency in the 21st Century; A Comparison of the U.S. and Europe ch 5. For Canada, see S Ben-Ishai and S Schwartz 'Bankruptcy for the Poor? (2007) 45(3) Osgoode Hall LJ 471. A recent Australian study identifies a group of low income individuals who have lost employment for whom bankruptcy may not provide a fresh start. See P Ali, L O'Brien & I (Ian) Ramsay, 'Bankruptcy and Debtor Rehabilitation: An Australian Empirical Study' (2017) 40 Melbourne L Rev. 688, 712–16, 733–34. In France, about 45 percent of individuals processed by the Overindebtedness Commissions are channelled to rétablissement personnel since they have no repayment capacity or assets. See Banque de France, Enquête typologique 2017 sur le surendettement des ménages <http://particuliers.banque-france.fr/enquete-typologique-2017-sur-le-surendettement-des-menages>

[3] Policymakers sometimes refer to the NINA debtor. Ronald Mann suggests that this should be extended to include 'those who have no substantial income or assets'. Mann, n2 (fn82).

[4] See World Bank, Report on the Treatment of the Insolvency of Natural Persons (J Kilborn, C Booth, J Niemi, I Ramsay and J Garrido, 2013) para 439 'One of the most pressing problems is the treatment of debtors who cannot generate significant disposable income for the duration of the plan.. Significant numbers of debtors in all insolvency systems for natural persons fall into this category.'

[5] See, e.g., Cyprus, discussed in Ramsay above note 2 at 168.

administrative proceeding with low fees for access' for those people 'in irretrievable distress'. The process would be 'a simple one-page form that debtors could complete without an attorney's assistance', in which public expenses 'are focused on vigilant efforts to detect and punish fraud'.[6]

The 'global proliferation'[7] of individual bankruptcy systems throughout the world during recent decades raises the important question of the appropriate institutional framework which will minimize overall social costs, and retain public confidence.[8] Individual bankruptcy cases are not a high stakes game and NINA debtors represent a significant percentage of debtors. At the same time, individual bankruptcy may raise legal, budgeting and social issues that are not always simple. The choice of institutional structure raises issues

---

[6.] See K Porter & R Mann, 'Saving Up for Bankruptcy' (2010) 98 Geo LJ 289,338. And see R Mann, 'Making Sense of Nation-Level Bankruptcy Filing Rates' in J Niemi, I Ramsay & W Whitford, (eds) Consumer Credit, Debt and Bankruptcy: Comparative and International Perspectives (Oxford, Hart, 2009) 243–44, 'The evidence points to bankruptcy simplification. The time has come to abandon the complicated structures laden with bureaucratic hurdles.. At least for the desperately insolvent, with no substantial income or assets, the best process is one that is stripped down to its most central elements.. the system should function as an administrative process designed to provide a service at the lowest possible transaction cost.. the system should provide complete and unconditional relief as quickly as practicable. This should occur within days or weeks after the filing.. Finally the system should impose stern criminal sanctions for fraud.. A simple and expedient process will collapse if it is tainted by fraud.'

Angela Littwin in discussing the impact of BAPCPA on bankruptcy costs notes: 'To make matters worse, clients who had particularly low incomes, were elderly, spoke little English or were otherwise not technologically savvy required additional resources to shepherd them through post-BAPCPA bankruptcy. This is a particular problem because disadvantaged clients are less able to afford these costs than others, and most of the attorneys who discussed this issue appeared to serve mainly this type of client.' A Littwin, 'Adapting to BAPCPA' (2016) 90 American Bankruptcy Law Journal 183, 223. See also A Littwin, 'The Affordability Paradox: How Consumer Bankruptcy's Greatest Weakness May Account for Its Surprising Success' (2011) 53 Wm & Mary L Rev 1933.

[7.] See F Trentmann, Empire of Things: How We Became a World of Consumers, from the Fifteenth Century to the Twenty First (London, Allen Lane, 2016) 432: 'The global proliferation of bankruptcy laws, finally, is a recognition that overindebtedness is a problem in all affluent societies, including social market and welfare states.'

[8.] See World Bank, above n4, II.2 'The Institutional Context'.

of public administration and governance and the balance of public and private actors. The World Bank suggest that institutional frameworks represent a continuum ranging from the situation where an administrative agency dominates the process to court-based systems serviced by publicly funded or private intermediaries.[9] Two further contemporary observations are relevant. Many countries are unwilling to invest significant public resources in consumer bankruptcy systems, posing the question of how to finance low-income bankruptcy, and there is a tendency therefore towards increased routinization of processing of individual bankruptcy cases.

Against this background, this chapter focuses on one jurisdiction's response to the issue of the NINA debtor, the English Debt Relief Order (DRO), a low-cost, means-tested, administrative procedure only accessible online. Introduced in 2009, its objectives are to provide access to debt relief and financial inclusion for those unable to pay for bankruptcy and for whom bankruptcy might be a disproportionate remedy.[10] It is delivered through a partnership between the English Insolvency Service and accredited debt advice agencies. The term Debt Relief Order rather than bankruptcy was intended to reduce the stigma associated with bankruptcy, encouraging those in irretrievable distress to seek a remedy. The media dubbed it 'bankruptcy light'[11] and it

---

[9] *Ibid.* para 159.

[10] The DRO provisions were enacted within Part V of the Tribunals, Courts and Enforcement Act 2007 and brought into force in 2009. When introducing the DRO the government stated that 'it deals with those who cannot pay their debts and are unable to access current procedures of debt relief.. [it seeks] to promote financial inclusion' Hansard, HL vol 687, col 766 (November 29,2006). Lady Justice Hale has described the procedure as 'a new and simplified way of wiping the slate clean for debtors who are too poor to go bankrupt'. *Secretary of State v. Payne* [2011] UKSC 60,63.

[11] See, e.g., James Andrews, 'Bankruptcy light soars –and it could get a lot worse: How to beat bad debt,' *Daily Mirror* April 29, 2016; Daily Mail, 'Bankruptcy light orders up 40% as graduates battle to find jobs and pay off debts.'

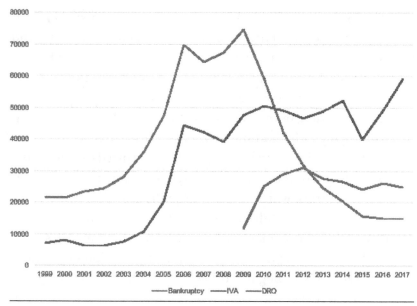

Figure 18.1 Bankruptcy, IVAs, (1999-2017), DROs (2009-2017).

is now the most frequently used 'straight bankruptcy' remedy (see Figure 18.1). The idea for a DRO originated with a New Zealand proposal for a 'No Asset Procedure' for consumer debtors in the early 2000s.[12] Ireland[13] subsequently introduced a variation on the English procedure and the No- Asset procedure has been transplanted to emerging and developing economies including

---

[12.] See New Zealand Ministry of Economic Development, No Asset Procedure Paper (Wellington, Ministry of Economic Development, 2002) 3, discussed in T Telfer, 'New Zealand Bankruptcy Law Reform: The New Role of the Official Assignee and the Prospects for a No-Asset Regime' in Niemi, Ramsay and Whitford ch 12. 263–67. See also T Keeper, 'New Zealand's No Asset Procedure: A Fresh Start at No Cost?' (2014) 14 QUT L Rev 79

[13.] Personal Insolvency Act 2012 (as amended) Part 3 chapter 1. Scotland introduced a 'Low-Income Low-Asset' bankruptcy procedure in 2007, subsequently replacing it with a 'Minimal Asset' procedure in 2015. See now Bankruptcy (Scotland) Act 2016 s 2(2) and Schedule 1.

Kenya,[14] India[15] and South Africa.[16] In contrast, no such procedure exists in several European countries such as Germany and Sweden, where a mandatory repayment plan of several years remains a condition of discharge, notwithstanding the fact that many individuals have no repayment capacity.

A central finding of this chapter is that although the DRO promised bankruptcy simplification it has in fact resulted in a more complex access procedure than bankruptcy. This occurred because of the relatively restrictive means test, liability limits and other overinclusive access controls, which increased significantly processing costs. The intermediary debt advice agencies, rather than the Insolvency Service or debtors, bear many of these costs which are in turn spread among the public and private sources of debt advice funding in England and Wales.[17] This English solution for the NINA reflected partly the influential role of the relevant government departments in the establishment of the scheme for whom the introduction of the DRO solved problems which they faced in addressing debt cases. Civil servants played a central role in reform, setting the agenda, framing the policy options and drafting the legislation. This story suggests

[14.] See Kenya, Insolvency Act 2015 ss343 and following. Section 345 sets out the means tested procedure in s345. In South Africa see National Credit Amendment Bill, 2018.

[15.] See the Insolvency and Bankruptcy Code 2016 chapter II Fresh Start Process. Reports leading up to reform had identified the DRO as a useful model: '[T]he innovative amendment of the DRO in the UK is a process of quick settlement between debtor.. and creditors leading to automatic discharge in a year without the label of insolvent attaching to the debtor. A DRO kind of a mechanism will be very useful in the Indian context considering the large number of poor debtors who could benefit from it.' S Ramann, R Sane & S Thomas, 'Reforming Personal Insolvency Law in India' 20.

(Indira Gandhi Institute of Development Research, Mumbai, Dec. 2015) https://ifrogs.org/PDF/WP-2015-035.pdf For a general background to the Indian reforms see A Feibelman, 'Anticipating the Function and Impact India's New Personal Insolvency and Bankruptcy Regime' ssrn https://papers.ssrn.com/sol3/papers.cfm?abstract_id=3092042

[16.] See Draft National Credit Amendment Bill 2018 https://pmg.org.za/call-for-comment/628/

[17.] See below section 2 for an outline of the funding of debt advice agencies involved in the Debt Relief Order.

that although the *idea* of bankruptcy simplification might be widely accepted internationally, any actual procedure will reflect the politics and institutional history of particular jurisdictions. This chapter contributes therefore to understanding why particular institutional frameworks for individual bankruptcy emerge and change.[18]

Part 2 outlines briefly the DRO process. Part 3 analyses the legislative background of the Order as a response to problems faced by the Ministry of Justice, responsible for the courts in England and Wales, and the Insolvency Service, the English executive agency responsible for administering the vast majority of individual bankrupts. These institutions played important roles in setting the agenda and framing the issues for reform, against the background of UK Treasury requirements that the Insolvency Service should cover its costs. This part describes the arguments marshalled for the DRO as a 'bankruptcy light' remedy which framed the policy process and discusses why the DRO developed its particular institutional form. Part 4 discusses briefly experience with the Order and contrasts it with existing bankruptcy practice in England and Wales. This suggests that the arguments for the DRO as an alternative 'bankruptcy light' remedy are not convincing, and that the DRO represents a more rigorous process of scrutiny than bankruptcy for many debtors. Part 5 provides brief comparative perspectives on bankruptcy simplification, comparing the relevance of the English experience for U.S. proposals for a simplified administrative bankruptcy, and suggests a future comparative research agenda.

II. Outline of the DRO Process

A debtor[19] must make an online application to the Insolvency Service through a limited number of intermediaries accredited by competent

---

[18.] Existing explanations include the influence of interest groups, legal origins or the influence of ideas, See discussion in 1 Ramsay, above n2, 11.

[19.] The process is only available to individual debtors and creditors may not initiate the process.

authorities[20] (see Table 18.1). These are Debt Advice Agencies whose work is funded through a combination of fair share financing,[21] a debt advice levy imposed on creditors by the Financial Conduct Authority,[22] and public or charitable funding.[23] These agencies act as screening agencies checking the eligibility of the debtor using credit reference data.[24] Debtor access is limited to individuals with non-exempt assets below £1,000,[25] a vehicle valued at less than 1,000, unsecured debts less than £20,000, and no more than £50 in surplus income, determined by reference to the reasonable domestic needs of the individual and her family, which is in practice determined by the 'common financial statement'.[26]

---

[20] See Debt Relief Orders (Designation of Competent Authorities) Regulations 2009.Citizens Advice is the major intermediary (See Table 1). See discussion below, section 3, 4.1 of its role.

[21] Stepchange represents this model.

[22] Specialist Debt Advice is funded through a levy on creditors by the Financial Conduct Authority. The levy is related to the amount of credit extended. See CP17/38: Regulatory fees and levies: policy proposals for 2018/19, The current levy is £48million. This money is disbursed through the Money Advice Service, established under the Financial Services and Markets Act 2000 which since amendments in 2012 is responsible for co-ordinating debt advice in England and Wales. See Financial Services and Markets Act 2000 (as amended) s3S. See www.moneyadviceservice.org.uk/en/corporate/money-advice-service-and-funding-of-debt-advice-services.

[23] Local authorities, for example, may fund specialist debt advice provided by Citizens Advice. One intermediary, Christians against Poverty, is financed through donations which may be made through churches. See Christians against Poverty, Annual Report, 2016 available at <https://capuk.org/downloads/finance/accounts_2016.pdf>. Approved intermediaries may also work in Law Centres which provide money advice and may be able to bring test cases. Legal aid is limited now in debt cases since the enactment of the Legal Aid, Sentencing and Punishment of Offenders Act 2012 which as part of austerity measures substantially cut back the availability of legal aid. See the House of Commons Justice Committee Report, Impact of changes to civil legal aid under Part 1 of the Legal Aid, Sentencing and Punishment of Offenders Act 2012. Accessible at <https://publications.parliament.uk/pa/cm201415/cmselect/cmjust/311/311.pdf>.

[24] The three main credit reference agencies, Experian, Equifax and CallCredit, provide free access to data for approved intermediaries. The formal checks are found in Insolvency Rules 5A.7. – Prescribed verification checks – conditions in paras 1–8 of Schedule 4ZA

[25] Insolvency Rules 1986/1925 Part 1 Preliminary 5A.10. – Particular descriptions of property to be excluded for the purpose of determining the value of a person's property.

[26] The Schedule defines 'monthly surplus income' as 'the amount by which a person's monthly income exceeds the amount necessary for the reasonable domestic needs of himself and his family'. Sch 4Z (2) This is generally calculated using

Table 18.1 Main Competent Authorities and Approved Intermediaries, 2013-2014

Competent authority	No of intermediaries	No of DRO apps
Citizens Advice	1,337 (72%)	14,520 (53%)
Institute of Money Advisers	287 (16%)	3,703(14%)
National Debtline	12 (1%)	1,227 (4%)
Payplan	12(1%)	269 (1%)
Stepchange Debt Charity	31(2%)	4,962 (18%)
Christians against Poverty	7 (0.4)	1,097 (4%)
Other	165 (9%)	1,547 (6%)
Total	1,851	27,329

Source: Insolvency Service.

Individuals must pay £90 for access to the DRO with £10 going to the approved intermediary. The bankruptcy access fee is £680. The DRO fee may be paid in instalments, but it must be paid before accessing the procedure.[27] Access to a DRO is barred to individuals who have entered into a transaction at an undervalue or given a preference within the previous two years,[28] and debtor behaviour may be

---

the Common Financial Statement (now known as the Standard Financial Statement).The Common Financial Statement was first developed by the Money Advice Trust (a debt charity) and the British Bankers Association in November 2002 for debt management plans. The Bankers Association agreed that if a debtor's expenditure was within the guidelines of the statement they would accept the plan. Scotland has conferred statutory force on its use as the exclusive tool for determining surplus income. It does not have statutory force in England and Wales but The Money Advice Service has co-ordinated an agreement with a wide variety of groups on the use of the statement and 'it is intended that the SFS will become the only format used by the debt advice sector, replacing the many alternative financial statements currently in use.' https://sfs.moneyadviceservice.org.uk/en/what-is-the-standard-financial-statement.

[27.] Contrast therefore with, e.g., the Canadian summary procedure where individuals can pay the fees in instalments during the nine-month discharge period and if necessary for another 12 months after discharge.

[28.] S 251 (c) (5) Part 1 Schedule 4ZC 9,10. The explanatory notes indicate that the rationale for this prohibition is 'to avoid a situation where the debtor has disposed

sanctioned through a Debt Restriction Order.[29] Creditors can oppose the making of an order. A debtor must inform the Insolvency service of any change in her financial status (e.g. increase in income) during the one-year period.[30] This may result in the Order being revoked. The use of the term 'Debt Relief' rather than bankruptcy is intended to avoid the stigma of bankruptcy which might deter some applicants.[31] The order can only be accessed every six years.

III. The Legislative Background to the English DRO

The growth of consumer overindebtedness during the 1980s and 90s raised the question of the appropriate forms of debt relief for the consumer debtor. Government committees had proposed that the central form of relief for consumer debtors should be a revised administration order, a court administered remedy originally introduced in 1883. Under the proposals, a debtor would make a partial

---

of his assets in order to meet the permitted criterion for obtaining a debt relief order and to protect the position of creditors'.

[29.] A restriction order may be made either through the court or an undertaking by the debtor to the Insolvency Service. It will continue the bankruptcy restrictions on a debtor such as the requirement that an individual must declare her status if making an application for a loan, as well as statutory disabilities attached to bankruptcy. A broad discretion exists to make such an order where it is appropriate structured by a list of factors such as 'incurring, before the date of the determination of the application for the debt relief order, a debt which the debtor had no reasonable expectation of being able to pay' See Schedule 4ZB (2)(h).

[30.] S251J (5).

[31.] A 2004 research paper on administration orders found that some of the people we interviewed were very resistant to the idea of bankruptcy, and were deterred by the stigma they would face given the relatively small sums of money they owed.. A simplified debt procedure would therefore seem more appropriate for people on very low incomes that are unlikely to increase. This could be called something other than bankruptcy, to overcome the stigma that people feel and differentiate it from the full bankruptcy procedure. E Kempson & S Collard Managing Multiple Debts: Experiences of County Court Administration Orders among Debtors, Creditors and Advisors DCA Research Series 1/04, 76 (2004).

repayment over a period of three years with a write off of any residual debt after this period.[32] This proposal, although enacted by
Parliament in 1990,[33] was never implemented by the relevant government department, the Ministry of Justice (then the Lord Chancellor's
Department), partly through fear of increased court costs. During
the 1990s consumer bankruptcies increased substantially notwithstanding the significant upfront fee to access bankruptcy. In 2002,
the New Labour government reduced the bankruptcy discharge
period from three years to one year as part of a policy to promote
entrepreneurialism. During the parliamentary debates MPs, briefed
by Citizens Advice,[34] had pressed unsuccessfully for the removal of

---

[32] See Ramsay n2, 81–84.

[33] See s13 Courts and Legal Services Act 1990.

[34] Citizens Advice was established during the second world war to assist citizens
with gaining knowledge of their rights. It became in the 1960s and 1970s a significant source of consumer advice and is now a primary source of legal advice to consumers on modest incomes and represents the largest independent network of free
advice centres in Europe. Citizens Advice is a national charity which is funded by a
number of government departments with a core grant and grants for specific purposes, such as money advice. Its services are delivered through approximately 600
sites by 300 independent local bureaux, independent charities funded through local
authorities, charitable donations and grants from CA. The national central office
provides expertise but trained volunteers comprise the largest percentage of workers in the local bureaux. Its website indicates that 'of the 28,500 people who work for
the service, over 22,000 of them are volunteers and nearly 6,500 are paid staff.' The
top five issues for advice are social benefits and tax credits, debt, consumer, housing
and employment.
  Citizens Advice performs a dual advice and campaigning role. The 2015–2016
Annual Report states: 'We support people to develop the skills they need to help
themselves and we use our evidence on the issues that our clients face to bring
about policy changes that benefit everyone.' For a recent overview see S Kirwan, M
McDermot and J Clarke, 'Imagining and practising citizenship in austere times: the
work of Citizens Advice' (2016) 20 Citizenship Studies 764–78.
  Collections of individual case studies feed into its campaigning and policy
role. This knowledge-acquisition role has led Jones to characterize it as part of a
'shadow state' which assists citizens to learn about their rights but also contributes
to a knowledge acquisition process by the state about the impact of its policies. R
Jones, 'Learning Beyond the State: The Pedagogical Spaces of the CAB service' (2011)
14(6) Citizenship Studies 725. Jones refers to the following definition of the shadow
state by Wolch (1990) The shadow state: government and voluntary sector in transition New York, the Foundation Center xvi 'para-state apparatus comprised of

the fee for individuals with limited means.[35] The bankruptcy deposit fee had also been challenged unsuccessfully in a test case as a contravention of human rights law.[36] The court concluded that that no fundamental human right of access to the courts was challenged by a mandatory bankruptcy administration fee. The court did however express concern for the plight of an individual denied access to debt relief because of cost, but indicated that this was an issue for Parliament. The court was signaling, in traditional English judicial fashion, that 'something ought to be done'.[37]

---

multiple voluntary sector organizations, administered outside of traditional democratic politics and charged with major collective service responsibilities previously shouldered by the public sector, yet remaining within the purview of state control'.

[35] See Citizens Advice, Insolvency: A Second Chance: A Response by the CAB Service to the Insolvency Services White Paper 13/11/2001; Opposition members briefed by Citizens Advice raised the issue of fees during the Parliamentary passage of the Bill. See, e.g., J Walley MP 'Citizens Advice Bureaus have already circulated their concerns to many members of Parliament. They are concerned about whether those on means tested benefits and in hardship will be exempt from the bankruptcy deposit fee.. Many of our constituents cannot afford to take advantage of some of the Bill's proposals'. HC Parl Deb Second Reading Enterprise Bill Col 69.

[36] Specifically, a common law right to access to courts and article 6(1) of the European Convention for the Protection of Human Rights and Fundamental Freedoms. See *R v. Lord Chancellor ex parte Lightfoot* [2000] QB 597. This case was brought by the Public Law Project, with support and information provided by the Money Advice Association, the Law Centres Federation, the Federation of Independent Advice Centres and the National Association of Citizens' Advice Bureaux. The debtor in this case was a casualty of the economic recession of the early 1990s, and had also experienced marriage breakdown. Her primary debt was the negative equity of £40,000 owing to the mortgagee. The European Court of Human Rights rejected an appeal from this decision.

Simon Brown LJ in the Court of Appeal did note that 'the appellant, Mrs Lightfoot, is unable to pay this deposit. She has debts of nearly £60,000 and no significant assets. She simply cannot raise the money. Nor is she alone in this predicament. Rather it appears that large numbers of debtors are similarly placed. It is, indeed, apparently for this reason that the great majority of those wishing to petition for bankruptcy do not in fact do so. To them, therefore, is denied what Lord Jauncey of Tullichettle in In re Smith (A Bankrupt); Ex parte Braintree District Council [1990] 2 A.C. 215, 237 called 'the importance of the rehabilitation of the individual insolvent'. They face instead a lifetime of unrelieved indebtedness.' *Ibid.* 617.

[37] Simon Brown LJ concluded that 'it is not difficult to recognise the hardship and worry that many will suffer through their financial exclusion from the undoubted benefits of this rehabilitation scheme and, in the more compassionate times in

The New Labour government had committed in 1997 to reform the administration order. It also established an ambitious over-indebtedness task force in 2004.[38] This involved a large number of initiatives by central and local government departments to reduce overindebtedness and provide support for those who became over-indebted.[39] Several initiatives were promised in this document under the category 'The Justice System and Debt.' Government departments and their civil servants play a significant role in the development of English bankruptcy law[40] and personal insolvency engages two Ministries, the Ministry of Justice,[41] responsible for court administration and the then Department of Trade and Industry,[42] within which sits the executive agency, the Insolvency Service.[43] Understanding the priorities of the two Ministries explains the particular approach, and framing of reform, and the structure of the DRO procedure.

A research report commissioned by the Ministry of Justice in 2004 painted a picture of a failing administration order in the

---

which we now live, it may be hoped that the competing interests will be considered anew and perhaps a fresh balance struck.' *Ibid*. 631. Chadwick LJ commented that 'If that consequence is now thought unacceptable, it is for Parliament to alter the law or for the Lord Chancellor, as the rule-making body, to make an amendment to the rules. It is not for the court to give effect to whatever view it might hold as to the appropriate social policy in this field under the guise of discovering some hitherto unrecognised fundamental constitutional right.' *Ibid*. at 635.

[38.] See the subsequent interdepartmental strategy paper, 'Tackling Overindebtedness' (DTI, DWP, 2004) which included reference to the proposed Debt Relief Order http://webarchive.nationalarchives.gov.uk/20090609023014/www.berr.gov.uk/files/file18559.pdf.

[39.] The strategy is reviewed critically by the National Audit Office in Helping Overindebted Consumers Report by the Comptroller and Auditor General HC 292 (2009–2010).

[40.] See for example the discussion of earlier English reforms by Halliday and Carruthers in T Halliday & B Carruthers, Rescuing Business: The Making of Corporate Bankruptcy Law in England and the United States (Oxford, OUP, 1998) Part 1, 3.

[41.] Then known as the Department of Constitutional Affairs and previously the Lord Chancellor's Office.

[42.] Now the Department for Business, Energy and Industrial Strategy.

[43.] These Ministries are regularly renamed so that the Ministry of Justice succeeded the Department of Constitutional Affairs, which succeeded the Lord Chancellor's Office. The current Department for Business, Energy & Industrial Strategy succeeded the Department of Business Innovation and Skills.

county court with high levels of default in repayment, and inconsistent application of the possibility of composition. Users of the order were primarily female lone parents, 70% of whom were unemployed.[44] The Ministry of Justice (then Department of Constitutional Affairs) proposed therefore the introduction of a NINA process[45] as part of the solution to the problem of the administration order in the county court and the prohibitive costs of a bankruptcy petition for low-income debtors.[46] The DRO represented an alternative for 'those with no disposable income or assets and little prospect of getting any in the foreseeable future (especially those on long term low-income)'.[47] The introduction of the NINA would divert a proportion of administration cases from the courts to the new procedure and also some bankruptcy cases, currently processed through the courts.[48] The Ministry rejected administration of the NINA procedure through the courts since this would be costly and fell outside the central role of the courts in dispute

---

[44] See E Kempson & S Collard, Managing Multiple Debts: Experiences of County Court Administration Orders among Debtors, Creditors and Advisors (London, Department of Constitutional Affairs, 2004) discussed in Ramsay n 2,85.

[45] See Department of Constitutional Affairs, 'A Choice of Paths': Better options to manage over-indebtedness CP23/04 para 35 'The Government is therefore developing a "No income No assets debt relief scheme" (NINA) which would be administered by the Insolvency Service to provide debt relief to the can't pay group.' http://webarchive.nationalarchives.gov.uk/20040722013541/www.dca.gov.uk/consult/debt/debt.pdf

[46] Ibid. para 32.

[47] Ibid. para 22. The subsequent Insolvency Service consultation indicated that 'The type of person at whom the scheme is aimed cannot pay even a portion of their debt within a reasonable timeframe. Such people are often living on very low incomes, and whilst at the time they borrowed the money they had every intention of paying it back, they simply lack the means to do so.' The Insolvency Service, 'Relief for the Indebted: An Alternative to Bankruptcy (2005) 4. http://webarchive.nationalarchives.gov.uk/20080610165612/www.insolvency.gov.uk/insolvencyprofessionandlegislation/con_doc_register/consultationpaperwithnewannex1.pdf

[48] The Legislative Impact Analysis estimated that 14% of individuals currently presenting their own bankruptcy petition would be eligible for relief under the DRO, thus freeing up court time.

settlement.[49] Ministry of Justice officials had picked up the idea of the DRO from proposals for a 'No-Asset' procedure in New Zealand designed for 'consumer debtors' whom it was assumed would have few assets and limited repayment capacity.

The summary of responses to the NINA consultation by the Ministry of Justice paper indicated that some consultees preferred the abolition of the bankruptcy deposit to the creation of a NINA procedure. However the Ministry simply responded that it was not convinced of the option of waiving the petition deposit, concluded that there was broad support for a NINA scheme, and handed over responsibility for its development to the Insolvency Service.[50]

The Insolvency Service, an executive agency within the Department of Business, processes and acts as trustee in bankruptcies which are not profitable for the private sector. It has done so since its creation in 1883. These cases now represent approximately 80–90% of individual bankruptcies, with a small percentage of individual small-business bankruptcies handled by the private sector.[51] The Insolvency Service follows the new public management model where government agencies operate along business lines and on a cost-recovery basis in relation to the processing of bankruptcies.[52] Since

---

[49.] 'Choice of Paths' above n 38, para 34.

[50.] See the summary of responses at http://webarchive.nationalarchives.gov.uk/20070101085734/www.dca.gov.uk/consult/debt/responses.pdf

[51.] In 2015 15,845 bankruptcies were processed by the Insolvency Service, 2,545 by private insolvency practitioners. Including DROs with bankruptcies as a form of bankruptcy light, private processing accounts for approximately 6% of bankruptcies. Of course, IPs will deal with IVAs. Research by R3 (The Insolvency Practitioners Association) of their members suggested that the average insolvency handled by a private practitioner involves unsecured debt of £109,780 and assets of £43,590; the bankrupt is usually self-employed with an average estimated income of £28,080. See R 3 'Closing the Gap' www.r3.org.uk/media/R3_Gender_Insolvency_June_2016.pdf

[52.] See Financial Memorandum between the DBIS and the Insolvency Service, 2004. The Service finances its bankruptcy processing costs from fee income: investigation and enforcement and redundancy payment recovery are funded from government grants and successful litigation.

the great majority of bankruptcy cases have no assets this is increasingly not a sustainable funding model.[53] A continuing challenge has been to reduce the costs associated with processing small bankruptcies which offer no dividend. During the 1990s the Service developed a summary process which involved a relatively light- touch investigation of the majority of bankrupts, and a bankruptcy discharge after two rather than three years.

The introduction of the DRO would not necessarily reduce the costs of the Insolvency Service if it were required to determine and check eligibility of debtors for the process. The Service proposed therefore the assistance of debt advice agencies[54] as competent authorities in processing the online applications. Debt advice agencies would benefit, it was argued, from the existence of the DRO through a reduction in the need for continuing negotiations with creditors to write off debts or make token payments. They would be able to close the file.[55]

---

[53] See discussion in House of Commons Business, Innovation and Skills Committee The Insolvency Service Sixth Report of Session 2012–2013 Report, together with formal minutes, oral and written evidence. (HMSO, London, 2013).

[54] 'In order to keep costs to as low a level as possible, we think there would be a need to involve the debt advice sector (which would act as an intermediary to assess whether a case is suitable before the debtor applies to the official receiver) and for the facility to apply for a debt relief order to be available only online.' Above n 47, para 6.

[55] Ibid. para 44. 'We are aware that intermediaries would need to be properly resourced to fulfil this task. We do feel that the availability of a scheme such as that which is proposed should, overall, represent a time saving for debt advisers. In cases at present where the debtor has nothing to offer his creditors, debt advisers spend large amounts of time negotiating and attempting to persuade creditors that the debt should be written off. They also devote time to assisting debtors to apply for grants in order to petition for bankruptcy and then assisting with queries arising out of any proceedings that ensue. The proposed scheme would remove the need for much of this work, but we recognise that the availability of a new form of debt relief may, at least in the short term, result in an increased workload for debt advisers while they become accustomed to the procedure and while clients who might not previously have sought advice seek a resolution to their problems.'

The Service then refers to how advisors view the setting up of an administration order as a method of effectively closing a case 'once an order has been set up a case can be effectively closed. In contrast, other multiple debt cases involve negotiations with a number of creditors and can remain open for a year or more'.

Several themes appear in the consultation,[56] the subsequent working group on the DRO[57] and the legislative impact analysis of the DRO in the omnibus Tribunals Courts and Enforcement Bill 2007. First, the idea of the approved intermediary, intended to make the system more accessible and efficient, received broad support from both creditors, intermediaries and the debt advice sector, although the latter raised concerns about funding the process and ensuring their independence. The approved intermediary was viewed as crucial to the success and legitimacy of the process, although the New Zealand model did not incorporate this aspect. Second, a majority favoured a moderate fee for the process although some debt advisors demurred arguing that since the scheme was aimed at those with no income or assets it was 'nonsensical' to require a fee.[58] The government did not really engage with the argument that the process might be funded by a creditor levy or through general taxation. The Insolvency Service was clear that the process must be self-funding. The Legislative Impact analysis for the Tribunals Courts and Enforcement Act also rejected the alternative of waiving the fees for

---

[56.] The consultation received 70 responses. They included creditors, including public creditors, and their trade associations (such as the Finance and Leasing Association), debt advisers, and professional intermediaries such as PWC. The idea of the approved intermediary received overwhelming support (50 in favour, two opposed) with a general view that it would make the system easier to function and would provide 'useful face-to-face contact'. But the debt advice agencies demonstrated two concerns: a possible loss of independence, and the need for extra resources required for processing DROs. The Insolvency Service, 'Relief for the Indebted – -an alternative to bankruptcy. Summary of Responses and Government Reply' (November, 2005) 16–17

[57.] The Working Group consisted of Citizens Advice Bureaux, Institute of Money Advisers, Advice Services Commission, National Debtline/Money Advice Trust, Advice UK, CCCS (now Stepchange) and the Legal Services Commission. A summary of the intermediary working group discussions can be found at the following page of the webarchive of the Insolvency Service <http://webarchive.nationalarchives.gov.uk/20090903115335/www.insolvency.gov.uk/insolvencyprofessionandlegislation/DebtRelief.htm>. The working group concluded that 'IMs are required to enable the DRO process. Without the IMs, there would be no link between the applying debtor and the INSS, and hence the system would not be workable.'

[58.] Above n 45,11.

bankruptcy arguing that bankruptcy was a disproportionate remedy for this group of debtors, that it would be unfair for other creditors to cross-subsidise these cases, and 'inappropriate' that it should be met out of general taxation.[59] A recurring theme was that although the DRO would impose costs on the Debt Advice sector, this would be offset by a reduction in the need for continued correspondence with creditors, and agencies would be able to provide debtors with access to a new remedy.

In summary, the Debt Advice sector had lobbied for abolition of the bankruptcy fee for low-income debtors. The response of the DRO drew its initial inspiration from a transplant from a foreign jurisdiction but the agenda of reform and the consequent structure and financing were driven by the interests of the Ministry of Justice and the Insolvency Service in removing debt administration from the courts and reducing the costs of the Service to ensure that it met the Treasury imperative of cost-recovery. The framing of the debate marginalized the possibility of abolition of the bankruptcy fee. The reduction in Insolvency Service costs could only be achieved by convincing the debt advice sector to play a 'partnership'[60] role in the process. Embedding the debt advice agencies in the process might also justify further government funding for debt advice, a continuing concern in an era of austerity.[61]

[59.] Tribunals Courts and Enforcement Bill: Regulatory Impact Assessment at 90 available at http://webarchive.nationalarchives.gov.uk/20081106064111/www.dca.gov.uk//risk/tce_bill.pdf. This repeated the earlier statement by the Insolvency Service in the 2005 Consultation. Above n 47, para 7.

[60.] See Intermediary Guidance Notes, DRO2, 3. The Insolvency Service Guidance Notes describe the intermediary as an 'agent' between the debtor and the Insolvency Service, playing a 'pivotal position' in the process. Citizens Advice indicate that their role within the DRO should not compromise its partnership agreement with Government that it 'will always act independently and in the best interests of our clients, and not as an agent of government'.

[61.] The Insolvency Service argued in the Working Group that the statutory requirement to consult debt advisors could benefit the sector and in addition 'may help safeguard existing funding (perhaps even encouraging more). One debt advisor on the working group did recognize that it would confer a larger statutory role on debt advice agencies.

Creditors could be reassured that given the 'robust entry criteria'[62] to the process (screening by approved debt advisers, preferences barring access, once every six years, obligation to inform of changes during the one year period, limits on the discharge, the possibility of a Debt Restriction Order) individuals would be genuine 'can't pays' and creditors did not need to continue chasing a debt. The intention was to create a simplified procedure, but the ultimate legislation, which probably reflected departmental concerns about potential abuse, includes a battery of provisions to ensure a proper 'balance' is achieved between debt relief and moral hazard concerns. Such controls might be justified by a concern to maintain a credible system, as suggested by Katherine Porter and Ronald Mann in the quotation at the beginning of this chapter.[63]

Little parliamentary discussion took place concerning the DRO provisions during the passage of the Tribunals Courts and Enforcement Bill.[64] Since the DRO was part of a larger set of government

---

Kirwan, McDermot and Clarke identify three pressures on the contemporary CABx, the increased demands caused by austerity, the pressures on funding, and the reductions in legal aid. See generally S Kirwan, M McDermot and J Clarke, (n34).

[62] Legislative Impact Analysis para 5.36. For creditor concerns, see, e.g., D Atkinson, 'Alarm at "quickie" bankruptcy plan; debts of up to £15,000 could be written off after a year with no need for court', Mail on Sunday, Nov 28, 2006, 5; D Atkinson, 'Debtors may hide assets', Mail on Sunday, Mar. 30, 2008, 67.

[63] n6). The City of London Law Society commented on a subsequent consultation on DROs that '[t]here is clearly a moral hazard risk in making the DRO process available to an individual with few or no assets, whatever the size of their debt, as this may simply encourage reckless borrowing'. City Of London Law Society Insolvency Committee, Response to the Insolvency Service call for evidence on Insolvency Proceedings: Review of debt relief orders and the bankruptcy petition limit Consultation www.citysolicitors.org.uk/index.php?option=com_content&view=-category&id=132 2. See also written evidence of the Insolvency Practices Council Memorandum submitted to Tribunals Courts and Enforcement Bill, 2007 concerning the DRO 'We are concerned that, in the absence of adequate verification of debtors' circumstances, the DRO procedure may be vulnerable to fraudulent claims.'

[64] On second reading in the House of Commons 5 March Col 1318 Mr Heald MP quoted NACAB input that 'in particular, the Debt Relief Order proposals have the potential to help a substantial proportion of CAB clients, many of whom are vulnerable and on low incomes.' See National Association of Citizens Advice Bureaux, Deeper in Debt: The Profile of CAB clients (2006) which indicated that half of their debt clients had less than £20 to offer their creditors and on average 'it would take

reforms, it benefited from the dominance of the executive in the UK parliamentary system, with little opportunity for substantial parliamentary changes. Throughout the development of the DRO evidence of comparative experience (by the consultees or the Insolvency Service) was modest.[65]

The English process suggests the important role of civil servants in the Westminster-style legislative process in framing a reform agenda. My account draws support from Joe Spooner's detailed analysis of the subsequent introduction of the DRO procedure in Ireland.[66] This took place against the background of the bailout of Ireland in the wake of the world financial crisis and the collapse of the Irish housing market. He argues that initial proposals for a relatively debtor friendly law were watered down in the 'quiet politics'[67] of departmental framing of detailed legislation with the result that relief under the Irish DRO is cabined more restrictively than the English procedure.[68] Although these Irish changes reflected the political pressure of both creditor interests and the International Financial

---

CAB debt clients who were able to make a repayment to their non-priority creditors 77 years to repay the debts at the amount offered' <16 www.citizensadvice.org.uk/about-us/policy/policy-research-topics/debt-and-money-policy-research/deeper-in-debt/>.

[65] A brief reference was made to the New Zealand scheme in the 2005 Insolvency Paper along with a reference to the Australian process where the Australian Insolvency Service subsidizes personal insolvency law by providing free access where there are no assets to pay a trustee fee, justified by the public good from reduction of externalities (such as costs to health care, and social security) from debt. In the early 2000s the Insolvency and Trustee Service Australia proposed to introduce a fee but this was rejected on the basis that the 'personal insolvency system provides an overriding general community benefit, not just relief for the debtor, so the cost of processing the petitions.. should be met by taxpayers, not individual debtors.' See Insolvency and Trustee Service Australia, Cost Recovery Impact Statement 17–18 (2005). A fee was introduced in 2014 but was then removed after criticism that it impeded access to bankruptcy. See www.afsa.gov.au/insolvency/how-we-can-help/fees-and-charges-0

[66] See J Spooner, 'The Quiet-Loud-Quiet Politics of Post-Crisis Consumer Bankruptcy Law Reform: the case of Ireland and the Troika' (2018) MLR (forthcoming).

[67] See P Culpepper, Quiet Politics and Business Power: Corporate Control in Europe and Japan (Cambridge, Cambridge University Press, 2011).

[68] For example, the 'once in a lifetime' approach, a qualified insolvency test (no likelihood of becoming solvent within a 3-year period), debtor must not have

Institutions, they also reflected civil servant influence. The English situation differs from Ireland since the DRO was a modification of an existing bankruptcy system rather than the introduction of a completely new law, which often induces caution, and the English legislation was enacted before the financial crisis of 2008.

IV. Implementation of the DRO

The primary objectives of the NINA process are simplification and cost reduction, thus extending access to debt relief. However, its implementation has thrown up many legal issues such as the scope of the moratorium,[69] the scope of excluded debts,[70] the nature of Insolvency Service decision-making under the DRO,[71] the construction of the preference provision,[72] the application to annual utility or Council tax bills which may be paid by instalments,[73] and the treatment of amounts received by the debtor during the moratorium. The Insolvency Service also issues intermediary guidance and meets with competent authorities on a regular basis to discuss emerging issues.[74]

---

arranged her financial affairs within past 6 months to become eligible for a DRN, three-year moratorium period.

[69.] See, e.g., R. (on the application of Payne) v. Secretary of State for Work and Pensions [2011] UKSC 60 (application of moratorium to government attempts to recover overpayment of welfare benefits). The moratorium will not prevent a landlord evicting the debtor. See Places for People Homes Ltd v. Sharples [2011] EWCA Civ 813 (CA). See J Spooner, 'Seeking Shelter in Personal Insolvency Law: Recession, Eviction, and Bankruptcy's Social Safety net' (2017) 44 (3) Journal of Law and Society 374.

[70.] For example, is a parking charge penalty a fine and therefore an excluded debt?

[71.] See R (Howard) v. Official Receiver (QBD) [2013] EWHC 1839 (In adjudicating on DRO applications is the Official Receiver acting in a judicial or administrative manner).

[72.] See, e.g., Islington LBC v. C [2012] BPIR 363.

[73.] See Kaye v. South Oxfordshire District Council [2013] EWHC 4165; Severn Trent Water Ltd v. Said (2015, unreported, Coventry County Court).

[74.] See Insolvency Service, Intermediary Guidance Notes version 16 www.gov.uk/government/publications/intermediary-guidance-notes-v15-dro2-guidance-for-approved-intermediaries.

The government estimated the potential uptake for the DRO as 43,000 after two years.[75] However only approximately 30,000 individuals used a DRO in 2012 and this remains the current level, notwithstanding an increase in qualifying liabilities from £15,000 to £20,000 in 2015.[76] Women represent almost two-thirds of applicants and many are sole parents. The majority are unemployed. They owe debts to central and local state creditors and public utilities as well as private creditors.[77] Comparison of the causes of bankruptcy and DROs (Tables 18.2 and 18.3) indicates the higher percentage of illness/accidents as a primary cause for DROs, and the dominance of factors such as significant reduction in income and increase in expense.

No comprehensive evaluation of the DRO programme has been undertaken, notwithstanding government promises to do so, but a government review in 2015 which collected input from intermediaries, concluded that 'the DRO competent authority and intermediary model is working well and . . . DROs have a very significant impact on the wellbeing of debtors'.[78] Feedback from

---

[75.] See Legislative Impact Analysis (n58) at 89. This was based partly on a survey of individuals who sought advice on debt problems with Citizens Advice Bureaux. The earlier Insolvency Service paper in 2004 (n 46, para 26) had predicted an uptake of 36,000.

[76.] And notwithstanding media predictions that the introduction of the DRO would result in 'soaring' insolvencies. See D Atkinson, 'Insolvencies to Soar with Quickie rules' The Mail on Sunday, April 5, 2009.

[77.] An early survey by the Insolvency Service noted that the profile of debtors accessing the DRO system was primarily low income, predominantly unemployed individuals with an average of six creditors; over 53% of debt was owed to banks, building societies and credit card companies. See Insolvency Service, (2010) 'Debt Relief Orders: initial evaluation report',3 http://webarchive.nationalarchives.gov.uk/20110119225508/www.insolvency.gov.uk/insolvencyprofessionandlegislation/con_doc_register/DRO%20interim%20evaluation%20report%20-FINAL.pdf. More informal data since the recession suggest that public creditors may now be more significant. See, e.g., A Pardo, J Lane, P Lane, D Hertzberg, Citizens Advice, Unsecured and Insecure (2015). This paper argues that over the past five years there has been a significant shift in problems 'away from mainstream credit issues towards problems with arrears on council tax, rent and energy bills. Five years ago, credit cards were the main debt issue we saw. Now council tax arrears top the list.'

[78.] See Department of Business, Innovation and Skills, 'Insolvency Proceedings: Debt Relief Orders and the bankruptcy petition limit – Call for Evidence (London,

Table 18.2 Causes of Bankruptcy as recorded by Official Receiver 2015

	Non-Trading Cases (n =11,095) %	All cases (n =14,905) %
Business Related Failure	–	25
Living Beyond Means	19	14
Relationship Breakdown	16	12
Loss of Employment	12	9
Illness/Accident	11	8
Reduction in household income	24	18
Speculation	1	1
Other	17	13

In 955 cases the cause was recorded as 'unknown/non-surrender'. These cases are not included in the table.

Source: Insolvency Service, Bankruptcies by age gender and cause of insolvency 2015 (www. gov.uk/government/statistics/individual-insolvencies-by-location-age-and-gender-england-and-wales-2015) (last accessed 19/12/2016).

Table 18.3 Causes of DRO: 2015

Business failure	180	0.74
Illness/accident	5,540	22.9
Increase in expense	2,885	11.9
Living beyond means	3,760	15.5
Loss of employment	2,795	11.5
Relationship breakdown	3,430	14.8
Reduction in household income	8,080	33.3
Other	1,595	6.5
Unknown	225	0.9

Source: N cases = 24,175, multiple causes cited in some cases. Source Insolvency Service.

clients of the approved intermediaries indicate that the DRO had the immediate effect of improving their mental and physical health, family relationships and reduced stress.[79] However, little evidence exists concerning the economic and financial long term impact of a DRO.[80]

A. The Central Role of Intermediaries in the DRO 'partnership'

The Insolvency Service is the decision-making body for DROs[81] but devotes modest resources to the DRO and covers its costs through the user fee.[82] It does not actively monitor debtors during the moratorium period.

The system relies heavily on the intermediaries. Citizens Advice, the dominant intermediary, operates a specialist unit for processing DROs,[83] in addition to processing cases through local bureaux, and introduced a central unit which provides expert legal advice to local

---

DBIS, 2015) 2. https://assets.publishing.service.gov.uk/government/uploads/system/uploads/attachment_data/file/398279/Analysis_of_responses_for_internet_-_revised_version_-_23_January_2015.pdf.

[79.] National Debtline survey of 30 clients who had completed the moratorium period within the last 6 months. See Money Advice Trust, 'Insolvency Service – DROs & the Bankruptcy Petition Limit' (2014).

[80.] Citizens Advice provide one example of an individual stressed by debt who was able to come off benefits move back into work and be promoted. See Citizens Advice, 'Response to the Insolvency Service, "Debt Relief Orders and the Bankruptcy Petition Limit: Call for Evidence"' (2014). The Intermediary Christians against Poverty conducted a study of their clients which suggested that the DRO had been successful. See CAP, The Freedom Report (2017) https://capuk.org/downloads/policy_and_government/the_freedom_report.pdf The study had an 18% response rate.

[81.] The Act makes it the decision-making body but also contains several presumptions which require the Service to assume the correctness of an application if it appears so on the record. See Insolvency Act 1986 s251C-D. See discussion of the judicial role of the Insolvency Service in DROs in *Regina (Howard) v. Official Receiver* [2013] EWHC 1839 (admin).

[82.] See Insolvency Service Annual Report and Accounts 2015–2016, Financial Statements 6 (HC 482) which indicates a surplus of £415,000 in 2015–2016. The Insolvency Service has a single division at Plymouth which administers DROs.

[83.] Established in 2014, this includes about 17 approved intermediaries who take references from local CABx throughout England and Wales.

bureaux in complex cases.[84] This latter unit meets with the Insolvency Service periodically to discuss current legal issues concerning the interpretation of DRO provisions, and the intermediary guidance. Both units are funded by the creditor levy distributed through the Money Advice Service. Citizens Advice has also initiated test cases on the interpretation of the DRO.

The DRO promised cost savings for debt advisors but the major intermediaries in a review in 2014 indicate that the fee does not cover the costs of processing DROs. Step Change (funded through the fair share model) argued that 'the current £10 payment to competent authorities for each DRO is nowhere close to the actual cost of advising on and processing a DRO application. This funding situation is not sustainable in the long term. . .'[85] Citizens Advice was more muted noting simply that 'the income generated via DRO application fees does not fully cover the costs of providing the competent authority role.'[86] A recent inquiry claims that the average cost of processing a DRO is £300.[87] My preliminary research suggests that processing a DRO takes up significant time and costs for intermediaries because of the need to check credit reference data,[88] ensure that all debts and assets are included and stated correctly,[89] and do not exceed the relevant ceilings. Possible

---

[84.] This service is now operated by Shelter, the primary housing charity in the U.K.. See www.nhas.org.uk/news/article/shelter-to-offer-specialist-debt-advice-service

[85.] Indicating a shortfall of £890,000 in the annual costs of processing DROs. Response by Step Change Debt Charity to the Insolvency Service Consultation Paper: Insolvency Proceedings: Debt relief orders and the bankruptcy petition limit (2014) 7.

[86.] Citizens Advice, 'Debt Relief Orders and the bankruptcy petition limit: Call for evidence: Citizens Advice response to the Insolvency Service, 9. The Money Advice Trust, another intermediary financed primarily by creditor contributions, pointed to the high costs of ensuring a debtor qualified for the DRO but noted that it 'provides reassurance for creditors. They can be confident that applying for a DRO is not an easy option'. Money Advice Trust at 13.

[87.] See P Wyman, 'Independent Review of the Funding of Debt Advice in England, Wales, Scotland and Northern Ireland' (2018) 26. The basis for this calculation is not clear.

[88.] This may still be done by post rather than online.

[89.] Thus, if an outstanding balance is stated as £500 but is in fact £600, only £500 will be written off.

preferences must be identified. Issues with rent arrears may require attention. Significant numbers of individuals applying for a DRO may be in vulnerable situations and require face-to-face advice in the DRO approval process.[90] Whether these short-term costs for intermediaries are being outweighed by savings in the long-term costs of continuing negotiations with creditors has not been tested. The DRO permitted the government to retain the integrity of its cost-recovery model, an imperative of central government, while passing on much of the costs to agencies which are funded through a mixture of public funds and creditor levies.

Screening by a limited number of approved intermediaries does ensure that only qualified debtors apply since almost no applications are rejected by the Insolvency Service.[91] It may heighten the legitimacy of the system and reduce calls to introduce other controls. This English model contrasts with New Zealand where the absence of screening agencies results in a high percentage of rejected applications by the state Insolvency Trustee service (see Table 18.4).[92] Few DROs are revoked (0.9%) under the Insolvency Service's discretionary power.[93] The Insolvency Service guidance indicates that revocation is unlikely where small increases occur to a debtor's income.[94]

Limiting access through approved intermediaries may however increase access costs. An advisor who is not an approved

---

[90] Compare with Littwin's comments in 'Adapting to BAPCPA' n6.

[91] Data provided to me by the Insolvency Service indicate that about 1% of applications are rejected by the Insolvency Service with further information requested in about 5 percent of cases.

[92] See also New Zealand Insolvency & Trustee Service, Insolvency Statistics and Debtor Profile Report (2017–2018) where the most common cause of rejection is "incomplete statement of affairs". https://www.insolvency.govt.nz/assets/pdf/Statistical-Data-Reports/ITS-Statistical-Data-Report-17-18.pdf

[93] Data provided by Insolvency Service. See Insolvency Act s 251 L for the various grounds under which the Insolvency Service 'may' revoke an order.

[94] '[A]pplicants are clearly required to comply with the legislation, they should not overly worry about small increases in income affecting their eligibility. Provided the increase in benefits or income does not permanently increase their income such that the parameter is breached, no further action will be taken by the Official Receiver.' See Insolvency Service Guide for Intermediaries 6 www.gov.uk/government/publications/intermediary-guidance-notes-v15-dro2-guidance-for-approved-intermediaries.

Table 18.4 Accepted and Rejected Files NZ No Asset Procedure, 2007-2017

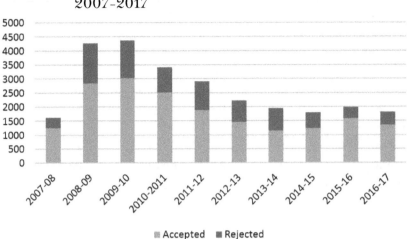

intermediary may have to refer an individual to another agency, and the profit-making debt management sector lacks incentives to promote this alternative. Anecdotal evidence also suggests that the existence of the £90 fee may restrict access for some low-income debtors.[95]

B. Comparison of the DRO Process to Bankruptcy

A primary reason for rejecting the policy of a reduced bankruptcy fee for those on low incomes was that bankruptcy was a disproportionate remedy. However, a comparison of the two procedures suggests that the DRO process may impose more rigorous requirements than bankruptcy (see Table 18.5). First, both a DRO and debtor applications for bankruptcy are now administrative rather than court based

---

[95.] See Christians against Poverty press release at https://capuk.org/fileserver/downloads/press/DROrelease17.pdf. Research in Australia also found that the introduction of a fee of AUS$120 for bankruptcy resulted in many individuals having to delay or forego access to bankruptcy. See Financial Counselling Australia, 'Too Poor to go Bankrupt: The Impact of the New Fee for Lodging a Debtor's Petition (2014). www.financialcounsellingaustralia.org.au/Corporate/News/FCA-Releases-Too-Poor-to-Go-Bankrupt

Table 18.5 Comparison of DROs with Bankruptcy

Access online	Yes	Yes
Court application necessary	No	No
Application through approved intermediary	No	Yes
Decision by Insolvency Service	Yes	Yes
Discharge period one year	Yes	Yes
Investigation of bankrupt?	Post-bankruptcy	Pre-bankruptcy
Restrictions on filing	Once every 6 years	
Cost	£680	£90
Preference bar access	No	Yes
Sanction of behaviour	Yes BRO	Yes DRO
Trustee over property	Yes	No
Credit file	6 years	6 years

procedures and may be completed online. Second, a DRO can be applied for only every six years whereas no such restriction applies to bankruptcy. Third, preferential payments are treated differently under DRO provisions. A preferential payment (without any need to demonstrate an intent to prefer) bars a DRO application, but does not prevent a bankruptcy petition being filed. The official rationale for this approach to DROs is to prevent individuals transferring away their property and then applying for an order.[96] The use of a bright line rule on preferences to achieve this objective may have been intended to reduce administration costs but this sanction will catch many small fry in its net, where individuals may have made some modest payments to family members. In addition the courts have indicated that in practice a desire to prefer should be read into

---

[96.] The explanatory notes indicate that the rationale is 'to avoid a situation where the debtor has disposed of his assets in order to meet the permitted criterion for obtaining a debt relief order and to protect the position of creditors.'

the section, creating uncertainty in application.[97] The preference provision also conflicts with the approach of the major debt advice agencies in drawing up budgets for clients. These agencies prioritize certain debt repayments for example to landlords and utilities. A literal application of the rule would permit a challenge of any subsequent DRO.[98] Debt advisors criticized the reach of the preference provision in the governmental review in 2014.[99] The rather clumsy strict preference provision seems animated by a fear of moral hazard, and a concern by government policymakers to allay any creditor fears of debtors avoiding repayment.

Third, a DRO releases an individual only from the qualifying debts listed in the order. Bankruptcy releases an individual from all bankruptcy debts, defined more broadly than debts in a DRO.[100]

Fourth, an individual receiving income or property during the moratorium period may be subject to the order being revoked.

[97.] See *Islington LBC v C* [2012] BPIR 363. In this case, a debtor had prioritised payments to a landlord to clear arrears of rent and avoid repossession. District Judge Hart concluded that a desire to prefer must be read into the section, '[o]therwise, almost any payment by the debtor to a qualifying creditor in the two years prior to the DRO application being determined would amount to a preference and rule out the possibility of a DRO being made. It is very unlikely that very many DROs could ever be made in the circumstances.. a payment to a landlord is likely to be motivated by a desire to avoid possession proceedings, rather than by a desire to better the position of the landlord' id 366.

[98.] As in the case above. The Insolvency Service guidance indicates that 'preference transactions are typically (but not restricted to) payments to friends or family members.' They provide no authority for this statement. See The Insolvency Service, Intermediary Guidance Notes DRO2 (2016) 39. It seems that payments to friends and family are more likely to lead to decline of an order rather than payments to priority creditors See CA response to the Insolvency Service 'Debt Relief Orders and the bankruptcy petition: Call for evidence', 21.

[99.] The Money Advice Trust's submission to the 2014 review claimed that 'there are many instances where we have had clients who have applied for a DRO but have either been declined or have not gone ahead with their application because of issues such as preference payments.. It seems unfair that some clients do not qualify for a DRO as a result of taking action (often entirely innocently) such as repaying a family member or friend before repaying creditors. We would expect most people would be likely to do the same in a similar situation.' Money Advice Trust, 'DROs and the Bankruptcy Petition Limit', 17.

[100.] Contingent liabilities are not included, presumably because of the cost of assessing them.

The Insolvency Service exercises a discretion as to revocation.[101] Although only a small percentage of orders are revoked the possibility of revocation because of an increase in income or assets raises the question of whether this reduces incentives for individuals to seek employment.

Fifth, a contrast exists between the DRO and bankruptcy in the timing and nature of investigation of the debtors conduct. Bankrupts are subject to investigation by the Insolvency Service after they have filed for bankruptcy. In practice evidence exists that this may be a relatively light-touch experience for many debtors. In 2012 I noted that two-thirds of bankrupts are interviewed briefly by phone[102] and anecdotal commentary suggests that the actual experience of debtors with the Insolvency Service is less draconian than they feared.[103] In contrast, the bulk of investigation of a debtor in a DRO is undertaken by an approved intermediary. The DRO shifts the weight of

---

[101.] The Insolvency Service Intermediary Guidance indicates at 6 that the 'decision to revoke is discretionary and where the value of the property acquired is modest, the Official Receiver will not revoke for all cases where the applicant is open and honest and the value of the asset in question is less than £1000, provided that the total sum involved does not exceed 50% of the applicant's total liabilities.' However, if the debtor receives a lumps sum 'which is associated with a permanent increase in income, bringing the applicant's surplus income to over £50 per month then this will lead to revocation'. *Ibid.* 7.

[102.] I D C Ramsay, 'A Tale of Two Debtors: Responding to the Shock of Over-indebtedness in France and England-A Story from the Trente Piteuses (202) 75(2) MLR 180, n168.

[103.] See, e.g., DD Wray, 'Here's what it's like to go bankrupt at 30'. Buzzfeed www.buzzfeed.com/danieldylanwray/heres-what-its-like-to-file-bankruptcy-at-30?utm_term=.brvAegVex#.njeB8K389 'My official receiver was great: She was kind and I felt she was going out of her way to help me rather than trip me up. The purpose of the interview with the official receiver is to work out how and why you got into the situation and to work out your current income and outgoings, with the idea that you may be assigned an income payment agreement (IPA) to continue to make reduced payments to your creditors (the people you owe money to).

Because I had continued to make all my repayments and had got into debt in a pretty traditional and genuine way, it seemed like I was in fairly good shape. The overwhelming feeling that soon took hold was that if you're not fraudulent and haven't simply taken out a massive loan, spent it, repaid nothing, and then declared bankruptcy, then you're generally going to be OK.'

investigation to the pre-filing stage and advisors will be careful to ensure accuracy since their client risks losing £90 if the strict criteria of the DRO are not met. Notwithstanding this pre-filing investigation by an approved intermediary an individual must wait a year before discharge.

Sixth, a debtor's assets do not vest in a trustee in a DRO since by definition they have few assets. However the majority of bankrupts also have no or limited assets and a very small percentage of bankruptcies are likely to offer a dividend to creditors after payment of the OR administration fee. Seventh, the requirement of access to the DRO through a limited number of competent authorities with approved intermediaries, may increase access costs for individuals and be one reason for the failure of DRO numbers to meet government predictions. Finally, both bankruptcies and DROs will remain on a credit file for six years and will appear on the insolvency register.[104]

The relevant Ministries argued that bankruptcy was a disproportionate remedy for lower income debtors. But in practice this conclusion appears questionable.

C. Summary

The idea of bankruptcy simplification through an administrative No Income-No Asset Procedure is attractive as a method of minimizing the overall social costs of overindebtedness. This brief description of the English approach suggests that the actual implementation has resulted in legislation which is not as simple as proponents might have expected and represents a screening process at least as rigorous as bankruptcy for most debtors. The DRO, a process established for the 'deserving poor' seems to be more stringent than bankruptcy, raising questions about equality of access to debt relief. However, the increased costs of screening are borne by the Debt Advice sector, and the credit reference agencies, rather than the debtor or the

---

[104] In the case of a DRO for a period of three months after completion of the DRO.

Insolvency Service. Funding of the process is partly underwritten financially by creditors through the creditor levy which finances debt advice, and specialist Citizens Advice DRO unit. This role of creditors in funding the DRO is ironic in the light of the opposition to such an approach in the initial consultations on the DRO. The DRO is a form of public-private partnership in its delivery. If it is an effective system (little research exists on long term effects of the DRO 'fresh start') it is primarily because of the relatively well developed institutional structure of bankruptcy administration and debt advice in England and Wales.

The DRO process, although apparently simple, is suffused with law and continuing legal issues of interpretation, requiring legal knowledge. Intermediaries play a significant role in processing debtors in this administrative system and in the application and development of the legal provisions. They also provide legitimacy to the process. This chapter is not directed towards reform of the DRO but it could be a more effective and less costly remedy if the level of liabilities were substantially increased and access barred only where there was likelihood of a significant dividend to creditors.[105]

V. Comparative Thoughts: Administrative Justice and U.S. Bankruptcy Simplification

In 2003 we highlighted the topic of 'administrative versus judicialized systems for implementing law',[106] as a topic in the comparative study of consumer bankruptcy. We suggested that future comparative research could attempt to explain why different systems for implementing consumer bankruptcy law have emerged in different

---

[105] Joe Spooner and I argued for this in the 2014 review. See I Ramsay & J Spooner, 'Insolvency Proceedings: Debt Relief Orders and the Bankruptcy Petition Limit' <https://papers.ssrn.com/sol3/papers.cfm?abstract_id=2601349>.

[106] See J Niemi, I Ramsay & W Whitford (eds) Consumer Bankruptcy in Global Perspective (Hart, Oxford, 2003) 11.

countries, and to draw judgments about whether an administrative or judicialised system is most effective. Systems of debt relief for consumers are increasingly systems of administrative justice,[107] but this general description masks substantial differences in terms of the role of institutions and intermediaries, their origins, objectives and values. The over indebtedness commissions in France, composed of representatives of the central and local state, creditors and consumers, and managed by the Bank of France, are distinct in origin and operation to the Swedish enforcement office (the KFM), originally a tax collection agency, and now striving to balance increased productivity with more debt relief.[108]

Future comparative research might compare these systems within distinct models and normative ideals of administrative justice. The treatment of NINAs is a useful site for research, since many proposals for NINA programmes assume an administrative model. Jerry Mashaw, in a study of the U.S. disability entitlement programme, identified three models of administrative justice: bureaucratic rationality, professional treatment and moral judgment.[109] These ideals responded to different critiques of the U.S. disability system – that it was inconsistent and poorly managed, that it failed to serve the client in providing rehabilitation, and that it operated unfairly without adequate attention to 'due process'. These models are not mutually exclusive so that any administrative system may contain a combination of aspects of these models. Mashaw's model permits analysis of potential trade-offs between normative values in an administrative system, and identification of the influence of different groups on a system.

[107.] World Bank above n4 paras 161, 163.

[108.] For a discussion of the development of the French system see Ramsay above n2 ch4 and for Sweden, ch5, 139. See also B Larsson & B Jacobsson, 'Discretion in the 'Backyard of Law: Case Handling of Debt Relief in Sweden' (2013) 3(1) Professions and Professionalism 1.

[109.] J. Mashaw, Bureaucratic Justice: Managing Social Security Disability Claims (New Haven, Yale, 1983) 26 et seq. See an updated and modified model based on Mashaw in M. Adler, 'A Socio-Legal Approach to Administrative Justice' (2003) 25 Law & Policy 323.

The English system of DROs represents a model of bureaucratic rationality, stressing the application of rules, driven by computerization, modestly tempered by professional treatment of debtors by the intermediaries.

At first sight the U.S. model of consumer bankruptcy administration might not seem to fit the description of a system of administrative justice with its assumption of state administration, given the central role of courts, and the 'primacy [of] lawyers rather than administrators'.[110] However, commentators recognize that the contemporary U.S. system of consumer bankruptcy is *in fact* an administrative system. The 'overwhelming majority of consumer bankruptcy cases are non-adversarial in nature',[111] and this has been the case for 'at least fifty years'.[112] Judges rarely deal with chapter 7 cases which are processed in a routinized manner, often by para-legal staff.

The recognition of the administrative nature of U.S. consumer bankruptcy raises the question of its relationship to Mashaw's categories. Bureaucratic rationality motivated the continuing attempts since the 1930s to introduce an administrative agency to process consumer bankruptcies in the U.S..[113] In 1970 the National Bankruptcy Review Commission adopted the findings of the Brookings Commission that much of the bankruptcy system was in fact administrative rather than judicial in nature,[114] and that 'there is no reason to involve judges in handling of papers and procedures for many thousands of cases in which no contest arises.'[115] The introduction of a Federal Bankruptcy Agency could process more swiftly the large number of uncontested

---

[110] D Skeel, Debt's Dominion: A History of Bankruptcy Law in America (Princeton, Princeton U Press, 2004) 47

[111] *Id.* 1982.

[112] Littwin, above n 0, 2011 citing data which indicate that even after BAPCPA 'chapter 7 remains a non-adversarial process.'

[113] Littwin, n 2 1981–1986. The Brookings Commission described the administration of bankruptcy in 1964 as a 'multimillion-dollar loosely connected structure' which would benefit from greater administrative co-ordination' D Stanley & M Girth, Bankruptcy: Problem, Process, Reform (Washington, DC, Brookings, 1971) 111.

[114] See Report of the Commission on the Bankruptcy Laws of the United States as summarized in (1973–1974) 29 Bus Law 75, 88.

[115] *Id.* 89.

cases, provide greater uniformity in administration, and offer budget and counselling services: debtors would not need legal representation within this system, substantially reducing bankruptcy costs. The idea of budget counselling intended to achieve better rehabilitation for debtors introduced an element of professional treatment, based on a model of the debtor as poor debt managers.[116]

The story of the political failure of these initiatives is well known. Bankruptcy judges and lawyers mounted a fierce opposition to the introduction of an administrative agency processing bankruptcies, evoking images of a 'despot state' – a 'huge bureaucracy with tentacles reaching into every area of the country and marked with all the weaknesses of inept officialism, expensive red tape and corruption.[117] Creditors also opposed an administrative system fearing the possibility of a bankruptcy explosion. The success of lawyers in defeating the administrative agency concept represents the continuing historical influence of legal professionals on bankruptcy policymaking in the U.S.. David Skeel argues that the early role of professional lawyers in bankruptcy administration in the U.S. resulted in a path dependency, entrenching the role of lawyers and courts, which raised the political costs for subsequent attempts to introduce administrative regulation of bankruptcy procedures in the 1930s and the 1960s.[118]

The U.S. is unlikely to adopt a model of public processing of debtors similar to England and Wales. However, this should not blind us to the fact that the U.S. system is an administrative system, with the administrative infrastructure provided by lawyers, and para-legals, overseen by both the judiciary and the Federal Trustee service which now has extensive powers over the system.[119] The U.S. system lacks the appearance of a centralized and unified 'top-down' government

---

[116.] The Bankruptcy Commission cited the Brookings study which concluded that the leading reason for bankruptcy was 'poor debt management'. See Stanley & Girth (n111) 47.

[117.] Asa Herzog a distinguished bankruptcy judge quoted in E Posner, 'The Political Economy of the Bankruptcy Reform Act of 1978 (1997) Michigan L Rev 47,78.

[118.] D Skeel, Debt's Dominion: A History of Bankruptcy Law in America (Princeton, Princeton U Press, 2001) 43–47.

[119.] Ramsay n2, 62–66.

bureaucracy but remains a loosely structured 'infrastructural power', represented by 'the positive capacity of the state to 'penetrate civil society' and implement policies throughout a given territory', using private actors (for example chapter 7 trustees) to achieve public objectives.[120] For example, the 2005 amendments to the BAPCPA harness the role of lawyers as gatekeepers, imposing penalties if they do not adequately monitor information provided by their client. Trends towards bureaucratic rationality may be accelerated by the increasing use of online technology. However, the existence of 'local legal culture'[121] indicates that the U.S. system does not fit snugly into a bureaucratic rationality model. Varying interpretations of appropriate professional treatment exist. Jean Braucher's important study of U.S. consumer bankruptcy lawyers demonstrated how lawyers' financial interests and social attitudes affected their advice and that varied models of client counselling existed.[122] She found that some lawyers played 'the role of a helping professional, part teacher, part social worker, part financial adviser'; some saw their role as a consumer advocate.'[123]

Intermediaries in this system might be analogized to 'street level bureaucrats'[124] who have a level of discretion in the implementation

---

[120.] William Novak, 'The Myth of the Weak American State' (2008) 113 The American Historical Review 752, 763. Novak argues that historians have underestimated the important infrastructural role of the state in U.S. history, because of the influence of European writers such as Max Weber who associated the modern state with 'unification, centralization, rationalization, organization, administration and bureaucratization'. Novak argues that although the U.S. state may appear dispersed and disorganized, perhaps deliberately to avoid becoming a 'despot state', it has significant 'infrastructural power'. W Novak, 'The Myth of the weak American state' (2008) 113 The American Historical Review 752.

[121.] '[S]ystematic and persistent variations in local legal practices as a consequence of a complex of perceptions and expectations shared by many practitioners and officials in a particular locality and differing in identifiable ways from the practices, perceptions, and expectations existing in other localities subject to the same or a similar formal regime.' See T Sullivan, E Warren & J Westbrook, 'Consumer Bankruptcy in the United States: A Study of Alleged Abuse and of Local Legal Culture' (1997) 20 Journal of Consumer Policy 223, 244.

[122.] See J Braucher, 'Lawyers and Consumer Bankruptcy: One Code, Many Cultures' (1993) 67 Am Bankr L J 501.

[123.] Id.

[124.] See M Lipsky, Street-level Bureaucracy: Dilemmas of the Individual in Public Services. (New York, NY: Russell Sage Foundation, 1980).

of law and policy: their interpretation may be the policy.[125] While the concept of the street level bureaucrat was coined to describe intermediaries in public services addressing problems between the individual and the state, it might be extended to consumer bankruptcy practice which is often a high volume and routinized procedure.

Angela Littwin, recognizing the administrative nature of the U.S. bankruptcy system, argues that unlike other redistributive programmes in the U.S., such as the 'Kafkaesque' social security administration, consumer bankruptcy administration represents an effective system because of 'the existence of the paid bar, strong bankruptcy judges and the prestige associated with the corporate bar'.[126] Procedural barriers, unmet legal needs and poor quality decision-making characterize social security administration in the U.S.. In contrast, she argues that bankruptcy administration is characterized by high quality decision makers, and the benefits of paid professionals. Lawyers act as consumer advocates, lobbyists for the system, and represent a professional corps which sustains the workability of the bankruptcy system.[127] She points, for example, to the Bankruptcy Rules Committee where bankruptcy lawyers and judges ironed out potential problems in the implementation of BAPCPA.

Littwin's arguments concerning U.S. consumer bankruptcy administration underline three points for future comparative analysis. First, the institutional structure of consumer bankruptcy is a key aspect in determining the credibility and legitimacy of the system. Second, both the English DRO and U.S. bankruptcy system harness civil society actors in bankruptcy administration. Third, intermediaries play a key role in both systems. The English experience suggests that even with bankruptcy simplification, intermediaries make the system work more effectively and ensure its credibility.[128] Citizens

---

[125.] See S Laws 'What is Owed: Debt: Bankruptcy and American Citizenship' PhD thesis, Univ of Minnesota, 2011) suggesting that chapter 7 trustees might be conceptualized as street level bureaucrats.

[126.] Littwin (n6)1988.

[127.] Id 2009–2022.

[128.] And see comments of Jay Westbrook on the need for lawyers in the U.S. system. J Westbrook, 'The Retreat of American Bankruptcy Law' (2017) 17 QUT LRev. 40, 56.

Advice functions in England and Wales as a lawyer, debt advisor, emotional supporter and processor for clients.[129] Debt problems are complex requiring a knowledge of bankruptcy law, consumer law, social security, housing law and budgeting.[130] Citizens Advice also acts as a lobbyist for change in the interests of debtors using sample cases to develop policy briefs on many topics. It participates in discussions on rule development through the intermediary guidance process. It thus appears to perform similar functions to private lawyers, judges and their organizations in the U.S.. An empirical study of the quality of decision-making by private lawyers and Citizens Advice agencies in relation to debt concluded that debt advisers in Citizens Advice were operating at a higher level of quality than private lawyers.[131] Social support programmes in the UK have also becomes stigmatized as residual, means tested institutions with similar stories of Kafkaesque bureaucracies,[132] but accessing administrative debt relief does not seem to be viewed in this light by its users who generally praise the role of Citizens Advice and the Insolvency Service.

These observations suggest the value of further comparative analysis of consumer bankruptcy systems as systems of administrative justice. Comparative institutional analysis of the law in action might puncture myths, undermine simple comparisons between private and public systems, and heighten understanding.

VI. Conclusion

This chapter outlined the response of one jurisdiction to addressing the issue of the NINA or LILA debtor. The cautious English approach

---

[129.] See, e.g., S Kirwan, 'Advice on the Law but Not Legal Advice So Much: Weaving Law and Life into Debt Advice' in S Kirwan (ed.) 'Advising in Austerity: Reflections on Challenging Times for Advice Agencies' (Bristol, Policy Press, 2017) 147–55.

[130.] See, e.g., the topics covered in Child Poverty Action Group, Debt Advice Handbook (11th ed., 2015).

[131.] R Moorhead et al., 'Contesting Professionalism: Legal Aid and NonLawyers in England and Wales (2003) 37 Law and Society Rev 765, 796.

[132.] Epitomised in the film I Daniel Blake (2016).

increased the costs of the process although they were masked by being borne by intermediaries rather than debtors. The English approach illustrates Jay Westbrook's caveat that although bankruptcy simplification is desirable, the moral ambiguity of bankruptcy often 'causes lawmakers to fill it with exceptions and qualifications'[133] leading to greater complexity and the consequent need for trained intermediaries, such as lawyers in the U.S. system.

Further comparative analysis of the institutional administration of consumer bankruptcies and its financing, should permit more generalization about why particular bankruptcy institutions emerge and change, the influence of different groups over this structure and the relative role of a variety of intermediaries – lawyers, accountants, debt advice agencies – in ensuring the effectiveness of these bankruptcy systems. Existing institutional structures in those countries with established bankruptcy systems are likely to have a patterning effect on any future reforms to address NINA or LILA debtors. Law reform projects in those jurisdictions which propose to introduce individual bankruptcy laws need also pay close attention to the importance of institutional structure in any transplantation of ideas, such as 'No Asset Procedures'.

---

[133] n122, 56.

Bankruptcy for Banks
A Tribute (and a Little Plea) to Jay Westbrook
David A. Skeel, Jr.*

J ay Westbrook articles are fun to read. When the latest reprint
arrives, I always read at least a few pages, and usually read it
all, no matter the topic. Jay is of course one of the top private
law scholars of the past generation. But the promise of clever
metaphors and unexpected connections is what pulls me in first.
Who else would call the executory contract rules "psychedelic" or
dismiss an aspect of their use as "like discussing a sunset after
dark?"[1]

This is a tribute, so I'll take my time getting to my assigned
topic: a conversation with Jay about possible "bankruptcy for banks"
legislation.

* * *

* S. Samuel Arsht Professor of Corporate Law, University of Pennsylvania Law
School. Reproduced with permission from Norton Journal of Bankruptcy Law and
Practice, Vol. 27 no. 5 (Oct. 2018), with permission of Thomas Reuters. Copyright ©
2018. Further use without the permission of Thomas Reuters is prohibited. For further information about this publication, please visit https://legal.thomsonreuters.
com/en/products/law-books or call 800.328.9352.
[1.] Jay Lawrence Westbrook, A Functional Analysis of Executory Contracts, 74 Tex.
L. Rev. 227, 228, 243 (1989).

Thirty years ago, when I first encountered Jay's work, I was primed to view it with suspicion. Law and economics was in its adolescence, and there was a sharp divide between its advocates and its critics. Law and economics scholars viewed bankruptcy's role as limited to avoiding the "race to the courthouse" that might ensue in the absence of bankruptcy, due to creditors' inability to coordinate.[2] Although bankruptcy is needed to solve the creditors' collective action problems, it should not otherwise interfere with the parties' nonbankruptcy rights. Bankruptcy's role is primarily procedural, as one of the pioneers of this perspective put it.[3] Critics of this perspective—call them progressives—insisted on a more robust role for bankruptcy. Bankruptcy should seek to facilitate reorganization, and it needs to mediate among the diverse interests of the stakeholders of the troubled debtor.[4]

Jay was a pillar of the progressive camp. Jay cheerfully and consistently critiqued the law and economics perspective.[5] As a child of law and economics, and having employed it in much of my own writing (and having bracketed any tensions with my literature background), I took up residence on the opposite side of the bankruptcy divide.

Yet I found that I liked Jay's work a great deal, even agreed with some of it. Jay and his co-authors Teresa Sullivan and Elizabeth Warren had already published As We Forgive Our Debtors,[6] the first of the books that emerged from their landmark study of consumer bankruptcy, and The Fragile Middle Class would appear a few years later.[7]

---

[2] Our foundation text was Thomas Jackson, The Logic and Limits of Bankruptcy (1986).

[3] Douglas G. Baird, Bankruptcy's Uncontested Axioms, 108 Yale L.J. 573 (1998).

[4] Their foundation text, written by Jay's most illustrious protégée, was Elizabeth Warren, Bankruptcy Policy, 54 U. Chi. L. Rev. 815 (1987).

[5] For a more recent example, see Jay Lawrence Westbrook & Elizabeth Warren, Contracting Out of Bankruptcy: An Empirical Intervention, 118 Harv. L. Rev. 1197 (2005).

[6] Teresa A. Sullivan, Elizabeth Warren, & Jay Lawrence Westbrook, As We Forgive Our Debtors: Bankruptcy and Consumer Credit in America (1989).

[7] Teresa A. Sullivan, Elizabeth Warren, & Jay Lawrence Westbrook, The Fragile Middle Class: Americans in Debt (2000).

Law and economics scholars grumbled that Jay and his co-authors had cherry-picked their data—after all, how else could it so strongly confirm the vulnerability of bankruptcy debtors?—but none questioned the seriousness and significance of the project. Jay and his co-authors had examined thousands of consumer bankruptcy filings, producing the most extensive empirical analysis of U.S. consumer bankruptcy ever, long before empirical legal scholarship became fashionable.

Another article that Jay published during this period spoke more directly to corporate bankruptcy scholars. In *A Functional Analysis of Executory Contracts*, Jay sought to reconceptualize the handling of executory contracts in bankruptcy.[8] From the very first sentence, Jay lures the reader in: "Bankruptcy is that volume of the law that might have been written by Lewis Carroll," he writes, "every conventional legal principle refracted through the prism of insolvency."[9] "In no chapter of that volume," he continues, decades before we learned LSD may be good for us, "has the law become more psychedelic than in the one titled "executory contracts.""[10]

According to the standard view, which derived from an article by Vern Countryman, a key predecessor of Jay's and his fellow bankruptcy progressives,[11] a contract is executory if the performance of the contract is sufficiently incomplete that failure by either party to complete its performance would constitute a material breach by that party. Under the Bankruptcy Code, the debtor can either "assume" or "reject" a contract that qualifies as executory.[12] Jay saw both the traditional definition and the Code's terminology as fraught with problems. The Countryman test suggested, for instance, that a debtor could not reject a contract that one party had performed, even if rejection was in the best interests of the debtor and its estate.

[8.] Westbrook, *supra* note 1, 74 Tex. L. Rev. 227.

[9.] 74 Tex. L. Rev. at 228.

[10.] 74 Tex. L. Rev. at 228.

[11.] Jay solutes Countryman at the outset of the article, calling his executory contract articles "a brilliant accomplishment." 74 Tex. L. Rev. at 230.

[12.] 11 U.S.C.A. 365.

Jay advocated that lawmakers scrap the existing executory contract apparatus, and replace it with a functional approach. From a functionalist perspective, he argued, there is nothing special about the supposed "power" to assume or reject contracts, and the executoriness concept is irrelevant.[13] This rejection of formalism and commitment to pragmatic, functional analysis is one of the signature features of Jay's jurisprudence. It also hints at the subtle links that connect Westbrookian jurisprudence to legal realists such as Karl Llewellyn and, especially, William Douglas.

* * *

The 2005 amendments to the Bankruptcy Code were so unpopular among bankruptcy scholars and professionals that we often found ourselves being asked a difficult question: Could we name one good provision in the 2005 amendments? Were there any provisions that made bankruptcy better? On more than one occasion, when I heard a colleague respond to this question, the answer they gave was, yes, the 2005 reforms did include one important innovation: chapter 15.

Chapter 15 is a small cluster of provisions governing cross-border bankruptcy filings. It gives broad authority for U.S. bankruptcy courts to permit cross-border filings and provides flexible rules for determining the extent to which courts should incorporate, through principles of comity, the rulings and rules of other countries. It is hard to imagine a better fit with Jay's jurisprudence. The fit is not altogether accidental: Jay was a very early promoter (and I suspect drafter) of the principles that coalesced in chapter 15.[14]

Jay's involvement was an outgrowth—or so I surmise, not having been there and Jay not having published memoirs—of his long involvement in cross-border insolvency projects. Jay's bankruptcy globetrotting dates back more than thirty years, to an era that

---

[13] Westbrook, *supra* note 1, 74 Tex. L. Rev. at 281.

[14] Jay has written extensively about chapter 15. See, e.g., Jay Lawrence Westbrook, chapter 15 Comes of Age, Ann. Rev. Insolv. L. 173 (2013).

comfortably predates American scholars' recognition of the importance of international issues. Jay has participated in numerous international projects to develop model bankruptcy principles or laws.

I first experienced Jay's international status at a conference in Geneva shortly after the turn of the new century. Three or four dozen insolvency scholars and professionals, including many of the world's leading experts, gathered in a lovely Geneva hotel to discuss a wide range of bankruptcy issues. From the first session or two, I noticed how often the international experts in the room looked toward Jay when a knotty issue emerged, especially if the issue was one that chapter 11 addresses. Jay was a cheerful advocate for the chapter 11 approach to financial distress—particularly the emphasis on reorganization—though he repeatedly emphasized that chapter 11 isn't the only, and may not be the best, approach.

* * *

Given his enthusiasm for chapter 11, which he has vigorously defended in the academic literature,[15] Jay's hostility to the recent proposal to enact "bankruptcy for banks" legislation may seem surprising.[16] The proposal would add a handful of provisions to existing bankruptcy law to better accommodate the insolvency of a large financial institution. Why would anyone be against this—particularly an enthusiast for chapter 11?

There's a logic to Jay's opposition, of course, but before I unveil it and conclude with a little plea for Jay to reconsider, I will briefly describe the proposal and its discontents, including Jay and some of participants in this celebration.

---

[15] Elizabeth Warren & Jay Lawrence Westbrook, The Success of chapter 11: A Challenge to the Critics, 107 Mich. L. Rev. 603 (2009).

[16] Jay's hostility is reflected in the letter he and several colleagues recently wrote urging lawmakers to eschew bankruptcy for banks. Edward Janger, John A.E. Pottow & Jay Lawrence Westbrook, Frying Pan to Fire: Bankruptcy for Sifis is a Very Risky Choice (2017).

In the first few years after the Dodd–Frank Act was enacted in 2010, the Federal Deposit Insurance Corporation (FDIC) and Federal Reserve developed a strategy known as "Single Point of Entry" or "SPOE" for resolving the failure of a systemically important financial institution under Title II of the legislation. Under SPOE, the FDIC would transfer the assets, short-term debt and secured debt of the holding company of a distressed financial institution to a newly formed bridge institution, leaving behind its stock and long-term debt.[17] The newly recapitalized bridge institution would be fully solvent, and could contribute liquidity to troubled subsidiaries as necessary. The transaction would be effected quickly, minimizing disruption.

The lawmakers who debated the Dodd-Frank Act would have been incredulous—or at the least, would have feigned incredulity—had they been told that SPOE would be the strategy of choice for Title II. By its terms, Title II calls for liquidation, whereas SPOE is a recapitalization. Title II's liquidation requirement was a terrible idea.[18] It would have discouraged regulators from ever using Title II. As a result, the SPOE alternative quickly caught on. By 2011, U.S. regulators and UK regulators had published a joint op-ed extolling SPOE.[19] The Fed and FDIC subsequently outlined the SPOE approach in a request for comments,[20] and they have imposed so-called total loss-absorbing capacity (TLAC) requirements to ensure large financial institutions have plenty of long term debt to use for a recapitalization if necessary.[21]

[17.] See, e.g., David A. Skeel, Jr., Single Point of Entry and the Bankruptcy Alternative, in Across The Great Divide: New Perspectives On The Financial Crisis, 313 (Martin N. Baily & John B. Taylor, eds. 2013).

[18.] See, e.g., Dodd–Frank Act section 204(a).

[19.] Martin J. Gruenberg (chairman, FDIC) & Paul Tucker (deputy governor, financial stability, Bank of England), Global Banks Need Global Solutions When They Fail, Fin. Times, Dec. 10, 2012.

[20.] Request for Comments Regarding Resolution of Systemically Important Financial Institutions: The Single Point of Entry Strategy, 78 Fed. Reg. 76,614 (Dec. 18, 2013).

[21.] Federal Reserve, Total Loss-Absorbing Capacity, Long-Term Debt, and Clean Holding Company Requirements for Systemically Important U.S. Bank Holding Companies and Intermediate Holding Companies of Systemically Important Foreign Banking Organizations (Jan. 24, 2017).

Bankruptcy for banks—aka the Financial Institution Bankruptcy Act (FIBA) or chapter 14—would adapt SPOE for bankruptcy. I should perhaps add that I have been an active and enthusiastic member of the working group that created the chapter 14 proposal that inspired FIBA.

The proposed FIBA legislation[22] consists of a handful of provisions that would authorize the bankruptcy court to approve the transfer of a holding company's assets to a new bridge institution, would define the required notice, and would insulate the transaction from fraudulent conveyance attacks. As of this writing, versions of the legislation have passed the House multiple times but have not been voted on in the Senate.

One can plausibly argue that bankruptcy for banks, or something like it, is necessary to satisfy one of the Dodd-Frank's core requirements. Title I of Dodd-Frank instructs the largest financial institutions to prepare rapid resolution plans—often called "living wills"—detailing how the financial institution could be resolved in bankruptcy without causing systemic instability.[23] It is not clear if this objective can be achieved under current bankruptcy law. Bankruptcy for banks would facilitate an SPOE-style strategy that provides more confidence that large financial institutions could be resolved effectively in bankruptcy, as the living will provision requires.

Although bankruptcy for banks appears to have broad support in Congress, it is more controversial among bankruptcy scholars. Several of the common objections are somewhat puzzling. One posits that Title II is better than bankruptcy for banks, so bankruptcy for banks is a bad idea. Even if Title II is indeed superior in some respects (its enthusiasts often point to the federal funding provided by Title II, for instance), the conclusion that bankruptcy for banks therefore needs to be prevented is a non sequitur. At most, it suggests that

---

[22.] Which Adam Levitin cleverly lampoons as "FIB" in his critique for the Westbrook celebration. Adam Levitin, Bankruptcy's Lorelei: The Dangerous Allure of Financial Institution Bankruptcy, 97 N.C. L. Rev. (forthcoming, 2019).

[23.] Dodd–Frank Act section 165(d)(1).

Title II should not be repealed, as some versions of the bankruptcy for banks legislation have proposed. It is not, however, an argument against bankruptcy for banks legislation.[24] In my view, the optimal approach would include both Title II and bankruptcy for banks.

The other puzzling tendency is critics' condemnation of features of bankruptcy for banks that also are features of the use of SPOE in Title II—the approach these same critics seem to favor. Critics argue that bankruptcy for banks would privilege derivatives and other short-term debt, thus perpetuating the perverse pre-2008 incentive to use derivatives. This is true—I consider to be one of the chief downsides of bankruptcy for banks—but it is just as true of SPOE resolution in Title II. SPOE is precisely the same approach in this regard. A problem with bankruptcy for banks is also a problem for SPOE.[25]

If we set the more puzzling objections aside, three major objections remain. The first is that bankruptcy is ill-suited for resolving a large financial institution, because financial institution resolution needs to be done quickly and secretly, rather than through the more cumbersome, rule-of-law-oriented procedures that characterize bankruptcy for banks.[26] SPOE, as incorporated into bankruptcy, is an alien graft that will inevitably be rejected. Second, unlike bank regulators, who can easily coordinate with their foreign counterparts, bankruptcy judges operate in isolation. The absence of coordination would make bankruptcy for banks ineffective for financial institutions with substantial foreign operations.[27] Finally, the SPOE or bankruptcy for banks process will require enormous amounts of

---

[24] I suppose one could argue that managers might use bankruptcy for banks precipitously, and that this would prove destructive. But the prospect of precipitous bankruptcy filings seems remote, and critics do not generally make the argument.

[25] Stephen Lubben's critique is more consistent this regard. Stephen Lubben, A Functional Analysis of SIFI Insolvency (Feb. 13, 2018). He is skeptical both of SPOE and bankruptcy for banks. A Functional Analysis of SIFI Insolvency at 11 (concluding that "SPOE has something of the character of a parlor trick"). Although I ultimately disagree, this strikes me as a plausible conclusion.

[26] Adam Levitin makes this argument in his essay for the Westbrook celebration. Levitin, 97 N.C. L. Rev., *supra* note 22.

[27] Levitin makes this argument, as well as do others.

funding, which will need to come from the federal government. Title II provides for this funding, whereas bankruptcy for banks does not.

Though not intended as such, Jay's prior work provides a response to several of these arguments. During the 2008 crisis, when the government effected the bailouts of Chrysler and General Motors through a creative use of the bankruptcy process, Jay pointed out that, although bankruptcy ordinarily is a somewhat leisurely process, "rough justice in the interest of speed is a common trade-off in the world of bankruptcy."[28] Judges need not ignore "public interest" considerations, Jay argued, such as the prospect that a debtor's collapse could "leav[e] the rest of us to try to help our fellow citizens recover from the blast." In each case, the same can be said about bankruptcy for banks.

In his work on cross-border insolvency, Jay has noted the increasing tendency of bankruptcy judges to interact with their counterparts in other countries.[29] It is not a stretch, in my view, to envision interaction between these same bankruptcy judges and foreign bank regulators—interactions that might take place informally, outside the context of an actual case.

Although I haven't finished addressing the objections, this is a good place to pause and revisit the question why Jay is so hostile to bankruptcy for banks. Many years ago, after reading a book chapter I'd written about removal of the Securities and Exchange Commission (SEC) from the central role it had in bankruptcy prior to 1978, Jay wrote me a note reminiscing about his own experience in the earlier era, and suggesting that the SEC had been more effective than I had implied. Jay clearly retained a fondness for the more regulator-centric process that had been put in place by his New Deal predecessors.

[28.] Jay Westbrook, Commentary: What Bankruptcy Could Do for GM, CNN.Com (June 1, 2009), available at www.cnn.com/2009/US/06/01/westbrook.gm/index.html.

[29.] See, e.g., Westbrook, *supra* note 14, Ann. Rev. Insolv. L. 173 (2013) at 187 (noting that chapter 15 and various model laws authorize communication between judges and administrators).

I suspect the same fondness for—and confidence in—regulators also has shaped Jay's thinking about bankruptcy for banks. Although my own inclinations still tend more toward the market side of the market-regulator spectrum than Jay's, I fully acknowledge that there is an important role for regulators, especially in the financial institution context. Regulators are involved in the oversight of large financial institutions long before there is any hint of financial distress. Regulators are thus likely to be well-informed about an institution that encounters financial distress from the moment the trouble begins. A bankruptcy judge, by contrast, would have little or no contact with the institution until the moment it filed for bankruptcy.

If bank regulators were given a robust role in the process, this would draw bankruptcy for banks a little closer to the regulator-centric process Jay prefers. An obvious way to do this would be to authorize regulators to file the bankruptcy case, rather than simply leaving this to the financial institution itself.[30] If regulators believed resolution was necessary, but concluded that bankruptcy for banks would work, they could file the bankruptcy petition unilaterally or encourage the institution to do so.

The most important remaining issue is funding. Although I do not think the financial institution's funding needs would be as enormous as some bankruptcy for banks critics contend, I agree that a source of federal funding should be provided.[31] My own preference is that the Federal Reserve's emergency funding authority be expanded to include funding in the bankruptcy for banks context.

Here, then, is my plea: that Jay offer a tiny, weeny hint that he might just support bankruptcy for banks if lawmakers gave bank regulators a robust role in the process, if they also added a significant source of federal funding as a financial backstop, and if they

---

[30.] As the chapter 14 proposal advocates. The legislation currently in Congress does not authorize regulators to file the petition.

[31.] I have developed these arguments in detail elsewhere. David Skeel, Financing Systemically Important Financial Institutions in Bankruptcy, in Making Failure Feasible: How Bankruptcy Reform Can End "Too Big to Fail" (Kenneth E. Scott, Thomas H. Jackson, & John B. Taylor, eds., Hoover Institution Press 2015).

promised to leave Title ll in place. This beefed up regime does not seem so far removed from the inclinations that run through Jay's writing.

Jay may well say no. But even if he does, he'll have a smile on his face, as he always does. And why not, given the remarkable career he's had.

EPILOGUE

Remarks of Lord Hoffmann[*]

I'm honoured and delighted to be here, especially because I think I am the only person at this symposium who is not a bankruptcy lawyer. In the course of a 24-year career as a judge I have had two or three accidental encounters with bankruptcy law but no one would call me a bankruptcy lawyer any more than they would call me a tax lawyer or a patent lawyer or a tort lawyer or a constitutional lawyer, each of which subjects probably took up more of my time than bankruptcy law. But one of those brushes with bankruptcy law was not so much accidental as serendipitous, because it led to my getting to know Jay.

By way of prologue, I should say that this is not the first time that I have come between American lawyers and their food. About 30 years ago, when I was a fairly new judge in the Chancery Division, which does corporate bankruptcy, I was invited to the annual convention of American bankruptcy lawyers which that year was in San Diego. There I found I was scheduled to speak at breakfast. So I addressed some 200 judges and their spouses tucking into their bacon and eggs on British bankruptcy. I don't think it was a great success.

My next encounter with U.S. bankruptcy was some time in 1990, when it was my turn to hear urgent applications. There was an application to appointed administrators to a bankrupt company which

---

[*] Rt. Hon. Leonard H. Hoffmann, Lord of Appeal in Ordinary, United Kingdom House of Lords (Ret.).

had been run by Robert Maxwell, a well-known British crook who had committed suicide the week before by jumping off his luxury yacht into the Atlantic. It was also in chapter ɪɪ in New York, where most of the assets were. I'd never had anything to do with cross-border insolvency before, but it seemed just intuitively a good idea to have some co-operation across the Atlantic and I authorised my administrators to negotiate an agreement with the U.S. bankruptcy court. It was a happy accident because I got to know the judge at the American end, the late and very much lamented Tina Brozman. So I learned at first hand the importance of co-operation between courts to achieve the best possible outcome. One example is that when, a year or so later, I had an application by a London bank for an anti-suit injunction to restrain the administrators from suing it in New York to set aside a pre-bankruptcy payment, I refused. I said the New York judge was the best person to decide what proceedings should be brought in her own court. I had complete confidence in Tina's decision and in due course she actually declined jurisdiction.

The result of all this was that Tina and I had an agreeable couple of years being paraded at various international bankruptcy conferences as models of international judicial co-operation, including the judicial gathering in Vienna which launched the UNCITRAL project that produced the Model Law. And that was how I got to know Jay. It was he who provided a scholarly but entirely practical basis for what had previously been just my general common sense feeling there should ideally be a single bankruptcy proceeding and that this was to prevent huge avoidable losses of money, jobs and general human welfare. Jay has been described in the epigraph to this symposium as a universal pragmatist. He does believe in the universality of bankruptcy proceedings and he is a pragmatist, because he understands the nitty-gritty of the economic consequences of bankruptcy. But there is more to it than that. If you are going to be principled as well as pragmatic, you have to be inventive and imaginative. You have to have the imagination to see how things could be done better without departing from principle. I read and admired his work; he invited me to spend a week here in Austin meeting people and attending some classes and then again, more recently, coming to a conference he had organised.

This was the background to the opinion which I wrote for our Supreme Court, presided over by the late Lord Bingham, in the Cambridge Gas case. (I should say that our Supreme Court has had three names over the past few years; it used to be called the House of Lords and in another guise, hearing appeals from British overseas islands, it is still called the Privy Council, but it is the same people doing the same job, so I shall just call it the Supreme Court.) Although I wrote the opinion, it was the unanimous judgment of the Court. It was an opinion very much influenced by Jay's views on bankruptcy universalism. But one of the things which I think made the decision acceptable to my colleagues was that the losing side had no merits. They were shareholders who had failed to persuade the New York bankruptcy judge that they should be allowed to put the assets into a phoenix company and leave the creditors with whatever sum they chose to pay. Now they were trying to defeat that judgment by claiming that their offshore company which held the assets was not subject to U.S. jurisdiction. Incidentally, there is a lesson there for U.S. bankruptcy judges and lawyers. If the debtor company has assets offshore, don't entertain a chapter 11 petition unless the offshore entities formally submit to the jurisdiction.

That was in 2006. In 2009, I retired from the bench. In the Rubin case in 2010, the English Court of Appeal enthusiastically followed Cambridge Gas and gave effect to the order of the NY bankruptcy court requiring the perpetrators of a scam on U.S. consumers to repay money to the company. In 2012 the Supreme Court reversed that decision. An English court, it said, had no power to make an order in assistance of a foreign court unless specifically authorised by statute. The Model Law, which by then had come into force, was not specific enough. Cambridge Gas, which asserted that such a power existed at common law, was overruled.

Why did this happen? The reasons lie, I think, partly in personalities and partly in English legal culture. Lawrence Collins, who wrote the leading Supreme Court judgment in Rubin, is a distinguished legal scholar. He used to teach at Cambridge and he now teaches every year in the winter semester at NYU. He is the editor and now largely the author of Dicey on the Conflict of Laws, which has been for over a century the leading English textbook on private international law. But he is a very different kind of scholar from Jay. While Jay is constantly producing imaginative solutions to practical problems, Lawrence distils the authority of the texts. He could easily have been a biblical or Talmudic scholar. The notion of bankruptcy exceptionalism, in which the orders of bankruptcy courts do not have to be classified as in rem or in personam and meet the jurisdictional requirements of one or the other, is anathema to him. Imaginative solutions are dangerous and if it is not in Dicey it does not exist.

That is the personal side. The other important factor is the sovereignty of parliament. The English courts are constantly aware of the boundary between changes in the law which they can properly make and changes which should be left to Parliament. Until the governmental nervous breakdown and paralysis which has followed the Brexit vote, it was generally the case that the government has a majority in Parliament and could secure the passage of whatevssser legislation it thought necessary. From a judicial point of view, this has been admirable and made for a quiet life for judges. The great social issues which occupy the Supreme Court of the United States, such as race discrimination, sex discrimination, capital punishment, abortion, gay marriage and such like, have all been settled by legislation in the United Kingdom and never trouble the courts. As a result, while everyone knows the identities, views and food preferences of the judges of the U.S. Supreme Court, in the United Kingdom hardly anyone knows who we are. I like it that way. But the boundary between improvements to the law which judges can make and what should be left to Parliament is a matter of judgment. Sometimes the sensible thing is to develop the law and leave it to Parliament, if it thinks fit, to change it back again.

In the Rubin case, and even more in the later case of Singularis, the Supreme Court were very preoccupied with the constitutional propriety of asserting a common law power to assist foreign bankruptcy courts. But I am bound to say that this seems to me, in the bankruptcy context, a singularly unpractical attitude. Lord Neuberger, then President of the Court, gave a talk to triple III last summer in which he said that he was all for universalism in a global economy but it had to be done by Parliament. But there is not the slightest chance of it being done by Parliament. That would require a further international convention. That is not easy. It took over 40 years to negotiate a European Bankruptcy Convention, which was then scuppered at the last minute by the British Government because they were annoyed with the French for not allowing the import of British beef during the mad cow disease epidemic. If that is what governments do, it is surely time for the courts to be grown ups and take responsibility for the economic consequences of what they are doing.

So I come before you in the character of a defeated general, whose positions have been overrun while he was away from the battlefields. But, as Senator Warren told us last night, you don't give up fighting. Perhaps someday my colleagues or their successors will be persuaded to read Jay's work and see the light. Meanwhile, I can only apologise on behalf of my country and thank him for the privilege of knowing him and being with you today.

INDEX

Note: Page numbers in *italics* refer to illustrations; Page numbers followed by "n" refer to notes.

Securities Investor Protection
Corporation (SIPC), 140, 361, 382
liquidation, 276, 280, 372n104
Shenzhen Bar Association, 227
Shenzhen Special Economic Zone,
227–28
SIFI. *See* systemically important
financial institution (SIFI)
single point of entry (SPOE), 147, 150,
153, 289n70, 366–69, 628–30
SIPA. *See* Securities Investor Protection
Act (SIPA)
SIPC. *See* Securities Investor Protection
Corporation (SIPC)
Skeel, David A., Jr., 318, 617, 623
Slovakia
Centre for Legal Aid, 211
fear of abuse in consumer
bankruptcy (2006–2017), 206–11
Slovak Bankruptcy Statistics, 211n55
Snidal, Duncan, 38n18, 40
soft law, 4
gap-filling, 50–51
role in international commercial
laws, 33–55
Solomons v. Ross (1764), 63–64
South Africa
common law, 426
customary international law in, 473
Debt Relief Order, 588
sovereignty effects of international
commercial laws, 44–49
Spain, criteria of the insolvency
proceedings, 423
SPE. *See* special-purpose entity (SPE)
special-purpose entity (SPE), 305, 306
SPOE. *See* single point of entry
(SPOE)
Spooner, Joe, 602
Standard & Poor's, 97–98
Stanley, David T., 240
State Department, 53
state insurance receiverships, 276, 280
state of insolvency, 429
Statute of the International Court of
Justice, 440
Statutists, 454
stealth financial institutions, 153
Stegold, Thomas, 179
Stone, John, 197
structured dismissal, 325–26

substantive law approach to choice of
law in multistate insolvency, 402–3
sufficient connection, 399
Sullivan, Teresa A., 233–35, 237, 241–43,
260
Fragile Middle Class, The, 624
We Forgive Our Debtors, 624
Sullivan, Terry, 1, 7
Sun Capital, 338
systemically important financial
institution (SIFI), 2, 135–61, 269, 274,
320
duct tape for, 149–50
insolvency, functional analysis of,
353–85
chapter 14, 367–68
court problems, 374–80
Dodd-Frank's OLA solution,
363–66
facing facts, 380–84
fundamentals, 358–63
problem, 356–70
single point of entry, 366–69
SIFI-specific response to Lehman,
141–43
systemic risk in, 152–54
systemic financial risk, 152–54, 266
bankruptcy as public policy forum,
315–20
political nature of, 313–15
systemic spillovers, reduction of,
294–96

Taiwan Consumer Insolvency Act of
2008, 228n139
TARP. *See* Toxic Asset Relief Program
(TARP)
Taxpayer Protection and Responsible
Resolution Act, 278n31
TFEU, art. 107, 522
Thorne, Deborah, 247–48
TLAC. *See* total loss-absorbing capacity
(TLAC)
TLOs. *See* Transnational Legal Orders
(TLOs)
Toronto-Dominion Bank (TD Bank),
13n8
total loss-absorbing capacity (TLAC),
628
Toxic Asset Relief Program (TARP),
158n40

Jay Westbrook (left), Douglas Whaley, and James Kunetka, circa 1967.

CPSIA information can be obtained
at www.ICGtesting.com
Printed in the USA
BVHW051048140223
658482BV00014B/337

9 781607 855477